The Adolescent in the Family

Adolescence can be a difficult time for all concerned. Issues such as youth employment, sexual behaviour and drug abuse have made it a matter of great concern to the community at large, whether as parents, politicians or those working with adolescents in education and welfare. In addition, many parents fear that these problems could affect their own families.

Patricia Noller and Victor Callan explore the complex needs of adolescents, emphasising the importance of the family environment in helping adolescents to cope with the many difficulties and changes they face during this period of their lives. The central theme is that adolescents, through conflict and negotiation, establish new but different relationships with their parents, relationships that can endure for a lifetime. The authors provide wide coverage of the key issues of adolescence, such as identity, separation from the family, and conflict, and look closely at the difficulties produced by events such as the divorce and re-marriage of parents, and social problems such as long-term unemployment.

With its positive approach to the family and adolescents, this clear, concise and helpful book will be invaluable both to parents and to the many professionals whose work involves them with adolescents.

Patricia Noller is Reader and Victor J. Callan is Associate Professor in the Department of Psychology, University of Queensland. They have written extensively on the family, and are the joint authors of *Marriage and the Family* (1987).

Adolescence and Society

Series editor: John C. Coleman

The Trust for the Study of Adolescence

The general aim of the series is to make accessible to a wide readership the growing evidence relating to adolescent development. Much of this material is published in relatively inaccessible professional journals, and the goals of the books in this series will be to summarise, review, and place in context current work in the field so as to interest and engage both an undergraduate and professional audience.

The intention of the authors is to raise the profile of adolescent studies among professionals and in institutes of higher education. By publishing relatively short, readable books on interesting topics to do with youth and society, the series will make people more aware of the relevance of the subject of adolescence to a wide range of social concerns.

The books will not put forward any one theoretical viewpoint. The authors will outline the most prominent theories in the field, and will include a balanced and critical assessment of each of these. Whilst some of the books may have a clinical or applied slant, the majority will concentrate on normal development.

The readership will rest primarily in two major areas: the undergraduate market, particularly in the fields of psychology, sociology, and education; and the professional training market, with particular emphasis on social work, clinical and educational psychology, counselling, youth work, nursing, and teacher training.

Also available in this series

Identity in Adolescence
Jane Kroger

The Nature of Adolescence (second edition)
John C. Coleman and Leo Hendry

The Adolescent in the Family

Patricia Noller

and

Victor Callan

London and New York

First published 1991
by Routledge
11 New Fetter Lane, London EC4P 4EE

Simultaneously published in the USA and Canada
by Routledge
a division of Routledge, Chapman and Hall, Inc.
29 West 35th Street, New York, NY 10001

© 1991 Patricia Noller and Victor Callan

Typeset by LaserScript Limited, Mitcham, Surrey
Printed and bound in Great Britain by Mackays of Chatham PLC, Kent

British Library Cataloguing in Publication Data
Noller, Patricia
   The adolescent in the family. – (Adolescence in society).
   1. Adolescents. Psychology
   I. Title II. Callan, Victor, *1954*– III. Series
   155.5

Library of Congress Cataloging in Publication Data
Noller, Patricia
   The adolescent in the family / Patricia Noller and Victor Callan.
   p.   cm.– (Adolescence and society)
   Includes bibliographical references.
   1. Parent and child. 2. Teenagers–Family relationships.   3. Adolescent
   psychology.   I. Callan, Victor J., 1954–   . II. Title. III. Series.
   HQ755.85.N65 1991
   306.874–dc20

                                                              90–33412
                                                              CIP

ISBN 0-415-01089-6
ISBN 0-415-01090-X

Contents

Illustrations

Preface

Adolescence has always been a controversial area of theory and research, and never more so than over the last twenty years. While adolescence was once just an area of academic discussion, many developments have made adolescence an area of great concern to members of the community at large, whether they be parents, politicians or those working with adolescents in education and/or welfare. With political and social issues such as youth unemployment, drug use and abuse and streetkids, almost everyone is aware of the problems facing particular groups of young people. In addition, many parents fear that these problems could affect their own family.

While once psychodynamic interpretations of adolescence with their emphasis on 'Sturm und Drang' (or Storm and Stress) clearly dominated our perceptions of what adolescence was like, there was an implicit belief that the family played little part in the lives of adolescents who were only interested in being involved with and pleasing their peer groups. Parents were very much seen as the outsiders. Today there is a much greater understanding of the complexity of the needs of adolescents and their strong desire to be close to both their parents and their friends. Adolescents are expected to establish their independence through renegotiating their relationships with their parents to involve more freedom and flexibility. While most adolescents are prepared to take on the new responsibilities associated with growing up, they also need the help and support of their parents as they work through this process. Sometimes the supportive environment is not there for the adolescents, because of family conflict, the breakup of marriages and societal problems such as high levels of youth unemployment. In this situation, a wide range of problems can result.

We have written this book for those who want to understand the part a supportive family can play in helping adolescents cope with the physical and emotional changes associated with this period of their lives. In particular, we have developed the theme that adolescents, through conflict and negotiation, establish new but different relationships with their parents, relationships that can endure for a life-time.

Parents will find a lot of encouragement in this book and may also be helped in relating better to their adolescents. They will also see the consequences of resorting to styles of parenting involving high levels of coercion and control. For those parents who have experienced a divorce, we have pointed to the importance of partners maintaining a good relationship with each other and with their children. At the same time, they will realise the many difficulties in supporting adolescents through a cycle of separation, divorce and re-marriage.

Others who may find help in reading this book would be those who live and work with adolescents away from the family environment: teachers, welfare workers, social workers, church leaders, psychologists and psychiatrists may all find material in this book that will help them to understand young people better. We have attempted here to bring together the best research available, much of which is generally restricted to academic journals devoted to adolescents. We believe this information belongs with the public. We hope you find reading about adolescents and their needs and problems as interesting and enjoyable as the task of writing this book has been.

Patricia Noller
and
Victor Callan

Acknowledgements

Firstly we would like to thank John Coleman for his invitation to contribute to this series, and for his support and encouragement throughout the process of preparing this book. Despite the distance between Brighton and Brisbane, he has been an excellent editor and advisor.

We would also like to thank the Psychology Department of the University of Queensland for once again supporting us in our research and writing about the family and adolescents. We would also like to specifically mention the parents and adolescents who have helped us in our research, the students who have been involved in some of the research projects, and the research assistants who have been involved in this project over the last two years.

Finally we would like to thank Charles and Margaret and our families for their continued support and interest in our work, and for their patience with us as we struggle with getting our ideas on paper. Twenty-one-year-old Alison Noller does not believe her mother knows enough about adolescents to write such a book, while the parents of five-year-old Alison Callan still believe their daughter will be the perfect adolescent, whatever that entails.

Patricia Noller
and
Victor Callan

Chapter one

Theoretical perspectives and controversies about adolescents

Adolescence is all about growing up and becoming an adult. Typically, the term refers to the time between one's childhood and adulthood, beginning with the physical and emotional changes characteristic of puberty. While the end of adolescence is probably not as clearly specified as the beginning, it is characterised by such events as the adolescent leaving home, beginning a career or getting married. As Stone and Church (1968) suggest, one of the difficulties for parents and adolescents is that 'readiness for adulthood comes about about two years later than the adolescent claims and about two years before the parent will admit' (p.447).

While adolescents may move away from their family towards their friends, relationships with their families are important for most adolescents both during adolescence and for the rest of their lives. For this reason, we want to argue quite strongly that any serious consideration of the adolescent experience has to include the type of focus on the family that we will be attempting in this book. We will be taking the view that the quality of family relationships is crucial in determining the competence and confidence with which young people face this major transition from childhood to adulthood. We believe that family relationships affect the success with which young people negotiate the major tasks of adolescence, the extent to which they become involved in the problem behaviours generally associated with this time, and their ability to establish meaningful close relationships that are likely to last. The aspects of the family that seem to be particularly important are the encouragement of autonomy and independence, the degree of control desired by parents, the amount of conflict among family members, the closeness of family bonds and the love and support available to the adolescents.

How many young people have the continuous, tumultuous experiences frequently depicted as a feature of adolescence? Offer and Sabshin (1984) claim that only about 21 per cent of their large sample of teenagers experienced such a tumultuous adolescence. About the same percentage were confident throughout the period and seemed to have very few problems. About 35 per cent 'moved through the period in spurts emotionally and mentally'. As we shall show later, the style of parenting is one very important determinant of the extent to which adolescents are likely to have major problems.

On the other hand, these figures do not allow us to deny that most adolescents are subject to conflict, confusion and stress. They are frequently unsure about themselves and about the direction of their lives. They are likely to experience periods of strong self-doubt, and feel quite uncertain about how quickly they want to grow up, or whether growing up will only make things worse. To further complicate the situation, such confusion is not always expressed as uncertainty, but rather as certainty, over-confidence, brashness and even anger at those who refuse to agree with them. Adolescents can also be unpredictable, so that within minutes they change from mature and adult-like behaviours to throwing childish temper tantrums. Parents find such unpredictability and moodiness very difficult to handle.

Many parents dread the onset of adolescence. Those parents who have 'been through it' often warn parents complaining about younger children that 'they've hardly started yet' or 'they don't know they're alive'. No wonder we hear proud parents of primary school children saying, 'You must come and meet our son, while he's still nice'. Rarely do we hear the parents of adolescents making similar invitations.

Research tends to support the views in the general community that raising adolescents can be difficult. For instance, Olson and his colleagues (1983), in a large cross-sectional study of families over the life-cycle found that adolescence was clearly the most stressful stage of the family life-cycle. Marital and family satisfaction, family pride and marital communication were all lower for families with adolescents than for any other group of families, and family stress was higher than at any other stage.

The theme of this book is the adolescent and the role played by the family in helping adolescents cope with the transition to adulthood. The family has a major role in shaping the identity of adolescents and their willingness to explore alternatives. Importantly, there is a significant body of theory about family functioning that points to the vital role played by the family in the development and adjustment of adolescents.

Understanding the functioning of families

How families function is conceptualized in a number of different ways, varying from a focus on the normal family (e.g. Olson *et al.*, 1983) or on the pathological family (Walsh, 1982). There are a number of models of family functioning, including Olson's Circumplex Model (Olson,

Sprenkle & Russell, 1979), Beavers' Systems Model (Beavers, 1981; Beavers & Voeller, 1983) and the McMaster Model (Epstein, Bishop & Baldwin, 1982; Epstein, Bishop & Levin, 1978). These models generally have two aims: to describe the most important dimensions of family functioning and to describe the dimensions which are most effective in discriminating between healthy and poorly functioning families.

Although the models are quite different in some ways, there is also a great deal of overlap and agreement. It is this agreement which has become our major focus here and elsewhere. In general, theorists agree that families should provide their members with moderate levels of cohesion (or closeness or connectedness) as well as moderate levels of flexibility about roles and rules. In addition, autonomy should be encouraged, and communication should be clear and direct.

For example, in the study by Olson and his colleagues (1983), families with adolescents showed high levels of stress and low levels of satisfaction. These researchers found, however, that those adolescent families with low levels of stress and high levels of satisfaction were balanced in terms of their cohesion and adaptability. That is, families that cope well with the transition to adulthood are close and supportive, but also flexible in their approach to solving family problems.

In another model of families, Beavers identifies two main dimensions: competence and family style. The dimension of competence includes power structure, degree of negotiation and encouragement of autonomy. The style dimension involves the extent to which the family is inward-focused (centripetal) or outward-focused (centrifugal). Healthy families are balanced on style, with some activities being family-centred and others involving outsiders and the community. Extremes of style are only evident in unhealthy families who are low in competence. These families tend to be either strongly centripetal, with intense family loyalties and activities generally centred in the family, or strongly centrifugal with weak family bonds and activities centred outside the family.

Beavers' ideas are of special interest to researchers and practitioners, because he sees family style as relevant to the type of psychopathology likely to develop in some family members. Adolescents in centripetal families are more likely to develop internally focused symptoms such as depression or schizophrenia. Those in centrifugal families are more likely to develop externally focused symptoms such as delinquent behaviours, psychopathy and general acting-out.

For Epstein, in the McMaster model, the healthy family is one where closeness is moderate and the control of behaviour is flexible. All necessary roles are assigned to competent individuals who are accountable for their performance and communication is clear and direct. Emotions are expressed at levels appropriate to the situation and problem-solving is effective. All of these models of the healthy family fit with the concerns of adolescence researchers for family environments where individuality and autonomy are encouraged, control is moderate and flexible and adolescents are likely to receive all the love and support they need.

Some major tasks for the adolescent

There are several developmental milestones through which adolescents must pass in order to achieve adulthood and healthy psychosocial functioning. As we shall show, each of these tasks is accomplished most effectively in families where autonomy is encouraged, the parents' level of control is low to moderate, conflict is generally low and members of the family feel supported and loved.

One task of adolescence could be labelled as emancipation from parents. This emancipation is accomplished gradually, but even so, not necessarily without stress and tension for both the parents and the adolescent. Psychosexual differentiation is also part of adolescence. The adolescent learns to deal with and control new capacities for physical sexual activity. Adolescents need to understand their sexuality, and the part it plays in close relationships. They also need to define their gender identity, grappling as well with the sex roles that are acceptable for their own and the opposite sex.

Adolescence also involves gaining the skills which are necessary for economic independence and for establishing a career. Adolescents cannot be truly independent until they are able to support themselves. They need to decide on the level of education they wish to achieve in order to pursue job opportunities. All of these tasks add to a sense of separation from parents.

We would like to argue that through the negotiation of these and other tasks, adolescents pass a further milestone of developing a realistic, stable, positive identity. This task is particularly important, since it can only be achieved if the other tasks have first been successfully negotiated. All of these tasks are basic to our discussion of adolescents and the family.

These milestones have probably always been part of the transition to adulthood. Recent social changes, however, have made such tasks more difficult, at least for some adolescents. Emancipation from parents is complicated by the increased need for higher education, the lack of job opportunities for many young people, increased levels of family breakdown and the tendency for some young people to move out of home into situations which are less than ideal. Sexual differentiation is

4

being affected by changing societal standards, more alternatives, a greater push to express one's sexuality and more opportunities to engage in sexual behaviours and explore sexual alternatives. Career goals for many adolescents are being badly affected by the lack of jobs, the intense competition throughout high school and higher education, as well as more existential concerns about the future of this world they are inheriting. Many ask whether there is any point in studying and working hard, when the world may not be here ten years from now. Finally, the challenge of establishing one's identity is being complicated by similar factors, as well as by the adolescents' disillusionment with the values of their parents. Today's adolescents are more concerned than most of their parents ever were, about the environment, the conservation of resources and heritage, the uses of nuclear power, personal freedom and the ideals of social and racial equality.

In sum, adolescence involves a series of milestones that include establishing individual sexual, social and work lives and a positive sense of identity. Parents want adolescents to be independent, but also to like themselves as young adults. Much of this volume is about these milestones, and the role of the family in producing independent, happy young people. The search for independence and a positive identity, however, is not without risks, as we shall see later.

Becoming independent from parents

Terms such as 'breaking away' or 'breaking free' are often used to describe the changes in the relationship between parents and their adolescents. As we will emphasise throughout this volume, however, for many adolescents there is no real break in their relationship with their parents, but rather a gradual movement toward more autonomy and independence. Of course, this change is unlikely to occur without some anxiety, and some anger and distress to both parents and adolescents. Parents resist changes to family rules that have worked very well in the past, while adolescents seem to want all the rules changed at once.

Early adolescence is an extremely important developmental period. There is increased stress from the onset of puberty. The transition from primary to secondary school is associated with increasing levels of conflict and more and more arguments with parents (Petersen & Taylor, 1980), with relationships improving between middle and late adolescence. From our perspective, while high levels of continued conflict are associated with bad outcomes, conflict in early adolescence can help the adolescent achieve some of the necessary changes in roles and relationships. Parents and adolescents then settle into the new situation under the new rules. In this new situation, adolescents want more freedom to make decisions about their appearance, their social lives, their eating habits and what they watch on television or listen to on the radio. We will talk more about these changes later.

One common problem is that adolescents want considerable independence and autonomy while still living at home. Again, the family is important in determining how successfully this autonomy is achieved. Where parents accept and encourage their adolescents to gain independence, minimal conflict is likely. Where parents resist their adolescents' strivings toward independence, trying to maintain total control, high levels of conflict are likely to ensue. In such a family climate, adolescents may even rebel against what they perceive to be the unreasonableness of their parents, and leave home.

There are different styles or types of independence. In a useful discussion of independence, Steinberg and Silverberg (1986) highlight very different aspects of autonomy. According to them, each of these styles is important to adolescents. Emotional autonomy is a process of individuation. The adolescent lets go of childish views that their parents are infallible or perfect and reduces his or her childish dependence on them. As might be expected, realising that they are separate from parents and that parents can be wrong, frequently leads to conflict between adolescents and parents. Adolescents who, in the past, generally accepted their parents' advice may start to argue and become defiant. Parents who were once seen as 'knowing-it-all' may become the 'know-alls' who think they know everything but, according to their adolescents, really don't know very much. Parents who recognise the source of such defiance, and the importance of adolescents giving up their childish dependence on them, will be less troubled by these periods of conflict.

A second feature of establishing autonomy is dealing with peer pressure, particularly pressure to get involved in the use of alcohol or drugs, or to engage in anti-social behaviours. There is an interesting cycle of changes in parent–peer relations. Preadolescents accept their parents' standards, and resist peer pressure by falling back on the rules and guidelines adopted from home. Early and middle adolescents, on the other hand, begin to reject the views of their parents and try out new rules. At this stage they appear to be more influenced by peer pressure. Older adolescents, however, complete the cycle in that they have frequently learned a lot about how the world works. As a result, they don't necessarily assume that their parents are always wrong and their peers are always right. They may even accept that their parents have some (if only a little) wisdom and experience. Thus, they seem less likely than younger adolescents either to reject their parents' views out of hand or to be overinfluenced by their peers.

As the research by Steinberg and Silverberg (1986) also indicates, autonomy from parents and resistance to peer pressure are negatively related. The more autonomous an individual feels from their parents, the more susceptible they are to peer pressure. Becoming autonomous from parents at too early an age may make adolescents more at risk of pressure from peers to engage in deviant behaviours. On the other hand, there is also evidence that adolescents who come from families where the parents are too controlling are also at risk (Burt, Cohen & Bjorck, 1988).

Other discussions of autonomy (e.g. Newman & Murray, 1983) point to the roles of behavioural and value autonomy. Behavioural autonomy involves the ability to make decisions about daily routines and personal preferences. Value autonomy involves thinking through values and making decisions about what is important. Behavioural and emotional autonomy generally precede value autonomy in adolescence, since separateness and confidence are essential to decisions about one's values. Some aspects of autonomy are also related to the development of identity in adolescents, an issue we will explore later.

Becoming independent from parents can also involve leaving home. The pattern today is very different from the past when young people generally lived with their parents until they left home to get married. With the increasing emphasis on autonomy, teenagers are likely to move out of home, to share a house with friends, to move in with a girlfriend or boyfriend, and, over a number of years, may even have several cohabiting relationships before getting married. Some young people even move back home in between relationships or house-sharing, especially if they are short of money or need to save. With more marriages breaking down, mature sons or daughters are even moving back home after a divorce, at least until they 'get back on their feet'. For some young people, however, returning home is not a satisfactory option, no matter how great their need. Going back may place financial pressures on the family, create conflict between parents and children or lead to physical abuse. Under these conditions, some adolescents feel that they can never go back home.

Unfortunately, many adolescents who leave home early are likely to end up living in poverty, or even homeless. These are times of high youth unemployment, combined with a lack of cheap housing. In desperation, these adolescents may seek a living through drugs, prostitution, or crime.

Sexual development and differentiation

As mentioned earlier, another important milestone for adolescents is the emergence of their sexuality. Coming to terms with one's sexual feelings and establishing a positive sexual identity are important aspects of individuation. Many changes are taking place in the young person's body that prepare the adolescent for sex and reproduction. There is also very rapid physical growth in both height and weight. If you've had the experience of visiting a friend's family and seeing their teenagers before and after a growth spurt, you will know how dramatic the changes can be. The sexual development of adolescents is an anxious stage for both the parents and the teenager. Parents worry about their adolescents having sex, getting pregnant and even becoming teenage parents. They are concerned about whether their child has the maturity to make responsible decisions about their sexual activity, and whether they are able to cope with the emotional demands of a sexual relationship. Parents are also in a dilemma about their role in preparing their child for sexual activity. Should they provide advice about contraceptives, or say nothing for fear of encouraging sexual experimentation? In the 1980s, there was also the spectre of AIDS and the possibility of infection through sexual activity with a person who is HIV positive. Fear of AIDS in the 80s and 90s is putting pressure on families, and the community, to educate teenagers about safe practices. In addition, parents realise that the pressures towards early sexual activity are much stronger than they used to be. With the more general rejection of religion and associated moral teaching, and constant exposure to sexually explicit material through television, movies and songs, there are clear pressures to become sexually involved even while still at high school.

As they accept their emerging sexuality, adolescents need to consider their own sexual orientation or preference. For most, the preference is for heterosexual relationships; however, homosexuality and bisexuality are more common choices in the 1980s than previously. While there is still stigma, there is less need for secrecy than used to be the case. Parents, on the other hand, are still likely to be devastated by the knowledge that their child is involved in homosexual activity.

Changing sex roles now mean that females, more so than before, can consider all careers as appropriate for women. In addition, young males are now expected to care for themselves and participate in household chores, whether single or married. While sex roles adopted during adolescence may not necessarily apply throughout life, young people do need to think about such issues.

Career and educational choices

Adolescence is a time for making choices about educational and career goals. Once again, these choices will not necessarily be final, but can have an important impact on the young person's future. Probably the most crucial choice is whether or not to finish school. Those who finish school seem to have a higher probablility of becoming employed. They are also more likely to get further education and training, soon after leaving school and later in life. While in recent times it was possible to gain mature age entry to educational institutions without the necessary qualifications, competition for tertiary places is now more intense. Such 'second chances' of mature entry are now very limited.

Young people who don't finish school and who leave home early probably run the greatest risk of ending up on the streets. Of course, these decisions to drop out of school or leave home may not be made by the adolescent, but by the family. If the family does not place a high value on education or does not have the financial resources to keep young people in school after the period of compulsory education, then parents may insist that the adolescent leave. Sometimes the issue is further complicated by the fact that there are jobs available for the young people while they are under 18 years of age. The jobs tend to be poorly paid, and adolescents are likely to be put off once they turn 18. Becoming unemployed at 18, with no qualifications, can be a devastating experience.

Those young people who have opportunities for further education need help in choosing the kind of training they would like to pursue. Making career decisions that take into account interests, abilities, willingness to study and financial resources requires help from a professional counsellor or vocational guidance person. Some adolescents may also need help in sorting out their own interests from the expectations of parents. For example, a student may feel pressure to train in pharmacy because of expectations that they will carry on with the family business. However, they may really hate science subjects and prefer to be an English teacher.

Identity development at adolescence

How adolescents succeed or fail in developing a clear sense of identity, is an important theme of this book. Erikson's (1963; 1968) eight stages of development provide a useful theoretical basis for concerns about identity and autonomy in adolescence. He argues that the establishment of a firm sense of ego identity provides a crucial bridge between childhood and adulthood, and is a requirement for the successful resolution of the following stage of initiating intimacy and the formation of stable intimate relationships.

Newman and Murray (1983) define identity as 'like a blueprint for future commitments and life choices. It is a set of beliefs and goals about one's relationship with family members, lovers and friends, one's roles as worker, citizen and religious believer and one's aspirations for achievement' (p.294). There is a progressive strengthening of the sense of identity throughout adolescence. Significantly, the adolescent should considers a range of identity alternatives rather than settling for the most

9

obvious choices (such as those of parents or other authority figures). How the young person evaluates his or her identity is also crucial. Ideally, the sense of self-acceptance and personal uniqueness are high and the adolescent is confident and positive about the future.

The formation of an identity occurs through two related processes: personal exploration and psychological differentiation (Campbell, Adams & Dobson, 1984). Personal exploration involves examining attitudes, values and opinions, comparing these with alternatives and making a commitment to particular values and positions. Psychological differentiation, on the other hand, involves a gradually increasing awareness of the kind of person you are and of your separateness from others. At this point, individual adolescents become more conscious of their similarities to and differences from others.

Identity is also formed through a series of decisions which have particular implications for identity formation. Such decisions might include whether to go to college or university, whether and whom to date, how much effort to put into study and leisure, whether to take drugs and whether to stay at home with parents or to move away. Many of these decisions, of course, also have implications for the rest of a person's life. Making these decisions and forming a clear identity are important because of the increased level of self-esteem, increased stability of the self-concept and lower levels of anxiety which emerge as a consequence of identity formation (Bernard, 1981).

There are also a number of different aspects of identity, including personal identity, sexual identity, religious identity and political identity. Identity development includes decisions about how I relate to others, what kinds of work and activity I like, whether I like taking risks. One adolescent's identity, for example, might include the following aspects: 'I am a warm person who gets on well with other people, I like to enjoy myself and I don't really like working hard. I like work which is active (I couldn't bear to sit at a desk all day!) but where I can set my own pace. I don't really like study much, so I don't want a career where I would need to study for further qualifications. I like outside activities, and enjoy taking risks in sporting activities. I look forward to getting married and having a family some day, but am not in any particular hurry. I would like to have a good time first.'

Another young person of similar age may have a quite different identity. 'I am a fairly quiet, shy person. I don't like going around in a big group, and prefer going out with one or two friends to a concert or a movie. I like to have a fair amount of time on my own. I love reading and study and hope to get to the top of my chosen career of law. I don't like team sports or rough games and get my exercise by swimming and jogging, generally alone. I have a pretty serious approach to life and want to be of service to my fellow human beings. I am fairly religious and go to church each Sunday. I'm not much interested in politics, at this stage. I hope to marry but that will have to wait until I have finished my study and established myself in a practice'.

Identity status

Basic to these differences in identity are the family experiences of adolescents, their individual personalities and whether or not they have experienced an identity crisis. In a theory of identity status, Marcia (1966; 1976) describes four different statuses which are defined in terms of whether the individual has experienced some form of identity crisis and whether there is commitment to a specific identity. Crisis involves some serious consideration of alternative possibilities such as different ideologies or life goals, while commitment involves the relatively firm choice of a specific identity (see Figure 1.1).

Figure 1.1 Types of identity status

		Committed to Identity	
		Yes	No
Identity Crisis	Yes	Identity Achievement	Moratorium
	No	Foreclosure	Diffusion

The four identity statuses are:

Identity achievement – individuals in this group have gone through a period of crisis and have developed relatively firm commitments;

Moratorium – individuals in this group are currently in a state of crisis and are actively exploring and seeking to make identity-related choices;

Foreclosure – individuals in this group have never experienced a crisis although they have committed themselves to particular goals and values which generally reflect wishes of authority figures;

Identity diffusion – individuals in this group do not have firm commitments and are not actively exploring or trying to form some commitments; these adolescents or adults may or may not have been through a crisis period, but whether they have or not, there has been no clear resolution of their identity or commitments.

Some writers, like Waterman (1982), argue that changes in identity status can be either developmentally progressive or regressive. Progressive changes involve either spending time actively thinking about and evaluating identity alternatives or developing personally meaningful commitments. Presumably, in order to make meaningful commitments, however, some period of reflection is essential. A change from some other status to the identity diffusion status is generally viewed as developmentally regressive, since identity concerns are put aside, at least temporarily, without any satisfactory resolution.

The greatest gains in identity formation seem to occur during college years (Adams & Fitch, 1982; Waterman & Goldman, 1976). Studies show significant increases in the number of students in the identity achievement status and decreases in the moratorium, diffusion and forelosure status groups. These findings are just what would be expected if adolescents are generally moving toward the identity achieved status.

Decreases in foreclosure status suggest that some students, at least, come to reject the views of their parents that they had previously adopted as their own. For example, experiences in college can undermine the traditional religious beliefs of students without helping the students to explore alternatives and establish new belief systems. (See Waterman, 1982.) While the move from the foreclosure status to the identity achieved status is seen as positive, moving from the foreclosure to the diffusion status is generally seen as regressive.

It also seems clear that identity development does not occur evenly across different areas of identity. Meilman (1979) and Archer (1981) both explored this issue. Foreclosure is most frequent in areas of sex role attitudes, vocational choice, and religious beliefs; diffusion, on the other hand, is most common in the area of political ideology. Many students have little interest in politics and only the really interested students tend to be in the identity achieved status. In our own work (Noller & Bagi, 1985; Noller & Callan, in press) politics is much more of an issue for older adolescents than for the younger ones.

Identity status and adjustment

One reason for emphasising the importance of identity status is the evidence for clear relationships between identity status in adolescents and their overall psychological adjustment (Bernard, 1981; Donovan, 1975). Identity achievers are the healthiest of the four status groups in their general adjustment and also in their relationships with both peers and authority figures. Thus families which encourage identity exploration and achievement are also likely to produce adolescents with healthy psychological adjustment

Identity achievers tend to be nurturant with their peers and to be high in internal control and self-esteem and low in anxiety, particularly if they are males. Identity achievers also seem more capable of forming close, stable relationships than the other groups of adolescents. Foreclosures, on the other hand, tend to be well adjusted, not very anxious, but distant from their peers. They are inclined to be manipulative and controlling to get their own way. Those in the diffusion status are not very open with their peers and overly compliant in peer presssure situations. They often pretend to agree even when they don't. The most negative relationships with peers involve those in the moratorium status who tend to be hostile to their peers (Campbell, Adams & Dobson, 1984).

The four identity status groups also differ with regard to their relationships with authority figures. Those in the identity achievement status tend to be cooperative with authority figures and those in the foreclosure status tend to be in awe of authority figures. After all, these are the young people who have adopted the values and attitudes of their authority figures, without much questioning of their positions. While those in the diffusion status group have normal MMPI profiles, they tend to be fearful of authority figures (Donovan, 1975). Moratoriums are less well-adjusted and more anxious than any of the other groups probably because they are still working through identity issues. They also tend to be involved in power struggles with authority figures, as they seek to work out and test their own positions on a range of issues.

Sex differences in identity formation and status

As mentioned earlier, there is some evidence that the progression through the stages of identity may be different for males and females. Adolescents need to establish priorities, and decide what issues are important to their identity. In Hodgson's (1977) study, for example, male identity was focused on issues of individual competence and knowledge, with males being more advanced in the resolution of these identity issues. Female identity, on the other hand, centred on issues of relating to others, with women being more advanced in the achievement of intimacy than men. Furthermore, the large body of literature relating to the intimacy problems experienced by adult males shows that such differences persist way beyond adolescence (e.g. Balswick, 1988; McGill, 1986).

There is also evidence that males and females are influenced in their progress toward identity formation by traditional sex role stereotypes. Kahn and his associates (1985) found that dependency clearly represented a part of the female but not the male identity. The identity of women seems intertwined with concerns about intimacy and relationships. Once again, males are primarily concerned about their competence and achievement, while relationships are the primary concern of females.

Not only is there a different emphasis for males and females, based on traditional sex-role stereotypes, but both males and females seem to value masculine attributes most highly. In fact, both men and women incorporate highly valued masculine characteristics such as assertiveness, independence and autonomy into their identities. They devalue feminine charateristics such as understanding and warmth, seeing them as less important than the masculine characteristics. On the other hand, high self-esteem for both males and females is associated with androgyny (high levels of both masculinity and femininity). (See Orlofsky, 1977.) It seems that feminine characteristics are valued, provided they are accompanied by masculine characteristics.

Identity status and close relationships

Identity status also affects young people's relationships. As Erikson argued, those who have a firm sense of their own identity are likely to relate best to others, particularly in intimate relationships. Identity status is related to measures of depth and mutuality in interpersonal relationships. Identity achievements and moratoriums are more likely to be involved in intimate relationships. Foreclosures and diffusions, on the other hand, tend to be involved in stereotyped relationships involving little depth and mutuality. Diffusions are also most likely to be involved in isolated relationships, or relationships which are not embedded in a larger group of friends (Orlofsky *et al.*, 1973).

Some interesting studies have traced the effects of adolescent identity on close relationships. Kahn and his colleagues (1985) provide data about a group of art students. They examined students' identity development during their time in college, as well as collecting information about their personal, family and professional life in the 18 years since leaving college. Marital status 18 years later was related to identity status in college, but in different ways for men and women. For men, there was a strong relationship between identity status and staying single, with most of those scoring low on the identity scale in college reporting that they had never married. For women, there was no relationship between identity status and whether they had married or not, but there was a clear relationship between identity status and marital stability. Women who scored low on the identity scale were more likely to experience a divorce. Thus, it seems that having a clear sense of identity does have important implications for long-term relationships for both men and women, although the consequences are different for each sex. These findings highlight the importance of establishing a clear sense of identity during adolescence, before becoming involved in long-term close relationships.

Special problems of achieving identity in the late twentieth century

Are changes occurring in society and in the nuclear family making the task of identity formation in adolescence a more difficult one? Wearing (1985) suggests, for example, that Erikson's (1971) concept of identity achievement is really only applicable to white middle-class males, and not to women or to working-class youth. These latter groups do not have the luxury of tertiary education and the consequent long period that provides for working through identity issues. Wearing suggests that the identity of working-class males may be centred, not on a career but rather on 'mateship, sexual prowess and sporting achievement' (p.18). In addition, in a situation of high unemployment, putting the emphasis on work as a crucial aspect of the identity is likely to be counterproductive for many young people. The situation is further complicated by the fact that current economic circumstances also make a high degree of autonomy and independence from the parents difficult, if not impossible, to achieve. Moreover, the high level of change in today's society makes flexibility more important than stability. Wearing suggests that the tasks of adolescence may need to be redefined in line with the greater level of diffusion which may be adaptive in the 1980s and beyond.

Others also argue that societal changes are making life more difficult for adolescents and their families. Quinn, Newfield and Protinsky (1985), for example, focus particularly on the lack of 'rites of passage' for adolescents in contemporary culture. There is a related lack of consensus about when adolescence begins and ends and about the appropriate allocation of rights, privileges and responsibilities at different ages. This uncertainty prolongs the struggle for identity, leads to excessive demands to be treated like adults and to disruptions to the emotional development of many adolescents.

Another view (e.g. Newman & Murray, 1983), is that societal changes have made a strong sense of personal identity even more crucial to the adolescent. Because society's expectations about entry into adulthood have become more flexible (e.g. greater tolerance of singleness, childlessness, homosexuality, and different patterns of family and career), it becomes even more important for an individual to take responsibility for the course of his or her own life and the fulfilment of personal goals. Assuming such responsibility is easier for those with a strong and well-formed personal identity.

Effects of family environments on adolescent development

As we have already noted, family factors affect the development of autonomy and the adolescents' willingness to explore their identity. Families, however, differ in the extent to which they provide an environment which encourages this. Adolescents have to renegotiate relationships with parents towards more autonomy and freedom and less parental domination. Even this renegotiation of relationships is more difficult in some families than in others.

Writers like Newman and Murray (1983) see the parents' use of power in the family as a crucial determinant of the willingness of adolescents to be involved in identity exploration. The extent to which the parents use coercive power is particularly important (see Figure 1.2).

Figure 1.2 Effects of parenting style on adolescents

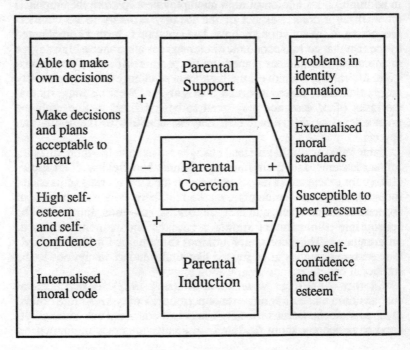

Adolescents whose parents are authoritarian and coercive in their relationships with them are (a) less likely to engage in exploring identity alternatives, (b) more likely to adopt external, rather than internalized moral standards, (c) likely to have lower self-confidence and self-esteem, and (d) likely to have problems in using their own judgment as a guide to behaviour. These adolescents are also likely to have problems with many aspects of autonomy because they will have a less developed sense of their own identity. These adolescents are generally less confident about their competence and more susceptible to peer pressure because they have learned to rely on external sources of approval and guidance.

Adolescents whose parents adopt an inductive, democratic style, on the other hand, are able to make their own decisions and formulate appropriate plans. Curiously though, these adolescents also make decisions and plans which are more satisfactory to their parents. They also seek the help and guidance of their parents. The paradox is that such democratic homes tend to produce adolescents who strongly identify with their parents and, in turn, have internalised their parents' rules and values.

Families influence the identity exploration of their adolescents by emphasising either the importance of autonomy and independence for individuals, or family togetherness, closeness and loyalty. In families where there is an emphasis on independence, there is more possibility of identity exploration, especially for females. (See Grotevant & Cooper, 1985.) Daughters are less likely to engage in identity exploration when they respect their mothers' views and are open and responsive to those views. It seems likely that these young girls would probably settle into the foreclosure status, adopting the views of their parents without exploring other alternatives. Sons explore their identities when they are open and responsive to their fathers' views and know that their fathers respect their opinions and attitudes. (See also Campbell, Adams & Dobson, 1984.)

Adolescents in different identity status groups have different relationships with their parents (Adams & Jones, 1983; Campbell, Adams & Dobson, 1984). Foreclosures seem to differ from identity diffusions in terms of their closeness to their parents. Foreclosures have the closest relationships with parents while those in the identity diffusions status tend to be distant from their families. These young people see their parents as indifferent to them, not understanding them and rejecting them.

Conflict is more characteristic of the families of adolescents in the moratorium and identity achievement groups. These young people tend to criticise their parents. Tensions betwen the parents and adolescents seem to be mainly about the young person's attempts at individuation.

Parents struggle with letting their adolescents be autonomous and independent. A balance between closeness to parents and a sense of autonomy seems to be important for healthy adolescent development. It also seems clear that achieving a stable identity is likely to involve at least some conflict with parents.

Adolescents who are encouraged to be assertive and to adopt their own points of view (Hauser *et al.*, 1984) also tend to have higher levels of ego development. These adolescents, however, still want the love and support of their parents, even while striving for goals like individuation and autonomy. As adolescents negotiate with parents and the family environment changes, parents come to show greater respect for the opinions of the growing adolescents. Certainly, older adolescents seem to change their relationships with their parents, developing interactions which involve less conflict and more control (Jacob, 1974; Steinberg & Hill, 1978) .

What happens when adolescents fail to negotiate these new relationships? Where these negotiations fail, and parents are highly critical and rejecting, the adolescents involved are likely to adopt a negative identity (Harris & Howard, 1984). They try to get their parents' attention or to punish them through behaving badly. Sadly, beneath the defiance is growing depression caused by their internalising the rejection of their parents.

The message is that families which best promote adolescent identity exploration and adjustment also emphasise both individuality and connectedness. Parents and adolescents work together at redefining the parent–adolescent relationship as a more mutual and equal one. The adolescent does not necessarily have to leave the relationship, or break away from it. It is the balance between closeness in the family, and the encouragement of individuality and autonomy that becomes the crucial factor (Campbell, Adams & Dobson, 1984; Cooper, Grotevant & Condon, 1984).

While some results are strong, any conclusions about the variables that most affect identity formation can only be tentative, on account of a range of methodological and conceptual factors. Even if the family members' reports could be assumed to be accurate, it is unwise to conclude that certain family variables are the cause of adolescents' problems. For example, effects may be attributable to the type of behaviour adolescents elicit from their parents, rather than caused directly by what the parents do to the adolescents. It is far easier to provide a supportive, child-centred environment when children identify strongly with parents and follow family traditions without question. Parents may have difficulty responding to adolescents at particular stages of development. It is clear that many of the studies of adolescents lack both a longitudinal and a bidirectional perspective. That is, they fail to take into account that children have effects on parents, as well as parents having effects on children.

The effects of family disruption on adolescent development

In this volume we devote a full chapter to the impact of divorce on adolescents. In the general community it is widely accepted that young people from broken homes have more identity-related problems than other children. Research findings, however, are more mixed than is generally realised. Oshman and Manosevitz (1976) found significantly lower scores on a scale measuring identity for those experiencing father absence from about ten years of age onwards. Jordan (1970) found that college males with identity-related problems were more likely to come from broken homes. Others report conflicting findings. As we have already noted, a combination of emotional attachment to parents and the encouragement of independence by parents seems to be associated with healthy identity development in adolescence. Maintaining close emotional attachment and the security associated with it may be more difficult for parents in families which have experienced a divorce or separation. Single parents may also have problems allowing their adolescents the autonomy they need, particularly where they have invested in their child or children the emotional attachment that would normally belong to the spouse.

There is also evidence for increased problems for adolescents in stepfamilies (Garbarino, Sebes & Schellenbach, 1984). There are several explanations for this finding. One possibility is that the adolescent or the family is still suffering damage from the earlier crisis of divorce. For example, they may have felt rejected by the parent who left the family, or be angry with their natural parents for not being able to sort out their differences. Another possibility is that step-parents have a lower genetic investment than parents, and that the adolescent is somehow conscious of this lower investment and reacts to it. However, we will address the consequences of such rejection in other parts of the book.

Family variables and adolescent adjustment

What helps or hinders an adolescent's ability to deal with the stresses associated with this period of their lives? In general, adolescents are better adjusted when the family is seen as cohesive, expressive and organised and independence is encouraged (Moos & Moos, 1981a & b). On the other hand, they tend to be less well adjusted when they see their family as high in conflict and very controlling (Burt, Cohen & Bjorck, 1988).

19

Some theorists argue that the stresses related to adolescence arise from the adolescents' lack of interpersonal skills to cope with all the changes necessary to move toward greater independence and autonomy (Hartup, 1979; Montemayor, 1983). On the other hand, in supportive families, they are likely to develop better social and coping skills and more positive identities (Cooper *et al.*, 1982). Where parents consistently demonstrate good coping and problem-solving skills, and encourage the adolescents to solve their own problems, adolescents are likely to cope much better, be more confident about their ability to cope and consequently have higher self-esteem. In these circumstances, they are more likely to develop a positive cycle, involving growing confidence, rather than a negative cycle of rebellion or depression.

Methodological issues in studying adolescents

As we shall see, in trying to understand adolescents and their families, researchers have asked a wide range of questions about the experiences of adolescents, about their families, and about the type of communication and relationships in these families. A central finding has been that different types of family environments have different impacts on adolescent development. Our task here is to describe the range of possible measures, highlighting both their advantages and limitations. In our view, there is no best method for studying adolescents. However, we do favour methods that provide a multiple perspective on the family, gaining data from each family member.

Choosing the appropriate method

A large number of methodologies are used in studying adolescents and their families. The choice of an appropriate method depends on the research question. The method should also suit the particular population being studied (e.g. social class). Researchers should also consider who are the appropriate informants (adolescents, parents or both) and whether they are primarily interested in insider or outsider views of the family. The best methods also gain the cooperation of family members, using research tasks that are likely to get all family members involved.

While there is a tendency for observational methods to be preferred to self-report methods, it is difficult to argue that one method is clearly more valid than the other. There is no doubt that self-report methods have problems because of their reliance on the subjects' awareness of emotional reactions and attitudes, and the subjects' willingness to report those reactions accurately. Observational methods, on the other hand, suffer from problems of ecological validity. Can we really be sure that the behaviours observed in a five- or ten-minute staged interaction are the behaviours we would see if we could be 'flies on the wall' in actual interactions? The problems of observational studies are at least as serious as those of self-report studies. We are not, by any means, arguing that such research is not useful, but researchers have to do the best they can and then recognise the limitations and weaknesses of their methods.

The crucial issue in deciding on a method is the research question. For example, if a researcher is interested in the processes families of adolescents use in making decisions, then an observational study is probably the most appropriate. Families can be videotaped while performing a decision-making task (such as planning a holiday) and these videotapes can then be coded to examine the decision-making processes. Family members are unlikely to be able to report accurately on such processes. On the other hand, if the research question concerns the patterns of communication in the family – for example, who usually talks to whom about what – the answer will not be found in a five-minute videotaped interaction. A self-report questionnaire involving questions about the frequency of conversations between family members on various topics is the way to answer such a question. Alternatively, family members could be asked to keep diaries of their conversations (Dickson-Markman & Markman, 1988) or they could be rung each night and asked to provide a list of the conversations they have had during the previous 24-hour period (e.g. Montemayor & Hanson, 1985). These latter methods are probably less susceptible to distortions of perception and memory than self-report inventories, but it may be necessary to collect data across a fairly large span of time to ensure that they are typical.

Choosing a method suitable for a particular population

One of the problems with many psychological instruments is that they deal with concepts more familiar to the middle class, and use language more applicable to the middle class. Hence, self-report instruments may be quite appropriate for studies involving middle-class adolescents in colleges or universities, but inappropriate for working-class adolescents or for adolescents with learning difficulties or emotional problems. Researchers should ensure that their instruments are appropriate to their population through extensive piloting of instruments, so that concepts not understood can be explained further, words not readily understood can be changed and the length of the instrument can be adjusted to suit.

Researchers can also help subjects who are not fluent readers by sitting with them and by reading the items aloud, if that is needed. Subjects are unlikely to give their best responses if much of their energy is going into reading the items. Telephone methods or interviews may be more appropriate where reading is likely to be a problem for some subjects.

Who should be the informants?

Researchers also need to consider whose perspective on the family they want. The parents' perspective? The adolescents' perspective? Do they want to compare several perspectives? Some studies have gathered information from various family members and then compared the findings.

Garbarino, Sebes and Schellenbach (1984) compared parents' and adolescents' reports of abuse in the family. They used the Adolescent Abuse Inventory (Sebes, 1983), a 26-item self-report measure designed to assess parental attitudes towards maltreatment. This instrument also assesses the likelihood that parents would act abusively in response to provocative behaviours on the part of their adolescents. Parental behaviours were selected from four categories: 'hands-on' abuse (physical and sexual), 'hands-off' abuse (verbal or psychological), neglect, and 'appropriate parenting behaviours'. Each item contains a vignette of problematic adolescent behaviour and a probable parental response. Parents were then asked three questions: how often their adolescent had behaved similarly in the past year, how they would rate the parent's behaviour (from very bad to very good) and how likely they would be to respond in the same way as the parent in the vignette. Sebes (1983) reports that adolescents classifications of the family as abusive or not, were very strongly related to parents' responses on the Adolescent Abuse Inventory. Garbarino *et al.* (1984) also found that adolescent reports of the family were more valid than parental reports.

In our own research (Callan & Noller, 1986; Noller & Bagi, 1985; Noller & Callan, 1986; 1988) we have also compared reports by various family members as well as other families and objective raters. We have found a general tendency for adolescents to rate the family more negatively than other family members whether responding to a self-report inventory (FACES II) or making ratings of family members from videotaped interactions. We have explained this in terms of the generational stake hypothesis. (See Chapter 2.) Parents, who have a large investment in their children, are likely to have a stake in seeing the family positively. Adolescents, on the other hand, who are beginning to distance themselves from the family, are likely to be more negative in their evaluations. Each generation seems to view family interaction in terms of its own particular bias. In addition, adolescents' ratings of their families are more highly correlated with those of outsiders than are ratings made by their parents (Noller & Callan, 1988).

Insider versus outsider views of the family

Related to the issue of who are the best informants is the question of whether insider or outsider views of the family and family processes should be obtained. This issue is also discussed extensively elsewhere (Huston & Robins, 1982; Noller & Guthrie, in press) and will be dealt with only briefly here. An important point is that the insider and outsider views of the family are highly likely to be different, and do not answer the same questions. If family members are asked to make ratings of their own interactions on a videotape, they will make those ratings in the context of a whole history of relationships with family members. On the other hand, when outsiders make ratings of family members on videotapes, the only context they have for making those ratings is what is happening on the videotape in front of them. How can we expect these two sets of ratings to be similar, and how can we expect to check the validity of family members' reports by using outsiders? If we are interested in family members' views of one another, then those are the data we should collect. If we are interested in outsiders' views of family members, then those are the data we should collect. The relationship between the two sets of ratings is an interesting and important empirical question, but is not a validity question. Both sets of data will give us a more complete picture of the behaviour in which we are interested.

Choosing a task

A final issue concerns the choice of a task in studies of adolescents and their families. Such tasks should encourage adolescent involvement, since the adolescents are likely to be even more anxious and self-conscious than their parents. In addition, the decision to participate is likely to be made by the parents, and the researcher needs to obtain the support of the adolescent. It may be very important for the researcher to show a real interest in the adolescents and their attitudes, opinions and issues, if they want to get the best response from these young people.

Summary

This book is about adolescents and their families. We have argued that adolescents do not break free from their families but rather negotiate new roles and relationships which are more equal and more mutual. How well the adolescent negotiates these new relationships and accomplishes the important tasks of adolescence depends on the characteristics of the family. As family theorists have argued, healthy adolescent development is most likely to occur in families where the encouragement of autonomy is high, control is flexible, and is balanced by support and acceptance from parents and other family members. While adolescents strive for independence, they also need the love and support of their parents. We have also focused on the four important developmental tasks which the adolescent must accomplish: emancipation from parents, psychosexual differentiation, acquiring the skills necessary for future economic independence and establishing career goals, and identity exploration and achievement. We have seen that for various reasons, these tasks have become more difficult and more complex over time. We have also considered the role of the family in identity formation and looked at the type of family environment which is conducive to identity achievement on the part of adolescents. As would be expected, families which encourage both closeness and individual autonomy seem to be the ones that best provide this environment.

In addition, we have also considered some of the methodologies used in studying the families of adolescents. We have reviewed briefly some important issues, including which methodologies are important for which research questions, who are the appropriate informants, whether outsider or insider ratings are more appropriate and issues to be considered when selecting tasks. Our belief is that all methodologies have various advantages and disadvantages, and one's choice of methodology depends on the research question being explored. Research on adolescents and the family has involved a variety of methodologies which have been used in exploring complex relationships.

The rest of this volume involves taking up some of these issues in more detail. In Chapter 2, we examine the changing relationships between parents and their adolescents, and consider the popular notion of the 'generation gap'. In Chapter 3, we discuss family communication, particularly asking about the style of communication in families which best contributes to healthy adolescent development. In Chapter 4, we will examine, in more detail than here, various aspects of family environments and the impact of different types of environments on the growing adolescent. Autonomy and control, closeness and intimacy, punishment and violence, sex-role socialisation, attitudes to achievement and creativity, marital discord and stability and the family's relationships with the outside world of school and work are all considered. In Chapter 5, we follow the adolescent leaving home, seeking a job or getting married. Our focus is on the range of factors behind leaving home, and the adolescents' relationships with their parents after they have left the family home. In Chapter 6, we consider the special case of family disruption that occurs when parents divorce. For adolescents, there is the shared trauma with their parents, anger and shame and their need to establish new roles and relationships with their own parents and possible step-parents. Finally, in Chapter 7, we consider the common problems of adolescence such as smoking, drug and alcohol abuse and teenage pregnancy, especially the link between these behaviours and a lack of family support. Once again, we show that adolescents who are less likely to engage in various problem behaviours come from families which encourage autonomy, provide them with love and support and use flexible control. Such adolescents value their parents above their peers. Finally we sketch out some helpful hints for parents struggling with their adolescents over these and other issues.

Chapter two

The generation gap

If you ask parents to explain the cause of many of the problems they are having with their adolescents, quite often they blame 'the generation gap'. While parents probably mean somewhat different things when they refer to the gap, it is often about differences in the attitudes of parents and adolescents. Parents and adolescents either fail to talk to each other about these differences, or the differences come to a head when the adolescent does something that parents are quite unhappy about.

As we can have attitudes about almost anything, there is a strong likelihood that even the closest parent and adolescent will have differences of opinion. The more well-recognised differences are in attitudes about dress, appearance, friendships, responsibilities and money. Many issues may seem trivial, but to many adolescents getting their own way in such areas is very important to them, and reflects their need to be seen as mature and independent.

We feel that it is important to look at the generation gap because it is used so often by parents and adolescents to explain why they are not getting on with each other. We are especially interested in examining the size of the generation gap and the factors that have brought it about, or which have made families immediately fall back on the gap as a seemingly acceptable explanation for unhappy relationships between parents and their children. The problem is that the idea of a gap may become too easy an explanation, so that the real cause of the problem is never dealt with. The generation gap is also often seen as beyond change, with many parents deciding to suffer with these problems until the adolescent becomes older and wiser.

There are other reasons why we need to investigate the generation gap. Towards understanding the relationship between adolescents and their families, many family therapists are increasingly turning their attention to getting the attitudes not only of the adolescents, but also of their parents and others inside or outside the family. In helping disturbed adolescents and their families, family therapists once only focused their attention on the adolescent. However, the acceptance of more systemic approaches to family therapy now means that professional counselling often involves some contact with most members of the family. Similarly, in an attempt to achieve a better understanding of the families, researchers are also seeking out the perceptions and attitudes of parents, adolescents, siblings and outsiders. Like family therapists, they recognise the need to consider the views of different members of the family.

Within more systemic models of the family, therapists are interested in each family member's perception of the problem, its causes, the nature of family functioning and relationships within the family. A major focus is the ability of the family system to change in order to deal with the problems of the adolescent, their needs and feelings. Generally, it is not too difficult to gain the perceptions of all family members, and important outsiders (e.g. teachers). One result is a wider set of attitudes about the organisation of the family, levels of communication, and the emotional bonds between adolescents, parents and others. Information also emerges about the ability of the family to deal with stresses related to developmental and situational strains upon its members.

A systemic approach, however, typically reveals a range of attitudes about the family. Many attitudes may overlap, but others can diverge quite considerably. For instance, although they belong to the same family, mothers, fathers, adolescents and other children have individual needs, likes and dislikes, and their own insider view of what it is like to be in the family. While the opinions of family members can be quite similar (see Jessop's (1981) review), each individual has views which may be at odds with other members of the family.

These differences are often attributed to a generation gap. Also the common belief is that reducing the gap solves the problem. For the family researcher, the existence of low levels of agreement between family members raises many possible explanations, only one of which is the generation gap. In this chapter we focus especially on the range of theoretical and methodological issues that may explain why the generation gap is presumed to exist. Due to many factors we argue that the gap is not as large as generally believed.

In assessing an adolescent's behavioural or emotional problem, agreement among family members about the problem is one way of checking the nature of the problem. For example, if parents and adolescents agree that the problem is related to the teenager's attitudes towards his stepfather, the family therapist can use this as a starting point, or even accept it as an objective point of view. What if opinions differ, and parents and adolescents blame quite separate issues, or see conflicts and arguments very differently? If opinions differ, you might assume that one family member is more objective than others. If this approach is taken, it probably comes down to a rule of majority-wins or the views of more powerful figures in the family (fathers and mothers) are believed more than those of the adolescent. Ultimately, as Beavers (1976) argues, most family therapists should expect differences in the opinions of family members, as differences in attitudes and perceptions are expressions of individuality which are characteristic of healthy, normal families. However, often we seem to forget this positive side of family disagreements.

Issues like objectivity, the generation gap and the validity of the reports of different members of the family are old ones in discussions about family life. These issues are taken up here because of our interest in adolescents and their relationships with their families. Very often families blame their problems on the existence of a generation gap. Families may sometimes too readily attribute their problems to some form of generation gap, and its use has probably got a little out of control.

The apparent size of the generation gap poses somewhat of a challenge to the role of parents as primary socialisers of children (see Tedin, 1974; Goodnow, 1985). If parents are the major socialisers, why then do adolescents show such dissimilar attitudes to those of their parents? More similarity in the attitudes of parents and adolescents would suggest some reciprocal flow of influence. Not only do parents influence their children, but adolescents also socialise their parents. They encourage them to adopt new opinions and attitudes. However, the apparent lack of similarity in the attitudes of parents and adolescents implies that they do not influence each other as much as argued in theories of socialisation and social learning.

Explaining the generation gap

Theories of adolescent development provide varying predictions about the extent to which parents and adolescents should have similar attitudes or make similar evaluations of family life. Theories describing adolescence as a period of tremendous turmoil, personal doubt and chaos in the family would predict considerable differences in the attitudes of adolescents and parents (see Chapter 1). It can be argued that these predictions are generally supported. There are low levels of parent–adolescent agreement on a wide variety of topics (see reviews by Niemi, 1968; Jessop, 1981). As would be expected, agreement is especially low on threatening topics and conflict-laden ones (e.g. attitudes to use of alcohol and other drugs, rules in the home). Similarly, within his theoretical writings, Erikson (1959) argues for the existence of differences in what the adolescent sees as his or her attitudes, and their parents' attitudes, because of a need to establish their own sense of ego identity.

Other theorists argue that adolescence involves a period of re-negotiation and a gradual change in the parent–adolescent relationship (see Chapter 1). Rather than completely separating from parents, and being under the total influence of peers, adolescents seek disengagement but still maintain a close working relationship with parents. Rather than adversaries separated from each other by an ever-widening generation gap, parents are still a major source of support. A lot of the evidence for the generation gap comes from studies of the attitudes of parents and adolescents. Several studies of the actual attitudes of parents and adolescents show that parents and adolescents may differ in their attitudes on 50 to 80 per cent of attitude items (e.g. about authority, drugs, work, school, dress, sex, war, politics). However, the most important point is that differences are often minor. Although differences are statistically significant, they are small, and their attitudes are typically side by side on a continuum rather than at opposite ends on various attitude scales (e.g. Lerner, Pendorf & Emery, 1971; Lerner, Karson, Meisels & Knapp, 1975).

Within the more recent theories of adolescence, the differences between parents and adolescents would tend to be explained by changes in the parent–adolescent relationship that allows the maturing adolescent to be more in control, and to be assertively independent (Olson, McCubbin, Barnes, Larsen, Muxen & Wilson, 1983). The fact that differences occur is not the critical issue. Rather, within the normal family, discussions of such differences in opinion are necessary for the development of self-esteem and stronger ego development among adolescents. Adolescents with higher levels of ego development come from families where different perspectives are shared, but where they are also challenged by their parents within a supportive family climate that encourages them to be curious (Grotevant & Cooper, 1986; Powers *et al.*, 1983). It is not the fact that differences exist that is critical to adolescent development, but rather how accepting parents are of these differences. Put another way, it may be that it is parents' willingness to accept, as well as to discuss and analyse the existence of a generation gap, that impacts on the adolescent's level of competence and ego identity.

Our task in the rest of this chapter is to examine various theoretical and methodological reasons that may explain the poor match between the attitudes of parents and their adolescents. It is clear that several factors are at work, but possibly the most widely researched explanation is the existence of different generational stakes.

The generational stake

In early reviews of parents' and adolescents' accounts of family life,

Niemi (1968, 1974) concluded that neither parents nor adolescents provide objectively accurate accounts of the lives of families. He believed that there was a small tendency for parents to overestimate the socially desirable features of families. In fact, Niemi argued that parents were more biased in their perceptions than adolescents, and adolescents were better reporters of what really was happening in the family. Adolescents were believed to be less biased because they have lower levels of emotional investment in their families. In contrast, children and building a happy family are major parts of the lives of parents. By the time children become teenagers, parents have devoted a dozen or more years to nurturing, guiding and caring for them.

Within societies that are pro-family and child-centred, every parent is encouraged to be proud of their children and their family. Being a responsible parent is a major part of the traditional male and female role, while being a good and successful parent is still central to the self-esteem of many adults. Therefore, when asked their attitudes about the amount of conflict in their family, parents may give more positive accounts than do their adolescents because they have a greater emotional investment in their families (Noller & Callan, 1986).

There are, however, other factors at work. Adolescents are attempting to alter their status as family members. Striving for more independence, they want more control and responsibility over decisions that directly affect them. The majority of them report that they feel close to their parents, and while they want to be more independent, they also expect a life-long close relationship with their parents (Maccoby & Martin, 1983; Pipp *et al.*, 1985). Indeed, both parents and adolescents judge their families as being close, and their perceptions about the levels of closeness in their families are much more similar than perceptions about most other issues (Callan & Noller, 1986; Richardson *et al.*, 1984). Nevertheless, having an adolescent is a stressful period for parents and families. Marital and family satisfaction, family pride and family cohesion tend to be low, and levels of family stress are high (see Chapter 1). While adolescents and parents do agree about the extent of closeness within the family, adolescents still rate these levels of closeness as being somewhat lower than do parents.

One explanation already offered is that parents have an emotional investment in their families that makes them adopt a more positive, biased view of family life. With adolescents, however, a number of factors may make them more negative about the family than parents. Wanting to be more independent, adolescents become less involved and less interested in the family (see Chapters 1 and 3). In doing so, adolescents also become more like outsiders and see the family from a different perspective. Interestingly, this sense of independence probably shows up in the perceptions that parents and adolescents have about expressions of power in the family. Parents and adolescents generally disagree on such power-related issues, both tending to perceive themselves as having more influence than the other thinks to be the case (Jessop, 1981).

Even early adolescents who are beginning to seek more independence seem to adopt this outsider perspective (see Callan & Noller, 1986). They are still very much insiders in that their interests and activities centre on the family, but they are also outsiders as they become more involved in activities with friends. As Jones and Nisbett (1971) note, the outside observer who is less involved in a situation can provide more accurate judgments than insider actors involved in the situation. Adolescents are outsiders with lower levels of investment in the family than their parents. From this different perspective, with less stake in the importance of feeling that they must live in a happy family, their perceptions differ from those of parents.

Bengtson and his colleagues (Bengtson & Kuypers, 1971; Bengtson & Troll, 1978) also make similar points. Each generation views family life in terms of its own bias or stake. They argue that adolescents are very involved in the development or creation of their own attitudes and ideologies. They are highly motivated to establish themselves as individuals in their own right, with their own values, lifestyles, needs and expectations. In contrast, at this time parents are very concerned about the investment they have in the validation of their values and strategies for coping with life. They want their adolescents to listen to them, and to accept their attitudes about life, and the strategies for dealing with various challenges and decisions. If adolescents accept their values and opinions, parents can then feel that their own attitudes are well-chosen and worth passing on.

Basic to the interpretation of a developmental or generational stake is that each generation misattributes attitudes to the other, but in quite opposite ways. Late adolescents exaggerate differences between their attitudes and those of their parents, while parents minimise differences. The true picture of the family, according to Bengtson and Troll, lies between the two extreme descriptions. Parents minimise differences because, as argued earlier, they have a large investment in their families. In addition, this minimisation strategy used by parents may be motivated by feelings of having less control over adolescents or by a recognition of their own mortality. That is, ageing parents, towards justifying their own actions, want their adolescents to carry on attitudes that have been important to them during their lives (i.e. 'generativity needs'). Some parents can have a tremendous stake in believing that their attitudes are also valued as much by their children.

As mentioned earlier, the attitudes of parents and adolescents do differ, but the size of the differences is often quite small. Another factor adding to such differences in attitudes is the openness of parents and adolescents to social influences and new ideas. Arguably, adolescents have a world view which is more in tune with changes that are currently occurring around them (Furstenberg, 1971). Like their parents before them, they love crazes and fads, and they want to keep up with the latest in clothes and expressions. However, even so, social change is slow enough that adolescents' attitudes are still fairly similar to their parents' and those of previous generations. As others have argued, there is a level of 'family continuity' in attitudes so that parents and adolescents, despite social change, still have quite similar attitudes on many topics (Bengtson & Troll, 1978).

Other explanations

There are other factors inherent in the methodologies used to study the generation gap which may have contributed to the size of the dissimilarity in the measured opinions of parents and adolescents. The threat and salience of the topic that researchers put before parents and adolescents seem to influence judgements. Jessop (1981) argues that agreement between parents and adolescents is lower for threatening topics. For example, there is low agreement in the extent to which parents and adolescents believe that family members talk to each other about drugs. As others have noted (e.g. Lerner *et al.*, 1975), it seems reasonable that some adolescents are reluctant to discuss issues like drugs and sexual behaviour with their parents. Levels of agreement in attitudes are lower because opinions about threatening topics like drugs and sex are not shared as much as they should be.

The sense of threat associated with a topic may also depend on how specific we are about the topic. For example, while adolescents and parents did not agree on the general topic of 'drugs' or 'talk about drugs', Jessop found that they did agree more about the existence of a rule about drugs in the family. That is, researchers may be over-estimating the size of the generation gap because they are being too general in their attitude measures. They are not being specific enough about the exact topic that they want parents and adolescents to consider.

Avoiding discussion of some topics may help parents and adolescents maintain low levels of conflict and good parent–adolescent relations (Jessop, 1981). We discuss this issue in more detail elsewhere (see Chapters 3 and 4). Even if a topic is important to them, adolescents may not discuss something with both parents, or one parent in particular, because they believe that the issue is threatening to the parent. The mismatch between parent–adolescent attitudes about what families talk about may arise in part from family members never actually hearing the opinions of others about such threatening topics.

Again, however, this factor is only one of several reasons why parents and adolescents may seem to have different views. Another factor may be the salience of the issue to parents. Cashmore (1983) found that parents and children were more likely to agree on topics that were more important to parents. For such important topics, adolescents were also likely to perceive their parents' opinions more accurately.

Further support for the significance of the salience of a topic is revealed in research into the socialisation of political attitudes. Compared with many other attitudes, there is often quite considerable agreement between parents and adolescents in their political attitudes, perhaps because individuals often feel strongly about political issues and are more likely to voice their opinions (Tedin, 1974). Politics is a major topic of debate almost every day in the mass media. It is quite likely that a parent who feels strongly about some political ideology would try through healthy debate to encourage others to consider his or her views. Ultimately they could influence the attitudes of other family members or at least it is likely that adolescents would learn about their parents' specific political opinions.

The importance of a parent's advocacy about an issue emerges in studies of educational goals and aspirations. Where fathers openly encourage children to pursue goals that are important to them, there is a stronger match between fathers' and childrens' attitudes about education even when mothers and fathers have different attitudes (Smith, 1982). However, as others have found (Bengtson & Troll, 1978), mothers do have more general influence in many areas, possibly due to the larger number of opportunities they have to interact with adolescents. Adolescents of all ages believe that compared with fathers, mothers talk more frequently to them, disclose more, and are more willing to listen to their point of view (see Chapter 3). This closeness to adolescents may explain why many mothers may be better judges than fathers of the attitudes of their adolescents.

Levels of actual and perceived agreement

In looking at the match between parent–adolescent attitudes, we need to distinguish between levels of actual and perceived agreement between parents and adolescents. Lerner and his colleagues (1975), for instance, even suggest that we need to consider generational gaps rather than a single generation gap. There is both a real gap, and secondly, a perceived generation gap.

It seems that both are important in determining the extent to which parents really do influence the attitudes and behaviour of adolescents. The real gap or the actual agreement between parents and adolescents is the match between the views of parents about their position, and the views of adolescents about their position. The perceived gap or perceived agreement, in contrast, is the match between adolescents' perceptions of their own and their parents' attitudes. The comparison of parents' and adolescents' real attitudes allows a test of the generation gap, as most people would see it. A high degree of similarity would suggest no real generation gap, but a poor match would suggest otherwise. The use of perceptions, however, adds another dimension to this test: does the generation gap only exist in the minds of adolescents and parents?

In addition, besides actual and perceived agreement, there is the accuracy of various perceptions: that is, the match between parents' responses for themselves, and the responses adolescents think their parents would make (Cashmore & Goodnow, 1985). It is possible to compare actual agreement, perceived agreement and the accuracy of perceptions towards better understanding the actual levels of agreement between adolescents and their parents. It is quite possible that different sets of factors influence the actual level of agreement between parents and adolescents (i.e. actual agreement), the match between the responses adolescents give for themselves and their parents (i.e. perceived agreement), and the match between parents' actual responses and what adolescents think their parents would say (i.e. accuracy of perception).

Adolescents' perceptions of the opinions of their parents may be influenced by various informational features in the communication between adolescents and their parents. Factors that may be significant include the importance of the issue to parents, the frequency with which they have expressed their attitudes to their adolescents about various issues, and the extent to which both parents present similar attitudes. For instance, when both parents have the same attitudes, adolescents do seem to be more likely to match their parents' attitudes and to perceive the opinions of their parents more accurately (see Jennings & Niemi, 1974; Cashmore, 1983).

Differences for mothers and fathers

Comparisons of actual attitudes generally support the view that mothers' and adolescents' attitudes about family life are more similar than those of fathers and adolescents. Again, while the match in parent–adolescent attitudes is at best low to moderate for both parents, adolescents and their mothers have more similar attitudes (see Demo, Small & Savin-Williams, 1987). Similarly, in their investigation of the attitudes of parents and adolescents, Campbell, Adams & Dobson (1984) found that the amount of shared variance was greater between adolescents and mothers (ranging from 9 to 24 per cent) than between the adolescents and fathers (ranging from 1 to 15 per cent). However, it seems that there are differences within attitudes. In the same study, attitudes about the level of affection shown in the family were more similar for mothers and adolescents than fathers and adolescents. But adolescents' perceptions about levels of independence in the family were closer to those of fathers than mothers. In other studies (e.g. Gecas & Schwalbe, 1986) in which parents and adolescents rate the levels of support, control and involvement in family life, again differences also emerge for mothers and fathers. Mothers' reports of their levels of involvement and support are higher than reports by adolescents. Fathers' ratings of their control over adolescents are higher than adolescents' reports. Again, the match between adolescents' and parents' attitudes are at best only low.

There are also differences in the similarity of mother–adolescent and father–adolescent attitudes about alcohol. Male and female adolescents have attitudes about alcohol that are much more similar to the attitudes of their fathers than their mothers (Wilks & Callan, 1984). Probably because males drink more often, fathers are major models for adolescents as they establish their own attitudes to beer, wine and spirits, and develop their own preferences and drinking habits. There is also a generational difference at work here. Compared with their mothers, daughters are more likely to perceive the use of alcohol as an acceptable feature of the female role. Adolescent females, like young males, see alcohol as helping them have more fun, especially with their friends. The attitudes of their mothers are seen by many daughters as too traditional and conservative. The use of alcohol by young women is also another expression of their independence and autonomy, as well as a statement about the changes that are occurring in social norms about what is acceptable behaviour for young women.

The role of communication

It is often claimed that a lack of communication between parents and adolescents is basic to the generation gap. The gap is there because parents and adolescents don't talk enough to each other. There is some support for this view. Poor communication is often the basis of conflict and a lack of closeness in families, especially when parents don't value the opinions of their adolescents. Yet, as we have discussed here and elsewhere (Chapter 3), supportive communication in families is one factor that encourages better social and coping skills among adolescents. Supportive communication leads to more positive identities.

There are also clear differences which show mothers to be more open, understanding and accepting, and more able to negotiate agreements with their adolescents (see Chapter 3). Fathers clearly have a

35

more limited style of communication. It is likely that this better communicative relationship between mothers and adolescents is the reason that the attitudes of mothers are more related to the attitudes of their adolescents than are those of their fathers (Acock & Bengtson, 1980).

The same may be true of mothers being slightly better at predicting the attitudes of their daughters than are fathers (Thompson, Acock & Clark, 1985). We found that daughters believe that they disclose more to mothers, talk more often to them and they are more satisfied with the nature of their conversations with mothers than fathers (Noller & Callan, in press). However, the mismatch between parent–adolescent attitudes is no less for parents who believe that they have good rather than poor levels of communication with their adolescents (Thompson *et al.*, 1985).

It is quite possible that many of the topics researchers assume are talked about in families are not discussed at all. Furstenberg (1971) raised this issue many years ago when he suggested that we need to consider differences in the socioeconomic status of families, arguing for class differences in the extent to which parents make their opinions known to their children. A wide range of topics may need to be canvassed to gain an understanding of the nature of communication, but in several studies (e.g. Acock & Bengtson, 1980) lists of topics include very unusual ones that were initially canvassed for purposes other than testing the similarity of the attitudes of parents and their adolescents, and the nature of socialisation in families (e.g. attitudes include one's duty to work; whether the USA should be ready to answer any challenge to its power; that the government should not interfere with business). Researchers then argue that the low correspondence between parents and adolescents on these 'important' issues is significant, and highlights a generation gap. Parents and adolescents, however, may be only guessing as the issues are too general, not very important to them, and thus are not often raised in family conversations. While researchers may believe that these topics are important to parents and adolescents, they rarely test this assumption by asking parents and adolescents to rate the importance of the topic or the extent to which it is talked about in the family. This could easily be done in pilot studies.

Some misrepresentation by parents to adolescents of their real opinions could be another explanation for the lack of success that adolescents have in accurately describing the attitudes of parents. For example, most parents want their children to do well at school. They may want their adolescents to think that they believe in the need to study hard all the time so that they will not feel that they have let them down by encouraging poor attitudes to study. They may also present rather conservative attitudes about the value of education, and the importance of religion and institutional power in the hope that their children will not be influenced by disruptive, radical influences in society. Many parents see themselves as providing a stabilising force that allows adolescents to stay on the straight and narrow. Parents feel that giving information about conventional issues is an area of authority that they should have over adolescents (Smetana, 1988). As Acock and Bengtson (1980) conclude: 'Caution, and the presentation of traditional attitudes, may be the implicit socialisation agenda for many parents . . .' (p.512).

Finally, some adolescents may just continue to fail to get the message about what their parents think. Maybe the problem is in the parents' efforts to communicate their attitudes because of the difficulty in explaining accurately to anyone the beliefs and feelings associated with one's attitudes. Even when they discover, after a fight, what are their parents' attitudes or that their parents' attitudes are not the same as their own, perceptions of similarity in attitudes may be difficult to change. 'One-off' conflicts over some issue may be insufficient to alert adolescents to what their parents really think. It may only be on issues where there is frequent conflict that adolescents finally get the message.

Implications of the generation gap

The family plays a major role in the socialisation of children and adolescents. We believe that parents influence children as role models, while also using their position of authority to shape the attitudes of adolescents. However, if parents are important socialisers of their children, we should expect to find more similarity in the attitudes of parents and adolescents than appears to be the case. The lack of similarity between parent–adolescent attitudes also challenges the arguments about the existence of a type of 'reverse socialisation'. That is, a better match between the attitudes of parents and adolescents would point to the possible influence that adolescents have in shaping the attitudes of their parents.

The general lack of correspondence between parents' and adolescents' attitudes challenges arguments about the role of parents as primary socialisers. However, the higher levels of agreement between adolescents' perceptions of what parents think and parents' attitudes suggests that socialisation influences are at work. It is not what parents think, but what adolescents think they think, that best predicts adolescents' own attitudes. The opinions adolescents attribute to their parents are strong predictors of adolescents' own attitudes. The actual opinions of parents might have little influence on the socialisation of adolescents, when compared with the influence of adolescents' perceptions of what they believe their parents think or do. Thus, socialisation theories may need to consider attributions and perceptions much more than before towards understanding any intergenerational transmission of values and attitudes.

Nevertheless, we have attempted to consider several factors that could contribute to the apparent mismatch between parents and adolescents in their own positions and attitudes. Table 2.1 presents a typology of these factors in terms of the different needs, perceptions and emotional investments of parents and adolescents. As this suggests, there are many psychological and generational issues, as well as the methodological problems outlined earlier in the existing research, that may have contributed to the fairly low reported correspondence between parents' and adolescents' attitudes on a wide range of topics.

Table 2.1 Factors related to the size of the generation gap

Type of factor	Parents	Adolescents
Needs	Generativity needs	Needs for independence
	Need to see that time put into family has led to positive outcomes	Need to keep up with fads and crazes
Perceptions	Have status and independence	Want status and independence
	Family compares well to other families	Family compares poorly to other families
	Overestimate positive aspects of families	Underestimate positive aspects of families
	Adopt an insider perspective	Adopt an outsider perspective
Emotions	Considerable emotional investment in families	Less emotional investment in families
	Feel less in control of their adolescents	Feel more in control of their lives
Methodological problems	Specificity of attitudes	Specificity of attitudes
	Level of threat	Level of threat
	Real or perceived attitudes	Real of perceived attitudes

In particular, as frequently argued, the generation gap may be largely due to the different experiences and vested interests of parents and adolescents. Both parents and adolescents may have a 'generational stake'. Parents need to see the family and relationships between family members as better than they really are since they have an emotional investment which may not encourage a hard-nosed objective account of the relationships between family members. It is less of a challenge to the self-esteem of adolescents to be critical of their families. In addition, their needs for independence probably further encourage more negative attitudes about the family.

We have also argued that the size of the generation gap, as evidenced by the low levels of similarity between the attitudes of adolescents and parents, may be caused in part by methodological problems. There are differences in the importance of topics to parents and adolescents, and differences in how much parents may express certain attitudes in front of their adolescents. Also parents are very likely to differ in the importance they place in adolescents adopting their opinions.

There are many issues that need to be examined in future research before we can fully understand the extent to which parents do influence the types of attitudes adopted by adolescents. Longitudinal studies would allow us to better understand any two-way process of social influence between parents and their adolescents. The untangling of these effects is definitely being helped by a greater recognition of the two types of generation gaps – not only at the level of actual agreement between parents and adolescents, but also the perceived level of agreement and the accuracy of perceptions. More research needs to gain actual opinions of adolescents and their perceptions of their parents' attitudes, plus their parents' actual attitudes and their perceptions of their adolescents' attitudes. There is a need for a wider range of specific attitudes to be examined. Parents and adolescents should provide ratings of the frequency that topics are discussed, and the importance of topics to them and their perceptions of their importance to other members of the family. As realised some time ago in studies of the relationship between attitudes and behaviour, greater attention must be given to measuring specific attitudes rather than the very general ones tapped so far. We also need to stop using second-hand data about the general attitudes of parents and adolescents which were obtained by investigators to answer very different research questions.

Rather than global ratings of whether parents and adolescents talk about an issue, we need to obtain more specific evaluations of the quality and levels of affect that are present in parent–adolescent communication. Ratings of the certainty that one's perceptions were accurate would add another dimension, as would more attention to differences between families (e.g. by social class, age and sex of adolescents, marital happiness of parents). We need to use more reliable measures to examine individual differences between family members in levels of closeness and adaptability. In exploring the impact of these variables, it is also possible that the effects may be dependent on whether we are looking at actual agreement or perceived agreement and on the accuracy of the perceptions of parents and adolescents.

In summary, research into the similarity of parent–adolescent opinions has generally supported the widely-held view of a generation gap. These differences in attitudes are seen to be at the centre of many conflicts between parents and adolescents, and adolescents and other figures of authority in our society. There is some match in the actual attitudes of parents and their adolescents, but as most studies reveal, the match is low to moderate rather than high. Importantly, levels of parent–adolescent concordance are nowhere near the levels that would be predicted if we believe that parents are major socialisers of the attitudes of their children. However, if we are to seriously examine the extent of the so-called generation gap, it is time researchers adopted more care in the methods they use. Also, theoretically they need to recognise two types of generation gaps, and that different factors may be influencing levels of correspondence between parents and adolescents on actual attitudes, perceived attitudes, as well as the accuracy of their perceptions.

Chapter three

Communication in families with adolescents

Communication is a crucial aspect of family life, affecting the quality of the relationship between the parents and the healthy functioning of both individual family members and the family as a whole. In particular, supportive communication in the family encourages the development of more positive identities among adolescents and higher levels of social and coping skills.

As Barnes and Olson (1985) showed, families with better parent–adolescent communication are more close and loving. They have a more flexible approach to solving family problems, and are more satisfied than families where parent–adolescent communication is poor. There is an intriguing paradox, however, in family functioning and adolescent development. Democratic parenting, where parents and children communicate and negotiate, seems to foster a sense of independence in the adolescent, and at the same time increases the bonds of affection and closeness between parents and children. Thus, families where there is positive communication between parents and children are most likely to produce adolescents who can stand on their own feet, and who function very effectively as independent adults.

Communication is important in all aspects of family life, and it is important that family members share their thoughts, feelings and attitudes. For example, disclosure of likes and dislikes about food and clothing, vacation activities and other issues are important. Adolescents who are unable to disclose these thoughts to parents can become frustrated and unhappy.

Too often family members are unwilling to share their true feelings with each other. As a consequence they may feel resentful because their feelings are not being taken into account. Adolescents can be particularly unwilling to share their feelings and parents often don't encourage their disclosures. When adolescents do share, parents may also be unwilling to understand and accept the adolescent's needs and attitudes. The problem is that when adolescents are not consulted or their wishes are ignored, they find other ways of sabotaging family life and creating problems for the rest of the family.

Sex differences in communication in the family

There are clear differences between adolescent males and females in the nature of their communication with parents. Communication with mothers is also different from that with fathers. Daughters communicate more with parents than sons, and adolescents talk more with their mothers across a wider range of topics than they do with their fathers. There is also evidence that communication with mothers is generally viewed more positively by adolescents, despite the fact that they also report more conflict with their mothers than their fathers.

Youniss and Smollar (1985) studied adolescents aged 15 to 18. They asked about six different areas: school–career, societal views, intra-family issues, friendship, sex and marriage, doubts and fears. They were interested in differences between families in how well they communicate with each other. For example, how open and understanding are parents and adolescents of each other's points of view? To what extent do they tend to be guarded or cautious in what they say to one another? How do they deal with disagreements, and are such disagreements generally settled to the satisfaction of both parents and adolescents? To what extent do parents impose (or try to impose) their solutions on the adolescents?

What emerged is that male and female teenagers have quite different views of their communication with each parent. Daughters, in particular, report stronger relationships with mothers than fathers. Mothers are seen as more open, understanding and accepting. They are interested in the day-to-day problems of their teenagers, and they are better at negotiating agreements with their children. Fathers, on the other hand, are seen as more judgmental, less willing to be involved in important discussions of feelings, self-doubts and problems. In addition, fathers are seen as more likely to try to impose their authority on the adolescents. Adolescents claim that they are more likely, as a result, to limit their communication with fathers, and to become more defensive and guarded towards them. Even males who are identified with their fathers generally believe that their mothers understand them better emotionally (Offer, 1969).

In two studies, we have also followed up these findings, and have expanded them in several areas. In our first study (Noller & Bagi, 1985) we examined differences in communication between parents and adolescents who attended university. Communication was assessed across 14 topic areas (e.g. sex roles, relationships, sexual information, politics, future plans). Since we were also interested in *how* families communicate, we also assessed communication across six process dimensions. These included the frequency of conversations about the topic, the extent to which the adolescent disclosed their real feelings, the extent to which the parents recognised and accepted the adolescent's disclosures, who initiated the conversations, who tended to dominate and how satisfied the adolescent was with their interactions with each parent. The only dimensions where there were clear differences related to sex of parent and sex of adolescent were the frequency of conversations and the extent to which the adolescents disclosed their real feelings. In Table 3.1 are presented the mean ratings by the adolescents of their communication with mothers and fathers for the topics and dimensions where there were differences in their ratings of each parent.

Table 3.1 Adolescents' perceptions of communication with mothers and fathers

Topic	Mother	Father
Frequency		
Social issues	3.19	2.33
Interests	4.32	2.79
Sex-roles	3.03	2.01
Family sex-roles	2.59	1.98
Relationships	3.15	2.12
Sex attitudes	2.78	1.75
Politics	2.75	3.41
Sex information	1.93	1.36
Sex problems	1.54	1.21
General problems	4.15	3.24
Self-disclosure		
Interests	4.80	4.10
Sex-roles	4.10	3.50
Relationships	3.92	3.27
Sex information	3.42	2.45
Sex problems	3.32	2.32

Note: Ratings were on a 6-point scale from 1 = rarely discuss this to 6 = frequent long discussions; and 1 = have not disclosed any feelings to 6 = have disclosed all aspects of my views and feelings.

Daughters reported more frequent discussions with their mothers about sexual attitudes and relationships and more disclosure to her about interests, family sex-roles, their relationships with others, sexual information, sexual problems and general problems. Daughters not only disclosed more to their mothers than sons, but also more to their fathers, particularly about their attitudes to the rules in society, general problems and their own plans for the future. Adolescents talked more to mothers than fathers over nine of the fourteen areas. Results confirmed that in most families, mothers are quite active in communicating with their adolescents, but fathers are much less involved. In view of this finding, it was also not surprising that mothers were better than fathers at predicting their adolescents' responses to the questionnaire (Parent–Adolescent Communication Inventory, Noller & Bagi, 1985).

In a follow-up study, Noller & Callan (in press) obtained data using the same instrument from adolescents who ranged in age from 12 to 17 years. These younger adolescents, unlike the older adolescents discussed in the earlier study, saw their mothers as both initiating more discussions with them and recognising and accepting their opinions more than their fathers. In addition, females tended to be more satisfied with their interactions with mothers than fathers. Males were only moderately satisfied with their interactions with both parents. They didn't distinguish between mothers and fathers to the same extent as the females. Age differences were practically nonexistent, except between the younger adolescents and the student sample. These findings again support the view that adolescents, especially daughters, generally have more positive interactions with their mothers than their fathers throughout adolescence.

In other research (e.g. Barnes & Olson, 1985; Olson *et al.*, 1983) adolescents also report more openness in their communication with mothers than fathers. Also, mothers consistently describe their communication with their adolescents as more open than do fathers. Adolescents report few problems in communicating with each of their parents, and have about the same number of problems with mothers as with fathers. Mothers and fathers also report equal levels of problems in their communication with their adolescents. Incidentally, parents tended to report more problems than the adolescents.

There are also differences in the extent to which adolescent sons and daughters disclose to each parent. For example, Davidson and his associates (1980) found that females reveal more general and personal information, while males claim that they tell their parents more about their sexuality. Other work (e.g. Mulcahey, 1973; Sparks, 1976) shows that males disclose more about work and study, and attitudes and opinions; females disclose more about aspects of their personalities. As we also found, adolescents report that they disclose more to their mothers than their fathers (Jourard, 1971; Komarovsky, 1974). These findings fit with the adolescents' perceptions that their mothers understand them better and are more willing to recognise and accept their differing points of view.

The self-esteem of adolescents also affects their self-disclosure to their parents. Adolescents who are high in self-esteem, and believe that they are valued by other family members, are more likely to self-disclose than are those who feel vulnerable and insecure, having low self-esteem and believing that they are not valued or wanted.

In general, adolescents seem more negative about the communication in the family than do their parents. Adolescents report less openness and, sometimes, more problems than their parents (Barnes & Olson, 1985). Other writers have also found a tendency for adolescents to present a more negative view of the family than do their parents (Cooper & Ayers-Lopez, 1985; Niemi, 1968). These differences in ratings between parents and adolescents are likely to be the result of two kinds of perceptual biases (see Callan & Noller, 1986): the parents' needs to present the family in a good light, and the adolescents' needs to develop a separate identity and to distance themselves from their parents and from the family. (See also Chapter 2.)

Conflict in families with adolescents

As we have already indicated, one of the most frequently debated topics in the adolescent literature is the level of conflict between parents and adolescents. As Jurkovic and Ulrici (1985) note, the truth is likely to be somewhere between the two extreme positions,which either claim that adolescence always involves turmoil and stress or, alternatively, that most adolescents proceed calmly to adulthood with no problems. Some, like Jurkovic and Ulrici (1985), criticise the tendency in early research to assume that the high levels of intergenerational conflict found in clinical populations apply to all adolescents. On the other hand, they do not go as far as some theorists who assert that adolescent rebellion and the generation gap are mythical constructions (Offer, 1969). Rather, they comment:

> While we generally agree that tensions between the generations have clearly been exaggerated, closer inspection of the self-report and observational findings suggests that maturational changes in normal adolescents are coincident with increased familial conflict and rigidity. Difficulties in adaptation, however, are followed by an increasingly pleasant mode of adolescent–parent relating, marked in part by a greater balance of power.
>
> (Jurkovic & Ulrici 1985: 239)

There is evidence that adolescents do have more conflict with mothers than fathers. They also report that mothers understand them better and that they have more positive interactions with their mothers than with their fathers. Thus, the higher level of conflict with mothers is likely to be related to the fact that the adolescents tend to have more frequent and more meaningful communication with their mothers than with their fathers.

The majority of arguments between parents and adolescents seem to be about day-to-day living and relationships within the family: personal hygiene, disobedience, school work, social activities and friendships, chores around the house and conflicts with siblings (Caplow, Bahr, Chadwick, Hill & Williamson, 1982; Csikszentmihalyi & Larson, 1984; Montemayor, 1982; 1983). Interestingly, Montemayor (1983) even presents data to show that the arguments between parents and adolescents in the 1970s and 1980s are basically about the same topics that parents and adolescents argued about in the 1920s.

Conflicts between parents and their adolescents tend to be about minor matters like dress and social life (see review by Montemayor, 1983). For instance, Ellis-Schwabe and Thornburg (1986) found that the parent with whom the adolescents are most likely to be in conflict depends on the type of conflict. Adolescents argue with mothers about personal manners, choice of friends, and clothes. With fathers, they argue about money, use of leisure time and attitudes to school. Responsibilities within the home tend to be a source of conflict with both parents.

On the other hand, parents and adolescents tend not to argue about some topics of greatest difference between them such as sex, drugs, religion and politics (Bengtson & Starr, 1975). For example, there seems to be a general lack of sex-related communication in families, with mothers being primarily responsible for what communication about sex occurs, even with sons (Fox & Inazu, 1979). A real paradox exists over communication about sex, since so little seems to occur, even though parents want to be seen as active resource agents for sex education with their own children, and adolescents report that they would like to have better sex-related communication with their parents. (See also Chapter 2.) Parents and adolescents want to talk more about sex and human sexuality but do not know how to do it. Given that parents often don't want outside educational services to give sex education to their children, because of fear of the children acquiring different values from those of their parents, it is important that more resources go into helping parents and adolescents to open up to one another on this important topic. In our research, as mentioned earlier, we have also found very little commun-ication about sex between parents and adolescents, although more communication about sex did occur between mothers and daughters than between other dyads.

One of the over-arching conflicts of adolescence concerns the different perspectives of parents and their offspring about how much control parents should have over various aspects of the lives of their adolescents. Adolescents appear to regard an increasing range of issues, that were once considered as under parental control, to be now under their own control. For example, adolescents have become less accepting of parents' attempts to influence them with regard to social events, dress styles and choice of friends. In fact, even young children resist parents' attempts to control their choice of friends. (See Tisak, 1986.) Children of all ages seem to react strongly to parents' criticisms of friends, and strong reactions by parents may only push children closer towards those particular friends.

Smetana (1988) compared parents' and adolescents' ideas about what areas (moral issues, conventional issues, personal issues) should come under parental control. Families with preadolescents were more likely to see issues as subject to parents' authority than were families with adolescents, suggesting some changes as the children get older. On the other hand, as would be expected, parents perceive issues as more under their authority than children. Moral and conventional issues were seen to be legitimate areas of parental control but parents often wanted to retain control in personal areas as well. Shifts in perceptions about parents' authority during adolescence primarily occur with personal issues, not moral or conventional ones. It is no wonder that so much of the conflict between parents and their adolescents is about these issues. An added problem is that some issues which parents see as moral (e.g. sexual behaviour) are seen by the adolescents as personal ones.

Being criticised by parents

Adolescents have been asked about the extent to which their parents criticise their behaviour and attitudes (e.g. Harris & Howard, 1984). Both girls and boys report being criticised for being disobedient, breaking family rules, being lazy or not ambitious enough, and being messy or sloppy. Girls tend to be criticised more frequently for being foolish, unappreciative, quarrelsome and stubborn. Boys, on the other hand, tend to be criticised for being disobedient, not applying themselves to tasks, being impulsive, being unsociable and having undesirable friends. Apparently, parents of adolescent boys are likely to find not applying oneself and being lazy particularly unacceptable. Yet parents of girls are likely to find being disobedient and hard to get along with particularly unacceptable. As traditional sex roles indicate, males are expected to be hardworking, successful breadwinners, while females ae expected to be submissive, unambitious and nurturant.

Mothers and fathers also differ in the behaviours they see as unacceptable in their children. In Harris and Howard's study, mothers tended to reject sons who were messy, not appreciative, and not sociable, while fathers were more likely to reject daughters who were not loving and affectionate. Fathers had little tolerance for foolish or silly behaviour, whether sons or daughters were being foolish.

Interestingly, Harris and Howard divided the adolescents into four groups, depending on whether they saw their parents as very accepting or not very accepting, and whether they saw themselves as being frequently or rarely criticised. Adolescents with the most positive self-image had parents who were accepting and not very critical. Those adolescents with the most negative self-image were the ones whose parents were highly critical and not very accepting. In other words, the greater the level of parents' criticism and the less their acceptance, the more negative was the adolescent's self-image. Where parent–adolescent communication consists mainly of criticisms, the adolescent develops a negative self-image which leads to more negative behaviours and more criticism and rejection from the parents. A vicious cycle is likely to be set up which can be very difficult to change.

Value conflicts between parents and adolescents

Research generally suggests that parents and their adolescents hold similar values (Coleman, 1978). Differences that do exist relate to minor issues such as tastes in dress, music and films. On the other hand, these issues may not always be minor. Modern rock music, for example, is often characterised by lyrics about drug use and promiscuous sexual behaviour, however subtly. What can happen is that parents and adolescents fight out deeper value differences in the guise of arguments about trivia.

It seems fairly clear, however, that adolescents tend to see their parents' views as more different from their own than they actually are. We have discused this issue in more detail in Chapter 2. For instance, Acock and Bengtson (1980) explored the question of whether parents' stated views on social and political issues, or the views attributed to them by their offspring had the greatest impact on adolescents. While adolescents' perceptions of parents' positions were generally good predictors of the adolescents' own opinions, adolescents over-emphasised the similarity of their parents' positions and the extent to which their parents' opinions were different from their own. In addition, adolescents were generally not very accurate in predicting their parents' responses to questions about social and political issues. To these authors, the 'generation gap' is far more apparent in the minds of the adolescents – the responses they attribute to their parents – than it is in the actual responses of parents and their children. Children consistently perceive their parents' attitudes as more traditional or conservative than they actually are.

Mothers have more impact on their children's beliefs than fathers, irrespective of the gender of the child. With both actual attitudes (Acock & Bengtson, 1978) and perceived attitudes (Acock & Bengtson, 1980), the mother's influence seems to be stronger than the father's. However, fathers do have an impact in some areas. Talk about politics seems to occur mainly between the father and the adolescent (Noller & Bagi, 1985) and it is likely that the father's views play an important role in the development of the adolescent's political beliefs. However, the impact of the mother should not be underestimated.

Parents also seem to play an important role in influencing the attitudes of their adolescents about religious beliefs (Hoge, Petrillo & Smith, 1982). However, whether this influence serves to convince or dissuade the adolescent to follow their parents' belief depends mainly on the quality of the parent–adolescent relationship (Hauser, 1981). Where the parent–adolescent relationship is primarily positive and cooperative, the adolescent is more likely to follow the beliefs of the parents. Harking back to the identity issues discussed in Chapter 1, however, it is important to consider whether the adolescent accepts the parents' views without taking them as their own (that is, forecloses) or is able to achieve a religious identity. Whether the relationship between the parents and the adolescent is such that the adolescent is encouraged to deal openly with doubts and questions, is likely to be important.

Some value discrepancies are related to the differing roles and life stages of parents and adolescents. Feather (1978), for example, found that parents, who tend to be primarily concerned with seeing their offspring embark on a secure future, seem to place a great deal of importance on values like responsibility, family, self-respect and national security. Adolescents, on the other hand, who are more concerned with short-term goals, tend to emphasise excitement, pleasure and the value of close companionship.

Daughters are more likely to follow the value orientations of their parents than are sons. It is worth noting again that daughters are more likely than sons to be in the foreclosure status of identity. (See Chapter 1.) In addition, the foreclosure status seems more adaptive for daughters than for sons. Daughters seem to show greater emotional dependence than do sons and this may be at least one of the reasons why they are more likely to adopt their parents' values.

Conflict with siblings

Conflict between siblings is a little-researched topic but violence between siblings seems fairly pervasive. According to Straus, Gelles and

Steinmetz (1980), 62 per cent of senior high school students admit hitting a sibling in the past year. Sibling aggression is also related to aggression outside the family (Gully *et al.*, 1981). Those who hit their siblings are more likely to be violent outside the family as well.

For highly aggressive boys, it is siblings who play the central role in triggering their aggressive behaviour (see Patterson, 1982). Younger siblings are generally dealt with more aggressively than older ones. Siblings are also more likely than peers to reciprocate negative behaviours such as hitting, thus setting up a coercive cycle of escalation. Each violent behaviour is likely to be followed by an even more violent and aggressive behaviour, until parents intervene or someone is hurt.

Montemayor and Hanson (1985) compared adolescents' reports of conflicts with parents and their reports of conflicts with siblings. To minimise the problems caused by distortions of memory, adolescents were interviewed over the telephone about the conflicts which had occurred the previous day. More than half of all conflicts occurred with siblings. Most arguments were with mothers or same-sex siblings. While the conflicts with parents were mainly about rules, a greater proportion of interpersonal conflicts took place with siblings. According to the adolescents, arguments with parents and siblings were least likely to be resolved through negotiation and were most often resolved by withdrawal. As disagreements with parents and siblings occurred equally frequently, Montemayor and Hanson maintain that the close living conditions, competition, and personal characteristics of family members interacting with each other are possibly the primary causes of most of the problems between adolescents, parents and siblings.

Disagreements with parents and siblings are largely about interpersonal issues, and are resolved in similar ways. These findings challenge claims that adolescents' arguments with their parents are about the need for independence, especially given the high levels of similarity between arguments with parents and those with siblings. One might expect, nevertheless that if most of the arguments with parents are about rules, presumably adolescents are wanting to exert their independence by flouting those rules, or, at least, trying to have them changed.

Relationships with peers

Another important issue is the adolescent's orientation to parents versus peers. Discussion of this issue involves extreme positions. Some theorists present the situation as 'a power battle between the influence of parents and peers' (Cooper & Ayers-Lopez, 1985, p.10). Adolescents are seen as either rebelling against the values and standards of their parents and being totally concerned with the opinions of their peers, or submitting totally to the demands of their parents and not progressing towards independence. This question of peer versus parental influence, however, reflects a false dichotomy to us and others (e.g. Mussen, Conger & Kagan, 1974). A more moderate position seems closer to the truth. Adolescents do seem to become more peer-oriented, but they are also concerned with maintaining the love and support of their parents and value their parents' opinions across a number of areas.

As Jurkovic and Ulrici (1985) suggest, the role of the family is not replaced by peers, but rather most adolescents move comfortably between these two generational groups and members of each are probably more similar than different in basic values and attitudes. Maintaining good relationships with parents seems important since positive and supportive relationships with parents do override the effects of poor peer relationships. Bronfenbrenner (1986) also argues against the segregation of parents and children which often happens in our society, since adolescents then have to face societal pressures without the support and guidance of their parents.

It seems clear that children disclose increasingly more to peers during adolescence. Self-disclosure to parents and peers changes as a function of pubertal status, especially for boys. In an early study, Rivenbark (1971) found that for boys, the least amount of disclosure to parents occurred at eighth grade which coincides with the average peak rate of growth. A slight decrease for girls in disclosure to parents occurs at the same time as the average peak rate of growth which is at 12 years of age (sixth grade). Assertiveness towards parents on the part of boys depends on their physical maturity, with boys interrupting their parents more as they proceed through puberty (Steinberg & Hill, 1978). As well, the peak period of pubertal change is associated with high levels of conflict between mothers and sons, and little involvement by sons in family activities (Hill *et al.*, 1985). Mothers are especially dissatisfied with their relationships with their adolescents at this stage. These changes in parent–adolescent relationships could be because the adolescents feel differently about themselves, or because the parents change their perception of the adolescent following this growth spurt. If adolescents become more confident and parents become more anxious at this stage, more conflict is likely to ensue.

Although peers become more important for adolescents and they spend a lot of their time talking with peers, there is little evidence that the peer group actually becomes more important than the family during adolescence. Fasick (1984) argues for a more comprehensive model of youth socialisation that recognizes the joint influences of parents and peers, particularly in the middle classes. Even the most peer-oriented of adolescent girls perceive their parents as more loving than friends, and generally like their families. In addition, teenagers orient more towards parents than peers when parents are perceived as having expertise in particular areas (Floyd & South, 1972).

Biddle and his colleagues (Biddle, Bank & Marlin, 1980) maintain that the impact of parents comes from expressing normative standards, while the impact of peers is through the modelling of behaviour. In other words, parents remind the adolescent about the standards generally accepted by the community as a whole, while their peers may model quite different behaviours. The adolescents may sometimes have to make choices between accepting the standards espoused by their parents and joining in with their friends. For example, parents may see demonstrations and street marches as inappropriate, while their peers may want to be involved and 'where the action is'. What the adolescent decides to do may depend on the strength of their feelings about the particular political issue (e.g. conservation, farm subsidies, nuclear power), as well as their relationships with their parents and their peers.

Some researchers have examined the types of interactions that occur between adolescents and their parents versus their peers. Hunter (1984; 1985), for example, was particularly interested in the occurrence of unilateral (directive or didactic) versus mutual interactions with parents and peers. A further question of interest was the relationship between the way an adolescent interacts with parents and the way they interact with peers. Both mothers and fathers are more directive and didactic with adolescents than are friends. In fact, parents spend more time explaining their own positions than listening to their adolescents and trying to understand their positions. Interactions with friends are generally more mutual than those with parents, with friends doing just what their parents failed to do, listening and trying to understand. Adolescents' interactions with parents seem to have little impact on their interactions with friends, especially for females. Adolescents with directive parents are as likely as those with nondirective parents to have mutual interactions with their friends.

It is also important to keep in mind that not all adolescents have highly mutual and intimate relationships with peers. In fact, there are large individual differences between adolescents in their ability to establish and maintain friendships (Coie & Dodge, 1983) and these differences are related to their level of social skills (Gottman, 1983). Much more work needs to be done to explore the variables affecting individual adolescents' problems and their satisfactions in both their peer and family relationships.

There are also differences between males and females in the relationships they have with their peers. The friendships of females tend to be one to one. They involve the self-disclosure of intimate material. The peer relationships of boys, on the other hand, are more likely to involve groups and shared activities, with little emphasis on self-disclosure

(Hunter & Youniss, 1982; Johnson & Aries, 1983). The interests of male adolescents are often focused on status and achievement, while those of females involve people and relationships, again following our traditional societal expectations.

These sex differences in friendships seem to persist way beyond adolescence and to impact on relationships such as marriage (Balswick, 1988; McGill, 1986). Males, especially those whose marriages are not particularly happy, tend to disclose little to their wives, and also disclose little to their same-sex friends. Females, on the other hand, disclose more to their spouses as well as to their same-sex friends. (See Gottman & Levenson, 1988 for a discussion of this issue.)

Table 3.2 Teenagers seeking parental advice over two decades

Issues	1976		1982	
	Males %	Females %	Males %	Females %
On what to spend money	31	55	54	60
Whom to date	4	17	14	13
Personal problems	37	35	49	18
Courses to take	33	44	59	64
Future occupation	43	64	65	56
Social events	4	10	8	11
College or not?	51	70	65	64
Books to read	8	8	14	7
Magazines to buy	4	6	8	2
How often to date	12	57	14	27
Drinking parties	18	26	19	18
Future spouse	27	42	35	24
Going steady?	14	32	15	16
How intimate on date	8	17	11	9
Info about sex	24	43	38	40

Source: Sebald (1986)

While it is generally assumed that adolescents of every generation are more oriented to their peers than their parents, and that the situation is relatively stable and unaffected by environmental factors, this does not seem to be the case. In an interesting comparison, Sebald (1986) examined the peer versus parent orientation of male and female adolescents across three decades, the 1960s, 1970s and 1980s. In the 1960s, girls were highly parent-oriented and boys were highly peer-oriented, while in the 1980s, the two sexes were much more similar. In addition, over the period there was a noticeable move back towards parents from the strong peer orientation generally evident in the 1960s. Thus, cultural norms prevailing at a particular time are likely to affect the extent to which adolescents focus on their peers versus their parents. In Table 3.2 we present some of Sebald's data about the extent to which adolescents consulted their parents for advice across two cohorts, the seventies and the eighties.

Variables affecting communication and conflict in the family

Variables linked with communication and conflict in families include structural variables such as social class and ethnicity, religiosity and the age of the adolescent. Middle-class families have more constructive communication and less conflict between parents and adolescents. Families from minority backgrounds tend to be more cohesive and to place less emphasis on autonomy and individuation. Religious families tend to have more positive and constructive communication than non church-related families. Families with early and late adolescents tend to have fewer communication problems than families of middle adolescents.

Social class and ethnicity

Studies of middle-class families indicate less overall discord than in working-class families (Jacob, 1974). Middle-class parents also use a more inductive parenting style with their children and emphasise independence in their socialisation (Baumrind, 1980; Kohn, 1969). There also seem to be stronger parental alliances and less disagreement between middle-class parents. Most of those in Offer and Sabshin's (1984) sample who experienced a tumultuous adolescence were from the group in the lowest social class represented in their study.

On the other hand, Henggeler and Tavormina (1980) found that working-class mothers claim they are more affectionate than do middle-class mothers, although raters judged the middle-class mothers to engage in more affectionate behaviour in a sample of interaction. Perhaps the two groups of mothers express their affection in different ways, and the coding system reflects the middle-class definitions more closely. The fact that researchers are generally middle class can create problems in designing and interpreting research, as we noted in Chapter 1.

One's ethnic background also affects the nature of parent–child interaction. Family ties for many ethnic groups tend to be stronger and families are generally more cohesive (Burns & Goodnow, 1979; Goodnow, 1981). Where adolescents seek greater autonomy than cultural practices allow, conflict is likely to ensue. Adolescents frequently report conflicts about having friends outside the ethnic group, being allowed to go out, being allowed to date and having to spend time visiting family when they would prefer to be with their peers. The issue of ethnic background will be taken up again in discussions of decision-making in families with adolescents.

Religiosity

Several studies have linked the level of religiosity in the family (frequency of church attendance, Bible-reading, saying grace etc.) with the type of communication occurring among family members. Bagi (1983) found differences in communication between religious and non-religious families in the frequency and extent of self-disclosure across a number of topic areas. Adolescents in religious families were more likely than other adolescents to talk to their mothers about issues related to philosophy of life, social issues, relationships and sexual attitudes. Similarly, adolescents in the religious families were more likely than other adolescents to talk to their fathers about social issues, philosophy of life, relationships and general problems but the extent to which they disclosed their real feelings and attitudes to their fathers was no different from other adolescents. Discussions with both parents were more frequent for the high religious group and covered a broader range of topics and higher levels of self-disclosure. It seems that religiosity facilitates parent–adolescent communication, at least for some topics of discussion.

Age

Conflict with parents tends to increase in early adolescence and then to decline over time. Relationships generally improve between middle and late adolescence. During this period, adolescents gain more influence in the family, while the influence of the parents declines.

Parents are more directive with mid-adolescents than with younger or older adolescents (Hunter, 1985). Parents of these 14- and 15-year-olds may be more strongly motivated to impress their views and values on the adolescents before they get any older. It is also possible that these adolescents are objecting more to the parents' control attempts and thus eliciting more directives. Other researchers have found this age group of adolescents to be a major problem for parents (Baranowski, 1981; Lapsley *et al.*, 1984; Noller & Callan, 1986; Steinberg, 1981).

A further interesting but not much researched aspect of communication in the family is the impact of the presence of the spouse on parents' interactions with their offspring. Some researchers have investigated these differences in parent–child interactions and demonstrated the interconnectedness of parent–child and spousal relationships.

Change in parental behaviour in the presence of the spouse depends on the quality of marital communication, especially for the father. In a recent study, Gjerde (1986) compared parent–adolescent interaction in the presence of the spouse (triad) and without the spouse present (dyad). Fathers of sons were less involved, less egalitarian, more critical and more antagonistic when the mother was present than when they talked alone with their sons. In contrast, mothers' interactions with sons were more positive when the spouse was present Mothers were more responsive, secure, affective and consistent when their spouses were present than when they were not. The presence of the spouse, therefore, seems to enhance mother's interactions with sons, but spoils father's interactions with sons. The presence of the spouse had little effect on interactions with daughters. Given that observations were taken in all conditions, the effect of the presence of the spouse in interactions with sons is different from the effect of the presence of just any observer.

It is not clear why adolescent males should elicit more positive behaviour from mothers when the father is present and more negative behaviour from fathers in the presence of mothers. One explanation is that the fathers may be trying to present themselves in front of the mothers as more strict with the son than they actually like to be. In doing so, they preserve the traditional patriarchal image. Mothers, on the other hand, may feel more comfortable in expressing love and affection to their sons when someone else is present and there is less risk of the positivity being interpreted sexually. Unfortunately, adolescent behaviour was not assessed in this study, so it was not possible to see whether the adolescents were also behaving differently and thus eliciting different behaviours, depending on whether one or both parents were present.

Decision-making in families with adolescents

Decision-making is a problem in adolescence for two related reasons. Firstly, adolescents are generally wanting to have more control over their lives and to make most of the decisions that directly affect them. At the same time, adolescent decisions can have far-reaching consequences for both themselves and their families. There are major decisions about whether to continue education, what kind of career to pursue, which peer group to spend most time with, whom to date and/or marry, whether to be involved in sexual activity and with whom, and whether to continue to live at home or to move out. Parents get anxious about the young person's ability to make decisions such as these. They try to have more influence than the adolescent sees as reasonable. Parents may also have more realistic ideas about the likely consequences of such decisions than do their adolescents. Ironically, parents who try to make decisions for their adolescents or who try to have too strong an influence may lose what influence they have, and may even alienate their offspring. The problem is further exacerbated by the adolescents' lack of communication about their activities, since without any information, parents are likely to get even more anxious. Again, this anxiety may only serve to increase the chances that the adolescent will make the decisions the parent fears most.

Poole & Gelder (1985) explored the perceptions of family decision-making of fifteen-year-olds. These adolescents generally saw themselves as making most of the decisions affecting their lives, although the influences of the family were still evident, depending on sex, social class and ethnic background. Female adolescents considered the mother's opinion as more important than did adolescent boys while the boys tended to be more influenced by their fathers' opinions than were girls. Females made more decisions for themselves than boys, despite the evidence that girls tend to be dominated by boys in mixed-sex decision-making tasks with peers. Perhaps parents trust the girls more, especially given that the girls are more likely to have values similar to those of their parents.

There are also class differences in attitudes about the decision-making of adolescents. Forming one's own opinions and taking note of the opinions of other family members, including both parents, were considered more important by high socioeconomic groups than by low socioeconomic groups. Families from ethnic backgrounds are more cohesive than Australian families. They are less willing to encourage autonomy in their adolescents and set less store by the opinions of outsiders. In addition, native-born Australian adolescents, particularly boys, claimed a larger network of friends than adolescents of immigrant background. Having a larger network probably gives these adolescents access to a wider range of opinions about various issues. This exposure may add to their level of cognitive development and increase their confidence in forming and expressing opinions different from those of their parents.

Whether parents or peers are thought to be the most important influence on decision-making for adolescents, depends on the relationship a young person has with both their parents and their peers, and the particular type of decision being made. Wilks (1986) found that university students considered their parents as the most important influences in their lives, but that parents tended to be more important in future-oriented decisions such as educational and vocational choices (see also Sebald & White, 1980). Peers were more important in current decisions such as social activities, hobbies and reading material.

Both parents and peers tend to agree that parents' opinions are more important when considering educational and vocational choices, as well as decisions about money. Of course, parents' involvement may be important in these areas because they are also likely to be important sources of financial support. Parents are also considered important in decisions about choosing a spouse, although many subjects were not sure whose opinion should count the most here. While most young people would want their parents to approve of their choice of partner, whether they would actually give up a partner that the parents didn't like is another question altogether.

Friends were the clearly preferred reference group for decisions about social events, books to read, clubs to join, hobbies to pursue and clothes to wear, and parents supported the use of the peer group as a reference for most of these decisions. There are still many areas of potential conflict, however, since fathers thought that they should be consulted about dress and both parents thought that they should be used as guides about alcohol use, dating and sex. The adolescents, on the other hand, considered that their friends were more important sources of advice in these areas. In addition, when problems arose these tended to be discussed more with their closest friend than with their parents.

Effects of parent–adolescent communication

Self-esteem

In considering communication between parents and adolescents, it is important to ask what type of communication promotes or inhibits the development of positive attitudes towards the self. While this issue will be taken up in greater detail later (Chapter 4), it is worth considering some studies briefly here. A number of studies have shown positive relationships between parental support or nurturance and self-esteem (Buri, Kirchner & Walsh, 1987; Gecas & Schwalbe, 1986; Hoelter & Harper, 1987; see also Rollins & Thomas, 1979 for a review of early research). Self-esteem is positively related to the use of support and induction techniques by parents and negatively related to their use of coercion.

Where parents coerce their children into doing what they want, they are likely to have negative effects on their children's self-esteem. The primary messages coming from coercive techniques are that the adolescent is not competent, cannot be trusted, is motivated by negative goals and does not know what is good for him or her. The adolescent cannot cope without the parent. In contrast, the main messages coming from the parent's use of supportive and inductive techniques are quite the opposite: that the adolescent is competent and able to decide, that with encouragement he or she will behave appropriately and wisely. In addition these adolescents are likely to get the message they can be trusted and seek to do what is best. No wonder these different styles of parenting have very different effects on self-esteem.

Openshaw, Thomas and Rollins (1984) investigated whether symbolic interactionist theory or social learning theory offers the most useful explanation of parental effects on adolescent self-esteem. To Symbolic Interactionists, adolescent self-esteem is related to the reflected appraisals adolescents receive from their parents; that is, the extent to which their parents' behaviour toward them confirms them as worthwhile and lovable individuals. Social learning theorists, on the other hand, would claim that adolescents model the self-esteem of their parents. That is, adolescents who have parents who behave confidently will also behave confidently, while those who have parents who lack confidence and doubt their own abilities will show the same self-doubt in their own behaviour. The research suggests that the self-esteem of adolescents is more strongly related to their perceptions of the support they received from their parents than it was to the self-esteem of their parents. Support for the symbolic interactionist model is stronger than for the social learning model.

Adolescent self-esteem is more closely related to the actual support adolescents receive from their parents (as coded by outsiders) than to the adolescents' perceptions of support (Gecas & Schwalbe, 1986). Adolescents' perceptions of the support and nurturance they receive from their parents are more highly correlated with adolescent self-esteem than are parents' reports of their parenting behaviours. It seems likely that adolescents' self-esteem reflects what they believe their parents think of them. Those who believe their parents think highly of them will tend to have high self-esteem, while those who believe their parents view them negatively will tend to have low self-esteem. Also, perceptions of fathers' support and nurturance are more strongly related to self-esteem in adolescents than are perceptions of mothers' nurturance, particularly for boys. Perhaps the father is still seen as the most powerful figure in the family and thus his perceptions of the adolescent are seen as more important. A further possibility is that mothers are generally supportive and nurturant of their children, and there is little discrimination between them. Differences between fathers in the level of support and nurturance would then be more salient.

There are differences in self-esteem in adolescents related to the sex of the adolescent. The self-esteem of males is most strongly affected by the balance between the amount of control exerted by the parent and the extent to which the adolescent is encouraged to be autonomous and independent (Gecas & Schwalbe, 1986; Openshaw *et al.*, 1984). Boys high in self-esteem are encouraged to be independent and their parents do not exert a lot of control. Those low in self-esteem are strongly controlled by parents, and are not encouraged to be independent.

The self-esteem of girls, on the other hand, is most affected by the parents' support and nurturance. It is hardly affected at all by control or autonomy. Girls whose parents are supportive are high in self-esteem whereas when parents are rejecting and unsupportive, adolescent girls are low in self-esteem.

As might be expected, there is evidence (e.g. Eskilson, Wiley, Muehlbauer & Dodder, 1986) that high levels of pressure to succeed from parents negatively affect adolescents' self-esteem. Given that parental pressure doesn't seem to improve academic performance, it seems likely that most adolescents would be better without it. Feeling able to meet the goals set by parents, on the other hand, contributes positively to self-esteem. Thus, pressure from parents can have more positive effects if it is related to realistic goals that are clearly attainable by the adolescent. A further negative effect of considerable pressure from parents was found by Eskilson and her colleagues. They showed that adolescents under high pressure from their parents to achieve were more likely to get involved in deviant behaviours such as alcohol abuse, drug-taking and vandalism. The relationship between problem behaviours of adolescents and family interaction patterns is discussed in detail in Chapter 7.

Discipline and control

Extremes of discipline tend to have negative effects on adolescents. Both physical punishment and discipline which is lax, neglectful and inconsistent have negative effects on adolescent functioning. Boys who are physically punished experience such negative consequences as poor internalization of control, low self-confidence, social isolation and covert resentment or rebellion (Douvan & Adelson, 1966). Healthy families, on the other hand, are characterised by a quasi-democratic approach (Jurkovic & Ulrici, 1985).

The use of power assertion techniques also hinders the development of higher moral reasoning in adolescents and leads to a moral code based on fear of detection and punishment. On the other hand, effective family communication facilitates the development of higher moral reasoning in adolescents (Hollstein, 1972; Stanley, 1978). The use of inductive disciplinary techniques by parents, combined with the expression of affection, is highly correlated with an internalised moral code (Hoffman, 1980) where adolescents behave morally because they want to. Adolescents with an externalised moral code are likely to be more influenced by their peer group and more concerned about getting caught than about behaving appropriately.

Observations of family discussions about moral dilemmas (Jurkovic & Prentice, 1974) have also shown that moral maturity in adolescents depends on the way their parents interact with them. Where parents are hostile and dominating, teenagers are likely to develop an immature, externalised approach to moral situations. Where parents use inductive techniques and encourage the adolescent to think through the likely impact of their behaviour on themselves and others, the adolescents are more likely to develop a mature, internalised moral code.

Conflict between parents

Another difficult situation for adolescents is where they become involved in triangulated relationships and drawn into the conflicts between their parents. Such involvement has a negative effect on adolescent development, at least for 15- and 17-year-old girls (Bell & Bell, 1982). These relationships can take a number of different forms. Adolescents may become involved in mediating between their parents, or even in taking sides with one parent against the other. They may also become involved in distracting their parents from fighting by engaging in bad behaviour, such as fighting with siblings, whenever their parents get involved in conflict. They may even be blamed for the conflict between their parents and seen as the prime cause. Obviously these situations are much worse for adolescents where the parents' marriage is clearly unhappy, and arguments between them occur regularly. Kleiman (1981), for instance, found better psychosocial adjustment in families where there are clear boundaries between the parental and child subsystems, with no inappropriate intergenerational alliances such as alliance between an adolescent child and one of their parents.

Summary

In this chapter we have focused on communication in families with adolescents. Positive, effective communication in the family is clearly a crucial determinant of healthy family functioning and the well-being of adolescents. Parent–adolescent communication is affected by sex of parent and adolescent, age of adolescent, social class, ethnic background and religiosity. There are also differences in patterns of communication with mothers and fathers. Adolescents report more communication and higher levels of self-disclosure to their mothers, as well as more conflict with them.

Most parent–adolescent conflict tends to be about relatively trivial issues like their dress, manners, and music. Adolescents see themselves as making most of the important decisions affecting their lives. Parents and adolescents avoid conflicts about issues such as sex and drugs, and tend to discuss such issues very little.

A crucial issue is who should control various aspects of the adolescents' lives. Conflict occurs because adolescents come to regard an increasing number of areas that were once considered as under parental control, as under personal control. In general, adolescents continue to see moral and conventional issues as legitimate areas of parental control although there is not always agreement about which issues are the moral ones. Adolescents who receive high levels of acceptance and low levels of criticism from their parents have higher self-esteem. Those receiving low levels of parental acceptance and high levels of criticism tend to be low in self-esteem. Similarly, the use of physical punishment, rather than induction and reasoning, tends to lead to lower levels of self-esteem in adolescents.

In general, we lean towards a moderate view about adolescence. Relationships between adolescents and their families are not always stressful, and most adolescents do not completely break away from their families. Rather, parent–adolescent relationships do become strained, at least for a time, as adolescents work toward the development of more equal and more positive relationships. These relationships, then, generally last for the rest of their lives. In addition, adolescents tend to become more peer-oriented, although most continue to value their relationships with their parents highly. The research into communication during adolescence that we have discussed generally supports the view that most parent–adolescent relationships are happy, but there are some inevitable tensions as adolescents establish their own identities.

Chapter four

Family environments and adolescent development

Given the close nature of relationships in families, the amount of time individuals spend with each other in their families and the undoubted impact that the family has on preparing individuals for adult life, it is clear that the family is a very important aspect of the environment in which individuals grow. Studies comparing the impact of the family environment with the impact of other environments on adolescents (e.g. school and peers) tend to indicate the central importance of the family environment (Greenberg, Siegel & Leitch, 1983; Hunter & Youniss, 1982; Siddique & D'Arcy, 1984). In addition, different types of families provide different types of environments which may have positive or negative effects on individual family members. These family members may 'flourish, struggle or wither' depending, at least in part, on the type of family environment in which they find themselves.

Today much more emphasis is placed on the type of environment in which children are socialised and much less emphasis is given to the precepts or rules taught to children (see Berg, 1985). One important reason for this change is that in the late twentieth century we are much more aware of the subtle or implicit messages that children can receive in their families, and which may have a much greater impact than the rules taught to them. For example, a child's self-esteem can be badly affected if he or she is continually receiving messages suggesting incompetence, stupidity or 'badness'. Adolescence may be a time when parents are especially likely to put more pressure on their offspring because they begin to see more clearly their 'finished product'. As they look at how their adolescent copes with independence and exposure to the community, they also evaluate their success as parents.

How stable are family environments anyway – do parents provide similar environments for children over time, or are there large variations according to the age of the children? Roberts and his associates (1984) obtained information about parents' child-rearing methods when their child was three years of age and again when the same child was twelve.

63

Over time, parents were remarkably consistent in their child-rearing goals and practices. The main differences seemed to be that older children were given more independence and opportunities for achievement, and less affection and physical punishment.

Family environments are studied across a range of dimensions, some of which will be examined in this chapter. Firstly, we will concentrate on parenting style and family functioning which affect the relationships between parents and adolescents. Variables such as family cohesion and adaptability, family organisation, family control, family conflict and violence and family socialisation practices are discussed. While some of these variables have already been considered briefly in terms of their relationship to identity formation in adolescence (Chapter 1) and to family communication and self-esteem (Chapter 3), they will be considered here more in terms of their impact on the overall family environment. We will also examine the effects on relationships between adolescents and their parents of structural variables such as the sex of adolescent, size of the family, and the spacing of children. The impact of father or mother absence because of separation or divorce is discussed in Chapter 6.

Secondly, we will examine the implications for the growing adolescent of sex-role attitudes in the family, particularly in terms of attitudes to changing sex-roles, expectations about relationships and attitudes to achievement, education and careers. Thirdly, we will examine the effects of other family system variables such as marital discord, maternal employment or study, and parents' attitudes to children's work around the home. Finally, the family's attitudes to the outside world will be reviewed. Here we include attidudes to the wider society in general, to the local community, to authority figures such as teachers and police, and to the world of work.

Parenting style and family functioning

Family cohesion or closeness

According to the large study carried out by Olson and his colleagues, families are most cohesive in the early stages of the family life-cycle, and least cohesive in the adolescent and launching stages. While levels of cohesion increase again at the 'empty nest' and retirement stages, families are never again quite as close as in the early stages.

Not only is family cohesion lower in adolescence, but adolescents report less family cohesion than do their parents. Some theorists, including Olson, would argue that family closeness at adolescence can be problematic since close families may have difficulty in allowing adolescents the autonomy they need. On the other hand, adolescents do see family closeness as important. When we asked young people about the level of closeness they wanted in their families, most wanted the family to be quite close, although not as close as their parents did (Noller & Callan, 1986). As we have emphasised before, adolescents may be distancing themselves from their families, but they still want the love and support of their parents. In Table 4.1 we present the mean levels of actual and desired cohesion and adaptability for mothers, fathers and adolescents.

Table 4.1 Ratings by parents and adolescents of real and ideal adaptability and cohesion

	Mother	Father	Adolescent
Real adaptability			
13-year-olds	44.5	45.0	42.1
14-year-olds	46.0	44.6	41.4
15-year-olds	44.9	45.2	40.9
16-year-olds	44.9	45.2	40.9
17-year-olds	43.3	43.7	39.3
Ideal adaptability			
13-year-olds	54.1	52.9	56.6
14-year-olds	54.7	52.3	53.4
15-year-olds	54.2	53.1	54.3
16-year-olds	53.7	52.7	55.1
17-year-olds	53.2	50.3	52.3
Real cohesion			
13-year-olds	61.5	61.8	59.4
14-year-olds	63.9	60.5	58.6
15-year-olds	59.6	59.5	52.9
16-year-olds	59.3	58.9	53.9
17-year-olds	55.6	54.4	49.8
Ideal cohesion			
13-year-olds	66.9	67.8	65.1
14-year-olds	68.7	67.8	61.0
15-year-olds	67.3	67.8	61.0
16-year-olds	68.4	67.1	63.1
17-year-olds	65.5	63.8	59.5

Note: The highest possible score for adaptability is 60.

The highest possible score for cohesion is 90.

Using the Moos Family Environment Scales, Burt, Cohen and Bjorck (1988) examined the relationship between measures of family environment and adolescents' anxiety, self-esteem and depression. Where the family was perceived as cohesive, organized and allowing members to express their feelings openly, family members tended to be less depressed and anxious, and to have higher self-esteem. Again, cohesion is an important aspect of family relationships, even for adolescents.

As we shall see later, the balance between closeness and control, rather than just the level of closeness, may be one of the more important aspects of the family environment during adolescence. Families that can provide a close, supportive environment to the adolescent, while at the same time encouraging autonomy and independence, seem to produce adolescents who can cope best with the transition to adulthood.

Adaptability, autonomy and control

In the study by Olson and his colleagues (1983), the tendency to see the family as more or less adaptable depending on the life-cycle stage was not clear. Adaptability decreased from the newly married group and reached a low during the adolescent stage. It is obviously much easier for families to be adaptable when there is just a young couple or a young couple and small children. Routines and rules become more important as children get older, and the family may become quite rigid. Adolescents are likely to demand change in these rules and routines, and the family system, rather than becoming more flexible, seems to resist change and become more rigid. It is interesting to note that the adolescents in Olson's study tended to view their families as less flexible than did their parents. One would expect that adolescents who are pushing for change in the system and finding resistance, would rate the family as more rigid than parents afraid of losing control of their teenagers.

Burt and his colleagues (1988) found that perceptions of the family as conflictual and controlling were related to lower levels of self-esteem and higher levels of depression in adolescents. They also checked, using a longitudinal study over six months, to see whether they could establish clearly that the parenting style was the cause of the low self-esteem and depression. They found little evidence that perceptions of conflict and control at the earlier time were related to anxiety, depression and self-esteem at the later time. Given the short time-frame used, however, the findings are hardly conclusive. Studies with much longer time-frames are clearly needed to answer such crucial questions.

As we noted earlier (see Chapter 1), the extent to which adolescents are encouraged to be autonomous and have parents who are not highly controlling seems to be strongly related to identity achievement, particularly for females (Adams & Jones, 1983). Adolescent females high in identity status report that their mothers encourage independence and autonomy. 'Diffused females' rate mothers high on control and regulation, as well as very high on encouragement of independence. These latter mothers seem to want their adolescent daughters to be independent, but also want to control the process by which they achieve such independence. It is no wonder that these adolescents generally struggle to achieve an independent identity.

Normal adolescent girls who score high on measures of psychological and social functioning tend to come from families that are lower in control and organization and higher in cohesiveness, expressiveness and independence (Bell & Bell, 1982). The evidence seems fairly clear that the best environment for adolescents involves limited control combined with encouragement to be independent and autonomous. The ability of the family to adjust to the adolescent's needs rather than to be rigid and inflexible is also important.

Figure 4.1 Factors associated with adolescent rebellion

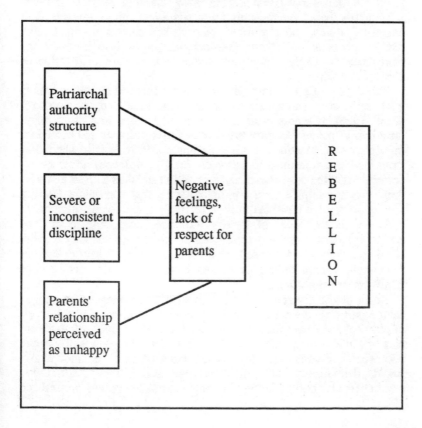

Punishment and violence

Rebellion is most likely to occur when the authority structure of the family is patriarchal and unequal, discipline is severe or inconsistent and the parents' marriage is perceived as unhappy (Balswick & Macrides, 1975). These relationships are presented graphically in Figure 4.1. When adolescents see discipline in the family as extreme (strict or permissive), they regard their parents less positively and have less respect for them (Balswick & Macrides, 1975; Middleton & Putney, 1963). Severe punishment by the parents is especially likely to have these negative effects on the quality of the parent–adolescent relationship.

There is considerable support for the negative relationship between punishment and feelings towards parents. For example, Baumrind (1971) contends that high levels of discipline, with its accompanying unjust, arbitrary, and restrictive parental demands generates rebelliousness and hostility, and even fear, towards parents. Ironically, Smith (1970) has shown that parents' power and influence over children is primarily based on the children's positive feelings towards their parents. Children who admire and respect their parents are much more likely to cooperate with them. Thus parents who overuse discipline and punishment are likely to minimise, rather than increase, their influence over their children.

The degree of punishment and perceived parental control seems to lower self-esteem and generate hostility in the adolescents (Amoroso & Ware, 1986). It seems clear that close supervision and other manifestations of parental control provoke negative attitudes and behaviour in adolescents. Martin and his colleagues (1987) found, when they examined the relationship between family violence, adolescents' perceptions of the outcomes of family conflict and their satisfaction with family relationships after a conflict episode, that nonviolent families seemed to resolve conflicts more effectively than violent families. In addition, as the level of family violence increased, so did the adolescent's anger towards their parents, while their satisfaction with family relationships decreased. These adolescents are likely to harbour resentment against their parents and look for ways to get revenge (Dreikurs & Soltz, 1964).

Being physically abused has a number of consequences for adolescents, apart from the actual physical damage. The effects of high levels of physical abuse are presented in Figure 4.2. High levels of abuse are part of a downward spiral for adolescents involving low self-esteem, poor social relationships, lack of empathy, drug or alcohol abuse, suicide, delinquency and homicide (Garbarino & Gilliam, 1980). Other researchers also point to acting-out behaviours, depression, generalised anxiety, extreme adjustment problems, emotional and thought disturbances, helplessness and dependency; poor school performance, aggression and lack of empathy for others; and less pleasure in life (Farber & Joseph, 1985; Galambos & Dixon, 1984; Herrenkohl, 1977).

Figure 4.2 Effects of physical abuse on adolescents

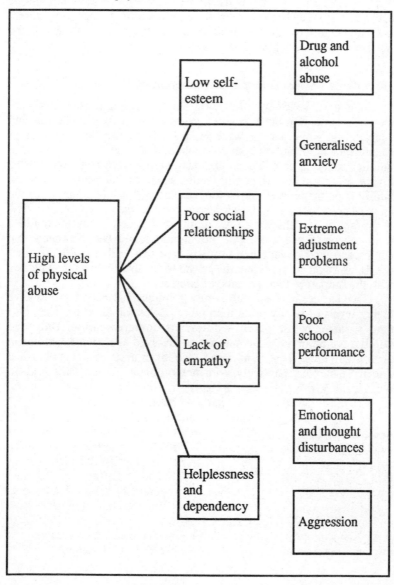

Are there any ways that we as a society can protect our kids from these kinds of abuses and their long-term consequences? The techniques used so far tend to involve media campaigns to increase community awareness of the problem. While arousing public awareness is important, there are problems with such campaigns. They may give the impression that abuse of children is even more common than it is, and therefore make it seem more justifiable in the eyes of some abusers. A better strategy may be the provision of programmes to increase parents' skills and to provide them with alternative solutions for dealing with the 'misbehaviour' of their adolescents.

The balance between cohesion and adaptability

In the study reported by Olson and his colleagues, adolescents were more likely to rate their families as extreme on both cohesion and adaptability, while parents were more likely to rate their families as balanced or moderate on both cohesion and adaptability. The fact that families balanced on cohesion and adaptability were most likely to be low in stress and high in coping skills, suggests that being a balanced family is particularly effective for families with adolescents. Thus the more extreme ratings by the adolescents reflect the more negative view of the family (see Chapter 2.) According to the adolescents, the families were too close and too rigid. We should remember, however, that adolescents tend to want their families to be extremely flexible. In other words, as might be expected, they want to be able to do as they please, with the support of their parents, of course.

As well as dealing best with family problems, balanced families have higher levels of family pride than other adolescent families. They also tend to have better parent–adolescent communication. Balanced families are more religious, but not as involved as extreme families in church activities. These families are also lower in stress and tend to deal directly, rather than passively, with their problems. These findings again point to the positive effects of a family environment which is warm and supportive for the adolescents, but only moderate in control.

We have used the dimensions of cohesion and adaptability to explore the kinds of families adolescents prefer. These Australian youngsters wanted their families to be highly adaptable (even chaotic) and quite cohesive, and more adaptable and less cohesive than did their parents (see Noller & Callan, 1986). (See Table 4.1.) Differences between parents and adolescents, however, were generally small. Adolescents want independence and autonomy, but within the context of supportive and cohesive family relationships. As Grotevant and Cooper (1986) also argue, the appropriate balance between connectedness and autonomy in the family best promotes psychological health in adolescents.

On the other hand, our findings also point to possible reasons for tension in these families. Adolescents are wanting very high levels of freedom and flexibility, and at the same time, wanting their parents to love and support them as they try out new ideas and new ways of behaving. Many parents must find this a tall order!

Effects of family environment on creativity

Family environments can even have an effect on the creativity of family members. Carl Rogers (1954) maintained that individuals whose pre-school environments provided both psychological safety and psychological freedom would show the highest levels of potential for creativity. Psychological safety involves receiving unconditional love and empathy without external evaluation. Psychological freedom is the permission to express oneself through art and other symbolic forms without restraint. As Harrington and his colleagues (1987) point out, these formulations are not all that different from those of other theorists (e.g. Erik Erikson, 1963) who emphasise the need for the child to develop basic trust in others and the world.

Harrington, Block & Block (1987) tested Rogers' (1954) theory of creativity-fostering environments, in an interesting longitudinal study. They found relationships between the kinds of preschool parenting practices suggested by Rogers and creative potential at both the preschool stage and in the early adolescent years (about seven years later). There were also clear relationships between preschool parenting practices and creative potential in adolescence, even after controling for the potentially confounding effects of sex, preschool intelligence and preschool creative potential. Those children who were most likely to be creative came from families which provided high levels of acceptance and support. These families also encouraged children to experiment with ways of expressing themselves through various forms of art.

Effects of structural variables on family environments

An interesting study of middle-class families by Richardson and her associates (1986) examined the effects of the sex of the adolescent, family size and the spacing of siblings on the quantity and quality of parent–adolescent contact and the parents' use of discipline. Daughters reported spending more time with their parents than did sons, particularly with their mothers. This greater amount of time with mothers was especially true for daughters in larger families. Perhaps daughters in large families spend more time helping their mothers. Time spent with fathers, on the other hand, was not related to any of the variables considered in the study, except for spacing of children. Adolescents,

71

either much older or younger than siblings, reported spending more time with their fathers. Quality of contact with parents was not affected by sex, family size or spacing, with adolescents generally reporting spending time that was perceived as satisfying with both parents.

Adolescents' perceptions of the discipline used by parents seems to be more affected by spacing than by the actual size of families (see Kidwell, 1981). Adolescents with an average spacing of fewer than three and a half years from their siblings describe their fathers as more strict, while those with wider spacings see the use of discipline in the family as fairer. Parents may believe that they need to be more strict when there are several children closer together in age all competing for the attention of parents and likely to get into mischief. Rules can be more relaxed when there is only one child, or children are at very different stages in the life-cycle.

Sex-role socialisation in the family

Recent developments in Western society have called for changes in the sex-role socialisation of both males and females. Females are being encouraged to consider careers outside the traditional female roles of caring and nurturing, and to combine a career with family responsibilities. Males are being challenged to be more involved in close relationships, especially marriage and parenting and to be more expressive of their feelings (Balswick, 1988; McGill, 1986). An interesting question involves the extent to which sex-role socialisation in the family is changing to prepare adolescents for the new expectations.

The evidence from some studies, however, shows that sex-roles are difficult to change. For example, Emihovich, Gaier and Cronin (1984) found that, while females are generally expected to be more like men, males are not being encouraged to adopt more feminine behaviours. Arguments in the press about the on-field antics (e.g. kissing and hugging) of cricketers and soccer players after getting wickets or scoring goals illustrates this point. In the family, even younger males are unwilling to give up expectations about being the primary breadwinner, in order to assume greater responsibility for children. As Emihovich *et al.* (1984) put it, men have difficulty surrendering the 'ideal of violence'.

General sex-role attitudes

Emihovich and her associates also explored two other questions in their study: do fathers' general sex-role beliefs influence their attitudes about the sex-roles they would like their sons to adopt; and do the wishes of fathers' about the sex-role attitudes they hope their sons will hold influence the attitudes their sons actually hold? Results showed that fathers' beliefs and expectations clearly influenced their sons' beliefs. Most of these middle-class, well-educated men held very traditional views about sex-roles. Fewer than 20 per cent advocated greater involvement by men in child care, and some expressed fears that 'boys were becoming too feminized', and that they were in danger of forgetting what it means to 'act like a man' (p.867). Given the strong relationships between fathers' and sons' attitudes, the prospects for change are not good.

What about the extent to which mothers and daughters agree in their sex-role attitudes? Notar and McDaniel (1986) measured young women's attitudes about domestic roles, employment, childrearing, marriage, sexual behaviour, dating and women's rights. These 19–20-year-old daughters believed there was strong agreement between themselves and their mothers about freedom of employment for women, marriage as an option rather than a priority for women, and shared parenting. There was less perceived agreement about economic and social freedom for women, the sharing of dating expenses and what sexual behaviour is appropriate. Mothers were generally seen as opposed to men taking over child-care and housework. If mothers are continuing to bring up both their sons and daughters to traditional sex-roles, change is not likely to accelerate. It is no wonder that working women do most of the chores around the home as well as holding down full-time jobs (Glezer, 1984; Scanzoni & Fox, 1980).

Most of the young women in Notar and McDaniel's study claimed to have good relationships with their mothers, including good communication, being close, and being able to confide in them. Most also reported discussing women's issues with their mothers, irrespective of whether they regarded themselves or their mothers as feminists. While some of the young women claimed that feminism had a negative impact on their relationship with their mothers, most reported that the women's movement had little or no effect. These discussions between mothers and their daughters seem to be keeping the daughters' views more traditional, rather than liberalising the views of the mothers and causing them to rethink their sex-role socialisation practices. As we mentioned earlier (see Chapter 2), parents and adolescents do differ in their atitudes, but at the same time, although significant, the differences are often small. They are rarely at opposite poles of attitude scales, although at different points. Also, as we argued earlier, the effects of social change are really quite slow, and although they may have somewhat different attitudes from their mothers, daughters' attitudes are generally still quite traditional.

Interpersonal conflicts

Sex-role socialisation also affects the way males and females approach interpersonal conflicts. Stereotyped views about sex-roles can lead to difficulties in problem-solving. For both males and females, there are sex differences in children's expectations of parents' responses to sons and daughters. In their study, Dino, Barnett & Howard (1984) had children from 4th to 8th grade rate a set of responses to hypothetical situations in which a child had described an interpersonal problem to his or her parent. Ratings involved how likely it was that the parent would make a particular response, and how helpful that response would be. Irrespective of age, children expected fathers to respond to sons with instrumental responses and mothers to respond to daughters with expressive responses. That is fathers of sons are expected to suggest ways of resolving the problem rather than try to understand the son's perspective. Mothers of daughters, on the other hand, are expected to try to understand the daughter's feelings and perspective rather than to suggest ways of solving the problem. Expectations based on sex-role stereotypes are clearly evident even with these primary school children. These very different styles of problem-solving are likely to affect later problem-solving in close relationships, like their own marriages. Males who model their fathers are less likely to understand their wives' needs to talk about problems in the relationship and to work through such issues. (See Noller & Fitzpatrick (1988) for a discussion of differences in the approaches of husbands and wives to solving problems in marriages.)

Attitudes to achievement

Attitudes to achievement are also affected by sex-role socialisation. A good example is mathematics which is seen as stereotypically male, despite the fact that males and females do equally well in maths courses. Because there are fewer female role models in mathematics, women can become caught up in a mathematical mystique (Fox, Brody & Tobin, 1980). They believe that they cannot possibly do well in mathematics. Unfortunately, such beliefs are likely to become self-fulfilling prophecies and may lead to females performing less well at maths.

Where female students are exposed to female models who are competent in mathematics, they take more courses in mathematics and are more likely to do well in those courses (Brody & Fox, 1980; Tobin & Fox, 1980). Females may do better in mathematics in single-sex schools because they have more exposure to competent female role models (such as female teachers and senior students) in these girls' schools.

Do parents have different attitudes about the maths performance of sons and daughters, and how do these attitudes affect their children's performance in mathematics and their interest in the area? Parsons, Adler and Kaczala (1982) examined how parents influenced their children's expectations about their success in maths and their perceptions of their mathematical ability. Fathers and mothers had very different attitudes. Fathers were more positive than mothers towards maths and their own ability at maths, although there was no relationship between these differences and their children's self-concepts for maths or their expectations about how well they would perform.

While parents of sons and daughters gave similar ratings of their children's ability in maths, parents of daughters believed that maths was more difficult and hence they had to work harder to do well. These findings fit with those of other studies showing that females generally believe they have to make more effort to do well across a range of areas (Frieze *et al.*, 1978). This study of parents' beliefs about maths ability indicates that mothers and fathers probably both reinforce this view in their children. In addition, children's beliefs about how good they are at maths are more strongly related to their parents' beliefs than to their own past performance. Even females who are performing well at maths can lack confidence because of sex-role stereotypes.

Children's household work

Sex-role beliefs are also expressed through the expectations about household work. There tends to be clear segregation of tasks by sex (see White & Brinkerhoff, 1981; Zill & Peterson, 1982). Girls generally spend more time than boys on household tasks. They do much more general housework in the kitchen, bathroom and laundry. Boys, on the other hand, are more likely to be involved in lawn-mowing, snow-shovelling, dealing with garbage and farm work. Both sexes are expected to keep their rooms clean, to tidy up after themselves and to care for pets. Table 4.2 is adapted from data presented by Amato (1987a). It is clear from that these data that females of high school age are more likely than males to be expected to keep their rooms clean and tidy and to take responsibility for housework. On the other hand males are more likely to take responsibility for taking out garbage, mowing the lawn and washing the car. Sex stereotyping of tasks increases with age although, as Goodnow (1988) points out, it is not clear whether parents or adolescents push for this change.

Another intriguing trend noted by Goodnow is that males are more likely to earn money by doing jobs around the house such as cleaning the car, and by doing tasks such as mowing the lawn for other households. There seems to be an implicit message that while men may work for money, women should work for love. It looks as though females are being prepared for the role of full-time housekeeper without monetary rewards.

Table 4.2 Percentage of secondary school children reporting responsibility for 10 household tasks

Task	Males	Females
Tidying up bedroom	68	87
Cleaning bedroom	63	75
Changing sheets	30	60
Washing or drying dishes	16	47
Sweeping or vacuuming	6	23
Taking out garbage	44	8
Mowing the lawn	65	14
Washing car	44	18
Cooking	9	19
Making bed	65	91

There is some evidence that socioeconomic variables such as class and education affect the household tasks of males and females. Where parents are well-educated, both boys and girls are likely to engage in activities such as cooking cakes and pies, and girls are more likely to be involved in 'masculine' activities such as woodwork (Zill & Peterson, 1982). On the other hand, children from lower-class families are likely to carry out more basic and essential tasks such as ironing or changing beds. These effects could be partly due to the impact of education, but may also reflect the differing economic situations of the two types of families.

On the other hand, there is also evidence that lower-class parents generally expect less from their children than do middle-class parents. Sex-roles are also relevant, however, since Newson and Newson (1976) found that 'working class boys seem especially able to escape responsibility if they want to' (p.249). Such effects may be related to the belief that mothers and daughters should be responsible for tasks around the home, or that males don't need to learn such tasks because they will eventually have wives to run their homes for them. Whatever, the reasons centre on the different beliefs held by middle- and working-class parents about what males and females should do in and around the home.

Family environments and adolescent development

The effects of conflict and unhappy marriages on the family environment

As might be expected, the environment of a family is affected by how happy the parents are with their relationship, and even by whether the mother stays at home or is in full- or part-time employment. Olson's research shows that marital and family satisfaction are at their lowest during the adolescent stage. The satisfaction of both parents seems to decline as the oldest child becomes an adolescent. While the husband's satisfaction begins to increase again as the oldest child leaves home, satisfaction does not really increase for the wife until all the children have left home. The difference in reactions of husbands and wives may be related to wives having more problems in adjusting to the departure of children. Alternatively, it may be related to the strains wives experience in having adult children at home.

How much marital unhappiness and conflict do adolescents report? Amato (1987b) interviewed 200 children aged between eight and nine years and 200 adolescents aged between 15 and 16 years. Adolescents were more likely to report frequent fighting between their parents (19 per cent) than were younger children (8 per cent) although almost half reported that their parents never or hardly ever fought. Adolescents were also more likely to report that they didn't care about their parents' fighting (16 per cent) or that they believed fighting to be normal (14 per cent). They were also less worried about the possibility of their parents separating than were the younger children. (See also Chapter 6.) Some adolescents were worried, angry or generally upset about the conflict between their parents, and particularly disliked being dragged into arguments between their parents as allies or protectors.

A close, satisfying relationship between parents is generally reflected in a warm and supportive family climate. Conflict between the parents is likely to result in a generally unsatisfactory home environment. Fighting between parents is clearly unpleasant for children, and in the long term, the consequences can be serious for them. Conflict between parents is related to behaviour problems in children and adolescents. There is evidence of low self-esteem, poor school performance and emotional problems in children from families high in conflict (Emery & O'Leary, 1984; Ochiltree & Amato, 1983; Porter & O'Leary, 1980).

Conflict between parents may have negative effects on their children for two reasons (Amato, 1987a): (a) the arguments between the parents create a stressful family environment, and (b) the unhappy marriage often 'spills over' into the parent–adolescent relationship, producing deterioration in that relationship as well. Conflict between the parents may also be over how to rear children. One parent may be too restrictive or too permissive. What often happens is that the permissive parent becomes èven more permissive to try and counteract the effects of the restrictive parent, while the restrictive parent becomes even more restrictive to counteract the effects of the permissive parent. Poor relationships between the parent and the adolescent may have negative effects on the marital relationship which, in turn, may have even more negative effects on the parent–child relationship. The evidence certainly points to lower marital satisfaction during the child-bearing years, a factor which could be related to disagreements about child-rearing.

While it is generally clear that there is a relationship between unhappy marriages and children having more behaviour problems, it is not clear whether marital conflict is a direct cause of behaviour problems or whether it acts in combination with other developmental stressors (O'Leary & Emery, 1984; Smith & Forehand, 1986). In the latter study, marital discord was related to perceived parent–adolescent conflict, but only for mothers and daughters. These researchers suggest that marital problems may make it difficult for a mother to accept her adolescent daughter's strivings toward independence. Mothers may fear the prospect of being left alone in their unhappiness. Mother–daughter conflict may be generated by the unhappy mother putting increasing demands on the daughter and trying to control the daughter's behaviour.

Satisfaction with financial management is also lowest at the adolescent stage, reflecting the strain that adolescent children can place on the resources of a family (Olson *et al.*, 1983). Adolescents are likely to cost more because they eat more and their clothes are more expensive. They are also likely to be fussier about clothes. Finding clothes that are 'in' but also in a reasonable price range can be quite a challenge for any parent. Many adolescents also want to be involved in a range of activities: sporting teams, coaching, music lessons, magazine subscriptions, movies, musical gigs and so on, all of which cost money. All of these costs are additional to the high costs involved in obtaining a basic education.

There is some evidence of problems in the communication of husbands and wives who have adolescents. In Olson's study (Olson *et al.*, 1983), husbands were generally more satisfied with the communication in the marriage than wives. It is likely, as these writers suggest, that wives are wanting more communication from their husbands at this time and they are dissatisfied with their husbands' responses to these demands. Adolescents are also very demanding of their parents' time, particularly demanding attention from their mothers. These demands may interfere with the communication between their parents. Certainly, some parents find that they have more trouble communicating with each other when their children are up as late as they are in the evening, or even later. These conditions can also put a strain on the parents' sexual relationship.

Stresses in families with adolescents

Families with adolescents report that the greatest stresses come from the increase in the number of outside activities with which children are involved. There are also financial problems related to basics such as food, clothing and power, to purchases such as cars, and to increases in the number of chores left undone. Finally, when adolescents leave high school, there are even more financial demands including the costs of education, and the costs of supporting adolescents as they move in and out of the home to go to college, or to change jobs. (See Chapter 5.)

Effects of maternal employment on adolescents

As Montemayor (Montemayor, 1984a; Montemayor & Clayton, 1983) has shown, adolescents with working mothers spend less time with their parents and more time with peers than those whose mothers do not work outside the home. Male adolescents with working mothers also tend to spend more time alone than other adolescent males. In addition, maternal employment also affects the level of conflict between mothers and their adolescent sons, perhaps because mothers provide less supervision but expect more cooperation in family chores. There is increasing evidence that maternal employment outside the home has negative effects on sons (Bronfenbrenner & Crouter, 1982; Hoffman, 1980).

Steinberg (1986) identifies the lack of parental monitoring as a crucial variable in the susceptibility of 'latch-key' children to undesirable influences from peers. Children whose parents know where they are and keep track of them are much less likely to become involved in antisocial activities. Again, males are more susceptible to these undesirable influences than females, and are also less likely to take notice of their parents' attempts to keep up with their movements.

The family and the outside world

As Bronfenbrenner (1986) notes in his review of research about the effects of external conditions on intrafamilial processes, the family is affected by a number of external factors. Included among these factors are the daily environment of the child (e.g. day care, school and peer group), the environment of the parents (e.g. work and recreation), and characteristics of the general community like community values, and the actual physical environment in which the community is situated. Further effects for families can come from economic pressures (unemployment, recession, depression), from natural disasters such as flood, fire and famine, from epidemics such as the poliomyelitis epidemic of the early

1940s or the AIDS epidemic of the 1980s and 1990s, as well as many other factors.

External factors affect the family environment through making it less stable. The stability of the family environment is important to psychological adjustment. Pulkkinen (1984) examined the effects of the stability vs instability of the family on the development of 8- to 14-year-olds. Instability was measured by the number of moves the family had made, parents' absences from the family, changes in arrangements about day care and schooling, changes in family structure and changes in the employment of the mother. Instability was associated with anxiety, aggressiveness and submissiveness in children and adolescents. Of course, one problem with interpreting studies of this type is the possibility that personality factors in the parents contribute to both the instability of the family environment and the negative effects on the family. Alternatively, both personality and environmental factors may contribute to the unsatisfactory parenting. Genetic factors may also be implicated although work in this area is highly controversial and there are numerous of methodological problems.

There is evidence that the age of the child at the time of any upheaval in the family is an important predictor of the effects of that upheaval. This effect is best illustrated by the findings of Elder's (1974) study of the children of the Great Depression. Those who were already adolescents at the time of the onset of the Depression were positively affected by the period of deprivation and difficulty, while those who were preschoolers were adversely affected. Adolescent boys, particularly those from the middle class, who suffered serious deprivation during the Great Depression had higher levels of achievement motivation and a clearer sense of career goals. Both boys and girls from the deprived group were also generally more satisfied with their lives. Elder explains these results in terms of the mobilization of family resources which had to occur, and the fact that these teenagers had to take on added responsibilities both inside and outside of the home. These experiences effectively trained the adolescents in initiative, responsibility and co-operation, all important attributes for success in personal and work contexts.

While a number of studies have examined the effect of family environment on school performance, few studies have examined the linkages between home and school in a more reciprocal way. Smith (1968) manipulated the strength of home–school linkages and found evidence for increases in academic achievement when these links were stronger. Since her studies involved only low-income families, predominantly black, there is clearly need for the work to be replicated with other samples.

In another noteworthy study, Epstein (1983) examined the transition to high school of a large group of 8th graders, particularly looking at the effect of opportunities for communication and decision-making in both home and school settings. Students who had participated in the decision-making processes that affected them, coped most effectively with the move to high school. They not only displayed more initiative and independence, but the effects were also seen in their academic performance. While the effects of family experiences were more important than school activities, the latter helped to counteract a lack of home experience.

The settings in which parents work can also affect their child-rearing values. Adults in highly supervised jobs (more characteristic of the working class) value conformity in their children They are more likely to use physical punishment to get obedience. On the other hand, parents with a high degree of freedom and little supervision in their jobs (more characteristic of the middle classes) are more likely to value autonomy and independence in children, and to value conformity and compliance much less (Miller *et al.*, 1979; Petersen, Lee & Ellis, 1982).

Some studies have looked at the effects of 'work absorption' by fathers on the family. Heath (1977), for example, found that the more absorbed fathers were in their work, the more irritable and impatient they were with their children. Job satisfaction tends to have the opposite effect. It increases the use of induction or reasoning in dealing with the children, and decreases the use of coercion by fathers (Kemper & Reichler, 1976).

The father's unemployment can also have negative effects on the family (Elder, Caspi & Van Nguyen, 1986; Elder, Van Nguyen & Caspi, 1985). If the father reacts to the situation with irritability, or the child responds to the situation by behaving in irritating ways, then the chances of long-term negative consequences for the child are higher. If there are also high levels of marital conflict following the unemployment, then long-term consequences are even more likely. Other negative family outcomes of prolonged unemployment include increased child mal-treatment and abuse as well as increased susceptibility to disease (Farran & Margolis, 1983; Steinberg, Catalano & Dooley, 1981). Possible reasons for the increased susceptibility to disease include reduced use of health prevention services and increased stress (Bronfenbrenner, 1986). A further possibility is reduced resistance to infection because of a less nutritious diet. Thus a whole range of variables which are external to the family can have important indirect effects on the family environment through their effects on one or other of the parents, on the parents' attitudes and goals in child-rearing, or on the economic state of the family.

Bronfenbrenner (1986) also argues that the early work experiences of adolescents are very important in the development of positive attitudes to work and employment. Studies by Steinberg and his colleagues have shown the quite negative effects of being involved in paid employment during the high school years (Greenberger, Steinberg & Vaux, 1981; Steinberg *et al.*, 1982). Such job involvement was related to less involvement with the family, greater use of tobacco and marijuana, and poor work attitudes. There is mixed evidence about whether adolescents learn to be more responsible through engaging in employment at this early stage. (See Chapter 5.)

A further important question concerns the effects on the family of the community in which they live. A carefully controlled series of studies by Rutter and his colleagues (Quinton, 1980; Rutter, 1981; Rutter *et al.*, 1975; Rutter & Madge, 1976; Rutter & Quinton, 1977) have shown that in some areas, particularly in the city, families are much more vulnerable to mental disorder than are families from other areas. However, the effects seem strongly related to the high levels of disruption to city families living in the 'vulnerable' areas. Why particular areas have such effects on families is not clear but the negative effect of city living on families has been shown quite conclusively for delinquency rates to decline once the family moved out of London (see Rutter & Giller, 1983).

Community effects on the family also come through the media. There is considerable concern about the effects of television on consumerism and materialism, on aggression and violence, on sexual attitudes and behaviour, and on behaviours such as smoking and drinking. Some writers like Strouse and Fabes (1985) discuss the impact of informal sources of sexual learning, such as television, on adolescents' attitudes to sex and sexual behaviour. They conclude that most brief sex education programmes 'cannot, in isolation, counteract the barrage of sexual messages from negative sexual models' (1985, p.261).

While pressure from the anti-smoking groups and the recognition of the negative effects of smoking on health has minimised adolescents' exposure to cigarette advertising, there is not nearly the same pressure to limit alcohol advertising. Adolescents are continually subjected to alcohol advertisements, usually endorsed by very famous cricket and rugby league heroes, on television, in glossy magazines, around sporting fields and on billboards. Nor is advertising the only problem. Alcohol is consumed on most television shows and movies, and very often in the context of release from stress. To drink alcohol whenever you feel stressed is not a healthy message for adolescents to receive.

In the next section, we will take up a related issue of the extent to which family themes prepare an individual for a role in society, and what happens when the family and the society are out of step with one another. Our special focus is the family theme.

Family themes

Family themes have important implications for participation in society. As we have noted earlier, while families used to be expected to teach rules to children, today much more emphasis is placed on the nature of the socialisation environment (see Berg, 1985). The argument is, that on the basis of the attitudes to self and others that have predominated in the family, each person develops a world view which provides the framework from which they interpret everything that happens. Berger and Kellner (1964) described the family as a 'reality-constructing institution' while Berg goes a step further in claiming that each family has its own unique view of the world.

Berg argues that these family themes (e.g. the rest of the world is wrong and we are right) are not subject to question when the child is young but are merely accepted as truths. They can be all-pervasive in their impact on the child. These family themes act as filters through which the world is viewed and which affect the child's interpretation of other people, events and ideas. A crucial issue is the extent to which the family themes correspond with societal meanings, and the degree to which these themes prepare the adolescent to take his place in the outside world.

In Berg's view, there are three types of families in terms of their attitudes to the outside world: opaque (or closed) families, transparent families and translucent families. Opaque families, who in systems theory terms have a closed boundary, attempt to maintain their belief systems by censoring information and ideas and preventing them from entering the family system. The world tends to be polarised into 'we' and 'they', with 'they' being undesirable because they are lower class, less well educated or have different political or religious beliefs, or different ethnic origins. Transparent families, on the other hand, take a very relativistic view of the world. They have no values and do not filter the input from the world. Any behaviour is appropriate, depending on the circumstances.

The translucent family seeks to maintain its views and to pass them on to the offspring through defending the reasonableness of their views and the compatability of those views with those of others. Not all views are accepted. Some are clearly rejected, but they are explained, rather than explained away. As Berg (1985) goes on to say, 'The translucent family is sufficiently meaning circumscribed so as to be said to have it own values, yet with standards which are amenable to defense without the need to "write off" the outside world.' (p.614). The translucent family is the most effective, and the most able to prepare young people to be satisfactory and successful members of society. The problem with the opaque family is that when the adolescent detects any flaw in the family's world view, he or she is likely to reject it totally, and family members with it. The transparent family, on the other hand, does not provide its members with the skills to evaluate the world as they find it and to work out a realistic belief position for themselves.

Attitudes to authority figures

Related to the family theme are attitudes to authority figures. Amoroso and Ware (1986) conducted a study relating home environment variables to adolescents' perceptions of themselves and authority figures such as teachers and police. Five factors of family environment emerged: extent of punishment, amount of chores at home, perceived parental control, absence of parents and parents' own attitudes toward authority figures. While all five family environment variables were related to adolescent attitudes, by far the most important effect was for adolescents' perceptions of the amount of punishment they received, and their perceptions of their parents' attitudes to authority. As we have already noted, a negative relationship exists between the use of punishment by parents and how positively their children feel towards them. Both extent of punishment and perceived parental control are related to the adolescents' negative views of themselves, suggesting once again, that negative parenting style may affect adolescent behaviour through its effects on self-esteem.

These same researchers also found positive relationships between parents' expectations that adolescents take responsibility for work around the home and their positive evaluations of both teachers and police. Perhaps those who have learned to take responsibility at home are more likely to evaluate positively those who are taking responsibility in the community. In addition, the parents' attitudes to external authority figures were highly correlated with those of their adolescents, although the direction of the effect is unclear. While it is likely that these relationships reflect the effects of parents on their children through teaching and modelling, it is also possible that the adolescents project their own views onto their parents. Given the data discussed earlier about the ways adolescents assume that their parents' views are more different from their own than they actually are, the projection explanation seems unlikely.

Summary

In this chapter we have considered the various factors which affect the environment in which adolescents grow up. The stability of the family environment is very important. Healthy adolescents come from family environments which provide a balance between closeness and intimacy on the one hand, and the autonomy of family members on the other. While flexible sex-role attitudes seem necessary to allow adolescents the maximum number of choices about how they spend their lives, many family environments are still very traditional. While females are offered more educational opportunities than in the past, they are still socialised to participate in very traditional kinds of families. It is expected that the husband will be the primary breadwinner, and the wife will be the one that provides services for the rest of the family. While women are generally encouraged to be more like men, men are not encouraged to adopt more traditionally feminine traits.

Relationships between the family and the school, the family and the parents' work environments and the family and the community are also very important. Adolescents tend to be more successful academically when the links between the family and the school are strong. The environment in which the parents work affects their child-rearing goals, particularly the extent to which they emphasise obedience and conformity versus initiative and independence. In addition, parents with high job satisfaction are likely to be more effective than those who are absorbed in their work and have little time for family activities. Unemployment also has negative effects on the family through the marital conflict which often ensues, and the economic stresses on the family.

Finally, community attitudes also have an impact on the family. At least some of this impact is negative as family standards and values are often undermined by the media and other aspects of society. Families need to help their adolescents to deal with differences between the family and society in more constructive ways. The family environment should prepare the adolescent to take his or her place as a useful and productive member of society.

Chapter five

Leaving the family

For adolescents who leave school, quite often the next step is also to get a job and possibly to move out of home. Most look forward to the chance to leave home, but it is increasingly the case that leaving home does not mean forever. Rather, young people leave home and return home as there are changes in their jobs, friends and financial situation. Other adolescents have little choice about leaving as they must go to another town or city to further their education and training or to take up a job. There are also other adolescents who have no choice about leaving in that they must leave to escape family conflict, and intolerable family situations that may have degenerated to violence and emotional abuse.

The theme of 'breaking away' is a common one in plays and movies about growing-up. Often set in some small country town, we see the maturing teenager and their friends deciding to leave family, friends and familiar surroundings to get jobs or to study in some large city. There is the conflict about leaving their boyfriends and girlfriends and school friends to move to the city. 'Breaking away' is also a time when those close to adolescents feel that they can be most helpful to them. At the same time, while parents, teachers and those concerned about the adolescent feel that their own experiences have given them a good grounding in the necessary survival skills, adolescents can be very reluctant to follow, or even listen to, the advice of their elders. 'It's my life, and I'll do what I want to' is a difficult message for parents to accept from their teenagers, especially as they feel that decisions about how to spend one's life – good jobs, where to live, how to spend and save money – are things that they really know about. As we have mentioned elsewhere, parents may not feel very competent at telling their adolescents about sex and contraception, but they do feel equipped to help their children with decisions about the right job, the best place to do further study, the best car to buy and what they should save their money for.

Leaving the family home to study, work or even to marry obviously further establishes the adolescent's sense of independence and separateness from the family. Physically and psychologically through their career choices the adolescent can choose to further distance themselves from their parents, siblings and school and other friends. At the same time, it is wrong to assume that adolescents no longer love or need their parents and families (see Chapter 1). We have repeatedly made this point. Rather, as they show by regular visits, telephone calls, the occasional letter, and the times when they come home to visit or even to live, most children want the lifelong support of parents especially as they make important decisions about their own lives.

Moving away from the family to get a job, to study or to be more independent means a lot of different things to adolescents. There can be more economic independence, more personal freedom, more control over their own lives and less control by their parents. There is less supervision and contact with parents. Significantly, adolescents are forced to live with the consequences of their own good and bad decisions.

Adolescents from happy families undoubtedly continue to feel close emotional ties with their families. They miss home, the attention of parents, and the sense that someone is close by if a problem comes up. The relationship between feeling close to one's parents, but also wanting to be less under their influence is a complex one. For instance, adolescents who adjust better to life away from home have more secure, supportive relationships with their parents (Sullivan & Sullivan, 1980). Feeling close to parents is important to adolescent adjustment. However, better adjustment is also predicted by the extent to which adolescents feel that they, rather than others, are in control of their lives (Anderson & Fleming, 1986). Adolescents need to know that they have the support and love of their parents, but also they need to feel that they are in control of their own lives.

Some adolescents have little choice about leaving home because of long-running conflict with their families. For them, leaving home is much less planned and is often under very unhappy and stressful circumstances. They can move in with friends, and get jobs to support themselves. Others become streetkids. The streets give them freedom, fun, and a lot of companionship and support from other teenagers who are very much like them. As streetkids with little or no income, however, they are at risk of being recruited for petty and more serious crime.

At night these runaways look for accommodation wherever it is available – at refuges, hostels, in industrial garbage bins, in abandoned warehouses or local parks. Most live on unemployment benefits, and to support drug habits their crimes can escalate from shop-lifting and purse snatching, to more serious crimes like breaking and entering, assault with a deadly weapon, to prostitution and drug running. In our major cities everywhere the number of streetkids is obviously on the increase.

As family researchers we see the community response in the number of seminars and large number of conferences arranged in the last few years to direct and coordinate better welfare and other resources towards meeting the needs of streetkids. The media have played an important role in alerting communities to the despair, alienation, poverty and ruthlessness often typical of this lifestyle. As again demonstrated by one recent programme on streetkids by the Australian Broadcasting Commission, the Australian public is still not aware of the level of physical and sexual abuse that drives children and adolescents onto the streets.

Table 5.1 Factors behind leaving home

Factor	Positive outcome
Independence	Positive identity development and self-esteem
Family conflict	Escape family violence, financial independence
To marry	Intimate loving relationship, more independence
To get a job or to be educated/trained	Independence, financial security

In this section we first consider some of the major reasons for adolescents' leaving home. As Table 5.1 indicates, a major factor is the need to establish lives more independent of their families. If adolescents can do this successfully, they will have stronger personal identities and better self-esteem than adolescents who fail to deal with the demands of living independently (see Chapter 1). Other factors associated with leaving home include family conflict, getting jobs or wanting to live with or marry their partner. The good outcomes, in terms of adolescent identity development and increased independence, are when adolescents leave home to go on to further study, and to do jobs and meet people who satisfy various social–psychological and other needs, and who help them establish lives which allow them to grow as individuals. The bad outcomes seem to be more likely for adolescents who run away from family conflict, sexual abuse, incest and violence. For them, there are much greater risks in being unemployed, being isolated and lonely, and of living in poverty. Their lives may also be at considerable risk as a result of heroin and other addictions, alcoholism, violent crime or AIDS, if they become the victims of child prostitution.

Wanting to be more independent

Most adolescents want to be independent and free to make their own decisions. These needs are well recognised in theoretical discussions of adolescents (see Coleman, 1980), and are mentioned by adolescents themselves in many studies (Callan & Noller, 1987; Youniss & Smollar, 1985).

The push for independence, however, is often associated with increased levels of conflict between parents and adolescents. Among 18- and 19-year-old adolescent males who leave home, independence is cited ahead of the need to continue study elsewhere, to want to live with friends or with a boyfriend or girlfriend. The need to be independent is as important as conflict as a reason for leaving home, although not as important as job opportunities (Young, 1987). For 18- and 19-year-old females, to be more independent is fourth in importance to them, being behind leaving due to family conflict, to get married or to cohabit, or to get a job. In addition, as Young's analysis of reasons for leaving also reveals, in comparison with young people of the 1970s, leaving home to be independent has increased in importance more than any of these factors.

The adolescent's need for more independence can mean family arguments and conflicts. The vast majority of parents nevertheless do seem to want their teenagers to be more mature and independent, and they are happy for this sense of autonomy to develop while teenagers are at home. Indeed, most parents would agree that they would rather be nearby to monitor, as it were, the growth of this independence. They accept the increased involvement of the adolescent with peers, sports and activities outside the family. New roles, tasks and demands do add to adolescents' sense of competence and self-esteem (Amato, 1987a; Maccoby & Martin, 1983). In turn, adolescents who try out these new roles have higher social skills, more social confidence and like themselves more.

Family conflict

In national opinion polls, adolescents cite family problems, only after having to go to school, as the worst thing in life. In these same polls, however, family relationships are rated as among the best things in life (Austrialian National Opinion Polls [ANOP], 1984). Although most adolescents deal quite well with the demands of living in families, going to school, and in meeting the expectations of teachers, parents and friends, there are times when all adolescents will disagree with their parents and will have family fights.

Family conflict is increasing as a major reason for leaving home. In the 1970s, surveys revealed conflict with parents to be a a minor factor for leaving home. For adolescent males family conflict is now the third most often cited reason, behind getting jobs and the need for independence (Maas, 1986). It is also third in importance among adolescent females as the reason for leaving home. At the same time, young people who leave home because of fights and conflict with their family stay away for the shortest amounts of time, an average of about a year (Young, 1987).

One reason for the frequent early returns is that the adolescents' departure is often unplanned. It is more in response to rather explosive arguments or even violence, rather than due to a series of minor issues that become more significant over time. Parents and adolescents use the time to 'cool down'. Often there is the understanding that the adolescent is welcome back home whenever they want to come back. Adolescents return when arguments are settled or forgotten, or even if they are not, to satisfy the wishes of one parent who wants the family to be reunited.

There is some evidence that adolescents who leave home because of fights and conflict with parents and siblings do not cope as well with life outside the family as those who leave for other reasons (e.g. work, independence, marriage). There could be several explanations for this. Possibly the family environment has not prepared them as well as adolescents who leave because of other factors. These adolescents may not be as self-confident and socially-skilled, while those who leave with the blessings and support of their parents tend to have their support if major problems occur that might affect their continued independence.

Levels of conflict in families do increase during adolescence, being highest during the adolescence of the eldest offspring (Olson *et al.*, 1983). However, as we have pointed out elsewhere, this does not imply that families with adolescents are always in conflict or that adolescents are always hot-headed and totally impulsive (see also reviews by Coleman, 1978; Hall, 1987; Montemayor, 1983). Adolescents do fight with their parents, but they often have as many or more fights with their siblings. At best they may only have a few arguments in an average week with various family members, and almost always these fights are short-lived. Importantly, the majority of disputes are about mundane, trivial issues, which can be fairly easily resolved.

As Table 5.2 shows, arguments occur about a wide range of issues, and they are very similar for adolescents of both sexes. There are disputes about taking more responsibility, appearance, spending more time with the family and in turn, arguments about what they prefer to do with their friends. Adolescents tend to fight more with some members of the family than with others. Arguments generally occur more often with mothers than fathers (see Papini & Sebby, 1988; Smith &

Forehand, 1986). Adolescents have more disputes with their mothers, but they also report that their most meaningful communication is also with them (see Chapter 3 for more detail). Next come arguments with same-sexed siblings. Fathers are very much less involved in conflict, probably as they are not present or just not interested in the day-to-day issues that are the source of arguments with the adolescent.

Table 5.2 Most common arguments with parents according to adolescents (1960s–1980s)

Focus of Arguments	
Males	*Females*
Responsibilities, especially completion of jobs and chores	Responsibilities, especially completion of jobs and chores
Eating dinner with the family	Being home enough
Cleanliness	Clothing and appearance
Using the family car	Using the family car
Arguing	Arguing
The spending of money	Types of friends
Number of times I go out on school nights	Following family rules
The time I get in at night	The time I get in at night

Source: Adapted from Montemayor (1983)

Adolescents are experiencing new and different feelings that they need to accept and cope with, and like all people, they have their self-doubts. There are a large number of issues that can be a cause of stress and self-doubt to adolescents – biological changes, their physical appearance, moodiness, needs for independence, freedom and autonomy, attitudes and priorities that differ from parents, and their emerging opinions about the right way to express their own sexuality. We know from adolescents that many arguments with parents are about rules, the use of time (study, school, help at home, going out) and cars, alcohol, and spending money (Caplow *et al.*, 1982; Ellis-Schwabe & Thornburg, 1986; Papini & Sebby, 1988). Whoever is their adversary, in the vast majority of families arguments don't end with adolescents leaving home or being thrown out by their parents. Families become flexible and adjust to the developmental challenges facing their various members. Parents are not isolated from these developmental changes. For example, they are also experiencing their 'middlescence', as they adjust to ageing, various financial demands and changes in their expectations. In some families it is probably the parents' difficulties in

91

adjusting to these demands that are more the source of their impatience with adolescents than the actual behaviour or attitudes of their children.

Research studies generally indicate that being in conflict with parents does stress adolescents. Family conflict is linked with adolescents' moving away from home, the higher chances of adolescents' becoming juvenile delinquents, failing at school, joining religious cults, committing suicide, and indulging in a wide variety of problem behaviours (see reviews by Hall, 1987; Montemayor, 1983, 1986). However, there are somewhat disparate reports of the levels of conflict within families with adolescents, probably as a result of the methods used by researchers.

It is well accepted that high levels of conflict, to the extent of adolescents being physically or sexually abused, is predictive of a variety of emotional and behavioural problems. In most non-clinical families this high level of conflict does not occur often. The self-reports of parents and adolescents show that there is conflict (Rutter *et al.*, 1976), but at the same time, conflict is seen as a normal consequence of different personalities living together in the same family. In such normal families, puberty is linked with increased levels of conflict in families, especially between adolescents and their mothers (Steinberg, 1981; 1986). It may be that adolescents find it easier to try out their autonomy with mothers rather than fathers. As mentioned earlier, it is clear that mothers are more likely to listen to the opinions of their adolescents than are fathers. They also become the disciplinarians for these minor problems (Montemayor, 1986). This happens because fathers are just not present or when they are, they are not very good communicators with adolescents of all ages. They self-disclose less than do mothers, and even sons prefer to talk to mothers than fathers about what generally are traditional father–son topics of conversation (Noller & Callan, in press). As others have labelled it, the adolescent–father relationship is quite 'emotionally neutral' (Youniss & Smollar, 1985).

A number of different methods are used to determine the real level of conflict in families with adolescents. Some investigators have contacted adolescents by telephone two or three times during the week to ask about conflict-laden events that may have occurred the previous day (Montemayor, 1982; 1983). Adolescents report that arguments occur about twice a week, rating arguments as being moderately upsetting, and as lasting an average of 11 minutes. Others have observed families to learn about the nature of parent–adolescent conflict. Videotaped interactions (Inoff-Germain *et al.*, 1988) of families discussing problem situations reveal marked differences between male and female adolescents in their levels of aggressive behaviours. Among male adolescents who have greater adjustment problems, there is more inflexibility, defiance towards both parents and anger especially directed at mothers.

92

The more parents try to exercise control, the more adolescent sons direct their anger at parents.

Interestingly, this apparent modelling of parents' verbal aggression by adolescents to resolve conflict is cited in other fields as a risk factor in the etiology and maintenance of adolescent psychopathology (e.g. Kashini, Burbach & Rosenberg, 1988). For female adolescents in the same study, those with behavioural problems and more concern about their self-image were more likely to respond rather inflexibly. They did not concentrate on the family interaction and replied angrily to any efforts by their mothers to use controlling behaviours. This was not the case, however, when fathers used similar behaviours.

Recently, some theorists have argued that not all family fights and conflicts adversely affect the development of healthy adolescents. At the right level, disputes between parents and adolescents can even assist adolescent development. In particular, there is some evidence that arguments among family members assist adolescent identity development. Healthy debate and involved, but controlled, disagreements with parents encourage adolescents to explore their sense of separateness and identity (Grotevant & Cooper, 1986) and lead to healthy ego development (Hauser *et al.*, 1984). It is possible that normal levels of disagreement may actually challenge and assist adolescents in the development of healthy personal identities.

While a little bit of disagreement is normal, and almost expected to occur in families with adolescents, families obviously need help with conflict that is extreme enough to create an unbearable, stressful environment for members of the family. In particular, families where relations are angry, rejecting and violent are often those unable to appropriately manage new episodes of intrafamilial conflict.

Leaving home to get married

Traditionally, marriage has been the major reason for young people leaving home. Today, marriage is still the major factor for young adults in their twenties leaving home (Young, 1987), and although not the major reason, to cohabit or marry are still important factors for young people. However, the majority of 15–19-year-olds live with their parents rather than marry or cohabit. Only about 10 to 20 per cent of this age group choose to live independently of their parents, either alone, with a partner or with friends.

Leaving home is a major transition for the adolescent and their family. Leaving home to live with friends allows adolescents more opportunities to go out, to date, and to establish intimate, meaningful relationships with opposite-sexed partners. At the same time, many parents are upset by the decision of their adolescent to move out in order to cohabit or to get married. Essentially, they are seen by parents as too young to make such major decisions about their lives. Because of the conflict that can be caused between adolescents and their parents about adolescents' personal relationships, it is important to consider what adolescents actually think about love, dating, cohabitation and marriage.

Dating and establishing close relationships with the opposite sex are challenges being confronted by adolescents, whether living at home or not. In terms of social exchange theory, it is clear that early in a dating relationship adolescents are exploring various behavioural options towards achieving a rewarding exchange. In particular, each person brings into the relationship various rewards and costs, and over time there is an exchange of behaviours between partners that can be both rewarding and costly (see Thibaut & Kelley, 1959).

An important rule determining their dating relationships is equity (Walster, Walster & Berscheid, 1978) – the more a person contributes to the relationship, the more that person should get out of it. Models of partner selection like the one outlined in Figure 5.1 point to relationships continuing if there is a good match in the features that initially bring partners together (e.g. similarity in values, physical attractiveness, levels of self-disclosure). Especially critical is the similarity in the amount of importance each partner attributes to certain characteristics (e.g. religion, ethnic group, social class, level of education, sex-role beliefs). Relationships don't normally continue if a partner is very concerned about the other partner's religion, socioeconomic status or ethnicity. Peers also influence the progress of the relationship, especially if they like the adolescent's choice of partner (e.g. 'she's really cute!'; 'what a nice guy!'). Parents' opinions are important, mothers in particular having more influence on their adolescent's choice of partner than fathers (Jedlicka, 1984).

When dating relationships end, many adolescents choose to scale-down the romance rather than make a complete break (see Duck, 1982). Nevertheless, adolescents seem to be no better or worse than married couples in ending relationships. Like the end of many marriages, breaking-up can be uncontrolled, stressful and painful (Baxter, 1984; Duck & Miell, 1984). Often young people choose less emotionally-laden indirect strategies (e.g. avoidance, scaling-down) rather than directly telling their partner that it's over. Helping the breakup of many teenage romances is the opportunity to avoid the partner because of school holidays or doing different subjects when school resumes (see Hill, Rubin & Peplau, 1979; Huston *et al.*, 1981).

As shown in our earlier reviews of adolescents and personal relationships (Callan, 1985; Callan & Noller, 1987), even though the overwhelming majority of adolescents expect to marry, some are still somewhat cynical and suspicious of marriage. Adolescents still anticipate

Figure 5.1 Stages in selecting a partner

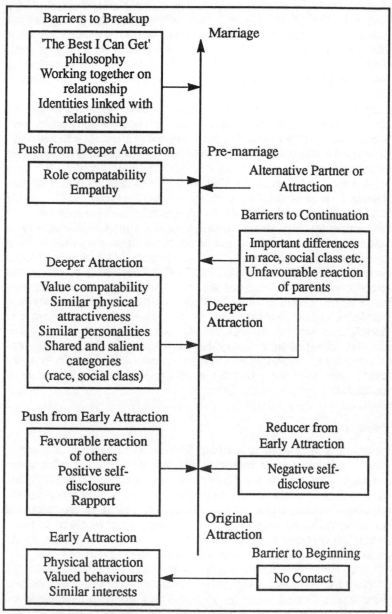

Source: Adapted from Callan & Noller (1987)

being married someday, and judge marriage as life-long and important to their personal development and happiness (Carmichael, 1984; Krupinski, 1981; Poole, 1983). Young (1980) found that the majority of young men and women believed that being married was more important than achievement. However, marriage during adoles- cence or in one's early twenties is seen as risky, and early marriage is regarded by adolescents as a barrier to expressing their individuality and personal development.

More and more young couples are choosing to leave home and cohabit prior to marriage. Cohabitation is cited by couples in most societies as a preparation rather than permanent alternative to marriage. In many Western societies, like Great Britain, Australia and the United States, about 4 to 8 per cent of couples are living together, the level being some 3 to 4 times higher than the 1970s (Spanier, 1983). There are at least 5 types of cohabiting relationships (Macklin, 1983), varying from one extreme of a friendly temporary relationship based on needs for companionship, to cohabitation as a permanent alternative to marriage. In some countries, like Sweden and Denmark, cohabitation is no longer considered as a 'trial marriage', but rather a distinct alternative to marriage (van de Kaa, 1987). About 40 to 50 per cent of adolescents in many Northern and Western European countries may never marry, choosing singlehood or non-marital cohabitation. It is interesting to note, however, that despite the trend to cohabit prior to marriage, as several reviews reveal (see Freeman & Lyon, 1983; Macklin, 1983), there are very few differences in the problems and satisfactions of cohabiting and married couples. Cohabitation does not make it any more likely that the marriages will be happier and more successful.

Choosing a career

As several studies reveal (e.g. Evans & Poole, 1987; Prediger & Sawyer, 1986), both adolescents and their parents are very concerned about future job opportunities and the importance of adolescents making good choices about careers. Adolescents have to deal with a complex and important decision that is based on their abilities, interests and personalities. Unfortunately, many students are not prepared to make these career-related decisions. In addition, in many countries career guidance programmes in secondary schools do not exist.

There are several theories basic to career guidance that consider the development of career interests by adolescents (see Osipow, 1983 for more detail). Donald Super (1953, 1980) in a life-span developmental theory of career development proposes that the individual not only develops a self-concept, but also a vocational concept of the self. The young person begins to favour some jobs or vocations ahead of others. Within Super's model of the development of a vocational self-concept, there are four stages: crystallisation (14–18 years), specification (18–21 years), implementation (21–24 years) and stabilisation (25–35 years of age). During the crystallisation phase, the adolescent makes decisions about their education and training that match their preferences. These decisions allow them to test the match between abilities and vocational preferences.

Other theories, like the one by Ginzberg and his colleagues (1951), also highlight adolescence as an important developmental stage in the establishment of career preferences. In this three-stage theory, the individual moves from a fantasy period (up to age 11), to a tentative period (11 to 18 years) during adolescence. From childhood, through adolescence to adulthood there is a change from a play to a work orientation in which more attention is given by the growing adolescent to whether their abilities and values suit particular careers.

A lot of attention is given to the factors that encourage adolescents, whether in a crystallisation stage or tentative period, to seek information and to explore certain careers. It is clear that parents, teachers and career counsellors play a major role. While many of these figures give advice and information, and act as role models, we have much to learn about their importance to adolescents as they make career choices.

As a number of writers point out, career exploration is a type of problem-solving behaviour which provides adolescents with information about themselves and the work environment they have to choose, then enter and adjust to. Grotevant and Cooper (1986), for example, argue that exploring a wide range of possible careers helps adolescents learn about occupations that are more congruent with their personalities. This argument combines features of various developmental theories noted earlier, focusing especially on the interaction between the individual and contextual factors. For instance, Holland (1973; 1985) argues that vocational outcomes are predicted from a person's knowledge about their personality type (e.g. realistic, investigative, artistic, social, enterprising, conventional) and the experiences, challenges and opportunities provided by various occupational encounters. He suggests that people search for environments that allow them to exercise their skills and abilities, to express their attitudes and values, and to take up appealing problems and challenges.

In a test of the developmental origins of congruence in adolescence, Grotevant and his associates (1986) examined whether adolescents who explore a wider range of career options made choices about careers that were actually more congruent with their interests and personalities. While results supported their prediction, other factors like the prestige of jobs, their complexity, and whether positions were currently dominated by a particular sex were also relevant. Others, like Krau (1987), have found evidence from middle to late adolescence of a shift in value preferences related to jobs and careers. These changes in the adolescents' value hierarchy occur as they move away from the influence of their school environment, to being more under the influence of the work environment. These changing values are in turn a push towards further exploring the match between their personalities and values, and the type of career they wish to follow.

Two issues mentioned briefly so far – the gender composition of jobs and values – are also cited among the major factors determining the different career paths after leaving school of male and female adolescents (see Poole, 1984). There is still a widespread belief among adolescents, and employers as well, that because of their different personality orientations (instrumental versus expressive), one sex is better suited than the other for certain jobs and types of work. Many occupations are strongly sex-role stereotyped, while the lack of appropriate female role models in traditional male occupations helps to maintain the attitude that there are male and female occupations. In addition, there is a conventional wisdom, somewhat supported by research, that males and females have different value systems. For example, adolescent females feel that being able to 'make a contribution' or the 'challenge of a job' are more important to their career choices than the income or status of jobs (Barnett, 1975). Adolescent males, in contrast, prefer jobs associated with power, profit, money and prestige, compared with adolescent females' interests in positions that are person-oriented.

Such sex-typed attitudes about careers are difficult to change. Generally, career intervention programmes with high school females show negligible effects, even when interventions involve the use of women in nontraditional careers as role models (see Wilson, 1981; Brooks & Holahan, 1985). Adolescent males and females have very fixed ideas about the occupations which are most appropriate for them to follow after leaving school.

The role of parents in helping adolescents choose a career cannot be underestimated. The behaviour and performance of adolescents at school is related to the quality of the parent–adolescent relationship (see Forehand *et al.*, 1986). Career choice is also an extension of the direct and indirect influence parents have over their adolescents. There is considerable evidence that adolescents prefer occupations related to the occupational status of their father's job (Connell *et al.*, 1983; Poole & Cooney, 1985). Adolescents from higher socioeconomic status groups are more likely to see themselves in upper income occupations. Overall, adolescents often have unrealistic expectations, in that regardless of their parents' occupations or their own abilities, they aspire to professional more than other careers (see Poole, 1983).

In an interesting study of British adolescents and their families, Breakwell and her colleagues (1988) examined various direct and indirect forms of parental influence on adolescents' motivation to train for careers in the areas of the new technology. The majority of school-aged adolescents believed that parents made some overt attempts to influence their choice of jobs. However, many (about 40 per cent) felt that parents had not significantly tried to influence them. Adolescents' wish to train for technological positions, however, was in part associated with the degree to which their own parents had some contact, especially through their own jobs, with the current technology. These parents may transfer to adolescents a value for technology or through the presence of computers and other forms of new technology in the home, may indirectly encourage more favourable attitudes towards technological occupations.

Various professionals in the area of career guidance point to pressures exerted on adolescents, especially by parents who have minimal secondary school education. It is clear that some parents truly struggle in their attempts to understand a world of careers and educational opportunities that is very foreign to them. Often from their own childhood they still harbour some distaste of the value of education. As a result, students can resist considering careers that are outside the experience of parents, especially careers that involve some innovation or change. The worst scenario is that adolescents make career choices that suggest randomness, peer pressure and a tendency to choose subjects at the tertiary level that are less demanding.

Being unemployed

One of the major reasons for adolescents leaving home is to get a job. Having a job represents psychologically and economically a further step towards autonomy and independence. Often to take up a job, the adolescent may have to leave home, and move away from the supports of close friends and family.

From the mid-1970s, economic recessions and high rates of unemployment unfortunately have meant that many adolescents never gain full-time employment or else there are long periods of unemployment between jobs. From large-scale surveys (e.g. Ochiltree & Amato, 1985) we know that up to 61 per cent of adolescents fear being unemployed after they leave school. It is clear that adolescents, like adults, have self-concepts that are influenced by the levels of success they experience in their day-to-day lives. Self-concepts and levels of self-esteem are affected by how people react towards them, and by how much success they have in what they do. Having a job is a major criterion used in our society to differentiate between those who are a success or a failure, and who are accepted or not in society. Importantly, adolescents also believe this to be the case (see Watson, 1985).

Being unemployed has a significant negative effect on the self-esteem of young people (see reviews by Feather, 1985; Furnham, 1985; O'Brien, 1986). Unemployed youth are more depressed than other youth, they have poor self-reported health and less personal control over their lives. Long-term unemployed youth, compared with teenagers whose unemployment is more short-term, report heavier smoking, reduced involvement in sport, and to some extent, more use of illegal drugs. Males in particular show evidence of losing social contact, while females respond to lengthy unemployment with a greater use of alcohol and more need for medical help.

Most probably because of the experiences related to unemployment, adolescents develop lower levels of self-esteem, and feel less in control of the direction of their lives. Often associated with long periods of unemployment is the rejection associated with failed job applications, and the criticisms of parents, friends and the mass media. While employed friends live rather independent lives, unemployed adolescents are financially limited in what they can do and spend by the level of their unemployment benefits. Unemployment may prevent adolescents from developing a sense of competence and belief in themselves. Long periods of unemployment lead to conflict with parents who, frustrated by their adolescent's lack of success, further challenge their child's competence. Alternatively, the relationship between low self-esteem and youth unemployment can be discussed from another direction: adolescents low in self-esteem and high in depression probably do not present very well in their job applications and interviews. Having generally low expectations about their own abilities and chances of success, they compare unfavourably with adolescents who are happier about themselves and more in control of the direction of their lives.

Some evidence for the former explanation – that unemployment causes lower self-esteem and more external locus of control – is provided in research by the first author. In a longitudinal study (Patton & Noller, 1984), adolescents who left high school, but stayed unemployed, were compared with those who either returned to school the next year or who left school and were successfully employed. Being unemployed altered the way adolescents perceived themselves. When all at school, the three groups of adolescents did not differ in their levels of self-esteem, depression or locus of control. On a second testing in the following year, compared with other youth, the unemployed group had lower levels of self-esteem, higher depression and they believed that they were less in control of their lives. Other longitudinal research (Feather & O'Brien, 1986) supports these findings for the period after adolescents had left school. Unemployed school leavers were more stressed and depressed than those who got jobs. They also saw themselves as less competent, active and pleasant. However, Feather and O'Brien also found these differences prior to the adolescents leaving school.

There are at least two major explanations for the relationship between unemployment and psychological problems. The phase or stage explanation suggests that the unemployed, over time, experience a number of reactions. Initially there is shock at losing the job; then pessimism and anxiety as their efforts to find another position fail; and finally there is an attitude of fatalism as the individual adjusts to being unemployed for the long-term (see Fryer & Payne, 1986). Despite little empirical support, this stage view is still widely held by professionals and members of the community because of its common-sense appeal.

An alternative explanation, with more empirical support, is the deprivation approach. In this approach, the negative effects of unemployment are due to the loss of the functions of employment. A job provides income, but also many latent consequences (see Jahoda, 1981) that include some routine and structure in an adolescent's day, contacts and experiences with people outside of their families, exposure to goals and purposes, a definition of their status and worth, and the benefits of being active. According to Jahoda (1981), for instance, unemployed adolescents suffer both because they are not as free as their peers to plan their lives, but more importantly, because there is an absence of interpersonal contacts, routine, activity and role definition that harms the adolescent's psychological well-being.

Studies into the impact of unemployment have to consider a large number of conceptual and methodological issues. There are a large number of variables at work that could affect the well-being of young people who experience either short- or long-term unemployment after they leave school. Among these factors are the emotional reactions of adolescents, their levels of self-esteem and depression prior to unemployment, their job expectations, the need to be employed, and the attributions they make about their periods of unemployment. These factors need to be measured both prior to, during and after unemployment with samples of adolescents representative of a wide range of socioeconomic groups and cultural backgrounds.

Adolescents are not a homogeneous group, and it is likely that sub-groups of school leavers will respond differently to unemployment because of a wide range of individual, situational and cultural factors, and whether unemployment is short- or long-term. At the same time it is unlikely that the employed are a homogeneous group of adolescents. They may differ in their levels of self-esteem and depression due to factors independent of the work environment. In addition, not all jobs are fulfilling or enhance one's psychological well-being. Thus we need to consider differences even among employed school leavers due to the nature of their jobs, levels of pay, opportunities to develop new skills, work conditions and levels of job satisfaction.

Part-time work

Unable to find full-time employment, many adolescents gain some form of part-time position which supplements the dole, the tertiary allowance for students or financial support from parents. While still at high school or college, they work at pizza restaurants, McDonalds or large shopping centres on weekends or evenings. Some two-thirds of 17–18-year-old adolescents in the USA work part-time in such jobs, while in other countries (e.g. Australia, Great Britain, Canada) about 20–40 percent of 16–18-year-olds get part-time wages. Proponents of part-time employment point to the opportunities for adolescents to gain further independence through having their own money, learning about work roles, improving interpersonal and vocational skills and developing more mature attitudes about work (see Hamilton & Crouter, 1980; Greenberger & Steinberg, 1986).

For instance, Schill and his associates (1985) found that high school students who did part-time work had higher grades, were from higher socioeconomic groups, and had a parent in a professional job. However, as in many such studies, the direction of these effects is unclear. For example, does part-time employment encourage students to learn skills that help them gain better grades? Or do employers use adolescents' academic performance as a screening device in deciding whom they should employ?

Critics of part-time employment for adolescents still at school cite many examples of the exploitation by employers of adolescents. There is the meaninglessness of the tasks given to them, with the majority of jobs not providing opportunities for developing vocational skills. There is little input by employers into the formal training of adolescent workers, and little recognition is given of the skills, academic ability or social maturity of the young worker (Greenberger & Steinberg, 1981; Greenberger, Steinberg & Ruggiero, 1982). There are even undesirable outcomes such as work stress, cynicism about work and the abuse of drugs in the form of cigarettes, alcohol and marihuana. In short, while part-time work provides many benefits, general life experiences outside of part-time employment may be perceived as providing similar or even better opportunities.

Critics of the movement towards greater part-time employment for adolescents also argue that adolescents who do not work have more opportunities to interact with their families and peers, developing important social skills. At the same time, they have fewer experiences that could damage their health and well-being.

What really seems to be critical is the type of learning context employers are willing to provide for adolescent workers. Dead-end jobs and tasks that do not challenge adolescents or encourage them to develop more mature work-related attitudes are unfortunately more the norm than the exception. Rather, governments and employers need to consider the long-term benefits of providing part-time work that at least encourages adolescents to use their talents and abilities, and which may involve some career training. We don't know nearly enough about the most suitable match between the needs of adolescents still at school, and the type of part-time jobs that will encourage better personal and job-related skills.

Homeless youth

Family problems are among the major reasons for homelessness among adolescents. In several surveys (Wilson & Arnold, 1986; Hancock & Burke, 1983), large proportions of young people cite family problems and family breakdown as one of the factors behind leaving home. Often the basis of conflict between older adolescents and parents is the frustration they and their parents feel about adolescents being unemployed for long periods. Homelessness is also associated with being in lower socioeconomic status families, drug and alcohol abuse, feelings of isolation, low self-esteem and criminal activity (Burke, Hancock & Newton, 1984; Report of the Senate Standing Committee on Social Welfare, 1982).

There is a lot of debate about who these runaways are. There is some evidence that these adolescents are insecure, unhappy, impulsive and unable to confront the normal difficulties in growing-up (Brennan, Huiziner & Elliott, 1978). At the same time, runaway behaviour is often unplanned but necessary in order to avoid violent or very stressful family environments (Young, 1987). Compared with adolescents living at home, for instance, homeless youth perceive their parents as being more controlling, punitive and less supportive (Turley, 1988).

There are two terms most often applied to runaways living away from home in search of somewhere to live – homeless youth and streetkids. While the terms are often used interchangeably, especially by the media, important differences do exist. Both groups are similar in living itinerant lives, and seeking temporary or emergency accommodation. Both groups are usually influenced in decisions to run away by family problems and conflict, and financial difficulties associated with living in the city. They face similar problems due to poor education and limited survival skills. Also a minority in both groups continue to attend school without any contact with their families.

Among the differences between the two groups are their ages. Homeless youth tend to be aged 16–25 years, but streetkids are more likely adolescents between 13 and 18 years of age. Streetkids do have a home that they can go back to, and often they return home to leave again at another time. Homeless youth are a larger group who always need somewhere to live. As a result the latter need emergency shelter for as long as possible. Streetkids, however, usually return home after a brief stay in shelters or refuges.

There is obviously a great need for welfare workers, parents, educators and politicians to get together about this issue of homelessness. There need to be large community efforts to help these young people with a wider variety of accommodation (e.g. refuges, hostels, board with volunteer families), training to help their chances of getting jobs, counselling support towards dealing with alcohol and drug abuse, and towards developing improved coping skills. In many countries (e.g. Australia, United Kingdom) government-supported inquiries have pointed to the needs of these homeless adolescents, and many services are being provided for them. Unfortunately, the risk with such minorities is that in times of economic hardship for all, it is these fringe groups that are the first to suffer when governments cut back funding support.

Conclusion

Only a minority of young people leave home while still teenagers. We have little real understanding of the life of those young adolescents who live independently of their parents, whether by choice or as a result of family conflict or violence. Strivings for independence and autonomy are seen as major needs for all adolescents, but the expression of these needs is almost always discussed in terms of a stable parent–adolescent relationship with adolescents still being at home. What about adolescents who leave school early, and seek outside employment or marry, and others who leave because of unbearable levels of tension and conflict at home?

The unemployed and the homeless obviously face many challenges. Often without the support of their families they don't fare too well. They suffer isolation, low self-esteem, depression and are more at risk of alcohol and drug-related problems. On the other hand, adolescents who leave home with the support of parents do considerably better. Not only can they fall back on their parents, but the maintenance of close relationships assists their ability to cope.

The problem of homelessness focuses the need to help adolescents and parents more in dealing appropriately with the tension and conflict that occurs in families. As research into divorce reveals (see Chapter 6), adolescents seem to have a tremendous capacity to cope, if they have the support of at least one parent, siblings or peers. Homeless youth and streetkids, however, are not under the same roof as any parent. Relationships with parents are not good, and when they do return home, they tend to leave again at another time. Evidence of family support and involvement producing higher levels of competence, better coping skills and independence should alert us to the need to help families deal more successfully with conflict, either between parents or with their adolescents. The result of such efforts should be less isolated youth, fewer teenagers living in poverty, and more adolescents making a successful transition to adulthood.

Chapter six

Separation, divorce and re-marriage

Many changes have occurred in how people perceive the family, marriage, divorce and remarriage. Getting a divorce is now seen as a reasonable alternative to continuing an unhappy marriage. Despite the increase in divorce, however, we know relatively little about how a breakup affects adolescents. How do children and adolescents cope with the end of the family as they know it, and the separation and divorce? Do they believe that their parents don't love them or care about them any more? And do they adjust to having new fathers or mothers if their parents ultimately remarry?

Once few marriages ended in divorce as couples believed that, despite their differences, they should stay together for the sake of their children. It was felt that young children in particular were harmed for ever if the family broke-up. Divorcees were seen as immoral, sexually promiscuous and a threat to happy families. Divorce laws made getting a divorce expensive, lengthy and highly public. As a result of these and other factors, divorces were quite infrequent.

From the 1970s, general reforms in the divorce laws allowed couples to end unhappy marriages more easily than before. 'No-fault' or 'mutual-consent' divorce was adopted in many contexts. For countries like Great Britain, Europe, the United States and Australia, between 30 and 45 per cent of couples married from the 1960s to the present are likely to divorce. In larger countries like the United States, over one million children a year experience the divorce or separation of their parents. In smaller countries like Australia, about 50,000 children annually are involved in the separation or divorce of their parents. These figures in themselves highlight the significance of high divorce rates to most communities. The sense of urgency associated with researching the impact of divorce on children has been linked both to the rising rates of divorce, and to our lack of understanding about the psychological consequences to children of the separation and remarriage of their parents.

Rates of divorce in the 1980s are quite high across most modern urbanised societies. The Swedes and Danes are most likely to divorce (45 per cent); in England, Wales and the United States, rates are about 40 per cent; and in Australia about 35 per cent of couples split up (McDonald, 1980; van de Kaa, 1987). Couples now put forward their case for divorce on the basis of irretrievable breakdown, generally shown by at least a 12-month separation. For most couples the process through family law courts or similar bodies is less legalised and briefer. Decisions are more strongly guided by the welfare of children, and the need for negotiation between the parents. The judge, however, is often still a central figure, especially in disputes about property, custody and maintenance. Nevertheless, in many countries the system of counselling and negotiation is still far from ideal, especially in terms of the women's share of property and the requirements upon husbands to meet maintenance arrangements (see Scutt & Graham, 1984).

Adolescents and divorce

Divorces can be economically disastrous for families. The changes in income are most marked for wives. More women than men report significantly lower incomes after divorce (Albrecht, 1980). Related to lower standards of living is the strong likelihood that they have custody for dependent children and economic responsibility for raising them. The economic demands on women are often more considerable than they should be, because many ex-husbands fail to provide the level of maintenance agreed upon in the courts. It is clear that divorce also has large emotional costs. There are changes to the lives of both partners, and the stress caused by the separation and divorce can present itself later in symptoms of psychological disturbance, alcoholism and even suicide (e.g. Bloom, Asher & White, 1978; Yoder & Nichols, 1980).

Adolescents are not oblivious to the problems of their parents. Many separations occur after years of the parents and adolescents coping with problems that have stressed each of them physically and emotionally. Adolescents see fights, verbal and physical abuse, and maybe the excessive drinking of parents. They live in homes where parents have over several years been leading emotionally and physically quite separate lives. Quite often they are so caught up in the drama of accusation and blame that they are forced to take sides. 'Can I be on both sides at once?' The frequent answer is 'no'.

For most adolescents, their parents' divorce results in one parent becoming primarily responsible for their health and welfare. The other parent, most often the father, is seen only every few weeks, monthly or not at all. If the custodial parent remarries, adolescents find themselves being raised by adults who are not their biological parents. They may gain new brothers and sisters who are complete strangers to them. In addition, divorce can alter the status of children, especially young adolescents. They are expected to assume the responsibility of household roles and the care of young children. Patterns of interaction with the custodial parent change (Montemayor, 1984b), and some parents seem to expect more maturity (Weiss, 1979). There is some evidence, at least from family interactions (e.g. Anderson, Hetherington & Clingempeel, 1986), that after the divorce adolescents demonstrate relationships with the sole parent more characterised by sharing and the acceptance of additional responsibilities.

Divorce as an additional challenge

It is clear that for most adolescents the adolescent–parent relationship is not dominated by major disputes with parents about their behaviour or needs (see Petersen, 1988). Earlier we have described what many theorists have proposed, and some researchers have investigated, as the major challenges of adolescence, and the reasons why some teenagers are less successful in coping than others (see Chapter 1). Young people can be stressed by the divorce of parents, and these stresses occur on top of existing problems at school, with friends or in their acceptance of themselves. The separation may also take away from adolescents the parent they love the most. Alternatively, the separation can reduce tension in the family, and bring the adolescent into a relationship with one parent that is more supportive and loving than in the past. That is, separation and divorce have many different outcomes which may aid or hinder the adolescents' success in dealing with the developmental tasks that they will naturally experience. There is no single scenario, and there is obviously considerable variability in how adolescents respond to divorce. There are both short- and more long-term effects, gender and age differences, while pre-existing factors (e.g. existing psycho-pathology in a divorcing parent) do seem to influence the post-divorce adjustment of children.

The effects of the divorce of parents also reveal themselves in other interesting ways. A fairly consistent finding is that adolescents after the divorce of parents are more concerned about the success of their future marriages (Wallerstein & Kelly, 1980). 'What makes a good marriage, and is marriage for me?' may be among the questions they ask themselves. Compared with adolescents whose parents do not separate, they have more negative opinions about the value of marriage (Booth, Brinkerhoff & White, 1984; Long, 1987). In addition, there is some evidence that adolescents of divorced parents, especially female adolescents, have less satisfactory relationships with the opposite sex (Hetherington, 1972; Long, 1987).

There are several explanations for these findings. One reason is that adolescents who are in unhappy marriages are more suspicious of personal relationships, and about marriage in particular. Their concerns are possibly justified in that adolescents from divorced marriages are more at risk of a first marriage ending in separation or divorce compared with adolescents of never-divorced parents (Mueller & Pope, 1977). At the same time, young people are generally more suspicious of marriage than ever before.

Adolescents' adjustment to divorce

Each adolescent can be expected to react differently to the divorce of their parents. Adjustment to a parent's separation may depend upon the adolescent's personality, their coping capacities, levels of socio-emotional maturity, and the nature of the post-divorce relationship between parents. It is also fairly clear that adolescents respond some-what differently than younger children to the separation of parents. For instance, in the 'Children and Divorce' project (Wallerstein & Kelly, 1978; 1980), preschool children ($3\frac{1}{2}$ to 6 years) were confused about what had happened. They were afraid of being abandoned by parents, while many hoped that their parents would eventually get together again. They would think, for example, that dad will come back, and everything will be normal again. Younger children also show higher levels of self-blame, believing that they caused mum or dad to leave the family. In contrast, this egocentric type of thinking is less typical of older children. In the same study, 13- to 18-years-olds reported being angry, ashamed and embarrassed about the breakup of their families. At the same time, many had decided about who was responsible for the divorce, and it was not them, but one or both of their parents who were to blame. Many avoided getting into conflicts of loyalty, and looked to peers and teachers for support during the separation.

Compared with younger children, Wallerstein and Kelly found that adolescents' attitudes about the breakup of the family are more realistic and objective (see also Reinhard, 1977). Indeed, their objectivity prob-ably assists their adjustment to the divorce. At the same time, as with older children, adolescents face several other challenges associated with the separation. The maturity of older children makes them more aware of their own emotions and those of their parents. They can feel pressured to get involved, and are more directly exposed to the turmoil being experienced by parents. For instance, in a follow-up of her sample, Wallerstein (1985) found that even 10 years after the separation, child-ren who were now young adults (19–20 years of age) were still burdened by memories of their parents' divorce. In addition, they were apprehen-sive about repeating their parents' unhappiness in their own marriages.

Important to an adolescent's level of adjustment are their perceptions of the amount of conflict between parents after the separation. Adolescents who judge the family to be happier and less conflictual since the separation tend to be more psychologically well-adjusted than adolescents who believe that the family situation is worse or where levels of conflict are still quite high (Dunlop & Burns, 1988).

All age groups, from 2-year-olds to 18-year-olds, show substantial negative effects from the divorce. As several writers point out, these negative outcomes for all age groups are really more significant than the subtle effects at different ages (see Clingempeel & Reppucci, 1982; Emery, 1982). As five year follow-ups of children reveal, no age group stands out as having significantly more problems in adjusting to the breakup of their parents' marriage than other age groups (Hetherington, 1979; Hodges & Bloom 1984). There are different responses to separation and divorce, in that younger children show more acting-out behaviours. Adolescents are more likely to report being depressed. With all ages, however, these reactions are short-term, and seem to decline within a year. Whether preschoolers or adolescents, children feel sad, unhappy and upset by the unhappy marriages and subsequent divorce of their parents. Even young adults (Burns, 1980; Farber, Primavera & Felner, 1984) are upset and disturbed about the divorce of their parents.

Table 6.1 Adolescents' feelings about the separation, and mothers' perceptions of their feelings

	Time since the separation			
	2 years or less	3–5	6 or more	Total
Adolescents' feelings				
negative	69	69	23	43
neutral	31	25	10	18
positive	23	12	3	9
don't know	8	6	72	44
Mothers' perceptions of adolescents' feelings				
negative	54	75	32	41
neutral	15	50	72	56
positive	46	19	3	15
don't know	8	0	5	4

Source: Adapted from Amato (1987a)

It seems that mothers at least are fairly good judges of the impact of the breakup upon their adolescents. As Table 6.1 indicates, in Amato's study mothers were fairly accurate in perceiving how their adolescents felt when the father left the family. When it was six or more years since his departure, mothers tended to believe that their adolescents had adopted quite a neutral attitude, but adolescents themselves were more likely to respond that they did not know how they now felt about the breakup.

Few adolescents believe that their parents offer them a good explanation of the reasons for the breakup of the marriage (see Johnstone & Campbell, 1988). Adolescents often talk about being angry at being 'kept in the dark' about the possibility that parents might separate (Dunlop & Burns, 1988). When it finally happens they are surprised, hurt and embarrassed about not being told about what was happening. Indeed, adolescents claim that, rather than being protected by their parents, they would have liked them to have confided in their children. On the other hand, parents may not confide in their older children because they don't feel they can do it very well, or because they feel that they will only upset them. They may not want adolescents to get caught up in the fights between parents. However, parents who do talk to older children about the tensions in the marriage believe that such opportunities do allow them to reassure adolescents that they do still care deeply about them (Johnstone & Campbell, 1988).

Many writers argue that many of the long-term emotional and behavioural problems among children and adolescents are a result of continued high levels of conflict between parents after the divorce. Children and adolescents involved in a divorce which is high in conflict do have more behavioural problems than children who experience the death of a parent (Dunlop & Burns, 1988; Emery, 1982). Also these children have more problems than those of parents who have less conflict-laden divorces. However, it is clear that many of these effects need to be investigated with larger samples of adolescents of different ages and both sexes.

Small samples sizes hinder any interpretations about the relationship between the age and sex of children, and their adjustment to divorce. More sex than age differences do emerge when we consider levels of adjustment. Boys do seem to be more vulnerable to post-divorce problems than are girls (see Block, Block & Gjerde, 1986; Hetherington, Cox & Cox, 1978). Boys from divorced homes present as more dependent, less masculine in their preferences, they have more school-related problems, and higher levels of impulsiveness and aggression. The strength of these sex differences varies from clinical to more representative samples, being weaker in the latter type of study (see

Emery, 1982). In addition, there is some evidence that although females seem to adjust better in the short-term to the divorce than boys, they may suffer more long-term problems. Hetherington (1972) points to the more troubled relationships adolescent females from broken homes have with the opposite sex, while others note their higher chances of emotional problems (Wallerstein & Kelly, 1978). Adolescent females also seek more counselling about their parents' divorce than do males (Farber *et al.*, 1984). However, in the general population females are more likely to seek counselling, and are more willing to admit that they need professional advice. It is quite likely that males are just more reluctant to seek counselling about a parent's divorce or any other personal problem.

There are many methodological problems in studies dealing with the impact of divorce on the adjustment of children and adolescents. There is biased sampling, in that most children are from clinic populations. In addition, many measures lack reliability and validity (see Emery, 1982). There is little use of control groups of non-divorced children, who are matched by age, sex, socioeconomic status and cultural background with children who are experiencing a divorce. Most studies have very small samples, being not even large enough to consider age or sex differences. Indeed, it may be the case that many methodological issues like these have resulted in researchers over-estimating the negative effects of divorce on children and adolescents. When researchers have used non-clinic samples (e.g. Dunlop & Burns, 1988), they have not found differences in the adjustment of adolescents from intact and separated families. However, even such samples obtained outside of clinics are far from representative of the general population of divorced children. They do not represent the wide range of ages, social classes and ethnic differences that exist among children.

There are few longitudinal studies with large samples that have considered the influence of the age and sex of the child on post-divorce outcome. Even larger retrospective clinical studies have not considered the impact of age of the child on post-divorce adjustment. Significantly, retrospective data, besides being prone to memories biased against discussing painful events, do not allow researchers to link a cause with an outcome. There is a real need for more research into the long-term adjustment of adolescents to the separation and divorce of parents, and the factors that assist adolescents in adjusting better to the breakdown of their families.

Visits by the non-custodial parent

The extent which fathers visit children after the divorce depends upon the father's attitudes towards the divorce, the age of the children and the children's attitudes to his visits. Children of all ages are generally dissatisfied about the arrangement made through the courts concerning their fathers' visits. Typically, fathers are allowed frequent short visits, which usually involve every second weekend. The courts seem unwilling to increase fathers' levels of contact, despite evidence from longitudinal studies that frequent contact between the non-custodial parent (typically the father) and children improves the post-divorce adjustment of children of all ages (Hetherington, *et al.*, 1978; Wallerstein & Kelly, 1976). Pre-adolescent boys, in particular, seem to gain from frequent contact with their fathers after the divorce. The positive effects of fathers' visits do not apply, however, in cases where the level of post-divorce conflict between parents is still quite high.

Young children generally want to see their fathers, and they seem to have higher levels of adjustment if they have frequent contact with them after the divorce. However, fathers' visits are perceived quite differently by adolescents. Many fathers also see these visits as being more of a problem. As might be expected, visits sometimes conflict with other activities adolescents have organised with their friends. In addition, the nature of visits can be somewhat challenging. As fathers may only see their teenagers on occasional weekends or over school vacations, the contact is often intense, involving many activities in a fairly short period of time. The high level of personal contact, especially over a weekend or single day, can be quite an interpersonal challenge to both the parent and the adolescent. For example, adolescent females report feeling uneasy visiting their fathers because of expectations about closeness and intimacy arising from the short time they have with them. They would not be expected to be so affectionate if dad still lived at home with them (Springer & Wallerstein, 1983). Under normal circumstances, having a full day alone with their fathers would be a rather exceptional occasion.

A frequent solution to weekends of intense personal contact between adolescents and the non-custodial parent is the longer visit over the school holidays. Arrangements may be such that adolescents take friends with them. Also, as a parent may be working during the day, the level of contact is not as intense.

While such solutions are tried by parents, little is known about the best arrangements for adolescents of different ages, personalities and needs. There is very likely a complex interaction between the adolescent's age, personality and self-image, and their coping mechanisms and psychosocial needs that determine the best post-divorce arrangement. Joint custody, in which both parents have equal authority for the children's care and welfare, is one option (see Clingempeel & Reppucci, 1982; Schwartz, 1987). However, while supporters point to its benefits in maintaining the children's relationships with both parents, critics argue that joint custody adds to the likelihood of adolescents having conflicts of loyalty.

Relationships with siblings

It is important to mention the supportive role that siblings play in helping each other cope with the divorce. Rarely are siblings separated from one another, and if any relationship stays fairly stable, it is the relationship between the children of the divorced parents. The supportive role played by brothers and sisters during the breakup is emerging in some longitudinal studies (e.g. Wallerstein, 1985). The shared experience of the divorce creates an enduring relationship between siblings that can survive throughout adolescence and into young adulthood. Often adolescents believe that it is a brother or sister that has helped them the most in coping with the breakup of the family, especially when parents themselves are not coping well with the loss of a partner.

The post-divorce relationship with the custodial parent

In about 9 out of 10 cases, mothers are the custodial parent. Reports now emerging from longitudinal studies reveal that the mother–daughter relationship often stays warm, loving and egalitarian after the divorce. The mother–son relationship, however, is sometimes quite troublesome. Some researchers even suggest that, in many cases, fathers should be given custody over adolescent sons, and mothers custody over daughters. Alternatively, if possible, joint custody should be allowed in order to introduce some of the authority and control that sons seem to expect from fathers. Such arrangements, of course, separate siblings from each other, an outcome not favourably regarded by the courts or the community. However, often such arrangements do emerge after a divorce in a rather informal way, especially with older children. It is not always the case that adolescents want to live with the same-sex parent, so that for a variety of personal reasons, they choose to be mostly with the other parent.

Some reviews describe the family atmosphere after a divorce as 'chaotic' (e.g. Montemayor, 1984b). Divorced mothers and their adolescents have less time together, in a household that is more disorganised than prior to the separation. There are take-away rather than home-cooked meals as mothers work outside the home and adjust to additional role demands. Rather than chaos, others point to a general level of disorganisation. There are role changes of the parent and adolescents, problems in doing routine tasks (preparing meals, eating together, being taken to school on time), and difficulties in meeting outside schedules. The immediate period after the divorce is obviously a difficult time for adolescents and parents. Yet this situation, while less satisfactory in some aspects, is still preferred to the tense situation between parents or parents and adolescents before the divorce. In some studies (e.g. Dunlop & Burns, 1988), up to 89 per cent of adolescents believe that their parents' decision to split was the correct one.

After the divorce, some parents complain about poor relationships with their adolescents. There are poor levels of communication, less time with them, and problems often about discipline. Mothers report being nagged by adolescents, especially their sons. In some studies, mothers in divorced families are described by adolescent sons as competitive, and not having any influence over them (Block *et al.*, 1986). In contrast, adolescent girls describe mothers as warm, protective, egalitarian and nonevaluative.

At the heart of some of these problems is that mothers are not supported by the noncustodial parent. Mothers and their adolescents have to adjust to a lower standard of living, and, in many cases without maintenance, a standard below the poverty line. Living independent single lives, a majority of noncustodial fathers do not have regular contact with their children (Weir, Silvesto & Bennington, 1984). When partners do meet, they discuss issues about their children that tend not to be loaded with conflict, like birthdays, vacations and holiday arrangements and the achievements of the children (Goldsmith, 1980). They avoid issues like school fees, medical or dental bills or the behavioural problems of a particular child. Fathers believe that they visit more often, but mothers report many fewer visits by fathers. Again, this can be another source of conflict between parents.

After the divorce, many parents begin a series of negotiations with adolescents about suitable arrangements for the efficient running of the household. With the separation and the divorce, Weiss (1979) suggests that adolescents actually benefit in assuming more responsibility, and being free of the tension associated with fights between parents. In time, many develop a more egalitarian relationship with the custodial parent.

Investigations into the allocation of roles in various households reveal that adolescents shoulder some of the physical burden of housework and the care of young children. There are different expectations, however, in mother-headed and father-headed families. In lone-father families, adolescents are more likely to take responsibility for housework, shopping and general tasks (English & King, 1983).

It is often asserted, more on the basis of anecdotal than empirical evidence, that adolescents become more mature as a result of their parents' separation and divorce. To keep some normal level of functioning in the family, parents push for changes in the parent–adolescent relationship that give adolescents more authority and control. Changes like these in the parent–adolescent relationship normally occur with puberty (Steinberg, 1981; 1986; see also Chapter 1). In other research (e.g. Dunlop & Burns, 1988), however, teenagers of divorced and intact families are found to be basically similar on various measures of maturity. Rather, the age of adolescents is a better predictor of maturity than whether the family has one or both parents living at home. At the same time, as Dunlop and Burns show in various case studies, some adolescents believe that their parents' divorce caused them to grow up more quickly, and to accept more independence and responsibility for their own welfare (see also Reinhard, 1977; McLoughlin & Whitfield, 1985). This issue of an increased level of maturity among adolescents needs to be further explored. A major task is the need for better measures of the concept of maturity. It is also important to recognise differences within divorced families themselves that may cause adolescents to be more mature or even to play down their maturity in order to get some sympathetic response from their parents.

In many communities there is a lot of concern about the effects of the absence of fathers on families. Fathers are believed to provide role models for adolescents of both sexes, especially for sons. In two-parent families Lueptow (1980), for instance, argues that fathers are more important than mothers as models of sex appropriate behaviour, for both sons and daughters. Also fathers are perceived by parents to be a major source of authority and control over teenage boys, as well as being supporters of a mother's actions towards rebellious adolescents. When fathers are absent, divorced women report a greater use of restrictive and more power-oriented strategies (Santrock, 1975; Hetherington, 1981).

Many divorced mothers and their sons do seem to have rather unsatisfactory relationships with each other. The absence of fathers increases levels of deviance and acting-out behaviours of some adolescent boys (Dornbusch *et al.*, 1985). In contrast, mother–daughter relationships are more similar in single-parent and two-parent families (Fox & Inazu, 1982).

It is wrong, however, to claim that the noncustodial parent, outside of much of the chaos of this post-divorce phase of family life, maintains a steady happy relationship with the children. In a five year follow-up, Wallerstein and Kelly (1980) found that father–daughter relationships were fairly stable over time. Warm and close relationships continued, while poor relationships remained poor. Father–son relationships, however, were twice as likely to change. Good relationships improved, but poorer relationships deteriorated.

There were also some interesting age effects. There was more deterioration in the father–adolescent relationship among boys and girls who were 9 to 12 years of age at the time of the divorce. During the five years after the separation, fathers had many problems in relating to adolescents. Fathers complained that adolescents needed to be almost continuously entertained. While demanding their time, they set about challenging the status of the father as parent and disciplinarian. Fathers and adolescents had differing opinions about the role of the non-custodial parent. The result was that fathers were often frustrated and angry about their lack of authority. Afraid of being rejected, they would not challenge attitudes or behaviours that they found unacceptable when their adolescents were staying with them. In addition, mothers who were upset about fathers' visiting rights, or who held grudges about various post-divorce arrangements, were more likely to complain in front of adolescents than younger children.

Living in a blended family

Especially among the younger divorced, the chances of getting married again are quite high. The young, the less educated and the childless are most likely to re-marry (Spanier & Glick, 1980). For most divorced partners, however, re-marriage is not immediate. In the 1960s, about 70 to 80 per cent of divorced adults in their twenties and thirties re-married within six years of the divorce. In the mid 1980s, on the other hand, only about 20 per cent did so. More suspicious of marriage, the divorced either live single lives or cohabit with one or several partners. As various longitudinal studies of the divorced reveal (e.g. Spanier & Furstenberg, 1982), time heals the emotional scars left by a divorce. Time, rather than a second marriage, is also the better predictor of higher psychological adjustment among the divorced.

For the divorced parent and their adolescents, another marriage means the establishment of several new relationships. Most often it is the divorced mother who takes her adolescents into this new family. There are four times the number of children living with a stepfather than a stepmother (see Bachrach, 1983). Children and younger adolescents are more likely to become part of another family in which there is a new father, and possibly stepbrothers and stepsisters. If the stepfather also had a previous marriage, they must accept sharing him, their mother and the household with his children during weekends or holidays. In short, a wide range of complex family structures can emerge with re-marriages, depending upon the number of previous marriages for each partner, the presence of children from these marriages, and the ages and location of children. In the majority of households where partners have re-married, at least one spouse has children from a previous marriage (Cherlin & McCarthy, 1985). According to some estimates, about one in every six children under 18 years of age is a stepchild (Mills, 1984).

There is considerable diversity and complexity in blended or reconstituted family arrangements. An individual may be a parent to their own children from another marriage, a step-parent to their

117

partner's children, as well as the biological parent of children born to the new marriage. Older children may come and go, moving between two households, college and their own friends. Step-parents are not the biological parents, but through marriage they do accept the legal status of parents and the responsibility for children. Some people become parents for the first time through re-marriage. If they do not have biological children, just like any new parent, they must confront the 'trial and error' learning that is often an integral feature of first parenthood. Even if they are parents to children from another marriage, they may not have experienced the responsibilities and demands of rearing adolescent children.

Table 6.2 Challenges confronting step-parents

Competition with ex-spouse in relationship with adolescents

Criticism from spouse and relatives about performance as a parent

Problem of how to discipline but also maintain love of stepchildren

Financial strain of raising adolescents in possibly two separate families

Negative stereotypes about step-parents

Developing trusting, intimate relationships with a stepchild

Dealing with the complex structure of blended families, and its impact on communication channels, stress and interpersonal relationahips

A lack of institutionalised guidelines about normative behaviour in stepfamilies

A lack of research and reading material available on the similar but also different challenges for parents and step-parents

---

A number of issues can make the lives of step-parents and step-children somewhat more difficult than those of intact families. We have outlined some of the challenges in particular facing step-parents in Table 6.2. Step-parents and stepchildren often complain that their role is poorly defined, especially on issues like their authority and the use of discipline. Does a step-parent have the same authority over a stepchild as they do over any natural children? Who should the adolescent believe about the appropriateness of an attitude or behaviour, the natural father or the stepfather? Adolescents can find themselves bargaining for independence and autonomy with two sets of fathers and mothers, with differences emerging across households in parents' expectations about the adolescent's status and role in the family. Any negotiations between parents and adolescents might also be coloured by unresolved feelings of anger, guilt or grief about the divorce. Unfortunately, the need to deal with these issues can increase the potential for conflict in families (see Cherlin, 1981; Chilman, 1983).

Traditionally, the image of stepchildren and step-parents has not been a good one. Community-based stereotypes portray both as having a number of personality problems. Unfortunately, early research tended to support these stereotypes. More recently, however, several findings have been challenged on the basis of both methodological and theoretical grounds (see Ganong & Coleman, 1984; Chilman, 1983). For example, research has not examined the range of variables that influence adjustment in stepfamilies (e.g. age and sex of children, marital quality, contact with the biological parent, prior experience of the step-parent), nor have researchers generally used the control group of single-marriage families. Rather, clinical writers have been more astute in presenting the complex personal, structural and interpersonal environments which are typical of stepfamilies. In particular, clinicians have given more attention to differences between stepmother and stepfather households, adolescent stepchildren who do and do not have stepsiblings, and adolescents who live permanently in one household, and those in more than one home.

Studies which have compared adolescents in stepfamilies and first-marriage families have found that mothers, fathers and adolescents have similar scores on levels of cohesion and adaptability (see Pink & Wampler, 1985). However, members of stepfamilies describe family life as less cohesive and less adaptable, although these levels of cohesion and adaptability still place families midway between normal and clinical families on measures of family functioning. In the stepfamilies, adolescents had less regard for their stepfathers. These perceptions are shared by stepfathers, who have less regard for the adolescents they care for as stepchildren.

Nevertheless, there is evidence that many stepfathers, rather than stepmothers, achieve better relationships more quickly with stepchildren of all ages. Stepmothers have more difficulty with adolescent stepchildren, but fewer problems with younger stepchildren. One explanation might be evidence that stepfathers play an important supportive role to the mother rather than a directive one on their own. Thus they are less likely to be directly involved in demanding certain behaviours from the adolescents or in being in open conflict with them.

Partly in an attempt to demonstrate their commitment and love for their stepchildren, there is an emerging trend in some countries for up to a half of step-parents to officially adopt stepchildren (Harper, 1983; 1984). Supporters of this movement point to adoption as a further way in which stepfathers show their love for their stepchildren. Undoubtedly, especially for many adolescents who may rarely see their biological fathers, adoption may strengthen their attachment to new fathers. Critics of this movement, however, question the need to make adolescents sever important ties with biological fathers. Adoption gives the child the surname of the stepfather, and as a result, many biological relatives (e.g. father, grandparents) no longer have any legal obligation for the welfare of the adolescent. In addition, there is the risk that some stepfathers are using adoption as a coping strategy when they can no longer cope with regular reminders about the biological father.

As mentioned earlier, there are various methodological problems that challenge the validity of many findings about the adjustment of step-children. To date, many studies of adolescents and college-age students do not show any differences between stepchildren and children in intact families on a variety of measures of psychological adjustment (Bernard, 1956; Oshman & Manosevitz, 1976; Parish & Dostal, 1980; Lutz, 1983). Although there is some evidence to the contrary, most studies fail to find differences in the self-image or psychological characteristics of adolescents in stepfamilies and other family structures. Unfortunately, many studies fail to accept that intact, divorced and step-parent families do differ in income, family size, the workforce involvement of mothers and in socioeconomic status. Significantly, it appears that many differences between these various family structures do diminish once demographic and socioeconomic factors are controlled (e.g. Guidubaldi & Perry, 1985). Similarly, when such controls are introduced in studies of adolescents in two-parent, step-parent and divorced families (Kurdek & Sinclair, 1988), no differences emerge in adolescents' self-reports of psychological symptoms, and school problems. In sum, while there are unique problems in adjusting to the loss of one parent and the arrival of another in the household, for most adolescents these problems are not serious enough to make them any less adjusted than adolescents in non-divorced households. But as individual case studies do reveal, we cannot forget that some adolescents are very negatively affected by the loss of a parent through a divorce, never adjusting to the demands of dealing with a new father or mother in their lives.

Conclusions

There are many serious methodological shortcomings in almost all of the research so far into adolescent adjustment to divorce and remarriage. At their worst, studies have not compared divorced families with control groups of intact families nor differentiated between adolescents in single-parent families because of the divorce or death of a parent. Even the better longitudinal studies have small samples, providing highly qualitative data from adolescents located through clinic referrals. There is a desperate need for more longitudinal research using large samples of children of both sexes and all ages from both divorced and non-divorced families.

Previous studies using clinical samples are often not comparable, because of differences in the socioeconomic status of families and different measures of adjustment and well-being. A wide variety of measures of adolescent adjustment are also employed, and many measures are not high on reliability or validity. Also adolescents are interviewed at different phases of the process of their parents' separation and divorce. As a result, studies are comparing adolescents at different stages of adjustment after the divorce.

Despite evidence that a parent's divorce stresses many adolescents, within a year or so after the divorce the majority of adolescents show good levels of adjustment. Indeed, compared with their parents, adolescents seem to bounce back more quickly. The post-divorce period, nevertheless, is still very challenging, especially with the emergence of a different type of relationship with their custodial mothers. Mothers carry the burden of caring for younger children and running the household. But there is evidence of many adolescents being mature, responsible and supportive of mothers. Many adolescents feel that the divorce of their parents has made them grow up a little quicker, but there are also cases where adolescents have reacted to the divorce with feelings of helplessness and insecurity. Adolescent males, in particular, seem to have a more difficult post-divorce transition, missing fathers and challenging the authority of their mothers.

There is sufficient evidence to suggest that most children and adolescents adjust well to the divorce of their parents. The degree of conflict between parents, not the divorce, is what can really affect adolescents' levels of adjustment. What we need to know more about are the developmental strengths, coping strategies and personality characteristics that help adolescents cope with the breakups of families. It is also obvious from research findings on adolescent adjustment to divorce that those using more objective, quantitative measures, and those employing in-depth interviews, gain somewhat different, even contradictory findings about the divorce experience for adolescents. Quantitative measures do play down how divorce is subjectively experienced by adolescents. More qualitative methods, however, are somewhat more open to bias and distortion (see Chapter 1). It is clear, as some researchers have shown (e.g. Dunlop & Burns, 1988), that both methods can be used to capture the impact of divorce. Especially when there are no differences between adolescents from divorced and intact families on various scales of personality and adjustment, case reports still remind us of individual cases where children have been seriously upset and disturbed by the breakup of the family. A minority of adolescents are distressed about the divorce for some time, but we know very little about the characteristics of adolescents who are more at risk of problems in adjusting to changes in their family life. Besides the need to use multiple research methods, there is also a need to gain corroborative information from the variety of other people who see the adolescent, including teachers, friends, natural and step-parents.

The majority of stepchildren have good levels of adjustment. Most report having a satisfactory relationship with the new step-parent, who very often is the stepfather. There are challenges for both the stepchild, the step-parent and the biological parents, and not surprisingly, there is some evidence of less closeness and adaptability between adolescents and parents in reconstituted families compared with intact families. These general conclusions, however, are very much open to further research. A deficit family model approach in which non-nuclear families are seen as atypical and dysfunctional has guided most research. This model has probably favoured interpretations indicating lower levels of adjustment among children of divorce and remarriage. In contrast, the bulk of null findings should now encourage investigators to use alternative theories (e.g. family systems theory, social learning, role theory), that may be much more appropriate conceptualisations of adolescents' experience after the breakup of their families.

Chapter seven

The family and adolescent issues

As we have said many times before, despite the fact that the peer group assumes new importance in adolescence, the family is still central to the health and well-being of the young person. In fact, Sheppard, Wright and Goodstadt (1985) go so far as to say that: 'The peer group, contrary to what is commonly believed, has little or no influence as long as the family remains strong. Peers take over only when parents abdicate' (p. 951). While this comment reflects an extreme view, it is undoubtedly clear from all the research that we have reviewed that most adolescents want to maintain, as far as possible, close positive relationships with their parents, and want their support and help. Parents who have positive relationships with their children can remain more influential than the peer group throughout adolescence. In fact, teenagers frequently use the standards of one group or the other, depending on what type of decision they are making (Glynn, 1981). For example, peers may be the reference group for music and dress, while parents are the reference group for long-term decisions about education and careers.

Various problems such as smoking, alcohol and drug abuse, teenage pregnancy and psychopathology are generally associated with the teenage years. In this chapter, we will look at the effects of both the family and the peer group on the extent to which these problems are likely to occur. We will begin by discussing the so-called battle between parents and peers and then look at the effects of various socialisation processes such as control, closeness, conflict and communication. We will also discuss the impact of the parents' own behaviour on the way the adolescent behaves and explore the effects of the parents' and the adolescents' personality on the likelihood of adolescents being involved in problem behaviours. Finally, we will examine ways of helping parents cope better with the problems of the teenage years.

Parents versus the peer group

There is quite a bit of evidence that the support of the family is crucial to adolescents, and that those who do not have strong support from parents are more likely to become involved in undesirable behaviours. Adolescents who rely on the peer group, rather than the family, for their main support are particularly vulnerable to peer pressure to engage in problem behaviours such as smoking cigarettes, drinking alcohol or using illegal drugs (Sheppard *et al.*, 1985). (These relationships are presented graphically in Figure 7.1.)

Figure 7.1 Effects for adolescents of reliance on family vs. peer group

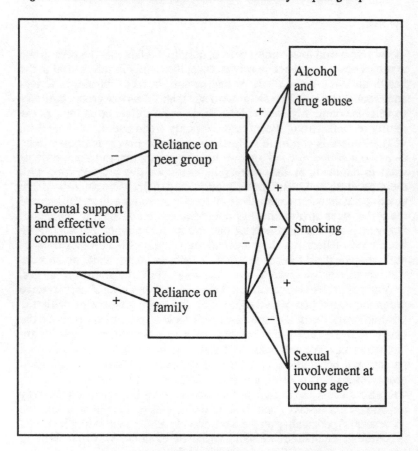

For example, Johnson (1986) examined the relative influence of parents and peers on adolescents' use and abuse of alcohol. The more involved adolescents were in their peer group, the more likely they were

to drink alcohol. These findings suggest how important it is for parents to stay by their adolescent and support them, rather than throwing them out of the home or withdrawing love and support in some other way. If parents fail to support their adolescents, the young people can become more involved with their peer group and even more committed to peer group values.

Commitment to the peer group

The more the adolescent is committed to the goals of the youth culture, the more they are likely to get involved in whatever problem behaviours are part of that culture. If their particular peer group is involved in alcohol or drugs, then those adolescents are likely to experience problems with alcohol or drugs. If they perceive their peer group as approving a particular behaviour, such as binge drinking, then they are likely to increase their own alcohol use. Even knowing that their peer group has no sanctions against alcohol use can increase that behaviour for those young people committed to a particular peer group.

While knowing that their peer group disapproves of a particular behaviour is likely to decrease involvement in that behaviour, knowing that parents disapprove can increase involvement in a behaviour, particularly for those young people who feel rejected and unsure of the love and concern of their parents. For example, young people who have poor relationships with their parents and who are involved in a peer group where members are heavy users of alcohol are highly likely to drink too much alcohol. McLaughlin and his colleagues (1985) compared peer and parental use of alcohol, along with the personality variables of tolerance of deviance and emotional maladjustment as predictors of teenage alcohol use in 7th and 10th grade boys and girls. Irrespective of grade or sex, the strongest predictor of alcohol use was the extent to which members of the peer group used alcohol. Tolerance of deviance and parental alcohol use were also related to adolescent use, but not as strongly as peer use. Similar findings hold for smoking. Adolescents are also more likely to smoke if parents, siblings and peers are smokers (Biglan *et al.*, 1983). Having opposite-sex friends who smoke also increases the chances of taking up smoking.

Taking up smoking seems generally to be prompted by peers, although some adolescents seem to be more primed to smoking than others. These adolescents have often thought more about the possibility of smoking before the first cigarette is offered and accept the initial offer with less hesitation (Friedman, Lichtenstein & Biglan, 1985). Few adolescents report that they started smoking alone, while about 90 per cent claim that they started smoking with same-sex friends. This study points to many other features of a first smoke. Another smoker is generally present, and there is frequently another person experimenting with smoking at the same time. While most adolescents claim that they are not pressured to smoke, 76 per cent admit smoking is suggested by another person and in 63 per cent of cases someone else actually offers a cigarette. About a quarter report being teased when they refuse or hesitate, and another quarter believe that taking the cigarette is necessary in order to be liked by their friends. Thus, there seem to be implicit pressures to smoke in these situations, although we must be careful not to take the responsibility away from the individual who is clearly still able to refuse. In the same study, nonsmokers asked about how they avoided taking the first cigarette said that they either politely said no, or else left the situation.

Just as the peer group is an important predictor of tobacco and alcohol use, it is also an important predictor of drug use. If adolescents are part of a peer group in which drug use is common, then they will be more likely to use drugs. In a rather polemical paper, Sheppard and her colleagues (1985) argue that adolescents who are interested in using drugs may seek out a peer group which supports that interest, as well as overestimate the prevalence of drug users in their community – the 'everyone is doing it' syndrome. In fact, Sheppard's data suggest that many young people are never offered cannabis, and many who are, simply refuse without feeling undue pressure to accept. These authors believe strongly that the responsibility for using drugs should be on the user, and that adolescents should be encouraged to realise that they do have a choice, and that they have the responsibility to say 'no' when pressured to conform in performing illegal or undesirable behaviours. Data collected by Meier, Burkett & Hickman (1984) also suggest that adolescents interested in using drugs tend to choose users as peers, and that this chosen peer group then serves to increase their usage, as well as to minimise the chances that sanctions will have any impact on them.

Young people who have sexual intercourse in their early teens are also more likely to have friends their parents don't like, to be more of a problem to their parents and to be more peer-oriented than the average adolescent. Girls engaging in sexual intercourse are also more likely to come from single-parent families and to be looking for affection. Overall then, the peer group can have strong influences on smoking, drinking and sexual behaviour. The strength of the impact, however, depends on the relative strength of commitment to the peer group and the quality of the parent–adolescent relationship. Parents will have more influence, and the peers less influence, when the parent–adolescent relationship is positive and cooperative.

Attachment to parents

Attachment to parents is related to the extent to which adolescents get involved in health-risk behaviours such as smoking and drinking. For example, adolescents who take up smoking are less strongly attached to their mothers than nonsmokers, and are more attached to their fathers and their friends (Skinner *et al.*, 1985). While attachment to friends would be expected, given that we have already shown that involvement with the peer group tends to encourage, rather than constrain, deviant behaviour, the researchers were not able to explain the effects of attachment to father. Fathers of smokers were more likely to also smoke, and this may have had some effect on the smoking behaviour of those who were strongly attached.

Since the study reported by Skinner and his colleagues (1985) was longitudinal, they were able to look at changes over time related to stopping smoking. Those who stopped were more closely bonded to their parents on the second occasion, although bonding to friends had not changed. Those who had continued smoking were less strongly bonded to their parents on the second occasion. Smokers who continued, reported associating more with smokers both initially and later. Other factors related to giving up smoking were becoming more religious and having a father who had cut back on smoking. These findings again support the likelihood that those who are closely identified with their fathers are likely to model their smoking on him. These young people are also more likely to stop smoking when their father expresses his concern about smoking by cutting back his own intake of cigarettes.

Drug-taking is affected by the quality of relationships with parents. In fact, these relationships can even predict changing patterns of drug use over a two year period (Norem-Hebeisen *et al.*, 1984). These researchers found that increasing drug use between grades 9 and 11 was associated with the adolescents' perceptions of parental disapproval and of receiving few expressions of caring and affection from their parents. These teenagers also described their fathers as angry with them and rejecting of them. Both parents also seemed to be continually and increasingly trying to control the teenagers' comings and goings. The adolescents who did not use drugs reported more positive relationships with their parents between the 9th and 11th grades, with more affirmation from both mothers and fathers and less hostility between themselves and their fathers.

Parental supervision

While adolescents tend to react negatively to parents who try to control them too much, some parental supervision seems to be important to their well-being, and particularly minimises the chances of their becoming involved in problem behaviours. Those who spend a lot of time unsupervised are more likely to engage in a range of such behaviours. For example, females are less likely to smoke if they are subjected to more parental supervision and if they associate less with female friends who smoke.

Illicit drug use is also related to amount of supervision, and is particularly high among young adults who are often on their own or who are living away from home with friends (Thorne & DeBlassie, 1985)). Of course, an important question concerns whether these young people use drugs more because they are away from home or leave home in order to be free to use drugs. It is clear, however, that being at home and being under some supervision reduces involvement in drugs.

Socialisation practices in the family

Given that the quality of the parent–adolescent relationship is so strongly related to the involvement of adolescents in problem behaviours, parents' socialisation practices are highly likely to be relevant. A range of family factors are related to drug use and abuse (see Jurich and his colleagues (1985)). Conflict between the parents, absence of one or both parents when the child was growing up, little closeness between parent and child, parental rejection and hostility, lack of communication in the family, problematic discipline procedures in the family, and the parents' own use of drugs, all have been implicated as causes of adolescent drug abuse. In this section, we will discuss the relationship between family functioning or socialisation practices and the adolescent's involvement in a range of problem behaviours.

Closeness and cohesion

An important issue is the level of closeness in the family. There are concerns, in fact, about whether families can be too close (Beavers & Voeller, 1983; Olson *et al.*, 1983) and what may be the consequences of too much closeness (see Steinhauer, 1987 for a discussion of this issue). Epstein and his colleagues (1978) describe an extreme level of symbiotic (or enmeshed) involvement as 'so intense that the boundaries between the two or more individuals are blurred' and 'extreme involvement that blurs individual differentiation' (p.26). The main issue is whether individuals are clearly differentiated (able to separate self from nonself) and able to function as separate autonomous beings. The assumption of many theorists seems to be that high closeness always involves low or nonexistent autonomy (e.g. Bowen, 1978; Minuchin,

1974). Of course, the relationship between autonomy and closeness is an empirical question and should be treated as such. We suspect, however, as Beavers and Voeller comment, that capable families are able to respect individual choice, as well as being able to maintain high levels of closeness (Lewis, Beavers, Gossett & Phillips, 1976).

Individuation and autonomy are as crucial to the adolescent's development of a separate sense of self, appropriate levels of self-esteem and healthy, constructive relationships with others. Enmeshed individuals are likely to rely excessively on primitive defences such as projection and introjection, especially in stressful situations (Steinhauer, 1987). This reliance leads to confusion of the individual's own feelings, thoughts and needs with those of the parent, and to generally destructive family relationships involving a great deal of acting-out and manipulation. A further concern is that those who are enmeshed as adolescents are likely to continue the pattern into their own families, and their children are also at great risk of being enmeshed.

On the other hand, those adolescents who experience warmth and closeness in their families are less likely to be over-influenced by the peer group and to be involved in problem behaviours. Jurich and his colleagues (1985), for example, found that families that were warm and close had fewer problems with adolescent drug use and abuse. Those adolescents who do not experience warmth and closeness in the family tend to look to their peer group and to engage in smoking, drinking and marihuana use to gain that support and acceptance (Sheppard *et al.*, 1985). They may also get involved in sexual relationships early as a way of finding the warmth and affection that is missing from their family relationships. As we shall see in the next section, however, there is also evidence that the balance between support and control in the family is more important than the level of closeness per se.

Balance between support and control

Adolescent patterns of alcohol consumption are related to the balance between support and control in the family (Barnes *et al.*, 1986). Alcohol problems among adolescents are particularly prominent where mothers are low in both support and control and at their lowest when mothers are high in support and low or medium in control. Alcohol problems also occur at high levels when fathers are low in support and high in control and at low levels when fathers are high in support and exert a medium level of control.

Support and control in the family also predict drug use, particularly for girls (Block, Block & Keyes, 1988). Parents of daughters who are more likely to become drug users are highly permissive with these daughters. They also make little attempt to inculcate traditional values, providing, instead, a rather unconventional family environment where the children are permitted to be highly expressive emotionally, and to challenge both parents and teachers. These daughters are encouraged towards early independence but are not pushed to achieve. The families and homes are generally noisy and poorly organized and manners are not expected.

It seems that families that are either too authoritarian or too permissive are most likely to have problems with drug abuse. The relationships between the level of control in the family and adolescent problem behaviours is presented in Figure 7.2. Jurich *et al.* (1985) compared a drug-using group (infrequent or occasional use of legal or nonaddictive drugs) with a drug-abusing group (almost daily ingestion of dangerous drugs).

Figure 7.2 Relationship between level of control in the family and problem behaviour of adolescents

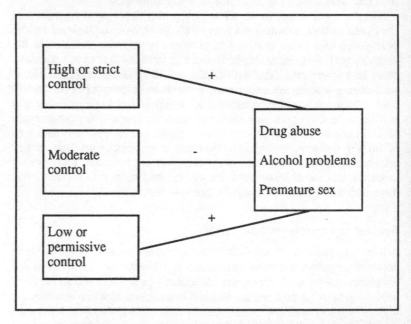

Parents of drug-abusers were less likely to be democratic in their parenting and were more likely to use either authoritarian discipline techniques or laissez-faire techniques. Authoritarian techniques are likely to increase parent–adolescent conflict and adolescent frustration, and to lead to acting-out on the part of the adolescent. Laissez-faire discipline, on the other hand, allows the adolescent more freedom than he or she can handle responsibly and may encourage a hedonistic use of drugs.

Having permissive parents also increases the chances of adolescents' being involved in sexual intercourse at an early age and of becoming teenage parents. Two factors are likely to be relevant here: the lack of parental supervision and the permissive parents' failure to discuss the issues with the adolescent, to inculcate standards and to point out the possible consequences of their behaviour.

In addition, power and control are relevant to the development of psychopathology in an adolescent family member. Again, a balanced level of control seems most appropriate. Psychopathology is most likely to occur in families where there is excessive dominance of one partner over other members (Rodick & Henggeler, 1982) or in families where mothers have difficulty taking the role of a parent and are too permissive (Barton, Alexander & Turner, 1988).

Inappropriate hierarchies (e.g. Hetherington, Stouwie & Ridberg, 1971) and inappropriate coalitions in the family have also been implicated. Inappropriate hierarchies occur where children, rather than parents, dominate decision-making in the family and parents have little or no control. Inappropriate coalitions occur when the parents do not operate as a unit, but either the mother or the father continually sides with one or more of the children against the other parent. Minuchin (1974) particularly emphasises the need for clear separation between the parent subsystem and the child subsystem and the importance of parents taking a clear leadership role. Children should not be encouraged to behave like parents, and parents should not abdicate their roles and behave like children.

On the other hand, it is also important that family roles and rules are not upheld too rigidly. Adaptability is very important to family functioning (see also Chapters 1 and 4). Parents need to be continually assessing roles and rules in the family to see whether they are still appropriate. Rules and roles in the family need to be altered in response to developmental changes in family members. Rules that were appropriate to a family with primary school children are often not appropriate to high school children. Rules that were appropriate to high school children may not be suitable for adolescents who are working or attending university. Rules may also need to change with changes in external circumstances such as moving house or involvement in outside activities. Roles and rules must be able to accommodate to each individual's unique situation and special needs.

Communication and conflict

Family communication is relevant to the adolescent's involvement in

131

problem behaviours in several ways. The quality of the communication in the family dictates the quality of the relationships between the parents and the adolescent, which, as we have already seen, affects the child's bonding to the parent and his or her involvement in the peer group. Those families where communication is positive and effective are less likely to be involved in problem behaviours. For example, poor parent–child relationships and parent–child communication are related to involvement in alcohol, drug abuse and sexual intercourse for young people.

Good communication is likely to mean that the adolescent confides in the parents and looks to them as a source of information. This willingness to confide is likely to be particularly relevant for sexual behaviour where there seems to be a serious lack of accurate information among teenagers. Adolescents who are able to talk to their parents about sex tend to be more knowledgeable than those who cannot discuss such issues with their parents (Rothenberg, 1980). In most families, however, parents are the least important sources of sex information, especially for sons. Given what we have said earlier about the lack of communication about sex in the family (see Chapter 3), we would not expect parents to be important sources of sexual information for their kids. A further problem is that parents do not always know the answers to the questions adolescents ask about sex (Fox & Inazu, 1980; Rothenberg, 1980), and adolescents often think they know everything when they don't. Providing good reading material for adolescents can be another way of ensuring that they have accurate information.

Morrison (1985) cites studies indicating quite clearly that adolescents are 'a mine of misinformation' about sexuality and conception. For example, adolescents often cite the time of the month as a reason for not using contraception, yet they are often wrong about which time of the month is 'safe'. Other amazing beliefs cited in studies of teenagers include 'if a girl truly doesn't want a baby, she won't get pregnant' (Sorenson, 1973) and 'a woman must have an orgasm in order to get pregnant' (Reichelt & Werley, 1975). Some adolescent girls do not understand that fertility begins when they start menstruating, and some believe that it is not possible to get pregnant the first time they have intercourse. While those who have had some form of sex education tend to have more accurate knowledge than those who do not, the appalling ignorance among adolescents does not seem to be totally alleviated by such classes (Morrison, 1985). The ideal is probably classes attended with parents, followed by discussion between parents and their own children. Unfortunately, given the reticence among family members to talk about sex, it is likely that adolescence is too late and discussion about sex needs to start much earlier. As we know, adolescents who have good relationships with their parents are also more likely to confide in them about any problems with alcohol, drugs or relationships. If adolescents are able to talk to their parents and respect their parents' advice and opinions they are likely to have fewer prob- lems in these areas and to be prepared to seek help when they need it.

Another reason why good communication is important is that families with effective communication have less conflict at both the marital and family levels, with high levels of conflict being related to adolescent psychopathology and delinquency. In addition, where family conflict is high, adolescents are likely to leave home earlier and thus be more prone to involvement in undesirable activities such as drug abuse and prostitution.

A number of studies point to a relationship between marital conflict and conduct disorders in boys. Rutter (1971) found that where the parents' marriage was rated as good, boys were not involved in antisocial behaviour. On the other hand, almost 40 per cent of those whose parents' marriages were rated as very poor were engaging in antisocial activities. The boys most at risk were those whose parents' marriage was rated as very poor and whose relationships with both parents were unsatisfactory. Having a good relationship with one of their parents halved their chances of being involved in antisocial behaviours.

A child in a family where marital conflict is high and the opposite-sex parent is very dominant is especially at risk for an internalizing disorder such as depression. For instance, a daughter, in a family where there is high marital conflict and the father is very dominant, is likely to be torn between identifying with the mother (because she is the same sex) and the father (because he is the more powerful). The conflict will be even stronger if the father treats the mother with contempt. Such a scenario is likely to lead to low self-esteem and depression in the daughter (see Martin, 1987).

While adolescents whose parents have a healthy relationship tend to develop strong positive identities and separate fairly smoothly from their parents, those whose parents are in conflict may have more separation problems. Martin suggests that separation from the parents may be particularly difficult if one of the parents is too involved with the adolescent, or if one or both parents is maladjusted. Conflicted parent–child relationships can also make separation difficult, rather than easy, for the adolescent because of the guilt, anxiety, resentment and anger that the adolescent feels toward the parent.

While conflict increases the strains on the family, how adolescents try to cope with this stress and conflict has a greater impact on their behaviour than the presence of the stress. Adolescents who experience a build-up of family stressors and strains are more likely to get involved in smoking, drinking or drugs than other adolescents (McCubbin,

Needle & Wilson, 1985). Those who are most at risk for heavy involvement in behaviours that put their health at risk, are those who tend to 'ventilate' or externalise in response to stress – blaming others, getting angry, yelling and complaining. On the other hand, those who cope with these strains by talking with their parents and trying to work out difficult issues with family members are much less likely to engage in these health-risk behaviours as a means of coping. Thus the quality of their communication with their parents is again likely to be crucial.

Family conflict, along with other communication problems, is implicated in both the development and maintenance of psychopathology in adolescents (Goldstein & Strachan, 1987). For instance, families of schizophrenics have a tendency to communicate with less clarity and accuracy than normal families, both with one another and with the schizophrenic patient (see also Alexander & Parsons, 1982; Klein, Alexander & Parsons, 1977). There is also evidence for less facilitative information exchange and extremes of conflict (Barton, Alexander & Turner, 1988). Goldstein and Strachan (1987) note that, across a number of studies, parents of schizophrenics tend to have difficulty maintaining a shared focus of attention, communicating meaning clearly and accurately and taking the perspective of another person.

Using a longitudinal design, Goldstein and his colleagues (Doane, West, Goldstein, Rodnick & Jones, 1981; Goldstein, Judd, Rodnick, Alkire & Gould, 1968) were able to demonstrate that communication problems were present in the family before the onset of a schizophrenia spectrum disorder (includes other schizotypal disorders). In a 15-year follow-up, they showed that schizophrenia spectrum disorders were most likely in families where parents had difficulty communicating clearly, used a negative affective style and were high in emotional expressiveness (harsh criticism and intrusiveness).

Some theorists also argue (e.g. Beavers & Voeller, 1983) that different types of problematic family interaction (or different family styles) produce different types of psychopathology in adolescents. According to Beavers and his colleagues, families which are extremely family-focused and have little interaction with the outside world (families he called centripetal) are likely to produce adolescents with internalizing disorders such as depression or schizophrenia. On the other hand, families which are focused strongly on the outside world, with only loose bonds between family members (families he called centrifugal) are likely to produce adolescents with externalizing disorders, that is, delinquent and conduct-disordered young people.

Effective communication in the family also provides the adolescent with models of social competence, as well as training in skills such as self-disclosure and problem-solving. There are several indications, for example, of a relationship between loneliness and an individual's social competence (Perlman & Peplau, 1981). Lonely people tend to avoid social situations, and have difficulty taking the initiative in conversations, making friends, introducing themselves to others and making phone calls to arrange social activities. Those whose parents have not provided them with good models in these areas, and have not helped them to overcome any reticence to initiate social contacts are more likely to be lonely and to have problems doing anything about that loneliness.

Learning appropriate patterns of self-disclosure in the family is also likely to decrease the chances of adolescents being lonely. Teenagers who learn to self-disclose in the family are more likely to self-disclose to their peers. In addition, teenagers who are more willing to self-disclose to their peers are also less likely to feel lonely (Franzoi & Davis, 1985).

For several reasons, loneliness seems to be a particularly acute problem among adolescents. During this time, teenagers attempt to achieve individuation, emphasise autonomy and freedom, and have problems of self-identity. They are involved in a search for meaningfulness, are developing their cognitive processes and often find themselves in a 'social limbo' (Mijuskovic, 1986). While adolescents who have more problems making friends are likely to be lonelier, those with more close friends are not necessarily less lonely (Medora, 1983; Medora & Woodward, 1986). Loneliness is also related to happiness, with those who are less lonely reporting themselves as happier. While we would expect the lonely to be less happy, they also tend to be consistently more negative in their outlook, so the results about happiness may reflect the possibility that this negative outlook increases their chances of being lonely. There is also evidence of negativity among lonely students who describe themselves as 'angry, self-enclosed, empty and awkward' (Russell *et al.*, 1978).

Adolescents model the social skills of parents with whom they have a positive relationship. High-school students report being more likely to self-disclose to parents who are warm and loving. Those who disclose to parents are also more likely to disclose to peers and thus be less lonely. There is also evidence that mothers' social competence directly affects the social competence of their children. Filsinger and Lamke (1983), for example, show that mothers who are anxious and socially withdrawing tend to have adolescents who behave similarly. These adolescents are also likely to be low in social self-esteem and to have problems with intimate relationships. These are the adolescents who are most likely to be lonely and unhappy.

Personality factors

Some personality factors in parents and adolescents predict problem behaviours in the adolescent. A notable study by Brook and her colleagues (e.g. Brook, Whiteman & Gordon, 1983; Brook, Whiteman, Gordon & Cohen, 1986) showed that parents who are conventional and warm and provide a structured environment for their children are less likely than other parents to have adolescents who use drugs. On the other hand, Brook and her colleagues have found evidence for drug-prone personalities in adolescents which lead to higher levels of drug usage, even when the family and peer environments are positive. Such personality traits include tolerance of deviance, rebelliousness, lack of conventionality, sensation-seeking, depression and obsessiveness. Teenagers with these personality traits are more likely to be involved in drug abuse. On the other hand, where the family environment is negative, adolescents tend to be involved in higher levels of drug use, even when they do not have 'drug-prone personalities' and their peer group is conventional. Drug use is more likely, however, where more than one of these factors are operating. For example, a lack of maternal warmth combined with unconventionality in the adolescent is more likely than either of the aspects separately to increase the level of drug use. The presence of several positive characteristics (e.g. warmth in the mother–child relationship and conventionality in the adolescent) is more likely to decrease the level of drug use.

The parent's personality seems to have an indirect effect on the child via the child's relationship with the parent. If the parent's personality is conducive to a warm, positive parent–child relationship, then the chances of involvement in problem behaviours are lower than if the parent's personality leads to a hostile, rejecting parent–child relationship, although the effects for relationships with the mother are stronger than those for the father. The mother who is both psychologically stable and conventional is more likely to have a relationship with the adolescent which is very affectionate and not marred by too much conflict. This positive relationship increases the probability that the adolescent will also be conventional and psychologically stable and therefore less likely to be involved in activities such as drug abuse.

Effects of the parents' own behaviour

Alcohol consumption and drinking patterns among adolescents tend to reflect the drinking patterns of adults in the same sociocultural milieu (Barnes, Farrell & Cairns, 1986). Drinking by adolescents is also affected by the drinking patterns of their parents. While parents who are heavy drinkers are more likely to have heavy drinkers among their adolescent children, abstaining mothers are also more likely to have heavy-drinking adolescents than are mothers who drink moderately. Adolescents are also more likely to smoke when their parents, siblings and peers are smokers (Biglan *et al.*, 1983) and they are also likely to have more problems giving up smoking when those closest to them smoke.

Other members of the families of drug abusers are more likely to use drugs than are the members of the families of adolescents who do not abuse drugs. Adolescents are especially likely to be influenced to abuse drugs when a powerful family member such as a parent uses drugs (Jurich *et al.*, 1985). These findings support the work of other researchers which shows that adolescent drug-takers are more likely to have one or more parents with alcohol problems (Barnes, 1977; Bratter, 1975) or who are heavy users of prescription drugs (Josephson & Caroll, 1974). In addition, adolescents who use drugs are much more likely than non-users to have parents who use drugs, including alcohol and tobacco (McDermott, 1984). Two explanations are possible, of course: a social learning explanation would see the parents as modelling drug-taking behaviour for their family members, while family theorists, on the other hand, would be more likely to suggest that environments where one or both parents are heavy users of drugs or alcohol are likely to be stressful and difficult environments in which to raise young people. The level of stress is likely to increase the probability that the adolescent will use drugs as a means of coping with the higher level of stress.

The adolescents' perceptions of their parents as permissive or nonpermissive in their attitudes towards drugs are also important predictors of drug use, with teenagers who perceive their parents as holding permissive attitudes being more likely to use drugs. In addition, parental attitude seems to be at least as important as the parents' actual behaviour in predicting drug use. Of course, the parents' own use of drugs may be a powerful indicator to a young person that the parent has permissive attitudes towards drugs.

Helping parents cope with adolescents' problems

Helping professionals are often called on to assist parents in coping with problems with their adolescent offspring. Parents are frequently confused about what style of parenting is appropriate for adolescents, and about the best way of reacting to their problem behaviours. Parents are usually anxious to know what action they can take, without making the situation worse. In this section, we will try to tie together the things we have been saying in terms of advice to parents about handling adolescents. It is important to recognise that we are trying to present general principles that seem to emerge, and that these may not apply in some cases.

It is clear from much that we have said that most adolescents want and need close, warm relationships with their parents. Constructive, helpful parenting aims to provide such a relationship. Adolescents who feel comfortable about their relationship with their parents are more likely to reflect their parents' values, to disclose to them and to cooperate with them. Obtaining adolescents' cooperation is much more crucial than obtaining their obedience. Where adolescents cooperate with their parents, obedience becomes a non-issue.

Authoritarian parenting-styles may increase conformity and obedience in the short-term, but adolescents with authoritarian parents are at risk for developing more external styles where they lack internal controls on their own behaviour and are more concerned about getting caught than about doing what is right for its own sake. Adolescents with external styles are also more likely to blame others when things go wrong and are less likely to take responsibility for their own decisions and behaviours.

Authoritarian parenting can also lead to rebellion and a complete breakdown of the parent–adolescent relationship. These parents are likely to believe that the answer to their problems with their adolescents is to be more and more controlling. The more strict and rigid their controls become, however, the more reactant their adolescents will become and the lower the chances that they will do what their parents want. In addition the adolescents will become more determined to free themselves from the 'tyranny' of their parents. Many kids are on the street because of this type of breakdown in their relationships with their parents.

Adolescents cope much better when they feel accepted by their parents and able to talk about their problems and issues and to negotiate changes in roles and rules. Many problems stem from the difficulties parents and adolescents have in communicating their feelings and needs and working out mutually acceptable solutions. Adolescents also need to be able to come to their parents for important information and to discuss issues with them. An accepting environment also helps adolescents to engage in the more basic tasks of identity exploration and development.

Parents need to be flexible in their dealings with adolescents. They must be prepared to change role expectations and rules when they are no longer appropriate. The emphasis on consistency so often found in the popular literature about child-rearing needs to be discussed here. It is important that adolescents know what the important family rules are, and that they are not punished for something one week that they got away with the week before. However, they should also expect that parents will be prepared to take into account their individual needs and circumstances and to negotiate changes. For example, if a family rule which says that all family members should be present at breakfast precludes a family member from training for the school swimming team as she would like to, then such a rule may need to be revised.

A further important consideration is that adolescents who are able to talk with their parents about their issues and rely on them for emotional support are likely to rely less on the peer group for both their emotional support and for guidance as to what behaviour is appropriate. Those whose main focus is on the peer group are more likely to be pressured into using less constructive means of coping such as drinking or drugs. In addition, the build-up of unresolved stressors and strains on the adolescent makes them increasingly at risk for using health-risk behaviours. Parenting styles encouraging the development of problem-solving approaches which involve talking to family members and trying to find ways of resolving the issues are much more constructive.

It is important for both adolescents and their parents to recognise that adolescents have to be responsible for their own behaviour, and not blame others or circumstances when they get involved in undesirable behaviours. The only real protection an adolescent has when confronted with the opportunity to engage in illegal, immoral or undesirable behaviours is the ability to say no and to withstand pressure. Parents, therefore, should emphasise internal rather than external controls and discourage inappropriate attributions of blame to external sources. Blaming peers or circumstances for excessive drinking of alcohol, for example, does not help the adolescent to take control of their drinking and take appropriate steps to decrease their indulgence. Parents should also be careful that the implicit messages sent to the adolescent are ones which encourage good judgment and competence.

Implicit messages related to smoking, drinking, drug abuse and sexual behaviour are also important. Adolescents are not likely to respect parents who expect a high standard of behaviour from their children, while indulging in problem behaviours themselves. The heavy drinking father, for example, is unlikely to be able to persuade his adolescents that drinking is not the best answer to stress if he, himself, continually uses alcohol for that purpose. The mother who regularly takes prescription drugs to deal with stress is also giving family members a clear message that such behaviour is appropriate.

Attitudes to the opposite sex are modelled in similar ways. Fathers who talk about women as though they are merely servants or sex objects are unlikely to engender healthy self-esteem in their daughters, or encourage their sons to treat women as equals. Wives who accept abuse from their husbands as though it is their due also provide poor role models for their daughters. Mothers who continually make negative or disparaging comments about men are likely to have negative effects on the sex role attitudes and close relationships of both their sons and their daughters. Sons are likely to have low self-esteem from hearing their sex continually degraded, while girls are likely to take on their mothers' negative opinions of the opposite sex. In situations such as these, the modelling of the parents is likely to have very powerful effects on their adolescents.

Attitudes to work and unemployment are also learned in the family and some adolescents are likely to learn destructive attitudes of one sort or another. Some may blame themselves inappropriately for situations which have more to do with government economic policy than with individuals. Others may learn to look to external authorities such as governments to solve their own and their family's problems and not realise that there are things they can do to help themselves. Either of these attitudes can be causes for concern. It is not appropriate for adolescents to be blamed for not working when no jobs are available, and governments must be prepared to provide backup services in such situations. On the other hand, young people should not be encouraged to expect governments to supply all their needs.

We began by discussing the controversy in the literature about whether adolescence is a time of storm and stress for families or whether most adolescents make a smooth transition from childhood to adulthood. We have opted for the relational view which suggests that adolescents renegotiate their relationships with their parents during adolescence. The achievement of new relationships on the basis of greater mutual respect and equality is likely to cause some problems in the short term for both parents and adolescents, and require a certain amount of patience on the part of both. Those who are able to manage the transition, however, will generally find that their relationships with their parents or children will be even more rewarding than before, and that these relationships will then continue indefinitely. Perhaps some of the ideas we have presented will help to make these transitions more painless and rewarding.

References

Acock, A.C., Bengtson, V.L. (1978) 'On the relative influence of mothers and fathers: A covariance analysis of political and religious socialisation', *Journal of Marriage and the Family* 40: 519–30.

Acock, A.C., Bengtson, V.L. (1980) 'Socialisation and attribution processes: Actual versus perceived similarity among parents and youth', *Journal of Marriage and the Family* 42: 501–15.

Adams, G.R. & Fitch, S.A. (1982) 'Ego state and identity status development: A cross-sequential analysis', *Journal of Personality and Social Psychology* 43: 574–83.

Adams, G.R. & Jones, R.M. (1983) 'Female adolescents' identity development: Age comparisons and perceived child-rearing experience', *Developmental Psychology* 19: 249–56.

Albrecht, S.L. (1980) 'Reactions and adjustments to divorce: Differences in the experiences of males and females', *Family Relations* 29: 59–68.

Alexander, J. & Parsons, B.V. (1982) *Functional Family Therapy*, Monterey, CA: Brooks/Cole.

Amato, P. (1987a) *Children in Australian Families: the growth of competence*, Melbourne: Prentice-Hall.

Amato, P. (1987b) 'Children's reactions to parental separation and divorce: The views of children and custodial mothers', *Australian Journal of Social Issues* 22: 610–23.

Amoroso, D.M. & Ware, E.E. (1986) 'Adolescents' perception of aspects of the home environment and their attitudes towards parents, self and external authority', *Adolescence* 21 (81): 191–204.

Anderson, E.R., Hetherington, E.M., & Clingempeel, W.G. (1986) 'Pubertal status and its influence on the adaptation to remarriage', Paper presented at the First Conference on Social Research into Adolescence, Madison, Wisconsin.

Anderson, S.A. & Fleming, W.M. (1986) 'Late adolescents' home-leaving strategies: Predicting ego identity and college adjustment', *Adolescence* 21: 453–59.

Archer, S.L. (1981) 'Ego identity development among early and mid-adolescents', Paper presented at The Eastern Psychological Association, New York, April.

References

Australian National Opinion Polls (ANOP) (1984) *A Study of Young Australians*, Canberra: Department of the Special Minister of State.

Bachrach, C. (1983) 'Children in families: Characteristics of biological, step-, and adopted children', *Journal of Marriage and the Family* 45: 171–79.

Bagi, S. (1983) 'Parent–adolescent communication', Unpublished honours thesis, University of Queensland.

Balswick, J. (1988) *The Inexpressive Male*, Lexington, MA: Lexington Books.

Balswick, J.O. & Macrides, C. (1975) 'Parental stimulus for adolescent rebellion', *Adolescence* 10 (38): 253–66.

Baranowski, M. (1981) 'Adolescents' attempted influence on parental behaviors', *Adolescence* 13: 585–603.

Barnes, G.M. (1977) 'The development of adolescent drinking behaviour: An evaluation review of the impact of the socialization process within the family', *Adolescence* 12: 571–91.

Barnes, G.M., Farrell, M.P., & Cairns, A. (1986) 'Parental socialization factors and adolescent drinking behaviours', *Journal of Marriage and the Family* 48: 27–36.

Barnes, H.L. & Olson, D.H. (1985) 'Parent–adolescent communication and the circumplex model', *Child Development* 56: 437–47.

Barnett, R.C. (1975) 'Sex differences and age trends in occupational preference and occupational prestige', *Journal of Counselling Psychology* 22 (1): 35–8.

Barton, C., Alexander, J.F., & Turner, C.W. (1988) 'Defensive communication in normal and delinquent families: The impact of context and social role', *Journal of Family Psychology* 1: 390–405.

Baumrind, D. (1971) 'Current patterns of parental authority', *Developmental Psychology Monograph* 4: 1–102.

Baumrind, D. (1980) 'New directions in socialization research', *American Psychologist* 35(7): 639–52.

Baxter, L.A. (1984) 'Trajectories of relationship disengagement', *Journal of Social and Personal Relationships* 1: 29–48.

Beavers, W.R. (1976) 'A theoretical basis for family evaluation', in J.M. Lewis, W.R. Beavers, J.T. Gossett, & V.A. Phillips (eds) *No Single Thread: psychological health in family systems* (46–82), New York: Brunner/Hazel.

Beavers, W.R. (1981) 'A systems model of family for family therapists', *Journal of Marital and Family Therapy* 7: 299–307.

Beavers, W.R. & Voeller, M.N. (1983) 'Family models: Comparing and contrasting the Olson circumplex model with the Beavers systems model', *Family Process* 22: 85–98.

Bell, L. & Bell, D. (1982) 'Family climate and the role of the female adolescent: Determinants of adolescent functioning', *Family Relations* 31: 519–27.

Belsky, J. (1979) 'The interaction of parental and spousal behavior during infancy in traditional nuclear families', *Journal of Marriage and the Family* 41: 749–55.

Bengtson, V.L. & Kuypers, J.A. (1971) 'Generational differences and the developmental stake', *Aging and Human Development* 2: 249–60.

Bengtson, V.L. & Starr, J.M. (1975) 'Contrast and consensus: A generational analysis of youth in the 1970's', in R.J. Havinghurst & P.H. Dreyer (eds),

Youth: The Seventy-Fourth Yearbook of the National Society for the Study of Education, Chicago: University of Chicago Press.

Bengtson, V.L., & Troll, L. (1978) 'Youth and their parents: Feedback and intergenerational influence in socialization' in R.M. Lerner & G.B. Spanier (eds), *Childrens' Influences on Marital and Family Interaction: a life-span perspective* (106–30), New York: Academic Press.

Berg, D. (1985) 'Reality construction at the family/society interface: The internalization of family themes and values', *Adolescence* 20(79): 605–18.

Berger, P.L. & Kellner, H. (1964) 'Marriage and the construction of reality', *Diogenes* 46: 1–24.

Bernard, H.S. (1981) 'Identity formation during late adolescence: A review of some empirical findings', *Adolescence* 16: 349–58.

Bernard, J. (1956) *Remarriage: a study of marriage,* New York: Holt, Rinehart and Winston.

Biddle, B.J., Bank, B.J., & Marlin, M.M. (1980) 'Parental and peer influence on adolescents', *Social Forces* 58: 1057–79.

Biglan, A., Severson, H.H., McConnell, S., & Bavry, J. (1983) 'Social influences and adolescent smoking: A first look behind the barn', *Health Education* 14: 14–18.

Block, J., Block, J.H., & Gjerde, P.F. (1986) 'The personality of children prior to divorce: A prospective study', *Child Development* 57: 827–40.

Block, J., Block, J.H., & Keyes, S. (1988) 'Longitudinally foretelling drug usage in adolescence: Early childhood personality and environmental precursors', *Child Development* 59: 336–55.

Bloom, B.L., Asher, S.J., & White, S.W. (1978) 'Marital disruption as a stressor: A review and analysis', *Psychological Bulletin* 85: 867–94.

Booth, A., Brinkerhoff, D.B., & White, L.K. (1984) 'The impact of parental divorce on courtship', *Journal of Marriage and the Family* 46: 85–94.

Bowen, M. (1978) *Family Therapy in Clinical Practice,* New York: Jason Aronson.

Bratter, T.E. (1975) 'Wealthy families and their drug abusing adolescents', *Journal of Family Counselling* 3: 72–6.

Breakwell, G.M., Fife-Schaw, C., & Devereux, J. (1988) 'Parental influence and teenagers' motivation to train for technological jobs', *Journal of Occupational Psychology* 61: 79–88.

Brennan, T., Huiziner, D., & Elliott, D. (1978) *The Social Psychology of Runaways,* Lexington, MA: Lexington Books.

Brody, L. & Fox, L.H. (1980) 'An accelerated intervention program for mathematically gifted girls', in L.H. Fox, L. Brody, & D. Tobin (eds), *Women and the Mathematical Mystique,* Baltimore: Johns Hopkins University Press.

Bronfenbrenner, U. (1986) 'Ecology of the family as a context for human development: Research perspectives', *Developmental Psychology* 22(6): 723–42.

Bronfenbrenner, U. & Crouter, A.C. (1982) 'Work & family through time and space', in S.B. Kamerman & C.D. Hayes (eds), *Families that Work: children in a changing world,* Washington, DC: National Academy Press.

References

Brook, J.S., Whiteman, M., & Gordon, A.S. (1983) 'Stages of drug use in adolescence: Personality, peer, and family correlates', *Developmental Psychology* 19: 269–77.

Brook, J.S., Whiteman, M., Gordon, A.S., & Cohen, P. (1986) 'Some models and mechanisms for explaining the impact of maternal and adolescent characteristics on adolescent stage of drug use', *Developmental Psychology* 22: 460–7.

Brooks, L. & Holahan, W. (1985) 'The effects of a nontraditional role-modeling intervention on sex typing of occupational preferences and career salience in adolescent females', *Journal of Vocational Behavior* 26: 264–76.

Buri, J.R., Kirchner, P.A., & Walsh, J.M. (1987) 'Familial correlates of self-esteem in young American adults', *Journal of Social Psychology* 127(6): 583–8.

Burke, T., Hancock, L., & Newton, P. (1984) *A Roof over their Heads: housing issues and families in Australia*, Melbourne: Institute of Family Studies.

Burns, A. (1980) *Breaking up: separation and divorce in Australia*, Melbourne: Nelson.

Burns, A. & Goodnow, J. (1979) *Children and Families in Australia*, Sydney: Allen & Unwin.

Burt, C.E., Cohen, L.H., & Bjorck, J.P. (1988) 'Perceived family environment as a moderator of young adolescents' life stress adjustment', *American Journal of Community Psychology* 16(1): 101–22.

Callan, V.J. (1985) *Choices about Children*, Melbourne: Longman Cheshire.

Callan, V.J. & Noller, P. (1986) 'Perceptions of communicative relationships in families with adolescents', *Journal of Marriage and the Family* 48: 813–20.

Callan, V.J. & Noller, P. (1987) *Marriage and the Family*, Australia: Methuen.

Campbell, E., Adams, G.R., & Dobson, W.R. (1984) 'Familial correlates of identity formation in late adolescence: A study of the predictive utility of connectedness and individuality in family relations', *Journal of Youth and Adolescence* 13: 509–25.

Caplow, T., Bahr, H.M., Chadwick, B.A., Hill, R., & Williamson, M.H. (1982) *Middletown Families*, Minneapolis: University of Minnesota Press.

Carmichael, G. (1984) 'The transition to marriage: trends in age at first marriage and proportions marrying in Australia', in Australian Institute of Family Studies, *Australian Family Research Conference*, vol.1, Melbourne: Institute of Family Studies.

Cashmore, J. (1983) *Factors in agreement between parents and children on values and sources of skill*, Unpublished Ph.D. thesis, Macquarie University.

Cashmore, J.A. & Goodnow, J.J. (1985) 'Agreement between generations: A two-process approach', *Child Development* 56: 493–501.

Cherlin, A. (1981) *Marriage, Divorce and Remarriage*, Cambridge, MA: Harvard University Press.

Cherlin, A. & McCarthy, J. (1985) 'Remarried couple households: data from the June 1980 current population survey', *Journal of Marriage and the Family* 47: 23–30.

Chilman, C.S. (1980) 'Social and psychological research concerning adolescent childbearing: 1970–1980', *Journal of Marriage and the Family* 42: 793–805.

Chilman, C.S. (1983) 'Remarriage and stepfamilies: Research results and implications', in E.D. Macklin & R.H. Rubin (eds), *Contemporary Families and Alternative Lifestyles* (147–63), Beverly Hills: Sage.

Clingempeel, W.G. & Reppucci, N.D. (1982) 'Joint custody after divorce: Major issues and goals for research', *Psychological Bulletin* 91: 102–27.

Coie, J.D. & Dodge, K.A. (1983) 'Continuities and changes in children's social status: A five year longitudinal study', *Merrill-Palmer Quarterly* 29: 261–82.

Coleman, J.C. (1978) 'Current contradictions in adolescent theory', *Journal of Youth and Adolescence* 7: 1–11.

Coleman, J.C. (1980) *The Nature of Adolescence*, London: Methuen.

Connell, R.W., Ashenden, D.J., Kessler, S., & Dowset, G.W. (1983) *Making the Difference: schools, families and social division*, Sydney: Allen & Unwin.

Cooper, C.R. & Ayers-Lopez, S. (1985) 'Family and peer systems in early adolescence: New models of the role of relationships in development', *Journal of Early Adolescence* 5(1): 9–21.

Cooper, C.R., Grotevant, H.D., & Condon, S.M. (1984) 'Individuality and connectedness: Both foster adolescent identity formation and role-taking skills', in H.D. Grotevant & C.R. Cooper (eds), *Adolescent Development in the Family: new directions for child development*, San Francisco: Jossey-Bass.

Cooper, C.R., Grotevant, H.D., Moore, M.S., & Condon, S.M. (1982) 'Family support and conflict: Both foster adolescent identity and role taking', Paper presented at the American Psychological Association, Washington, DC.

Csikszentmihalyi, M. & Larson, R. (1984) *Being Adolescent*, New York: Basic Books.

Davidson, B., Balswick, J.O., & Halverson, C.F. (1980) 'Factor analysis of self-disclosure for adolescents', *Adolescence* 15(60): 947–57.

Demo, D.H., Small, S.A., & Savin-Williams, R.C. (1987) 'Family relations and the self-esteem of adolescents and their parents', *Journal of Marriage and the Family* 49: 705–15.

Dickson-Markman, F. & Markman, H. (1988) 'The effect of others on marriage', in P. Noller & M.A. Fitzpatrick (eds), *Perspectives on Marital Interaction* (294–322), Clevedon & Philadelphia: Multilingual Matters.

Dino, G.A., Barnett, M.A., & Howard, J.A. (1984) 'Children's expectations of sex differences in parents' responses to sons and daughters encountering interpersonal problems', *Sex Roles* 11(7–8): 709–17.

Doane, J.A., West, K.L., Goldstein, M.J., Rodnick, E.H., & Jones, J.E. (1981) 'Parental communication deviance and affective style as predictors of subsequent schizophrenia spectrum disorders in vulnerable adolescents', *Archives of General Psychiatry* 38: 679–85.

Donovan, J.M. (1975) 'Identity status and interpersonal style', *Journal of Youth and Adolescence* 4: 37–55.

Dornbusch, S.M., Carlsmith, J.M., Bushwall, S.J., Ritter, P.L., Leiderman, H., Hastorf, A.H., & Gross, R.T. (1985) 'Single parents, extended households, and the control of adolescents', *Child Development* 56: 326–41.

Douvan, E. & Adelson, J. (1966) *The Adolescent Experience*, New York: Wiley.

Dreikurs, A., & Soltz, V. (1964) *Children: The Challenge*, Chicago: Alfred

Adler Institute.

Duck, S.W. (1982) 'A topography of relationship disengagement and dissolution', in S.W. Duck (ed.), *Personal Relationships 4: dissolving personal relationships*, New York: Academic Press.

Duck, S.W. & Miell, D.E. (1984) 'Towards a comprehension of friendship development and breakdown', in H. Tajfel, C. Fraser, & J. Jaspers (eds), *The Social Dimension: European developments in social psychology*, vol.1, London: Academic Press.

Dunlop, R. & Burns, R. (1988) *'Don't feel the world is caving in': adolescents in divorcing families*, Melbourne: Australian Institute of Family Studies.

Elder, G.H. (Jr) (1974) *Children of the Great Depression*, Chicago: University of Chicago Press.

Elder, G.H. (Jr), Van Nguyen, T., & Caspi, A. (1985) 'Sinking family hardship to children's lives', *Child Development* 56: 361–75.

Elder, G.H. (Jr), Caspi, A., & Van Nguyen, T. (1986) 'Resourceful and vulnerable children: Family influences in stressful times', in R.K. Silbereisen & K. Eyferth (eds), *Development in Context: integrative perspectives of youth development*, New York: Springer.

Ellis-Schwabe, M. & Thornburg, H.D. (1986) 'Conflict areas between parents and their adolescents', *The Journal of Psychology* 120: 59–68.

Emery, R.E. (1982) 'Interparental conflict and the children of discord and divorce', *Psychological Bulletin* 92: 310–30.

Emery, R.E. & O'Leary, K.D. (1984) 'Marital discord and child behavior problems in a nonclinical sample', *Journal of Abnormal Child Psychology* 12: 411–20.

Emihovich, C.A., Gaier, E.L., & Cronin, M.C. (1984) 'Sex-role expectation changes by fathers for their sons', *Sex Roles*, 11(9–10): 861–8.

English, B.A. & King, R.J. (1983) *Families in Australia*, Kensington: Family Research Unit, University of New South Wales.

Epstein, J.L. (1983) 'Longitudinal effects of family–school–person interactions on student outcomes', *Research in Sociology of Education and Socialization* 4: 101–27.

Epstein, N.B., Bishop, D.S., & Levin, S. (1978) 'The McMaster model of family functioning', *Journal of Marriage and Family Counselling* 40: 585–93.

Epstein, N.B., Bishop, D.S., & Baldwin, L.M. (1982) 'McMaster model of family functioning', in F. Walsh, *Normal Family Processes*, New York: Guilford Press.

Erikson, E.H. (1959) *Childhood and Society*, New York: Norton.

Erikson, E.H. (1963) 'Youth: Fidelity and diversity', in E.H. Erikson (ed.), *Youth: Challenge and Change*, New York: Basic Books.

Erikson, E.H. (1968) *Identity: Youth and Crisis*, New York: Norton.

Erikson, E.H. (1971) *Identity: Youth, and Crisis*, London: Faber & Faber.

Eskilson, A., Wiley, M.G., Muehlbauer, G., & Dodder, L. (1986) 'Parental pressure, self-esteem and adolescent reported deviance: bending the twig too far', *Adolescence* 21(83): 501–15.

Evans, G.T. & Poole, M.E. (1987) 'Adolescent concerns: A classification for life skills areas', *Australian Journal of Education* 31: 55–72.

Farber, E. & Joseph, J. (1985) 'The maltreated adolescent: Patterns of physical abuse', *International Journal of Child Abuse and Neglect* 9: 201–6.

Farber, S.S., Primavera, J., & Felner, R.D. (1984) 'Older adolescents and parental divorce: Adjustment problems and mediators of coping', *Journal of Divorce* 7: 59–75.

Farran, D.C. & Margolis, L.H. (1983) 'The impact of paternal job loss on the family', Paper presented at the Biennial Meeting of the Society for Research in Child Development, Detroit, Michigan.

Fasick, F.A. (1984) 'Parents, peers, youth culture and autonomy in adolescence', *Adolescence* 19(73): 143–57.

Feather, N.T. (1978) 'Family resemblances in conversation: Are daughters more similar to parents than sons are?', *Journal of Personality* 46: 260–78.

Feather, N.T. (1985) 'The psychological impact of unemployment: empirical findings and theoretical approaches', in N.T. Feather (ed.), *Australian Psychology: Review of Research* (265–95), Sydney: Allen & Unwin.

Feather, N.T. & O'Brien, G.E. (1986) 'A longitudinal study of the effects of employment and unemployment on school leavers', *Journal of Occupational Psychology* 59: 121–44.

Filsinger, E.E. & Lamke, L.K. (1983) 'The lineage transmission of interpersonal competence', *Journal of Marriage and the Family* 45: 75–80.

Floyd, H.H. & South, D.R. (1972) 'Dilemma of youth: The choice of parents or peers as a frame of reference for behaviour', *Journal of Marriage and the Family* 34: 626–33.

Forehand, R., Long, N., Brody, G.H., & Fauber, R. (1986) 'Home predictors of young adolescents' school behavior and academic performance', *Child Development* 57: 1528–33.

Fox, G.L. & Inazu, J.K. (1979) 'The effects of mother–daughter communication on daughters' sexual and contraceptual knowledge and behaviour', Paper presented at the annual meeting of the Population Association of America, Philadelphia.

Fox, G.L. & Inazu, J.K. (1980) 'Patterns and outcomes of mother–daughter communication upon sexuality', *Journal of Social Issues* 36: 7–29.

Fox, G.L. & Inazu, J.K. (1982) 'The influence of mother's marital history on the mother–daughter relationship in black and white households', *Journal of Marriage and the Family* 44: 143–53.

Fox, L.H., Brody, L., & Tobin, D. (eds) (1980) *Women and the Mathematical Mystique*, Baltimore: Johns Hopkins University Press.

Franzoi, S.L. & Davis, M.H. (1985) 'Adolescent self-disclosure and loneliness: Private self-consciousness and parental influences', *Journal of Personality and Social Psychology* 48: 768–80.

Freeman, M.D. & Lyon, C.M. (1983) *Cohabitation without Marriage: an essay in law and social policy*, London: Gower.

Friedman, L., Lichtenstein, E., & Biglan, A. (1985) 'Smoking onset among teens: An empirical analysis of initial situations', *Addictive Behaviours* 10: 1–13.

Frieze, I.H., Fisher, J., Hanusa, B., McHugh, M., & Valle, V. (1978) 'Attributing the causes of success and failure: Internal and external barriers to achievement in women', in J. Sherman & F. Denmard (eds), *Psychology of Women: future directions for research*, New York: Psychological Dimensions.

Fryer, D. & Payne, R. (1986) 'Being unemployed: A review of the literature on the psychological experience of unemployment', in *International Review of Industrial and Organisational Psychology*, New York: Wiley.

Furnham, A. (1985) 'Youth unemployment: A review of the literature', *Journal of Adolescence* 8: 109–24.

Furstenberg, F.F. (1971) 'The transmission of mobility orientation in the family', *Social Forces* 49: 595–603.

Galambos, N.L. & Dixon, R.A. (1984) 'Adolescent abuse and the development of personal sense of control', *Child Abuse and Neglect* 8: 285–93.

Ganong, L.H. & Coleman, M. (1984) 'The effects of remarriage on children: a review of the empirical literature', *Family Relations* 33: 389–406.

Garbarino, J. & Gilliam, G. (1980) *Understanding Abusive Families*, Lexington, MA: Lexington.

Garbarino, J., Sebes, J., & Schellenbach, C. (1984) 'Families at risk for destructive parent–child relations in adolescence', *Child Development* 55: 174–83.

Gecas, V. & Schwalbe, M.L. (1986) 'Parental behaviour and adolescent self-esteem', *Journal of Marriage and the Family* 48: 37–46.

Ginzberg, E., Ginsburg, S.W., Axelrad, S., & Herma, J.R. (1951) *Occupational Choice: an approach to a general theory*, New York: Columbia University Press.

Gjerde, P.F. (1986) 'The interpersonal structure of family interaction settings: parent–adolescent relations in dyads and triads', *Developmental Psychology* 22(3): 297–304.

Glezer, H. (1984) 'Antecedents and correlates of marriage and family attitudes in young Australian men and women', Paper presented at the Proceedings of the XXth International Committee on Family Research Seminar, Institute of Family Studies, Melbourne.

Glynn, T. (1981) *Drugs and the Family: research issues* 29, Washington: Dept of Health and Human Services.

Goldsmith, J. (1980) 'Relationships between former spouses: descriptive findings', *Journal of Divorce* 4:1–20.

Goldstein, M.J. (1985) 'Family factors that antedate the onset of schizophrenia and related disorders: The results of a fifteen year prospective longitudinal study', *Acta Psychiatrica Scandinavica* 71: 7–18.

Goldstein, M.J., Judd, L.L., Rodnick, E.H., Alkire, A.A., & Gould, E. (1968) 'A method for studying social influence and coping patterns within families of disturbed adolescents', *Journal of Nervous and Mental Diseases* 147: 233–51.

Goldstein, M.J. & Strachan, A.M. (1987) 'The family and schizophrenia', in T. Jacob (ed.), *Family Interaction and Psychopathology: theories, methods, and findings* (481–508), New York: Plenum Press.

Goodnow, J.J. (1981) 'Expectations about child development and schooling in two groups of mothers: Australian-born and Lebanese-born', *ERDC Report*, Canberra, A.C.T.

Goodnow, J.J. (1985) 'Parents' ideas about parenting and development: A review of issues and recent work', in M. Lamb, A. Brown, & B. Rogoff (eds), *Advances in Developmental Psychology* (193–242), New Jersey: L.E.A. Publishers.

Goodnow, J.J. (1988) 'Children's household work: Its nature and functions', *Psychological Bulletin* 103(1): 5–26.

Gottman, J.M. (1983) 'How children become friends', *Monograph of the Society for Research in Child Development*, 48(3 serial No. 201).

Gottman, J.M. & Levenson, R.W. (1988) 'The social psychophysiology of marriage', in P. Noller & M.A. Fitzpatrick (eds), *Perspectives on Marital Interaction*, Clevedon & Philadelphia: Multilingual Matters.

Greenberg, M., Siegel, J., & Leitch, C. (1983) 'The nature and importance of attachment relationships to parent and peers during adolescence', *Journal of Youth and Adolescence* 12: 373–86.

Greenberger, E. & Steinberg, L. (1981) 'The workplace as a context for the socialisation of youth', *Journal of Youth and Adolescence* 10: 185–210.

Greenberger, E. & Steinberg, L. (1986) *When Teenagers Work: the psychological and social costs of adolescent employment*, New York: Basic Books.

Greenberger, E., Steinberg, L.D., & Ruggiero, M. (1982) 'A job is a job is a job ... or is it?', *Work and Occupations* 9: 76–96.

Greenberger, E., Steinberg, L.D., & Vaux, A. (1981) 'Adolescents who work: Health and behavioral consequences of job stress', *Developmental Psychology* 6: 691–703.

Grotevant, H.D. & Cooper, C.R. (1985) 'Patterns of interaction in family relationships and the development of identity exploration in adolescence', *Child Development* 56: 415–28.

Grotevant, H.D. & Cooper, C.R. (1986) 'Individuation in family relationships: A perspective on individual differences in the development of identity and role-taking skill in adolescence', *Human Development* 29: 82–100.

Grotevant, H.D., Cooper, C.R., & Kramer, K. (1986) 'Exploration as a predictor of congruence in adolescents' career choices', *Journal of Vocational Behavior* 29: 201–15.

Guidubaldi, J. & Perry, J.D. (1985) 'Divorce and mental health sequelae for children', *Journal of the American Academy of Child Psychiatry* 24: 531–7.

Gully, K.J., Dengerink, H.A., Pepping, M., & Bergstrom, D. (1981) 'Research note: Sibling contribution to violent behavior', *Journal of Marriage and the Family* 43: 333–7.

Hall, J.A. (1987) 'Parent–adolescent conflict: An empirical review', *Adolescence* 22: 767–89.

Hamilton, S.F. & Crouter, A.C. (1980) 'Work and growth: A review of research on the impact of work experience on adolescent development', *Journal of Youth and Adolescence* 9: 48–68.

Hancock, L. & Burke, T. (1983) *Youth Housing Policy*, Canberra: Australian Housing Research Council.

Harper, P. (1983) 'Who is my family? Who cares for me? Legal status and relationships of children and their families', *Australian Journal of Social Issues* 18: 90–7.

References

Harper, P. (1984) 'Children in stepfamilies: their legal and family status', in *Institute of Family Studies Policy Background Paper*, No. 4, Melbourne: Institute of Family Studies.

Harrington, D.M., Block, J.H., & Block, J. (1987) 'Testing aspects of Carl Rogers' theory of creative environments: Child rearing antecedents of creative potential in young adolescents', *Journal of Personality and Social Psychology* 52: 851–6.

Harris, I.D. & Howard, K.I. (1984) 'Parental criticism and the adolescent experience', Journal of Youth and Adolescence 13: 113–21.

Hartup, W.W. (1979) 'The social worlds of childhood', *American Psychologist* 34: 944–50.

Hauser, J. (1981) 'Adolescents and religion', *Adolescence* 16: 309–20.

Hauser, S.T., Powers, S.I., Noam, G.G., Jacobson, A.M., Wiess, B., & Follansbee, D.J. (1984) 'Familial contexts of adolescent ego development', *Child Development* 55: 195–213.

Heath, D.B. (1977) 'Some possible effects of occupation on the maturing of professional men', *Journal of Vocational Behavior* 11: 262–81.

Henggeler, S.W. & Tavormina, J.B. (1980) 'Social class and race differences in family interaction: Pathological, normative, or confounding methodological factors?', *Journal of Genetic Psychology* 137: 211–22.

Herrenkohl, R. (1977) 'Research: Too much too late?', in M. Lauderdale, R. Anderson, & S. Cramer (eds), *Child Abuse and Neglect: issues of innovation and implementation* (174–84). Washington, DC: US Dept of Health and Human Services.

Hetherington, E.M. (1972) 'Effects of father absence on personality development in adolescent daughters', *Developmental Psychology* 7: 313–26.

Hetherington, E.M. (1979) 'Divorce: A child's perspective', *American Psychologist* 34: 851–8.

Hetherington, E.M. (1981) 'Children and divorce', in R.W. Henderson (ed.), *Parent–Child Interaction: theory, research and prospects*, New York: Academic Press.

Hetherington, E.M., Cox, M., & Cox, R. (1978) 'The aftermath of divorce', in J.H. Stevens & M. Mathews (eds), *Mother–Child, Father–Child Relationships*, Washington, DC: National Association for the Education of Young Children.

Hetherington, E.M., Stouwie, R., & Ridberg, E.H. (1971) 'Patterns of family interaction and child rearing attitudes related to three dimensions of juvenile delinquency', *Journal of Abnormal Psychology* 77: 160–76.

Hill, C.T., Rubin, Z., & Peplau, L.A. (1979) 'Breakups before marriage: the end of 103 affairs', in G. Levinger & O.C. Moles (eds), *Divorce and Separation: Contexts, Causes, and Consequences*, New York: Basic Books.

Hill, J.P., Holmbeck, G.N., Marlow, L., Green, T.M., & Lynch, M.E. (1985) 'Pubertal status and parent–child relations in families of seventh grade boys', *Journal of Early Adolescence* 5(1): 31–44.

Hodges, W.F. & Bloom, B.L. (1984) 'Parents' report of children's adjustment to marital separation: A longitudinal study', *Journal of Divorce* 8: 33–50.

Hodgson, J.W. (1977) 'Sex differences in processes of identity and intimacy development', unpublished doctoral dissertation, The Pennsylvania State University.

Hoelter, J. & Harper, L. (1987) 'Structural and interpersonal family influences on adolescent self-conception', *Journal of Marriage and the Family* 49: 129–39.

Hoffman, L.W. (1980) 'The effects of maternal employment on the academic attitudes and performance of school-age children', *School Psychology Review*, 319–35.

Hoge, D.R., Petrillo, G.H., & Smith, E.L. (1982) 'Transmission of religious and social values from parent to teenage children', *Journal of Marriage and the Family* 44: 569–80.

Holland, J.L. (1973) *Making Vocational Choices*, Englewood Cliffs, NJ: Prentice-Hall.

Holland, J.L. (1985) *Making Vocational Choices: a theory of vocational personalities and work environments* (2nd edn), Englewood Cliffs, NJ: Prentice-Hall.

Hollstein, C.E. (1972) 'The relation of children's moral judgment level to that of their parents and to communication patterns in the family', in R.C. Smart & M.S. Smart (eds), *Readings in Child Development and Relationships*, New York: MacMillan.

Hunter, F.T. (1984) 'Socializing procedures in parent–child and friendship relations during adolescence', *Developmental Psychology* 20(6): 1092–9.

Hunter, F.T. (1985) 'Individual adolescents' perceptions of interactions with friends and parents', *Journal of Early Adolescence* 5: 295–305.

Hunter, F.T. & Youniss, J. (1982) 'Changes in functions of three relations during adolescence', *Developmental Psychology* 18: 806–11.

Huston, T.L. & Robins, E. (1982) 'Conceptual and methodological issues in studying close relationships', *Journal of Marriage and the Family* 44: 901–25.

Huston, T.L., Surra, C.A., Fitzgerald, N.M., & Cate, R.M. (1981) 'From courtship to marriage: mate selection as an interpersonal process', in S. Duck & R. Gilmour (eds), *Personal Relationships 2: developing personal relationships*, London: Academic Press.

Inoff-Germain, G., Nottelmann, E.D., Arnold, G.S., & Susman, E.J. (1988) 'Adolescent aggression and parent–adolescent conflict: Relations between observed family interactions and measures of the adolescents' general functioning', *Journal of Early Adolescence* 8: 17–36.

Jacob, T. (1974) 'Patterns of family conflict and dominance as a function of child age and social class', *Developmental Psychology* 10: 1–12.

Jahoda, M. (1981) 'Work, employment and unemployment: values, theories and approaches in social research', *American Psychologist* 36: 184–91.

Jedlicka, D. (1984) 'Indirect parental influence on mate choice: test of the psychoanalytic theory', *Journal of Marriage and the Family* 46: 65–70.

Jennings, M.K. & Niemi, R.G. (1974) *The Political Character of Adolescence: the influence of families and schools*, Princeton: Princeton University Press.

Jessop, D.J. (1981) 'Family relationships as viewed by parents and adolescents: A specification', *Journal of Marriage and the Family* 43: 95–107.

References

Johnson, F.L. & Aries, E.J. (1983) 'Conversational patterns among same-sex pairs of late-adolescent close friends', *Journal of Genetic Psychology* 142: 225–38.

Johnson, K.A. (1986) 'Informal control networks and adolescent orientations towards alcohol use', *Adolescence* 21: 767–84.

Johnstone, J.R. & Campbell, L.E. (1988) *Impasses of Divorce: the dynamics and resolutions of family conflict*, New York: Free Press.

Jones, E.E. & Nisbett, R.E. (1971) *The Actor and the Observer: divergent perceptions of the causes of behaviour*, Morristown, NJ: General Learning Press.

Jordan, D. (1970) 'Parental antecedents of ego identity formation', unpublished master's thesis, State University of New York, Buffalo.

Josephson, E. & Carroll, E.E. (1974) *Drug Use: epidemiological and sociological approaches*, New York: Halstead.

Jourard, S.M. (1971) *Self-disclosure: an experimental analysis of the transparent self*, New York: Wiley.

Jurich, A.P., Polson, C.J., Jurich, J.A., & Bates, R.A. (1985) 'Family factors in the lives of drug users and abusers', *Adolescence* 20: 143–59.

Jurkovic, G.J. & Prentice, N.M. (1974) 'Dimensions of moral interaction and moral judgment in delinquent and nondelinquent families', *Journal of Consulting and Clinical Psychology* 42: 256–62.

Jurkovic, G.J. & Ulrici, D. (1985) 'Empirical perspectives on adolescents and their families', in L. L'Abate (ed.), *The Handbook of Family Psychology and Therapy*, vol. 1, Homewood, IL: Dorsey Press.

Kahn, S., Zimmerman, G., Csikszentmihalyi, M., & Getzels, J.W. (1985) 'Relations between identity in young adulthood and intimacy at midlife', *Journal of Personality and Social Psychology* 49: 1316–22.

Kashini, J.H., Burbach, D.J., & Rosenberg, T.K. (1988) 'Perception of family conflict resolution and depressive symptomatology in adolescents', *Journal of the American Academy of Child and Adolescent Psychiatry* 27: 42–8.

Kemper, T. & Reichler, M. (1976) 'Marital satisfaction and conjugal power as determinants of intensity and frequency of rewards and punishments administered by parents', *Journal of Genetic Psychology* 129: 221–34.

Kidwell, J.S. (1981) 'Number of siblings, sibling spacing, sex and birth order: Their effects on perceived parent–adolescent relationships', *Journal of Marriage and the Family* 43: 315–32.

Kleiman, J.I. (1981) 'Optimal and normal family functioning', *American Journal of Family Therapy* 9: 37–44.

Klein, N.C., Alexander, J.F., & Parsons, B.V. (1977) 'Impact of family systems intervention on recidivism and sibling delinquency-model of primary prevention and program evaluation', *Journal of Consulting and Clinical Psychology* 45: 469–74.

Kohn, M.L. (1969) *Class and Conformity: a study in values*, Homewood, IL: Dorsey.

Komarovsky, M. (1974) 'Patterns of self-disclosure of male undergraduates', *Journal of Marriage and the Family* 36(4): 677–86.

Krau, E. (1987) 'The crystallization of work in adolescence: A sociocultural approach', *Journal of Vocational Behavior* 30: 103–23.

Krupinski, J. (1981) 'The family of the future: The Australian teenage view', *Journal of Comparative Family Studies* 12: 461–74.

Kurdek, L. & Sinclair, R. (1988) 'Adjustment of young adolescents in two-parent nuclear, stepfather and mother custody families', *Journal of Consulting and Clinical Psychology* 56: 91–6.

Lapsley, D.K., Harwell, M.R., Olson, L.M., Flannery, D., & Quintana, S.M. (1984) 'Moral judgment, personality and attitude to authority in early and late adolescence', *Journal of Youth and Adolescence* 13(6): 527–42.

Lerner, R.M., Karson, M., Meisels, M., & Knapp, J.R. (1975) 'Actual and perceived attitudes of late adolescents and their parents: The phenomenon of the generational gaps', *Journal of Genetic Psychology* 126: 195–207.

Lerner, R.M., Pendorf, J., & Emery, A. (1971) 'Attitudes of adolescents and adults toward contemporary issues', *Psychological Reports* 28: 139–45.

Lewis, J.M., Beavers, W.R., Gossett, J.T., & Phillips, V.A. (1976) *No Single Thread: psychological health in family systems*, New York: Brunner/Mazel.

Long, B.H. (1987) 'Perceptions of parental discord and parental separations in the United States: Effects on daughters' attitudes toward marriage and courtship progress', *Journal of Social Psychology* 127: 573–82.

Lueptow, L.B. (1980) 'Social structure, social change and parental influence in adolescent sex-role socialisation: 1974–1975', *Journal of Marriage and the Family* 42: 93–104.

Lutz, P. (1983) 'The stepfamily: An adolescent perspective', *Family Relations* 32: 367–75.

Maas, F. (1986) 'Family conflict and leaving home', *The Bulletin of the National Clearing House for Youth Studies* 5: 9–13.

Maccoby, E. & Martin, J.A. (1983) 'Socialisation in the context of the family: Parent–child interaction', in P.H. Mussen (ed.), *Handbook of Child Psychology*, vol. 4 (1–101), New York: Wiley.

Macklin, E.D. (1983) 'Nonmarital heterosexual cohabitation: an overview', in E.D. Macklin & H. Rubin (eds), *Contemporary Families and Alternative Lifestyles: handbook of research and theory*, Beverly Hills: Sage.

Marcia, J.E. (1966) 'Development and validation of ego-identity status', *Journal of Personality and Social Psychology* 3: 551–8.

Marcia, J.E. (1976) 'Identity six years after: A follow-up study', *Journal of Youth and Adolescence* 5: 145–60.

Martin, B. (1987) 'Development perspectives on family theory and psychopathology', in T. Jacob (ed.), *Family Interaction and Psychopathology: theories, methods and findings*, New York Plenum.

Martin, M.J., Schumm, W.R., Bugaighis, M.A., Jurich, A.P., & Bollman, S.R. (1987) 'Family violence and adolescents' perceptions of outcomes of family conflict', *Journal of Marriage and the Family* 49: 165–71.

McCubbin, H.I., Needle, R.H., & Wilson, M. (1985) 'Adolescent health risk behaviours: Family stress and adolescent coping as critical factors', *Family Relations* 34: 51–62.

McDermott, D. (1984) 'The relationship of parental drug use and parents' attitude concerning adolescent drug use to adolescent drug use', *Adolescence* 19: 89–97.

References

McDonald, P. (1980) 'Trends in marriage and divorce in the USA and Australia compared', *Family Matters: AIFS Newsletter* 21: 27–8.

McGill, M.E. (1986) *The McGill Report on Male Intimacy*, New York: Harper & Row.

McLaughlin, R.J., Baer, P.E., Burnside, M.A., & Pokorny, A.D. (1985) 'Psychosocial correlates of alcohol use at two age levels during adolescence', *Journal of Studies on Alcohol* 46: 212–18.

McLoughlin, D. & Whitfield, R. (1985) 'Adolescents and divorce', *Marriage Guidance* (Spring): 2–8.

Medora, N.P. (1983) 'Variables affecting loneliness among individuals undergoing treatment in alcohol rehabilitation centers', Unpublished doctoral dissertation, University of Nebraska, Lincoln.

Medora, N. & Woodward, J.C. (1986) 'Loneliness among adolescent college students at a midwestern university', *Adolescence* 21: 391–402.

Meier, R.R., Burkett, S.R., & Hickman, C.A. (1984) 'Sanctions, peers and deviance: Preliminary models of a social control process', *The Sociological Quarterly* 25: 67–82.

Meilman, P.W. (1979) 'Cross-sectional age changes in ego identity status during adolescence', *Developmental Psychology* 15: 230–1.

Middleton, R. & Putney, S. (1963) 'Political expression of adolescent rebellion', *American Journal of Sociology* 67: 527–37.

Mijuskovic, B. (1986) 'Loneliness: Counseling adolescents', *Adolescence* 21: 941–50.

Miller, J.A., Schooler, C., Kohn, M.L., & Miller, K.A. (1979) 'Women and work: The psychological effects of occupational conditions', *American Journal of Sociology* 85: 66–94.

Mills, D.M. (1984) 'A model of stepfamily development', *Family Relations* 33: 365–72.

Minuchin, S. (1974) *Families and Family Therapy*, Cambridge, MA: Harvard University Press.

Montemayor, R. (1982) 'The relationship between parent–adolescent conflict and the amount of time adolescents spend alone and with parents and peers', *Child Development* 53: 1512–19.

Montemayor, R. (1983) 'Parents and adolescents in conflict: All families some of the time and some families most of the time', *Journal of Early Adolescence* 3: 83–103.

Montemayor, R. (1984a) 'Maternal employment and adolescents' relations with parents, siblings, and peers', *Journal of Youth and Adolescence* 13: 543–57.

Montemayor, R. (1984b) 'Picking up the pieces: The effects of parental divorce on adolescents with some suggestions for school-based intervention programs', *Journal of Early Adolescence* 4: 289–314.

Montemayor, R. (1986) 'Family variation in parent–adolescent storm and stress', *Journal of Adolescent Research* 1: 15–31.

Montemayor, R. & Clayton, M.D. (1983) 'Maternal employment and adolescent development', *Theory into Practice* 22: 112–18.

Montemayor, R. & Hanson, E. (1985) 'A naturalistic view of conflict between adolescents and their parents and siblings', *Journal of Early Adolescence* 5: 23–30.

Moos, R. (1974) *Family Environment Scale*, California: Consulting Psychologists Press.

Moos, R. & Moos, B. (1981a) 'A typology of family social environments', *Family Process* 15: 357–71.

Moos, R. & Moos, B. (1981b) *Family Environment Scale Manual*, Palo Alto: Consulting Psychologists Press.

Morrison, D.M. (1985) 'Adolescent contraceptive behaviour: A review', *Psychological Bulletin* 98: 538–68.

Mueller, C.W. & Pope, H. (1977) 'Marital instability: A study of transmission between generations', *Journal of Marriage and the Family* 39: 83–93.

Mulcahey, G.A. (1973) 'Sex differences in patterns of self-disclosure among adolescents: A developmental perspective', *Journal of Youth and Adolescence* 2: 343–56.

Mussen, P.H., Conger, J.J., & Kagan, J. (1974) *Child Development and Personality* (4th edn), New York: Harper & Row.

Newman, B.A. & Murray, C.I. (1983) 'Identity and family relations in early adolescence', *Journal of Early Adolescence* 3: 293–303.

Newson, J., & Newson, E. (1976) *Seven Years Old in the Home Environment*, London: Allen & Unwin.

Niemi, R.G. (1968) *A Methodological Study of Political Socialisation in the Family*, Ann Arbor: University Microfilms.

Niemi, R.G. (1974) *How family members perceive each other: political and social attitudes in two generations*, New Haven: Yale University.

Noller, P. & Bagi, S. (1985) Parent–adolescent communication, *Journal of Adolescence* 8: 125–44.

Noller, P. & Callan, V.J. (1986) 'Adolescent and parent perceptions of family cohesion and adaptability', *Journal of Adolescence* 9: 97–106.

Noller, P. & Callan, V.J. (1988) 'Understanding parent–adolescent interactions: Perceptions of family members and outsiders', *Developmental Psychology* 24: 707–14.

Noller, P., & Callan, V.J. (in press) 'Adolescents' perceptions of the nature of their communication with parents', *Journal of Youth and Adolescence*.

Noller, P. & Fitzpatrick, M.A. (eds) (1988) *Perspectives on Marital Interaction*, Clevedon & Philadelphia: Multilingual Matters.

Noller, P. & Guthrie, D.M. (in press) 'Methodological issues in studying communication in close relationships', in W.H. Jones & D. Perlman (eds), *Advances in Personal Relationships*, vol. 3, London: Jessica Kingsley.

Norem-Hebeisen, A., Johnson, D.W., Anderson, D., & Johnson, R. (1984) 'Predictors and concomitants of changes in drug use patterns among teenagers', *The Journal of Social Psychology* 124: 43–50.

Notar, M. & McDaniel, S.A. (1986) 'Feminist attitudes and mother–daughter relationships in adolescence', *Adolescence* 21(81): 11–21.

O'Brien, G.E. (1986) *Psychology of Work and Unemployment*, Chichester: John Wiley & Sons.

Ochiltree, G. & Amato, P.R. (1983) 'Family conflict and child competence', Paper presented at the Proceedings of the Family Research Conference, vol. VI: Family Life, Melbourne: Institute of Family Studies.

Ochiltree, G. & Amato, P. (1985) *The Child's Eye View of Family Life*,

Melbourne: Institute of Family Studies.

Offer, D. (1969) *The Psychological World of the Teenager*, New York: Basic Books.

Offer, D., & Sabshin, M. (eds) (1984) *Normality and the Life Cycle*, New York: Basic Books.

O'Leary, K.D. & Emery, R.E. (1984) 'Marital discord and child behavior problems', in M.D. Levine & P. Satz (eds), *Middle Childhood: Development and Dysfunction* (345–64), Baltimore, MD: University Park Press.

Olson, D.H., McCubbin, H., Barnes, H.L., Larsen, A., Muxen, M., & Wilson, M. (1983) *Families: What Makes Them Work?*, Beverly Hills, CA: Sage.

Olson, D.H., Sprenkle, D.H., & Russell, C.S. (1979) 'Circumplex model of marital and family systems, 1: Cohesion and adaptability dimensions, family types and clinical applications', *Family Process* 18: 3–27.

Openshaw, D.K., Thomas, D.L., & Rollins, B.C. (1984) 'Parental influences on adolescent self-esteem', *Journal of Early Adolescence* 4(3): 259–74.

Orlofsky, J.L. (1977) 'Sex-role orientation, identity formation, and self-esteem in college men and women', *Sex Roles* 3: 561–75.

Orlofsky, J.L., Marcia, J.E., & Lesser, I. (1973) 'Ego identity status and the intimacy versus isolation crisis of young adulthood', *Journal of Personality and Social Psychology* 27: 211–19.

Oshman, H. & Manosevitz, M. (1976) 'The impact of the identity crisis on the adjustment of late adolescent males', *Journal of Youth and Adolescence* 3: 207–16.

Osipow, S.H. (1983) *Theories of Career Development* (3rd edn), Englewood Cliffs, NJ: Prentice-Hall.

Papini, D.R. & Sebby, R.A. (1988) 'Variations in conflictual family issues by adolescent pubertal status, gender and family member', *Journal of Early Adolescence* 8: 1–15.

Paris, T. & Dostal, J. (1980) 'Evaluations of self and parent figures by children from intact, divorced, and reconstituted families', *Journal of Youth and Adolescence* 9: 347–51.

Parsons, J.E., Adler, T.F., & Kaczala, C.M. (1982) 'Socialization of achievement attitudes and beliefs: Parental influences', *Child Development* 53: 310–21.

Patterson, G.R. (1982) *Coercive Family Processes*, Eugene, OR: Castalia.

Patton, W. & Noller, P. (1984) 'Unemployment and youth: A longitudinal study', *Australian Journal of Psychology* 36: 399–413.

Perlman, D. & Peplau, L.A. (1981) 'Toward a social psychology of loneliness', in S.Duck & R. Gilmour (eds), *Personal Relationships 3: personal relationships in disorder* (31–56), London: Academic Press.

Petersen, A.C. (1988) 'Adolescent development', *Annual Review of Psychology* 39: 583–607.

Petersen, A.C. & Taylor, B. (1980) 'The biological approach to adolescence: Biological change and psychological adaption', in J. Adelson, *Handbook of Adolescent Psychology*, New York: Wiley.

Petersen, L.R., Lee, G.R., & Ellis, G.J. (1982) 'Social structure, socialization values and disciplinary techniques', *Journal of Marriage and the Family* 44: 131–42.

Pink, J.E. & Wampler, K.S. (1985) 'Problem areas in stepfamilies: Cohesion, adaptability and the stepfather–adolescent relationship', *Family Relations* 33: 365–72.

Pipp, S., Shaver, P., Jennings, S., Lamborn, S., & Fischer, K.W. (1985) 'Adolescents' theories about the development of their relationships with parents', *Journal of Personality and Social Psychology* 48: 991–1001.

Poole, M.E. (1983) *Youth: Expectations and Transitions*, Melbourne: Routledge & Kegan Paul.

Poole, M.E. (1984) 'Realities and constraints: Pathways for female school leavers', *Australian Journal of Social Issues* 19(1): 43–59.

Poole, M.E. & Cooney, G.H. (1985) 'Careers: Adolescent awareness and exploration of possibilities for self', *Journal of Vocational Behavior* 26: 251–63.

Poole, M.E. & Gelder, A.J. (1985) 'Family cohesiveness and adolescent autonomy in decision-making', *Australian Journal of Sex, Marriage and Family* 5(2): 65–75.

Porter, B., & O'Leary, K.D. (1980) 'Marital discord and child behavior problems', *Journal of Abnormal Child Psychology* 8: 287–95.

Powers, S.I., Hauser, S.T., Schwartz, J.M., Noam, G.G., & Jacobson, A.M. (1983) 'Adolescent ego development and family interaction: A structural–developmental perspective', in H.D. Grotevant & C.R. Cooper (eds), *Adolescent Development in the Family: new directions for child development* (5–25), San Francisco: Jossey-Bass.

Prediger, D. & Sawyer, K. (1986) 'Ten years of career development: A nationwide study of high-school students', *Journal of Counselling and Development* 65: 45–9.

Pulkkinen, L. (1984) *Youth and Home Ecology*, Helsinki: Otava.

Quinn, W.H., Newfield, M.A., & Protinsky, H.O. (1985) 'Rites of passage in families with adolescents', *Family Process* 24: 101–11.

Quinton, D. (1980) 'Family life in the inner city: Myth and reality', in M. Marland (ed.), *Education for the Inner City* (45–67), London: Heinemann.

Reichelt, P.A. & Werley, H.H. (1975) 'Contraception, abortion and venereal disease: Teenagers' knowledge and the effect of education', *Family Planning Perspectives* 7: 83–8.

Reinhard, D.W. (1977) 'The reaction of adolescent boys and girls to the divorce of their parents', *Journal of Clinical Child Psychology* 6: 21–3.

Report of the Senate Standing Committee on Social Welfare (1982) *Homeless Youth*, Canberra: Australian Government Publishing Service.

Richardson, R.A., Abramowitz, R.H., Asp, C.E., & Petersen, A.C. (1986) 'Parent–child relationships in early adolescence: Effects of family structure', *Journal of Marriage and the Family*, 48: 805–11.

Richardson, R.A., Galambos, N.L., Schulenberg, J.E., & Petersen, A.C. (1984) 'Young adolescents' perceptions of the family environment', *Journal of Early Adolescence* 4: 131–53.

Rivenbark, W.H. (1971) 'Self-disclosure patterns among adolescents', *Psychological Reports* 28: 35–42.

Roberts, G.C., Block, J.H., & Block, J. (1984) 'Continuity and change in parents' child rearing practices', *Child Development* 55: 586–97.

References

Rodick, J.D. & Henggeler, S.W. (1982) 'Parent–adolescent interaction and adolescent emancipation', in S.W. Henggeler (ed.), *Delinquency and Adolescent Psychopathology: a family-ecological systems approach*, Littleman, MA: Wright-PSG.

Rogers, C.R. (1954) 'Towards a theory of creativity', *ETC: A Review of General Semantics* 11: 249–60.

Rollins, B.C. & Thomas, D.L. (1979) 'Parental support, power and control techniques in the socialization of children', in W.R. Burr, R. Hill, F.I.Nye, & I.L. Reiss (eds), *Contemporary Theories about the Family*, vol. 1, New York: Free Press.

Rothenberg, P.B. (1980) 'Communication about sex and birth control between mothers and their adolescent children', *Population and Environment* 3: 35–50.

Russell, D., Peplau, L.A., & Ferguson, M.L. (1978) 'Developing a measure of loneliness', *Journal of Personality Assessment* 42: 290–4.

Rutter, M. (1971) 'Parent–child separation: Psychological effects on children', *Journal of Child Psychology & Psychiatry* (12): 233–60.

Rutter, M. (1981) 'The city and the child', *American Journal of Orthopsychiatry* 51: 610–25.

Rutter, M., Cox, A., Tupling, C., Berger, M., & Yule, W. (1975) 'Attainment and adjustment in two geographic areas, 1: The prevalence of psychiatric disorder', *British Journal of Psychiatry* 126: 493–509.

Rutter, M. & Giller, H.J. (1983) *Juvenile Delinquency: trends and perspectives*, New York: Penguin Books.

Rutter, M., Graham, P., Chadwick, O.F., & Yule, W. (1976) 'Adolescent turmoil: Fact or fiction?', *Journal of Child Psychology and Psychiatry* 17: 35–56.

Rutter, M. & Madge, W. (1976) *Cycles of Disadvantage*, London: Heinemann.

Rutter, M. & Quinton, D. (1977) 'Psychiatric disorder: Ecological factors and concepts of causation', in H. McGurk (ed.) *Ecological Factors in Human Development* (173–87), Amsterdam: North-Holland.

Santrock, J.W. (1975) 'Father absence, perceived maternal behaviour, and moral development in boys', *Child Development* 46: 753–7.

Scanzoni, J. & Fox, G.L. (1980) 'Sex roles, family and society: The seventies and beyond', *Journal of Marriage and the Family* 42: 20–33.

Schill, W.J., McCartin, R., & Meyer, K. (1985) 'Youth unemployment: Its relationship to academic and family variables', *Journal of Vocational Behaviour* 26: 155–63.

Schwartz, L.L. (1987) 'Joint custody: Is it right for all children?', *Journal of Family Psychology* 1: 120–34.

Scutt, J.A. & Graham, D. (1984) *For Richer, for Poorer: Money, Marriage and Property Rights*, Melbourne: Penguin.

Sebald, H. (1986) 'Adolescents' shifting orientation toward parents and peers: A curvilinear trend over recent decades', *Journal of Marriage and the Family* 48: 5–13.

Sebald, H. & White, B. (1980) 'Teenagers' divided reference groups: Uneven alignment with parents and peers', *Adolescence* 15: 979–84.

Sebes, J.M. (1983) 'Determining risk for abuse in families with adolescents: the development of a criterion measure', unpublished doctoral dissertation, Pennsylvania State University, Pennsylvania.

Sheppard, M.A., Wright, D., & Goodstadt, M.S. (1985) 'Peer pressure and drug use – exploding the myth', *Adolescence* 20: 949–58.

Siddique, C.M. & D'Arcy, C. (1984) 'Adolescence, stress and psychological well-being', *Journal of Youth and Adolescence* 13(6): 459–73.

Skinner, W.F., Massey, J.L., Krohn, M.D., & Lauer, R.M. (1985) 'Social influences and constraints on the initiation and cessation of adolescent tobacco use', *Journal of Behavioural Medicine* 8: 353–76.

Smetana, J.G. (1988) 'Adolescents' and parents' conceptions of parental authority', *Child Development* 59: 321–35.

Smith, K.A. & Forehand, R. (1986) 'Parent–adolescent conflict: Comparison and prediction of the perceptions of mothers, fathers and daughters', *Journal of Early Adolescence* 6: 353–67.

Smith, M.B. (1968) 'School and home: Focus on achievement', in A.H. Passow (ed.) *Developing Programs for the Educationally Disadvantaged*, New York: Teachers College Press.

Smith, T.E. (1970) 'Foundations of parental influence upon adolescents: An application of social power theory', *American Sociological Review* 35: 860–73.

Smith, T.E. (1982) 'The case for parental transmission of educational goals: The importance of accurate offspring perceptions', *Journal of Marriage and the Family* 44: 661–74.

Sorenson, R.C. (1973) *Adolescent Sexuality in Contemporary America*, Cleveland: World Publishing Co.

Spanier, G.B. (1983) 'Married and unmarried cohabitation in the United States: 1980', *Journal of Marriage and the Family* 45: 277–88.

Spanier, G.B. & Furstenberg, F.F. (1982) 'Remarriage after divorce: a longitudinal analysis of well-being', *Journal of Marriage and the Family* 44: 709–20.

Spanier, G.B. & Glick, P.C. (1980) 'Paths to remarriage', *Journal of Divorce* 3: 283–98.

Sparks, D.C. (1976) 'Self-disclosure and its relationship to self-concept among students in a selected high school', unpublished doctoral dissertation, University of Michigan.

Springer, C. & Wallerstein, J.S. (1983) 'Young adolescents' responses to their parents' divorces', in L.A. Kurdek (ed.) *Children and Divorce* (15–28), San Francisco: Jossey-Bass.

Stanley, S. (1978) 'Family education: A means of enhancing the moral atmosphere of the family and the moral development of adolescents', *Journal of Counseling Psychology* 25: 110–18.

Steinberg, L.D. (1981) 'Transformations in family relations at puberty', *Developmental Psychology* 7: 833–40.

Steinberg, L.D. (1986) *Latchkey children and susceptibility to peer pressure: An ecological analysis*, Unpublished Manuscript, University of Wisconsin, Dept of Child and Family Studies.

References

Steinberg, L.D. (1986) *Adolescence*, New York: Alfred A. Knopf.

Steinberg, L.D. (1987) 'Impact of puberty on family relations: Effects of pubertal status and pubertal timing', *Developmental Psychology* 23: 451–60.

Steinberg, L.D., Catalano, R., & Dooley, D. (1981) 'Economic antecedents of child abuse and neglect', *Child Development* 52: 975–85.

Steinberg, L.D., Greenberger, E., Garduque, L., Ruggiero, M., & Vaux, A. (1982) 'The effects of working on adolescent development', *Developmental Psychology* 18: 385–95.

Steinberg, L.D. & Hill, J.P. (1978) 'Patterns of family interaction as a function of age, the onset of puberty, and formal thinking', *Developmental Psychology* 14(6): 683–4.

Steinberg, L.D. & Silverberg, S.B. (1986) 'The vicissitudes of autonomy in early adolescence', *Child Development* 57: 841–51.

Steinhauer, P.D. (1987) 'The family as a small group: The process model of family functioning' in T. Jacob (ed.), *Family Interaction and Psychopathology: Theories, Methods, and Findings* (67–115), New York: Plenum Press.

Stone, L.J. & Church, J. (1968) *Childhood and Adolescence: a psychology of the growing person* (2nd edn), New York: Random House.

Straus, M.A., Gelles, R.J., & Steinmetz, S.K. (1980) *Behind Closed Doors: violence in the American family*, New York: Anchor.

Strouse, J., & Fabes, A. (1985) 'Formal versus informal sources of sex education: Competing forces in the sexual socialization of adolescents', *Adolescence* 20(78): 252–63.

Sullivan, K. & Sullivan, A. (1980) 'Adolescent–parent separation', *Developmental Psychology* 16: 93–104.

Super, D.E. (1953) 'A theory of vocational development, *American Psychologist* 8: 185–90.

Super, D.E. (1980) 'A life-span life-space approach to career development', *Journal of Vocational Behavior* 16: 282–98.

Tedin, K.L. (1974) 'The influence of parents on the political attitudes of adolescents', *American Political Science Review* 68: 1579–92.

Thibaut, J.W. & Kelley, H.H. (1959) *The Social Psychology of Groups*, New York: Wiley.

Thompson, L., Acock, A.C., & Clark, K. (1985) 'Do parents know their children? The ability of mothers and fathers to gauge the attitudes of their young adult children', *Family Relations* 34: 315–20.

Thorne, C.R. & DeBlassie, R.R. (1985) 'Adolescent substance abuse', *Adolescence* 22: 335–47.

Tisak, M. (1986) 'Children's conceptions of parental authority', *Child Development* 57: 166–76.

Tobin, D. & Fox, L.H. (1980) 'Career interests and career education: A key to change', in L.H. Fox, L. Brody, & D. Tobin (eds) *Women and the Mathematical Mystique*, Baltimore: Johns Hopkins University Press.

Turley, P. (1988) 'Homeless young people: A psychological study', *The Bulletin of the National Clearing House for Youth Studies* 7: 23–7.

van de Kaa, D. (1987) 'Europe's second demographic transition', *Population Bulletin* 42(1).

Wallerstein, J.S. (1985) 'Children of divorce: Preliminary report of a ten-year follow-up of older children and adolescents', *Journal of the American Academy of Child Psychiatry* 24: 545–53.

Wallerstein, J.S. & Kelly, J.B. (1976) 'The effects of parental divorce: experiences of the child in later latency', *American Journal of Orthopsychiatry* 46: 256–69.

Wallerstein, J.S. & Kelly, J.B. (1978) 'Effects of divorce on the visiting father–child relationship', *American Journal of Psychiatry* 137: 1534–9.

Wallerstein, J.S. & Kelly, J.B. (1980) *Surviving the Breakup: how children and parents cope with divorce*, New York: Basic Books.

Walsh, F. (ed.) (1982) *Normal Family Processes*, New York: Guilford Press.

Walster, E., Walster, G.W., & Berscheid, E. (1978) *Equity: theory and research*, Boston: Allyn & Bacon.

Waterman, A.S. (1982) 'Identity development from adolescence to adulthood: An extension of theory and a review of research', *Developmental Psychology* 18: 341–58.

Waterman, A.S. & Goldman, J. (1976) 'A longitudinal study of ego identity development at a liberal arts college', *Journal of Youth and Adolescence* 5: 361–70.

Watson, I. (1985) *Double Depression: schooling, unemployment and family life in the eighties*, Sydney: Allen & Unwin.

Wearing, B.M. (1985) 'The impact of changing patterns of family living on identity formation in late adolescence', *Australian Journal of Sex, Marriage and Family* 5: 16–24.

Weir, R., Silvesto, R., & Bennington, L. (1984) 'A study of access patterns between three groups differing in their post-separation conflict', in Institute of Family Studies *Australian Family Research Conference* vol. 2, Melbourne: Institute of Family Studies.

Weiss, R.S. (1979) 'Growing up a little faster: The experience of growing up in a single-parent household', *Journal of Social Issues* 35: 97–111.

West, D. (1982) *Delinquency: its roots, careers and prospects*, London: Heinemann.

White, L.K. & Brinkerhoff, D.B. (1981) 'The sexual division of labor: Evidence from childhood', *Social Forces* 60: 170–81.

Wilks, J. (1986) 'The relative importance of parents and friends in adolescent decision making', *Journal of Youth and Adolescence* 15(4): 323–35.

Wilks, J. & Callan, V.J. (1984) 'Similarity of university students and their parents' attitudes toward alcohol', *Journal of Studies on Alcohol* 45: 326–33.

Wilson, D.G. (1981) 'Videotape and guided fantasy strategies for the career counselling of college women', Paper presented at the American Psychological Association Convention, Los Angeles, CA.

Wilson, P. & Arnold, J. (1986) *Street Kids: Australia's alienated young*, Blackburn: Collins Dove.

Yoder, J.D. & Nichols, R.C. (1980) 'A life perspective comparison of married and divorced persons', *Journal of Marriage and the Family* 42: 413–19.

Young, C. (1980) 'Leaving home and lifestyle: a survey analysis of young adults', in D. Davis, G. Caldwell, M. Bennet, & D. Boorer (eds), *Living together: family patterns and lifestyles*, Canberra: Centre for Continuing

References

Education, Australian National University.

Young, C. (1987) *Young People Leaving Home in Australia: the trend toward independence,* Canberra: Australian Institute of Family Studies.

Youniss, J. & Smollar, J. (1985) *Adolescent relations with mothers, fathers, and friends,* Chicago: University of Chicago Press.

Zill, N. & Peterson, J.L. (1982) 'Learning to do things without help', in L.M. Laosa & I.E. Sigel (eds) *Families as Learning Environments for Children,* New York: Plenum Press.

Name index

163

Name index

Tavormina, J.B. 54
Taylor, B. 5
Tedin, K.L. 28, 33
Thibaut, J.W. 94
Thomas, D.L. 58–60
Thompson, L. 36
Thornburg, H.D. 46, 91
Thorne, C.R. 128
Tisak, M. 47
Tobin, D. 74
Troll, L. 31–3
Turley, P. 103
Turner, C.W. 131, 134

Ulrici, D. 45, 51, 60

van de Kaa, D. 96, 107
Van Nguyen, T. 81
Vaux, A. 82
Voeller, M.N. 3, 128, 134

Wallerstein, J.S. 108–9, 112–14, 116
Walsh, F. 2
Walsh, J.M. 58
Walster, E. and G.W. 94
Wampler, K.S. 119
Ware, E.E. 68, 84
Waterman, A.S. 12

Watson, I. 100
Wearing, B.M. 15
Weir, R. 115
Weiss, R.S. 108, 115
Werley, H.H. 132
West, D. 82
West, K.L. 134
White, B. 58
White, L.K. 75, 108
White, S.W. 107
Whiteman, M. 136
Whitfield, R. 116
Wiley, M.G. 60
Wilks, J. 35, 57–8
Williamson, M.H. 46, 91
Wilson, D.G. 98
Wilson, M. 2–3, 29, 66, 78–9, 128, 133–4
Wilson, P. 103
Woodward, J.C. 135
Wright, D. 123–4, 126, 129

Yoder, J.D. 107
Young, C. 89–90, 93, 96, 103
Youniss, J. 42, 53, 63, 89, 92

Zill, N. 75–6

Subject index

An Introduction to
Statistics in Psychology

An Introduction to Statistics in Psychology

A Complete Guide for Students

DENNIS HOWITT AND DUNCAN CRAMER

PRENTICE HALL
HARVESTER WHEATSHEAF
LONDON   NEW YORK   TORONTO   SYDNEY   TOKYO
SINGAPORE   MADRID   MEXICO CITY   MUNICH   PARIS

First published 1997 by
Prentice Hall/Harvester Wheatsheaf
Campus 400, Maylands Avenue
Hemel Hempstead
Hertfordshire, HP2 7EZ
A division of
Simon & Schuster International Group

Typeset in 10/12pt Times
by Dorwyn Ltd, Rowlands Castle, Hants

Printed and bound in Great Britain by
Redwood Books, Trowbridge, Wiltshire

Library of Congress Cataloging-in-Publication Data

Howitt, Dennis.
    An introduction to statistics in psychology : a complete guide for
students / Dennis Howitt and Duncan Cramer.
      p.   cm.
    Includes bibliographical references and index.
    ISBN 0–13–239823–0 (pbk.)
    1. Psychometrics.   I. Cramer, Duncan, 1948– . II. Title.
BF39.H74   1997
150'.15195—dc20   96–31825
                                              CIP

British Library Cataloguing in Publication Data

A catalogue record for this book is available from
the British Library

ISBN 0–13–239823–0 (pbk)

1 2 3 4 5   01 00 99 98 97

Contents

Introduction

Structure

This textbook is intended to cover most of the statistics that students need in a first-degree course in psychology.

- Part 1 covers basic descriptive statistics from tables and diagrams through to the correlation coefficient and simple regression.
- Part 2 covers basic inferential statistics – significance testing. So the significance of the correlation coefficient, the t-tests, and nonparametric testing are major features of Part 2.
- Part 3 covers the Analysis of Variance (ANOVA) up to the level at which the use of computers is recommended, not merely desirable.
- Part 4 covers more advanced correlational statistics such as partial correlation, multiple regression and factor analysis.

Package

The textbook is part of a package of materials for the teaching and learning of statistics as applied in psychological research. The package consists of the following three parts:

- This textbook, which provides an overview of the use of statistics in undergraduate laboratory work, practical work and final-year projects.
- A computer book explaining how computations are easy to carry out using a standard computer package. The student may learn to use SPSS for Windows. This is commonly available at universities and colleges throughout the world. It is now user-friendly and solves many of the problems associated with the analysis of psychological data. Computer packages make it feasible to include more advanced statistical techniques than are normally included in statistics textbooks for psychology students.

■ An instructors' manual. This includes exercises, problems, multiple-choice assessment materials, calculation worksheets, and templates for producing overhead transparencies.

Level of difficulty

Throughout, the package is designed to remain at a relatively simple level even where complex statistics are being explained. The material is aimed at the vast majority of students who, although having some mathematical skills, nevertheless do not relish complex formulae and abstract explanations of obscure mathematical procedures.

Flexibility

The textbook is designed as a menu of statistical techniques, not all of which need be sampled. Chapters 1 to 18 constitute a thorough but compact basic introduction to psychological statistics; they are suitable for use as a basic-level course as they cover descriptive statistics and common inferential statistics. Flexibility was another important feature planned for the package:

■ All instructors teach courses differently. The textbook covers most of the commonly taught techniques and many less common ones too. Instructors may omit some chapters without causing difficulties. The textbook contains pertinent basic and revision information within each chapter wherever possible. In other words, instructors will be able to select their favoured route through the material.

■ Some instructors prefer to teach statistics practically through the use of computers. This is made easy by this package which contains both a textbook and a computer manual.

■ Many students will have little difficulty in self-study of most chapters. Supervisors of student practical classes and projects may find this particularly appealing as they can direct students to appropriate parts of the textbook.

■ However, the flexibility is far greater than this. The package can serve as an introduction to statistics or as a textbook for an intermediate-level course. Not only is this simply better value for students; it means that the problems of transferring from one textbook to another are bypassed.

Professional relevance

It is increasingly obvious that the statistics taught to students and the statistics contained in journal articles and books are drawing apart. For that reason, the book contains introductions to techniques such as factor analysis, multiple regression and path analysis which are common in professional publications and generally easy to do using computer packages. Again, this section of the text-book may form part of an intermediate course.

Other features of the package

■ Tables of statistical significance have been simplified extensively. Students find some books hard and confusing to use because the statistical tables are so obscurely or badly presented.

■ Statistical formulae have been kept to a minimum. This is relatively easy since not too many formulae are necessary anyway.

■ Every calculation is illustrated with a step-by-step example for students to follow. Where hand calculation is too difficult, the student is advised when it is essential to use a computer package.

■ We have preferred to use methods and descriptions that communicate clearly and effectively to students even if they are at times not the most formally rigorous explanations. This introduces a degree of informality that might annoy the most statistically precise thinkers. We think it is for the greater good to avoid a too abstract approach.

■ We have tried to provide insight into the ways in which psychologists use statistics.

■ Practical advice on the learning and use of statistics in psychology is given at the end of every chapter of the textbook.

■ The package is excellent value for the student as it meets essentially all of their statistical needs for a first degree in psychology.

Acknowledgements

We are extremely grateful to Antoinette Hardy for help and advice from a student's perspective and for her careful checking of the manuscript. In addition, Rosemary Chapman's suggestions about student needs in statistics have been incorporated with our thanks.

Part 1

Descriptive statistics

Chapter 1

Why you need statistics

Types of data

1.1 Introduction

Imagine a world in which everything is the same; people are identical in all respects. They wear identical clothes; they eat the same meals; they are all the same height from birth; they all go to the same school with identical teachers, identical lessons and identical facilities; they all go on holiday in the same month; they all do the same job; they all live in identical houses; and the sun shines every day. They do not have sex as we know it since there are no sexes so everyone self-reproduces at the age of 30; their gardens have the same plants and the soil is exactly the same no matter whose garden; they all die on their 75th birthdays and are all buried in the same wooden boxes in identical plots of land. They are all equally clever and they all have identical personalities. Their genetic make-up never varies. Mathematically speaking all of these characteristics are constants. If this world seems less than ideal then have we got news for you – you need statistics. Only in a world of standardisation would you not need statistics – in a richly varying world statistics is essential.

If nothing varies, then everything that is to be known about people could be guessed from information obtained from a single person. No problems would arise in generalising since what is true of Sandra Green is true of everyone else – they're all called Sandra Green after all. Fortunately, the world is not like that. Variability is an essential characteristic of life and the social world in which we exist. The sheer quantity of variability has to be tamed when trying to make statements about the real world. Statistics is largely about making sense of variability.

Statistical techniques do three main things:

1. They provide ways of summarising the information that we collect from a multitude of sources. Statistics is partly about tabulating your research information or data as clearly and effectively as possible. As such it merely describes the information collected. This is achieved using tables and diagrams summarising data and simple formulae which turn fairly complex data into simple indexes that describe numerically the main features of the data.

3

This branch of statistics is called *descriptive statistics* for very obvious reasons – it describes the information you collect as accurately and succinctly as possible. The first few chapters of this book are largely devoted to descriptive statistics.

2.   Another branch of statistics is far less familiar to most of us: *inferential statistics*. This branch of statistics is really about economy of effort in research. There was a time when in order to find out about people, for example, everyone in the country would be contacted in order to collect information. This is done today when the government conducts a *census* of everyone in order to find out about the population of the country at a particular time. This is an enormous and time-consuming operation that cannot be conducted with any great frequency. But most of us are familiar with using relatively small *samples* in order to approximate the information that one would get by studying everybody. This is common in public opinion surveying where the answers of a sample of 1000 or so people may be used, say, to predict the outcome of a national election. Granted that sometimes samples can be misleading, nevertheless it is the principle of sampling that is important. *Inferential statistics* is about the confidence with which we can generalise from a sample to the entire population.

3.   The amount of data that a researcher can collect is potentially massive. Some statistical techniques enable the researcher to clarify trends in vast quantities of data using a number of powerful methods. Data simplification, data exploration or data reduction are among the names given to the process. Whatever the name the objective is the same – to make sense of large amounts of data that otherwise would be much too confusing. These *data exploration techniques* are mainly dealt with in the final few chapters.

1.2   Variables and measurement

The concept of a *variable* is basic but vitally important in statistics. It is also as easy as pie. *A variable is merely anything that varies and can be measured.* These measurements need *not* correspond very well with everyday notions of measurement such as weight, distance, and temperature. So the sex of people is a variable since it can be measured as either male or female – and sex varies between people. Similarly, eye colour is a variable because a set of people will include some with brown eyes, some with blue eyes and some with green eyes. Thus measurement can involve merely categorisation. Clinical psychologists might use different diagnostic categories such as schizophrenia, manic-depression and anxiety in research. These diagnostic categories constitute a variable since they are different mental and emotional problems to which people can be allocated. Such categorisation techniques are an important type of measurement in statistics.

Another type of measurement in statistics is more directly akin to everyday concepts of measurement in which numerical values are provided. These *numerical* values are assigned to variables such as weight, length, distance, temperature and the like – for example, 10 kilometres or 30 degrees. These numerical values are called *scores*. In psychological research many variables are measured and *quantified* in much the same way. Good examples are the many tests and scales used to assess intelligence, personality, attitudes and mental abilities. In most of these, people are assigned a number (or score) in order to describe, for example, how neurotic or how extraverted an individual is. Psychologists will speak of a person having an IQ of 112 or 93, for example, or they will say an individual has a low score of 6 on a measure of psychoticism. Usually these numbers are used as if they corresponded exactly to other forms of measurement such as weight or length. For these, we can make statements such as that a person has a weight of 60 kilograms or is 1.3 metres tall.

1.3   The major types of measurement

Traditionally, statistics textbooks for psychologists emphasise different types of measurement – usually using the phrase *scales of measurement*. However, *for virtually all practical purposes there are only two different types of measurement in statistics*. These have already been discussed, but to stress the point:

1. *Score/numerical measurement*:   This is the assignment of a *numerical* value to a measurement. This includes most physical and psychological measures. In psychological jargon these numerical measurements are called *scores*. We could record the IQ scores of five people as in Table 1.1. Each of the numerical values in the table indicates the named individual's *score* on the variable IQ. It is a simple point, but note that the numbers contain information that someone with an IQ of 150 has a higher intelligence than someone with an IQ of 80. In other words, the numbers *quantify* the variable.

2. *Nominal/category measurement*:   This is merely deciding to which category of a variable a particular case belongs. So, if we were measuring a person's job or occupation, we would have to decide whether or not he or she was a lorry driver, a professor of sociology, a debt collector, and so forth. This is called *nominal* measurement since usually the categories are described in words and, especially, given names. Thus the category 'lorry driver' is a name or verbal description of what sort of case should be placed in that

Table 1.1   **IQ scores of five named individuals**

Individual	IQ score
Stan	80
Mavis	130
Sanjit	150
Sharon	145
Peter	105

Table 1.2 **Frequencies of different occupations**

Occupational category	Number or frequency in set
Lorry drivers	27
Sociology professors	10
Debt collectors	15
Other occupations	48

category. Notice that there are no numbers involved in the process of categorisation as such. A person is either a lorry driver or not. *However, you need to be warned of a possible confusion that can occur.* If you have 100 people whose occupations are known you might wish to count how many are lorry drivers, how many are professors of sociology, and so forth. These counts could be entered into a data table like Table 1.2. Notice that the numbers this time merely correspond to a count of the *frequency* or number of cases falling into each of the four occupational categories. *They are not scores*, but frequencies. The numbers do not correspond to a single measurement but are the aggregate of many separate (nominal) measurements.

The distinction between numerical scores and frequencies is important so always take care to check whether what appears to be numerical scores in a table are not actually frequencies.

Make a habit of mentally labelling variables as numerical scores or nominal categories. Doing so is a big step forward in thinking statistically. This is all you really need to know about types of measurement. However, you should be aware that others use more complex systems. Read the following section to learn more about scales of measurement.

Formal measurement theory

You may find it unnecessary to learn the contents of this section in detail. However, it does contain terms with which you ought to be familiar since other people might make reference to them.

Many psychologists speak of four different scales of measurement. Conceptually they are distinct. Nevertheless, for most practical situations in psychologists' use of statistics the nominal category versus numerical scores distinction discussed above is sufficient.

The four 'theoretical' scales of measurement are as follows. Numbers 2, 3 and 4 are different types of *numerical* scores.

1. **Nominal** categorisation. This is the placing of cases into *named* categories – nominal clearly refers to names. It is exactly the same as our nominal measurement or categorisation process.

2. **Ordinal** (or rank) measurement. The assumption here is that the values of the numerical scores tell us little else other than which is the smallest, the next smallest and so forth up to the largest. In other words, we can place the scores in *order* (hence ordinal) from the smallest to the largest. It is sometimes called rank measurement since we can assign ranks to the first, second, third, fourth, fifth, etc. in order from the smallest to the largest numerical value. These ranks have the numerical value 1, 2, 3, 4, 5, etc. You will see examples of this later in the book, especially in Chapters 7 and 18. However, few psychologists collect data directly as ranks.

3. **Interval** or equal-interval measurement. The basic idea here is that in some cases the intervals between numbers on a numerical scale are equal in size. Thus, if we measure distance on a scale of centimetres then the distance between 0 and 1 centimetre on our scale is exactly the same as the difference between 4 and 5 centimetres or between 11 and 12 centimetres on that scale. This is obvious for some standard physical measurements such as temperature.

4. **Ratio** measurement. This is exactly the same as interval scale measurement with one important proviso. A ratio scale of measurement has an absolute zero point that is measured as 0. Most physical measurements such as distance and weight have zero points that are absolute. Thus zero on a tape measure is the smallest distance one can have – there is no distance between two coincident points. With this sort of scale of measurement it is possible to work out ratios between measures. So, for example, a town that is 20 kilometres away is twice as far away as a town that is only 10 kilometres away. A building that is 15 metres high is half the height of a building that is 30 metres high. (Not all physical measures have a zero that is absolute zero – this applies particularly to several measures of temperature. Temperatures measured in degrees Celsius or Fahrenheit have points that are labelled as zero. However, these zero points do not correspond to the lowest possible temperature you can have. It is then meaningless to say, for example, that it is twice as hot if the temperature is 20 degrees Celsius than if it were 10 degrees Celsius.)

It is very difficult to apply the last three types of measure to psychological measurements with certainty. Since most psychological scores do not have any directly observable physical basis, it is impossible to decide whether they consist of equal intervals or have an absolute zero. For many years this problem caused great controversy and confusion among psychologists. For the most part, much current usage of statistics in psychology ignores the distinctions between the three different types of numerical scores. This has the support of many statisticians. On the other hand, some psychologists prefer to emphasise that some data are best regarded as rankable and lack the qualities which are characteristic of interval/ratio data. They are more likely to use the statistical techniques to be found in Chapter 18 and the ranking correlation coefficient (Chapter 7) than others. In other words, for precisely the same data, different psychologists will adopt different statistical techniques. Usually this will make little difference to the outcomes of their statistical analyses. In general, it will cause you few, if any, problems if you ignore the three subdivisions of numerical score measurement in your practical use of statistics. The exceptions to this are discussed in Chapters 7 and 18. Since psychologists rarely if ever collect data in the form of ranks, Chapters 2 to 6 are unaffected by such considerations.

1.4   Notes and recommendations

- Always ask yourself what sort of measurement it is you are considering – is it a numerical score on a variable or is it putting individuals into categories?
- Never assume that a number is necessarily a numerical score. Without checking, it could be a *frequency* of observations in a named category.
- Clarity of thinking is a virtue in statistics – you will rarely be expected to demonstrate great creativity in your statistical work. Understanding precisely the meaning of terms is a positive advantage in statistics.

Chapter 2

Describing variables

Tables and diagrams

Preparation
Remind yourself what a variable is from Chapter 1. Similarly, if you are still not sure of the nominal (categorisation) form of measurement and the use of numerical scores in measurement then revise these too.

2.1   Introduction

You probably know a lot more about statistics than you think. The mass media regularly feature statistical tables and diagrams; children become familiar with statistical tables and diagrams at school. Skill with these methods is essential because researchers collect large amounts of data from numerous people. If we asked 100 people their age, sex, marital status (divorced, married, single, etc.), their number of children and their occupation this would yield 500 separate pieces of information. Although this is small fry compared to much research, it is not very helpful to present these 500 measurements in your research report. Such unprocessed information is called *raw data*. Statistical analysis has to be more than describing the raw ingredients. It requires structuring data in ways that *effectively communicate* the major trends. If you fail to structure your data, you may as well just give the reader copies of your questionnaires or observation schedules to interpret themselves.

There are very few rules regulating the production of tables and diagrams in statistics so long as they are clear and concise; they need to communicate quickly the important trends in the data. There is absolutely no point in using tables and diagrams that do not ease the task of communication. Probably the best way of deciding whether your tables and diagrams do their job well is to ask other people to decipher what they mean. Tables which are unclear to other people are generally useless.

The distinction between nominal (category) data and numerical scores discussed in the previous chapter is important in terms of the appropriate tables and diagrams to use.

Design consideration: One of the easiest mistakes to make in research is to allow participants in your research to give more than one answer to a question. So, for example, if you ask people to name their favourite television programmes and allow each person more than one answer you will find that the data can be very tricky to analyse thoroughly. Take our word for it for now: statistics in general do not handle multiple responses very well. Certainly it is possible to draw up tables and diagrams but some of the more advanced statistical procedures become difficult to apply. You will sometimes read comments to the effect that the totals in a table exceed the number of participants in the research. This is because the researcher has allowed multiple responses to a single variable. So only allow the participants in your research to give one piece of data for each variable you are measuring to avoid digging a pit for yourself. If you plan your data analysis in detail before you collect your data you should be able to anticipate any difficulties.

2.2   Choosing tables and diagrams

So long as you are able to decide whether your data are either numerical scores or nominal (category) data, there are few other choices to be made since the available tables and diagrams are essentially dependent upon this distinction.

Tables and diagrams for nominal (category) data

One of the main characteristics of tables and diagrams for nominal (category) data is that they have to show the *frequencies* of cases in each category used. While there may be as many categories as you wish, it is *not* the function of statistical analysis to communicate all of the data's detail; the task is to identify the major trends. For example, imagine you are researching the public's attitudes towards private health care. If you ask participants in your research their occupations then you might find that they mention tens if not hundreds of different job titles – newsagents, housepersons, company executives and so forth. Simply counting the frequencies with which different job titles are mentioned results in a vast number of categories. You need to think of relevant and meaningful ways of reducing this vast number into a smaller number of much broader categories that might reveal important trends. For example, since the research is about a health issue you might wish to form a category made up of those involved in health work – some might be dentists, some nurses, some doctors, some paramedics, and so forth. Instead of keeping these as different categories, they might be combined into a category 'health worker'. There are no hard-and-fast rules

Table 2.1   **Occupational status of participants in the research expressed as frequencies and percentage frequencies**

Occupation	Frequency	Percentage frequency
Nuns	17	21.25
Nursery teachers	3	3.75
Television presenters	23	28.75
Students	20	25.00
Other	17	21.25

about combining to form broader categories. The following might be useful rules of thumb:

1. Keep your number of categories low, especially when you have only small numbers of participants in your research.

2. Try to make your 'combined' categories meaningful and sensible in the light of the purposes of your research. It would be nonsense, for example, to categorise jobs by the letter of the alphabet with which they start – nurses, night watchpersons, nuns, nursery teachers, and national footballers. All of these have jobs that begin with the same letter but it is very difficult to see any other common thread which allows them to be combined together meaningfully.

In terms of drawing tables, all we do is to list the categories we have chosen and give the frequency of cases that fall into each of the categories (Table 2.1).

The frequencies are presented in two ways in this table – *simple* frequencies and *percentage* frequencies. A percentage frequency is merely the frequency expressed as a percentage of the total of the frequencies (or total number of cases, usually).

Notice also that one of the categories is called 'other'. This consists of those cases which do not fit into any of the main categories. It is, in other words, a 'rag bag' category or miscellany. Generally, all other things being equal, it is best to have a small number of cases in the 'other' category.

Calculation 2.1

Percentage frequencies

Many readers will not need this. But if you are a little rusty with simple maths, it might be helpful.

The percentage frequency for a particular category, say for students, is the frequency in that category expressed as a percentage of the total frequencies in the data table.

Step 1:   What is the category frequency? For students in Table 2.1:

Category frequency$_{[students]}$ = 20

Step 2:   Add up all of the frequencies in Table 2.1:

Total frequencies = nuns + nursery teachers + TV presenters + students + other

= 17 + 3 + 23+ 20 + 17 = 80

Step 3:

$$\text{Percentage frequency}_{[students]} = \frac{\text{Category frequency}_{[students]} \times 100}{\text{Total frequencies}}$$

$$= \frac{20 \times 100}{80}$$

$$= \frac{2000}{80}$$

$$= 25\%$$

One advantage of using computers is that they enable experimentation with different schemes of categorising data in order to decide which is best for your purposes. In this you would use initially narrow categories for coding your data. Then you can tell the computer which of these to combine into broader categories.

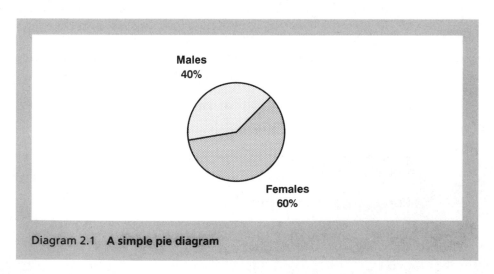

Diagram 2.1   **A simple pie diagram**

Sometimes it is preferable to turn frequency tables into diagrams. Good diagrams are quickly understood and add variety to the presentation. The main types of diagrams for nominal (category) data are *pie diagrams* and *bar charts*. A pie diagram is a very familiar form of presentation – it simply expresses each category as a slice of a pie which represents all cases (see Diagram 2.1).

Notice that the *number* of slices is small – a multitude of slices can be confusing. Each slice is clearly marked with its category name, and the percentage frequency in each category also appears.

Calculation 2.2

Slices for a pie diagram

There is nothing difficult in constructing a pie diagram. Our recommendation is that you turn each of your frequencies into a percentage frequency. Since there are 360° in a circle, if you multiply each percentage frequency by 3.6 you will obtain the angle in degrees of the slice of the pie which you need to mark out. In order to create the diagram you will require a protractor to measure the angles. However, graph packages for use on the computer would be standard at any university or college and do an impressive job.

In Table 2.1, 25.00% of cases were students. In order to turn this into the correct angle for the slice of the pie you simply need to multiply 25.00 × 3.6 to give an angle of 90 degrees.

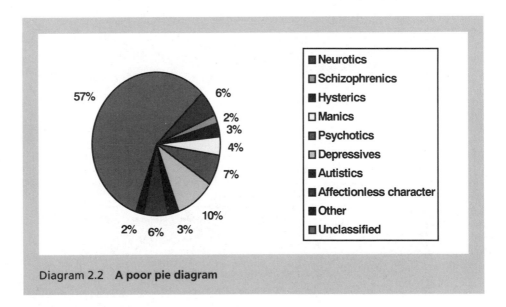

Diagram 2.2   **A poor pie diagram**

Diagram 2.2 shows a *bad* example of a pie diagram for purposes of comparison. There are several problems with this pie diagram: ·

1. There are too many small slices identified by different shading patterns and the 'legend' takes time to decode.

2. It is not too easily seen what each slice concerns and the relative sizes of the slices are difficult to judge. We have the size of the slices around the figure and a separate 'legend' or key to identify the components to help cope with the overcrowding problem. In other words, too many categories have resulted in a diagram which is far from easy to read – a cardinal sin in any statistical diagram.

A simple frequency table might be more effective in this case.

Another very familiar form of statistical diagram for nominal (category) data is the *bar chart*. Again these are very common in the media. Basically they are diagrams in which bars represent the size of each category. An example is shown in Diagram 2.3.

The relative lengths (or heights) of the bars quickly reveal the main trends in the data. With a bar chart there is very little to remember other than that the bars have a standard space separating them. The spaces indicate that the categories are not in a numerical order; they are frequencies of categories, *not* scores.

It is hard to go wrong with a bar chart (that is not a challenge!) so long as you remember the following:

1. The heights of the bars represent frequencies (number of cases) in a category.

2. Each bar should be clearly labelled as to the category it represents.

3. Too many bars make bar charts hard to follow.

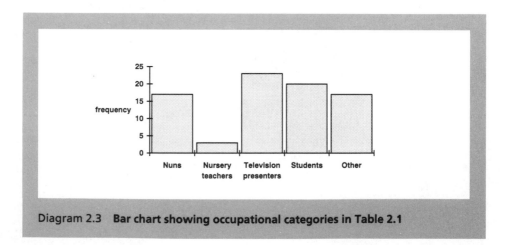

Diagram 2.3   **Bar chart showing occupational categories in Table 2.1**

4. Avoid having *many* empty or near-empty categories which represent very few cases. Generally, the information about substantial categories is the most important. (Small categories can be combined together as an 'other' category.)

5. Nevertheless, if *important* categories have very few entries then this needs recording. So, for example, a researcher who is particularly interested in opportunities for women surveys people in top management and finds very few women employed in such jobs. It is important to draw attention to this in the bar chart of males and females in top management. Once again, there are no hard and fast rules to guide you – common sense will take you a long way.

6. Make sure that the vertical axis (the heights of the bars) is clearly marked as being frequencies or percentage frequencies.

7. The bars should be of equal width.

In newspapers and on television you are likely to come across a variant of the bar chart called the *pictogram*. In this, the bars of the bar chart are replaced by varying sized drawings of something eye-catching to do with your categories. Thus, pictures of men or women of varying heights, for example, replace the bars. Pictograms are rarely used in professional presentations. The main reason is that pictures of things get wider as well as taller as they increase in size. This can misrepresent the relative sizes of the categories, given readers forget that it is only the height of the picture which counts.

Tables and diagrams for numerical score data

One crucial consideration when deciding what tables and diagrams to use for score data is the number of separate scores recorded for the variable in question. This can vary markedly. So, for example, age in the general population can range from newly born to over 100 years of age. If we merely recorded ages to the nearest whole year then a table or diagram may have entries for 100 different

Table 2.2 **Ages expressed as age bands**

Age range	Frequency
0–9 years	19
10–19 years	33
20–29 years	17
30–39 years	22
40–49 years	17
50 years and over	3

ages. Such a table or diagram would look horrendous. If we recorded age to the nearest month, then we could multiply this number of ages by twelve! Such scores can be grouped into bands or ranges of scores to allow effective tabulation (Table 2.2).

Many psychological variables have a much smaller range of numerical values. So, for example, it is fairly common to use questions which pre-specify just a few response alternatives. The so-called Likert-type questionnaire item is a good case in point. Typically this looks something like this:

Statistics is my favourite university subject:

| *Strongly agree* | *Agree* | *Neither agree nor disagree* | *Disagree* | *Strongly disagree* |

Participants completing this questionnaire circle the response alternative which best fits their personal opinion. It is conventional in this type of research to code these different response alternatives on a five-point scale from one to five. Thus strongly agree might be coded 1, neither agree nor disagree 3, and strongly disagree 5. This scale therefore has only five alternative values. Because of this small number of alternative answers, a table based on this question will be relatively simple. Indeed, if students are not too keen on statistics, you may well find that they select only the disagree and strongly disagree categories.

Tabulating such data is quite straightforward. Indeed you can merely report the numbers or frequencies of replies for each of the different categories or scores as in Table 2.3.

A *histogram* might be the best form of statistical diagram to represent these data. At first sight histograms look very much like bar charts but without gaps between the bars. This is because the histogram does not represent distinct unrelated categories but different points on a *numerical* measurement scale. So a histogram of the above data might look like Diagram 2.4.

But what if your data have numerous different possible values of the variable in question? One common difficulty for most psychological research is that the number of respondents tends to be small. The large number of possible different scores on the variable is therefore shared between very few respondents. Tables and diagrams should present major features of your data in a simple and easily

Table 2.3 **Distribution of students' attitudes towards statistics**

Response category	**Value**	**Frequency**
Strongly agree	1	17
Agree	2	14
Neither agree nor disagree	3	6
Disagree	4	2
Strongly disagree	5	1

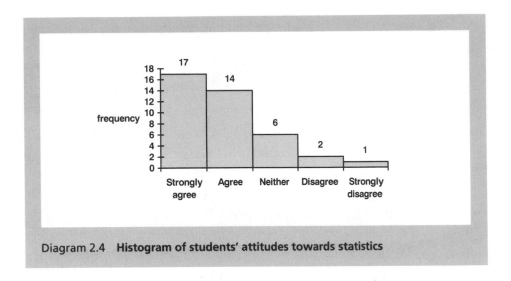

Diagram 2.4   **Histogram of students' attitudes towards statistics**

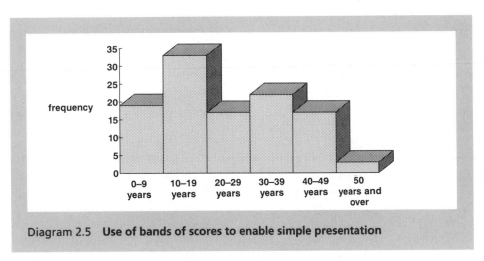

Diagram 2.5   **Use of bands of scores to enable simple presentation**

assimilated form. So sometimes you will have to use *bands of scores* rather than individual score values just as you did for Table 2.2 above. So if we asked 100 people their ages we could categorise their replies into bands such as 0–9 years, 10–19 years, 30–39 years, 40–49 years and a final category of those 50 years and over. By using bands we reduce the risk of empty parts of the table and allow any trends to become clear (Diagram 2.5).

How one chooses the bands to use is an important question. The answer is a bit of luck and judgement and a lot of trial and error. It is very time consuming to rejig the ranges of the bands when one is analysing the data by hand. One big advantage of computers is that they will recode your scores into bands repeatedly until you

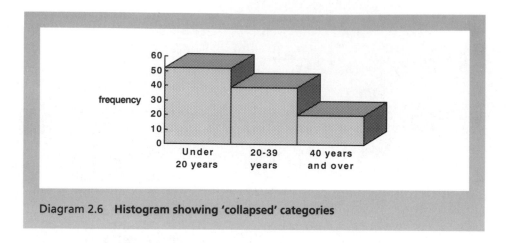

Diagram 2.6   **Histogram showing 'collapsed' categories**

have tables which seem to do the job as well as possible. The criterion is still whether the table communicates things effectively.

The one rule is that the bands ought to be of the same size – that is cover, for example, equal ranges of scores. Generally this is easy except at the upper and lower ends of the distribution. Perhaps you wish to use 'over 70' as your upper range. This, in modern practice, can be done as a bar of the same width as the others, but must be very carefully marked. (Strictly speaking the width of the band should represent the range of scores involved and the height reduced in the light of this. However, this is rarely done in modern psychological statistics.)

One might redefine the bands of scores and generate another histogram based on identical data but a different set of bands (Diagram 2.6).

It requires some thought to decide which of the diagrams is best for a particular purpose. There are no hard-and-fast rules.

2.3   Errors to avoid

There are a few mistakes that you can make in drawing up tables and diagrams:

1. *Do not* forget to head the table or diagram with a succinct description of what it concerns. You will notice that we have done our best throughout this chapter to supply each table and diagram with a clear title.

2. Label everything on the table or diagram as clearly as possible. What this means is that you have to mark your bar charts and histograms in a way that tells the reader what each bar means. Then you must indicate what the height of the bar refers to – probably either frequency or percentage frequency.

Note that this chapter has concentrated on describing a *single* variable as clearly as possible. In Chapter 6, methods of making tables and diagrams showing the relationships between two or more variables are described.

2.4   Notes and recommendations

- Try to make your tables and diagrams useful. It is not usually their purpose to record the data as you collected it in your research. Of course you can list your data in the appendix of projects that you carry out, but this is not useful as a way of illustrating trends. It is part of a researcher's job to make the data accessible to the reader in a structured form that is easily understood by the reader.

- Especially when using computers, it is very easy to generate *useless* tables and diagrams. This is usually because computer analysis encourages you not to examine your raw data in any detail. This implies that you should always regard your first analyses as tentative and merely a step towards something more ideal.

- If a table is not clear to you, it is unlikely to be any clearer to anyone else.

- Check each table and diagram for clear and full labelling of each part. Especially, check that frequencies are clearly marked as such.

- Check that there is a clear, helpful title to each table and diagram.

Chapter 3

Describing variables numerically

Averages, variation and spread

Preparation
Revise the meaning of nominal (category) data and numerical score data.

3.1   Introduction

Tables and diagrams take up a lot of space. It can be more efficient to use numerical indexes to describe the distributions of variables. For this reason, you will find relatively few pie charts and the like in published research. One numerical index is familiar to everyone – the numerical average (or arithmetic mean). Large amounts of data can be described adequately using just a few numerical indexes.

Table 3.1   **Two different sets of scores**

Variable A scores	Variable B scores
2	27
2	29
3	35
3	40
3	41
4	42
4	45
4	45
4	49
4	49
5	49
5	
5	

What are the major features of data that we might attempt to summarise in this way? Look at the two different sets of scores in Table 3.1. The major differences between these two sets of data are:

1. The sets of scores differ substantially in terms of their typical value – in one case the scores are relatively large (Variable B); in the other case the scores are much smaller (Variable A).

2. The sets of scores differ in their spread or variability – one set (Variable B) seems to have more spread or a greater variability than the other.

3. If we plot these two sets of scores as histograms then we also find that the shapes of the distributions differ markedly. Variable A is much steeper and less spread out than Variable B.

Each of these different features of a set of scores can be described using various indexes. They do *not* generally apply to nominal (category) variables.

3.2   Typical scores: mean, median and mode

Researchers sometimes speak about the *central tendency* of a set of scores. By this they are raising the issue of what are the most typical and likely scores in the distribution of measurements. We could speak of the average score but that can mislead us into thinking that the arithmetic mean is the average score when it is just one of several possibilities. There are three main measures of the typical scores – the *arithmetic mean*, the *mode* and the *median*. These are quite distinct concepts but generally simple enough in themselves.

The arithmetic mean

The arithmetic mean is calculated by summing all of the scores in a distribution and dividing by the number of scores. This is the everyday concept of average. In statistical notation we can express this mean as follows:

$$\overline{X}_{\text{[mean]}} = \frac{\Sigma X_{\text{[scores]}}}{N_{\text{[number-of-scores]}}}$$

As this is the first statistical formula we have presented, you should take very careful note of what each symbol means:

X is the statistical symbol for a score
Σ is the summation or sigma sign
ΣX means add up all of the scores X
N is the number of scores
$\overline{X}$ is the statistical symbol for the arithmetic mean of a set of scores

We have added a few comments in small square brackets [just like this]. Although mathematicians may not like them very much, you might find they help you interpret a formula a little more quickly.

Calculation 3.1

The numerical or arithmetic mean

To illustrate the calculation of the arithmetic mean we can use the following six scores:

$X_1 = 7$
$X_2 = 5$
$X_3 = 4$
$X_4 = 7$
$X_5 = 7$
$X_6 = 5$

The subscripts following the Xs above define a particular score.

$$\overline{X}_{[mean]} = \frac{\Sigma X_{[scores]}}{N_{[number-of-scores]}}$$

$$\overline{X} = \frac{X_1 + X_2 + X_3 + X_4 + X_5 + X_6}{N}$$

$$= \frac{7 + 5 + 4 + 7 + 7 + 5}{6}$$

$$= \frac{35}{6}$$

$$= 5.83$$

Although you probably do not need the formula to work out the arithmetic mean, it is useful at this stage to make sure that you understand how to decode the symbols. It is a simple example but contains several of the important elements of statistical formulae. It is good preparation to go through the calculation using the formula.

The mode

The mode is the most frequently occurring category of score. It is merely the most common score or most frequent category of scores. In other words, you can

Table 3.2   **Frequencies of scores**

Score	Frequency (*f*)
4	1
5	2
6	0
7	3

Table 3.3   **A bimodal frequency distribution**

Score	Frequency (*f*)
3	1
4	2
5	3
6	1
7	3
8	1

apply the mode to any category data and not just scores. In the above example where the scores were 7, 5, 4, 7, 7, and 5 we could represent the scores in terms of their frequencies of occurrence (Table 3.2).

Frequencies are often represented as *f* in statistics. It is very easy to see in this example that the most frequently occurring score is 7 with a frequency of 3. So the mode of this distribution is 7.

If we take the slightly different set of scores 7, 5, 4, 7, 7, 5, 3, 4, 6, 8, and 5, the frequency distribution of these scores is shown in Table 3.3. Here there is no single mode since scores 5 and 7 jointly have the highest frequency of 3. This sort of distribution is called *bimodal* and the two modes are 5 and 7. The general term *multimodal* implies that a frequency distribution has several modes.

The mode is the only measure in this chapter that applies to nominal (category) data as well as numerical score data.

The median

The median is the middle score of a set if they are organised from the smallest to the largest. Thus the scores 7, 5, 4, 7, 7, 5, 3, 4, 6, 8, and 5 become 3, 4, 4, 5, 5, 5, 6, 7, 7, 7, and 8 when put in order from the smallest to the largest. Since there are 11 scores and the median is the middle score from the smallest to the largest, the median has to be the sixth score, i.e. 5.

With odd numbers of scores all of which are different, the median is easily calculated since there is a single score that corresponds to the middle score in the set of scores. However, if there is an even number of all different scores in the set then sometimes the mid-point will not be a single score but two scores. So if you have 12 different scores placed in order from smallest to largest, the median will be somewhere between the sixth and seventh score from smallest. There is no such score, of course, by definition – the 6.5th score just does not exist. What we could do in these circumstances is to take the average of the sixth and seventh scores to give us an estimate of the median.

For the distribution of 40 scores shown in Table 3.4, the middle score from the smallest is somewhere between the 20th and 21st scores. Thus the median is somewhere between score 5 (the 20th score) and score 6 (the 21st score). One could give the average of these two as the median score – that is, the median is 5.5. For most purposes this is good enough.

You may find that computer programs give different values from this. The computer program is making adjustments since there may be several identical scores near the median but you need only a fraction of them to reach your mid-point score. So in the above example the 21st score comes in score category 6 although there are actually eight scores in that category. So in order to get that extra score we need take only one-eighth of score category 6. One-eighth equals 0.125 so the estimated median equals 5.125. To be frank, it is difficult to think of many circumstances in which this level of precision about the value of the median is required in psychological statistics. You ought to regard this feature of computer output as a bonus and adopt the simpler method for your hand calculations.

Table 3.4 **Frequency distribution of 40 scores**

Score	Frequency (*f*)
1	1
2	2
3	4
4	6
5	7
6	8
7	6
8	3
9	2
10	1
11	0
12	1

3.3 Comparison of mean, median and mode

Usually the mean, median and mode will give different values of the central tendency when applied to the same set of scores. It is only when a distribution is perfectly symmetrical *and* the distribution peaks in the middle that they coincide completely. Regard big differences between the mean, median and mode as a sign that your distribution of scores is rather asymmetrical or lopsided.

Distributions of scores do not have to be perfectly symmetrical for statistical analysis but it tends to make some calculations a little more accurate. It is difficult to say how much lack of symmetry there can be without it becoming a serious problem. There is more about this later, especially in Chapter 18 and Appendix A which makes some suggestions about how to test for asymmetry. This is done relatively rarely in our experience.

3.4 The spread of scores: variability

The concept of variability is essential in statistics. Variability is a non-technical term and is related to (but is *not* identical with) the statistical term *variance*. Variance is nothing more nor less than a mathematical formula that serves as a useful indicator of variability. But it is not the only way of assessing variability.

The following set of ages of 12 university students can be used to illustrate some different ways of measuring variability in our data:

18 years	21 years	23 years	18 years	19 years	19 years
19 years	33 years	18 years	19 years	19 years	20 years

These 12 students vary in age from 18 to 33 years. In other words, the range covers a 15-year period. The interval from youngest to oldest (or tallest to shortest, or fattest to thinnest) is called the *range* – a useful statistical concept. As a *statistical* concept, range is *always* expressed as a single number such as 20 centimetres and *never* as an interval, say, from 15 to 25 centimetres.

One trouble with range is that it can be heavily influenced by extreme cases. Thus the 33-year-old student in the above set of ages is having a big influence on the range of ages of the students. This is because he or she is much older than most of the students. For this reason, the *interquartile range* has advantages. To calculate the interquartile range we split the age distribution into quarters and take the range of the middle two quarters (or middle 50%), ignoring the extreme quarters. Since we have 12 students, we delete the three youngest (the three 18-year-olds) and the three oldest (aged 33, 23 and 21). This leaves us with the middle two quarters (the middle 50%) which includes five 19-year-olds and one 20-year-old. The range of this middle two quarters, or the interquartile range, is one year (from 19 years to 20 years). The interquartile range is sometimes a better indicator of the variability of, say, age than the full range because extreme ages are excluded.

Table 3.5   **Deviations from the mean**

Score – mean	Deviation from mean
18 – 20.5	–2.5
21 – 20.5	0.5
23 – 20.5	2.5
18 – 20.5	–2.5
19 – 20.5	–1.5
19 – 20.5	–1.5
19 – 20.5	–1.5
33 – 20.5	12.5
18 – 20.5	–2.5
19 – 20.5	–1.5
19 – 20.5	–1.5
20 – 20.5	–0.5

Useful as the range is, a lot of information is ignored. It does not take into account all of the scores in the set, merely the extreme ones. For this reason, measures of spread or variability have been developed which include the extent to which each of the scores in the set differs from the mean score of the set.

One such measure is the *mean deviation*. To calculate this we have to work out the mean of the set of scores and then how much each score in the set differs from that mean. These deviations are then added up to give the total of deviations from the mean. Finally we can divide by the number of scores to give the average or mean deviation from the mean of the set of scores. If we take the ages of the students listed above, we find that the total of the ages is 18 + 21 + 23 + 18 + 19 + 19 + 19 + 33 + 18 + 19 + 19 + 20 = 246. Divide this total by 12 and we get the average age in the set to be 20.5 years. Now if we subtract 20.5 years from each of the student's ages we get the figures in Table 3.5.

The average amount of deviation from the mean (ignoring the sign) is known as the mean deviation (for the above deviations this would give a value of 2.6 years). Although frequently mentioned in statistical textbooks it has no practical applications in psychological statistics and is best forgotten. However, there is a very closely related concept, *variance*, that is much more useful and has widespread and extensive applications. Variance is calculated in an almost identical way to mean deviation but for one thing. When we draw up a table to calculate the variance, we *square* each deviation from the mean before summing the total of these squared deviations as shown in Table 3.6.

The total of the squared deviations from the mean is 193. If we divide this by the number of scores (12), it gives us the value of the variance, which equals 16.08 in this case.

Table 3.6   **Squared deviations from the mean**

Score – mean	Deviation from mean	Square of deviation from mean
18 – 20.5	–2.5	6.25
21 – 20.5	0.5	0.25
23 – 20.5	2.5	6.25
18 – 20.5	–2.5	6.25
19 – 20.5	–1.5	2.25
19 – 20.5	–1.5	2.25
19 – 20.5	–1.5	2.25
33 – 20.5	12.5	156.25
18 – 20.5	–2.5	6.25
19 – 20.5	–1.5	2.25
19 – 20.5	–1.5	2.25
20 – 20.5	–0.5	0.25
	Total = 0	Total = 193

Expressing the concept as a formula:

$$\text{Variance} = \frac{\Sigma\,(X - \overline{X})^2}{N}$$

The above formula defines what variance is – it is the *defining formula*. The calculation of variance above corresponds to this formula. However, in statistics there are often quicker ways of doing calculations. These quicker methods involve *computational formulae*. The computational formula for variance is important and worth memorising as it occurs in many contexts.

Standard deviation (see Chapter 5) is a concept which computationally is very closely related to variance. Indeed, many textbooks deal with them at one and the same time. Unfortunately, this tends to confuse two very distinct concepts in our view and adds nothing to clarity.

Calculation 3.2

Variance using the computational formula

The computational formula for variance speeds the calculation since it saves us having to calculate the mean of the set of scores and subtract this mean from each of the scores. The formula is:

$$\text{Variance}_{\text{[computational formula]}} = \frac{\Sigma X^2 - \frac{(\Sigma X^2)}{N}}{N}$$

Take care with elements of this formula:

X = the general symbol for each member of a set of scores
Σ = sigma or the summation sign, i.e. add up all the things which follow
ΣX^2 = the sum of the square of each of the scores
$(\Sigma X)^2$ = sum all the scores and square that total
N = the number of scores

Step 1:   Applying this formula to our set of scores, it is useful to draw up a table (Table 3.7) consisting of our scores and some of the steps in the computation. N (number of scores) equals 12.

Table 3.7   **A set of scores and their squares for use in the computing formula for variance**

Score X	Squared score X^2
18	324
21	441
23	529
18	324
19	361
19	361
19	361
33	1089
18	324
19	361
19	361
20	400
$\Sigma X = 246$	$\Sigma X^2 = 5236$
$(\Sigma X)^2 = 246^2 = 60516$	

Step 2:   Substituting these values in the computational formula:

$$\text{Variance}_{\text{[computational formula]}} = \frac{\Sigma X^2 - \frac{(\Sigma X)^2}{N}}{N}$$

$$\text{Variance} = \frac{5236 - \frac{60516}{12}}{12}$$

$$= \frac{5236 - 5043}{12}$$

$$= \frac{193}{12}$$

$$= 16.08$$

So the variation in the scores is quite high.

There is a concept called the *variance estimate* (or estimated variance) which is closely related to variance. The difference is that variance estimate is your best guess as to the variance of a population of scores *if* you only have the data from a small set of scores from that population on which to base your estimate. The variance estimate is described in Chapter 11. It involves a slight amendment to the variance formula in that instead of dividing by N one divides by $N - 1$.

3.5 Notes and recommendations

■ Because they are routine ways of summarising the typical score and the spread of a set of scores, it is important always to report the following information for each of your variables:

  – mean, median and mode

  – range and variance

  – number of scores in the set of scores

■ *The above does not apply to nominal categories.* For these, the frequency of cases in each category exhausts the main possibilities.

■ It is worth trying to memorise the definitional and computational formulae for variance. You will be surprised how often these formulae reappear in statistics.

■ When using a computer, look carefully for variables that have zero variance. They can cause problems and generally ought to be omitted from your analyses (see Chapter 7). Normally the computer will not compute the calculations you ask for in these circumstances. The difficulty is that if all the scores of a variable are the same, it is impossible to calculate many statistical formulae. If you are calculating by hand, variables with all the scores the same are easier to spot.

Chapter 4

Shapes of distributions of scores

Preparation
Be clear about numerical scores and how they can be classified into ranges of scores (Chapter 2).

The final important characteristic of sets of scores is the particular shape of their distribution. It is useful for a researcher to be able to describe this shape succinctly. Obviously it is possible to find virtually any shape of distribution amongst the multitude of variables that could be measured. So, intuitively, it seems unrealistic to seek to describe just a few different shapes. But there are some advantages in doing so, as we shall see.

4.1 Histograms and frequency curves

Most of us have very little difficulty in understanding histograms; we know that they are plots of the frequency of scores (the vertical dimension) against a numerical scale (the horizontal dimension). Diagram 4.1 is an example of a histogram based on a relatively small set of scores. This histogram has quite severe steps from bar to bar. In other words, it is quite angular and not a smooth shape at all. Part of the reason for this is that the horizontal numerical scale moves along in discrete steps, so resulting in this pattern. Things would be different if we measured on a *continuous scale* on which every possible score could be represented to the smallest fraction. For example, we might decide to measure people's heights in centimetres to the nearest whole centimetre. But we know that heights do not really conform to this set of discrete steps or points; people who measure 120 centimetres actually differ in height by up to a centimetre from each other. Height can be measured in fractions of centimetres, not just whole centimetres. In other words height is a continuous measurement with infinitesimally small steps between measures so long as we have sufficiently precise measuring instruments.

So a histogram of heights measured in centimetre units is at best an approximation to reality. Within each of the blocks of the histogram is a possible

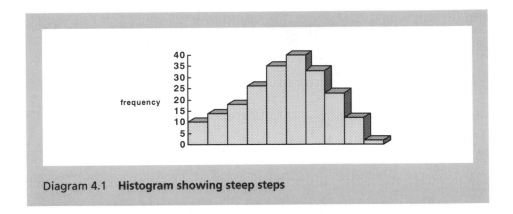

Diagram 4.1 **Histogram showing steep steps**

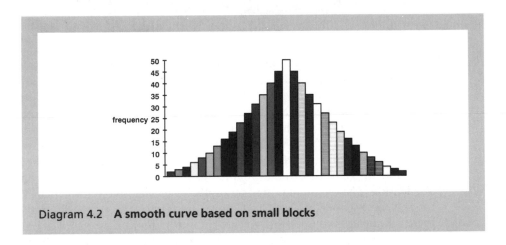

Diagram 4.2 **A smooth curve based on small blocks**

multitude of smaller steps. For this reason, it is conventional when drawing frequency curves for theoretical purposes to smooth out the blocks to a continuous curve. Essentially this is like taking much finer and precise measurements and redrawing the histogram. Instead of doing this literally we approximate it by drawing a smooth curve through imaginary sets of extremely small steps. When this is done our histogram is 'miraculously' turned into a continuous unstepped curve (Diagram 4.2).

A frequency curve can, of course, be of virtually any shape but one shape in particular is of concern in psychological statistics – the normal curve.

4.2 The normal curve

The normal curve describes a particular shape of the frequency curve. Although this shape is defined by a formula and can be described mathematically, for most purposes it is sufficient to regard it as a symmetrical bell-shape (Diagram 4.3).

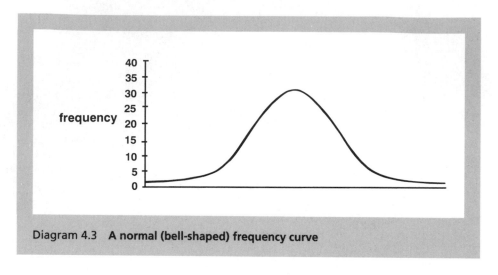

Diagram 4.3   **A normal (bell-shaped) frequency curve**

It is called the 'normal' curve because it was once believed that distributions in the natural world correspond to this shape. Even though it turns out that the normal curve is not universal, it is important because many distributions are more or less this shape – at least sufficiently so for most practical purposes. The crucial reason for its use in statistics is that theoreticians developed many statistical techniques on the assumption that the distributions of scores were bell-shaped or normal. It so happens that these assumptions which are useful in the development of statistical techniques have little bearing on their day-to-day application. The techniques may generally be applied to data which are only very roughly bell-shaped without too much inaccuracy. In run-of-the-mill psychological statistics, the question of whether a distribution is normal or bell-shaped is relatively unimportant. Exceptions to this will be mentioned as appropriate in later chapters.

Design consideration: One thing which may trouble you is the question of how precisely your data need fit this normal or bell-shaped ideal. Is it possible to depart much from the ideal without causing problems? The short answer is that usually a lot of deviation is possible without it affecting things too much. So, in the present context, you should not worry too much if the mean, median and mode do differ somewhat; for practical purposes you can disregard deviations from the ideal distribution, especially when dealing with, say, about 30 or more scores. Unfortunately, all of this involves a degree of subjective judgement since there are no useful ways of assessing what is an acceptable amount of deviation from the ideal when faced with the small amounts of data that student projects often involve.

Don't forget that for the perfectly symmetrical, bell-shaped (normal) curve the values of the mean, median and mode are identical. Disparities between the three are indications that you have an asymmetrical curve.

4.3   Distorted curves

The main concepts which deal with distortions in the normal curve are *skewness* and *kurtosis*.

Skewness

It is always worth examining the shape of your frequency distributions. Gross skewness is the exception to our rule-of-thumb that non-normality of data has little influence on statistical analyses. By skewness we mean the extent to which your frequency curve is lopsided rather than symmetrical. A mid-point of a frequency curve may be skewed either to the left or to the right of the range of scores (Diagrams 4.4 and 4.5).

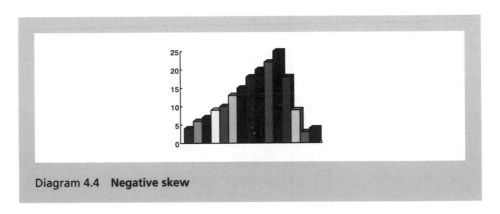

Diagram 4.4   **Negative skew**

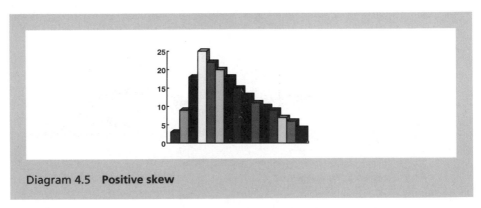

Diagram 4.5   **Positive skew**

There are special terms for left-handed and right-handed skew:

- *Negative skew:*
  (a) relatively more scores are to the left of the mode;
  (b) the mean and median are smaller than the mode.
- *Positive skew:*
  (a) relatively more scores are to the right of the mode;
  (b) the mean and median are bigger than the mode.

There is also an index of the amount of skew shown in your set of scores. With hand-calculated data analyses the best approach is usually to look at your frequency curve. With computer analyses the ease of obtaining the index of skewness makes more formal methods unnecessary. The index of skewness is positive for a positive skew and negative for a negative skew. Appendix A explains how to test for skewness in your data.

Kurtosis (or steepness/shallowness)

Some symmetrical curves may look rather like the normal bell-shaped curve except that they are excessively steep or excessively flat compared to the mathematically defined normal bell-shaped curve (Diagrams 4.6 and 4.7).

Kurtosis is the term used to identify the degree of steepness or shallowness of a distribution. There are technical words for different types of curve:

- a steep curve is called leptokurtic
- a normal curve is called mesokurtic
- a flat curve is called platykurtic.

Although they are terms beloved of statistics book writers, since the terms mean nothing more than steep, middling, and flat there seems to be good reason to drop the Greek words in favour of everyday English.

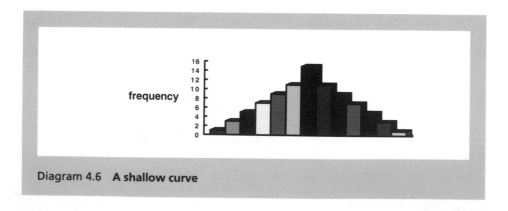

Diagram 4.6   **A shallow curve**

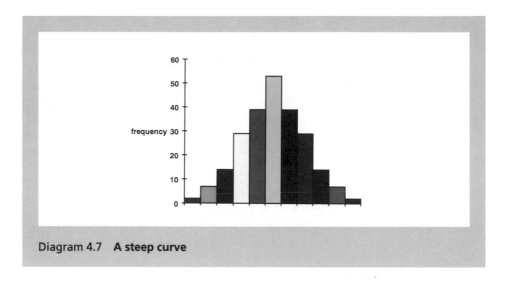

Diagram 4.7   **A steep curve**

It is possible to obtain indexes of the amount of shallowness or steepness of your distribution compared with the mathematically defined normal distribution. These are probably most useful as part of a computer analysis. For most purposes an inspection of the frequency curve of your data is sufficient in hand analyses. Knowing what the index means should help you cope with computer output; quite simply:

■ a positive value of kurtosis means that the curve is steep
■ a zero value of kurtosis means that the curve is middling
■ a negative value of kurtosis means that the curve is flat.

Steepness and shallowness have little or no bearing on the statistical techniques you use to analyse your data, quite unlike skewness.

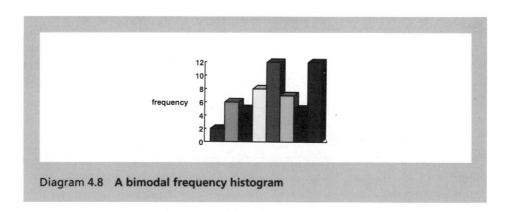

Diagram 4.8   **A bimodal frequency histogram**

4.4   Other frequency curves

Bimodal and multimodal frequency distributions

Of course, there is no rule that says that frequency curves have to peak in the middle and tail off to the left and right. As we have already explained, it is perfectly possible to have a frequency distribution with twin peaks (or even multiple peaks). Such twin-peaked distributions are called *bimodal* since they have two modes – most frequently occurring scores. Such a frequency curve might look like Diagram 4.8.

Cumulative frequency curves

There are any number of different ways of presenting a single set of data. Take, for example, the 50 scores in Table 4.1 for a measure of extraversion obtained from airline pilots.

One way of tabulating these extraversion scores is simply to count the number of pilots scoring at each value of extraversion from 1 to 5. This could be presented in several forms, e.g. Table 4.2, Table 4.3 and Diagram 4.9.

Table 4.1   **Extraversion scores of 50 airline pilots**

3	5	5	4	4	5	5	3	5	2
1	2	5	3	2	1	2	3	3	3
4	2	5	5	4	2	4	5	1	5
5	3	3	4	1	4	2	5	1	2
3	2	5	4	2	1	2	3	4	1

Table 4.2   **Frequency table based on data in Table 4.1**

Number scoring 1	7
Number scoring 2	11
Number scoring 3	10
Number scoring 4	9
Number scoring 5	13

Table 4.3   **Alternative layout for data in Table 4.1**

Number of pilots scoring				
1	2	3	4	5
7	11	10	9	13

Table 4.4   **Cumulative frequency distribution of pilots'
extraversion scores from Table 4.1**

1	7
2 or less	18
3 or less	28
4 or less	37
5 or less	50

Table 4.5   **Alternative style of cumulative frequency distribution
of pilots' extraversion scores from Table 4.1**

Number of pilots scoring				
1	2 or less	3 or less	4 or less	5 or less
7	18	28	37	50

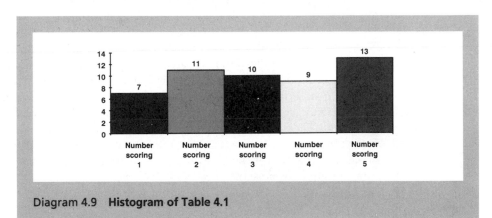

Diagram 4.9   **Histogram of Table 4.1**

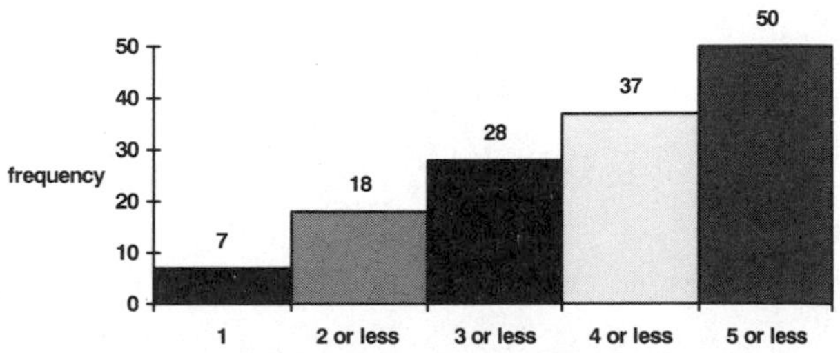

Diagram 4.10   **Cumulative histogram of the frequencies of pilots'
extraversion scores from Table 4.1**

Exactly the same distribution of scores could be represented using a *cumulative* frequency distribution. A simple frequency distribution merely indicates the number of people who achieved any particular score. A cumulative frequency distribution gives the number scoring, say, one, two or less, three or less, four or less, and five or less. In other words, the frequencies accumulate. Examples of cumulative frequency distributions are given in Table 4.4, Table 4.5 and Diagram 4.10 (see p. 37).

There is nothing difficult about cumulative frequencies – but you must label such tables and diagrams clearly or they can be very misleading.

Percentiles

Percentiles are merely a form of cumulative frequency distribution, but instead of being expressed in terms of accumulating scores from lowest to highest, the categorisation is in terms of whole numbers of percentages of people. In other words, the percentile is the score which a given percentage of scores equal or exceed. You do not necessarily have to report every percentage point and units of 10 might suffice for some purposes. Such a distribution would look something like Table 4.6.

The table shows that 10% of scores are equal to 7 or less and 80% of scores are equal to 61 or less. Note that the 50th percentile corresponds to the median score.

Percentiles are commonly used in standardisation tables of psychological tests and measures. For these it is often very useful to be able to describe a person's standing compared to the set of individuals on which the test or measure was initially researched. Thus if a particular person's neuroticism score is described as being at the 90th percentile it means that they are more neurotic than about 90% of people. In other words, percentiles are a quick method of expressing a person's scores relative to those of others.

Table 4.6   **Example of percentiles**

Percentile	Score
10th	7
20th	9
30th	14
40th	20
50th	39
60th	45
70th	50
80th	61
90th	70
100th	78

4.5   Notes and recommendations

■ The most important concept in this chapter is that of the normal curve or normal distribution. It is worth extra effort to memorise the idea that the normal curve is a bell-shaped symmetrical curve.

■ Be a little wary if you find that your scores on a variable are very *skewed* since this can lose precision in certain statistical analyses.

Chapter 5

Standard deviation

The standard unit of measurement in statistics

Preparation
Make sure you know the meaning of variables, scores, Σ and scales of measurement – especially nominal, interval and ratio (Chapter 1).

5.1 Introduction

Measurement ideally uses standard or universal units. It would be really stupid if, when we ask people how far it is to the nearest railway station, one person says 347 cow's lengths, another says 150 poodle jumps, and a third person says three times the distance between my doctor's house and my dentist's home. If you ask us how hot it was on midsummer's day you would be pretty annoyed if one of us said 27 degrees Howitt and the other said 530 degrees Cramer. We measure in standard units such as centimetres, degrees Celsius, kilograms, and so forth. The advantages of doing so are obvious – standard units of measurement allow us to communicate easily, precisely and effectively with other people.

It is much the same in statistics – the trouble is the perplexing variety of types of units possible because of the universality of statistics in many research disciplines. Some variables are measured in physical ways such as metres and kilograms. Others use more abstract units of measurement such as scores on an intelligence test or a personality inventory. Although it would be nice if statisticians had a standard unit of measurement, it is not intuitively obvious what this should be.

5.2 Theoretical background

Imagine a 30-centimetre rule – it will be marked in one-centimetre units from zero centimetres to 30 centimetres (Diagram 5.1). The standard unit of measurement here is the centimetre. But you could have a different sort of rule in which instead of the scale being from 0 to 30 centimetres, the mid-point of the scale is 0 and the scale is marked as –15, –14, –13, . . . , –1, 0, +1, . . . , +13, +14, +15 centimetres. This rule is essentially marked in deviation units (Diagram 5.2).

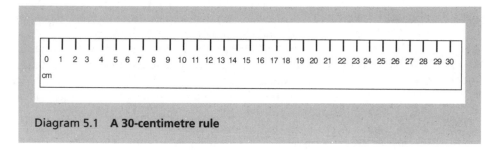

Diagram 5.1　**A 30-centimetre rule**

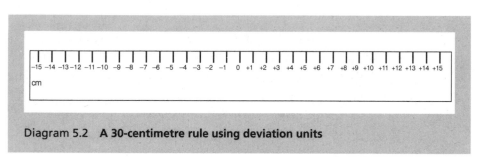

Diagram 5.2　**A 30-centimetre rule using deviation units**

The two rules use the same unit of measurement (the centimetre) but the deviation rule is marked with 0 in the middle, not at the left-hand side. In other words, the mid-point of the scale is marked as 0 deviation (from the mid-point). The standard deviation is similar to this rule in so far as it is based on *distances or deviations* from the average or mid-point.

As it is the standard unit of measurement in statistics, it is a pity that statisticians chose to call it standard deviation rather than 'standard statistical unit'. The latter phrase would better describe what it is. In contrast to a lot of measurements such as metres and kilograms, the standard deviation corresponds to no single standard of measurement that can be defined in *absolute terms* against a physical entity locked in a vault somewhere.

The standard deviation of a set of scores is measured *relative* to all of the scores in that set. Put as simply as possible, *the standard deviation is the 'average' amount by which scores differ from the mean or average score*. Now this is an odd idea – basing your standard measure on a set of scores rather than on an absolute standard. Nevertheless, it is an important concept to grasp. Don't jump ahead at this stage – there are a couple of twists in the logic yet. Perhaps you are imagining that if the scores were 4, 6, 3, and 7 then the mean is 20 divided by 4 (the number of scores), or 5. Each of the four scores deviates from the average by a certain amount – for example, 7 deviates from the mean of 5 by just 2. The sum of the deviations of our four scores from the mean of 5 is 1 + 1 + 2 + 2 which equals 6. Surely, then, the standard deviation is 6 divided by 4, which equals 1.5?

But this is *not* how statisticians work out the average deviation for their standard unit. Such an approach might seem logical but it turns out to be not very useful in practice. Instead *standard deviation uses a different type of average which most mortals would not even recognise as an average.*

The big difference is that standard deviation is calculated as the average *squared* deviation. What this implies is that instead of taking our four deviation scores $(1 + 1 + 2 + 2)$ we square each of them $(1^2 + 1^2 + 2^2 + 2^2)$ which gives $1 + 1 + 4 + 4 = 10$. If we divide this total deviation of 10 by the number of scores (4), this gives a value of 2.5. However, this is still not quite the end of the story since *we then have to calculate the square root of this peculiar average deviation from the mean.* Thus we take the 2.5 and work out its square root – that is, 1.58. In words, *the standard deviation is the square root of the average squared deviation from the mean.*

And that really is it – honest. It's a pity that one of the most important concepts in statistics is less than intuitively obvious, but there we are. To summarise:

1. The standard deviation is the standard unit of measurement in statistics.

2. The standard deviation is simply the 'average' amount that the scores on a variable deviate (or differ) from the mean of the set of scores. In essence, the standard deviation is the average deviation from the mean. Think of it like this since most of us will have little difficulty grasping it in these terms. Its peculiarities can be safely ignored for most purposes.

3. Although the standard deviation is an average, it is not the sort of average which most of us are used to. However, it is of greater use in statistical applications than any other way of calculating the average deviation from the mean.

The standard deviation gives greater numerical emphasis to scores which depart by larger amounts from the mean. The reason is that it involves *squared* deviations from the mean which give disproportionately more emphasis to larger deviations.

It should be stressed that the *standard deviation is not a unit-free measure.* If we measured a set of people's heights in centimetres, the standard deviation of their heights would also be a certain number of *centimetres*. If we measured 50 people's intelligences using an intelligence test, the standard deviation would be a certain number of IQ points. It might help you to remember this, although most people would merely say or write things like 'the standard deviation of height was 4.5' without mentioning the units of measurement.

Calculation 5.1

Standard deviation

The defining formula for standard deviation is as follows:

$$\text{Standard déviation} = \sqrt{\frac{\Sigma (X - \overline{X})^2}{N}}$$

or the computationally quicker formula is

$$\text{Standard deviation} = \sqrt{\dfrac{\Sigma X^2 - \dfrac{(\Sigma X)^2}{N}}{N}}$$

Table 5.1   **Steps in the calculation of the standard deviation**

Scores (X) (age in years)	Scores squared (X^2)
20	400
25	625
19	361
35	1225
19	361
17	289
15	225
30	900
27	729
$\Sigma X = 207$	$\Sigma X^2 = 5115$

Table 5.1 lists the ages of nine students (N = number of scores = 9) and shows steps in calculating the standard deviation. Substituting these values in the standard deviation formula:

$$\text{Standard deviation} = \sqrt{\dfrac{\Sigma X^2 - \dfrac{(\Sigma X)^2}{N}}{N}}$$

$$= \sqrt{\dfrac{5115 - \dfrac{(207)^2}{9}}{9}}$$

$$= \sqrt{\dfrac{5115 - 4761}{9}}$$

$$= \sqrt{\dfrac{354}{9}}$$

$$= \sqrt{39.3333}$$

$$= 6.27 \text{ years}$$

(You may have spotted that the standard deviation is simply the square root of the variance.)

The standard deviation is important in statistics for many reasons. The most important is that the *size* of the standard deviation is an indicator of how much variability there is in the scores for a particular variable. The bigger the standard deviation the more spread there is in the scores. However, this is merely to use standard deviation as a substitute for its close relative variance.

In this chapter, the standard deviation is discussed as a descriptive statistic; that is, it is used like the mean and median, for example, to characterise important features of a set of scores. Be careful to distinguish this from the *estimated* standard deviation which is discussed in Chapter 11. Estimated standard deviation is your best guess as to the standard deviation of a population of scores based on information known about only a small subset or sample of scores from that population. Estimated standard deviation involves a modification to the standard deviation formula so that the estimate is better – the formula is modified to read $N–1$ instead of just N.

5.3   Measuring the number of standard deviations – the z-score

Given that one of the aims of statisticians is to make life as simple as possible for themselves, they try to use the minimum number of concepts possible. Expressing standard statistical units in terms of standard deviations is just one step towards trying to express many measures in a consistent way. Another way of achieving consistency is to express all scores in terms of a *number* of standard deviations. That is, we can abandon the original units of measurements almost entirely if all scores are re-expressed as a number of standard deviations.

It's a bit like calculating all weights in terms of kilograms or all distances in terms of metres. So, for example, since there are 2.2 pounds in a kilogram, something which weighs 10 pounds converts to 4.5 kilograms. We simply divide the number of pounds weight by the number of pounds in a kilogram in order to express our weight in pounds in terms of our standard unit of weight, the kilogram.

It is very much like this in statistics. If we know that the size of the standard deviation is, say, 7, we know that a score which is 21 above the mean score is 21/7 or three standard deviations above the mean. A score which is 14 below the mean is 14/7 or two standard deviations below the mean. So, once the size of the standard deviation is known, all scores can be re-expressed in terms of the *number* of standard deviations they are from the mean. One big advantage of this is that unlike other standard units of measurement such as distance and weight, the *number* of standard deviations will apply no matter what the variable being measured is. Thus it is equally applicable if we are measuring time, anxiety, depression, height, or any other variable. So *the number of standard deviations is a universal scale* of measurement. But note the stress on the *number* of standard deviations.

Despite sounding a bit space-age and ultra-modern, the *z-score* is nothing other than the *number* of standard deviations a particular score lies above or below the mean of the set of scores – precisely the concept just discussed. So in order to work out the z-score for a particular score (*X*) on a variable we also need to know the mean of the set of scores on that variable and the value of the standard deviation of that set of scores. Sometimes it is referred to as the *standard score* since it allows all scores to be expressed in a standard form.

Calculation 5.2

Converting a score into a z-score

To convert the age of a 32-year-old to a z-score, given that the mean of the set of ages is 40 years and the standard deviation of age is 6 years, just apply the following formula:

$$\text{z-score} = \frac{X - \overline{X}}{\text{sd}}$$

where *X* stands for a particular score, $\overline{X}$ is the mean of the set of scores, and sd stands for standard deviation.

The z-score of any age (e.g. 32) can be obtained as follows:

$$\text{z-score}_{[\text{of a 32-year-old}]} = \frac{32 - 40}{6} = \frac{-8}{6} = -1.33$$

The value of –1.33 means that:

1. A 32-year-old is 1.33 standard deviations from the mean age of 40 for this set of age scores.

2. The negative sign (–) simply means that the 32-year-old is younger (lower) than the mean age for the set of age scores. A positive sign (or no sign) would mean that the person is older (higher) than the mean age of 40 years.

5.4   A use of z-scores

So z-scores are merely scores expressed in terms of the *number* of standard statistical units of measurement (standard deviations) they are from the mean of the set of scores. One big advantage of using these standard units of measurement is that variables measured in terms of many different units of measurement can be compared with each other and even combined.

A good example of this comes from a student project (Szostak, 1995). The researcher was interested in the amount of anxiety that child tennis players exhibited and its effect on their performance (serving faults) in competitive situations as compared with practice. One consideration was the amount of commitment that parents demonstrated to their children's tennis. Rather than base this simply on the extent to which parents claimed to be involved, she asked parents the amount of money they spent on their child's tennis, the amount of time they spent on their child's tennis, and so forth:

1. How much money do you spend *per week* on your child's *tennis coaching*?
2. How much money do you spend *per year* on your child's *tennis equipment*?
3. How much money do you spend *per year* on your child's *tennis clothing*?
4. How many *miles per week* on average do you spend travelling to tennis events?
5. How many *hours per week* on average do you spend watching your child *play tennis*?
6. How many *LTA tournaments* does your child participate in *per year*?

This is quite straightforward information to collect but it causes difficulties in analysing the data. The student wanted to combine these six different measures of commitment together to give an overall commitment score for each parent. However, the six items are based on radically different units of measurement – time, money and so forth. Her solution was simply to turn each parent's score on each of the questionnaire items into a z-score. This involves only the labour of working out the mean and standard deviation of the answers to each questionnaire and then turning each score into a z-score. These six z-scores are then added (including the + or – signs) to give a total score on the amount of commitment by each parent, which could be a positive or negative value since z-scores can be + or –.

This was an excellent strategy since this measure of parental commitment was the best predictor of a child performing poorly in competitive situations; the more parental commitment the worse the child does in real matches compared with practice.

There are plenty of other uses of the standard deviation in statistics as we will see.

5.5 The standard normal distribution

There is a remaining important use of standard deviation. Although it should now be obvious that there are some advantages in converting scores into standard units of measurement, you might get the impression that, in the end, the scores themselves on a variable contain information which the z-score does not fully capture. In particular, if one looks at a distribution of the original scores, it is possible to have a good idea of how a particular individual scores relative to other people. So, for example, if you know the distribution of weights in a set of people, it should be possible to say something about the weight of a particular person relative to other people. A histogram giving the weights of 38 children in a school class allows us to compare a child with a weight of say 42 kilograms with the rest of the class (Diagram 5.3).

We can see that a child of 42 kilograms is in the top four of the distribution – that is, in about the top 10% of the weight distribution. Counting the frequencies in the histogram tells us the percentage of the part of the distribution the child falls in. We can also work out that 34 out of 38 (about 90%) of the class are lighter than this particular child.

Surely this cannot be done if we work with standard deviations? In fact it is relatively straightforward to do so since there are ready-made tables to tell us precisely how a particular score (expressed as a z-score or number of standard deviations from the mean) compares with other scores. This is achieved by using a commonly available table which gives the frequency curve of z-scores assuming that this distribution is bell-shaped or 'normal'. This table is known as either the 'standard normal distribution' or the z-distribution. To be frank, some versions of the table are rather complicated but we have opted for the simplest and most generally useful possible. Many statistical tables are known as *tables of significance* for reasons which will become more apparent later on.

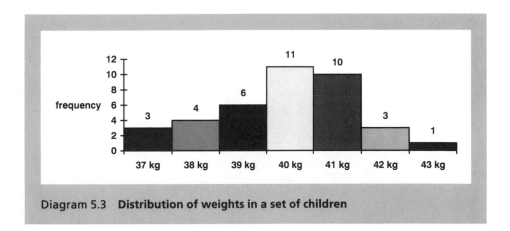

Diagram 5.3   **Distribution of weights in a set of children**

Significance Table 5.1   **The standard normal z-distribution: this gives the percentage of z-scores which are higher than the tabled values**

Z-Score	Percentage of scores higher than this particular z-score	Z-score	Percentage of scores higher than this particular z-score
−4.00	99.997%	0.00	50.00%
−3.00	99.87%	+0.10	46.02%
−2.90	99.81%	+0.20	42.07%
−2.80	99.74%	+0.30	38.21%
−2.70	99.65%	+0.40	34.46%
−2.60	99.53%	+0.50	30.85%
−2.50	99.38%	+0.60	27.43%
−2.40	99.18%	+0.70	24.20%
−2.30	98.93%	+0.80	21.19%
−2.20	98.61%	+0.90	18.41%
−2.10	98.21%	+1.00	15.87%
−2.00	97.72%	+1.10	13.57%
−1.96	97.50%	+1.20	11.51%
		+1.30	9.68%
SCORES ABOVE THIS POINT ARE IN THE		+1.40	8.08%
EXTREME 5% OF SCORES IN EITHER		+1.50	6.68%
DIRECTION FROM THE MEAN (I.E. THE		+1.60	5.48%
EXTREME 2.5% BELOW THE MEAN)			
		SCORES BELOW THIS POINT ARE IN THE	
−1.90	97.13%	EXTREME 5% ABOVE THE MEAN	
−1.80	96.41%		
−1.70	95.54%	+1.64	5.00%
−1.64	95.00%	+1.70	4.46%
		+1.80	3.59%
SCORES ABOVE THIS POINT ARE IN THE		+1.90	2.87%
EXTREME 5% BELOW THE MEAN			
		SCORES BELOW THIS POINT ARE IN THE	
−1.60	94.52%	EXTREME 5% OF SCORES IN EITHER	
−1.50	93.32%	DIRECTION FROM THE MEAN (I.E. THE	
−1.40	91.92%	EXTREME 2.5% ABOVE THE MEAN)	
−1.30	90.32%		
−1.20	88.49%	+1.96	2.50%
−1.10	86.43%	+2.00	2.28%
−1.00	84.13%	+2.10	1.79%
−0.90	81.59%	+2.20	1.39%
−0.80	78.81%	+2.30	1.07%
−0.70	75.80%	+2.40	0.82%
−0.60	72.57%	+2.50	0.62%
−0.50	69.15%	+2.60	0.47%
−0.40	65.54%	+2.70	0.35%
−0.30	61.79%	+2.80	0.26%
−0.20	57.93%	+2.90	0.19%
−0.10	53.98%	+3.00	0.13%
0.00	50.00%	+4.00	0.0003%

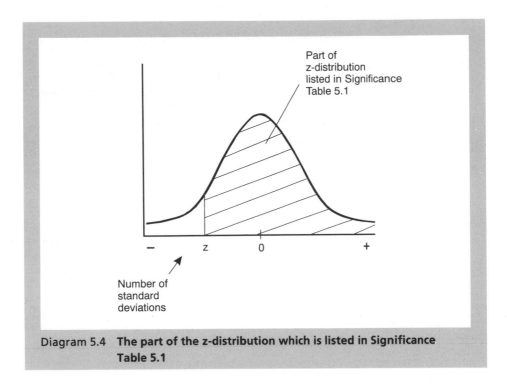

Diagram 5.4 **The part of the z-distribution which is listed in Significance Table 5.1**

Significance Table 5.1 gives the percentage number of scores which will be higher than a score with a given z-score. Basically this means that the table gives the proportion of the frequency distribution of z-scores which lie in the shaded portions in the example shown in Diagram 5.4. The table assumes that the distribution of scores is normal or bell-shaped. The table usually works sufficiently well even if the distribution departs somewhat from the normal shape.

Calculation 5.3

Using the table of the standard normal distribution

Significance Table 5.1 is easy to use. Imagine that you have the IQs of a set of 250 people. The mean $(\overline{X})$ of these IQs is 100 and you calculate that the standard deviation (sd) is 15. You could use this information to calculate the z-score of Darren Jones who scored 90 on the test:

$$z\text{-score} = \frac{X - \overline{X}}{sd}$$

$$= \frac{90 - 100}{15} = \frac{-10}{15} = -0.67 = -0.7 \text{ (to 1 decimal place)}$$

Taking a z-score of –0.7, Significance Table 5.1 tells us that 75.80% of people in the set would have IQs equal to or greater than Darren's. In other words, he is not particularly intelligent. If the z-score of Natalie Smith is +2.0 then this would mean that only 2.28% of scores are equal to or higher than Natalie's – she's very bright.

Of course, you could use the table to calculate the proportion of people with *lower* IQs than Darren and Natalie. Since the total number of scores = 100%, we can calculate that there are 100% – 75.80% = 24.20% of people with IQs equal to or smaller than his. For Natalie, there are 100% – 2.28% = 97.72% of scores equal to or lower than hers.

More about Significance Table 5.1

Significance Table 5.1 is just about as simple as we could make it. It is not quite the same as similar tables in other books:

1. We have given negative as well as positive values of z-scores.
2. We have only given z-scores to 1 decimal place with minor exceptions.
3. We have given percentages – many other versions of the table give *proportions* out of 1. In order to convert the values in Significance Table 5.1 into proportions, simply divide the percentage by 100 and delete the % sign.
4. We have introduced a number of 'cut-off points' or zones into the table. These basically isolate extreme parts of the distribution of z-scores and identify those z-scores which come into the extreme 5% of the distribution. If you like, these are the exceptionally high and exceptionally low z-scores. The importance of this might not be obvious right now but will be clearer later on. The extreme zones are described as 'significant'. We have indicated the extreme 5% in either direction (that is, the extreme 2.5% above and below the mean) as well as the extreme 5% in a particular direction.

5.6   An important feature of z-scores

Z-scores enable the researcher to say an enormous amount about a distribution of scores extremely succinctly. If we present the following information:

■ the mean of a distribution
■ the standard deviation of the distribution
■ that the distribution is roughly bell-shaped or normal

then we can use this information to make very clear statements about the relative position of any score on the variable in question. In other words, rather than present an entire frequency distribution, these three pieces of information are virtually all that is required. Indeed, the third assumption is rarely mentioned since in most applications it makes very little difference.

5.7 Notes and recommendations

■ Do not despair if you have problems in understanding standard deviation; it is one of the most abstract ideas in statistics but so fundamental that it cannot be avoided. It can take some time to absorb completely.

■ Remember that the standard deviation is a sort of average deviation from the mean and you will not go far wrong.

■ Remember that using z-scores is simply a way of putting variables on a standard unit of measurement irrespective of special characteristics of that variable.

■ Remember that virtually any numerical score variable can be summarised using the standard deviation and that virtually any measurement can be expressed as a z-score. The main exception to its use is measurements which are in *nominal* categories like occupation or eye colour. Certainly if a score is *interval or ratio* in nature, standard deviation and z-scores are appropriate.

Chapter 6

Relationships between two or more variables

Diagrams and tables

Preparation

You should be aware of the meaning of variables, scores and the different scales of measurement, especially the difference between nominal (category) measurement and numerical scores.

6.1 Introduction

Although it is fundamental and important to be able to describe the characteristics of each variable in your research both diagrammatically and numerically, *interrelationships* between variables are more characteristic of research in most areas of psychology and the social sciences. Public opinion polling is the most common use of single-variable statistics that most of us come across. Opinion pollsters ask a whole series of questions about political leaders and voting intentions which are generally reported separately. However, researchers often report relationships between two variables. So, for example, if one asks whether the voting intentions of men and women differ it is really to enquire whether there is a relationship between the variable 'sex' and the variable 'voting intention'. Similarly, if one asks whether the popularity of the President of the USA changed over time, this really implies that there may be a relationship between the variable 'time' and the variable 'popularity of the President'. Many of these questions seem so familiar to us that we regard them almost as common sense. Given this, we should not have any great difficulty in understanding the concept of interrelationships among variables.

Interrelationships between variables form the bedrock of virtually all psychological research. It is rare in psychology to have research questions which require data from only one variable at a time. Much of psychology concerns explanations of why things happen – what causes what – which clearly is about relationships between variables. This chapter describes some of the main graphical and tabular methods for presenting interrelationships between variables. Diagrams and tables often overlap in function as will become apparent in the following discussion.

Table 6.1 **Types of relationships based on nominal categories and numerical scores**

	Variable X = numerical scores	Variable X = nominal categories
Variable Y = numerical scores	Type A	Type C
Variable Y = nominal categories	Type C	Type B

6.2 The principles of diagrammatic and tabular presentation

Choosing appropriate techniques to show relationships between two variables requires an understanding of the difference between nominal category data and numerical score data. If we are considering the interrelationships between *two* variables (Variables X and Y) then the types of variables involved are as shown in Table 6.1.

Once you have decided to which category your pair of variables belongs, it is easy to suggest appropriate descriptive statistics. We have classified different situations as Type A, Type B and Type C. Thus Type B has both variables measured on the nominal category scale of measurement.

6.3 Type A: both variables numerical scores

Where both variables take the form of numerical scores, generally the best form of graphical presentation is the *scattergram* or scatterplot. This is a sort of graph in which the values on one variable are plotted against the values on the other variable. The most familiar form of graph is one which plots a variable against time. These are very familiar from newspapers, especially the financial sections (see Diagram 6.1).

Time is no different, statistically speaking, from a wide range of other numerical scores. Diagram 6.2 is an example of a scattergram from a psychological study. You will see that the essential features remain the same. In Diagram 6.2, the point marked with an arrow represents a case whose score on the X-variable is 8 and whose score on the Y-variable is 120. It is sometimes possible to see that the points of a scattergram fall more or less on a straight line. This line through the points of a scattergram is called the *regression line*. Diagram 6.2 includes the regression line for the points of the scattergram.

One complication you sometimes come across is where several points on the scattergram overlap completely. In these circumstances you may well see a number next to a point which corresponds to the number of overlapping points at that position on the scattergram.

In line with general mathematical notation, the horizontal axis or horizontal dimension is described as the X-axis and the vertical axis or vertical dimension is

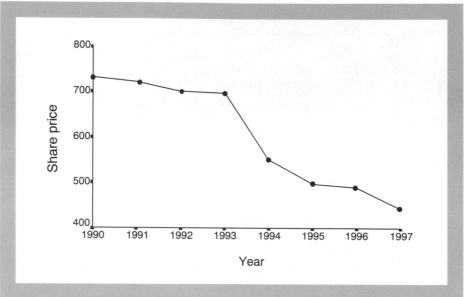

Diagram 6.1 **The dramatic fall in share prices in the Timeshare Office Company**

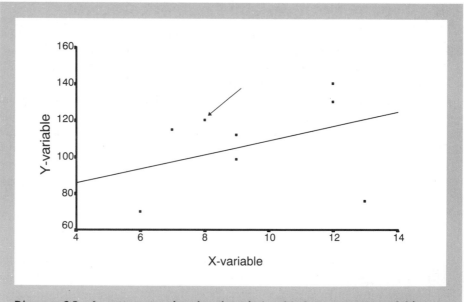

Diagram 6.2 **A scattergram showing the relationship between two variables**

Table 6.2   **Use of bands of scores to tabulate the relationship between two numeri-cal score variables**

		Variable Y				
		1–5	6–10	11–15	16–20	21–25
	0–9	15	7	6	3	4
	10–19	7	12	3	5	4
Variable X	20–29	4	9	19	8	4
	30–39	1	3	2	22	3
	40–49	3	2	3	19	25

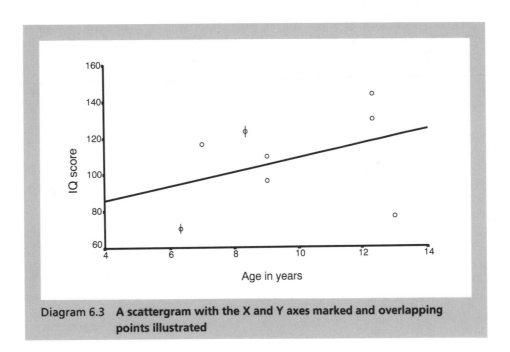

Diagram 6.3   **A scattergram with the X and Y axes marked and overlapping points illustrated**

called the Y-axis. It is helpful if you remember to label one set of scores the X-scores since these belong on the horizontal axis, and the other set of scores the Y-scores because these belong on the vertical axis (Diagram 6.3).

In Diagram 6.3, overlapping points are marked not with a number but with lines around the point on the scattergram. These are called 'sunflowers' – the number of 'petals' is the number of *additional* points overlapping the original point. Thus there are two positions with overlapping points, both of which have two overlaps; in each case, this indicates that there are *three* people with identical ages and IQs for that point.

Apart from cumbersomely listing all of your pairs of scores, it is often difficult to think of a succinct way of presenting data from pairs of numerical scores in tabular form. The main possibility is to categorise each of your score variables into 'bands' of scores and express the data in terms of *frequencies* of occurrence in these bands; a table like Table 6.2 (see p. 55) might be appropriate.

Such tables are known as 'crosstabulation' or 'contingency' tables. In Table 6.2 there does seem to be a relationship between Variable X and Variable Y. People with low scores on Variable X also tend to get low scores on Variable Y. High scorers on Variable X also tend to score highly on Variable Y. However, the trend in the table is less easily discerned than in the equivalent scattergram.

6.4 Type B: both variables nominal categories

Where both variables are in nominal categories it is necessary to report the frequencies in all of the possible groupings of the variables. If you have more than a few nominal categories, the tables or diagrams can be too big.

Take the imaginary data shown in Table 6.3 on relationship between a person's sex and whether they have been hospitalised at any time in their life for a psychiatric reason. These data are ideal for certain sorts of tables and diagrams because *there are few categories of each variable*. Thus a suitable table for summarising these data might look like Table 6.4 – it is called a contingency or crosstabulation table.

The numbers (frequencies) in each category are instantly obvious from this table. You might prefer to express the table in percentages rather than frequencies,

Table 6.3   **Sex and whether previously hospitalised for a set of 89 people**

Person	Sex	Previously hospitalised
1	Male	Yes
2	Male	No
3	Male	No
4	Male	Yes
5	Male	No
. . .	. . .	. . .
85	Female	Yes
86	Female	Yes
87	Female	No
88	Female	No
89	Female	Yes

Table 6.4   **Crosstabulation table of sex against hospitalisation**

	Male	Female
Previously hospitalised	$f = 20$	$f = 25$
Not previously hospitalised	$f = 30$	$f = 14$

Table 6.5   **Crosstabulation table with all frequencies expressed as a percentage of the total number of frequencies**

	Male	Female
Previously hospitalised	22.5%	28.1%
Not previously hospitalised	33.7%	15.7%

Table 6.6   **Crosstabulation table with hospitalisation expressed as a percentage of the male and female frequencies taken separately**

	Male	Female
Previously hospitalised	40.0%	64.1%
Not previously hospitalised	60.0%	35.9%

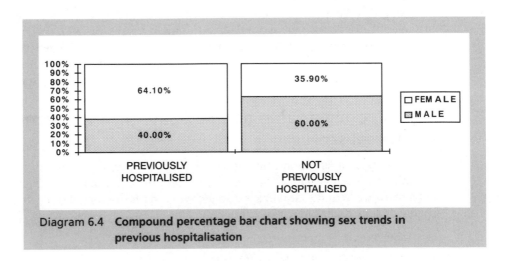

Diagram 6.4   **Compound percentage bar chart showing sex trends in previous hospitalisation**

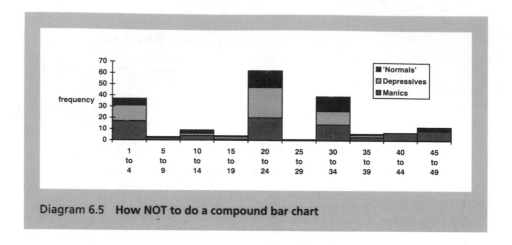

Diagram 6.5 **How NOT to do a compound bar chart**

but some thought needs to go into the choice of percentages. For example, you could express the frequencies as percentages of the total of males and females separately (Table 6.5).

You probably think that Table 6.5 is not much of an improvement in clarity. An alternative is to express the frequencies as percentages of males *and* percentages of females (Table 6.6). By presenting the percentages based on males and females separately, it is easier to see the trend for females to have had a previous psychiatric history.

The same data can be expressed as a *compound bar chart*. In a compound bar chart information is given about the subcategories based on a pair of variables. Diagram 6.4 shows one example in which the proportions are expressed as percentages of the males and females separately.

The golden rule for such data is to ensure that the number of categories is manageable. In particular, avoid having too many empty or near-empty categories. The compound bar chart shown in Diagram 6.5 is a particularly bad example and is *not to be copied*. This chart fails any reasonable clarity test and is too complex to decipher quickly.

6.5 Type C: one variable nominal categories, the other numerical scores

This final type of situation offers a wide variety of ways of presenting the relationships between variables. We have examined the compound bar chart so it is not surprising to find that there is also a *compound histogram*. To be effective, a compound histogram needs to consist of:

- a small number of *categories* for the nominal category variable, and
- a few *ranges* for the numerical scores.

Table 6.7   Crosstabulation table of anxiety against type of industry

| | Frequency of anxiety score | | | |
	0–3	4–7	8–11	12–15
Low tech industry	7	18	3	1
High tech industry	17	7	0	0

Table 6.8   Comparison of the statistical characteristics of anxiety in two different types of industry

	Mean	Median	Mode	Inter-quartile range	Variance
High tech industry	3.5	3.9	3	2.3–4.2	2.2
Low tech industry	5.3	4.7	6	3.9–6.3	3.2

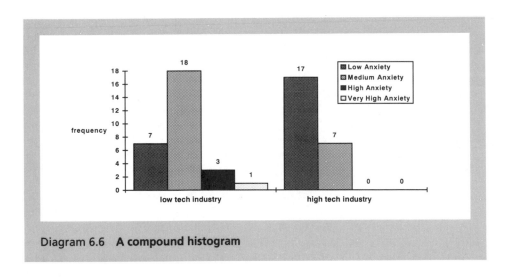

Diagram 6.6   A compound histogram

So, for example, if we wish to plot the relationship between managers' anxiety scores and whether they are managers in a high tech or a low tech industry, we might create a compound histogram like Diagram 6.6 in which there are only two values of the nominal variable (high tech and low tech) and four bands of anxiety score (low anxiety, medium anxiety, high anxiety and very high anxiety).

An alternative way of presenting such data is to use a crosstabulation table as in Table 6.7. Instead, however, it is almost as easy to draw up a table (Table 6.8)

which gives the mean, median, mode, etc., for the anxiety scores of the two different groups.

6.6   Notes and recommendations

■ Never assume that your tables and diagrams are good enough at the first attempt. They could probably be improved with a little care and adjustment.

■ Do not forget that tables and diagrams are there to present clearly the major trends in your data (or lack of them). There is not much point in having tables and diagrams which do not clarify your data.

■ Your tables and diagrams are not means of tabulating your unprocessed data. If you need to present your data in full then most of the methods to be found in this chapter will not help you much.

■ Labelling tables and diagrams clearly and succinctly is an important part of the task – without titling and labelling clearly you are probably wasting your time.

Chapter 7

Correlation coefficients

Pearson Correlation and Spearman's Rho

Preparation
Revise variance (Chapter 3) and the use of the scattergram to show the relationship between two variables (Chapter 6).

7.1 Introduction

Although the scattergram is an important statistical tool for showing relationships between two variables, it is space consuming. For many purposes it is more convenient to have the main features of the scattergram expressed as a single numerical index – the *correlation coefficient*. This is merely a numerical index which summarises some, but not all, of the key features of a scattergram. The commonest correlation coefficient is the Pearson Correlation, also known more grandly and obscurely as the Pearson Product Moment Correlation Coefficient. It includes two major pieces of information:

1. The closeness of the fit of the points of a scattergram to the best-fitting straight line through those points.

2. Information about whether the slope of the scattergram is positive or negative.

It therefore omits other information such as the scales of measurement of the two variables and specific information about individuals.

The correlation coefficient thus neatly summarises a great deal of information about a scattergram. It is especially useful when you have several variables which would involve drawing numerous scattergrams, one for each pair of variables. It most certainly does not replace the scattergram entirely but merely helps you to present your findings rather more concisely than other methods. Indeed, we recommend that you draw a scattergram for every correlation coefficient you calculate even if that scattergram is not intended for inclusion in your report.

Although the correlation coefficient is a basic descriptive statistic, it is elaborated in a number of sophisticated forms such as partial correlation, multiple correlation and factor analysis. It is of paramount importance in many forms of research, especially survey, questionnaire and similar forms of research.

7.2   Principles of the correlation coefficient

The correlation coefficient basically takes the following form:

$$r_{\text{[correlation coefficient]}} \quad = \quad +1.00$$
$$\text{or} \quad 0.00$$
$$\text{or} \quad -1.00$$
$$\text{or} \quad 0.30$$
$$\text{or} \quad -0.72, \text{ etc.}$$

So a correlation coefficient consists of two parts:

1. A positive or negative sign (although for positive values the sign is frequently omitted).
2. Any numerical value in the range of 0.00 to 1.00.

The + or – sign tells us something important about the slope of the regression line (i.e. the best-fitting straight line through the points on the scattergram). A positive value means that the slope is *from the bottom left to the top right* of the scattergram (Diagram 7.1). On the other hand, if the sign is negative (–) then the slope of the straight line goes *from upper left to lower right* on the scattergram (Diagram 7.2).

The numerical value of the correlation coefficient (0.50, 0.42, etc.) is an index of how close the points on the scattergram fit the best-fitting straight line.

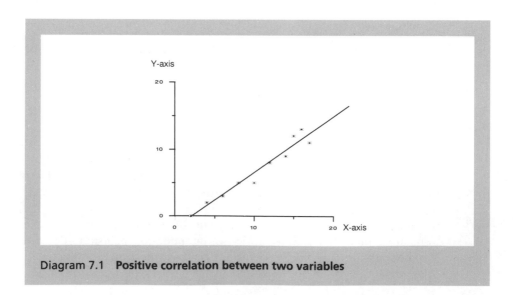

Diagram 7.1   **Positive correlation between two variables**

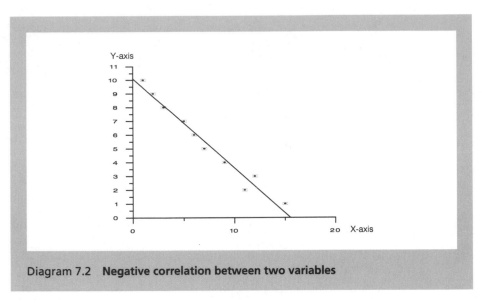

Diagram 7.2   **Negative correlation between two variables**

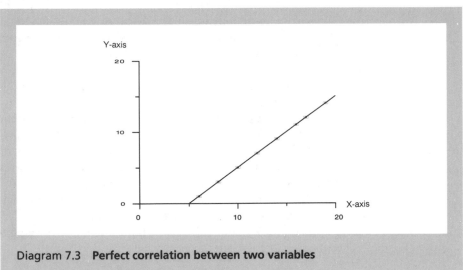

Diagram 7.3   **Perfect correlation between two variables**

A value of 1.00 means that the points of the scattergram all lie exactly on the best-fitting straight line (Diagram 7.3), unless that line is perfectly vertical or perfectly horizontal, in which case it means that there is no variation in the scores on one of the variables and so no correlation can be calculated.

A value of 0.00 means that the points of the scattergram are randomly scattered around the straight line. It is purely a matter of luck if any of them actually touch the straight line (Diagram 7.4). In this case the best-fitting straight line for this scattergram could be virtually any line you arbitrarily decide to draw

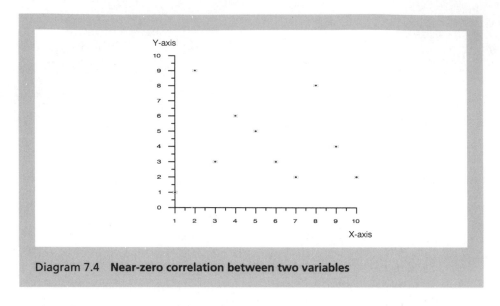

Diagram 7.4   Near-zero correlation between two variables

through the points. Conventionally it is drawn as a horizontal line, but any other angle of slope would do just as well since there is no discernible trend in the relationship between the two variables on the scattergram.

A value of 0.50 would mean that although the points on the scattergram are generally close to the best-fitting straight line, there is considerable spread of these points around that straight line.

The correlation coefficient is merely an index of the amount of variance of the scattergram points from the straight line. However, it is calculated in such a way that the *maximum* variance around that straight line results in a correlation of zero. In other words, the closer the relationship between the two variables, the higher is the correlation coefficient, up to a maximum value of 1.00.

To summarise, the components of the correlation coefficient are the sign (+ or –), which indicates the direction of the slope, and a numerical value which indicates how much variation there is around the best-fitting straight line through the points (i.e. the higher the numerical value the closer the fit).

Covariance

The actual computation of the correlation coefficient involves little more than an elaboration of the formula for variance:

$$\text{Variance} = \frac{\Sigma\,(X - \overline{X})^2}{N}$$

If you wished (you will see why in a moment), the formula for variance could be re-expressed as:

$$\text{Variance} = \frac{\Sigma (X - \overline{X})(X - \overline{X})}{N}$$

All we have done is to expand the formula so as not to use the square sign. (A square is simply a number multiplied by itself.)

In the formula for the correlation coefficient we use something called the *covariance*. This is almost exactly the same as the formula for variance, but instead of multiplying scores by themselves we multiply the score on one variable (X) by the score on the second variable (Y):

$$\text{Covariance}_{[\text{of variable X with variable Y}]} = \frac{\Sigma (X - \overline{X})(Y - \overline{Y})}{N}$$

where:

X = scores on variable X
$\overline{X}$ = mean score on variable X
Y = scores on variable Y
$\overline{Y}$ = mean score on variable Y
N = number of pairs of scores

We get a large positive value of covariance if there is a strong positive relationship between the two variables, and a big negative value if there is a strong negative relationship between the two variables. If there is no relationship between the variables then the covariance is zero. Notice that unlike variance the covariance can take positive or negative values.

However, the size of the covariance is affected by the size of the variances of the two separate variables involved. The larger the variances, the larger is the covariance, potentially. Obviously this would make comparisons difficult. So the covariance is adjusted by dividing by the square root of the product of the variances of the two separate variables. (Because N, the number of pairs of scores, in the variance and covariance formulae can be cancelled out in the correlation formula, the usual formula includes no division by the number of scores.) Once this adjustment is made to the covariance formula, we have the formula for the correlation coefficient:

$$r_{[\text{correlation coefficient}]} = \frac{\Sigma (X - \overline{X})(Y - \overline{Y})}{\sqrt{\Sigma (X - \overline{X})^2} \sqrt{\Sigma (Y - \overline{Y})^2}}$$

The lower part of the formula actually gives the largest possible value of the covariance of the two variables – that is, the theoretical covariance if the two variables lay perfectly on the straight line through the scattergram. Dividing the covariance by the maximum value it could take (if there was no spread of points away from the straight line through the scattergram) ensures that the correlation coefficient can never be greater than 1.00. The covariance formula also contains the necessary sign to indicate the slope of the relationship.

A slightly quicker computational formula which does not involve the calculation of the mean scores directly is as follows:

$$r_{\text{[correlation coefficient]}} = \frac{\Sigma XY - \dfrac{\Sigma X \, \Sigma Y}{N}}{\sqrt{\left(\Sigma X^2 - \dfrac{(\Sigma X)^2}{N}\right)\left(\Sigma Y^2 - \dfrac{(\Sigma Y)^2}{N}\right)}}$$

The resemblance of parts of this formula to the computational formula for variance should be fairly obvious. This is not surprising as the correlation coefficient is a measure of the *lack* of variation around a straight line through the scattergram.

Calculation 7.1

The Pearson Correlation coefficient

Our data for this calculation come from scores on the relationship between mathematical ability and musical ability for a group of 10 children (Table 7.1).

Table 7.1   **Scores on musical and mathematical ability for 10 children**

Individual	Music score	Mathematics score
Angela	2	8
Arthur	6	3
Peter	4	9
Mike	5	7
Barbara	7	2
Jane	7	3
Jean	2	9
Ruth	3	8
Alan	5	6
Theresa	4	7

It is always sound practice to draw the scattergram for any correlation coefficient you are calculating. For these data, the scattergram will be like Diagram 7.5. Notice that the slope of the scattergram is negative, as one could have deduced from the tendency for those who score highly on mathematical ability to have low scores on musical ability. You can also see not only that a straight line is a pretty good way of describing the trends in the points on the scattergram but that the points fit the straight line reasonably well. Thus we should expect a fairly high negative correlation from the correlation coefficient.

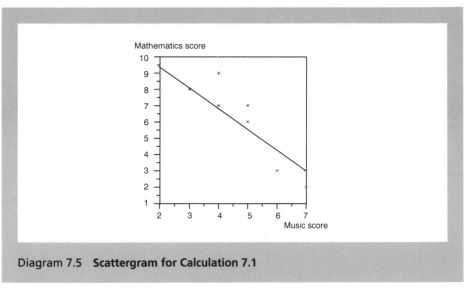

Diagram 7.5 **Scattergram for Calculation 7.1**

Step 1: Set the scores out in a table (Table 7.2) and follow the calculations as shown. Here N is the number of *pairs* of scores, i.e. 10.

Table 7.2 **Essential steps in the calculation of the correlation coefficient**

X-score (music)	*Y*-score (mathematics)	*X²*	*Y²*	*X × Y*
2	8	4	64	16
6	3	36	9	18
4	9	16	81	36
5	7	25	49	35
7	2	49	4	14
7	3	49	9	21
2	9	4	81	18
3	8	9	64	24
5	6	25	36	30
4	7	16	49	28
$\Sigma X = 45$	$\Sigma Y = 62$	$\Sigma X^2 = 233$	$\Sigma Y^2 = 446$	$\Sigma XY = 240$

Step 2: Substitute the values from Table 7.2 in the formula:

$$r_{[\text{correlation coefficient}]} = \frac{\Sigma XY - \dfrac{\Sigma X \, \Sigma Y}{N}}{\sqrt{\left(\Sigma X^2 - \dfrac{(\Sigma X)^2}{N}\right)\left(\Sigma Y^2 - \dfrac{(\Sigma Y)^2}{N}\right)}}$$

$$= \frac{240 - \frac{45 \times 62}{10}}{\sqrt{\left(233 - \frac{45^2}{10}\right)\left(446 - \frac{62^2}{10}\right)}}$$

$$= \frac{240 - \frac{2790}{10}}{\sqrt{\left(233 - \frac{2025}{10}\right)\left(446 - \frac{3844}{10}\right)}}$$

$$= \frac{240 - 279}{\sqrt{(233 - 202.5)(446 - 384.4)}}$$

$$= \frac{-39}{\sqrt{30.5 \times 61.6}}$$

$$= \frac{-39}{\sqrt{1878.8}}$$

$$= \frac{-39}{43.35}$$

$$= -0.90$$

So the value obtained for the correlation coefficient equals –0.90. This value is in line with what we suggested about the scattergram which serves as a rough check on our calculation. There is a very substantial negative relationship between mathematical and musical ability. In other words, the good mathematicians tended to be the poor musicians and vice versa. It is not claimed that they are good at music *because* they are poor at mathematics but merely that there is an inverse association between the two.

7.3   Some rules to check out

1.   You should make sure that a straight line is the best fit to the scattergram points. If the best-fitting line is a *curve* such as in Diagram 7.6 then you should not use the Pearson Correlation Coefficient. The reason for this is that the Pearson Correlation assumes a straight line which is a gross distortion if you have a curved (curvilinear) relationship.

2.   Make sure that your scattergram does not contain a few extreme cases which are unduly influencing the correlation coefficient (Diagram 7.7). In this

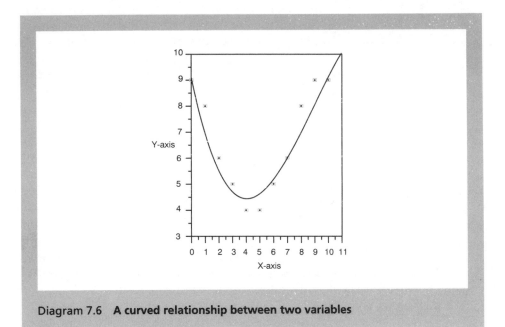

Diagram 7.6   **A curved relationship between two variables**

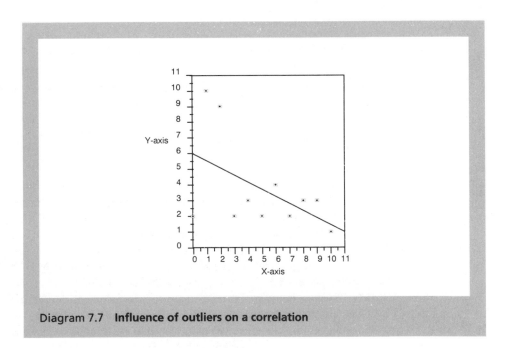

Diagram 7.7   **Influence of outliers on a correlation**

diagram you can see that the points at the top left of the scattergram are responsible for the apparent negative correlation between the two variables. Your eyes probably suggest that for virtually all the points on the scattergram there is no relationship at all. You could in these circumstances eliminate the 'outliers' (i.e. extreme, highly influential points) and recalculate the correlation coefficient based on the remaining, more typical group of scores. If the correlation remains significant with the same sign as before then your interpretation of your data is likely to remain broadly unchanged. However, there needs to be good reason for deleting the 'outliers'; this should not be done simply because the data as they stand do not support your ideas. It may be that something unusual had happened – perhaps an outlier arose from the responses of a slightly deaf person who could not hear the researcher's instructions, for example.

> **Design consideration:** It is typically argued that a correlation does not prove causality. Because two variables are related to each other is not reason to say anything other than that they are related. Statistical analysis is basically incapable of proving that one variable influenced the other variable directly. Questions such as whether one variable affected the other are addressed primarily through the nature of your research design and not through the statistical analysis as such. Conventionally psychologists have turned to laboratory experiments in which variables could be systematically manipulated by the researcher in order to be able to enhance their confidence in making causal interpretations about relationships between variables.

7.4 Coefficient of determination

The correlation coefficient is an index of how much variance two variables have in common. However, you need to square the correlation coefficient in order to know precisely how much variance is shared. The squared correlation coefficient is also known as the *coefficient of determination*.

The proportion of variance shared by two variables whose correlation coefficient is 0.5 equals 0.5^2 or 0.25. This is a proportion out of 1 so as a percentage it is $0.25 \times 100\% = 25\%$. A correlation coefficient of 0.8 means that $0.8^2 \times 100\%$ or 64% of the variance is shared. A correlation coefficient of 1.00 means that $1.00^2 \times 100\% = 100\%$ of the variance is shared. Since the coefficient of determination is based on *squaring* the correlation coefficient, it should be obvious that the amount of variance shared by the two variables declines increasingly rapidly as the correlation coefficient gets smaller (Table 7.3).

Table 7.3　**Variance shared by two variables**

Correlation coefficient	Variance shared by two variables
1.00	100%
0.90	81%
0.80	64%
0.70	49%
0.60	36%
0.50	25%
0.40	16%
0.30	9%
0.20	4%
0.10	1%
0.00	0%

7.5　Significance testing

Some readers who have previously studied statistics a little will be familiar with the notion of significance testing and might be wondering why this has not been dealt with for the correlation coefficient. The answer is that we will be dealing with it, but not until Chapter 10. In the present chapter we are merely presenting the correlation coefficient as a descriptive statistic which numerically summarises a scattergram between two variables. For those of you who wish to understand significance testing for the correlation coefficient, simply skip Chapter 8 on regression for now and proceed to Chapters 9 and 10.

7.6　Spearman's Rho: another correlation coefficient

Spearman's Rho is often written as r_s. We have not used this symbol in the following discussion although it is common in textbooks.

The Pearson Correlation Coefficient is the dominant correlation index in psychological statistics. There is another called Spearman's Rho which is not very different – practically identical, in truth. Instead of taking the scores directly from your data, the scores on a variable are ranked from smallest to largest. That is, the smallest score on Variable X is given rank 1, the second smallest score on Variable X is given rank 2, and so forth. The smallest score on Variable Y is given rank 1, the second smallest score on Variable Y is given rank 2, etc.

Table 7.4 **Ranking of a set of scores when tied (equal) scores are involved**

Scores	4	5	5	6	7	8	9	9	9	10
Ranks	1	2.5	2.5	4	5	6	8	8	8	10

Then Spearman's Rho is calculated like the Pearson Correlation Coefficient between the two sets of ranks as if the ranks were scores. A special procedure is used to deal with *tied ranks*, as follows.

Sometimes certain scores on a variable are identical. There might be two or three people who scored 7 on Variable X, for example. This situation is described as *tied scores* or *tied ranks*. The question is what to do about them. The conventional answer in psychological statistics is to pretend first of all that the tied scores can be separated by fractional amounts. Then we allocate the appropriate ranks to these 'separated' scores but give each of the tied scores the average rank that they would have received if they could be separated (Table 7.4).

The two scores of 5 are each given the rank 2.5 because if they were slightly different they would have been given ranks 2 and 3 respectively. But they can't be separated and so we average the ranks:

$$\frac{2 + 3}{2} = 2.5$$

which is the average of the two ranks and corresponds to what we entered into Table 7.4.

There are three scores of 9 which would have been allocated the ranks 7, 8, and 9 if the scores had been slightly different from each other. These three ranks are averaged to give an average rank of 8 which is entered as the rank for each of the three tied scores in Table 7.4.

There is a special computational formula (see Calculation 7.3 later in this chapter) which can be used which is quicker than applying the conventional Pearson Correlation formula to data in the form of ranks. It is nothing other than a special case of the Pearson Correlation formula. Most statistics textbooks provide this formula for routine use. Unfortunately this formula is only accurate when you have absolutely no tied ranks at all – otherwise it gives a slightly wrong answer! As tied ranks are common in psychological research it is dubious whether there is anything to be gained in using the special Spearman's Rho computational formula as opposed to the Pearson Correlation Coefficient applied to the ranks.

You may wonder why we have bothered to turn the scores into ranks before calculating the correlation coefficient. The reason is that ranks are commonly used in psychological statistics when the distributions of scores on a variable are markedly unsymmetrical and do not approximate (even poorly) a normal distribution. In the past it was quite fashionable to use rankings of scores instead of the scores themselves but we would suggest that you avoid ranking if possible. Use ranks only when your data seem extremely distorted from a normal distribution. We realise that others may argue differently. The reasons for this are explained in Chapter 18.

Calculation 7.2

Spearman's Rho with or without tied ranks

We could apply the Spearman Rho Correlation to the data on the relationship between mathematical ability and musical ability for a group of 10 children which we used previously. But we must rank the two sets of scores before applying the normal Pearson Correlation formula since there are tied ranks (see Table 7.5). In our calculation, N is the number of *pairs* of ranks, i.e. 10.

Table 7.5   **Steps in the calculation of Spearman's Rho correlation coefficient**

Person	Maths score X score	Music score Y score	Maths rank X_r	Maths rank squared X_r^2	Music rank Y_r	Music rank squared Y_r^2	Maths rank × music rank $X_r \times Y_r$
1	8	2	7.5	56.25	1.5	2.25	11.25
2	3	6	2.5	6.25	8	64.00	20.00
3	9	4	9.5	90.25	4.5	20.25	42.75
4	7	5	5.5	30.25	6.5	42.25	35.75
5	2	7	1	1.00	9.5	90.25	9.50
6	3	7	2.5	6.25	9.5	90.25	23.75
7	9	2	9.5	90.25	1.5	2.25	14.25
8	8	3	7.5	56.25	3	9.00	22.50
9	6	5	4	16.00	6.5	42.25	26.00
10	7	4	5.5	30.25	4.5	20.25	24.75
			ΣX_r $= 55$	ΣX_r^2 $= 383$	ΣY_r $= 55$	ΣY_r^2 $= 383$	$\Sigma X_r Y_r$ $= 230.50$

We then substitute the totals in the computational formula for the Pearson Correlation Coefficient, although now we call it Spearman's Rho:

$$r_{[\text{Spearman's Rho}]} = \frac{\Sigma X_r Y_r - \dfrac{\Sigma X_r \, \Sigma Y_r}{N}}{\sqrt{\left(\Sigma X_r^2 - \dfrac{(\Sigma X_r)^2}{N}\right)\left(\Sigma Y_r^2 - \dfrac{(\Sigma Y_r)^2}{N}\right)}}$$

$$= \frac{230.5 - \left(\frac{55 \times 55}{10}\right)}{\sqrt{\left(383 - \frac{55^2}{10}\right)\left(383 - \frac{55^2}{10}\right)}}$$

$$= \frac{230.5 - 302.5}{\sqrt{(383 - 302.5)\,(383 - 302.5)}}$$

$$= \frac{-72.00}{\sqrt{(80.5)\,(80.5)}}$$

$$= \frac{-72.00}{80.5}$$

$$= -0.89$$

So, Spearman's Rho gives a substantial negative correlation just as we would expect from these data. You can interpret the Spearman correlation coefficient more or less in the same way as the Pearson correlation coefficient so long as you remember that it is calculated using ranks.

It so happens in this case that the Spearman coefficient gives virtually the same numerical value as Pearson's applied to the same data. *This is fortuitous. Usually there is a discrepancy between the two.*

We referred earlier to a special computational formula which could be used to calculate Spearman's Rho when there are no ties. There seems little point in learning this formula, since a lack of tied ranks is not characteristic of psychological data. You may as well simply use the method of Calculation 7.2 irrespective of whether there are ties or not. For those who want to save a little time when there are no tied ranks, the procedure of Calculation 7.3 may be used.

Calculation 7.3

Spearman's Rho where there are no tied ranks

The formula used in this computation applies only when there are no tied scores. If there are any, the formula becomes increasingly inaccurate and the procedure of Calculation 7.2 should be applied. However, many psychologists use the formula whether or not there are tied ranks, despite the inaccuracy problem.

For illustrative purposes we will use the same data on maths ability and musical ability despite there being ties, as listed in Table 7.6. Once again, $N = 10$.

Table 7.6   **Steps in the calculation of Spearman's Rho correlation coefficient using the speedy formula**

Person	Maths score	Music score	Maths rank	Music rank	Maths rank – music rank	Square of previous column
	X score	Y score	X_r	Y_r	D (differ-ence)	D^2
1	8	2	7.5	1.5	6.0	36.00
2	3	6	2.5	8	–5.5	30.25
3	9	4	9.5	4.5	5	25.00
4	7	5	5.5	6.5	–1.0	1.00
5	2	7	1	9.5	–8.5	72.25
6	3	7	2.5	9.5	–7.0	49.00
7	9	2	9.5	1.5	8.0	64.00
8	8	3	7.5	3	4.5	20.25
9	6	5	4	6.5	–2.5	6.25
10	7	4	5.5	4.5	1.0	1.00
						ΣD^2 = 305

$$r_{[\text{Spearman's Rho}]} = 1 - \frac{6\Sigma D^2}{N(N^2-1)}$$

$$= 1 - \frac{6 \times 305}{10(10^2-1)}$$

$$= 1 - \frac{1830}{10 \times (100-1)}$$

$$= 1 - \frac{1830}{10 \times 99}$$

$$= 1 - \frac{1830}{990}$$

$$= 1 - 1.848$$

$$= -0.848$$

$$= -0.85 \text{ to two decimal places}$$

It should be noted that this value of Spearman's Rho is a little different from its correct value (–0.89) as we calculated it in Calculation 7.2. The reason for this difference is the inaccuracy of the speedy formula when there are tied scores. Although the difference is not major, you are strongly recommended not to incorporate this error. Otherwise the interpretation of the negative correlation is the same as we have previously discussed.

7.7   An example from the literature

Pearson Correlation coefficients are extremely common in published research. They can be found in a variety of contexts so choosing a typical example is virtually meaningless. The correlation coefficient is sometimes used as an indicator of the validity of a psychological test. So it might be used to indicate the relationship between a test of intelligence and children's performance in school. The test is a valid predictor of school performance if there is a substantial correlation between the test score and school performance.

The correlation coefficient is also very useful as an indicator of the reliability of a psychological test. This might mean the extent to which people's scores on the test are consistent over time. You can use the correlation coefficient to indicate whether those who perform well now on the test also performed well a year ago. For example, Gillis (1980) in the manual accompanying the Child Anxiety Scale indicates that he retested 127 US schoolchildren in the first to third grades immediately after the initial testing. The reliability coefficients (test–retest reliability) or the correlation coefficients between the two testings were:

> Grade 1 = 0.82
> Grade 2 = 0.85
> Grade 3 = 0.92

A sample of children retested after a week had a retest reliability coefficient of 0.81. It is clear from this that the reliability of the measure is good. This means that the children scoring the most highly one week also tend to get the highest scores the next week. It does not mean that the scores are identical from week to week – only that the relative scores are the same.

Practically all reliability and validity coefficients used in psychological testing are variants on much the same theme and are rarely much more complex than the correlation coefficient itself.

7.8   Notes and recommendations

Most of the major points have been covered already. But they bear repetition:

■ Check the scattergram for your correlation coefficient for signs of a nonlinear relationship – if you find one you should not be using the Pearson Correlation Coefficient. In these circumstances you should use coefficient eta which is designed for curvilinear relationships. However, eta is a relatively obscure statistic. It is mentioned again in Chapter 31.

■ Check the scattergram for outliers which may spuriously be producing a correlation when overwhelmingly the scattergram says that there is a poor relationship.

■ Examine the scattergram to see whether there is a positive or negative slope to the scatter and form a general impression of whether the correlation is good (the points fit the straight line well) or poor (the points are very widely scattered around the straight line). Obviously you will become more skilled at this with experience but it is useful as a rough computational check among other things.

■ Before concluding your analysis, check out Chapter 10 to decide whether or not to generalise from your set of data.

Chapter 8

Regression

Prediction with precision

Preparation
You should have a working knowledge about the scattergram (Chapter 6) of the relationship between two variables and understand the correlation coefficient (Chapter 7).

8.1 Introduction

Regression, like the correlation coefficient, numerically describes important features of a scattergram relating two variables together. However, it does it in a different way to the correlation coefficient. Among its important uses is that it allows the researcher to make predictions (for example, when choosing the best applicant for a job on the basis of an aptitude or ability test).

Assume that research has shown that a simple test of manual dexterity is capable of distinguishing between the better and not-so-good assembly workers in a precision components factory. Manual dexterity is a *predictor* variable and

Table 8.1 **Manual dexterity and number of units produced per hour**

Manual dexterity score	Number of units produced per hour
56	17
19	6
78	23
92	22
16	9
23	10
29	13
60	20
50	16
35	19

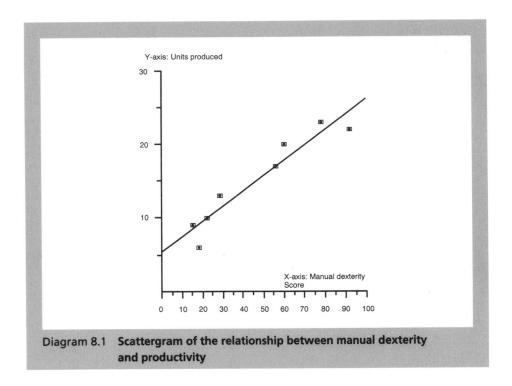

Y-axis: Units produced

X-axis: Manual dexterity Score

Diagram 8.1   **Scattergram of the relationship between manual dexterity and productivity**

job performance the *criterion* variable. So it should be possible to predict which applicants are likely to be the more productive employees from scores on this easily administered test of manual dexterity. Using the test might be a lot cheaper than employing people who do not make the grade. Imaginary data for such a study are shown in Table 8.1.

The scattergram (Diagram 8.1) shows imaginary data on the relationship between scores on the manual dexterity test and the number of units per hour the employee produces in the components factory. Notice that we have made scores on the manual dexterity test the horizontal dimension (*X*-axis) and the number of units produced per hour the vertical dimension (*Y*-axis). In regression in order to keep the number of formulae to the minimum, *the horizontal dimension (X-axis) should always be used to represent the variable from which the prediction is being made, and the vertical dimension (Y-axis) should always represent what is being predicted.* It is clear from the scattergram that the number of units produced by workers is fairly closely related to scores on the manual dexterity test. If we draw a straight line as best we can through the points on the scattergram, this line could be used as a basis for making predictions about the most likely score on work productivity from the aptitude test score of manual dexterity. *This line through the points on a scattergram is called the regression line.* In order to predict the likeliest number of units per hour corresponding to a score of 70 on the manual dexterity test, we simply draw (i) a right angle from

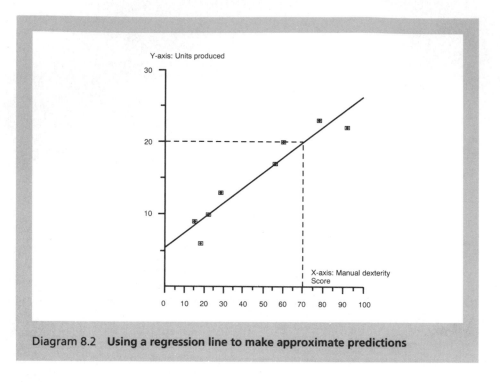

Y-axis: Units produced

X-axis: Manual dexterity
Score

Diagram 8.2   Using a regression line to make approximate predictions

the score 70 on the horizontal axis (manual dexterity test score) to the regression line, and then (ii) a right angle from the vertical axis to meet this point. In this way we can find the productivity score which best corresponds to a particular manual dexterity score (Diagram 8.2). Estimating from this scattergram and regression line, it appears that the best prediction from a manual dexterity score of 70 is a productivity rate of about 19 or 20.

There is only one major problem with this procedure – the prediction depends on the particular line drawn through the points on the scattergram. You might draw a somewhat different line from the one we did. Subjective factors such as these are not desirable and it would be better to have a method which was not affected in this way. So mathematical ways of determining the regression line have been developed. Fortunately, the computations are generally straightforward.

8.2   Theoretical background and regression equations

The line through a set of points on a scattergram is called the *regression line*. In order to establish an objective criterion, the regression line is chosen which gives the closest fit to the points on the scattergram. In other words, the procedure ensures that there is a minimum sum of distances of the regression line to the points in the scattergram. So, in theory, one could keep trying different possible regression lines until one is found which has the minimum deviation of the points from it.

The sum of the deviations (*d*'s) of the scattergram points from the regression line should be minimal. Actually, the precise criterion is the sum of the *squared* deviations. This is known as the *least squares solution*. But it would be really tedious work drawing different regression lines, then calculating the sum of the squared deviations for each of these in order to decide which regression line has the smallest sum of squared deviations. Fortunately things are not done like that and trial-and-error is not involved at all. The formulae for regression do all of that work for you.

In order to specify the regression line for any scattergram, you quantify two things:

1. The point at which the regression line cuts the vertical axis – this is a number of units of measurement from the zero point of the vertical axis. It can take a positive or negative value, denoting whether the vertical axis is cut above or below its zero point. It is normally denoted in regression as point *a* or the *intercept*.

2. The *slope* of the regression line or, in other words, the gradient of the best-fitting line through the points on the scattergram. Just as with the correlation coefficient, this slope may be positive in the sense that it goes up from

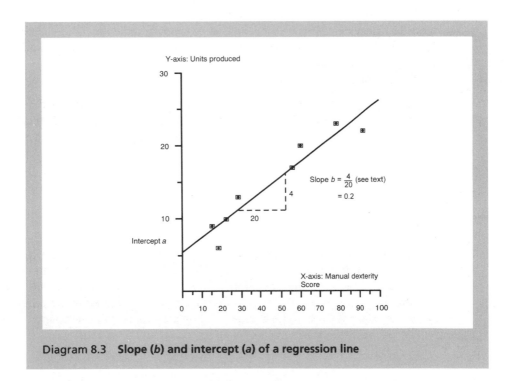

Diagram 8.3 **Slope (*b*) and intercept (*a*) of a regression line**

bottom left to top right or it can be negative in that it goes downwards from top left to bottom right. The slope is normally denoted by the letter b.

The intercept and slope are both shown in Diagram 8.3. To work out the slope, we have drawn a horizontal dashed line from $X = 30$ to $X = 50$ (length 20) and a vertical dashed line up to the regression line (length about 4 up the Y-axis). The slope b is the increase (+) or decrease (−) of the units produced (in this case +4) divided by the increase in the manual dexterity score (in this case 20), i.e. +0.2.

The slope is simply the number of units that the regression line moves up the vertical axis for each unit it moves along the horizontal axis. In other words, you mark a single step along the horizontal axis and work out how much increase this represents on the vertical axis. So, for example, if you read that the slope of a scattergram is 2.00, this means that for every increase of 1.00 on the horizontal axis (X-axis) there is an increase of 2.00 on the vertical axis (Y-axis). If there is a slope of −0.5 then this means that for every increase of 1 on the horizontal axis (X-axis) there is a *decrease* of 0.5 on the vertical axis (Y-axis).

In our example, for every increase of 1 in the manual dexterity score, there is an increase of 0.2 (more accurately, 0.21) in the job performance measure (units produced per hour). We have estimated this value from the scattergram – it may not be exactly the answer that we would have obtained had we used mathematically more precise methods. This increase defines the slope. (Note that you do not work with angles – merely distances on the vertical and horizontal axes.)

Fortunately, the application of two relatively simple formulae (see Calculation 8.1) provides all the information we need to calculate the slope and the intercept. A third formula is used to make our predictions from the horizontal axis to the vertical axis.

The major differences between correlation and regression are:

1. Regression retains the original units of measurement so direct comparisons between regression analyses based on different variables are difficult. Correlation coefficients can readily be compared as they are essentially on a standardised measurement scale and free of the original units of measurement.

2. The correlation coefficient does *not* specify the slope of a scattergram. Correlation indicates the amount of spread or variability of the points around the regression line in the scattergram.

Design consideration: There are always two regression lines between two variables: that from which Variable A is predicted from Variable B, and that from which Variable B is predicted from Variable A. They almost invariably have different slopes. However, life is made simpler if we always have the predictor on the horizontal axis and the criterion to be predicted on the vertical axis. You need to be careful what you are trying to predict and from what.

In other words, correlation and regression have somewhat different functions despite their close similarities.

Calculation 8.1

Regression equations

To facilitate comparison, we will take the data used in the computation of the correlation coefficient (Chapter 7). The data concern the relationship between mathematical and musical ability for a group of 10 individuals. The 10 scores need to be set out in a table like Table 8.2 and the various intermediate calculations carried out. However, it is important with regression to make the X scores the predictor variable; the Y scores are the criterion variable. N is the number of *pairs* of scores, i.e. 10. (Strictly speaking the Y^2 and ΣY^2 calculations are not necessary for regression but are included here because they highlight the similarities between the correlation and regression calculations.)

Table 8.2   **Important steps in calculating the regression equation**

Person	Maths score *X* score	Music score *Y* score	*X²*	*Y²*	*XY*
1	8	2	64	4	16
2	3	6	9	36	18
3	9	4	81	16	36
4	7	5	49	25	35
5	2	7	4	49	14
6	3	7	9	49	21
7	9	2	81	4	18
8	8	3	64	9	24
9	6	5	36	25	30
10	7	4	49	16	28
	ΣX $= 62$	ΣY $= 45$	ΣX^2 $= 446$	ΣY^2 $= 233$	ΣXY $= 240$

The slope (b) of the regression line is given by the following formula:

$$b = \frac{\Sigma XY - \left(\dfrac{\Sigma X \, \Sigma Y}{N}\right)}{\Sigma X^2 - \dfrac{(\Sigma X)^2}{N}}$$

Thus, substituting the values from the table in the above formula:

$$b_{[slope]} = \frac{240 - \left(\frac{62 \times 45}{10}\right)}{446 - \frac{(62)^2}{10}}$$

$$= \frac{240 - \frac{2790}{10}}{446 - \frac{3844}{10}}$$

$$= \frac{240 - 279}{446 - 384.4}$$

$$= \frac{-39}{61.6}$$

$$= -0.63$$

This tells us that the slope of the regression line is negative – it moves downwards from top left to bottom right. Furthermore, for every unit one moves along the horizontal axis, the regression line moves 0.63 units *down* the vertical axis since in this case it is a *negative* slope.

We can now substitute in the following formula to get the cutting point or intercept (*a*) of the regression line on the vertical axis:

$$a_{[intercept \ on \ vertical \ axis]} = \frac{\Sigma Y - b \Sigma X}{N}$$

$$= \frac{45 - (-0.63 \times 62)}{10}$$

$$= \frac{45 - (-39.06)}{10}$$

$$= \frac{84.06}{10} = 8.41$$

This value for *a* is the point on the vertical axis (musical ability) cut by the regression line.

If one wishes to predict the most likely score on the vertical axis from a particular score on the horizontal axis, one simply substitutes the appropriate values in the following formula:

$$Y_{[predicted \ score]} = a_{[intercept]} + b_{[slope]} \times X_{[known \ score]}$$

Thus if we wished to predict musical ability for a score of 8 on mathematical ability, given that we know the slope (b) is –0.63 and the intercept is 8.41, we simply substitute these values in the formula:

$$Y_{\text{[predicted score]}} = a_{\text{[intercept]}} + b_{\text{[slope]}} \times X_{\text{[known score]}}$$

$$= 8.41 + (-0.63 \times 8)$$

$$= 8.41 + (-5.04)$$

$$= 3.37$$

This is the *best* prediction – it does not mean that people with a score of 8 on mathematical ability inevitably get a score of 3.37 on musical ability. It is just our most intelligent estimate.

Design consideration: The use of regression in prediction is a fraught issue not because of the statistical methods but because of the characteristics of the data used. In particular, note that our predictions about job performance are based on data from the people already in the job. So, for example, those with the best manual dexterity might have developed these skills on the job rather than having them when they were interviewed. Thus it may not be that manual dexterity determines job performance but that they are both influenced by other (unknown) factors. Similarly, if we found that age was a negative predictor of how quickly people get promoted in a banking corporation, this may simply reflect a bias against older people in the profession rather than greater ability of younger people.

8.3   Standard error: how accurate are the predicted score and the regression equations?

You may prefer to leave studying the following material until you have had the opportunity to study Chapter 11.

The accuracy of the predicted score on the criterion is dependent on the closeness of the scattergram points to the regression line; if there is a strong correlation between the variables there is little error in the prediction. Examining the scattergram between two variables will give you an idea of the variability around the regression line and hence the precision of the estimated or predicted scores.

Statisticians prefer to calculate what they call the standard error to indicate how certain one can be about aspects of regression such as the prediction, the intercept or cut-off points, and the slope. A standard error is much the same as the standard deviation except it applies to the *means* of samples rather than individual scores. So the standard error of something is the average deviation of sample means from the mean of the sample means. Don't worry too much if you don't understand the concept quite yet, since we come back to it in Chapters 11 and 12. *Just regard standard error of an estimate as the average amount by which an estimate is likely to be wrong.* As you might expect, since this is statistics, the average is calculated in an unexpected way, as it was for the standard deviation, which is little different.

> Standard error is discussed again in later chapters. Superficially, it may appear to be quite different from the ideas in this chapter. However, remember that whenever we use any characteristic of a sample as the basis for estimating the characteristic of a population, we are likely to be wrong to some extent. The standard error is merely the average amount by which the characteristics of *samples* from the population differ from the characteristic of the *whole* population.

Although the formulae for calculating the standard errors of the various aspects of the regression line are readily available, they add considerably to the computational labour involved in regression, so we recommend that you use a computer to relieve you of this computational chore.

The main standard errors involved in regression are:

■ the one for your predicted (or estimated) value on the criterion (this is known as the standard error of the estimate of y)

■ the one for the slope of the regression line (b)

■ the one for the intercept on the vertical axis (a).

Don't forget that the formulae for calculating these standard errors merely give you the average amount by which your estimate is wrong.

It might be more useful to estimate the likely range within which the true value of the prediction, slope or intercept is likely to fall. In other words, to be able to say that, for example, the predicted score on the criterion variable is likely to be between 2.7 and 3.3. In statistics, this likely range of the true value is known as the *confidence interval*. Actually there are several confidence intervals depending on how confident you wish to be that you have included the true value – the interval is obviously going to be wider if you wish to be *very* confident rather than just confident. In statistics one would routinely use the 95% confidence interval. This

95% confidence interval indicates the range of values within which the true value will fall 95% of the time. That is, we are likely to be wrong only 5% of times.

The following is a rule of thumb which is accurate enough for your purposes for now. Multiply the standard error by two. This gives you the amount which you need to *add and subtract* from the estimated value to cut off the middle 95% of the possible values – that is the 95% confidence interval. In other words, if the estimated value of the criterion (Y variable) is 6.00 and the standard error of this estimate is 0.26, then the 95% confidence interval is 6.00 plus or minus (2×0.26) which is 6.00 plus or minus 0.52. This gives us a 95% confidence interval of 5.48 to 6.52. Thus it is almost certain that the person's score will actually fall in the range of 5.48 to 6.52 although the most likely value is 6.00.

Exactly the same applies to the other aspects of regression. If the slope is 2.00 with a standard error of 0.10, then the 95% confidence interval is 2.00 plus or minus 2×0.10, which gives a confidence interval of 1.80 to 2.20.

The use of confidence intervals is not as common as it ought to be despite the fact that it gives us a realistic assessment of the precision of our estimates.

The above calculations of confidence intervals are approximate if you have fewer than about 30 pairs of scores. If you have between 16 and 29 pairs of scores the calculation will be more accurate if you multiply by 2.1 rather than 2.0. If you have between 12 and 15 pairs of scores then multiplying by 2.2 would improve the accuracy of the calculation. With fewer than 12 pairs the method gets a little more inaccurate. When you have become more knowledgeable about statistics, you could obtain precise confidence intervals by multiplying your standard error by the appropriate value of t from Significance Table 12.1 (Chapter 12). The appropriate value is in the row headed 'Degrees of freedom', corresponding to your number of pairs of scores minus 2 under the column for the 5% significance level (i.e. if you have 10 pairs of scores then you would multiply by 2.31).

8.4   Notes and recommendations

- Drawing the scattergram will invariably illuminate the trends in your data and strongly hint at the broad features of the regression calculations. It will also provide a visual check on your computations.

- These regression procedures assume that the best-fitting regression line is a straight line. If it looks as if the regression line ought to be curved or curvilinear, do not apply these numerical methods. Of course, even if a relationship is curvilinear you could use the curved-line scattergram to make graphically based predictions.

- It may be that you have more than one predictor variable that you wish to use – if so look at Chapter 28 on multiple regression.

Part 2

Significance testing

Chapter 9

Samples and populations

Generalising and inferring

Preparation
This chapter introduces some important new ideas. They can be understood by anyone with a general familiarity with Chapters 1–8.

Most research in psychology relies on just a small sample of data from which general statements are made. The terms *sample* and *population* are familiar to most of us, although the fine detail may be a little obscure. So far we have mainly discussed *sets* of data. This was deliberate since *everything that we have discussed in previous chapters is applicable to either samples or populations*. The next stage is to understand how we can use a sample of scores to make general statements or draw general conclusions that apply well beyond that sample. This is a branch of statistics called *inferential* statistics because it is about drawing inferences about all scores in the population from just a sample of those scores.

9.1 Theoretical considerations

We need to be careful when defining our terms. A *sample* is fairly obvious – it is just a small number of scores selected from the entirety of scores. A *population* is the entire set of scores. In other words, a sample is a small set or a subset taken from the full set or population of scores.

You need to notice some special features of the terminology we have used. We have mentioned a population of *scores* and a sample of *scores*. In other words, population and sample refer to scores on a variable. We do not deal with a population of people or even a sample of people. So, in statistical terms, all of the people living in Scotland do not constitute a population. Similarly, all of the people working in clothing factories in France or all of the goats on the Isle of Capri are not *statistical* populations. They may be populations for geographers or for everyday purposes, but they are not statistical populations. A statistical population is merely *all* of the scores on a particular variable.

This notion can take a little getting used to. However, there is another feature of statistical populations that can cause confusion. In some cases all of the scores are potentially obtainable, for example the ages of students entering psychology degrees in a particular year. However, often the population of scores is infinite and otherwise impossible to specify. An example of this might be the amount of time people take to react to an auditory signal in a laboratory. The number of possible measures of reaction time in these circumstances is bounded only by time and resources. No one could actually find out the population of scores other than by taking measurement after measurement – and then there is always another measurement to be taken. The notion of population in statistics is much more of a conceptual tool than something objective. Normally a psychologist will only have a few scores (his or her sample) and no direct knowledge of what all the scores or the population of scores are.

Thus the sample is usually known about in detail in research whereas the population generally is unknown. But the real question is what can we possibly say about the population based on our knowledge of this limited entity, the sample? Quite a lot. The use of sampling in public opinion polls, for example, is so familiar that we should need little convincing of the value of samples. Samples may only approximate the characteristics of the population but generally we accept that they are sufficient to base decisions on.

If we know nothing about the population other than the characteristics of a sample drawn from that population of scores, our best guess or inference about the characteristics of the population is the characteristics of the sample from that population. It does not necessarily have to be particularly precise since an informed guess has to be better than nothing. So, in general, if we know nothing else, our best guess as to the mean of the population is the mean of the sample, our best guess as to the mode of the population is the mode of the sample, and our best guess as to the variance of the population is the variance of the sample. It is a case of beggars not being able to be choosers.

In statistical inference, it is generally assumed that samples are drawn *at random* from the population. Such samples are called *random samples* from the population. The concept of randomness is sometimes misunderstood. Randomness is not the same as arbitrariness, informality, haphazardness or any other term that suggests a casual approach to drawing samples. A random sample of scores from a population entails selecting scores in such a way that each and every score in the population has an equal chance of being selected. In other words, a random sample favours the selection of no particular scores in the population. Although it is not difficult to draw a random sample, it does require a systematic approach. Any old sample you choose because you like the look of it is not a random sample.

There are a number of ways of drawing a random sample. Here are just a few:

1. Put the information about each member of the population on a slip of paper, put all of the slips into a hat, close your eyes, give the slips a long stir with

your hand and finally bring one slip out of the hat. This slip is the first member of the sample; repeat the process to get the second, third and subsequent members of the sample. *Technically the slip of paper should be returned to the container after being selected so it may be selected again. However, this is not done, largely because with a large population it would make little difference to the outcome.*

2. Number each member of the population. Then press the appropriate randomisation button on your scientific calculator to generate a random number. If it is not one of the numbers in your population, ignore it and press the button again. The member of the population corresponding to this number becomes a member of the sample. Computer programs are also available for generating random numbers.

3. Low-tech researchers might use the random number tables found in many statistics textbooks. Essentially what you do is merely to choose a random starting point in the table (a pin is recommended) and then choose numbers using a predetermined formula. For example, you could take the first three numbers after the pin, then a gap of seven numbers and then the three numbers following this, then a gap of seven numbers and then the three numbers following this, etc.

Do not laugh at these procedures – they are valid and convenient ways of choosing random samples.

9.2   The characteristics of random samples

In Table 9.1 there is a population of 100 scores – the mode is 2, the median is 6.00, and the mean is 5.52. Have a go at drawing random samples of, say, five

Table 9.1   **A population of 100 scores**

7	5	11	3	4	3	5	8	9	1
9	4	0	2	2	2	9	11	7	12
4	8	2	9	7	0	8	0	8	10
10	7	4	6	6	2	2	1	12	2
2	5	6	7	10	6	6	2	1	9
3	4	2	4	9	7	5	1	6	4
5	7	12	2	8	8	3	4	6	5
9	2	6	0	7	7	5	9	10	8
6	1	7	12	3	5	2	7	2	7
2	2	8	11	4	5	8	6	4	6

Table 9.2   **Means of 40 samples each of five scores taken at random from the population in Table 9.1**

2.20	5.60	4.80	5.00	8.40	6.80	4.60	6.60
4.00	3.00	5.00	5.60	8.80	5.60	4.60	6.80
3.00	8.20	8.20	3.80	5.40	6.00	4.80	5.20
3.20	5.20	3.00	5.00	5.40	4.80	6.00	7.40
5.00	2.00	3.60	4.60	5.60	4.60	4.40	6.00

scores from this population. Repeat the process until you have a lot of sets (or samples) of scores. For each sample calculate any of the statistics just mentioned – the mean is a particularly useful statistic.

We have drawn 40 samples from this population at random using a random sampling procedure from a computer program. The means of each of the 40 samples are shown in Table 9.2. It is noticeable that these means vary quite considerably. However, if we plot them graphically we find that sample means close to the population mean of 5.52 are relatively common. The average of the sample means is 5.20 which is close to the population mean. The minimum sample mean is 2.00 and the maximum is 8.80; these contrast with minimum and maximum values of 0 and 12 in the population. Sample means very different from this population mean become relatively uncommon the further away they go from the population mean.

We could calculate the standard deviation of these 40 sample means by entering each mean into the standard deviation formula:

$$\text{Standard deviation} = \sqrt{\frac{\Sigma X^2 - \frac{(\Sigma X)^2}{N}}{N}}$$

This gives us a standard deviation of sample means of 1.60. The standard deviation of sample means has a technical name, although the basic concept differs only in that it deals with means of samples and not scores. The special term is *standard error*.

So, in general, it would seem that sample means are a pretty good estimate of population means although not absolutely necessarily so.

All of this was based on samples of size 5. Table 9.3 shows the results of exactly the same exercise with samples of size 20.

Much the same trends appear with these larger samples but for the following:

1.   The spread of the sample means is reduced somewhat and they appear to cluster closer to the population mean. The minimum value is 4.25 and the maximum value is 6.85. The overall mean of these samples is 5.33, close to the population mean of 5.52.

Table 9.3   **Means of 40 samples each of size 20 taken at random from the population in Table 9.1**

4.50	5.70	5.90	5.15	4.25	5.25	5.60	5.00
5.35	5.90	6.85	5.55	5.30	5.60	5.70	4.55
6.35	6.30	4.40	5.25	4.65	5.30	4.80	5.65
4.85	5.35	5.70	4.35	5.25	5.10	6.45	5.05
5.50	6.15	5.65	5.05	5.15	5.10	4.65	4.95

2. The standard deviation of these means (i.e. the standard error) of larger samples is smaller. For Table 9.3 the standard deviation is 0.60.

3. The distribution of sample means is a steeper curve than for the smaller samples.

The conclusion of all this is that the larger sample size produces better estimates of the mean of the population. For statistics, this verges on common sense.

Great emphasis is placed on the extreme samples in a distribution. We have seen that samples from the above population differ from the population mean by varying amounts, that the majority of samples are close to that mean, and that the bigger the sample the closer to the population mean it is likely to be. There is a neat trick in statistics by which we try to define which sample means are very unlikely to occur through random sampling. It is true that in theory just about any sample mean is possible in random sampling, but those very different from the population mean are relatively rare. In statistics the extreme 5% of these samples are of special interest. Statisticians identify the extreme 2.5% of means on each side of the population mean for special consideration. Two 2.5's make 5%. These extreme samples come in the zone of relative rarity and are termed *significant*. Significance in statistics really means that we have a sample with characteristics very different from those of the population from which it was drawn. Significance at the 5% level of confidence merely means falling into the 5% of samples which are most different from the population. These extremes are, as we have seen, dependent on the size of sample being used.

9.3   Confidence intervals

There is another idea that is fundamental to some branches of statistics – *confidence interval of the mean*. In public opinion surveys you often read of the margin of error being a certain percentage. The margin of error is simply the amount for, say, voting intention which defines the middle 95% most likely sample means. This is expressed relative to the obtained sample mean. So when public opinion pollsters say that the margin of error is a certain percentage they are telling us the cut-off points from the obtained percentage which would include the middle 95% of sample means. The confidence interval in more general statistics is the range of means that cuts off the extreme 5% of sample means. So the 95% confidence interval merely gives the range of sample means which occupies the middle 95% of the distribution of sample means. The confidence interval will be larger for smaller samples, all other things being equal.

Finally, a little more jargon. The correct term for characteristics of samples such as their means, standard deviations, ranges and so forth is *statistics*. The same characteristics of populations are called *parameters*. In other words, you use the statistics from samples to estimate or infer the parameters of the population from which the sample came.

9.4   Notes and recommendations

■ The material in this chapter is not immediately applicable to research. Regard it as a conceptual basis for the understanding of inferential statistics.

■ You need to be a little patient since the implications of this chapter will not be appreciated until later.

Chapter 10

Statistical significance for the correlation coefficient

A practical introduction to statistical inference

Preparation

You must be familiar with correlation coefficients (Chapter 7) and populations and samples (Chapter 9).

Researchers have correlated two variables for a sample of 20 people. They obtained a correlation coefficient of 0.56. The problem is that they wish to generalise beyond this sample and make statements about the trends in the data which apply more widely. However, their analyses are based on just a small sample which might not be characteristic of the trends in the population.

10.1 Theoretical considerations

We can all sympathise with these researchers. The reason why they are concerned is straightforward. Imagine that Table 10.1 contains the *population* of pairs of scores. Overall, the correlation between the two variables in this population is 0.00. That is, there is absolutely no relationship between Variable X and Variable Y in the population.

However, what happens if we draw many samples of, say, eight pairs of scores at random from this population and calculate the correlation coefficients for *each* sample? Some of the correlation coefficients are indeed more or less zero but a few are substantially different from zero as we can see from Table 10.2. Plotted on a histogram, the distribution of these correlation coefficients looks like Diagram 10.1. It is more or less a normal distribution with a mean correlation of zero and most of the correlations being close to that zero point. However, some of the correlation coefficients are substantially different from 0.00. This shows that even where there is zero relationship between the two variables in the population, random samples can appear to have correlations which depart from 0.00.

Just about anything is possible in samples although only certain things are likely. Consequently, we try to stipulate which are the *likely* correlations in

Table 10.1 **An imaginary population of 60 pairs of scores with zero correlation between the pairs**

Pair	Variable X	Variable Y	Pair	Variable X	Variable Y	Pair	Variable X	Variable Y
01	14	12	02	5	11	03	12	5
04	3	13	05	14	9	06	10	14
07	5	12	08	17	17	09	4	8
10	15	5	11	3	3	12	19	12
13	16	7	14	14	9	15	12	13
16	13	8	17	15	11	18	15	7
19	12	17	20	11	14	21	5	13
22	12	11	23	11	9	24	15	14
25	5	12	26	15	9	27	12	13
28	6	13	29	14	7	30	18	13
31	12	1	32	19	12	33	12	19
34	11	14	35	12	17	36	13	9
37	14	12	38	15	5	39	18	13
40	17	11	41	3	12	42	16	9
43	16	12	44	11	9	45	18	2
46	12	14	47	12	14	48	15	11
49	16	12	50	12	14	51	8	14
52	5	11	53	7	8	54	16	8
55	13	13	56	12	15	57	18	2
58	3	1	59	7	8	60	11	6

samples of a given size and which are the *unlikely* ones (if the population correlation is zero). Actually all we say is that correlations in the *middle* 95% of the distribution of samples are likely if the population correlation is zero. Correlations in the extreme 5% (usually the extreme 2.5% in each direction) are unlikely in these circumstances. These are arbitrary cut-off points, but they are conventional in statistics and have long antecedents. It is also not an unreasonable cut-off for most purposes to suggest that if a sample has only a 1 in 20 chance of occurring then it is unlikely to represent the population value.

If a correlation is in the extreme 5% of the distribution of samples from a *population* where the correlation is zero, it is deemed *statistically significant*. We

Table 10.2　Two hundred correlation coefficients obtained by repeatedly random sampling eight pairs of scores from Table 10.1

−0.56	−0.30	0.36	0.54	−0.27	0.05	−0.33	−0.19	0.54	0.18
−0.54	0.11	0.25	−0.15	−0.57	−0.31	−0.24	0.17	−0.69	−0.19
−0.53	0.68	−0.22	−0.22	−0.26	−0.42	0.08	−0.30	−0.41	0.29
−0.45	−0.09	−0.06	−0.30	−0.72	−0.53	0.04	−0.66	0.65	−0.53
−0.39	−0.21	0.07	−0.80	−0.68	0.08	0.13	0.76	−0.04	0.18
−0.36	−0.19	0.29	0.24	0.38	−0.55	−0.40	0.50	−0.09	−0.30
−0.30	−0.56	0.68	−0.14	0.35	−0.28	0.56	−0.38	−0.16	0.15
−0.29	−0.23	−0.42	−0.27	0.01	0.43	0.01	−0.33	−0.20	0.49
−0.26	−0.41	−0.09	0.00	0.54	0.17	0.34	0.52	−0.11	0.67
−0.26	−0.16	−0.70	0.00	−0.17	0.40	0.03	−0.02	0.35	−0.01
−0.23	0.03	0.30	−0.52	−0.05	−0.26	−0.32	−0.37	−0.51	0.18
−0.20	−0.17	−0.43	−0.39	0.37	0.23	−0.10	0.32	0.02	0.52
−0.18	0.38	0.45	−0.50	−0.58	0.28	−0.34	−0.28	0.24	0.53
−0.17	−0.02	−0.34	−0.23	−0.54	0.25	−0.71	0.72	0.03	−0.13
−0.08	−0.30	−0.06	−0.10	−0.65	0.27	−0.04	0.32	−0.52	−0.42
−0.04	0.59	−0.29	−0.31	0.48	−0.48	0.02	−0.30	0.81	−0.23
0.10	−0.12	−0.51	−0.19	0.08	0.18	−0.27	−0.67	−0.69	0.50
0.15	−0.54	−0.15	0.05	0.01	0.52	0.19	0.19	0.07	0.27
0.34	−0.44	−0.11	−0.21	−0.02	−0.07	0.17	−0.30	−0.06	−0.49
0.57	−0.10	−0.23	0.01	−0.09	−0.27	0.22	−0.28	0.43	−0.34

should be sitting up and taking notice if this happens. In other words, statistical significance merely signals the statistically unusual or unlikely. In the above example, by examining Table 10.2 we find that the correlations 0.81, 0.76, 0.72, 0.68 and 0.68 and −0.80, −0.72, −0.71, −0.70, and −0.69 are in the extreme 5% of correlations away from zero. This extreme 5% is made up of the extreme 2.5% positive correlations and the extreme 2.5% negative correlations. Therefore, a correlation of between 0.68 and 1.00 or −0.69 and −1.00 is in the extreme 5% of correlations. This is the range which we describe as statistically significant. Statistical significance simply means that our sample falls in the relatively extreme part of the distribution of samples obtained if the null hypothesis (see next section) of no relationship between the two variables is true.

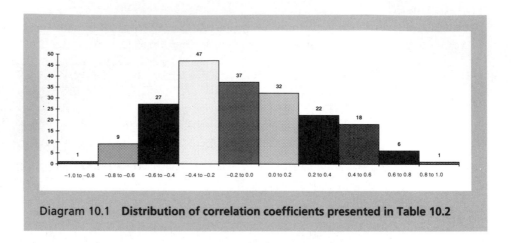

Diagram 10.1   Distribution of correlation coefficients presented in Table 10.2

These ranges of significant correlations mentioned above only apply to samples of size eight. A different size of sample from the same population results in a different spread of correlations obtained from repeated sampling. The spread is bigger if the samples are smaller and less if the samples are larger. In other words, there is more variation in the distribution of samples with small sample sizes than with larger ones.

On the face of things, all of this is merely a theoretical meandering of little value. We have assumed that the population correlation is zero. A major difficulty is that we are normally unaware of the population correlation since our information is based solely on a sample which may or may not represent the population very well. However, it is not quite the futile exercise it appears. Some information provided by a sample can be used to infer or estimate the characteristics of the population. For one thing, information about the variability or variance of the scores in the sample is used *to estimate the variability of scores in the population.*

10.2 Back to the real world: the null hypothesis

There is another vitally important concept in statistics – the hypothesis. Hypotheses in psychological statistics are usually presented as antithetical pairs – the *null hypothesis* and its corresponding *alternative hypothesis*:

1. The *null hypothesis* is essentially a statement that there is no relationship between two variables. The following are all examples of null hypotheses:

    (a) There is no relationship between brain size and intelligence
    (b) There is no relationship between gender and income
    (c) There is no relationship between baldness and virility
    (d) There is no relationship between children's self-esteem and that of their parent of the same sex

(e) There is no relationship between ageing and memory loss

(f) There is no relationship between the amount of carrots eaten and ability to see in the dark.

2. The *alternative hypothesis* simply states that there is a relationship between two variables. In its simplest forms the alternative hypothesis says only this:

(a) There is a relationship between the number of years of education people have and their income

(b) There is a relationship between people's gender and how much they talk about their emotional problems

(c) There is a relationship between people's mental instability and their artistic creativity

(d) There is a relationship between abuse in childhood and later psychological problems

(e) There is a relationship between birth order and social dominance

(f) There is a relationship between the degree of similarity of couples and their sexual attraction for each other.

So the difference between null and alternative hypotheses is merely the word 'no'. Of course, sometimes psychologists dress their hypotheses up in fancier language than this but the basic principle is unchanged. (Actually there is a complication – directional hypotheses – but these are dealt with in Chapter 17.)

The statistical reason for using the null hypothesis and alternative hypothesis is that they *clarify* the populations in statistical analyses. *In statistics, inferences are based on the characteristics of the population as defined by the null hypothesis.* Invariably the populations defined by the null hypothesis are ones in which there is no relation between a pair of variables. Thus, the population defined by the null hypothesis is one where the correlation between the two variables under consideration is 0.00. The characteristics of a sample can be used to assess whether it is likely that the correlation for the sample comes from a population in which the correlation is zero.

So the basic trick is to use certain of the characteristics of a sample together with the notion of the null hypothesis to define the characteristics of a population. Other characteristics of the sample are then used to estimate the likelihood that this sample comes from this particular population. To repeat and summarise:

1. The null hypothesis is used to define a population in which there is no relation between two variables.

2. Other characteristics, especially the variability of this population, are estimated or inferred from the known sample.

It is then possible to decide whether or not it is likely that the sample comes from this population defined by the null hypothesis. If it is *unlikely* that the sample comes from the null hypothesis-based population, the possibility that the null hypothesis is true is rejected. Instead the view that the alternative hypothesis is true is accepted. That is, the alternative hypothesis that there really is a relationship is preferred. This is the same thing as saying that we can safely generalise from our sample.

10.3 Pearson's Correlation Coefficient again

The null hypothesis for research involving the correlation coefficient is that there is *no* relationship between the two variables. In other words, the null hypothesis implies that the correlation coefficient between two variables is 0.00 in the population (defined by the null hypothesis). So what if, in a sample of 10 pairs of scores, the correlation is 0.94 as for the data in Table 10.3?

Is it likely that such a correlation would occur in a sample if it actually came from a population where the true correlation is zero? We are back to our basic problem of how likely it is that a correlation of 0.94 would occur if really there is no correlation in the population. We need to plot the distribution of correlations in random samples of 10 pairs drawn from this population. Unfortunately we do not have the population of scores, only a sample of scores. However, statisticians can use the variability of this sample of scores to estimate the variability in the population. Then the likely distribution of correlations in repeated samples of a given size drawn from the population with this amount of variability can be calculated. Mere mortals like ourselves do not have to get actively involved in this since it is fairly easy to capitalise on statisticians' efforts. They have provided tables which neatly summarise a great deal of hard work on their part.

Tables are available which, for any given size of sample, tell you the minimum size of a correlation coefficient which cuts the middle 95% of correlations from the extreme 5% of correlations (assuming the null hypothesis is true in the population). These cut-off points are usually called *critical values*:

1.   If the sample's correlation is in the middle 95% of correlations then we accept the null hypothesis that there is no relationship between the two variables.

Table 10.3   **A sample of 10 pairs of scores.**

Pair number	X-score	Y-score
1	5	4
2	2	1
3	7	8
4	5	6
5	0	2
6	1	0
7	4	3
8	2	2
9	8	9
10	6	7

2. However, if the correlation in the sample is in the extreme 5% of correlations then the alternative hypothesis is accepted (that there is a relationship between the two variables).

Significance Table 10.1 reveals that for a sample size of 10, a correlation has to be between −0.63 and −1.00 *or* between 0.63 and 1.00 to be sufficiently large as to be in the extreme 5% of correlations which support the alternative hypothesis. Correlations closer to 0.00 than these come in the middle 95% which are held to support the null hypothesis.

Significance Table 10.1 **5% Significance values of the Pearson Correlation Co-efficient (two-tailed test)**

Your value must be in the listed ranges for your sample size to be significant at the 5% level (i.e. to accept the hypothesis).

If your required sample size is not listed, then take the nearest *smaller* sample size. Alternatively extrapolate from listed values.

Sample size	Significant at 5% level: accept hypothesis			
5	−0.88 to −1.00	or	+0.88 to +1.00	
6	−0.81 to −1.00	or	+0.81 to +1.00	
7	−0.75 to −1.00	or	+0.75 to +1.00	
8	−0.71 to −1.00	or	+0.71 to +1.00	
9	−0.67 to −1.00	or	+0.67 to +1.00	
10	−0.63 to −1.00	or	+0.63 to +1.00	
11	−0.60 to −1.00	or	+0.60 to +1.00	
12	−0.58 to −1.00	or	+0.58 to +1.00	
13	−0.55 to −1.00	or	+0.55 to +1.00	
14	−0.53 to −1.00	or	+0.53 to +1.00	
15	−0.51 to −1.00	or	+0.51 to +1.00	
16	−0.50 to −1.00	or	+0.50 to +1.00	
17	−0.48 to −1.00	or	+0.48 to +1.00	
18	−0.47 to −1.00	or	+0.47 to +1.00	
19	−0.46 to −1.00	or	+0.46 to +1.00	
20	−0.44 to −1.00	or	+0.44 to +1.00	
25	−0.40 to −1.00	or	+0.40 to +1.00	
30	−0.36 to −1.00	or	+0.36 to +1.00	
40	−0.31 to −1.00	or	+0.31 to +1.00	
50	−0.28 to −1.00	or	+0.28 to +1.00	
60	−0.25 to −1.00	or	+0.25 to +1.00	
100	−0.20 to −1.00	or	+0.20 to +1.00	

The above table has been adapted and extended from Table VII of R.A. Fisher and F. Yates (1974). *Statistical Tables for Biological, Agricultural and Medical Research*. London: Longman. With the kind permission of the publisher.

Calculation 10.1

Statistical significance of a Pearson Correlation Coefficient

Having calculated your value of the Pearson Correlation Coefficient, make a note of the sample size and consult Significance Table 10.1. In the example in Chapter 7 (Calculation 7.1), the correlation between mathematical scores and musical scores was found to be –0.90 with a sample size of 10. If this correlation is in the range of correlations listed as being in the extreme 5% of correlations for this sample size, the correlation is described as being statistically significant at the 5% level of significance.

In this case, since our obtained value of the correlation coefficient is in the significant range of the correlation coefficient (–0.63 to –1.00 and 0.63 to 1.00), we reject the null hypothesis in favour of the alternative hypothesis that there is a relationship between mathematical and musical scores.

In our report of the study we would conclude by writing something to the following effect: 'There is a negative correlation of –0.90 between mathematical and musical scores which is statistically significant at the 5% level with a sample size of 10.'

The terms *Type 1 error* and *Type 2 error* frequently appear in statistics textbooks although they are relatively uncommon in reports and other publications. They refer to the risk that no matter what decision you make in statistics there is always a chance that you will be making the wrong decision.

A Type 1 error is deciding that the null hypothesis is false when it is actually true. A Type 2 error is deciding that the null hypothesis is true when it is actually false. Powerful statistical tests are those in which there is less chance of a Type 2 error.

Unfortunately, the terms are not particularly useful in the everyday application of statistics where it is hard enough making a decision let alone worrying about the chance that you have made a wrong decision. Given that statistics deals with probabilities and not certainties, there is always a chance that any decision you make is wrong.

10.4 The Spearman's Rho Correlation Coefficient

Virtually the same logic applies when testing the statistical significance of a ranked correlation coefficient. However, a slightly different table is used to assess the significance level (Significance Table 10.2).

Significance Table 10.2   **5% Significance values of the Spearman Correlation Co-efficient (two-tailed test)**

Your value must be in the listed ranges for your sample size to be significant at the 5% level (i.e. to accept the hypothesis).

If your required sample size is not listed, then take the nearest *smaller* sample size. Alternatively extrapolate from listed values.

Sample size	Significant at 5% level: accept hypothesis						
5			−1.00	*or*	+1.00		
6	−0.89	to	−1.00	*or*	+0.89	to	+1.00
7	−0.79	to	−1.00	*or*	+0.79	to	+1.00
8	−0.74	to	−1.00	*or*	+0.74	to	+1.00
9	−0.68	to	−1.00	*or*	+0.68	to	+1.00
10	−0.65	to	−1.00	*or*	+0.65	to	+1.00
11	−0.62	to	−1.00	*or*	+0.62	to	+1.00
12	−0.59	to	−1.00	*or*	+0.59	to	+1.00
13	−0.57	to	−1.00	*or*	+0.57	to	+1.00
14	−0.55	to	−1.00	*or*	+0.55	to	+1.00
15	−0.53	to	−1.00	*or*	+0.53	to	+1.00
16	−0.51	to	−1.00	*or*	+0.51	to	+1.00
17	−0.49	to	−1.00	*or*	+0.49	to	+1.00
18	−0.48	to	−1.00	*or*	+0.48	to	+1.00
19	−0.46	to	−1.00	*or*	+0.46	to	+1.00
20	−0.45	to	−1.00	*or*	+0.45	to	+1.00
25	−0.40	to	−1.00	*or*	+0.40	to	+1.00
30	−0.36	to	−1.00	*or*	+0.36	to	+1.00
40	−0.31	to	−1.00	*or*	+0.31	to	+1.00
50	−0.28	to	−1.00	*or*	+0.28	to	+1.00
60	−0.25	to	−1.00	*or*	+0.25	to	+1.00
100	−0.20	to	−1.00	*or*	+0.20	to	+1.00

The above table has been adapted and extended from G.J. Glasser and R.F. Winter (1961). Critical values of the coefficient of rank correlation for testing the hypothesis of independence. *Biometrika*, **48**, 444–448. With the kind permission of the Biometrika Trustees.

Calculation 10.2

Statistical significance of Spearman's Rho Correlation Coefficient

In Chapter 7 (Calculation 7.2) we calculated Spearman's Rho Correlation Coefficient between mathematical score and musical score. The correlation was found to be –0.89 with a sample size of 10. Significance Table 10.2 reveals that in order to be significant at the 5% level with a sample size of 10, correlations have to be in the range 0.65 to 1.00 *or* –0.65 to –1.00.

It follows from this that we accept the alternative hypothesis that mathematical and musical scores are related and reject the null hypothesis.

We can report a significant correlation: 'There is a negative correlation of –0.89 between mathematical and musical scores which is statistically significant at the 5% level with a sample size of 10.'

10.5 Notes and recommendations

■ There is nothing complex in the calculation of statistical significance for the correlation coefficients. However, statistical tables normally do not include every sample size. When a particular sample size is missing you can simply use the nearest (lower) tabulated value. Alternatively you could extrapolate from the nearest tabulated value above and the nearest tabulated value below your actual sample size.

■ It is a bad mistake to report a correlation without indicating whether it is statistically significant.

■ Chapter 16 explains how to report your significance levels in a more succinct form. Try to employ this sort of style as it eases the writing of research reports and looks professional.

■ Beware that some statistical textbooks provide significance tables which are distributed by degrees of freedom rather than sample size. For any given sample size, the degrees of freedom are *two* less. Thus, for a sample size of 10, the degrees of freedom are 10 – 2, or 8.

Chapter 11

Standard error

The standard deviation of the means of samples

Preparation
Review z-scores and standard deviation (Chapter 5) and sampling from populations (Chapter 9).

Most psychological research involves the use of samples drawn from a particular population. Just what are the characteristics of samples drawn from a population? In theory, it is possible to draw samples with virtually any mean score if we randomly sample from a population of scores. So is it possible to make any generalisations about the characteristics of randomly drawn samples from a population?

Standard error is one way of summarising the diversity of sample means drawn from a population. This chapter explains the concept of standard error. However, the practical use of standard error in psychological research will not become obvious until the next two chapters which deal with the *t*-tests. Nevertheless, it is essential to understand standard error before moving on to its practical applications.

11.1 Theoretical considerations

Table 11.1 contains a population of 25 scores with a mean of 4.20. We have selected, at random, samples of four scores until we have 20 samples. These are arbitrary decisions for illustrative purposes. For each of these 20 samples the mean has been calculated giving 20 separate sample means. These were as in Table 11.2.

The distribution of the sample means is called a *sampling distribution*. Clearly, in Table 11.2 the 20 sample means differ to varying degrees from each other and from the population mean of 4.20. In fact the average of the sample means is

Table 11.1 **A population of 25 scores**

5	7	9	4	6
2	6	3	2	7
1	7	5	4	3
3	6	1	2	4
2	5	3	3	4

Table 11.2 **Means of 20 samples each of four scores taken at random from the population of 25 scores in Table 11.1**

3.75	6.00	4.00	4.25
3.00	3.75	4.50	3.50
4.50	3.00	4.25	2.50
3.50	5.00	3.00	4.25
4.00	3.00	4.50	5.75

4.00. The standard deviation of these 20 sample means is 0.89. This was calculated using the normal formula for the standard deviation (see Calculation 5.1). There is a special name for the standard deviation formula when it is applied to a set of sample means – the *standard error*. Therefore the standard error is 0.89. The implication of this is that the standard error is directly comparable to the standard deviation. Consequently, the standard error is simply the average deviation of sample means from the mean of the sample means. Although this is clumsy to write down or say, it captures the essence of standard error effectively. (The average of sample means, if you have a lot of samples, will be more or less identical to the mean of the population. Thus, it is more usual to refer to the population mean rather than the average of sample means.)

If we sampled from the population of scores in Table 11.1 but using a different sample size, say samples of 12, we would get a rather different sampling distribution. In general, all other things being equal, the standard error of the means of bigger samples is less than that of smaller sized samples. This is merely a slightly convoluted way of supporting the commonsense belief that larger samples tend to be more precise estimates of the characteristics of populations than smaller samples are. In other words, we tend to be more convinced by large samples than small samples.

A frequency curve of the means of samples drawn from a population will tend to get taller and narrower as the sample size involved increases. It also tends to be normal in shape, i.e. bell-shaped. The more normal (bell-shaped) the population of scores on which the sampling is done, the more normal (bell-shaped) the frequency curve of the sample means.

11.2 Estimated standard deviation and standard error

The difficulty with the concept of standard error is that we rarely have information about anything other than a sample taken from the population. This might suggest that the standard error is unknowable. After all, if we only have a single sample mean, how on earth can we calculate the standard error? There is only one sample mean which obviously cannot vary from itself. Fortunately we can estimate the standard error from the characteristics of a sample of scores. The first stage in doing this involves estimating the *population* standard deviation from the standard deviation of a *sample* taken from that population. There is a relatively easy way of using the standard deviation of a sample of scores in order to estimate the standard deviation of the population. The formula is:

$$\text{Estimated standard deviation} = \sqrt{\frac{\Sigma X^2 - \frac{(\Sigma X)^2}{N}}{N-1}}$$

The above formula is exactly the same as the standard deviation computational formula given in Chapter 5 with one difference. You will see in the lower half of the formula the term $N - 1$. In our previous version of the formula, N occurred rather than $N - 1$. The point is that if we know the scores in a sample, we can use them to estimate the standard deviation of the scores in the population.

You may be wondering about the $N - 1$ in the above formula. The reason is that if we try to extrapolate the standard deviation of the whole population directly from the standard deviation of a sample from this population, we get things somewhat wrong. However, this is easily corrected by adjusting the standard deviation by dividing by $N - 1$ instead of N. The adjusted standard deviation formula gives the *estimated* standard deviation. We can also estimate the variance of the population from the characteristics of the sample:

$$\text{Estimated variance} = \frac{\Sigma X^2 - \frac{(\Sigma X)^2}{N}}{N-1}$$

These formulae for estimated standard deviation and estimated variance apply when you are using a sample to estimate the characteristics of a population. However, some researchers also use these estimating formulae (in which you divide by N – 1) in place of the variance and standard deviation formulae (in which you divide by N) when dealing with populations. Generally this makes little difference in practice since usually psychologists are working with samples and trying to estimate the characteristics of the population.

The term $N - 1$ is called the *degrees of freedom.*

There is a second step in estimating the standard error from the characteristics of a sample. The standard error involves sample *means*, not the *scores* involved in the standard deviation and estimated standard deviation. How does one move from scores to sample means? Fortunately a very simple relationship exists between the standard deviation of a population of scores and the standard error of samples of scores taken from that population. The standard error is obtained by dividing the population standard deviation by the *square root* of the sample size involved. This implies that the standard deviation of large samples taken from the population of scores is smaller than the standard deviation of small samples taken from the population. The formula is basically the same whether we are using the standard deviation of a known population or the estimated standard deviation of a population based on the standard deviation of a sample.

$$\text{(Estimated) standard error} = \frac{\text{(estimated) standard deviation of population}}{\sqrt{N}}$$

Obviously it is possible to combine the (estimated) standard deviation and the (estimated) standard error formulae together:

$$\text{(Estimated) standard error} = \frac{\sqrt{\dfrac{\Sigma X^2 - \dfrac{(\Sigma X)^2}{N}}{N - 1}}}{\sqrt{N}}$$

Calculation 11.1

Estimated standard error of sample means from scores for a single sample from the population

The following is a sample of six scores taken at random from the population: 5, 7, 3, 6, 4, 5.

Table 11.3   **Steps in calculating the standard error**

X (scores)	X^2 (squared scores)
5	25
7	49
3	9
6	36
4	16
5	25
$\Sigma X = 30$	$\Sigma X^2 = 160$

Step 1: Using this information we can estimate the standard error of samples of size 6 taken from the same population. Taking our six scores (X), we need to produce Table 11.3, where $N = 6$.

Step 2: Substitute these values in the standard error formula:

$$\text{(Estimated) standard error} = \frac{\sqrt{\dfrac{\Sigma X^2 - \dfrac{(\Sigma X)^2}{N}}{N-1}}}{\sqrt{N}}$$

$$= \frac{\sqrt{\dfrac{160 - \dfrac{30^2}{6}}{6-1}}}{\sqrt{6}}$$

$$= \frac{\sqrt{\dfrac{160 - \dfrac{900}{6}}{5}}}{2.449}$$

$$= \frac{\sqrt{\dfrac{160 - 150}{5}}}{2.449}$$

$$= \frac{\sqrt{\dfrac{10}{5}}}{2.449}$$

$$= \frac{\sqrt{2}}{2.449}$$

$$= \frac{1.414}{2.449}$$

$$= 0.58$$

Roughly speaking, this suggests that on average sample means differ from the population mean by 0.58.

The term standard *error* is used because it is the standard or average amount by which you would be wrong if you tried to estimate the mean of the population from the mean of a sample from that population.

11.3 Notes and recommendations

■ The standard error is often reported in computer output and in research publications. Very much like standard deviation, it can be used as an indicator of the variability in one's data. Variables with different standard errors essentially have different variances so long as the number of scores is the same for the two variables.

■ Standard error is almost always really *estimated* standard error in psychological statistics. However, usually this estimate is referred to simply as the standard error. This is a pity since it loses sight of the true nature of standard error.

Chapter 12

The *t*-test

Comparing two samples of correlated/related scores

Preparation
Review z-scores and standard deviation (Chapter 5) and standard error (Chapter 11).

12.1 Introduction

Many research projects involve comparisons between two groups of scores. Each group of scores is a sample from a population of scores. There is a test called the related (correlated) *t*-test which compares the means of two *related* samples of scores to see whether the means differ significantly. The meaning of related samples can be illustrated by the following examples:

1. People's scores on a psychological test of creativity are measured at two different points in time in order to see if any improvement has taken place (see Table 12.1). Notice that we have mentioned individuals by name to stress that they are being measured twice – they are *not* different individuals in the two conditions. Also, some of the data have been omitted.

Table 12.1 **Creativity scores measured at two different times**

	1 March	Six months later
Sam	17	19
Jack	14	17
. . .	. . .	. . .
Karl	12	19
Shahida	19	25
Mandy	10	13
Mean	$\overline{X}_1 = 15.09$	$\overline{X}_2 = 18.36$

Table 12.2   **Time of day and memory performance scores**

	Morning	Afternoon
Rebecca	9	15
Sharon	16	23
. . .	. . .	. . .
Neil	18	24
Mean	$\overline{X}_1 = 17.3$	$\overline{X}_2 = 22.1$

Table 12.3   **Reaction time in seconds for drug and no-drug conditions**

	'Nogloom'	Placebo
Jenny	0.27	0.25
David	0.15	0.18
. . .	. . .	. . .
Mean	$\overline{X}_1 = 0.22$	$\overline{X}_2 = 0.16$

2. A group of students' memory test scores are measured in the morning and in the afternoon in order to see whether memory is affected by time of day (Table 12.2).

3. A group of participants in an experiment are assessed in terms of their reaction time to a coloured light when they have taken the anti-depressant drug 'Nogloom' and when they have taken an inert control tablet (placebo) (see Table 12.3).

In each of the above experiments, the researcher wishes to know whether the means of the two conditions differ from each other. The question is whether the mean scores in the two conditions are sufficiently different from each other that they fall in the extreme 5% of cases. If they do, this allows us to generalise from the research findings. In other words, are the two means significantly different from each other?

The key characteristics of all of the above studies is that a group of participants is measured twice on a single variable in slightly different conditions or circumstances. So in the above studies, creativity has been measured twice, memory has been measured twice and reaction time has been measured twice. In other words, they are *repeated measures designs* for the obvious reason that participants have been measured more than once on the same variable. Repeated measures designs are also called *related measures designs* and *correlated scores designs*.

Design consideration: Repeated measures designs of the sort described in this chapter can be problematic. For example, since the participants in the research are measured under both the experimental and control conditions, it could be that their experiences in the experimental condition affect the way they behave in the control condition. Many of the problems can be overcome by *counterbalancing* conditions. By this we mean that a random selection of half of the participants in the research are put through the experimental condition first; the other half are put through the control condition first.

In our opening paragraph we mentioned the related (correlated) *t*-test. There are in fact two versions of the *t*-test – a correlated/related and an uncorrelated/ unrelated samples version. The latter is more likely to be of use to you simply because unrelated designs are commoner in psychological statistics. However, the correlated/related *t*-test is substantially simpler to understand and is useful as a learning aid prior to tackling the more difficult unrelated *t*-test, which is described in Chapter 13.

Design consideration: It is also possible to have a related design if you take pairs of subjects *matched* to be as similar as possible on factors which might be related to their scores on the dependent variable. So pairs of participants might be matched on sex and age so that each member of the pair in question is of the same sex and age group (or as close as possible). One member of the pair would be assigned *at random* to one experimental condition, the other member to the other experimental condition. Using the effects of time of day on memory research question (Table 12.2), the arrangement for a matched pairs or matched subjects design might be as in Table 12.4.

Table 12.4   **A matched pairs design testing memory score**

Matched pairs	Morning score	Afternoon score
Both male and under 20	16	17
Both female and under 20	21	25
Both male and over 20	14	20
Both female and over 20	10	14

The purpose of matching, like using the same person twice, is to reduce the influence of unwanted variables on the comparisons.

12.2　Dependent and independent variables

The scores in Tables 12.1–12.3 are scores on the *dependent variable*. They include the variables creativity, memory and reaction time in the above experiments.

However, there is another variable – the *independent variable*. This refers to the various conditions in which the measurements are being taken. In Table 12.1 measurements are being taken at two different points in time – on 1 March and six months later. The alternative hypothesis is that there *is* a relationship between the independent variable 'time of measurement' and the dependent variable 'creativity score'. Obviously, it is being assumed that creativity scores are *dependent* on the variable time.

12.3　Some basic revision

A *z*-score is simply the number of standard deviations a score is away from the mean of the set of scores. The formula is:

$$z\text{-score} = \frac{X - \overline{X}}{\text{sd}}$$

where X = a particular score, $\overline{X}$ = the mean of the set of scores, and sd = standard deviation of the set of scores.

Remember, once you have obtained the *z*-score, it is possible to use the table of the standard normal distribution (*z*-distribution) (Significance Table 12.1) to identify the relative position of the particular score compared to the rest of the set.

12.4　Theoretical considerations

As we have seen, the most important theoretical concept with any inferential statistical test is the null hypothesis. This states that there is *no* relationship between the two variables in the research. In the previous example the independent variable is time of day and the dependent variable is memory. The null hypothesis is that there is no relation between the independent variable time and the dependent variable memory. This implies, by definition, that the two samples, according to the null hypothesis, come from the same population. In other words, in the final analysis the overall trend is for pairs of samples drawn from this population to have identical means. However, that is the trend over many pairs of samples. The means of some pairs of samples will differ somewhat from each other simply because samples from even the same population tend to vary. Little differences will be more common than big differences.

Another important concept is that of the *t*-distribution. This is a theoretical statistical distribution which is similar to the *z*-distribution discussed in Chapter 5. There is also a *t*-score which is similar to the *z*-score. The *t*-score is based on analogous logic to the *z*-score. The major difference is that the *t*-score involves *standard error* and not standard deviation. As we saw in the previous chapter, the standard error is nothing other than the standard deviation of a set of sample means. Using the *z*-distribution, it is possible to work out the relative standing of any score compared to the rest of the set of scores. Exactly the same applies where one has the standard error of a set of sample means. One can calculate the relative extent to which a particular sample mean differs from the average sample mean. (The average sample mean with many samples will be the same as the mean of the population, so normally the population mean is referred to rather than the average of sample means.) The key formulae are as follows:

$$z = \frac{\text{particular score} - \text{sample mean of scores}}{\text{standard deviation of scores}}$$

$$t = \frac{\text{particular sample mean} - \text{average of sample means}}{\text{standard error of sample means}}$$

or

$$t = \frac{\text{particular sample mean} - \text{population mean}}{\text{standard error of sample means}}$$

As you can see, the form of each of these formulae is identical.

Both *z*- and *t*- refer to standard distributions which are symmetrical and bell-shaped. The *z*-distribution is a normal distribution – the standard normal distribution. Similarly, the *t*-distribution is also a normal distribution when large sample sizes are involved. In fact *z*- and *t*- are identical in these circumstances. As the sample size gets smaller, however, the *t*-distribution becomes a decidedly flatter distribution. Significance Table 12.1 (p. 122) is a table of the *t*-distribution which reports the value of the *t*-score needed to put a sample mean outside the middle 95% of sample means and into the extreme 5% of sample means that are held to be unlikely or *statistically significant* sample means. Notice that the table of the *t*-distribution is structured according to the *degrees of freedom*. Usually this is the sample size minus one if a single sample is used to *estimate* the standard error, otherwise it may be different.

The *t*-test can be applied to the data on the above population. Assume that for a given population, the population mean is 1.0. We have estimated the standard error by taking a known sample of 10 scores, calculating its estimated standard deviation and dividing by the square root of the sample size. All of these stages are combined in the following formula which was discussed in Chapter 11:

$$\text{(Estimated) standard error} = \frac{\sqrt{\dfrac{\Sigma X^2 - \dfrac{(\Sigma X)^2}{N}}{N-1}}}{\sqrt{N}}$$

This has given the (estimated) standard error to be 2.5. We can calculate if a sample with a mean of 8.0 ($N = 10$) is statistically unusual. We simply apply the t-test formula to the information we have:

$$t = \frac{\text{particular sample mean} - \text{population mean}}{\text{standard error of sample means}}$$

$$= \frac{8.0 - 1.0}{2.5}$$

$$= \frac{7.0}{2.5}$$

$$= 2.8$$

In other words, our sample mean is actually 2.8 standard errors *above* the average sample mean (i.e. population mean) of 1.0.

We can now use Significance Table 12.1. This table is distributed according to the number of degrees of freedom involved in the estimation of the population standard deviation. Since the sample size on which this estimate was based is 10, the degrees of freedom are 1 less than 10, i.e. $N - 1 = 9$ degrees of freedom. Significance Table 12.1 tells us that we need a t-score of 2.26 or more to place our particular sample mean in the extreme 5% of sample means drawn from the population. Our obtained t-score was 2.8. This means that our sample mean is within the extreme 5% of sample means, i.e. that it is statistically significantly different from the average of sample means drawn from this particular population.

Wonderful! But what has this got to do with our research problem which we set out at the beginning of this chapter? The above is simply about a single sample compared with a multitude of samples. What we need to know is whether or not *two* sample means are sufficiently different from each other that we can say that the difference is statistically significant. There is just one remaining statistical trick that statisticians employ in these circumstances. That is, *the two samples of scores are turned into a single sample by subtracting one set of scores from the other*. We calculate the difference between a person's score in one sample and their score in the other sample. This leaves us with a sample of difference scores (D) which constitutes the single sample we need. In other words, the standard error of a single sample is sufficient theory.

The stylised data in Table 12.5 show just what is done. The difference scores in the final column are the single sample of scores which we use in our standard error formula. For this particular sample of difference scores the mean is 4.0. According to the null hypothesis, the general trend should be zero difference between the two samples – that is, the mean of the difference scores would be zero if the sample reflected precisely the null hypothesis. Once again we are reliant on the null hypothesis to tell us what the population characteristics are. Since the null hypothesis has it that there is no difference between the *samples*,

Table 12.5   **Basic rearrangement of data for the related samples *t*-test**

Person	Sample 1 (X_1)	Sample 2 (X_2)	Difference $X_1 - X_2 = D$
A	9	5	4
B	7	2	5
C	7	3	4
D	11	6	5
E	7	5	2

there should be zero difference in the population, that is, the average difference score should be 0. (Since the difference between sample means under the null hypothesis that the two samples do not differ is zero by definition, this means that the population mean should be zero. In other words we can delete the population mean from the formula for *t*-scores.) We would of course expect some samples of difference scores to be above or below zero by varying amounts. The question is whether a mean difference of 4.0 is sufficiently different from zero to be statistically significant. If it comes in the middle 95% of the distribution of sample means then we accept the null hypothesis. If it comes in the extreme 5% then we describe it as significant and reject the null hypothesis in favour of the alternative hypothesis. We achieve this by using the *t*-test formula applied to the sample of difference scores. We then test the significance of *t* by comparing it to the values in Significance Table 12.1. For a sample of four, since the degrees of freedom are $N - 1$ which equals 3, the table tells us that we need a *t*-score of 3.18 at the minimum to put our sample mean in the significant extreme 5% of the distribution of sample means.

Calculation 12.1

The related/correlated samples *t*-test

The data are taken from an imaginary study which looked at the relationship between age of an infant and the amount of eye-contact it makes with its mother. The infants were six months old and nine months old at the time of testing – age is the independent variable. The dependent variable is the number of one-minute segments during which the infant made any eye-contact with its mother over a ten-minute session. The null hypothesis is that there is no relation between age and eye-contact. The data are given in Table 12.6 which includes the difference between the six-month and nine-month scores as well as the square of this difference. The number of cases, N, is the number of difference scores, i.e. 8.

Table 12.6   **Steps in calculating the related/correlated samples *t*-test (number of one-minute segments with eye-contact)**

Subject	Six months X_1	Nine months X_2	Difference $D = X_1 - X_2$	Difference² D^2
Baby Clara	3	7	−4	16
Baby Martin	5	6	−1	1
Baby Sally	5	3	2	4
Baby Angie	4	8	−4	16
Baby Trevor	3	5	−2	4
Baby Sam	7	9	−2	4
Baby Bobby	8	7	1	1
Baby Sid	7	9	−2	4
Sums of columns	ΣX_1 = 42	ΣX_2 = 54	ΣD = −12	ΣD^2 = 50
Means of columns	$\overline{X}_1$ = 5.25	$\overline{X}_2$ = 6.75	$\overline{D}$ = −1.5	

We can clearly see from Table 12.6 that the nine-month-old babies are spending more periods in eye-contact with their mothers, on average, than they did when they were six months old. The average difference in eye-contact is 1.5. The question remains, however, whether this difference is statistically significant.

Step 1:   The formula for the standard error of the difference (D) scores is as follows. It is exactly as for Calculation 11.1 except that we have substituted D for X.

$$\text{Standard error} = \frac{\sqrt{\dfrac{\Sigma D^2 - \dfrac{(\Sigma D)^2}{N}}{N-1}}}{\sqrt{N}}$$

Substituting the values from Table 12.6:

$$= \frac{\sqrt{\dfrac{50 - \dfrac{-12^2}{8}}{8-1}}}{\sqrt{8}}$$

$$= \frac{\sqrt{\dfrac{50 - \dfrac{144}{8}}{7}}}{2.828}$$

$$= \frac{\sqrt{\dfrac{50 - 18}{7}}}{2.828}$$

$$= \frac{\sqrt{\dfrac{32}{7}}}{2.828}$$

$$= \frac{\sqrt{4.571}}{2.828}$$

$$= \frac{2.138}{2.828}$$

$$= 0.756$$

Step 2:   We can now enter our previously calculated values in the following formula:

$$t\text{-score} = \frac{\overline{D}}{se}$$

where $\overline{D}$ is the average difference score and se is the standard error

$$= \frac{-1.5}{0.756}$$

$$= -1.98$$

Step 3:   If we look up this *t*-score in Significance Table 12.1 for $N - 1 = 7$ degrees of freedom, we find that we need a *t*-value of 2.37 or more (or –2.37 or less) to put our sample mean in the extreme 5% of sample means. In other words, our sample mean of –1.5 is in the middle 95% of sample means which are held to be statistically not significant. In these circumstances we prefer to believe that the null hypothesis is true. In other words, there is no significant difference between the babies' scores at six and nine months. We would write something like the following in our report: 'The hypothesis that eye-contact differs in six-month and nine-month old babies was not supported at the 5% level of significance.'

Warning comment

The distribution of the difference scores should not be markedly skewed if the *t*-test is to be used. Appendix A explains how to test for significant skewness. If the distribution of difference scores is markedly skewed, you might wish to consider the use of the Wilcoxon Matched Pairs Test (Chapter 18, Calculation 18.2).

Significance Table 12.1   **5% Significance values of related *t* (two-tailed test)**

Your value must be in the listed ranges for your degrees of freedom to be significant at the 5% level (i.e. to accept the hypothesis).

If your required degrees of freedom are not listed, then take the nearest *smaller* listed values. Alternatively extrapolate from listed values.

'More extreme' means that, for example, values in the ranges of +3.18 to infinity or –3.18 to (minus) infinity are statistically significant with 3 degrees of freedom.

Degrees of freedom (always $N - 1$ for related *t*-test)	Significant at 5% level Accept hypothesis
3	±3.18 or more extreme
4	±2.78 or more extreme
5	±2.57 or more extreme
6	±2.45 or more extreme
7	±2.37 or more extreme
8	±2.31 or more extreme
9	±2.26 or more extreme
10	±2.23 or more extreme
11	±2.20 or more extreme
12	±2.18 or more extreme
13	±2.16 or more extreme
14	±2.15 or more extreme
15	±2.13 or more extreme
18	±2.10 or more extreme
20	±2.09 or more extreme
25	±2.06 or more extreme
30	±2.04 or more extreme
40	±2.02 or more extreme
60	±2.00 or more extreme
∞	±1.96 or more extreme

The above table has been adapted and extended from Table III of R.A. Fisher and F. Yates (1974). *Statistical Tables for Biological, Agricultural and Medical Research*. London: Longman. With the kind permission of the publisher.

12.5 Cautionary note

Many psychologists act as if they believe that it is the design of the research which determines whether you should use a related test. Related designs are those, after all, in which people serve in both research conditions. It is assumed that there is a correlation between subjects' scores in the two conditions. What if there is no correlation between the two samples of scores ? The standard error becomes relatively large compared to the number of degrees of freedom so your research is less likely to be statistically significant (especially if the samples are small). So while trying to control for unwanted sources of error, if there is no correlation between the scores in the two conditions of the study, the researcher may simply reduce the likelihood of achieving statistical significance. The reason is that the researcher may have obtained non-significant findings simply because (a) they have reduced the error degrees of freedom, which therefore (b) increases the error estimate, thereby (c) reducing the significance level perhaps to insignificance. Some computer programs print out the correlation between the two variables as part of the correlated *t*-test output. If this correlation is not significant then you might be wise to think again about your test of significance. This situation is particularly likely to occur where you are using a matching procedure (as opposed to having the same people in both conditions). Unless your matching variables actually do correlate with the dependent variable, the matching can have no effect on reducing the error variance.

In the previous calculation, we found no significant change in eye-contact in older compared to younger babies. It is worth examining the correlation between the two sets of scores to see if the assumption of correlation is fulfilled. The correlation is 0.42 but we need a correlation of 0.71 or greater to be statistically significant. In other words the correlated scores do not really correlate – certainly not significantly. Even applying the uncorrelated version of the *t*-test described in the next chapter makes no difference. It still leaves the difference between the two age samples non-significant. We are not for one minute suggesting that if a related *t*-test fails to achieve significance you should replace it by an unrelated *t*-test, merely that you risk ignoring trends in your data which may be important. The most practical implication is that matching variables should relate to the dependent variable, otherwise there is no point in matching in the first place.

12.6 Notes and recommendations

■ The related or correlated *t*-test is merely a special case of the one-way analysis of variance for related samples (Chapter 21). Although it is frequently used in psychological research it tells us nothing more than the equivalent analysis of variance would do. Since the analysis of variance is generally a more flexible statistic allowing any number of groups of scores to be compared, it might be your preferred statistic. However, the common occurrence of the *t*-test in psychological research means that you need to have some idea about what it is.

■ The related *t*-test assumes that the distribution of the difference scores is not markedly skewed. If it is then the test may be unacceptably inaccurate. Appendix A explains how to test for skewness.

- If you compare many pairs of samples with each other in the same study using the *t*-test, you should consult Chapter 23 to find out about appropriate significance levels. There are better ways of making multiple comparisons, as they are called, but with appropriate adjustment to the critical values for signficance, multiple *t*-tests can be justified.

- If you find that your related *t*-test is not significant, it could be that your two samples of scores are not correlated together thus not meeting the assumptions of the related *t*-test.

- The *t*-table presented in this chapter applies whenever we have estimated the standard error from the characteristics of a sample. However, if we had actually known the population standard deviation and consequently the standard error was the actual standard error and not an estimate, we should not use the *t*-distribution table. In these rare (virtually unknown) circumstances, the distribution of the *t*-score formula is that for the *z*-scores.

- Although the correlated *t*-test can be used to compare any pairs of scores, it does not always make sense to do so. For example, you could use the correlated *t*-test to compare the weights and heights of people to see if the weight mean and the height mean differ. Unfortunately, it is a rather stupid thing to do since the numerical values involved relate to radically different things which are not comparable with each other. It is the comparison which is nonsensical in this case. The statistical test is not to blame. On the other hand, one could compare a sample of people's weights at different points in time quite meaningfully.

Chapter 13

The *t*-test

Comparing two groups of unrelated/uncorrelated scores

Preparation

This chapter will be easier if you have mastered the related t-test *of Chapter 12. Revise dependent and independent variables from that chapter.*

The *t*-test described in this chapter has various names. The unrelated *t*-test, the uncorrelated scores *t*-test and the independent samples *t*-test are the commonest variants. It is also known as the Student *t*-test after its inventor who used the pen-name Student.

13.1 Introduction

Often researchers compare two groups of scores from *two* separate groups of individuals to assess whether the average score of one group is higher than that of the other group. The possible research topics involved in such comparisons are limitless:

1. One might wish to compare an experimental group with a control group. For example, do volunteer women who are randomly assigned to a sex abstinence condition have more erotic dreams than those in the sexually active control group? The independent variable is sexual activity (which has two levels – sexually abstinent and sexually active) and the dependent variable is the number of erotic dreams in a month (see Table 13.1). The independent variable differentiates the two groups being compared. In the present example this is the amount of sexual activity (sexually abstinent versus sexually active). The dependent variable is the variable which might be influenced by

Table 13.1 **Number of erotic dreams per month in experimental and control groups**

Experimental group: sexually abstinent	Control group: sexually active
17	10
14	12
16	7

Table 13.2 **Decision time (seconds) in experienced and inexperienced managers**

Experienced managers	Inexperienced managers
24	167
32	133
27	74

Table 13.3 **Number of times bullied in a year in schools with different discipline policies**

Strict policy	Counselling
8	12
5	1
2	3

the independent variable. These variables correspond to the scores given in the main body of the table (i.e. number of erotic dreams).

2. A group of experienced managers may be compared with a group of inexperienced managers in terms of the amount of time which they take to make complex decisions. The independent variable is experience in management (which has two levels – experienced versus inexperienced) and the dependent variable is decision-making time (Table 13.2).

3. A researcher might compare the amount of bullying in two schools, one with a strict and punitive policy and the other with a policy of counselling on discipline infringements. A sample of children from each school is interviewed and the number of times they have been bullied in the previous school year obtained. The independent variable is policy on discipline (which has two levels – strict versus counselling); and the dependent variable is the number of times a child has been bullied in the previous school year (see Table 13.3).

The basic requirements for the unrelated/uncorrelated scores *t*-test are straightforward enough – two groups of scores coming from two distinct groups of people. The scores should be roughly similar in terms of the shapes of their distributions. Ideally both distributions should be bell-shaped and symmetrical. However, there can be marked deviance from this ideal and the test will remain sufficiently accurate.

The *t*-test is the name of a statistical technique which examines whether the two groups of scores have significantly *different* means – in other words, how likely is it that there could be a difference between the two groups as big as the one obtained if there is no difference in reality in the population?

13.2 Theoretical considerations

The basic theoretical assumption underlying the use of the *t*-test involves the characteristics of the null hypothesis. We explained null hypotheses in Chapter 10. The following explanation uses the same format for null hypotheses as we used in that chapter.

Null hypotheses are statements that there is no relationship between two variables. The two variables in question at the moment are the independent and dependent variables. *This is another way of saying that there is no difference between the means of the two groups (i.e. columns) of scores.* The simplest null hypotheses for the above three studies are:

1. There is no relationship between sexual activity and the number of erotic dreams women have.
2. Managerial experience is not related to speed of complex decision making.
3. The disciplinary style of a school is not related to the amount of bullying.

The alternative hypotheses to these null hypotheses can be obtained by simply deleting *no* or *not* from each of the above. Notice that the above way of writing the null hypothesis is relatively streamlined compared to what you often read in books and journals. So do not be surprised if you come across null hypotheses expressed in much more clumsy language such as:

4. Women who abstain from sex will have the same number of erotic dreams as women who are sexually active.
5. Erotic dreams do not occur at different frequencies in sexually active and sexually inactive women.

Styles 4 and 5 tend to obscure the fact that null hypotheses are fundamentally similar irrespective of the type of research under consideration.

The erotic dreams experiment will be used to illustrate the theoretical issues. There are two different samples of scores defined by the independent variable – one for the sexually abstinent group and the other for the sexually active group. The scores in Table 13.4 are the numbers of sexual dreams that each woman

Table 13.4 **Possible data from the sexual activity and erotic dreams experiment (dreams per seven days)**

Subject	Sexually abstinent condition	Subject	Sexually active condition
Lindsay	6	Janice	2
Claudine	7	Jennifer	5
Sharon	7	Joanne	4
Natalie	8	Anne-Marie	5
Sarah	9	Helen	6
Wendy	10	Amanda	6
Ruth	8	Sophie	5
Angela	9		

Table 13.5 **Imaginary population of scores for erotic dreams study**

Experimental group: sexually abstinent	Control group: sexually active
8	6
7	8
6	7
7	4
5	6
5	9
2	10
3	6
6	4
7	7
7	9
9	8
8	7
7	5
4	2
6	3
10	6
9	7
7	8
5	7
4	6
6	7
7	5
8	5
6	7

in the study has in a seven-day period. We can see that, on average, the sexually active women have fewer erotic dreams. Does this reflect a generalisable (significant) difference? The data might be as in Table 13.4. Apart from suggesting that Wendy's fantasy life is wonderful, the table indicates that sexual abstinence leads to an increase in erotic dreams.

The *null hypothesis* suggests that the scores in the two samples come from the same population since it claims that there is no relationship between the independent and dependent variables. That is, for all intents and purposes, the two samples can be construed as coming from a single population of scores; there is no difference between them due to the independent variable. Any differences between samples drawn from this null-hypothesis-defined population are due to chance factors rather than a true relationship between the independent and dependent variables. Table 13.5 is an imaginary population of scores from this null-hypothesis-defined population on the dependent variable 'number of erotic dreams'. The table also indicates whether the score is that of a sexually abstinent woman or a sexually active one. If the two columns of scores are examined carefully, there are no differences between the two sets of scores. In other words, they have the same average scores. Statistically, all of the scores in Table 13.5 can be regarded as coming from the same population. There is no relationship between sexual activity and the number of erotic dreams.

Given that the two samples (sexually abstinent and sexually active) come from the same population of scores on erotic dreams, in general we would expect no difference between pairs of samples drawn at random from this single population. Of course, sampling always introduces a chance element so some pairs of samples would be different but mostly the differences will cluster around zero.

Table 13.6   **Random samples of scores from population in Table 13.5 to represent experimental and control conditions**

Experimental group: sexually abstinent	Control group: sexually active
4	5
5	5
10	10
7	9
7	7
5	7
7	8
9	6
9	2
8	
$\overline{X}_1 = 7.100$	$\overline{X}_2 = 6.556$

Table 13.7   Forty pairs of random samples from the population in Table 13.5

Experimental group: sexually abstinent $N = 10$	Control group: sexually active $N = 9$	Difference (column 1 – column 2)
6.100	6.444	–0.344
6.300	5.444	0.856
6.000	6.556	–0.556
6.400	6.778	–0.378
6.600	6.111	0.489
5.700	6.111	–0.411
6.700	6.111	0.589
6.300	5.667	0.633
6.400	6.667	–0.267
5.900	5.778	0.122
6.400	6.556	–0.156
6.360	6.444	–0.084
6.400	6.778	–0.378
6.200	6.222	–0.022
5.600	5.889	–0.289
6.100	6.222	–0.122
6.800	6.667	0.133
6.100	6.222	–0.122
6.900	6.000	0.900
7.200	5.889	1.311
5.800	7.333	–1.533
6.700	6.889	–0.189
6.200	6.000	0.200
6.500	6.444	0.056
5.900	6.444	–0.544
6.000	6.333	–0.333
6.300	6.778	–0.478
6.100	5.778	0.322
6.000	6.000	0.000
6.000	6.667	–0.667
6.556	6.778	–0.222
6.700	5.778	0.922
5.600	7.000	–1.400
6.600	6.222	0.378
5.600	6.667	–1.067
5.900	7.222	–1.322
6.000	6.667	–0.667
7.000	6.556	0.444
6.400	6.556	–0.156
6.900	6.222	0.678

Overall, numerous pairs of samples will yield an *average* difference of zero. We are assuming that we consistently subtract the sexually active mean from the sexually abstinent mean (or vice versa – it doesn't matter so long as we always do the same thing) so that positive and negative differences cancel each other out.

Since in this case we know the population of scores under the null hypothesis, we could pick out samples of 10 scores at random from the population to represent the sexually abstinent sample and, say, nine scores from the population to represent the sexually active sample. (Obviously the sample sizes will vary and they do not have to be equal.) Any convenient randomisation procedure could be used to select the samples (e.g. computer generated, random number tables or numbers drawn from a hat). The two samples selected at random, together with their respective means, are listed in Table 13.6 (p. 129).

Examining Table 13.6, we can clearly see that there is a difference between the two sample means. This difference is 7.100 – 6.556 or 0.544. This difference between the two sample means has been obtained despite the fact that we know that there is no relationship between the independent variable and the dependent variable in the null-hypothesis-defined population. This is the nature of the random sampling process.

We can repeat this experiment by drawing more pairs of samples of these sizes from the null-hypothesis-defined population. This is shown for 40 new pairs of variables in Table 13.7.

Many of the differences between the pairs of means in Table 13.7 are very close to zero. This is just as we would expect since the independent and dependent variables are not related. Nevertheless, the means of some pairs of samples are somewhat different. In Table 13.7, 95% of the differences between the two means come in the range 0.922 to –1.400. (Given the small number of samples we have used, it is not surprising that this range is not symmetrical. If we had taken large numbers of samples, we would have expected more symmetry. Furthermore, had we used normally distributed scores, the symmetry may have been better.) The middle 95% of the distribution of differences between pairs of sample means are held clearly to support the null hypothesis. The extreme 5% beyond this middle range are held more likely to support the alternative hypothesis.

The standard deviation of the 40 'difference' scores gives the standard error of the differences. Don't forget we are dealing with *sample* means so the term standard error is the correct one. The value of the standard error is 0.63. This is the 'average' amount by which the differences between sample means is likely to deviate from the population mean difference of zero.

13.3 Standard deviation and standard error

The trouble with all of the above is that it is abstract theory. Normally we know nothing for certain about the populations from which our samples come. Fortunately, quite a lot can be inferred about the population given the null hypothesis and information from the samples:

1. Since the null hypothesis states that there is no relationship between the independent and dependent variables in the population, it follows that there should be no systematic difference between the scores in the pair of samples. That is, the average difference between the two means should be zero over many pairs of samples.

2. We can use the scores in a sample to estimate the standard deviation of the scores in the population. However, if we use our usual standard deviation formula the estimate tends to be somewhat too low. Consequently we have to modify our standard deviation formula (Chapter 5) when estimating the standard deviation of the population. The change is minimal – the N in the bottom half of the formula is changed to $N-1$:

$$\text{Estimated standard deviation} = \sqrt{\frac{\Sigma X^2 - \frac{(\Sigma X)^2}{N}}{N-1}}$$

The net effect of this adjustment is to increase the estimated standard deviation in the population – the amount of adjustment is greatest if we are working with small sample sizes for which subtracting 1 is a big adjustment.

But this only gives us the estimated standard deviation of the *scores* in the population. We really need to know about the standard deviation (i.e. standard error) of sample means taken from that population. Remember, there is a simple formula which converts the estimated standard deviation of the population to the estimated standard error of sample means drawn from that population – we simply divide the estimated standard deviation by the square root of the sample size. It so happens that the computationally most useful way of working out the standard error is as follows:

$$\text{Standard error} = \frac{\sqrt{\frac{\Sigma X^2 - \frac{(\Sigma X)^2}{N}}{N-1}}}{\sqrt{N}}$$

Still we haven't finished because this is the estimated standard error of *sample means*; we want the estimated standard error of *differences between pairs of sample means*. It makes intuitive sense that the standard error of differences between pairs of sample means is likely to be the sum of the standard errors of the two samples. After all, the standard error is merely the average amount by which a sample mean differs from the population mean of zero. So the standard error of the differences between pairs of sample means drawn from a population should be the two separate standard errors combined.

Well, that is virtually the procedure. However, the two different standard errors are added together in a funny sort of way:

$$se_{[of \text{ differences between sample means}]} = \sqrt{(se_1^2 + se_2^2)}$$

Finally, because the sample sizes used to estimate the two individual standard errors are not always the same, it is necessary to adjust the equation to account for this, otherwise you end up with the wrong answer. The computational formula for the estimated standard error of differences between pairs of sample means is as follows:

Standard error of differences between pairs of sample means

$$= \sqrt{\left(\frac{\left(\Sigma X_1^2 - \frac{(\Sigma X_1)^2}{N_1} \right) + \left(\Sigma X_2^2 - \frac{(\Sigma X_2)^2}{N_2} \right)}{N_1 + N_2 - 2} \right) \left(\frac{1}{N_1} + \frac{1}{N_2} \right)}$$

Although this looks appallingly complicated, the basic idea is fairly simple. It looks complex because of the adjustment for different sample sizes.

Now we simply use the *t*-test formula. The average difference between the pairs of sample means is zero assuming the null hypothesis to be true. The *t* formula is:

$$t = \frac{\text{sample 1 mean} - \text{sample 2 mean} - 0}{\text{standard error of differences between sample means}}$$

or

$$t = \frac{\text{difference between the two sample means} - 0}{\text{standard error of differences between sample means}}$$

Since in the above formula the population mean of difference between pairs of sample means is always zero, we can omit it:

$$t = \frac{\text{sample 1 mean} - \text{sample 2 mean}}{\text{standard error of differences between sample means}}$$

The formula expressed in full looks very complicated:

$$t = \frac{\overline{X}_1 - \overline{X}_2}{\sqrt{\left(\frac{\left(\Sigma X_1^2 - \frac{(\Sigma X_1)^2}{N_1} \right) + \left(\Sigma X_2^2 - \frac{(\Sigma X_2)^2}{N_2} \right)}{N_1 + N_2 - 2} \right) \left(\frac{1}{N_1} + \frac{1}{N_2} \right)}}$$

So *t* is the number of standard errors by which the difference between our two sample means differs from the population mean of zero. The distribution of *t* is rather like the distribution of *z* if you have a large sample – thus it approximates very closely the normal distribution. However, with smaller sample sizes the curve of *t* becomes increasingly flatter and more spread out than the normal curve. Consequently we need different *t*-distributions for different sample sizes.

Significance Table 13.1 gives values for the *t*-distributions. Notice that the distribution is dependent on the degrees of freedom which for this *t*-test is the total number of scores in the two samples combined minus 2.

Significance Table 13.1 **5% Significance values of unrelated *t* (two-tailed test)**

Your value must be in the listed ranges for your degrees of freedom to be significant at the 5% level (i.e. to accept the hypothesis).

If your required degrees of freedom are not listed, then take the nearest *smaller* listed values. Alternatively extrapolate from listed values.

'More extreme' means that, for example, values in the ranges of +3.18 to infinity or –3.18 to (minus) infinity are statistically significant with 3 degrees of freedom.

Degrees of freedom (always $N - 2$ for unrelated *t*-test)	Significant at 5% level Accept hypothesis
3	±3.18 or more extreme
4	±2.78 or more extreme
5	±2.57 or more extreme
6	±2.45 or more extreme
7	±2.37 or more extreme
8	±2.31 or more extreme
9	±2.26 or more extreme
10	±2.23 or more extreme
11	±2.20 or more extreme
12	±2.18 or more extreme
13	±2.16 or more extreme
14	±2.15 or more extreme
15	±2.13 or more extreme
18	±2.10 or more extreme
20	±2.09 or more extreme
25	±2.06 or more extreme
30	±2.04 or more extreme
40	±2.02 or more extreme
60	±2.00 or more extreme
∞	±1.96 or more extreme

The above table has been adapted and extended from Table III of R.A. Fisher and F. Yates (1974). *Statistical Tables for Biological, Agricultural and Medical Research*. London: Longman. With the kind permission of the publisher.

Calculation 13.11

The unrelated (uncorrelated) *t*-test

The calculation of the unrelated *t*-test uses the following formula:

$$t = \frac{\overline{X}_1 - \overline{X}_2}{\sqrt{\left(\dfrac{\left(\Sigma X_1^2 - \dfrac{(\Sigma X_1)^2}{N_1}\right) + \left(\Sigma X_2^2 - \dfrac{(\Sigma X_2)^2}{N_2}\right)}{N_1 + N_2 - 2}\right)\left(\dfrac{1}{N_1} + \dfrac{1}{N_2}\right)}}$$

Horrific, isn't it? Probably the worst formula that you are likely to use in psychological statistics. However, it contains little new. It is probably best to break the formula down into its component calculations and take things step-by-step. However, if you prefer to try to work directly with the above formula do not let us stand in your way.

The data are from an imaginary study involving the emotionality of children from lone-parent and children from two-parent families. The independent variable is family type which has two levels – the lone-parent type and the two-parent type. The dependent variable is emotionality on a standard psychological measure – the higher the score on this test, the more emotional is the child. The data are listed in Table 13.8.

Table 13.8   Emotionality scores in two-parent and lone-parent families

Two-parent family X_1	Lone-parent family X_2
12	6
18	9
14	4
10	13
19	14
8	9
15	8
11	12
10	11
13	9
15	
16	

A key thing to note is that we have called the scores for the two-parent family condition X_1 and those for the lone-parent family condition X_2.

Step 1:   Extend the data table by adding columns of squared scores, column totals, and sample sizes as in Table 13.9. The sample size for $X_1 = N_1 = 12$; the sample size for $X_2 = N_2 = 10$.

ΣX_1 = sum of scores for two-parent family sample
ΣX_1^2 = sum of squared scores for two-parent family sample
ΣX_2 = sum of scores for lone-parent family sample
ΣX_2^2 = sum of squared scores for lone-parent family sample

Table 13.9   **Table 13.8 extended to include steps in the calculation**

Two-parent family X_1	Square previous column X_1^2	Lone-parent family X_2	Square previous column X_2^2
12	144	6	36
18	324	9	81
14	196	4	16
10	100	13	169
19	361	14	196
8	64	9	81
15	225	8	64
11	121	12	144
10	100	11	121
13	169	9	81
15	225		
16	256		
$\Sigma X_1 = 161$	$\Sigma X_1^2 = 2285$	$\Sigma X_2 = 95$	$\Sigma X_2^2 = 989\,0$

Step 2:   Do each of the following calculations.

Calculation A:

$$A = \frac{\Sigma X_1}{N_1} - \frac{\Sigma X_2}{N_2}$$

$$= \frac{161}{12} - \frac{95}{10}$$

$$= 13.417 - 9.500$$

$$= 3.917$$

Calculation B:

$$B = \Sigma X_1^2 - \frac{(\Sigma X_1)^2}{N_1}$$

$$= 2285 - \frac{161^2}{12}$$

$$= 2285 - \frac{25921}{12}$$

$$= 2285 - 2160.0833$$

$$= 124.9167$$

Calculation C:

$$C = \Sigma X_2^2 \ - \ \frac{(\Sigma X_2)^2}{N_2}$$

$$= \ 989 \ - \ \frac{95^2}{10}$$

$$= \ 989 \ - \ \frac{9025}{10}$$

$$= \ 989 - 902.5$$

$$= \ 86.5$$

Calculation D:

$$D = \ N_1 + N_2 - 2$$

$$= \ 12 + 10 - 2$$

$$= \ 20$$

Calculation E:

$$E = \ \frac{1}{N_1} \ + \ \frac{1}{N_2}$$

$$= \ \frac{1}{12} \ + \ \frac{1}{10}$$

$$= \ 0.0833 + 0.1000$$

$$= \ 0.1833$$

Calculation F:

$$F = \ \left(\frac{B + C}{D} \right) \ \times E$$

$$= \ \left(\frac{124.9167 + 86.5000}{20} \right) \ \times 0.1833$$

$$= \ \left(\frac{211.4167}{20} \right) \ \times 0.1833$$

$$= \ 10.57083 \times 0.1833$$

$$= \ 1.938$$

Calculation G:

$$G = \sqrt{F}$$
$$= \sqrt{1.938}$$
$$= 1.392$$

Calculation t:

$$t = \frac{A}{G}$$
$$= \frac{3.917}{1.392}$$
$$= 2.81$$

Step 3: t is the t-score or the number of standard errors our sample data are away from the population mean of zero. We use Significance Table 13.1 to check the statistical significance of our value of 2.81 by checking against the row for degrees of freedom (i.e. $N_1 + N_2 - 2 = 20$ degrees of freedom). This table tells us that our value of t is in the extreme 5% of the distribution because it is larger than 2.09; so we reject the null hypothesis that family structure is unrelated to emotionality. Our study showed that emotionality is significantly greater in the two-parent family structure as opposed to the lone-parent family structure.

13.4 Cautionary note

You should not use the t-test if your samples are markedly skewed, especially if they are skewed in opposite directions. Appendix A explains how to test for skewness. You might consider using the Mann–Whitney U-test in these circumstances (Chapter 18, Calculation 18.3).

13.5 Notes and recommendations

■ The t-test is commonly used in psychological research. So it is important that you have an idea of what it does. However, it is only a special case of the analysis of variance (Chapter 20) which is a much more flexible statistic. Given the analysis of variance's ability to handle any number of samples, you might just prefer to use it instead of the t-test in most circumstances. To complicate matters, some use the t-test in the analysis of variance.

■ The t-test assumes that the variances of the two samples are similar so that they can be combined together to yield an overall estimate. However, if the variances of the two samples are significantly different from each other, you should not use this version of the *t*-test. The way to see if two variances are dissimilar is to use the variance ratio test described in Chapter 18.

■ If you wish to use the *t*-test but find that you fall foul of this *F*-ratio requirement, there is a version of the *t*-test which does not assume equal variances. The best way of doing such *t*-tests is to use a computer package which applies both tests to the same data. Unfortunately the calculation for the degrees of freedom is a little complex (you can have fractions involved in the values) and it goes a little beyond reasonable hand calculations. The calculation details are provided in Blalock (1972).

Chapter 14

Chi-square

Differences between samples of frequency data

Preparation

Crosstabulation/contingency tables; samples and populations.

> Often, chi-square is written as χ^2. However, we have avoided Greek letters as far as possible.

14.1 Introduction

If a researcher has several samples of data which involve *frequencies* rather than scores, a statistical test designed for frequency data must be used. The following are some examples of research of this sort:

1. Male and female schoolchildren are compared in terms of wanting to be psychologists when they leave school (Table 14.1).

2. The sexual orientations of a sample of religious men are compared with those of a non-religious sample (Table 14.2).

Table 14.1   **Relationship between sex and wanting to be a psychologist**

Intention	Male	Female
Wants to be a psychologist	$f = 17$	$f = 98$
Does not want to be a psychologist	$f = 67$	$f = 35$

Table 14.2   **Relationship between sexual orientation and religion**

Orientation	Religious	Non-religious
Heterosexual	57	105
Gay	13	27
Bisexual	8	17

Table 14.3   **Relationship between doll choice and ethnicity**

Choice	Black child	White child	Mixed-race child
Black doll	19	17	5
White doll	16	18	9

Table 14.4   **Stylised table for chi-square**

Category	Sample 1	Sample 2	Sample 3
Category 1	27	21	5
Category 2	19	20	19
Category 3	9	17	65

3. Choosing to play with either a black or a white doll in black and white children (Table 14.3).

In each of these examples, both variables consist of a relatively small number of categories. In other words, schematically each study approximates to the form shown in Table 14.4 in which the independent variable is the sample and the dependent variable consists of one of several categories.

The precise number of samples may vary from study to study and the number of categories of the dependent variable can be two or more. As a rule of thumb, *it is better to have just a few samples and a few categories*, since large tables can be difficult to interpret and generally require large numbers of participants or cases to be workable.

The 'cells' of Table 14.4 (called a *crosstabulation* or *contingency* table) contain the frequencies of individuals in that particular sample and that particular category. So the 'cell' which corresponds to Sample 2 and Category 3 contains the frequency 17. This means that in your data there are 17 cases in Sample 2 which also fit Category 3. In other words, a cell is the intersection of a row and a column.

The statistical question is whether the distribution of frequencies in the different samples is so varied that it is unlikely that these all come from the same population. As ever this population is the one defined by the null hypothesis (which suggests that there is no relationship between the independent and dependent variables).

14.2 Theoretical issues

Imagine a research study in which children are asked to choose between two television programmes, one violent and the other non-violent. Some of the children have been in trouble at school for fighting and the others have not been in trouble. The researcher wants to know if there is a relationship between the violence of the preferred television programme and having been in trouble for fighting at school. The data might look something like Table 14.5.

We can see from Table 14.5 that the fighters (sample 1) are relatively more likely to prefer the violent programme and the non-fighters (sample 2) are relatively more likely to prefer the non-violent programme. The frequencies obtained in the research are known as the *observed* frequencies. This merely refers to the fact that we obtain them from our empirical *observations* (that is, the data).

Assume that both of the samples come from the same population of data in which there is no relationship between the dependent and independent variables. This implies that any differences between the samples are merely due to the chance fluctuations of sampling. A useful index of how much the samples differ from each other is based on how different each sample is from the population distribution defined by the null hypothesis. As ever, since we do not know the population directly in most research, we have to estimate its characteristics from the characteristics of samples.

With the chi-square test, we simply *add* together the frequencies for whatever number of samples we have. These sums are then used as an estimate of the distribution of the different categories in the population. Since differences between the samples under the null hypothesis are solely due to chance factors, by combining samples together the best possible estimate of the characteristics of the population is obtained. In other words, we simply add together the characteristics of two or more samples to give us an estimate of the population distribution of the categories. The first stage of doing this is illustrated in Table 14.6.

Table 14.5   **Relationship between preferred TV programme and fighting**

Preference	Sample 1 Fighters	Sample 2 Non-fighters
Violent TV preferred	40	15
Non-violent TV preferred	30	70

Table 14.6 **Relationship between preferred TV programme and fighting including the marginal frequencies (column and row frequencies)**

Preference	Sample 1 Fighters	Sample 2 Non-fighters	Row frequencies
Violent TV preferred	40	15	55
Non-violent TV preferred	30	70	100
Column frequencies	70	85	Overall frequencies = 155

So in the null-hypothesis-defined population, we would expect 55 out of every 155 to prefer the violent programme and 100 out of 155 to prefer the non-violent programme. But we obtained 40 out of 70 preferring the violent programme in Sample 1, and 15 out of 85 preferring the violent programme in Sample 2. How do these figures match the expectations from the population defined by the null hypothesis? We need to calculate the expected frequencies of the cells in Table 14.6. This calculation is based on the assumption that the null hypothesis population frequencies are our best information as to the relative proportions preferring the violent and non-violent programmes if there truly was no difference between the samples.

Sample 1 contains 70 children; if the null hypothesis is true then we would expect 55 out of every 155 of these to prefer the violent programme. Thus our expected frequency of those preferring the violent programme in Sample 1 is:

$$70 \times \frac{55}{155} = 70 \times 0.354 = 24.84$$

Similarly, since we expect under the null hypothesis 100 out of every 155 to prefer the non-violent programme, then our expected frequency of those preferring the non-violent programme in Sample 1 out of the 70 children in that sample is

$$70 \times \frac{100}{155} = 70 \times 0.645 = 45.16$$

Notice that the sum of the expected frequencies for Sample 1 is the same as the number of children in that sample (24.84 + 45.16 = 70).

We can apply the same logic to Sample 2 which contains 85 children. We expect that 55 out of every 155 will prefer the violent programme and 100 out of every 155 will prefer the non-violent programme. The expected frequency preferring the violent programme in Sample 2 is:

$$85 \times \frac{55}{155} = 85 \times 0.354 = 30.16$$

Table 14.7   Contingency table including both observed and expected frequencies

Preference	Sample 1 Fighters	Sample 2 Non-fighters	Row frequencies
Violent TV preferred	Observed frequency = 40 *Expected frequency = 24.84*	Observed frequency = 15 *Expected frequency = 30.16*	55
Non-violent TV preferred	Observed frequency = 30 *Expected frequency = 45.16*	Observed frequency = 70 *Expected frequency = 54.84*	100
Column frequencies (i.e. sum of observed frequencies in column)	70	85	Overall frequencies = 155

The expected frequency preferring the non-violent programme in Sample 2 is:

$$85 \times \frac{100}{155} = 85 \times 0.645 = 54.84$$

We can enter these expected frequencies (population frequencies under the null hypothesis) into our table of frequencies (Table 14.7).

The chi-square statistic is based on the differences between the observed and the expected frequencies. It should be fairly obvious that the greater the disparity between the observed frequencies and the population frequencies under the null hypothesis, the less likely is the null hypothesis to be true. Thus if the samples are very different from each other, the differences between the observed and expected frequencies will be large. Chi-square involves calculating the overall disparity between the observed and expected frequencies over all the cells in the table. To be precise, the chi-square formula involves the squared deviations over the expected frequencies, but this is merely a slight diversion to make our formula fit a convenient statistical distribution which is called chi-square. The calculated value of chi-square is then compared with a table of critical values of chi-square (Significance Table 14.1) in order to estimate the probability of obtaining our pattern of frequencies by chance (if the null hypothesis of no differences between the samples was true). This table is organised according to degrees of freedom, which is always (number of columns of data – 1) × (number of rows of data – 1). This would be (2 – 1) × (2 – 1) or 1 for Table 14.7.

Significance Table 14.1   **5% and 1% significance values of chi-square (two-tailed test)**

Your value must be in the listed ranges for your degrees of freedom to be significant at the 5% level (column 2) or the 1% level (column 3) (i.e. to accept the hypothesis).

Degrees of freedom	Significant at 5% level Accept hypothesis	Significant at 1% level Accept hypothesis
1	3.8 or more	6.7 or more
2	6.0 or more	9.2 or more
3	7.8 or more	11.3 or more
4	9.5 or more	13.3 or more
5	11.1 or more	15.1 or more
6	12.6 or more	16.8 or more
7	14.1 or more	18.5 or more
8	15.5 or more	20.1 or more
9	16.9 or more	21.7 or more
10	18.3 or more	23.2 or more
11	19.7 or more	24.7 or more
12	21.0 or more	26.2 or more

The above table has been adapted and extended from Table IV of R.A. Fisher and F. Yates (1974). *Statistical Tables for Biological, Agricultural and Medical Research*. London: Longman. With the kind permission of the publisher.

Calculation 14.1

Chi-square

The calculation of chi-square involves several relatively simple but repetitive calculations. For each cell in the chi-square table you calculate the following:

$$\frac{(\text{observed frequency} - \text{expected frequency})^2}{\text{expected frequency}}$$

The only complication is that this small calculation is repeated for each of the cells in your crosstabulation or contingency table. The formula in full becomes:

$$\text{Chi-square} = \Sigma \ \frac{(O - E)^2}{E}$$

where O = observed frequency, and E = expected frequency.

The following is an imaginary piece of research in which teenage boys and girls were asked to name their favourite type of television programme from a list of three – (1) soap operas, (2) crime dramas, and (3) neither of these. The researcher suspects that sex may be related to programme preference (Table 14.8).

Table 14.8　**Relationship between favourite type of TV programme and sex of respondent**

Respondents	Soap opera	Crime drama	Neither	Totals
Males	Observed = 27	Observed = 14	Observed = 19	Row 1 = 60
Females	Observed = 17	Observed = 33	Observed = 9	Row 2 = 59
Totals	Column 1 = 44	Column 2 = 47	Column 3 = 28	Total = 119

We next need to calculate the expected frequencies for each of the cells in Table 14.8. One easy way of doing this is to multiply the row total and the column total for each particular cell and divide by the total number of observations (i.e. total frequencies). This is shown in Table 14.9.

Table 14.9　**Calculation of expected frequencies by multiplying appropriate row and column totals and then dividing by overall total**

Respondents	Soap opera	Crime drama	Neither	Totals
Males	Observed = 27 *Expected = 60 ×* *44/119 = 22.185*	Observed = 14 *Expected = 60 ×* *47/119 = 23.697*	Observed = 19 *Expected = 60 ×* *28/119 = 14.118*	Row 1 = 60
Females	Observed = 17 *Expected = 59 ×* *44/119 = 21.815*	Observed = 33 *Expected = 59 ×* *47/119 = 23.303*	Observed = 9 *Expected = 59 ×* *28/119 = 13.882*	Row 2 = 59
Totals	Column 1 = 44	Column 2 = 47	Column 3 = 28	Total = 119

We then simply substitute the above values in the chi-square formula:

$$\text{Chi-square} = \Sigma \; \frac{(O - E)^2}{E}$$

$$= \frac{(27 - 22.185)^2}{22.185} + \frac{(14 - 23.697)^2}{23.697} + \frac{(19 - 14.118)^2}{14.118} + \frac{(17 - 21.815)^2}{21.815} + \frac{(33 - 23.303)^2}{23.303} + \frac{(9 - 13.882)^2}{13.882}$$

$$= \frac{4.815^2}{22.185} + \frac{(-9.697)^2}{23.697} + \frac{4.882^2}{14.118} + \frac{(-4.815)^2}{21.815} + \frac{9.697^2}{23.303} + \frac{(-4.882)^2}{13.882}$$

$$= \frac{23.184}{22.185} + \frac{94.032}{23.697} + \frac{23.834}{14.118} + \frac{23.184}{21.815} + \frac{94.032}{23.303} + \frac{23.834}{13.882}$$

$$= 1.045 + 3.968 + 1.688 + 1.063 + 4.035 + 1.717$$

$$= 13.52$$

The degrees of freedom are the number of columns – 1 × the number of rows – 1 = (3 – 1) × (2 – 1) = 2 degrees of freedom.

We then check the table of the critical values of chi-square (Significance Table 14.1) in order to assess whether or not our samples differ amongst each other so much that they are unlikely to be produced by the population defined by the null hypothesis. The value must equal or exceed the tabulated value to be significant at the listed level of significance. Some tables will give you more degrees of freedom but you will be hard pressed to do a sensible chi-square that exceeds 12 degrees of freedom.

Our value of chi-square is well in excess of the minimum value of 6.0 needed to be significant at the 5% level for 2 degrees of freedom, so we reject the hypothesis that the samples came from the population defined by the null hypothesis. Thus we accept the hypothesis that there is a relationship between television programme preferences and sex.

14.3 Partitioning chi-square

There is no problem when the chi-square contingency table is just two columns and two rows. The chi-square in these circumstances tells you that your two samples are different from each other. But if you have, say, a 2 × 3 chi-square (e.g. you have two samples and three categories) then there is some uncertainty as to what a significant chi-square means – does it mean that all three samples are different from each other, that sample 1 and sample 2 are different, that sample 1 and sample 3 are different, or that sample 2 and sample 3 are different? In the television programmes example, although we obtained a significant overall chi-square, there is some doubt as to why we obtained this, The major differences between the sexes are between the soap opera and crime drama conditions rather than between the soap opera and the 'other' condition.

It is a perfectly respectable statistical procedure to break your large chi-square into a number of 2 × 2 chi-square tests to assess precisely where the significant differences lie. Thus in the TV programmes study you could generate *three* separate chi-squares from the 2 × 3 contingency table. These are illustrated in Table 14.10.

These three separate chi-squares each have just one degree of freedom (because they are 2 × 2 tables). If you calculate chi-square for each of these tables you hopefully should be able to decide precisely where the differences are between samples and conditions.

The only difficulty is the significance levels you use. Because you are doing three separate chi-squares, the normal significance level of 5% still operates but it is *divided between the three chi-squares* you have carried out. In other words we share the 5% between three to give us the 1.667% level for each – any of the three chi-squares would have to be significant at this level to be reported as being

Table 14.10   **Three partitioned sub-tables from the 2 × 3 Contingency Table 14.8**

(1) Soap Opera versus Crime Drama

Respondents	Soap opera	Crime drama	Totals
Males	27	14	Row 1 = 41
Females	17	33	Row 2 = 50
Totals	Column 1 = 44	Column 2 = 47	Total = 91

(2) Soap Opera versus Neither

Respondents	Soap opera	Neither	Totals
Males	27	19	Row 1 = 46
Females	17	9	Row 2 = 26
Totals	Column 1 = 44	Column 3 = 28	Total = 72

(3) Crime Drama versus Neither

Respondents	Crime drama	Neither	Totals
Males	14	19	Row 1 = 33
Females	33	9	Row 2 = 42
Totals	Column 2 = 47	Column 3 = 28	Total = 75

significant at the 5% level. Chi-square tables are not available for this precise level, so approximate by taking the 1% level of significance as the nearest available we have to the required level.

14.4 Important warnings

Chi-square is rather less user-friendly than is warranted by its popularity among psychologists. The following are warning signs not to use chi-square or to take very great care:

1. If the expected frequencies in any cell fall lower than 5 then chi-square becomes rather inaccurate. Some authors suggest that no more than a fifth of values should be below 5 but this is a more generous criterion. Some computers automatically print an alternative to chi-square if this assumption is breached.

2. Never do chi-square on percentages or anything else other than frequencies.

3. Always check that your total of frequencies is equal to the number of participants in your research. Chi-square should not be applied where

participants in the research are contributing more than one frequency each to the total of frequencies.

14.5 Alternatives to chi-square

The situation is only salvageable if your chi-square violates the expected cell-frequencies rule – none should fall below 5. Even then you cannot always save the day. The alternatives are as follows:

1. If you have a 2 × 2 or a 2 × 3 chi-square table then you can use the Fisher Exact Probability test which is not sensitive to small expected frequencies (see Calculation 14.2 below).

2. Apart from omitting very small samples or categories, sometimes you can save the day by combining samples and/or categories in order to avoid the small expected frequencies problem; by combining in this way you should increase the expected frequencies somewhat. So, for example, take the data set out in Table 14.11. It should be apparent that by combining two samples and/or two categories you are likely to increase the expected frequencies in the resulting chi-square table.

But you cannot simply combine categories or samples at a whim – the samples or categories have to be combined meaningfully. So if the research was on the relationship between the type of degree that students take and their hobbies, you might have the following categories and samples:

Category 1 – Socialising
Category 2 – Dancing
Category 3 – Stamp collecting
Sample 1 – English literature students
Sample 2 – Media studies students
Sample 3 – Physics students

Looking at these, it would seem reasonable to combine categories 1 and 2 together and samples 1 and 2 together since they seem to reflect relatively similar things. No other combinations would seem appropriate. For example, it is hard to justify combining dancing and stamp collecting.

Table 14.11 **A 3 × 3 contingency table**

Sample	Category 1	Category 2	Category 3
Sample 1	10	6	14
Sample 2	3	12	4
Sample 3	4	2	5

Calculation 14.2

The Fisher Exact Test

The Fisher Exact Test is not usually presented in introductory statistics books. We will only give the calculation of a 2 × 2 Fisher Exact Probability Test although there is a version for 2 × 3 tables. The reason for its inclusion is that much student work for practicals and projects has very small sample sizes. As a consequence, the assumptions of the chi-square test are frequently broken. The Fisher Exact Test is not subject to the same limitations as the chi-square and can be used when chi-square cannot. It is different from chi-square in that it calculates the exact probability rather than a critical value. Apart from that, a significant result is interpreted much as the equivalent chi-square would be, so we will not explain it further.

A number followed by ! is called a factorial. So 5! = 5 × 4 × 3 × 2 × 1 = 120. And 9! = 9 × 8 × 7 × 6 × 5 × 4 × 3 × 2 × 1 = 362880. Easy enough but it can lead to rather big numbers which make the calculation awkward to handle. Table 14.12 list factorials up to 15.

The Fisher Exact Test is applied to a 2 × 2 contingency table by extending the table to include the marginal row and column totals of frequencies as well as the overall total (see Table 14.13).

Table 14.12   **Factorials of numbers from 0 to 15**

Number	Factorial
0	1
1	1
2	2
3	6
4	24
5	120
6	720
7	5040
8	40320
9	362880
10	3628800
11	39916800
12	479001600
13	6227020800
14	87178291200
15	1307674368000

Table 14.13   **Symbols for the Fisher Exact Probability**

	Column 1	**Column 2**	**Row totals**
Row 1	a	b	$W (= a + b)$
Row 2	c	d	$X (= c + d)$
Column totals	$Y (= a + c)$	$Z (= b + d)$	Overall total $= N$

The formula for the exact probability is as follows:

$$\text{Exact probability} = \frac{W!\ X!\ Y!\ Z!}{N!\ a!\ b!\ c!\ d!}$$

Imagine you have collected data on a small group of exceptionally gifted children. You find that some have 'photographic' memories and others do not. You wish to know if there is a relationship between sex of subject and having a photographic memory (Table 14.14).

Table 14.14   **Steps in calculating the Fisher Exact Probability**

Respondents	**Photographic memory**	**No photographic memory**	**Row totals**
Males	$a = 2$	$b = 7$	$W (= a + b) =\ \ 9$
Females	$c = 4$	$d = 1$	$X (= c + d) =\ \ 5$
Column totals	$Y (= a + c) = 6$	$Z (= b + d) = 8$	Overall total $= 14$

Substituting in the formula:

$$\text{Exact probability} = \frac{9!\ 5!\ 6!\ 8!}{14!\ 2!\ 7!\ 4!\ 1!}$$

The values of each of these factorials can be obtained from Table 14.12:

$$\text{Exact probability} = \frac{362880 \times 120 \times 720 \times 40320}{87178291200 \times 2 \times 5040 \times 24 \times 1}$$

Unfortunately you will need a scientific calculator to do this calculation.

The alternative is to cancel wherever possible numbers in the upper part of the formula with those in the lower part:

Exact probability =

$$\frac{9 \times 8 \times 7 \times 6 \times 5 \times 4 \times 3 \times 2 \times 1 \times 5 \times 4 \times 3 \times 2 \times 1 \times 6 \times 5 \times 4 \times 3 \times 2 \times 1 \times 8 \times 7 \times 6 \times 5 \times 4 \times 3 \times 2 \times 1}{14 \times 13 \times 12 \times 11 \times 10 \times 9 \times 8 \times 7 \times 6 \times 5 \times 4 \times 3 \times 2 \times 1 \times 2 \times 1 \times 7 \times 6 \times 5 \times 4 \times 3 \times 2 \times 1 \times 4 \times 3 \times 2 \times 1 \times 1}$$

$$= \frac{5 \times 4 \times 3 \times 6 \times 5 \times 8}{14 \times 13 \times 12 \times 11 \times 10 \times 1}$$

$$= \frac{14400}{240240}$$

$$= 0.06$$

But to approximate our conventional two-tailed test this needs to be doubled to give a probability of 0.12. Therefore the exact probability equals the 12% significance level. Thus we cannot reject the null hypothesis at the 5% level.

Fisher Exact Test for 2 × 3 tables

This is calculated in a very similar way as for the Fisher 2 × 2 test, the difference being simply the increased numbers of cells (Table 14.15). The formula for the 2 × 3 exact probability is as follows:

$$\text{Exact probability} = \frac{W! \ X! \ K! \ L! \ M!}{N! \ a! \ b! \ c! \ d! \ e! \ f!}$$

Remember to double the answer to give the two-tailed test value. The calculation should be easy enough although it can be even more cumbersome than for the 2 × 2 Fisher Exact Test.

14.6 Chi-square and known populations

Sometimes but rarely in research we know the distribution in the population. If the population distribution of frequencies is known then it is possible to employ the 'single sample' chi-square. Usually the population frequencies are known as relative frequencies or percentages. So, for example, if you wished to know the likelihood of getting a sample of 40 university psychology students in which there are 30 female and 10 male students *if* you know that the population of psychology students is 90% female and 10% male, you simply use the latter proportions to calculate the expected frequencies of females and males in a sample of 40. If the sample were to reflect the population then 90% of the 40 should be female and 10% male. So the expected frequencies are 40 × 90/100 for females

Table 14.15   **Stages in the calculation of a 2 × 3 Fisher Exact test**

	Column 1	Column 2	Column 3	Row totals
Row 1	a	b	c	$W \ (= a + b + c)$
Row 2	d	e	f	$X \ (= d + e + f)$
Column totals	$K \ (= a + d)$	$L \ (= b + e)$	$M \ (= c + f)$	Overall total $= N$

and $40 \times 10/100$ for males = 36 females and 4 males. These are then entered into the chi-square formula, but note that there are only two cells. The degrees of freedom for the one-sample chi-square is the number of cells minus 1 (i.e. $2 - 1 = 1$).

Calculation 14.3

The one-sample chi-square

The research question is whether a sample of 80 babies of a certain age in foster care show the same level of smiling to their carer as a population of babies of the same age assessed on a developmental test. On this developmental test 50% of babies at this age show clear evidence of the smiling response, 40% clearly show no evidence, and for 10% it is impossible to make a judgement. This is the population from which the foster babies are considered to be a sample. It is found that 35 clearly showed evidence of smiling, 40 showed no clear evidence of smiling and the remaining 5 were impossible to classify.

We can use the population distribution to work out the expected frequency in the sample of 80 if this sample precisely matched the population. Thus 50% of the 80 (= 40) should be clear smilers, 40% of the 80 (= 32) should be clear non-smilers, and 10% of the 80 (= 8) should be impossible to classify. Table 14.16 gives the expected frequencies (i.e. population-based) and observed frequencies (i.e. sample-based).

These observed and expected frequencies are entered into the usual chi-square formula. The only difference is that the degrees of freedom are not quite the same – they are the number of conditions minus 1 (i.e. $3 - 1 = 2$ in the above example):

$$\text{Chi-square} = \Sigma \; \frac{(O - E)^2}{E}$$

$$= \frac{(35 - 40)^2}{40} + \frac{(40 - 32)^2}{32} + \frac{(5 - 8)^2}{8}$$

$$= \frac{(-5)^2}{40} + \frac{8^2}{32} + \frac{(-3)^2}{8}$$

Table 14.16 **Data for a one-sample chi-square**

	Clear smilers	**Clear non-smilers**	**Impossible to classify**
Observed frequency	35	40	5
Expected frequency	40	32	8

$$= \frac{25}{40} + \frac{64}{32} + \frac{9}{8}$$

$$= 0.625 + 2.000 + 1.125$$

$$= 3.75$$

But from Significance Table 14.1 we can see that this value of chi-square is far below the critical value of 6.0 required to be significant at the 5% level. Thus the sample of foster babies is not significantly different from the population of babies in terms of their smiling response.

14.7 Chi-square for related samples – the McNemar Test

It is possible to use chi-square to compare *related* samples of frequencies. Essentially this involves arranging the data in such a way that the chi-square contingency table only includes two categories – those who change from the first to the second occasion. For example, data are collected on whether or not teenage students wish to go to university; following a careers talk favouring university education the same informants are asked again whether they wish to go to university. The data can be tabulated as in Table 14.17.

We can see from this table that although some students did not change their minds as a consequence of the talk (30 wanted to go to university before the talk and did not change their minds, 32 did not want to go to university before the talk and did not change their minds), some students did change. Fifty changed their minds and wanted to go to university following the talk and 10 changed their minds and did not want to go to university after the talk.

The McNemar test simply uses the data on those who changed; non-changers are ignored. The logic of the test is that if the talk did not actually affect the teenagers, just as many would change their minds in one direction after the talk as change their minds in the other direction. That is, 50% should change towards wanting to go to university and 50% should change against wanting to go to university, *if the talk had no effect*. We simply create a new table (Table 14.18) which only includes changers and calculate chi-square on the basis that the null hypothesis of no effect would suggest that 50% of the changers should change in each direction.

Table 14.17   **Illustrative data for the McNemar Test**

	Before talk 'yes'	**Before talk 'no'**
After talk 'yes'	30	50
After talk 'no'	10	32

Table 14.18   **Table of those who changed in a positive or negative
direction based on Table 14.17**

	Positive changers	Negative changers
Observed frequency	50	10
Expected frequency	30	30

The calculation is now exactly like that for the one-sample chi-square. This gives us a chi-square value of 26.67 with 1 degree of freedom (since there are two conditions). This is very significant when checked against the critical values in Significance Table 14.1. Thus there appears to be more change towards wanting to go to university following the careers talk than change towards not wanting to go to university.

Yates's correction

A slightly outmoded statistical procedure when the expected frequencies in chi-square are small is to apply Yates's correction. This is intended to make such data fit the theoretical chi-square distribution a little better. Essentially all you do is to subtract 0.5 from each (observed frequency – expected frequency) in the chi-square formula prior to squaring that difference. With large expected frequencies this has virtually no effect. With small tables, it obviously reduces the size of chi-square and therefore its statistical significance. We have opted for not using it in our calculations. Really it is a matter of personal choice as far as convention goes.

Example from the literature

In a study of the selection of prison officers, Crighton and Towl (1994) found the relationship shown in Table 14.19 between the ethnicity of the candidate and whether or not they were selected during the recruitment process.

The interpretation of this table is that there is no significant relationship (p = n.s.) between selection and ethnicity. In other words, the table does not provide evidence of a selection bias in favour of white applicants, for example. While this

Table 14.19   **Relationship between ethnicity and selection**

	Selected	Not selected
Ethnic minority	1	3
Ethnic majority	17	45
Chi-squared = 0.43; p = n.s.		

is not an unreasonable conclusion based on the data if we ignore the small numbers of ethnic minority applicants, the statistical analysis itself is not appropriate. In particular, if you calculate the expected frequencies for the four cells you will find that 50% of the expected frequencies are less than 5, thus a rule has been violated. The Fisher Exact Test would be better for these data.

14.8 Notes and recommendations

■ Avoid as far as possible designing research with a multiplicity of categories and samples for chi-square. Large chi-squares with many cells are often difficult to interpret without numerous sub-analyses.

■ Always make sure that your chi-square is carried out on frequencies and that each participant contributes only one to the total frequencies.

■ Check for expected frequencies under 5; if you have any then take one of the escape routes described above if possible.

Recommended further reading

Maxwell, A.E. (1961). *Analysing Qualitative Data*. London: Methuen.

Chapter 15

Probability

Preparation

General familiarity with previous chapters.

15.1 Introduction

From time to time, researchers need to be able to calculate the probabilities associated with certain patterns of events. One of us remembers that as a student in class we carried out an experiment based on newspaper reports of a Russian study in which people appeared to be able to recognise colours through their finger-tips. So we designed an experiment in which a blindfolded person felt different colours in random order. Most of us did not do very well but some in the class seemed excellent. The media somehow heard about the study and a particularly good identifier in our experiment quickly took part in a live TV demonstration of her skills. She was appallingly bad at the task this time.

The reason why she was bad on television was that she had no special skills in the first place. It had been merely a matter of chance that she had done well in the laboratory. On the television programme, chance was not on her side and she turned out to be as bad as the rest of us. Actually, this reflects a commonly referred to phenomenon called *regression to the mean*. Choose a person (or group) because of their especially high (or alternatively especially low) scores and they will tend to score closer to the mean on the next administration of the test or measurement. This is because the test or measure is to a degree unreliable and by choosing exceptional scores you have to an extent capitalised on chance factors. With a completely unreliable test or measure, the reversion towards the mean will be dramatic. In our colour experiment the student did badly on TV because she had been selected totally on the basis of a criterion that was fundamentally unreliable – that is completely at random.

Similar problems occur in any investigation of individual paranormal or psychic powers. For example, a spiritual medium who addresses a crowd of 500 people is doing nothing spectacular if in Britain she claims to be speaking to a dead relative of someone and that relative is Mary or Martha or Margaret. The chances of someone in the 500 having such a relative are very high.

15.2 The principles of probability

When any of us use a test of significance we are utilising probability theory. This is because most statistical tests are based on it. Our working knowledge of probability in most branches of psychology does not have to be very great for us to function well. We have been using probability in previous chapters on significance testing when we talked about the 5% level of significance, the 1% level of significance, and the 95% confidence intervals. Basically what we meant by a 5% level of significance is that a particular event (or outcome) would occur on five occasions out of 100. Although we have adopted the percentage system of reporting probabilities in this book, statisticians would normally not write of a 5% probability. Instead they would express it as being out of a *single* event rather than 100 events. Thus:

- 0.05 (or just .05) is an alternative way of writing 5%
- 0.10 (or .10) is an alternative way of writing 10%
- 1.00 is an alternative way of writing 100%

The difficulty for some of us with this alternative, more formal, way of writing probability is that it leaves everything in decimals that does not appeal to the less mathematically skilled. However, you should be aware of the alternative notation since it appears in many research reports. Furthermore, much computer output can give probabilities to several decimal places which can be confusing. For example, what does a probability of 0.00001 mean? The answer is one chance in 100000 or a 0.001% probability ($\frac{1}{100000} \times 100 = 0.001\%$).

There are two rules of probability with which psychologists ought to be familiar. They are the *addition rule* and the *multiplication rule*.

1. The *addition rule* is quite straightforward. It merely states that for a number of mutually exclusive outcomes the sum of their probabilities adds up to 1.00. So if you have a set of 150 people of which 100 are women and 50 are men, the probability of picking a woman at random is 100/150 or 0.667. The probability of picking a man at random is 50/150 or 0.333. However, the probability of picking either a man or a woman at random is 0.667 + 0.333 or 1.00. In other words, it is certain that you will pick either a man or a woman. The assumption is that the categories or outcomes are mutually exclusive, meaning that a person cannot be in both the man and woman categories. Being a man excludes that person from also being a woman. In statistical probability theory, one of the two possible outcomes is usually denoted p and the other is denoted q, so $p + q = 1.00$. Outcomes that are not mutually exclusive include, for example, the categories man and young since a person could be a man and young.

2. The *multiplication rule* is about a set of events. It can be illustrated by our set of 150 men and women in which 100 are women and 50 are men. Again the

assumption is that the categories or outcomes are mutually exclusive. We could ask how likely it is that the first five people that we pick at random will all be women, given that the probability of choosing a woman on a single occasion is 0.667. The answer is that we multiply the probability associated with the first person being a woman by the probability that the second person will be a woman by the probability that the third person will be a woman by the probability that the fourth person will be a woman by the probability that the fifth person will be a woman:

$$\text{Probability of all five being women} = p \times p \times p \times p \times p$$

$$= 0.667 \times 0.667 \times 0.667 \times 0.667 \times 0.667 = 0.13$$

Therefore there is a 13% probability (0.13) that we will choose a sample of five women at random. That is not a particularly rare outcome. However, picking a sample of all men from our set of men and women is much rarer:

$$\text{Probability of all five being men} = q \times q \times q \times q \times q$$

$$= 0.333 \times 0.333 \times 0.333 \times 0.333 \times 0.333 = 0.004$$

Therefore there is a 0.4% probability (0.004) of choosing all men.

The multiplication rule as stated here assumes that once a person is selected for inclusion in the sample, he or she is replaced in the population and possibly selected again. This is called random sampling with replacement. However, normally we do not do this in psychological research, though if the population is big then not replacing the individual back into the population has negligible influence on the outcome. Virtually all statistical analyses assume replacement but it does not matter that people are usually not selected more than once for a study in psychological research.

15.3 Implications

Such theoretical considerations concerning probability theory have a number of implications for research. They ought to be carefully noted.

1. *Repeated significance testing* within the same study. It is tempting to carry out several statistical tests on data. Usually we find that a portion of these tests are statistically significant at the 5% level whereas a number are not. Indeed, even if there were absolutely no trends in the population, we would expect, by chance, 5% of our comparisons to be significant at the 5% level. This is the meaning of statistical significance, after all. The more statistical comparisons we make on our data the more significant findings we would

expect. If we did 20 comparisons we would expect one significant finding even if there are no trends in the population. In order to cope with this, the correct procedure is to make the statistical significance more stringent the more tests of significance we do. So if we did two tests then our significance level per test should be 5%/2 or 2.5%; if we did four comparisons our significance level would be 5%/4 or 1.25% significance per test. In other words, we simply divide the 5% significance level by the number of tests we are doing. Although this is the proper thing to do, few psychological reports actually do it. However, the consequence of not doing this is to find more significant findings than you should.

2. *Significance testing across different studies*. An application of the multiplication rule in assessing the value of replicating research shows the dramatic increase in significance that this can achieve. Replication means the essential repeating of a study at a later date and possibly in radically different circumstances such as other locations. Imagine that the significance level achieved in the original study is 5% ($p = 0.05$). If one finds the same significance level in the replication the probability of two studies producing this level of significance by chance is $p \times p$ or $0.05 \times 0.05 = 0.0025$ or 0.25%. This considerably enhances our confidence that the findings of the research are not the result of chance factors but reflect significant trends.

Calculation 15.1

The addition rule

A psychologist wishes to calculate the chance expectations of marks on a multiple choice test of general knowledge. Since a person could get some answers correct simply by sticking a pin into the answer paper, there has to be a minimum score below which the individual is doing no better than chance. If each question has four response alternatives then one would expect that by chance a person could get one in four or a quarter of the answers correct. That is intuitively obvious. But what if some questions have three alternative answers and others have four alternative answers? This is not quite so obvious but we simply apply the law of addition and add together the probabilities of being correct for all of the questions on the paper. This entails adding together probabilities of 0.33 and 0.25 since there are three or four alternative answers. So if there are 10 questions with three alternative answers and five questions with four alternative answers, the number of answers correct by chance is $(10 \times 0.33) + (5 \times 0.25)$ $= 3.3 + 1.25 = 4.55$.

Calculation 15.2

The multiplication rule

A psychologist studies a pair of twins who have been brought up separately and who have never met. The psychologist is surprised to find that the twins are alike on seven out of ten different characteristics. These characteristics are:

(a) They both marry women younger than themselves (0.9)

(b) They both marry brunettes (0.7)

(c) They both drive (0.7)

(d) They both swim (0.6)

(e) They have spent time in hospital (0.8)

(f) They both take foreign holidays (0.5)

(g) They both part their hair on the left (0.9)

However, they are different in the following ways:

(h) One attends church (0.4) and the other does not

(i) One has a doctorate (0.03) and the other does not

(j) One smokes (0.3) and the other does not

The similarities between the two men are impressive if it is exceptional for two randomly selected men to be similar on each of the items. The probabilities of each of the outcomes are presented in brackets above. These probabilities are the proportions of men in the general population demonstrating these characteristics. For many of the characteristics it seems quite likely that they will be similar. So two men taken at random from the general population are most likely to marry a younger woman. Since the probability of marrying a younger woman is 0.9, the probability of any two men marrying younger women is 0.9×0.9 or 0.81. The probability of two men taken at random both being drivers is 0.7×0.7 or 0.49. In fact the 10 characteristics listed above are shared by randomly selected pairs of men with the following probabilities:

(a) $0.9 \times 0.9 = 0.81$

(b) $0.7 \times 0.7 = 0.49$

(c) $0.6 \times 0.6 = 0.36$

(d) $0.6 \times 0.6 = 0.36$

(e) $0.8 \times 0.8 = 0.64$

(f) $0.5 \times 0.5 = 0.25$

(g) $0.9 \times 0.9 = 0.81$

(h) $0.4 \times 0.4 = 0.16$

(i) $0.03 \times 0.03 = 0.0009$

(j) $0.3 \times 0.3 = 0.09$

The sum of these probabilities is 3.97. Clearly the pair of twins are more alike than we might expect on the basis of chance. However, it might be that we would get a different answer if instead of taking the general population of men, we took men of the same age as the twins.

15.4 Notes and recommendations

■ Although probability theory is of crucial importance for mathematical statisticians, psychologists generally rely on an intuitive approach to the topic. That may be laziness on their part, but we have kept the coverage of probability minimal given the scope of this book. It can also be very deterring to anyone not too mathematically inclined. If you need to know more, especially if you need to estimate precisely the likelihood of a particular pattern or sequence of events occurring, we suggest that you consult books such as Kerlinger (1986) for more complete accounts of mathematical probability theory.

■ However, it is important to avoid basic mistakes such as repeated significance testing on the same data without adjusting your significance levels to allow for the multitude of tests. This is not necessary for tests designed for multiple testing such as those for the analysis of variance, some of which we discuss later (Chapter 23), as the adjustment is built in.

Chapter 16

Reporting significance levels succinctly

Preparation

You need to know about testing significance from Chapter 11 onwards.

16.1 Introduction

So far, the reporting of statistical significance in this book has been a relatively clumsy and long-winded affair. In contrast, a glance at any psychology journal will suggest that precious little space is devoted to reporting significance. Detailed expositions of the statistical significance of your analyses have no place in professional reports. Researchers can make life much simpler for themselves by adopting the 'standard' style of reporting statistical significance. Clarity is one great benefit; another is the loss of wordiness.

Although the 'standard' approach to reporting statistical significance does vary slightly, there is little difficulty with this. At a minimum, the following should be mentioned when reporting statistical significance:

1. The statistical distribution used (e.g. F, chi, r, z, t, etc.).

2. The degrees of freedom (df). Alternatively, for some statistical techniques you may report the sample size (N).

3. The value of the calculation (e.g. the value of your z-score or your chi-square).

4. The probability or significance level. Sometimes 'not significant', 'not sig.' or 'n.s.' is used.

5. If you have a one-tailed hypothesis then this should be also mentioned. Otherwise a two-tailed hypothesis is assumed. You can also state that you are using a two-tailed test. This is most useful when you have several analyses and some are one-tailed and others are two-tailed.

16.2 Shortened forms

In research reports, comments such as the following are to be found:

■ The hypothesis that drunks slur their words was supported ($t = 2.88$, degrees of freedom = 97, $p<0.01$).

- There was a trend for drunks to slur their words more than sober people (t = 2.88, df = 97, sig. = 1%).
- The null hypothesis that drunks do not slur their words more than sober people was rejected (t = 2.88, degrees of freedom = 97, p = 0.01).
- The analysis supported the hypothesis since drunks tended to slur their words the most often (t (97) = 2.88, p = 0.01, two-tailed test).
- The hypothesis that drunks slur their words was accepted (t (97) = 2.88, p = 0.005, 1-tail).

All of the above say more or less the same thing. The symbol t indicates that the t-test was used. The symbol < indicates that your probability level is even smaller than the given value. Thus $p<0.01$ means that the probability is, say, 0.008 or 0.005. That is, the test is statistically significant at better than the reported level of 0.01. Sometimes, the degrees of freedom are put in brackets after the symbol for the statistical test used, as in t (97) = 2.88. In all of the above examples, the hypothesis was supported and the null hypothesis rejected.

The following are examples of what might be written if the hypothesis was not supported by your data:

- The hypothesis that drunks slur their words was rejected (t = 0.56, degrees of freedom = 97, $p>.05$).
- Drunks and sober people did not differ in their average rates of slurring their speech (t = 0.56, df = 97, not sig.).
- The hypothesis that drunks slur their words was rejected in favour of the null hypothesis (t = 0.56, df = 97, $p>0.05$, not significant).

The last three statements mean much the same. The symbol > means that your probability is greater than the listed value. It is used to indicate that your calculation is not statistically significant at the stated level.

Notice throughout this chapter that the reported significance levels are not standardised on the 5% level of significance. It is possible, especially with computers, to obtain much more exact values of probability than the critical values used in tables of significance. While there is nothing at all technically wrong with using the more precise values if you have them to hand, there is one objection. Statistical significance can become a holy grail in statistics, supporting the view 'the smaller the probability the better'. Although significance is important, the size of the trends in your data is even more crucial. A significant result with a strong trend is the ideal which is not obtained simply by exploring the minutiae of probability.

One thing causes a lot of confusion in the significance levels given by computers. Sometimes values like $p<0.0000$ are listed. All that this means is that the probability level for the statistical test is less than 0.0001. In other words the significance level might be, say, 0.00003 or 0.0000004. These are very significant findings, statistically speaking. We would recommend that you report them slightly differently in your writings. Values such as 0.0001 or 0.001 are clearer to some readers. So change your final 0 in the string of zeros to 1.

16.3 Examples from the published literature

Example 1

' . . . a post hoc comparison was carried out between means of the adult molesters' and adult control groups' ratings using Student's t-test. A significant (t (49) = 2.96, $p<0.001$) difference was found between the two groups.' (Johnston and Johnston, 1986, p. 643)

The above excerpt is fairly typical of the ways in which psychologists summarise the results of their research. To the practised eye, it is not too difficult to decipher. However, some difficulties can be caused to the novice statistician. A little patience at first will help a lot. The extract contains the following major pieces of information:

1. The statistical test used was the t-test. The authors mention it by name but it is also identified by the t mentioned in the brackets. However, the phrase 'Student's t-test' might be confusing. Student was the pen-name of a researcher at the Guinness Brewery who invented the t-test. It is quite redundant nowadays – the name Student, not Guinness!

2. The degrees of freedom are the (49) contained in the brackets. If you check the original paper you will find that the combined sample size is 51. It should be obvious, then, that this is an unrelated or uncorrelated t-test since the degrees of freedom are clearly $N - 2$ in this case.

3. The value of the t-test is 2.96.

4. The difference between the two groups is statistically significant at the 0.001 or 0.1% level of probability. This is shown by $p<0.001$ in the above excerpt.

5. Post hoc merely means that the researchers decided to do the test after the data had been collected. They had not planned it prior to collecting the data.

6. No mention is made of whether this is a one-tailed or a two-tailed test so we would assume that it is a two-tailed significance level.

Obviously, there are a variety of ways of writing up the findings of any analysis. The following is a different way of saying much the same thing:

'* . . . a post hoc comparison between the means of the adult molesters' and adult control groups' ratings was significant (t = 2.96, d.f. = 49, p<0.001).'*

Example 2

'The relationship of gender of perpetrators and victims was examined. Perpetrators of female victims were more often male (13,900 of 24,947, 55.8%) while perpetrators of males were more often female (10,977 of 21,373, 51.4%, χ^2 (1) = 235.18, $p<0.001$).' (Rosenthal, 1988, p. 267)

The interpretation of this is as follows:

1. The chi-square test was used. χ^2 is the Greek symbol for chi-square.

2. The value of chi-square is 235.18.

3. It is statistically very significant as the probability level is less than 0.001 or less than 0.1%.

4. Chi-square is usually regarded as a directionless test. That is, the significance level reported is for a two-tailed test unless stated otherwise.

5. Although the significance level in this study seems impressive, just look at the sample sizes involved – over 46,000 children in total. The actual trends are relatively small – 55.8% versus 51.4%. This is a good example of when not to get excited about statistically significant findings.

An alternative way of saying much the same thing is:

'Female victims were offended against by males in 55.8% of cases (N = 24,947). For male victims, 51.4% of offenders were female (N = 21,373). Thus victims were more likely to be offended against by a member of the opposite sex (chi-square = 235.18, degrees of freedom = 1, p<0.1%).'

Example 3

'A 2 × 2 analysis of variance (ANOVA) with anger and sex of target as factors was conducted on the BP2 (after anger manipulation) scores. This analysis yielded a significant effect for anger, F (1, 116) = 43.76, $p<0.004$, with angered subjects revealing a larger increase in arousal (M = 6.01) than the nonangered subjects (M = 0.01).' (Donnerstein, 1980, p. 273)

This should be readily deciphered as:

1. A two-way analysis of variance with two different levels of each independent variable. One of the independent variables is anger (angered and non-angered conditions are the categories). The other independent variable is sex of the target of aggression. Something called BP2 (whatever that may be – it turns out to be blood pressure) is the dependent variable.

2. The mean BP2 score for the angered condition was 6.01 and the mean for the nonangered condition was 0.01. The author is using M as the symbol of the sample mean.

3. The test of significance is the F-ratio test. We know this because this is an analysis of variance but also because the statistic is stated to be F.

4. The value of F, the variance ratio, equals 43.76.

5. There are 1 and 116 degrees of freedom for the F-ratio for the main effect of the variable anger. The 1 degree of freedom is because there are two

different levels of the variable anger (df = $c - 1$ or the number of columns of data minus one). The 116 degrees of freedom means that there must have been 120 participants in the experiment. The degrees of freedom for a main effect is N – number of cells = $120 - (2 \times 2) = 120 - 4 = 116$. All of this is clarified in Chapter 22.

6.   The difference between the angered and nonangered conditions is statistically significant at the 0.4% level.

A slightly different style of describing these findings is:

'Blood pressure following the anger manipulation was included as the dependent variable on a 2 × 2 analysis of variance. The two independent variables were sex of the target of aggression and anger. There was a significant main effect for anger (F = 43.76, d.f. = 1, 116, p<0.4%). The greater mean increase in blood pressure was for the angered group (6.01) compared to the nonangered group (0.01).'

16.4 Notes and recommendations

■ Remember that the important pieces of information to report are:
   – the symbol for the statistic (t, T, r, etc.)
   – the value of the statistic for your analysis – two decimal places are enough
   – an indication of the degrees of freedom or the sample size involved (df =, N =)
   – the probability or significance level
   – whether a one-tailed test was used

■ Sometimes you will see symbols for statistical techniques that you have never heard of. Do not panic since it is usually possible to work out the sense of what is going on. Certainly if you have details of the sort described in this chapter, you know that a test of significance is involved.

■ Using the approaches described in this chapter creates a good impression and ensures that you include pertinent information. However, standardise on one of the variants in your report. Eventually if you submit papers to a journal for consideration, you should check out that journal's method of reporting significance.

■ Some statistical tests are regarded as being directionless. That is, their use always implies a two-tailed test. This is true of chi-square and the analysis of variance. These tests can only be one-tailed if the degrees of freedom equal one. Otherwise, the test is two-tailed. Even when the degrees of freedom equal one, only use a one-tailed test if you are satisfied that you have reached the basic requirements of one-tailed testing (see Chapter 17).

Chapter 17

One-tailed versus two-tailed significance testing

Preparation

Revise the null hypothesis and alternative hypothesis (Chapter 10) and significance testing.

17.1 Introduction

Sometimes researchers are so confident about the likely outcome of their research that they make pretty strong predictions about the relationship between their independent and dependent variables. So, for example, rather than say that the *independent variable* age is correlated with verbal ability, the researcher predicts that the *independent variable* age is *positively* correlated with the *dependent variable* verbal ability. In other words, it is predicted that the older participants in the research will have better verbal skills. Equally the researcher might predict a *negative* relationship between the independent and dependent variables.

It is conventional in psychological statistics to treat such *directional* predictions differently from *non-directional* predictions. Normally psychologists speak of a directional prediction being one-tailed whereas a non-directional prediction is two-tailed. The crucial point is that if you have a directional prediction (one-tailed test) the critical values of the significance test become slightly different.

In order to carry out a one-tailed test you need to be satisfied that you have met the criteria for one-tailed testing. These, as we will see, are rather stringent. In our experience, many one-tailed hypotheses put forward by students are little more than hunches and certainly not based on the required strong past-research or strong theory. In these circumstances it is unwise and wrong to carry out one-tailed testing. It would be best to regard the alternative hypothesis as non-directional and choose two-tailed significance testing exactly as we have done so far in this book. One-tailed testing is a contentious issue and you may be confronted with different points of view; some authorities reject it although it is fairly commonplace in psychological research.

17.2 Theoretical considerations

If we take a directional alternative hypothesis (such as that intelligence correlates positively with level of education) then it is necessary to revise our understanding of the null hypothesis somewhat. (The same is true if the directional alternative hypothesis suggests a negative relationship between the two variables.) In the case of the positively worded alternative hypothesis, the null hypothesis is:

Intelligence does not correlate *positively* with level of education.

Our previous style of null hypothesis would have left out the word *positively*. There are two different circumstances which support the null hypothesis that intelligence does not correlate *positively* with level of education:

If intelligence *does not correlate* at all with level of education, *or*
If intelligence correlates *negatively* with level of education.

That is, it is only research which shows a *positive* correlation between intelligence and education which supports the directional hypothesis – if we found an extreme negative correlation between intelligence and education this would lead to the rejection of the alternative hypothesis just as would zero or near-zero relationships. Because, in a sense, the dice is loaded against the directional alternative hypothesis, it is conventional to argue that we should not use the extremes of the sampling distribution in both directions for our test of significance for the directional hypothesis. Instead we should take the extreme samples in the positive direction (if it is positively worded) or the extreme samples in the negative direction (if it is negatively worded). In other words, our extreme 5% of samples which we define as significant should all be from one side of the sampling distribution, not 2.5% on each side as we would have done previously (see Diagram 17.1).

Because the 5% of extreme samples, which are defined as significant, are all on the same side of the distribution, you need a smaller value of your significance test to be in that extreme 5%. Part of the attraction of directional or one-tailed significance tests of this sort is that basically you can get the same level of significance with a smaller sample or smaller trend than would be required for a two-tailed test. Essentially the probability level can be halved – what would be significant at the 5% level with a two-tailed test is significant at the 2.5% level with a one-tailed test.

There is a big proviso to this. If you predicted a positive relationship but found what would normally be a significant negative relationship, with a one-tailed test you ought to ignore that negative relationship – it merely supports the null hypothesis. The temptation is, however, to ignore your original directional alternative hypothesis and pretend that you had not predicted the direction. Given that significant results are at a premium in psychology and are much more likely to get published, it is not surprising that psychologists seeking to publish their research might be tempted to 'adjust' their hypotheses slightly.

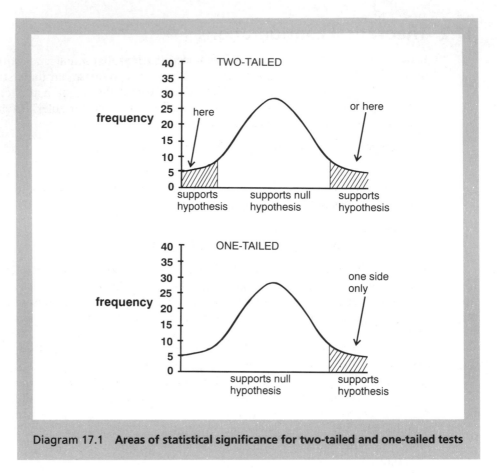

Diagram 17.1   Areas of statistical significance for two-tailed and one-tailed tests

It is noteworthy that the research literature contains very few tests of signifi-cance of directional hypotheses which are rejected when the trend in the data is strongly (and significantly with a two-tailed test) in the opposite direction to that predicted. The only example we know of was written by one of us.

17.3 Further requirements

There are a number of other rules which are supposed to be followed if one is to use a directional hypothesis. These include:

1. The prediction is based on strong and well-researched theory and not on a whim or intuition.

2. The prediction is based on previous similar research demonstrating consis-tent trends in the predicted direction.

3. One should make the above predictions in advance of any information about the trends in the data about which the prediction is to be made. That is, for

example, you do not look at your scattergrams and then predict the direction of the correlation between your variables. That would be manifestly cheating but a 'good' way otherwise of getting significant results with a one-tailed test when they would not quite reach significance with a two-tailed test.

There is another practical problem in the use of directional hypotheses. That is, if you have *more than two groups* of scores it is often very difficult to decide what the predicting trends between the groups would be. For this reason, many statistical techniques are commonly regarded as directionless when you have more than two groups of scores or subjects. This applies to techniques such as chi-square, the analysis of variance and other related tests.

Although this is clearly a controversial area, you will probably find that as a student you rarely if ever have sufficient justification for employing a one-tailed test. As you might have gathered, most of these criteria for selecting a one-tailed test are to a degree subjective which makes the use of one-tailed tests less objective than might be expected. We would recommend that you choose a two-tailed or directionless test unless there is a pressing and convincing reason to do otherwise. Otherwise the danger of loading things in favour of significant results is too great.

Appendix D gives significance tables for all of the statistical distributions discussed in this book for one-tailed testing at the 5% level of significance.

17.4 Notes and recommendations

■ Routinely make your alternative hypotheses two-tailed or directionless. This is especially the case when the implications of your research are of practical or policy significance. However, this may not be ideal if you are testing theoretical predictions when the direction of the hypothesis might be important. Nevertheless, it is a moot point whether you should take advantage of the 'less stringent' significance requirements of a one-tailed test.

■ If you believe that the well-established theoretical or empirical bases for predicting the direction of the outcomes are strong enough, then still be a little cautious about employing one-tailed tests. In particular, do not formulate your hypothesis *after* collecting or viewing your data.

■ You cannot be faulted for using two-tailed tests since they are less likely to show significant relationships. Thus they are described as being statistically more conservative. Student research often does not arise out of previous research or theory. Often the research is initiated before earlier research and theory have been reviewed. In these circumstances one-tailed tests are not warranted.

Chapter 18

Ranking tests

Nonparametric statistics

Preparation

Be aware of the t-tests for related and unrelated samples. Revise ranking (Chapter 7).

18.1 Introduction

From time to time any researcher will be faced with the distinction between parametric and nonparametric significance tests. The difference is quite straightforward. Many statistical techniques require that the details are known or estimates can be made of the characteristics of the population. These are known as *parametric* tests (a parameter is a characteristic of a population). Almost invariably, as we have seen, the population is the population defined by the null hypothesis. Generally speaking, the numerical scores we used had to roughly approximate the normal (bell-shaped) distribution in order for our decisions to be precise. The reason for this is that the statistician's theoretical assumptions, when developing the test, included the normal distribution of the data. It is widely accepted that the assumption of a bell-shaped or normal distribution of scores is a very broad criterion and that the distribution of scores on a variable would have to be very lop-sided (skew) in order for the outcomes to be seriously out of line. Appendix A explains how to test for such skewness.

But what if assumptions such as that of symmetry are so badly violated that the use of the test seems somewhat unacceptable? One traditional alternative approach is called *nonparametric* testing because it makes few or no assumptions about the distribution in the population. Many nonparametric tests of significance are based on rankings given to the original numerical scores – it is unusual for researchers to collect their data in the form of ranks in the first place.

Conventionally these tests for ranks are regarded as relatively easy computations for students – this is part of their appeal. Up to a point this can be true, but the difficulties are as follows:

1. They become disproportionately cumbersome with increasing amounts of data.

2. They also suffer from the difficulty that many psychological data are gathered using rather restricted ranges of scores. This often results in the same values appearing several times in a set of data. The tests based on ranks also become cumbersome with increased tied scores and, consequently, somewhat inaccurate.

3. Worst of all, the variety and flexibility of these nonparametric statistical techniques is nowhere as great as for parametric statistics. For this reason it is generally best to err towards using parametric statistics in our opinion. Certainly current research practice seems to increasingly disfavour nonparametric statistics.

18.2 Theoretical considerations

Ranking merely involves the ordering of a set of scores from the smallest to the largest. The smallest score is given the rank 1, the second smallest score is given the rank 2, the fiftieth smallest score is given the rank 50 and so on.

Since many nonparametric statistical techniques use ranks, the question is raised why this is so. The answer is very much the same as the reason for using the normal distribution as the basis for parametric statistics – it provides a standard distribution of scores with standard characteristics. It is much the same for the tests based on ranks. Although there are incalculable varieties in samples of data, for any given number of scores the ranks are always the same. So the ranks of 10 scores which represent the IQs of the 10 greatest geniuses of all time are exactly the same as the ranks for the scores on introversion of the 10 members of the local stamp collectors' club: 1, 2, 3, 4, 5, 6, 7, 8, 9 and 10.

Since all sets of 10 scores use exactly the same set of ranks, this considerably eases the statistician's calculations of the distribution of the ranks under the null hypothesis that there is no relationship between pairs of variables. Instead of an infinite variety of 10 scores, there is just this one set of 10 ranks on which to do one's calculations. Only sample size makes a difference to the ranks, not the precise numerical values of the scores themselves.

18.3 Nonparametric statistical tests

There is an extensive battery of nonparametric tests although many are interchangeable with each other or rather obscure with very limited applications. In this chapter we will consider only a small number of tests which you may come across during your university courses or general reading. We have discussed chi-square (for frequencies) and Spearman's Rho (for correlations) elsewhere in this book. The non-parametric tests discussed in this chapter are usually applicable in very much the same experimental designs as the parametric tests we have discussed elsewhere (see Table 18.1).

Table 18.1   **Similar parametric and nonparametric tests**

Parametric test	Nonparametric equivalent
Related t-test	Wilcoxon Matched Pairs test
	Sign test
Unrelated t-test	Mann–Whitney U-test

Tests for related samples

Two nonparametric tests are familiar in the literature – the sign test (which is not based on ranks) and the Wilcoxon Matched Pairs test (which is based on ranks). Because they would apply to data for the related t-test, we will use the data for the worked example in Chapter 12 to illustrate the application of both of these tests.

Calculation 18.1

The sign test

The sign test is like the related t-test in that it takes the differences between the two related samples of scores. However, instead of considering the *size* of the difference, the sign test merely uses the *sign* of the difference. In other words, it loses a lot of the information inherent in the size of the difference.

Step 1:   Delete from the analysis any case which has identical scores for both variables. They are ignored in the sign test. Take the second group of scores away from the first group (Table 18.2). Remember to include the sign of the difference (+ or –).

Table 18.2   **Steps in the calculation of the sign test**

Subject	Six months X_1	Nine months X_2	Difference $D = X_1 - X_2$
Baby Clara	3	7	–4
Baby Martin	5	6	–1
Baby Sally	5	3	+2
Baby Angie	4	8	–4
Baby Trevor	3	5	–2
Baby Sam	7	9	–2
Baby Bobby	8	7	+1
Baby Sid	7	9	–2

Significance Table 18.1   **5% Significance values for the sign test giving values of *T* (the smaller of the sums of signs) (two-tailed test)**

Your value must be in the listed ranges for your sample size to be significant at the 5% level (i.e. to accept the hypothesis).

Number of pairs of scores (ignoring any tied pairs)	Significant at 5% level Accept hypothesis
6–8	0 only
9–11	0 to 1
12–14	0 to 2
15–16	0 to 3
17–19	0 to 4
20–22	0 to 5
23–24	0 to 6
25–27	0 to 7
28–29	0 to 8
30–32	0 to 9
33–34	0 to 10
35–36	0 to 11
37–39	0 to 12
40–41	0 to 13
42–43	0 to 14
44–46	0 to 15
47–48	0 to 16
49–50	0 to 17

The above table has been adapted and extended from Table M of R.P. Runyon, A. Haber and K.A. Coleman (1994). *Behavioural Statistics: The Core*. New York: McGraw-Hill. With the kind permission of the publisher.

Step 2:   Count the *number* of scores which are positively signed and then count the *number* of scores which are negatively signed. (Don't forget that zero differences are ignored in the sign test.)

Step 3:   Take whichever is the smaller number – the number of positive signs or the number of negative signs.

Step 4:   Look up the significance of this smaller number in Significance Table 18.1. You need to find the row which contains the *sum* of the positive and negative signs (i.e. ignoring zero differences). Your value has to be in the tabulated range to be statistically significant.

   In our example, there are 6 negative and 2 positive signs; 2 is the smaller number. The sum of positive and negative signs is 8. Significance Table 18.1

gives the significant values of the smaller number of signs as 0 only. Therefore our value is not statistically unusual and we accept the null hypothesis.

If your number of pairs of scores is too many for the table, it would be a good approximation to use the one-sample chi-square formula (Calculation 14.3), given that you would expect equal numbers of positive and negative differences under the null hypothesis that 'the two samples do not differ'. That is, the distributions of the sign test and the McNemar Test (Section 14.7) for the significance of changes are the same.

Calculation 18.2

The Wilcoxon Matched Pairs test

The test is also known as the Wilcoxon Signed Ranks test. It is similar to the sign test except that when we have obtained the difference score we rank-order the differences ignoring the sign of the difference.

Step 1:   The difference scores are calculated and then ranked ignoring the sign of the difference (Table 18.3). Notice that where there are tied values of the differences, we have allocated the average of the ranks which would be given if it were possible to separate the scores. Thus the two difference scores which equal 1 are both given the rank 1.5 since if the scores did differ minutely one would be given the rank 1 and the other the rank 2. Take care: zero differences are ignored and are *not* ranked.

Table 18.3   **Steps in the calculation of the Wilcoxon Matched Pairs test**

Subject	Six months X_1	Nine months X_2	Difference $D = X_1 - X_2$	Rank of difference ignoring sign during ranking
Baby Clara	3	7	−4	7.5⁻
Baby Martin	5	6	−1	1.5⁻
Baby Sally	5	3	2	4.5⁺
Baby Angie	4	8	−4	7.5⁻
Baby Trevor	3	5	−2	4.5⁻
Baby Sam	7	9	−2	4.5⁻
Baby Bobby	8	7	1	1.5⁺
Baby Sid	7	9	−2	4.5⁻

Step 2: The ranks of the differences can now have the sign of the difference reattached – we have used superscripts after the rank to identify this in Table 18.3.

Step 3: The sum of the positive ranks is calculated $= 4.5 + 1.5 = 6$. The sum of the negative ranks is calculated $= 7.5 + 1.5 + 7.5 + 4.5 + 4.5 + 4.5 = 30$.

Step 4: We then decide which is the smaller of the two sums of ranks – in this case it is 6. This is normally designated T.

Step 5: We then find the significance values of T (the smaller of the two sums of ranks) from Significance Table 18.2. This is structured in terms of the number of pairs of scores used in the calculation, which is 8 in the present case. The critical value for a two-tailed test at the 5% level is 4 or less. Our value is 6 which is not statistically significant.

If your sample size is larger than Significance Table 18.2 deals with, Appendix B explains how to test for significance.

Significance Table 18.2 **5% Significance values for the Wilcoxon Matched Pairs test (two-tailed test)**

Your value must be in the listed ranges for your sample size to be significant at the 5% level (i.e. to accept the hypothesis).

Number of pairs of scores (ignoring any tied pairs)	Significant at 5% level Accept hypothesis
6	0 only
7	0 to 2
8	0 to 4
9	0 to 6
10	0 to 8
11	0 to 11
12	0 to 14
13	0 to 17
14	0 to 21
15	0 to 25
16	0 to 30
17	0 to 35
18	0 to 40
19	0 to 46
20	0 to 52
21	0 to 59
22	0 to 66
23	0 to 73
24	0 to 81
25	0 to 89

The above table has been adapted and extended from Table J of R.P. Runyon and A. Haber (1989). *Fundamentals of Behavioural Statistics*. New York: McGraw-Hill. With the kind permission of the publisher.

Generally speaking it is difficult to suggest circumstances in which the sign test is to be preferred over the Wilcoxon Matched Pairs test. The latter uses more of the information contained within the data and so is more likely to detect significant differences where they exist.

The sign test can be applied in virtually any circumstance in which the expected population distribution under the null hypothesis is 50% of one outcome and 50% of another. In other words, the table of significance of the sign test can be used to check for departures from this 50–50 expectation.

Tests for unrelated samples

The major nonparametric test for differences between two groups of unrelated or uncorrelated scores is the Mann–Whitney U-test.

Calculation 18.3

The Mann–Whitney U-test

The commonest nonparametric statistic for unrelated samples of scores is the Mann–Whitney U-test. This is used for similar research designs as the unrelated or uncorrelated scores *t*-test (Chapter 13). In other words, it can be used whenever you have two groups of scores which are independent of each other (i.e. they are usually based on different samples of people). We will use the identical data upon which we demonstrated the calculation of the unrelated / uncorrelated scores *t*-test (Chapter 13).

Step 1: Rank all of the scores from the smallest to the largest (Table 18.4). Scores which are equal are allocated the average of ranks that they would be given if there were tiny differences between the scores. *Be careful! All of your scores are ranked irrespective of the group they are in.* To avoid confusion, *use the first column for the larger group* of scores. If both groups are equal in size then either can be entered in the first column. Group size $N_1 = 12$ for the two-parent families and $N_2 = 10$ for the lone-parent families.

Step 2: Sum the ranks for the *larger* group of scores. This is R_1. (If the groups are equal in size then either can be selected.)

Step 3: The sum of ranks (R_1) of Group 1 (174.5) (the larger group) and its sample size N_1 ($N_1 = 12$) together with the sample size N_2 of Group 2 ($N_2 = 10$) are entered into the following formula which gives you the value of the statistic U:

Table 18.4   **Steps in the calculation of the Mann–Whitney U-test**

Two-parent families (X_1) (This column is for the larger group)	Rankings	Lone-parent families (X_2) (This column is for the smaller group)	Rankings
12	12.5	6	2
18	21	9	6
14	16.5	4	1
10	8.5	13	14.5
19	22	14	16.5
8	3.5	9	6
15	18.5	8	3.5
11	10.5	12	12.5
10	8.5	11	10.5
13	14.5	9	6
15	18.5		
16	20		
	$\Sigma R_1 = 174.5$ (note that this is the sum of ranks for the *larger* group)		

$$U = (N_1 \times N_2) + \frac{N_1 \times (N_1 + 1)}{2} - R_1$$

$$= (12 \times 10) + \frac{12 \times (12 + 1)}{2} - 174.5$$

$$= 120 + \frac{12 \times 13}{2} - 174.5$$

$$= 120 + \frac{156}{2} - 174.5$$

$$= 120 + 78 - 174.5$$

$$= 198 - 174.5$$

$$= 23.5$$

Step 4:   Check the significance of your value of U by consulting Significance Table 18.3. In order to use this table, you need to find your value of N_1 in the column headings and your value of N_2 in the row headings. (However, since the table is symmetrical it does not matter if you use the rows instead of the columns and vice versa.) The table gives the *two* ranges of values of U which

Significance Table 18.3   **5% Significance values for the Mann–Whitney U-test (two-tailed test)**

Your value must be in the listed ranges for your sample sizes to be significant at the 5% level (i.e. to accept the hypothesis).

Sample size for smaller group	Sample size for larger group											
	5	**6**	**7**	**8**	**9**	**10**	**11**	**12**	**13**	**14**	**15**	**20**
5	0–2	0–3	0–5	0–6	0–7	0–8	0–9	0–11	0–12	0–13	0–14	0–20
	23–25	27–30	30–35	34–40	38–45	42–50	46–55	49–60	53–65	57–70	61–75	80–100
6	0–3	0–5	0–6	0–8	0–10	0–11	0–13	0–14	0–16	0–17	0–19	0–27
	27–30	31–36	36–42	40–48	44–54	49–60	53–66	58–72	62–78	67–84	71–90	93–120
7	0–5	0–6	0–8	0–10	0–12	0–14	0–16	0–18	0–20	0–22	0–24	0–34
	30–35	36–42	41–49	46–56	51–63	56–70	61–77	66–84	71–91	76–98	81–105	106–140
8	0–6	0–8	0–10	0–13	0–15	0–17	0–19	0–22	0–24	0–26	0–29	0–41
	34–40	40–48	46–56	51–64	57–72	63–80	69–88	74–96	80–104	86–112	91–120	119–160
9	0–7	0–10	0–12	0–15	0–17	0–20	0–23	0–26	0–28	0–31	0–34	0–48
	38–45	44–54	51–63	57–72	64–81	70–90	76–99	82–108	89–117	95–126	101–135	132–180
10	0–8	0–11	0–14	0–17	0–20	0–23	0–26	0–29	0–33	0–36	0–39	0–55
	42–50	49–60	56–70	63–80	70–90	77–100	84–110	91–120	97–130	104–140	111–150	145–200
11	0–9	0–13	0–16	0–19	0–23	0–26	0–30	0–33	0–37	0–40	0–44	0–62
	46–55	53–66	61–77	69–88	76–99	84–110	91–121	99–132	106–143	114–154	121–165	158–220
12	0–11	0–14	0–18	0–22	0–26	0–29	0–33	0–37	0–41	0–45	0–49	0–69
	49–60	58–72	66–84	74–96	82–108	91–120	99–132	107–144	115–156	123–168	131–180	171–240
13	0–12	0–16	0–20	0–24	0–28	0–33	0–37	0–41	0–45	0–50	0–54	0–76
	53–65	62–78	71–91	80–104	89–117	97–130	106–143	115–156	124–169	132–182	141–195	184–260
14	0–13	0–17	0–22	0–26	0–31	0–36	0–40	0–45	0–50	0–55	0–59	0–83
	57–70	67–84	76–98	86–112	95–126	104–140	114–154	123–168	132–182	141–196	151–210	197–280
15	0–14	0–19	0–24	0–29	0–34	0–39	0–44	0–49	0–54	0–59	0–64	0–90
	61–75	71–90	81–105	91–120	101–135	111–150	121–165	131–180	141–195	151–210	161–225	210–300
20	0–20	0–27	0–34	0–41	0–48	0–55	0–62	0–69	0–76	0–83	0–90	0–127
	80–100	93–120	106–140	119–160	132–180	145–200	158–220	171–240	184–260	197–280	210–300	273–400

The above table has been adapted and extended from Table I of R.P. Runyon and A. Haber (1989). *Fundamentals of Behavioural Statistics*. New York: McGraw-Hill. With the kind permission of the publisher.

are significant. Your value must be in *either* of these two ranges to be statistically significant. (Appendix B explains what to do if your sample size exceeds the largest value in the table.)

The table tells us that for sample sizes of 12 and 10, the ranges are 0 to 29 or 91 to 120. Our value of 23.5 therefore is significant at the 5% level. In other words, we reject the null hypothesis that the independent variable is unrelated to the dependent variable in favour of the view that family structure has an influence on scores of the dependent variable.

18.4 Three or more groups of scores

The Kruskal–Wallis test and the Friedman test are essentially extensions of the Mann–Whitney U-test and the Wilcoxon Matched Pairs test respectively. Appendix C gives information on how to calculate these nonparametric statistics.

18.5 Notes and recommendations

- Often you will not require nonparametric tests of significance of the sort described in this chapter. The *t*-test will usually fit the task better.

- Only when you have marked symmetry problems in your data will you require the nonparametric tests. But even then remember that a version of the unrelated *t*-test is available to cope with some aspects of the problem (Chapter 13).

- The computations for the nonparametric tests may appear simpler. A big disadvantage is that when the sample sizes get large the problems in ranking escalate disproportionately.

- Some professional psychologists tend to advocate nonparametric techniques for entirely outmoded reasons.

- There is no guarantee that the nonparametric test will always do the job better when the assumptions of parametric tests are violated.

- There are large sample formulae for the nonparametric tests reported here for when your sample sizes are too big for the printed tables of significance. However, by the time this point is reached the computation is getting clumsy and can be better handled by a computer; also the advantages of the nonparametric tests are very reduced.

Recommended further reading

Mariscuilo, L.A., and McSweeney, M. (1977). *Nonparametric and Distribution-Free Methods for the Social Sciences*. Monterey, CA: Brooks/Cole Publishing Company.

Siegel, S., and Castellan, N.J. (1988). *Nonparametric Statistics for the Behavioral Sciences*. New York: McGraw-Hill.

Part 3

Introduction to analysis of variance

Chapter 19

The variance ratio test

The *F*-ratio to compare two variances

Preparation
Make sure that you understand variance and the variance estimate (Chapters 3 and 11). Familiarity with the t-test will help with some applications (Chapters 12 and 13).

19.1 The research problem

In a number of circumstances in research it is important to compare the variances of two samples of scores. The conventions of psychological research stress examining the sample *means* with each other. However, it is perfectly possible to find that despite the means of two groups being identical, their variances are radically different. Take the following simple experiment in which men and women are shown advertisements for tights, illustrated in Table 19.1. The dependent variable is the readers' degree of liking for the product rated on a

Table 19.1 **Data comparing men and women on ratings of tights**

Men	Women
5	1
4	6
4	7
3	2
5	6
4	7
3	5
6	7
5	2
5	6
	1
	2

scale from 1 to 7 (on which 1 means that they strongly disliked the advertisement and 7 means that they strongly liked the advertisement).

The big difference between the two groups is not in terms of their means – the men's mean is 4.4 whereas the women's mean is 4.3. This is a small and unimportant difference. What is more noticeable is that the women seem to be split into two camps. The women's scores tend to be large or small with little in the centre. There is more variance in the women's scores. Just how does one test to see whether the differences in variances are significant?

There are other circumstances in which we compare variances:

1. For the unrelated t-test, it is conventional to make sure that the two samples do not differ significantly in terms of their variances – if they do then it is better to opt for an 'unpooled' t-test (see Chapter 13).

2. Another major application is the analysis of variance in which variance estimates are compared (see Chapter 20).

The statistical test to use in all these circumstances is called the F-ratio test or the variance ratio test.

Significance Table 19.1 **5% Significance values of the *F*-distribution for testing differences in variance estimates between two samples (two-tailed test)**

Your value has to equal or be larger than the tabulated value to be significant at the 5% level for a two-tailed test (i.e. to accept the hypothesis).

Additional values are to be found in Significance Table 20.1, 21.1 or 22.1.

Degrees of freedom for smaller variance estimate (denominator)	Degrees of freedom for larger variance estimate (numerator)					
	5	7	10	20	50	∞
5	5.1 or more	4.9	4.7	4.6	4.4	4.4
6	4.4	4.1	4.1	3.9	3.8	3.7
7	4.0	3.8	3.6	3.4	3.3	3.2
8	3.7	3.5	3.3	3.2	3.0	2.9
10	3.3	3.1	3.0	2.8	2.6	2.5
12	3.1	2.9	2.8	2.5	2.4	2.3
15	2.9	2.7	2.6	2.3	2.2	2.1
20	2.7	2.5	2.4	2.1	2.0	1.8
30	2.5	2.3	2.2	1.9	1.8	1.6
50	2.4	2.2	2.0	1.8	1.6	1.4
100	2.3	2.1	1.9	1.7	1.5	1.3
∞	2.2	2.0	1.8	1.6	1.4	1.0

The above table has been adapted and extended from Table D of R.P. Runyon and A. Haber (1989). *Fundamentals of Behavioural Statistics*. New York: McGraw-Hill. With the kind permission of the publisher.

19.2 Theoretical issues and an application

The variance ratio simply compares two variances together in order to test whether they come from the same population. In other words, are the differences between the variances simply the result of chance sampling fluctuations? Of course, since we are comparing samples from a population we need the variance estimate formula. In the simpler applications of the variance ratio test (*F*-ratio) the variance estimate involves using the sample size minus one ($N - 1$) as the denominator (lower part) of the variance estimate formula. (This does not apply in quite the same way in the more advanced case of the analysis of variance, as we will see in Chapter 20 onwards.)

The variance ratio formula is as follows:

$$F = \frac{\text{larger variance estimate}}{\text{smaller variance estimate}}$$

There is a table of the *F* distribution (Significance Table 19.1) which is organised according to the degrees of freedom of the two variance estimates.

Calculation 19.1

The variance ratio (*F*-ratio)

Imagine a very simple piece of clinical research which involves the administration of electro convulsive therapy (ECT). There are two experimental conditions – in one case the electric current is passed through the left hemisphere of the brain and in the other case it is passed through the right hemisphere of the brain. The dependent variable is scores on a test of emotional stability

Table 19.2   **Emotional stability scores from a study of ECT to different hemispheres of the brain**

Left hemisphere	Right hemisphere
20	36
14	28
18	4
22	18
13	2
15	22
9	1
Mean = 15.9	Mean = 15.9

following treatment. Patients were assigned to one or other group at random. The scores following treatment were as listed in Table 19.2 (p. 187).

Quite clearly there is no difference in terms of the mean scores on emotional stability. Looking at the data, though, it looks as if ECT to the right hemisphere tends to push people to the extremes whereas ECT to the left hemisphere leaves a more compact distribution.

To calculate the variance ratio, the variance *estimates* of the two separate samples (left and right hemispheres) have to be calculated using the usual variance estimate formula. The following is the computational formula version of this:

$$\text{Estimated variance} = \frac{\Sigma X^2 - \frac{(\Sigma X)^2}{N}}{N-1}$$

Step 1: Calculate the variance of the first group of scores (i.e. the left hemisphere group), as in Table 19.3. The sample size (number of scores) is $N_1 = 7$.

Table 19.3   **Step 1 in the calculation of the variance estimate**

X_1 = left hemisphere	X_1^2
20	400
14	196
18	324
22	484
13	169
15	225
9	81
$\Sigma X_1 = 111$	$\Sigma X_1^2 = 1879$

Substituting in the formula:

$$\text{Variance estimate}_{[\text{group 1}]} = \frac{\Sigma X_1^2 - \frac{(\Sigma X_1)^2}{N_1}}{N_1 - 1}$$

$$= \frac{1879 - \frac{111^2}{7}}{7 - 1}$$

$$= \frac{1879 - \frac{12321}{7}}{6}$$

$$= \frac{1879 - 1760.143}{6}$$

$$= \frac{118.857}{6}$$

$$= 19.81 \text{ (degrees of freedom} = N_1 - 1 = 6)$$

Step 2:   The variance estimate of the right hemisphere group is calculated using the standard computational formula as in Table 19.4. The sample size $N_2 = 7$.

Table 19.4   **Step 2 in the calculation of the variance estimate**

X_2 = right hemisphere	X_2^2
36	1296
28	784
4	16
18	324
2	4
22	484
1	1
$\Sigma X_2 = 111$	$\Sigma X_2^2 = 2909$

Substituting in the formula:

$$\text{Variance estimate}_{[\text{group 2}]} = \frac{\Sigma X_2^2 - \frac{(\Sigma X_2)^2}{N_2}}{N_2 - 1}$$

$$= \frac{2909 - \frac{111^2}{7}}{7 - 1}$$

$$= \frac{2909 - \frac{12321}{7}}{6}$$

$$= \frac{2909 - 1760.143}{6}$$

$$= \frac{1148.857}{6}$$

$$= 191.48 \text{ (degrees of freedom} = N_2 - 1 = 6)$$

Step 3: The larger variance estimate is divided by the smaller:

$$F = \frac{\text{larger variance estimate}}{\text{smaller variance estimate}}$$

$$= \frac{191.48}{19.81}$$

$$= 9.67 \text{ (df larger variance estimate} = 6,$$
$$\text{df smaller variance estimate} = 6)$$

Step 4: We need to check whether or not a difference between the two variance estimates as large as this ratio implies would be likely if the samples came from the same population of scores. Significance Table 19.1 contains the critical values for the F-ratio. To use the table you find the intersection of the column for the degrees of freedom for the larger variance estimate and the degrees of freedom for the smaller variance estimate. Notice that the degrees of freedom we want are not listed for the numerator, so we take the next smaller listed value. Thus the table tells us we need a value of 4.39 at a minimum to be significant at the 5% level with a two-tailed test. Our calculated value of F is substantially in excess of the critical value. Thus we conclude that it is very unlikely that the two samples come from the same population of scores. We accept the hypothesis that the two sample variances are significantly different from each other.

19.3 Notes and recommendations

- Psychologists often fail to explore for differences in variances. It is good practice to routinely examine your data for them.

- The F-ratio is a necessary adjunct to applying the unrelated t-test correctly. Make sure that you check that the variances are indeed similar before using the t-test.

- Be very careful when you use the F-ratio in the analysis of variance (Chapter 20 onwards). The F-ratio in the analysis of variance is not quite the same. In this you do not always divide the larger variance estimate by the smaller variance estimate.

Chapter 20

Analysis of variance (ANOVA)

Introduction to the one-way unrelated or uncorrelated ANOVA

Preparation

It is pointless to start this chapter without a clear understanding of how to calculate the basic variance estimate formula and the computational formula for variance estimate. A working knowledge of the variance ratio test (F-ratio test) is also essential.

20.1 Introduction

Up to this point we have discussed research designs comparing the means of just *two* groups of scores. The analysis of variance (ANOVA) can do this but in addition can extend the comparison to three or more groups of scores. Analysis of variance takes many forms but is primarily used to analyse the results of experiments. Nevertheless, the simpler forms of ANOVA are routinely used in surveys and similar types of research. This chapter describes the one-way analysis of variance. This can be used whenever we wish to compare two or more groups in terms of their mean scores on a dependent variable. The scores must be independent (uncorrelated or unrelated). In other words each respondent contributes just one score to the statistical analysis. Stylistically, Table 20.1 is the sort of research design for which the (uncorrelated or unrelated) one-way analysis of variance is appropriate.

Table 20.1 **Stylised table of data for unrelated analysis of variance**

Group 1	Group 2	Group 3	Group 4
9	3	1	27
14	1	4	24
11	5	2	25
12	5	31	

The scores are those on the dependent variable. The groups are the independent variable. There are very few limitations on the research designs to which this is applicable:

1. It is possible to have any number of groups with the minimum being two.
2. The groups consist of independent samples of scores. For example the groups could be:
   - men versus women
   - an experimental versus one control group
   - four experimental groups and one control group
   - three different occupational types – managers, office personnel, and production workers.
3. The scores (the dependent variable) can be for virtually any variable. The main thing is that they are numerical scores suitable for calculating the mean and variance.
4. It is *not* necessary to have equal numbers of scores in each group. With other forms of analysis of variance, not having equal numbers can cause complications.

20.2 Some revision and some new material

You should be familiar with most of the following. Remember the formula for *variance*:

$$\text{Variance}_{[\text{definitional formula}]} = \frac{\Sigma (X - \overline{X})^2}{N}$$

If you wish to estimate the variance of a population from the variation in a sample from that population, you use the *variance estimate* formula which is:

$$\text{Variance estimate}_{[\text{definitional formula}]} = \frac{\Sigma (X - \overline{X})^2}{N - 1}$$

(By dividing by $N - 1$ we get an unbiased estimate of the population variance from the sample data.)

It is useful if you memorise the fact that the top part of the formula

$$\Sigma (X - \overline{X})^2$$

is called the *sum of squares*. It is the sum of the squared deviations from the mean. The phrase 'sum of squares' occurs repeatedly in all forms of the analysis of variance so cannot be escaped.

The bottom part of the variance formula (N) or variance estimate formula ($N - 1$) is called in the analysis of variance the *degrees of freedom*. It is a little complex in that its calculation can vary. Nevertheless, memorising that the phrase 'degrees of freedom' refers to the bottom part of the variance formulae is a useful start.

We can rewrite the above formulae as *computational formulae*:

$$\text{Variance estimate}_{[\text{computational formula}]} = \frac{\Sigma X^2 - \dfrac{(\Sigma X)^2}{N}}{N-1}$$

20.3 Theoretical considerations

The analysis of variance (ANOVA) involves very few new ideas. However, some basic concepts are used in a relatively novel way. Unfortunately, most textbooks confuse readers by presenting the analysis of variance rather obscurely. In particular, they use a variant of the computational formula for the calculation of the variance estimate which makes it very difficult to follow the logic of what is happening. This is a pity since the analysis of variance is relatively simple in many respects. The main problem is the number of steps which have to be coped with.

All measurement assumes that a score is made up of two components:

■ the 'true' value of the measurement

■ an 'error' component.

Most psychological measurements tend to have a large error component compared to the true component. Error results from all sorts of factors – tiredness, distraction, unclear instructions and so forth. Normally we cannot say precisely to what extent these factors influence our scores. It is further assumed that the 'true' and 'error' components add together to give the obtained scores (i.e. the data). So, for example, an obtained score of 15 might be made up of:

$$15_{[\text{obtained score}]} = 12_{[\text{true}]} + 3_{[\text{error}]}$$

or an obtained score of 20 might be made up as follows:

$$20 = 24 + (-4)$$

The error score may take a positive or negative value.

We have no certain knowledge about anything other than the obtained scores. *The true and error scores cannot be known directly. However, in some circumstances we can infer them through intelligent guesswork.*

In the analysis of variance, each score is separated into the two components – true scores and error scores. This is easier than it sounds. Look at Table 20.2 from some fictitious research. It is a study of the effects of two different hormones and an inert (placebo) control on depression scores in men.

Tables 20.3 and 20.4 give the best estimates possible of the 'true' scores and 'error' scores in Table 20.2. Try to work out the simple 'tricks' we have employed. All we did to produce these two new tables was the following:

Table 20.2 Stylised table of data for unrelated analysis of variance with means

Group 1 Hormone 1	Group 2 Hormone 2	Group 3 Placebo control
9	4	3
12	2	6
8	5	3
Mean = 9.667	Mean = 3.667	Mean = 4.000
		Overall mean = 5.778

Table 20.3 'True' scores based on the data in Table 20.2

Group 1 Hormone 1	Group 2 Hormone 2	Group 3 Placebo control
9.667	3.667	4.000
9.667	3.667	4.000
9.667	3.667	4.000
Mean = 9.667	Mean = 3.667	Mean = 4.000
		Overall mean = 5.778

Table 20.4 'Error' scores based on the data in Table 20.2

Group 1 Hormone 1	Group 2 Hormone 2	Group 3 Placebo control
−0.667	0.333	−1.000
2.333	−1.667	2.000
−1.667	1.333	−1.000
Mean = 0.000	Mean = 0.000	Mean = 0.000
		Overall mean = 0.000

1. In order to obtain a table of 'true' scores we have simply substituted the column mean for each group for the individual scores, the assumption being that the obtained scores deviate from the 'true' score because of the influence of varying amounts of error in the measurement. In statistical theory, error is assumed to be randomly distributed. Thus we have replaced all of the scores for Group 1 by the mean of 9.667. The column mean is simply the best estimate of what the 'true' score would be for the group *if we could get*

rid of the 'error' component. As all of the scores are the same, there is absolutely no error component in any of the conditions of Table 20.3. The assumption in this is that the variability within a column is due to error so the average score in a column is our best estimate of the 'true' score for that column. Notice that the column means are unchanged by this.

2. We have obtained the table of 'error' scores (Table 20.4) simply by subtracting the scores in the 'true' scores table (Table 20.3) away from the corresponding score in the original scores table (Table 20.2). What is not a 'true' score is an 'error' score by definition. Notice that the error scores show a mixture of positive and negative values, *and* that the sum of the error scores in each column (and the entire table for that matter) is zero. This is always the case with error scores so constitutes an important check on your calculations. An alternative way of obtaining the error scores is to take the column (or group) mean away from each score in the original data table.

So what do we do now that we have the 'true' scores and 'error' scores? The two derived sets of scores – the 'true' and the 'error' scores – are used separately to estimate the variance of the population of scores from which they are samples. (That is, the calculated variance estimate for the 'true' scores is an estimate of the 'true' variation in the population, and the calculated variance estimate of the 'error' scores is an estimate of the 'error' variation in the population.) Remember, the null hypothesis for this research would suggest that differences between the three groups are due to error rather than real differences related to the influence of the independent variable. The null hypothesis suggests that both the 'true' and 'error' variance estimates are similar since they are both the result of error. *If the null hypothesis is correct*, the variance estimate derived from the 'true' scores should be no different from the variance estimate derived from the 'error' scores. After all, under the null hypothesis the variation in the 'true' scores is due to error anyway. *If the alternative hypothesis is correct*, then there should be rather more variation in the 'true' scores than is typical in the 'error' scores.

We calculate the variance estimate of the 'true' scores and then calculate the variance estimate for the 'error' scores. Next the two variance estimates are examined to see whether they are significantly different using the *F*-ratio test (the variance ratio test). This involves the following calculation:

$$F = \frac{\text{variance estimate}_{\text{[of true scores]}}}{\text{variance estimate}_{\text{[of error scores]}}}$$

(The error variance is always at the bottom in the analysis of variance. This is different from the *F*-ratio test described in the previous chapter. This is because we want to know if the variance estimate of the true scores is *bigger* than the variance estimate of the 'error' scores. It is of little interest if the error variance is bigger than the true variance estimate.)

Significance Table 20.1   5% Significance values of the *F*-ratio for unrelated ANOVA

Your value has to equal or be larger than the tabulated value to be significant at the 5% level for a two-tailed test (i.e. to accept the hypothesis).

Additional values are to be found in Significance Table 19.1.

Degrees of freedom for error or within-cells mean square (or variance estimate)	Degrees of freedom for true or between-treatments mean square (or variance estimate)					
	1	2	3	4	5	∞
1	161 or more	200	216	225	230	254
2	18.5	19.0	19.2	19.3	19.3	19.5
3	10.1	9.6	9.3	9.1	9.0	8.5
4	7.7	6.9	6.6	6.4	6.3	5.6
5	6.6	5.8	5.4	5.2	5.1	4.4
6	6.0	5.1	4.8	4.5	4.4	3.7
7	5.6	4.7	4.4	4.1	4.0	3.2
8	5.3	4.5	4.1	3.8	3.7	2.9
9	5.1	4.3	3.9	3.6	3.5	2.7
10	5.0	4.1	3.7	3.5	3.3	2.5
13	4.7	3.8	3.4	3.2	3.0	2.2
15	4.5	3.7	3.3	3.1	2.9	2.1
20	4.4	3.5	3.1	2.9	2.7	1.8
30	4.2	3.3	2.9	2.7	2.5	1.6
60	4.0	3.2	2.8	2.5	2.4	1.4
∞	3.8	3.0	2.6	2.4	2.2	1.0

The above table has been adapted and extended from Table D of R.P. Runyon and A. Haber (1989). *Fundamentals of Behavioural Statistics*. New York: McGraw-Hill. With the kind permission of the publisher.

It is then a fairly straightforward matter to use Significance Table 20.1 for the *F*-distribution to decide whether or not these two variance estimates are significantly different from each other. We just need to be careful to use the appropriate numbers of degrees of freedom. The *F*-ratio calculation was demonstrated in Chapter 19. If the variance estimates are similar then the variance in 'true' scores is little different from the variance in the 'error' scores; since the estimated 'true' variance is much the same as the 'error' variance in this case, both can be regarded as 'error'. On the other hand, if the *F*-ratio is significant it means that the variation due to the 'true' scores is much greater than that due to 'error'; the 'true' scores represent reliable differences between groups rather than chance factors.

And that is just about it for the one-way analysis of variance. There is just one remaining issue – the *degrees of freedom*. If one were to work out the variance estimate of the original data in our study we would use the formula as given above:

$$\text{Variance estimate}_{[\text{original data}]} = \frac{\Sigma X^2 - \frac{(\Sigma X)^2}{N}}{N - 1}$$

where $N - 1$ is the number of degrees of freedom.

However, the calculation of the number of degrees of freedom varies in the analysis of variance (it is not always $N - 1$). With the 'true' and 'error' scores the degrees of freedom are a little more complex although easily calculated using formulae. But the idea of degrees of freedom can be understood at a more fundamental level with a little work.

20.4 Degrees of freedom

This section gives a detailed explanation of degrees of freedom. It might be convenient to ignore this section until you are a little more familiar with ANOVA.

Degrees of freedom refer to the distinct items of information contained in your data. By information we mean something which is new and not already known. For example, if we asked you what is the combined age of your two best friends and then asked you the age of the younger of the two, you would be crazy to accept a bet that we could tell you the age of your older best friend, the reason being that if you told us that the combined ages of your best friends was 37 years and that the younger was 16 years, any fool could work out that the older best friend must be 21 years. The age of your older best friend is contained within the first two pieces of information. The age of your older friend is redundant because you already know it from your previous information.

It is much the same sort of idea with degrees of freedom – which might be better termed the quantity of distinct information.

Table 20.5 'True' scores based on the data in Table 20.2

Group 1 Hormone 1	Group 2 Hormone 2	Group 3 Placebo control
9.667	3.667	4.000
9.667	3.667	4.000
9.667	3.667	4.000
Mean = 9.667	Mean = 3.667	Mean = 4.000
		Overall mean = 5.778

Table 20.6   Insertion of arbitrary values in the first column

Group 1	Group 2	Group 3
10.000	–	–
10.000	–	–
10.000	–	–
Mean = 10.000		
		Overall mean = 5.778

Table 20.7   Insertion of arbitrary values in the second column

Group 1	Group 2	Group 3
10.000	3.000	–
10.000	3.000	–
10.000	3.000	–
Mean = 10.000	Mean = 3.000	
		Overall mean = 5.778

Table 20.5 repeats the table of the 'true' scores that we calculated earlier as Table 20.3. The question is how many items of truly new information the table contains. You have to bear in mind that what we are looking at is the variance estimate of the scores which is basically their variation around the overall mean of 5.778. Don't forget that the overall mean of 5.778 is our best estimate of the population mean under the null hypothesis that the groups do not differ. Just how many of the scores in this table are we able to alter and still obtain this same overall mean of 5.778?

Well, for this table, we simply start scrubbing out the scores one-by-one and putting in any value we like. So *if we start with the first person in Group 1* we can arbitrarily set his or her score to 10.000 (or any other score you can think of). But, once we have done so, each score in Group 1 has to be changed to 10.000 because the columns of the 'true' score table have to have identical entries. Thus the first column has to look like the column in Table 20.6 (the dashes represent parts of the table we have not dealt with yet).

We have been free to vary just one score so far. We can now move on to the Group 2 column. Here we can arbitrarily put in a score of 3.000 to replace the first entry. Once we do this then the remaining two scores in the column have to be the same because this is the nature of 'true' tables – all the scores in a column have to be identical (Table 20.7).

Thus so far we have managed to vary only two scores independently. We can now move on to Group 3. We could start by entering, say, 5.000 to replace the

Table 20.8   Forced insertion of a particular value in the third column because of the requirement that the overall mean is 5.778

Group 1	Group 2	Group 3
10.000	3.000	4.333
10.000	3.000	4.333
10.000	3.000	4.333
Mean = 10.000	Mean = 3.000	Mean = 4.333
		Overall mean = 5.778

Table 20.9   'Error' scores based on the data in Table 20.2

Group 1	Group 2	Group 3
−0.667	0.333	−1.000
2.333	−1.667	2.000
−1.667	1.333	−1.000
Mean = 0.000	Mean = 0.000	Mean = 0.000
		Overall mean = 0.000

first score but there is a problem. The overall mean has to end up as 5.778 and the number 5.000 will not allow this to happen given that all of the scores in Group 3 would have to be 5.000. There is only one number which can be put in the Group 3 column which will give an overall mean of 5.778, that is 4.333 (Table 20.8).

We have not increased the number of scores we were free to vary by changing Group 3 – we have changed the scores but we had no freedom other than to put one particular score in their place.

Thus we have varied only *two* scores in the 'true' scores table – notice that this is one less than the number of groups we have. We speak of *the 'true' scores having two degrees of freedom.*

It is a similar process with the error table. The requirements this time are (a) that the column averages equal zero and (b) that the overall average equals zero. This is because they are error scores which must produce these characteristics – if they do not they cannot be error scores. Just how many of the scores can we vary this time and keep within these limitations? (We have 'adjusted' the column means to ignore a tiny amount of rounding error.)

The answer is six scores (Table 20.9). The first *two* scores in each group can be varied to any values you like. However, having done this the value of the third score has to be fixed in order that the column mean equals zero. Since there are three equal-size groups then there are *six degrees of freedom for the error table* in this case.

Just in case you are wondering, for the *original data* table the degrees of freedom correspond to the number of scores minus one. This is because there are no individual column constraints – the only constraint is that the overall mean has to be 5.778. The lack of column constraints means that the first eight scores could be given any value you like and only the final score is fixed by the requirement that the overall mean is 5.778. In other words, the variance estimate for the original data table uses $N - 1$ as the denominator – thus the formula is the usual variance estimate formula for a sample of scores.

Also note that the degrees of freedom for the 'error' and 'true' scores tables add up to $N - 1$.

Quick formulae for degrees of freedom

Anyone who has difficulty with the above explanation of degrees of freedom should take heart. Few of us would bother to work out the degrees of freedom from first principles. It is much easier to use simple formulae. For the one-way analysis of variance using unrelated samples, the degrees of freedom are as follows:

N = the number of scores in the table

degrees of freedom$_{[\text{original data}]} = N - 1$

degrees of freedom$_{[\text{'true' scores}]}$ = number of columns – 1

degrees of freedom$_{[\text{'error' scores}]} = N$ – number of columns

This is not cheating – most textbooks ignore the meaning of degrees of freedom and merely give the formulae anyway.

Calculation 20.1

Unrelated/uncorrelated one-way analysis of variance

Step-by-step, the following is the calculation of the analysis of variance.

Step 1: Draw up your data table using the format shown in Table 20.10. The degrees of freedom for this table is the number of scores minus one = $9 - 1 = 8$.

Table 20.10   **Data table for an unrelated analysis of variance**

Group 1 Hormone 1	Group 2 Hormone 2	Group 3 Placebo control
9	4	3
12	2	6
8	5	3
Mean = 9.667	Mean = 3.667	Mean = 4.000
		Overall mean = 5.778

Although this is not absolutely necessary you can calculate the variance estimate of your data table as a computational check – the sum of squares for the data table should equal the total of the sums of squares for the separate components. Thus, adding together the true and error sums of squares should give the total sum of squares for the data table. Similarly, the data degrees of freedom should equal the total of the true and error degrees of freedom. We will use the computational formula

$$\text{Variance estimate}_{[\text{original data}]} = \frac{\Sigma X^2 - \dfrac{(\Sigma X)^2}{N}}{\text{df}}$$

ΣX^2 means square each of the scores and then sum these individual calculations:

$$\Sigma X^2 = 9^2 + 4^2 + 3^2 + 12^2 + 2^2 + 6^2 + 8^2 + 5^2 + 3^2$$
$$= 81 + 16 + 9 + 144 + 4 + 36 + 64 + 25 + 9$$
$$= 388$$

$(\Sigma X)^2$ means add up all of the scores and then square the total:

$$(\Sigma X)^2 = (9 + 4 + 3 + 12 + 2 + 6 + 8 + 5 + 3)^2$$
$$= (52)^2$$
$$= 2704$$

The number of scores, N, equals 9. The degrees of freedom (df) equals $N - 1 = 9 - 1 = 8$. Substituting in the formula:

$$\text{Variance estimate}_{[\text{original data}]} = \frac{\Sigma X^2 - \dfrac{(\Sigma X)^2}{N}}{\text{df}}$$

$$= \frac{388 - \dfrac{2704}{9}}{8}$$

$$= \frac{388 - 300.444}{8}$$

$$= \frac{87.556}{8}$$

$$= 10.944$$

Step 2:   Draw up Table 20.11 of 'true' scores by replacing the scores in each column by the column mean.

Table 20.11 'True' scores based on the data in Table 20.10

Group 1	Group 2	Group 3
9.667	3.667	4.000
9.667	3.667	4.000
9.667	3.667	4.000
Mean = 9.667	Mean = 3.667	Mean = 4.000
		Overall mean = 5.778

ΣX^2 $= 9.667^2 + 3.667^2 + 4.000^2 + 9.667^2 + 3.667^2 + 4.000^2 + 9.667^2 + 3.667^2 + 4.000^2$

$= 93.451 + 13.447 + 16.000 + 93.451 + 13.447 + 16.000 + 93.451 + 13.447 + 16.000$

$= 368.694$

$(\Sigma X)^2 = (9.667 + 3.667 + 4.000 + 9.667 + 3.667 + 4.000 + 9.667 + 3.667 + 4.000)^2$

$= (52.000)^2$

$= 2704$

The number of scores, N, equals 9. The degrees of freedom (df) are given by:

Degrees of freedom$_{[\text{true scores}]}$ = number of columns – 1

$$= 3 - 1$$

$$= 2$$

We can now substitute in the formula:

$$\text{Variance estimate}_{[\text{true scores}]} = \frac{\Sigma X^2 - \dfrac{(\Sigma X)^2}{N}}{df}$$

$$= \frac{368.694 - \dfrac{2704}{9}}{2}$$

$$= \frac{368.694 - 300.444}{2}$$

$$= \frac{68.250}{2}$$

$$= 34.125$$

Table 20.12   'Error' scores based on the data in Table 20.10

Group 1	Group 2	Group 3
−0.667	0.333	−1.000
2.333	−1.667	2.000
−1.667	1.333	−1.000
Mean = 0.000	Mean = 0.000	Mean = 0.000
		Overall mean = 0.000

Step 3:   Draw up the table of the 'error' scores (Table 20.12) by subtracting the 'true' scores table from the original data table (Table 20.10). Remember all you have to do is to take the corresponding scores in the two tables when doing this subtraction. The alternative is to take the appropriate column mean away from each score in your data table.

$$\text{Variance estimate}_{[\text{original data}]} = \frac{\Sigma X^2 - \frac{(\Sigma X)^2}{N}}{\text{df}}$$

$\Sigma X^2 = (-0.667)^2 + 0.333^2 + (-1.000)^2 + 2.333^2 + (-1.667)^2 + 2.000^2 + (-1.667)^2 + 1.333^2 + (-1.000)^2$

$\quad = 0.445 + 0.111 + 1.000 + 5.443 + 2.779 + 4.000 + 2.779 + 1.777 + 1.000$

$\quad = 19.334$

$(\Sigma X)^2 = [(-0.667) + 0.333 + (-1.000) + 2.333 + (-1.667) + 2.000 + (-1.667) + 1.333 + (-1.000)]^2$

$\quad = 0$

The number of scores, N, equals 9. The degrees of freedom (df) equals N minus the number of columns, i.e. $9 - 3 = 6$. We can now substitute in the above formula:

$$\text{Variance estimate}_{[\text{error}]} = \frac{\Sigma X^2 - \frac{(\Sigma X)^2}{N}}{\text{df}}$$

$$= \frac{19.334 - \frac{0}{9}}{6}$$

$$= 3.222$$

Step 4:   We can now work out the F-ratio by dividing the variance estimate$_{[\text{true scores}]}$ by the variance estimate$_{[\text{error scores}]}$:

$$F\text{-ratio} = \frac{\text{variance estimate}_{[\text{true scores}]}}{\text{variance estimate}_{[\text{error scores}]}} = \frac{34.125}{3.222}$$

$$= 10.6 \text{ (degrees of freedom} = 2 \text{ for true and } 6 \text{ for error)}$$

From Significance Table 20.1 (p. 196), we need a value of F of 5.1 or more to be significant at the 5% level of significance. Since our value of 10.6 is substantially larger than this, we can reject the null hypothesis and accept the hypothesis that the groups are significantly different from each other at the 5% level of significance.

20.5 The analysis of variance summary table

The analysis of variance calculation can get very complicated with complex experimental designs. In preparation for this, it is useful to get into the habit of recording your analysis in an analysis of variance summary table. This systematically records major aspects of the calculation. Table 20.13 is appropriate to the above analysis. Notice that the sums of squares for 'true' and 'error' added together are the same as the sum of squares of the original data (allowing for rounding errors). Don't forget that the sum of squares is simply the upper part of the variance estimate formula. Similarly the degrees of freedom of 'true' and 'error' scores added together give the degrees of freedom for the original data. The degrees of freedom are the lower part of the variance estimate formula.

In Table 20.13, we have used the terminology from our explanation. This is not quite standard in discussions regarding the analysis of variance. It is more usual to see the analysis of variance summary table in the form of Table 20.14 which uses slightly different terms.

Tables 20.13 and 20.14 are equivalent except for the terminology and the style of reporting significance levels:

1. 'Mean square' is analysis of variance terminology for variance estimate. Unfortunately the name 'mean square' loses track of the fact that it is an estimate and suggests that it is something new.

Table 20.13   **Analysis of variance summary table for unrelated ANOVAs**

Source of variation	Sum of squares	Degrees of freedom	Variance estimate	*F*-ratio	Probability
'True' scores	68.250	2	34.125	10.6	5%
'Error' scores	19.334	6	3.222		
Original data	87.556	8	10.944		

Table 20.14   **Analysis of variance summary table for unrelated ANOVAs using alternative terminology**

Source of variation	Sum of squares	Degrees of freedom	Mean square	*F*-ratio
Between groups	68.250	2	34.125	10.6*
Within groups	19.334	6	3.222	
Total	87.556	8	10.944	

* Significant at 5% level.

2. 'Between' is another way of describing the variation due to the 'true' scores. The idea is that the variation of the 'true' scores is essentially the differences between the groups or experimental conditions. Sometimes these are called the 'treatments'.

3. 'Within' is just another way of describing the 'error' variation. It is called 'within' since the calculation of 'error' is based on the variation *within* a group or experimental condition.

4. Total is virtually self explanatory – it is the variation of the original scores which combine 'true' and 'error' components.

20.6 Notes and recommendations

■ The *t*-test is simply a special case of one-way ANOVA, so these tests can be used interchangeably when you have two groups of scores. They give identical significance levels.

■ Do not be too deterred by some of the strange terminology used in the analysis of variance. Words like treatments and levels of treatment merely reveal the agricultural origins of these statistical procedures; be warned that it gets worse. Levels of treatment simply refers to the number of different conditions for each independent variable. Thus if the independent variable has three different values it is said to have three different levels of the treatment.

■ The analysis of variance with just two conditions or sets of scores is relatively easy to interpret. You merely have to examine the difference between the means of the two conditions. It is not so easy where you have three or more groups. Your analysis may not be complete until you have employed a multiple comparisons procedure as in Chapter 23.

■ We have used computational procedures which are not identical to those in most textbooks. We have tried to explain the analysis of variance by referring to the basic notion of variance estimate. Virtually every textbook we have seen merely gives computational procedures alone.

Chapter 21

Analysis of variance for correlated scores or repeated measures

Preparation

You need a good understanding of the unrelated/uncorrelated analysis of variance (Chapter 20). In addition, the difference between correlated/related samples and unrelated/uncorrelated samples (or repeated measures) should be revised.

The analysis of variance reported in this chapter is also called the related, related scores, related samples, repeated measures and matched analysis of variance.

21.1 Introduction

Correlated or related research designs are held to be efficient forms of planning research. Generally these designs involve the same group of participants being assessed in two or more research conditions. The assumption is that by doing so many of the differences between people are 'allowed for' by having each person 'serve as their own control' – that is, appear in all of the research conditions.

The different sets of scores in the related or correlated analysis of variance are essentially different treatment conditions. We can describe them as either different levels of the treatment or different experimental conditions (Table 21.1).

The numerical scores are scores on the *dependent variable*. They can be any measures for which it is possible to calculate their means and variances meaningfully – in other words basically numerical scores. The treatments are the levels of the independent variable. There are very few limitations to the use of this research design:

1. It is possible to have any number of treatments with two being the minimum.

Table 21.1   **Stylised research design for the analysis of variance**

Case	Treatment 1	Treatment 2	Treatment 3	Treatment 4
Case 1 (John)	9	14	6	18
Case 2 (Heather)	7	12	9	15
Case 3 (Jane)	5	11	6	17
Case 4 (Tracy)	10	17	12	24
Case 5 (Paul)	8	15	7	19

Table 21.2   **Research design of IQ assessed sequentially over time**

Child	Age 5 years	Age 8 years	Age 10 years
John	120	125	130
Paula	93	90	100
Sharon	130	140	110
etc.			

Table 21.3   **Reaction time in seconds comparing two experimental conditions with two control conditions**

Subject	Four-letter words	Mild swear words	Neutral words	Nonsense syllables
Darren	0.3	0.5	0.2	0.2
Lisa	0.4	0.3	0.3	0.4
etc.				

2. The groups consist of related or correlated sets of scores, for example:

(a) children's IQs assessed at the age of 5 years, then again at 8 years and finally at 10 years (Table 21.2)

(b) two experimental conditions versus two control conditions so long as the same subjects are in each of the conditions. The research is a study of reaction time to recognising words. The two experimental conditions are very emotive words (four-letter words) and moderately emotive words (mild swear words). The two control conditions are using neutral words and using·nonsense syllables; the dependent variable is reaction time (Table 21.3)

(c) a group of weight watchers' weights before and after dieting. The dependent variable is their weight in pounds (Table 21.4).

3. It is necessary to have equal numbers of scores in each group since this is a related subjects or repeated measures design. Obviously in the above examples we have used small numbers of cases.

Table 21.4   **Weight in pounds before and after dieting**

Dieter	Before diet	After diet
Ben	130	120
Claudine	153	141
etc.		

Table 21.5   **Stylised ANOVA design using matched samples**

Matched set	Treatment 1	Treatment 2	Treatment 3	Treatment 4
Matched set 1	9	14	6	18
Matched set 2	7	12	9	15
Matched set 3	5	11	6	17
Matched set 4	10	17	12	24
Matched set 5	8	15	7	19

The related/correlated analysis of variance can also be applied when you have *matched sets* of people (Table 21.5). By this we mean that although there are different people in each of the treatment conditions, they are actually very similar. Each set is as alike as possible on specified variables such as age or intelligence. One member of each matched set is assigned at random to each of the treatment conditions. The variables forming the basis of the matching are believed or known to be correlated with the dependent variable. There is no point in matching if they are not. The purpose of matching is to reduce the amount of 'error' variation.

One advantage of using matched sets of people in experiments rather than the same person in several different treatment conditions is their lack of aware- ness of the other treatment conditions. That is, they only respond in one version of the experimental design and so cannot be affected by their ex- perience of the other conditions. Matching can be done on any variables you wish but it can get cumbersome if there are too many variables on which to match. So, for example, if you believed that age and sex were related to the dependent variable, you could control for these variables by using matched sets which contained people of the same sex and a very similar age. In this way variation due to sex and age is equally spread between the different treatments or conditions. Thus, Matched Set 1 might consist of four people matched in that they are all females in the age range 21 to 25 years. Each one of each of these is randomly assigned to one of the four treatment conditions. Matched Set 2 might consist of four males in the age range 16 to 20 years. Once again, one of each of these four people is randomly assigned to one of the four treatment conditions.

21.2 Theoretical considerations

It is a very small step from the uncorrelated to the correlated analysis of variance. All that is different in the correlated ANOVA is that the *error* scores are reduced (or adjusted) by removing from them the contribution made by *individual differences*. By an individual difference we mean the tendency of a particular person to score generally high or generally low irrespective of the research treatment or condition they are being tested in. So, for example, bright people will tend to score higher on tests involving intellectual skills no matter what the test is. Less bright people may tend to score relatively poorly no matter what the intellectual test is. In *uncorrelated* research designs there is no way of knowing the contribution of individual differences. In effect, the individual differences have to be lumped together with the rest of the variance which we have called error. But *repeated/related/correlated* designs allow us to subdivide the error variance into two sorts – (a) that which is explained (as individual differences), and (b) that which remains unexplained (or residual error variance). So far we have discussed error variance as if it were purely the result of chance factors but error variance is to some extent explicable in theory – the problem is that we do not know what causes it. If we can get an estimate of the contribution of an individual's particular characteristics to their scores in our research we should be able to revise the error scores so that they no longer contain any contribution from the individual difference of that participant. (Remember that individual differences are those characteristics of individuals which tend to encourage them to score generally high or generally low on the dependent variable.)

21.3 Examples

Once we have measured the same participant twice (or more) then it is possible to estimate the individual difference.Take the data from two individuals given in Table 21.6. Looking at these data we can see the participants' memory ability for both words and numbers. It is clear that Ann Jones tends to do better on these memory tasks irrespective of the precise nature of the task; John Smith generally does worse no matter the task. Although both of them seem to do better on memory for numbers, this does not alter the tendency for Ann Jones to

Table 21.6 **Individual differences for two people**

Subject	Memory for words	Memory for numbers	Row mean
Ann Jones	17	20	18.5
John Smith	11	14	12.5
		Overall mean = 15.5	

Table 21.7 **Pain relief scores from a drugs experiment**

Participant	Aspirin	'Product X'	Placebo	Row mean
Bob Robertson	7	8	6	7.000
Mavis Fletcher	5	10	3	6.000
Bob Polansky	6	6	4	5.333
Ann Harrison	9	9	2	6.667
Bert Entwistle	3	7	5	5.000
Column mean	6.000	8.000	4.000	Overall mean = 6.000

generally do better. This is not measurement error but a general characteristic of Ann Jones. On average, Ann Jones tends to score six points above John Smith or three points above the overall mean of 15.5 and John Smith tends to score three points below the overall mean of 15.5. In other words, we can give a numerical value to their individual difference relative to the overall mean.

A physiological psychologist is researching the effects of different pain relieving drugs on the amount of relief from pain people experience in a controlled trial. In one condition people are given aspirin, in another condition they are given the trial drug 'Product X', and in the third condition (the control condition) they are given a tablet which contains no active ingredient (this is known as a placebo). The amount of relief from pain experienced in these conditions is rated by each of the participants. The higher the score, the more pain relief. Just to be absolutely clear, participant 1 (Bob Robertson) gets a relief from pain score of 7 when given one aspirin, 8 when given 'Product X' and 6 when given the inactive placebo tablet (Table 21.7). It is obvious that Bob Robertson tends to get the most relief from pain (the row mean for Bob is the highest there is) whereas Bert Entwistle tends to get the least relief from pain (his row mean is the lowest there is).

The related/correlated scores analysis of variance is different in that we make adjustments for these tendencies for individuals to typically score generally high or generally low or generally in the middle. We simply subtract each person's row mean from the table's overall mean of 6.000 to find the amount of adjustment needed to each person's score in order to 'eliminate' individual differences from the scores. Thus for Bob Robertson we need to add –1 (i.e. 6.000 – 7.000) to each of his scores in order to overcome the tendency of his scores to be 1.000 higher than the overall mean (i.e. average score in the table). Do not forget that adding –1 is the same as subtracting 1. Table 21.8 shows the amount of adjustment needed to everyone's scores in order to eliminate individual differences.

Apart from the adjustment for individual differences, the rest of the analysis of variance is much as in Chapter 20.

Table 21.8   Amount of adjustment of Table 21.7 for individual differences

Participant	Overall mean	Row mean	Adjustment needed to error scores to allow for individual differences (overall mean minus row mean)
Bob Robertson	6.000	7.000	−1.000
Mavis Fletcher	6.000	6.000	0.000
Bob Polansky	6.000	5.333	0.667
Ann Harrison	6.000	6.667	−0.667
Bert Entwistle	6.000	5.000	1.000

Calculation 21.1

Correlated samples analysis of variance

The end point of our calculations is the analysis of variance summary table (Table 21.9). Hopefully by the time we reach the end of our explanation you will understand all of the entries in this table.

Step 1: To begin, you need to tabulate your data. We will use the fictitious relief from pain experiment described above. This is given in Table 21.10.

If you wish you may calculate the variance estimate of this table using the standard variance estimate formula. As this is generally only a check on your calculations it is unnecessary for our present purposes since it contains nothing new. If you do the calculation then you should find that the sum of

Table 21.9   Analysis of variance summary table

Source of variation	Sum of squares	Degrees of freedom	Mean square (or variance estimate)	F-ratio	Prob-ability (signifi-cance)
Between treatments (i.e. drugs)	40.00	2	20.00	5.10	5%
Between people (i.e. individual differences)	8.67	4	2.17		
Error (i.e. residual)	31.33	8	3.92		
Total	80.00	14			

Table 21.10   **Pain relief scores from a drugs experiment**

Participant	Aspirin	'Product X'	Placebo	Row mean
Bob Robertson	7	8	6	7.000
Mavis Fletcher	5	10	3	6.000
Bob Polansky	6	6	4	5.333
Ann Harrison	9	9	2	6.667
Bert Entwistle	3	7	5	5.000
Column mean	6.000	8.000	4.000	Overall mean = 6.000

Table 21.11   **'True' scores (obtained by replacing each score in a column by its column mean)**

Participant	Aspirin	'Product X'	Placebo	Row mean
Bob Robertson	6.000	8.000	4.000	6.000
Mavis Fletcher	6.000	8.000	4.000	6.000
Bob Polansky	6.000	8.000	4.000	6.000
Ann Harrison	6.000	8.000	4.000	6.000
Bert Entwistle	6.000	8.000	4.000	6.000
Column mean	6.000	8.000	4.000	Overall mean = 6.000

squares is 80 and the degrees of freedom 14 which would give a variance estimate value of 5.71 (i.e. 80 divided by 14). These pieces of information are entered into the analysis of variance summary table.

Step 2:   We then produce a table of the 'true' scores. Remember that 'true' scores are usually called the 'between' or 'between groups' scores in analysis of variance. To do this we simply substitute the column mean for each of the individual scores in that column so leaving no variation within the column – the only variation is between the columns. The results are given in Table 21.11.

The estimated variance of these data can be calculated using the standard formula:

$$\text{Estimated variance}_{[\text{true/between scores}]} = \frac{\Sigma X^2 - \dfrac{(\Sigma X)^2}{N}}{df}$$

$$\Sigma X^2 = 6.000^2 + 8.000^2 + 4.000^2 + 6.000^2 + 8.000^2$$
$$+ 4.000^2 + 6.000^2 + 8.000^2 + 4.000^2 + 6.000^2$$
$$+ 8.000^2 + 4.000^2 + 6.000^2 + 8.000^2 + 4.000^2$$

$$= \ 36.000 + 64.000 + 16.000 + 36.000 + 64.000$$
$$+ \ 16.000 + 36.000 + 64.000 + 16.000 + 36.000$$
$$+ \ 64.000 + 16.000 + 36.000 + 64.000 + 16.000$$
$$= \ 580$$

$$(\Sigma X)^2 = \ (6.000 + 8.000 + 4.000 + 6.000 + 8.000$$
$$+ \ 4.000 + 6.000 + 8.000 + 4.000 + 6.000$$
$$+ \ 8.000 + 4.000 + 6.000 + 8.000 + 4.000)^2$$
$$= \ (90)^2$$
$$= \ 8100$$

The number of scores, N, equals 15. The degrees of freedom (df) equals the number of columns of data minus $1 = 3 - 1 = 2$. Substituting in the formula:

$$\text{Estimated variance}_{[\text{true/between scores}]} = \frac{\Sigma X^2 - \dfrac{(\Sigma X)^2}{N}}{\text{df}}$$

$$= \frac{580 - \dfrac{8100}{15}}{2}$$

$$= \frac{580 - 540}{2}$$

$$= \frac{40}{2}$$

$$= 20.00$$

Table 21.12 'Error' scores (original data table minus true/between scores)

Participant	Aspirin	'Product X'	Placebo	Row mean
Bob Robertson	1.000	0.000	2.000	1.000
Mavis Fletcher	−1.000	2.000	−1.000	0.000
Bob Polansky	0.000	−2.000	0.000	−0.667
Ann Harrison	3.000	1.000	−2.000	0.667
Bert Entwistle	−3.000	−1.000	1.000	−1.000
Column mean	0.000	0.000	0.000	Overall mean = 0.000

Table 21.13 'Residual (error)' scores (obtained by subtracting individual differences or row means from Table 21.12)

Participant	Aspirin	'Product X'	Placebo	Row mean
Bob Robertson	0.000	–1.000	1.000	0.000
Mavis Fletcher	–1.000	2.000	–1.000	0.000
Bob Polansky	0.667	–1.333	0.667	0.000
Ann Harrison	2.333	0.333	–2.667	0.000
Bert Entwistle	–2.000	0.000	2.000	0.000
Column mean	0.000	0.000	0.000	Overall mean = 0.000

Step 3: The error table is now calculated as an intermediate stage. As ever, this is done by subtracting the true/between scores from the scores in the original data table (see Table 21.12, p. 213). Alternatively, we subtract the column mean from each of the scores in the data table.

This is essentially our table of 'error' scores but since the row means vary (Bert Entwistle's is –1.000 but Mavis Fletcher's is 0.000) then we still have to remove the effects of the individual differences. This we do simply by taking away the row mean from each of the error scores in the row. That is, we take 1.000 away from Bob Robertson's error scores, 0.000 from Mavis Fletcher's, –0.667 from Bob Polansky's, 0.667 from Ann Harrison's, and –1.000 from Bert Entwistle's. (Don't forget that subtracting a negative number is like adding a positive number.) This gives us a revised table of error scores without any individual differences. It is usually called the *residual* scores table in analysis of variance, but it is just a more refined set of error scores (Table 21.13).

Notice that both the column and row means now equal zero. This is because not only have the 'true' or between scores been removed from the table but the individual differences are now gone. We need to check out the degrees of freedom associated with this table. There are more constraints now because the row totals have to equal zero. Thus in the Aspirin column we can adjust four scores but the fifth score is fixed by the requirement that the mean equals zero. In the Product X condition we can again vary four scores. However, once we have made these changes, we cannot vary any of the scores in the placebo condition because the row means have to equal zero. In other words, there is a total of 8 degrees of freedom in the residual error scores.

The formula for the degrees of freedom is quite straightforward:

Degrees of freedom[residual error scores] =

(number of columns of error scores – 1) × (number of rows of error scores – 1)

The variance estimate of this residual error can be calculated using the standard formula:

$$\text{Variance estimate}_{[residual\ error\ scores]} = \frac{\Sigma X^2 - \frac{(\Sigma X)^2}{N}}{df}$$

$$
\begin{aligned}
\Sigma X^2 =\ & 0.000^2 + (-1.000)^2 + 1.000^2 + (-1.000)^2 + 2.000^2 \\
& + (-1.000)^2 + 0.667^2 + (-1.333)^2 + 0.667^2 + 2.333^2 \\
& + 0.333^2 + (-2.667)^2 + (-2.000)^2 + 0.000^2 + 2.000^2 \\
=\ & 0.000 + 1.000 + 1.000 + 1.000 + 4.000 \\
& + 1.000 + 0.445 + 1.777 + 0.445 + 5.443 \\
& + 0.111 + 7.113 + 4.000 + 0.000 + 4.000 \\
=\ & 31.334
\end{aligned}
$$

$$
\begin{aligned}
(\Sigma X)^2 =\ & [0.000 + (-1.000) + 1.000 + (-1.000) + 2.000 \\
& + (-1.000) + 0.667 + (-1.333) + 0.667 + 2.333 \\
& + 0.333 + (-2.667) + (-2.000) + 0.000 + 2.000]^2 \\
=\ & 0
\end{aligned}
$$

The number of scores, N, equals 15 as before. The degrees of freedom are given by:

Degrees of freedom = (number of columns − 1) × (number of rows − 1)

$$= (3 - 1) \times (5 - 1)$$

$$= 2 \times 4$$

$$= 8$$

Substituting in the formula:

$$\text{Variance estimate}_{[residual\ error\ scores]} = \frac{\Sigma X^2 - \frac{(\Sigma X)^2}{N}}{df}$$

$$= \frac{31.334 - \frac{0}{15}}{8}$$

$$= \frac{31.334}{8}$$

$$= 3.92$$

Step 4: This is not absolutely necessary, but the conventional approach to correlated/repeated measures analysis of variance calculates the variance estimate of the individual differences. This is usually described as the between-people variance estimate or 'blocks' variance estimate. (The word 'blocks' originates from the days when the analysis of variance was confined to agricultural research. Different amounts of fertiliser would be put on a single area of land and the fertility of these different 'blocks' assessed. The analysis of variance contains many terms referring to its agricultural origins such as split plots, randomised plots, levels of treatment and so forth.)

If you wish to calculate the between-people (or individual differences) variance estimate, you need to draw up Table 21.14 which consists of the individual differences component in each score (this is obtained by the difference between the row means and the overall mean in the original data). In other words, it is a table of the amount of adjustment required to everyone's scores in order to remove the effect of their individual characteristics.

We calculate the variance estimate of this using the usual variance estimate formula for the analysis of variance. The degrees of freedom are constrained by the fact that the column means have to equal zero and that all the scores in the row are the same. In the end this means that the degrees of freedom for this table are the number of rows minus 1. We have five rows so therefore the number of degrees of freedom is 4.

The sum of squares for Table 21.14 is 8.67 and the degrees of freedom = 4, therefore the variance estimate is 8.67/4 = 2.17. These values can be entered in the analysis of variance summary table. (Strictly speaking this is another unnecessary stage in the calculation but it does provide a check on the accuracy of your calculations.)

Step 5: We can enter the calculations into an analysis of variance summary table. It might be more conventional to see an analysis of variance summary table written in the form shown in Table 21.15. Some calculations are unnecessary and we have omitted them.

Table 21.14 **Between-people (individual difference) scores (obtained by taking the difference between the row means and overall mean in the original data)**

Participant	Aspirin	'Product X'	Placebo	Row mean
Bob Robertson	1.000	1.000	1.000	1.000
Mavis Fletcher	0.000	0.000	0.000	0.000
Bob Polansky	−0.667	−0.667	−0.667	−0.667
Ann Harrison	0.667	0.667	0.667	0.667
Bert Entwistle	−1.000	−1.000	−1.000	−1.000
Column mean	0.000	0.000	0.000	Overall mean = 0.000

Table 21.15   **Analysis of variance summary table**

Source of variation	Sum of squares	Degrees of freedom	Mean square (or variance estimate)	F-ratio
Between treatments (i.e. drugs)	40.00	2	20.00	5.10*
Between people (i.e. individual differences)	8.67	4	2.17	–
Error (i.e. residual)	31.33	8	3.92	–
Total	80.00	14	–	–

* Significant at 5% level.

Notice that the total sum of squares (80.00) is the same as the sum of the individual components of this total (40.00 + 8.67 + 31.33) and this applies also to the degrees of freedom. This can provide a useful check on the accuracy of your calculations.

The most important part of the table is the F-ratio. This is the between-groups variance estimate divided by the error (residual) variance estimate. In other words, it is 20.00/3.92 = 5.10. The statistical significance of this value has been assessed by the use of Significance Table 21.1 (p. 218). With 2 degrees of freedom for between treatments and 8 for the error, a minimum F-ratio of 4.5 is needed to be statistically significant. Thus the obtained F-ratio of 5.10 is significant at the 5% level.

The significant probability value of 5% tells us that the variance in the between-groups scores is substantially greater than the error (residual) variance. Thus the null hypothesis that the drugs have no effect on the amount of relief from pain is rejected and the hypothesis that the drugs treatments have an effect at the 5% level of significance is accepted.

21.4 Notes and recommendations

■ Working out this analysis of variance by hand is quite time consuming and extremely repetitive. Computers will save most people time.

■ Do not be too deterred by some of the strange terminology used in the analysis of variance. Words like blocks, split-plots and levels of treatment have their origins in agricultural research, as does ANOVA.

■ The analysis of variance in cases in which you have just two conditions or sets of scores is relatively easy to interpret. It is not so easy where you have three or more groups; then your analysis is not complete until you have employed a multiple comparisons procedure as in Chapter 23.

Significance Table 21.1   **5% Significance values of the *F*-ratio for related ANOVA (two-tailed test)**

Your value has to equal or be larger than the tabulated value to be significant at the 5% level for a two-tailed test (i.e. to accept the hypothesis).

Additional values are to be found in Significance Table 19.1.

Degrees of freedom for residual or residual error mean square (or variance estimate)	**Degrees of freedom for between-treatments mean square (or variance estimate)**					
	1	**2**	**3**	**4**	**5**	**∞**
1	161 or more	200	216	225	230	254
2	18.5	19.0	19.2	19.3	19.3	19.5
3	10.1	9.6	9.3	9.1	9.0	8.5
4	7.7	6.9	6.6	6.4	6.3	5.6
5	6.6	5.8	5.4	5.2	5.1	4.4
6	6.0	5.1	4.8	4.5	4.4	3.7
7	5.6	4.7	4.4	4.1	4.0	3.2
8	5.3	4.5	4.1	3.8	3.7	2.9
9	5.1	4.3	3.9	3.6	3.5	2.7
10	5.0	4.1	3.7	3.5	3.3	2.5
13	4.7	3.8	3.4	3.2	3.0	2.2
15	4.5	3.7	3.3	3.1	2.9	2.1
20	4.4	3.5	3.1	2.9	2.7	1.8
30	4.2	3.3	2.9	2.7	2.5	1.6
60	4.0	3.2	2.8	2.5	2.4	1.4
∞	3.8	3.0	2.6	2.4	2.2	1.0

The above table has been adapted and extended from Table D of R.P. Runyon and A. Haber (1989). *Fundamentals of Behavioural Statistics*. New York: McGraw-Hill. With the kind permission of the publisher.

Chapter 22

Two-way analysis of variance for unrelated/uncorrelated scores

Two experiments for the price of one?

Preparation

Chapter 20 on the one-way analysis of variance contains material essential to the full understanding of this chapter.

22.1 Introduction

Often researchers wish to assess the influence of more than a single independent variable at a time in experiments. The one-way analysis of variance deals with a single independent variable which can have two or more levels. However, analysis of variance copes with several *independent* variables in a research design. These are known as multifactorial ANOVAs. The number of 'ways' is the number of independent variables. Thus a two-way analysis of variance allows two independent variables to be included, three-way analysis of variance allows three independent variables and five-way analysis of variance means that there are five independent variables. *There is only one dependent variable no matter how many 'ways' in each analysis of variance. If you have two or more dependent variables each of these will entail a separate analysis of variance.* Although things can get very complicated conceptually, two-way analysis of variance is relatively straightforward and introduces just one major new concept – interaction.

In this chapter we will be concentrating on examples in which all of the scores are independent (uncorrelated). Each person therefore contributes just one score to the analysis. In other words, it is an *uncorrelated* design.

Generally speaking, the 'multivariate' analysis of variance is best suited to experimental research in which it is possible to allocate participants at random into the various conditions. Although this does not apply to the one-way analysis of variance, there are problems in using two-way and multi-way analyses of

Table 22.1 **Data for typical two-way analysis of variance: number of mistakes on video test**

	Sleep deprivation		
	4 hours	**12 hours**	**24 hours**
Alcohol	16	18	22
	12	16	24
	17	25	32
No alcohol	11	13	12
	9	8	14
	12	11	12

variance in survey and other non-experimental research. The difficulty is that calculations become more complex if you do not have equal numbers of scores in each of the cells or conditions. This is difficult to arrange in surveys. (It is possible to work with unequal numbers of scores in the different conditions, or cells, but these procedures tend to be a little cumbersome for hand calculation – see Chapter 24.)

So a typical research design for a two-way analysis of variance is the effect of the *independent variables* alcohol *and* sleep deprivation on the *dependent variable* of people's comprehension of complex video material expressed in terms of the number of mistakes made on a test of understanding of the video material. The research design and data might look like that shown in Table 22.1.

In a sense one could regard this experiment conceptually as two separate experiments, one studying the effects of sleep deprivation and the other studying the effects of alcohol. The effects of each of the two independent variables are called the *main* effects. Additionally the analysis normally looks for *interactions* which are basically findings which cannot be explained on the basis of the distinctive effects of alcohol level and sleep deprivation acting in combination. For example, it could be that people do especially badly if they have been deprived of a lot of sleep *and* have been given alcohol. They do more badly than the additive effects of alcohol and sleep deprivation would predict. Interactions are about the effects of specific combinations of variables. We will return to the concept of interaction later.

In the analysis of variance we sometimes talk of the *levels of a treatment* – this is simply the number of values that any independent variable can take. In the above example, the alcohol variable has two different values – that is, there are two levels of the treatment or variable alcohol. There are three levels of the treatment or variable sleep deprivation. Sometimes, a two-way ANOVA is identified in terms of the numbers of levels of treatment for each of the independent variables. So a 2 × 3 ANOVA has two different levels of the first variable and three for the second variable. This corresponds to the above example.

22.2 Theoretical considerations

Much of the two-way analysis of variance is easy if it is remembered that it largely involves two separate 'one-way' analyses of variance as if there were two separate experiments. Imagine an experiment in which one group of subjects is given iron supplements in their diet to see if it has any effect on their depression levels. In the belief that women have a greater need for iron than men, the researchers included sex as their other independent variable. The data are given in Table 22.2.

Table 22.2 represents a 2 × 2 ANOVA. Comparing the four condition means (cell means), the depression scores for females not receiving the supplement seem rather higher than those of any other groups. In other words, it would appear that the lack of the iron supplement has more effect on women. Certain sex and iron supplement conditions in combination have a great effect on depression scores. This suggests an interaction. That is, particular cells in the analysis have much higher or lower scores than can be explained simply in terms of the sex trends or dietary supplement trends acting separately.

The assumption in the two-way analysis of variance is that the variation in Table 22.2 comes from four sources:

■ 'error', plus

■ the main effect of sex, plus

■ the main effect of iron supplement, plus

■ the interaction of sex and iron supplement.

The first three components above are dealt with exactly as they were in the one-way unrelated analysis of variance. The slight difference is that instead of calculating the variance estimate for one independent variable we now calculate

Table 22.2   Data table for study of dietary supplements

	Iron supplement		No iron supplement		Row means
Males	3	Cell mean = 5.00	9	Cell mean = 7.00	Row mean = 6.00
	7		5		
	4		6		
	6		8		
Females	11	Cell mean = 9.00	19	Cell mean = 17.00	Row mean = 13.00
	7		16		
	10		18		
	8		15		
	Column mean = 7.00		Column mean = 12.00		Overall mean = 9.50

two variance estimates – one for each independent variable. However, the term *main effect* should not cause any confusion It is merely the effect of an independent variable acting alone as it would if the two-way design were turned into two separate one-way designs.

The interaction consists of any variation in the scores which is left after we have taken away the 'error' and main effects for the sex and iron supplements sub-experiments. That is, priority is given to finding main effects at the expense of interactions.

22.3 Steps in the analysis

Step 1

To produce an 'error' table we simply take our original data and subtract the cell mean from every score in the cell. Thus, for instance, we need to subtract 5.00 from each score in the cell for males receiving the iron supplement and 17.00 from each cell for the females not receiving the iron supplement, etc. In the present example the 'error' table is as in Table 22.3.

We calculate the 'error' variance estimate for this in the usual way. The formula, as ever, is:

$$\text{Variance estimate}_{[\text{'error'}]} = \frac{\Sigma X^2 - \dfrac{(\Sigma X)^2}{N}}{\text{df}}$$

The degrees of freedom (df), analogously to the one-way analysis of variance, are the number of scores minus the number of conditions or cells. This leaves 12 degrees of freedom (16 scores minus 4 conditions or cells).

Table 22.3 **'Error' scores for study of dietary supplements**

	Iron supplement		No iron supplement		Row means
Males	$3 - 5 = -2$	Cell mean = 0.00	$9 - 7 = 2$	Cell mean = 0.00	Row mean = 0.00
	$7 - 5 = 2$		$5 - 7 = -2$		
	$4 - 5 = -1$		$6 - 7 = -1$		
	$6 - 5 = 1$		$8 - 7 = 1$		
Females	$11 - 9 = 2$	Cell mean = 0.00	$19 - 17 = 2$	Cell mean = 0.00	Row mean = 0.00
	$7 - 9 = -2$		$16 - 17 = -1$		
	$10 - 9 = 1$		$18 - 17 = 1$		
	$8 - 9 = -1$		$15 - 17 = -2$		
	Column mean = 0.00		Column mean = 0.00		Overall mean = 0.00

Step 2

To produce a table of the main effects for the iron supplement treatment, simply substitute the column means from the original data for each of the scores in the columns. The 'iron supplement' mean was 7.00 so each iron supplement score is changed to 7.00 thus eliminating any other source of variation. Similarly, the 'no iron supplement' mean was 12.00 so each score is changed to 12.00 (see Table 22.4).

The variance estimate of the above scores can be calculated using the usual variance estimate formula. The degrees of freedom are calculated in the familiar way – the number of columns minus one (i.e. df = 1).

Step 3

To produce a table of the main effect of sex, remember that the independent variable sex is tabulated as the rows (not the columns). In other words, we substitute the row mean for the males and the row mean for the females for the respective scores (Table 22.5).

The variance estimate of the above scores can be calculated with the usual variance estimate formula. Even the degrees of freedom are calculated in the usual way. However, *as the table is on its side* compared to our usual method, the degrees of freedom are the number of *rows* minus one in this case (2 – 1 or 1 degree of freedom).

Table 22.4   **Main effect scores for study of dietary supplements**

Iron supplement	**No iron supplement**	**Row means**
7.00	12.00	Row mean = 9.50
7.00	12.00	
7.00	12.00	
7.00	12.00	
7.00	12.00	Row mean = 9.50
7.00	12.00	
7.00	12.00	
7.00	12.00	
Column mean = 7.00	Column mean = 12.00	Overall mean = 9.50

Table 22.5   **Main effect scores for study of dietary supplements**

Males	6.00	6.00	6.00	6.00	6.00	6.00	6.00	6.00	Row mean = 6.00
Females	13.00	13.00	13.00	13.00	13.00	13.00	13.00	13.00	Row mean = 13.00

The calculation of the main effects (variance estimates) for sex and the iron supplement follows exactly the same procedures as in the one-way analysis of variance.

Step 4

The remaining stage is to calculate the interaction. This is simply anything which is left over after we have eliminated 'error' and the main effects. So for any score, the interaction score is found by taking the score in your data and sub-tracting the 'error' score and the sex score and the iron supplement score.

Table 22.6 is our data table less the 'error' variance, in other words a table which replaces each score by its cell mean.

It is obvious that the row means for the males and females are not the same. The row mean for males is 6.00 and the row mean for females is 13.00. To get rid

Table 22.6   **Data table with 'error' removed**

	Iron supplement	No iron supplement	Row means
Males	5.00	7.00	Row mean = 6.00
	5.00	7.00	
	5.00	7.00	
	5.00	7.00	
Females	9.00	17.00	Row mean = 13.00
	9.00	17.00	
	9.00	17.00	
	9.00	17.00	
	Column mean = 7.00	Column mean = 12.00	Overall mean = 9.50

Table 22.7   **Data table with 'error' and sex removed**

	Iron supplement	No iron supplement	Row means
Males	−1.00	1.00	Row mean = 0.00
	−1.00	1.00	
	−1.00	1.00	
	−1.00	1.00	
Females	−4.00	4.00	Row mean = 0.00
	−4.00	4.00	
	−4.00	4.00	
	−4.00	4.00	
	Column mean = −2.50	Column mean = 2.50	Overall mean = 0.00

Table 22.8 Interaction table (i.e. data table with 'error', sex and iron supplement all removed)

	Iron supplement	No iron supplement	Row means
Males	1.5	−1.5	Row mean = 0.00
	1.5	−1.5	
	1.5	−1.5	
	1.5	−1.5	
Females	−1.5	1.5	Row mean = 0.00
	−1.5	1.5	
	−1.5	1.5	
	−1.5	1.5	
	Column mean = 0.00	Column mean = 0.00	Overall mean = 0.00

of the sex effect we can subtract 6.00 from each male score and 13.00 from each female score in the previous table. The results of this simple subtraction are found in Table 22.7.

You can see that the male and female main effect has been taken into account since now both row means are zero. That is, there remains no variation due to sex. But you can see that there remains variation due to iron treatment. Those getting the supplement now score −2.50 on average and those not getting the iron treatment score +2.50. To remove the variation due to the iron treatment subtract −2.50 from the iron supplement column and 2.50 from the non-iron supplement column (Table 22.8). Do not forget that *subtracting a negative number is like adding a positive number*.

Looking at Table 22.8, although the column and row means are zero throughout, the scores in the cells are not. This shows that there still remains a certain amount of variation in the scores even after 'error' and the two main effects have been taken away. That is, there is an interaction, which may or may not be significant. We have to check this using the *F*-ratio test.

What the interaction table implies is that women *without* the iron supplement and men *with* the iron supplement are getting the higher scores on the dependent variable.

We can calculate the variance estimate for the interaction by using the usual formula. Degrees of freedom need to be considered. The degrees of freedom for the above table of the interaction is limited by:

■ all scores in the cells having to be equal (i.e. no 'error' variance)
■ all marginal means (i.e. row and column means) having to equal zero.

In other words, there can be only one degree of freedom in this case.

There is a general formula for the degrees of freedom of the interaction:

Degrees of freedom$_{[interaction]}$ = (number of rows − 1) × (number of columns − 1)

Since there are two rows and two columns in this case, the degrees of freedom are:

$$(2 - 1) \times (2 - 1) = 1 \times 1 = 1$$

Step 5

All of the stages in the calculation are entered into an analysis of variance summary table (Table 22.9).

Notice that there are several *F*-ratios because you need to know whether there is a significant effect of sex, a significant effect of the iron supplement and a significant interaction of the sex and iron supplement variables. In each case you divide the appropriate mean square by the 'error' mean square. If you wish to check your understanding of the processes involved, see if you can obtain the above table by going through the individual calculations.

The significant interaction indicates that some of the cells or conditions are getting exceptionally high or low scores which cannot be accounted for on the basis of the two main effects acting independently of each other. In this case, it would appear that females getting the iron supplement and males not getting the iron supplement are actually getting higher scores than sex or supplement acting separately and independently of each other would produce. In order to interpret an interaction you have to remember that the effects of the independent variables are separately removed from the table (i.e. the main effects are removed first). It is only after this has been done that the interaction is calculated. In other words, ANOVA gives priority to main effects and sometimes it can confuse interactions for main effects. Table 22.10 presents data from the present experiment

Table 22.9   **Analysis of variance summary table**

Source of variation	Sums of squares	Degrees of freedom	Mean square	*F*-ratio
Main effects:				
Sex	196.00	1	196.00	58.96*
Iron supplement	100.00	1	100.00	30.00*
Interaction:				
Sex with iron supplement	36.00	1	36.00	10.81*
'Error'	40.00	12	3.33	–
Total (data)	372.00	15	–	–

* Significant at 5% level.

Table 22.10 **Alternative data table showing different trends**

	Iron supplement	No iron supplement	Row means
Males	Cell mean = 5.00	Cell mean = 5.00	Row mean = 5.00
Females	Cell mean = 5.00	Cell mean = 17.00	Row mean = 11.00
	Column mean = 5.00	Column mean = 11.00	

in which the cell means have been altered to emphasise the lack of main effects.

In this example, it is absolutely clear that all the variation in the cell means is to do with the female/no supplement condition. All the other three cell means are identical at 5.00. Quite clearly the males and females in the iron supplement condition have exactly the same average score. Similarly, males in the iron supplement and no supplement conditions are obtaining identical means. In other words, there seem to be no main effects at all. The females in the no-supplement condition are the only group getting exceptionally high scores.

This would suggest that there is an interaction but no main effects. However, if you do the analysis of variance on these data you will find that there are two main effects and an interaction! The reason for this is that the main effects are estimated before the interaction, so the exceptionally high row mean for females and the exceptionally high column mean for the no-supplement condition will lead to the interaction being mistaken for main effects as your ANOVA summary table might show significant main effects. So you need to examine your data with great care as you carry out your analysis of variance, otherwise you will observe main effects which are an artifact of the method and ignore interactions which are actually there! The analysis of variance may be tricky to execute but it can be even trickier for the novice to interpret properly – to be frank, many professional psychologists are unaware of the problems.

It is yet another example of the importance of close examination of the data alongside the statistical analysis itself.

Calculation 22.1

Two-way unrelated analysis of variance

Without a safety net we will attempt to analyse the sleep and alcohol experiment mentioned earlier. It is described as a 2 × 3 analysis of variance because one independent variable has two values and the other has three values (Table 22.11).

Table 22.11   **Data for sleep deprivation experiment: number of mistakes on video test**

	Sleep deprivation		
	4 hours	**12 hours**	**24 hours**
Alcohol	16	18	22
	12	16	24
	17	25	32
No alcohol	11	13	12
	9	8	14
	12	11	12

Table 22.12   **Data for sleep deprivation experiment with the addition of cell, column and row means**

		Sleep deprivation						Row means
		4 hours		**12 hours**		**24 hours**		
Alcohol	16	Cell mean	18	Cell mean	22	Cell mean		Row mean
	12	= 15.000	16	= 19.667	24	= 26.000		= 20.222
	17		25		32			
No	11	Cell mean	13	Cell mean	12	Cell mean		Row mean
alcohol	9	= 10.667	8	= 10.667	14	= 12.667		= 11.333
	12		11		12			
		Column mean		Column mean		Column mean		Overall mean
		= 12.833		= 15.167		= 19.333		= 15.777

Step 1 (Total Variance Estimate):   We enter the row and column means as well as the means of each of the six cells (Table 22.12).

$$\text{Variance estimate}_{[data]} = \frac{\Sigma X^2 - \dfrac{(\Sigma X)^2}{N}}{df}$$

$$\begin{aligned}
\Sigma X^2 &= 16^2 + 18^2 + 22^2 + 12^2 + 16^2 + 24^2 + 17^2 + 25^2 + 32^2 + 11^2 + 13^2 \\
&\quad + 12^2 + 9^2 + 8^2 + 14^2 + 12^2 + 11^2 + 12^2 \\
&= 256 + 324 + 484 + 144 + 256 + 576 + 289 + 625 + 1024 + 121 \\
&\quad + 169 + 144 + 81 + 64 + 196 + 144 + 121 + 144 \\
&= 5162
\end{aligned}$$

$$(\Sigma X)^2 = (16 + 18 + 22 + 12 + 16 + 24 + 17 + 25 + 32$$
$$+ 11 + 13 + 12 + 9 + 8 + 14 + 12 + 11 + 12)^2$$
$$= (284)^2$$
$$= 80656$$

The number of scores, N, equals 18. The degrees of freedom (df) equals the number of scores minus one, i.e. 17. Substituting in the formula:

$$\text{Variance estimate}_{[\text{data}]} = \frac{\Sigma X^2 - \dfrac{(\Sigma X)^2}{N}}{\text{df}}$$

$$= \frac{5162 - \dfrac{80656}{18}}{17}$$

$$= \frac{5162 - 4480.889}{17}$$

$$= \frac{681.111}{17}$$

$$= 40.065$$

The sum of squares here (i.e. 681.111) is called the *total* sum of squares in the ANOVA summary table. (Strictly speaking this calculation is unnecessary in that its only function is a computational check on your other calculations.)

Step 2 ('Error' Variance Estimate): Subtract the cell mean from each of the scores in a cell to obtain the 'error' scores (Table 22.13).

Table 22.13 **'Error' scores**

	Sleep deprivation			
	4 hours	**12 hours**	**24 hours**	**Row means**
Alcohol	1.000	−1.667	−4.000	Row mean
	−3.000	−3.667	−2.000	= 0.000
	2.000	5.333	6.000	
No alcohol	0.333	2.333	−0.667	Row mean
	−1.667	−2.667	1.333	= 0.000
	1.333	0.333	−0.667	
	Column mean = 0.000	Column mean = 0.000	Column mean = 0.000	Overall mean = 0.000

Apart from rounding errors, the cell means, the row means, the column means, and the overall mean are all zero – just as required of an 'error' table.

We calculate the 'error' variance estimate using the usual variance estimate formula:

$$\text{Variance estimate}_{['error' \text{ scores}]} = \frac{\Sigma X^2 - \frac{(\Sigma X)^2}{N}}{df}$$

$$\begin{aligned}
\Sigma X^2 = \ & 1.000^2 + (-1.667)^2 + (-4.000)^2 + (-3.000)^2 + (-3.667)^2 \\
& + (-2.000)^2 + 2.000^2 + 5.333^2 + 6.000^2 + 0.333^2 + 2.333^2 \\
& + (-0.667)^2 + (-1.667)^2 + (-2.667)^2 + 1.333^2 + 1.333^2 \\
& + 0.333^2 + (-0.667)^2
\end{aligned}$$

$$\begin{aligned}
= \ & 1.000 + 2.779 + 16.000 + 9.000 + 13.447 + 4.000 + 4.000 \\
& + 28.441 + 36.000 + 0.111 + 5.443 + 0.445 + 2.779 + 7.113 \\
& + 1.777 + 1.777 + 0.111 + 0.445
\end{aligned}$$

$$= 134.668$$

$$\begin{aligned}
(\Sigma X)^2 = \ & [1.000 + (-1.667) + (-4.000) + (-3.000) + (-3.667) + (-2.000) \\
& + 2.000 + 5.333 + 6.000 + 0.333 + 2.333 + (-0.667) + (-1.667) \\
& + (-2.667) + 1.333 + 1.333 + 0.333 + (-0.667)]^2
\end{aligned}$$

$$= 0$$

(notice that this calculation is unnecessary as it will always equal 0 for 'error' scores). The number of scores, N, equals 18. The degrees of freedom, df, equals the number of scores minus the number of cells, i.e. $18 - 6 = 12$. We can now substitute these values in the formula:

$$\text{Variance estimate}_{['error' \text{ scores}]} = \frac{\Sigma X^2 - \frac{(\Sigma X)^2}{N}}{df}$$

$$= \frac{134.668 - \frac{0}{18}}{12}$$

$$= \frac{134.668}{12}$$

$$= 11.222$$

Table 22.14 **Scores due to sleep deprivation**

	Sleep deprivation	
4 hours	**12 hours**	**24 hours**
12.833	15.167	19.333
12.833	15.167	19.333
12.833	15.167	19.333
12.833	15.167	19.333
12.833	15.167	19.333
12.833	15.167	
Column mean = 12.833	Column mean = 15.167	Column mean = 19.333

Step 3 (Sleep Deprivation Variance Estimate): We now derive our table containing the scores in the three sleep deprivation conditions (combining over alcohol and non-alcohol conditions) simply by replacing each score in the column by the column mean (Table 22.14).

$$\text{Variance estimate}_{[\text{‘sleep deprivation’ scores}]} = \frac{\Sigma X^2 - \dfrac{(\Sigma X)^2}{N}}{df}$$

$$\Sigma X^2 = 12.833^2 + 15.167^2 + 19.333^2 + 12.833^2 + 15.167^2 + 19.333^2$$
$$+ 12.833^2 + 15.167^2 + 19.333^2 + 12.833^2 + 15.167^2 + 19.333^2$$
$$+ 12.833^2 + 15.167^2 + 19.333^2 + 12.833^2 + 15.167^2 + 19.333^2$$

$$= 164.686 + 230.038 + 373.765 + 164.686 + 230.038 + 373.765$$
$$+ 164.686 + 230.038 + 373.765 + 164.686 + 230.038 + 373.765$$
$$+ 164.686 + 230.038 + 373.765 + 164.686 + 230.038 + 373.765$$

$$= 4610.934$$

$$(\Sigma X)^2 = (12.833 + 15.167 + 19.333 + 12.833 + 15.167 + 19.333 + 12.833$$
$$+ 15.167 + 19.333 + 12.833 + 15.167 + 19.333 + 12.833 + 15.167$$
$$+ 19.333 + 12.833 + 15.167 + 19.333)^2$$

$$= 284^2$$

$$= 80656$$

The number of scores, N, equals 18. The degrees of freedom, df, equals the number of columns minus one, i.e. $3 - 1 = 2$. We can now substitute these values in the formula:

Table 22.15　**Scores due to alcohol effect alone**

Alcohol	20.222	20.222	20.222
	20.222	20.222	20.222
	20.222	20.222	20.222
No alcohol	11.333	11.333	11.333
	11.333	11.333	11.333
	11.333	11.333	11.333

$$\text{Variance estimate}_{['sleep\ deprivation'\ scores]} = \frac{\Sigma X^2 - \dfrac{(\Sigma X)^2}{N}}{df}$$

$$= \frac{4610.934 - \dfrac{80656}{18}}{2}$$

$$= \frac{4610.934 - 4480.889}{2}$$

$$= \frac{130.045}{2}$$

$$= 65.023$$

Step 4 (Alcohol Variance Estimate):　The main effect for alcohol (or the table containing scores for the alcohol and no-alcohol comparison) is obtained by replacing each of the scores in the original data table by the row mean for alcohol or the row mean for no-alcohol as appropriate. In this way the sleep deprivation variable is ignored (Table 22.15).

The variance estimate of these 18 scores gives us the variance estimate for the independent variable alcohol. We calculate:

$$\text{Variance estimate}_{['alcohol'\ scores]} = \frac{\Sigma X^2 - \dfrac{(\Sigma X)^2}{N}}{df}$$

$$\Sigma X^2 = 20.222^2 + 20.222^2 + 20.222^2 + 20.222^2 + 20.222^2 + 20.222^2$$
$$+ 20.222^2 + 20.222^2 + 20.222^2 + 11.333^2 + 11.333^2 + 11.333^2$$
$$+ 11.333^2 + 11.333^2 + 11.333^2 + 11.333^2 + 11.333^2 + 11.333^2$$

$$= 408.929 + 408.929 + 408.929 + 408.929 + 408.929 + 408.929$$
$$+ 408.929 + 408.929 + 408.929 + 128.437 + 128.437 + 128.437$$

$$+ 128.437 + 128.437 + 128.437 + 128.437 + 128.437 + 128.437$$

$$= 4836.294$$

$$(\Sigma X)^2 = (20.222 + 20.222 + 20.222 + 20.222 + 20.222 + 20.222$$
$$+ 20.222 + 20.222 + 20.222 + 11.333 + 11.333 + 11.333$$
$$+ 11.333 + 11.333 + 11.333 + 11.333 + 11.333 + 11.333)^2$$

$$= (284)^2$$

$$= 80656$$

The number of scores, N, equals 18. The degrees of freedom, df, equals the number of rows minus one, i.e. $2 - 1 = 1$. We can now substitute these values in the formula:

$$\text{Variance estimate}_{\text{['alcohol' scores]}} = \frac{\Sigma X^2 - \frac{(\Sigma X)^2}{N}}{\text{df}}$$

$$= \frac{4836.294 - \frac{80656}{18}}{1}$$

$$= \frac{4836.294 - 4480.889}{1}$$

$$= \frac{355.405}{1}$$

$$= 355.405$$

Table 22.16 **Data minus 'error' (each data score replaced by its cell mean)**

	Sleep deprivation			
	4 hours	**12 hours**	**24 hours**	**Row means**
Alcohol	15.000	19.667	26.000	Row mean
	15.000	19.667	26.000	= 20.222
	15.000	19.667	26.000	
No alcohol	10.667	10.667	12.667	Row mean
	10.667	10.667	12.667	= 11.333
	10.667	10.667	12.667	
	Column mean = 12.833	Column mean = 15.167	Column mean = 19.333	Overall mean = 15.777

Table 22.17   Data minus 'error' and alcohol effect (row mean subtracted from each score in Table 22.16)

| | Sleep deprivation | | | |
	4 hours	12 hours	24 hours	Row means
Alcohol	−5.222	−0.555	5.778	Row mean
	−5.222	−0.555	5.778	= 0.000
	−5.222	−0.555	5.778	
No alcohol	−0.666	−0.666	1.334	Row mean
	−0.666	−0.666	1.334	= 0.000
	−0.666	−0.666	1.334	
	Column mean = −2.944	Column mean = −0.611	Column mean = 3.556	Overall mean = 0.000

Table 22.18   Interaction table: data minus 'error', alcohol and sleep deprivation (column mean subtracted from each score in Table 22.17)

| | Sleep deprivation | | | |
	4 hours	12 hours	24 hours	Row means
Alcohol	−2.278	0.056	2.222	Row mean
	−2.278	0.056	2.222	= 0.000
	−2.278	0.056	2.222	
No alcohol	2.278	−0.056	−2.222	Row mean
	2.278	−0.056	−2.222	= 0.000
	2.278	−0.056	−2.222	
	Column mean = 0.000	Column mean = 0.000	Column mean = 0.000	Overall mean = 0.000

Step 5 (Interaction Variance Estimate):   The final stage is to calculate the interaction. This is obtained by getting rid of 'error', getting rid of the effect of sleep deprivation and then getting rid of the effect of alcohol:

1.   Remove 'error' by simply replacing our data scores by the cell mean (Table 22.16, p. 233).

2.   Remove the effect of the alcohol versus no-alcohol treatment. This is done simply by subtracting the row mean (20.222) from each of the alcohol scores and the row mean (11.333) from each of the no-alcohol scores (Table 22.17).

3. Remove the effect of sleep deprivation by subtracting the column mean for each sleep deprivation condition from the scores in the *previous table*. In other words *subtract* –2.944, –0.611 or 3.556 as appropriate. (Do not forget that subtracting a negative number is like adding the absolute value of that number.) This leaves us with the interaction (Table 22.18).

The variance estimate from the interaction is computed using the usual formula.

$$\text{Variance estimate}_{[\text{'interaction' scores}]} = \frac{\Sigma X^2 - \dfrac{(\Sigma X)^2}{N}}{df}$$

$$\begin{aligned}
\Sigma X^2 = {} & (-2.278)^2 + 0.056^2 + 2.222^2 + (-2.278)^2 + 0.056^2 + 2.222^2 \\
& + (-2.278)^2 + 0.056^2 + 2.222^2 + 2.278^2 + (-0.056)^2 + (-2.222)^2 \\
& + 2.278^2 + (-0.056)^2 + (-2.222)^2 + 2.278^2 + (-0.056)^2 + (-2.222)^2
\end{aligned}$$

$$\begin{aligned}
= {} & 5.189 + 0.003 + 4.937 + 5.189 + 0.003 + 4.937 \\
& + 5.189 + 0.003 + 4.937 + 5.189 + 0.003 + 4.937 \\
& + 5.189 + 0.003 + 4.937 + 5.189 + 0.003 + 4.937
\end{aligned}$$

$$= 60.774$$

$$\begin{aligned}
(\Sigma X)^2 = {} & [(-2.278) + 0.056 + 2.222 + (-2.278) + 0.056 + 2.222 \\
& + (-2.278) + 0.056 + 2.222 + 2.278 + (-0.056) + (-2.222) \\
& + 2.278 + (-0.056) + (-2.222) + 2.278 + (-0.056) + (-2.222)]^2
\end{aligned}$$

$$= 0$$

(this is an unnecessary calculation as it will always equal 0). The number of scores, N, equals 18. The degrees of freedom, df, is given by the following formula:

$$\begin{aligned}
df = \text{degrees of freedom} & = (\text{number of rows} - 1) \times (\text{number of columns} - 1) \\
& = (2 - 1) \times (3 - 1) \\
& = 1 \times 2 \\
& = 2
\end{aligned}$$

We can now substitute the above values in the formula:

$$\text{Variance estimate}_{[\text{'interaction' scores}]} = \frac{\Sigma X^2 - \dfrac{(\Sigma X)^2}{N}}{df}$$

$$= \frac{60.774 - \dfrac{0}{18}}{2}$$

$$= \frac{60.774 - 0}{2}$$

$$= \frac{60.774}{2}$$

$$= 30.387$$

Step 6: Table 22.19 is the analysis of variance summary table. The F-ratios are always the mean square of either one of the main effects or the interaction divided by the variance estimate (mean square) due to 'error'. The significance of each F-ratio is checked against Significance Table 22.1. Care must be taken to use the appropriate degrees of freedom. For error in this case it is 12, which means that alcohol (with one degree of freedom) must have an F-ratio of 4.8 or more to be significant at the 5% level. Sleep deprivation and the interaction need to have a value of 3.9 or more to be significant at the 5% level. Thus the interaction is not significant, but sleep deprivation is.

The interpretation of the analysis of variance summary table in this case appears to be quite straightforward:

1. Alcohol has a significant influence on the number of mistakes in the understanding of the video.

2. The amount of sleep deprivation has a significant influence on the number of mistakes in the understanding of the video.

Table 22.19   **Analysis of variance summary table**

Source of variation	Sums of squares	Degrees of freedom	Mean square	*F*-ratio
Main effects:				
Sleep deprivation	130.045	2	65.023	5.79*·
Alcohol	355.405	1	355.405	31.67*
Interaction:				
Sleep deprivation with alcohol	60.774	2	30.387	2.71
'Error'	134.668	12	11.222	–
Total (data)	681.111	17	–	–

* Significant at 5% level.

Significance Table 22.1   **5% Significance values of the *F*-ratio for unrelated ANOVA**

Your value has to equal or be larger than the tabulated value to be significant at the 5% level for a two-tailed test (i.e. to accept the hypothesis).

Additional values are to be found in Significance Table 19.1.

Degrees of freedom for error or mean square (or variance estimate)	Degrees of freedom for between-treatments mean square (or variance estimate)					
	1	**2**	**3**	**4**	**5**	**∞**
1	161 or more	200	216	225	230	254
2	18.5	19.0	19.2	19.3	19.3	19.5
3	10.1	9.6	9.3	9.1	9.0	8.5
4	7.7	6.9	6.6	6.4	6.3	5.6
5	6.6	5.8	5.4	5.2	5.1	4.4
6	6.0	5.1	4.8	4.5	4.4	3.7
7	5.6	4.7	4.4	4.1	4.0	3.2
8	5.3	4.5	4.1	3.8	3.7	2.9
9	5.1	4.3	3.9	3.6	3.5	2.7
10	5.0	4.1	3.7	3.5	3.3	2.5
13	4.7	3.8	3.4	3.2	3.0	2.2
15	4.5	3.7	3.3	3.1	2.9	2.1
20	4.4	3.5	3.1	2.9	2.7	1.8
30	4.2	3.3	2.9	2.7	2.5	1.6
60	4.0	3.2	2.8	2.5	2.4	1.4
∞	3.8	3.0	2.6	2.4	2.2	1.0

The above table has been adapted and extended from Table D of R.P. Runyon and A. Haber (1989). *Fundamentals of Behavioural Statistics*. New York: McGraw-Hill. With the kind permission of the publisher.

3. There is apparently no significant interaction – that is, the differences between the conditions are fully accounted for by alcohol and sleep deprivation acting independently.

But this only tells us that there are significant differences; we have to check the column and row means in order to say precisely which condition produces the greatest number of mistakes. In other words, the analysis of variance summary table has to be interpreted in the light of the original data table with the column, row, and cell means all entered.

Carefully checking the data suggests that the above interpretation is rather too simplistic. It seems that sleep deprivation actually has little effect unless the person has been taking alcohol. The high cell means are associated with alcohol and sleep deprivation. In these circumstances, there is some doubt that the main effects explanation is good enough.

We would conclude, in these circumstances, 'Although, in the ANOVA, only the main effects were significant, there is reason to think that the main effects are actually the results of the interaction between the main effects. Careful examination of the cell means suggests that especially high scores are associated with taking alcohol and undergoing higher amounts of sleep deprivation. In contrast, those in the no-alcohol condition were affected only to a much smaller extent by having high amounts of sleep deprivation.'

This is tricky for a student to write up since it requires a rather subtle interpretation of the data which might exceed the statistical skills of the readers of their work.

22.4 More on interactions

A conventional way of illustrating interactions is through the use of graphs such as those in Diagrams 22.1 and 22.2. These graphs deal with the sleep and alcohol study just analysed. Notice that the means are given for each of the cells of the two-way ANOVA. Thus the vertical axis is a numerical scale commensurate with

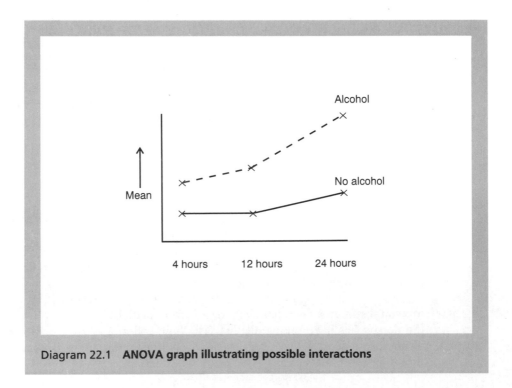

Diagram 22.1   ANOVA graph illustrating possible interactions

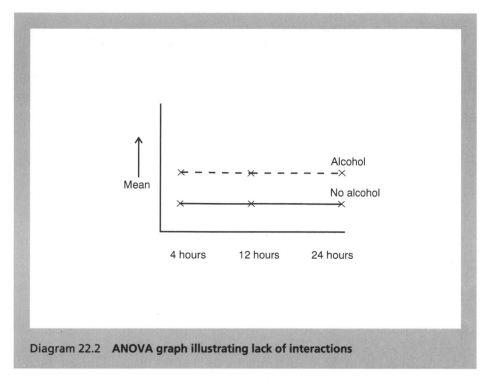

Diagram 22.2 ANOVA graph illustrating lack of interactions

the scale of the dependent variable; the horizontal axis simply records the different levels of *one* of the independent variables. In order to indicate the different levels of the second independent variable, the different cell means for each level are joined together by a distinctively different line.

The main point to remember is that main effects are assumed to be effects which can be added directly to the scores in the columns or rows for that level of the main effect and that the effect is assumed to be common and equal in all of the cells involved. This implies that:

1. If there is *no* interaction, then the lines through the points should move more or less parallel to each other.

2. If there *is* an interaction, then the lines through the points will not be parallel; they may touch, move together or move apart.

Diagram 22.2 illustrates the sort of pattern we might expect if there is no interaction between the independent variables.

22.5 Notes and recommendations

■ Only when you have a 2 × 2 unrelated analysis of variance is the interpretation of the data relatively straightforward. For 2 × 3 or larger analyses of variance you need to read Chapter 23 as well.

■ Although at heart simple enough, the two-way analysis of variance is cumbersome to calculate by hand and is probably best done on a computer if you have anything other than small amounts of data.

■ Analysis of variance always requires a degree of careful interpretation of the findings and cannot always be interpreted in a hard and fast way. This is a little disconcerting given its apparent mathematical sophistication.

■ Before calculating the analysis of variance proper, spend a good deal of effort trying to make sense of the pattern of column, row and cell means in your data table. This should alert you to the major trends in your data. You can use your interpretation in combination with the analysis of variance summary table to obtain as refined an interpretation of your data as possible.

Chapter 23

Multiple comparisons in ANOVA

Just where do the differences lie?

Preparation

You will need a working knowledge of Chapters 19, 20 and 21 on the analysis of variance. Chapter 14 introduces the problem of multiple comparisons in the context of partitioning chi-square tables.

23.1 Introduction

When in research there are *more than two levels* of an *independent* variable it is not always obvious where the differences between conditions lie. There is no problem when you have only two groups of scores to compare in a one-way or a 2 × 2 ANOVA. However, if there are three or more different levels of any independent variable the interpretation problems multiply. Take, for example, Table 23.1 of means for a one-way analysis of variance.

Although the analysis of variance for the data which are summarised in this table may well be statistically significant, there remains a very obvious problem. Groups 1 and 2 have virtually identical means and it is Group 3 which has the exceptionally large scores. Quite simply we would be tempted to assume that Group 1 and Group 2 do not differ significantly and that any differences are due

Table 23.1 **Sample means in a one-way ANOVA**

	Group 1	Group 2	Group 3
Mean	5.6	5.7	12.9

Table 23.2 **Sample means in another one-way ANOVA**

	Group 1	Group 2	Group 3
Mean	5.6	7.3	12.9

to Group 3. Our eyes are telling us that only parts of the data are contributing to the significant ANOVA.

Although the above example is very clear, it becomes a little more fraught if the data are less clear-cut than this (Table 23.2). In this case, it may well be that all three groups differ from each other. Just by looking at the means we cannot know for certain since they may just reflect sampling differences.

Obviously it is essential to test the significance of the differences between the means for all *three* possible *pairs* of sample means from the three groups. These are:

Group 1 with Group 2
Group 1 with Group 3
Group 2 with Group 3

If there had been *four* groups then the pairs of comparisons would be:

Group 1 with Group 2
Group 1 with Group 3
Group 1 with Group 4
Group 2 with Group 3
Group 2 with Group 4
Group 3 with Group 4

This is getting to be a lot of comparisons.

23.2 Methods

There are a number of different procedures which you could employ to deal with this problem. One traditional approach involves comparing each of the pairs of groups using a *t*-test (or you could use one-way analysis of variance for two groups). So for the four-group experiment there would be six separate *t*-tests to calculate (Group 1 with Group 2, Group 1 with Group 3, etc.).

The problem with this procedure (which is not so bad really) is the number of separate comparisons being made. The more comparisons you make between pairs of variables the more likely is a significant difference merely due to chance (always the risk in inferential statistics). Similar procedures apply to the multi-factor (two-way, etc.) analysis of variance. You can compare different levels of any of the main effect pairs simply by comparing their means using a *t*-test or the equivalent. However, the multiple comparison difficulty remains unless you make an adjustment.

To cope with this problem a relatively simple procedure, the Bonferroni method is used. It assumes that the significance level should be shared between the *number* of comparisons made. So if you are making four comparisons (i.e. conducting four separate *t*-tests) then the appropriate significance level for the individual tests is as follows:

$$\text{Significance level for each test} = \frac{\text{overall significance level}}{\text{number of comparisons}}$$

$$= \frac{5\%}{4}$$

$$= 1.25\%$$

In other words, a comparison actually needs to be significant at the 1.25% level according to the significance tables before we accept that it is significant at the *equivalent* of the 5% level. This essentially compensates for our generosity in doing many comparisons and reduces the risk of inadvertently capitalising on chance differences. (We adopted this procedure for chi-square in Chapter 14.) Although this is the proper thing to do, we have often seen examples of analyses which fail to make this adjustment. Some researchers tend to stick with the regular 5% level per comparison no matter how many they are doing, although sometimes they point out the dangers of multiple comparisons without making an appropriate adjustment.

So long as you adjust your critical values to allow for the number of comparisons made, there is nothing much wrong with using multiple *t*-tests. Indeed, this procedure, properly applied, is a slightly 'conservative' one in that it errs in favour of the null hypotheses. However, there are better procedures for making multiple comparisons which are especially convenient when using a computer. These include such procedures as the Scheffé Test and the Duncan Multiple Range Test. The advantage of these is that they report directly significance levels which are adjusted for the numbers of comparisons being made.

23.3 Planned versus *a posteriori (post hoc)* comparisons

In the fantasy world of statisticians there is a belief that researchers are meticulous in planning the last detail of their statistical analysis in advance of doing research. As such an ideal researcher, one would have planned in advance precisely what pairs of cells or conditions in the research are to be compared. These choices are based on the hypotheses and other considerations. In other words, they are planned comparisons. More usual, in our experience, is that the details of the statistical analysis are decided upon *after* the data have been collected. Psychological theory is often not so strong that we can predict from it the precise pattern of outcomes we expect. Comparisons decided upon after the data have been collected and tabulated are called *a posteriori* or *post hoc* comparisons.

Since properly planned comparisons are not the norm in psychological research, for simplicity we will just consider the more casual situation in which comparisons are made as the data is inspected. (Basically, if your number of planned comparisons is smaller than your number of experimental conditions, then they can be tested by the multiple *t*-test *without* adjusting the critical values.)

There are a number of tests which deal with the situation in which multiple comparisons are being made. These include Dunnett's Test, Duncan's Test and others. The Scheffé Test will serve as a model of the sorts of things achieved by many of these tests and is probably as good as any other similar test for general application. Some other tests are not quite so stringent in ensuring that the appropriate level of significance is achieved.

23.4 The Scheffé test for one-way ANOVA

Although this can be computed by hand without too much difficulty, the computer output of the Scheffé Test is particularly useful as it gives subsets of the groups (or conditions) in your experiment which do not differ significantly from each other. For example:

```
SUBSET 1
Group    Grp 3    Grp 1    Grp 2
mean     4.00     5.60     7.00
```

This means that Groups 1, 2 and 3 are not significantly different from each other. If you had significant differences between all three groups then you would have three subsets (Subset 1, Subset 2, and Subset 3) each of which contained just one group. If Groups 1 and 3 did not differ from each other but they both differed from Group 3 you would obtain something like

```
SUBSET 1
Group    Grp 3    Grp 1
mean     4.00     5.60

SUBSET 2
Group    Grp 2
mean     7.00
```

23.5 Multiple comparisons for multifactorial ANOVA

If your experimental design is multifactorial (that is, with two or more independent variables), multiple comparisons are tackled much as for the two-way ANOVA using exactly the same methods (including the adjusted multiple *t*-test procedure or the Scheffé Test). Of course, you would only need such a test if any of the independent variables (factors) has three or more different levels. Otherwise, the significance of the comparisons in the ANOVA is obvious from the ANOVA summary table since there are only two groups of scores to compare with each other (except for interactions).

If you have an independent variable with three or more different levels then multiple comparisons are important to tell you precisely where the significant differences lie. It would be possible to carry out multiple comparisons between every cell mean in the ANOVA but generally this would not be helpful. All one would do is to produce a table analogous to a one-way ANOVA by making the data in each cell of the multifactorial ANOVA into a column of the one-way ANOVA. The difficulty is that this multiplicity of comparisons would be practically uninterpretable since each cell consists of several sources of variation — the various main effects, for example.

It is much more useful and viable to employ multiple comparisons to compare the means of the several different levels of the independent variable(s). If there are four different levels of the independent variable, then one would essentially set out the table like a one-way ANOVA with four different levels of the independent variable. It is then possible to test the significance of the differences among the four means using, for example, the Scheffé Test.

23.6 Notes and recommendations

- ■ If you have more than two sets of scores in the analysis of variance (or any other test for that matter), it is important to employ one of the procedures for multiple comparisons.

- ■ Even simple procedures such as multiple t-tests are better than nothing, especially if the proper adjustment is made for the number of t-tests being carried out and you adjust the critical values accordingly.

- ■ Modern computer packages, especially SPSS, have a range of multiple comparison tests. It is a fine art to know which is the most appropriate for your particular circumstances. Usually it is expedient to compare the results from several tests; often they will give much the same results, especially where the trends in the data are clear.

Recommended further reading

Howell, D. (1987). *Statistical Methods for Psychology*. Boston: Duxbury Press.

Chapter 24

More on the analysis of variance

Special variants of the approach

Preparation

You need to be familiar with the two-way ANOVA (Chapter 22) and the related one-way ANOVA (Chapter 21).

24.1 Introduction

The analysis of variance designs covered so far are an excellent foundation for the statistical analysis of experiments and, sometimes, survey and similar data. However, ANOVA includes a substantial number of more complex and sometimes esoteric designs. Many of these are well beyond the needs of the majority of professional psychological researchers, let alone students. However, psychologists need to appreciate the range of applications of the analysis of variance just in case they are faced with a particularly unusual analysis problem.

In psychology, the complexity of experimental research is constrained by various features, for example:

1. A multitude of conditions in an experiment may involve an extremely high time commitment. Preparing complex sets of instructions for participants in the different experimental conditions, randomly assigning individuals to these groups and many other methodological considerations usually limit our level of ambition in research designs. In non-psychological disciplines, the logistics of experiments are different since the units may not be people but, for example, seedlings in pots containing one of several different composts, with different amounts of fertiliser, and one of several different growing temperatures.

2. People have memories and there is limited scope to use repeated measures designs. They may get a good idea of what the experiment is about if they are exposed to several treatments or they may have more and more practice on the dependent variable which influences their scores. Counterbalancing the order in which participants experience the different experimental conditions

can help but this gets progressively more complex as we venture much beyond two-way analysis of variance. (By counterbalancing we mean that the same numbers of participants in the research experience Condition A first as experience Condition B first.)

3. Interpreting ANOVA is more skilful than many researchers realise. Care is needed to interpret even a two-way analysis properly because main effects are prioritised in the calculation, which results in main effects being credited with variation which is really due to interaction.

In this chapter we will present a sort of compendium of the major analyses of variance which are readily carried out using computers but increasingly complex to carry out by hand. The main aspects covered include the following:

1. More than two independent variables
2. Mixed designs and repeated measures
3. Unequal sample sizes
4. Fixed versus random effects
5. Analysis of covariance (ANCOVA)

24.2 More than two independent variables

The sky's the limit to the number of independent variables *theoretically* possible in the analysis of variance. It is not simply the limits of our imagination that should encourage caution in going overboard in terms of the complexity of our designs. The problems of interpretation get somewhat more difficult the more independent variables there are. The complexity is largely the result of the number of possible *interactions*. Although there is just one interaction with a two-way analysis of variance, there are four with a three-way analysis of variance. As the number of variables increases the number of interactions increases in a rapidly accelerating fashion; remember that caution was expressed about the need for care when interpreting just a single interaction in Chapter 22. As far as possible, we would recommend any psychologist to be wary of going far beyond a two-way analysis of variance without very careful planning and without some experience with these less complex designs. That is not intended to be patronising but merely an indication of the need for building up skill in interpreting complex ANOVAs.

It is possible to disregard the interactions and simply analyse the different variables in the experiment as if they were merely several one-way experiments carried out at the same time. The interpretations would be simpler by doing this. However, this is rarely if ever done in psychological research and it is conventional always to consider interactions.

Imagine the following three-way or three-factor analysis of variance. The three independent variables are:

Table 24.1   **A stylised three-way analysis of variance study**

	Noisy conditions		Quiet conditions	
	Young	**Old**	**Young**	**Old**
Males	. . .	. . .	. . .	. . .
Females	. . .	. . .	. . .	. . .

Table 24.2   **Interaction of age and sex**

	Young	**Old**
Males	. . .	. . .
Females	. . .	. . .

1. Age – coded as either young or old

2. Sex – coded as either male or female

3. Noise – the research takes place in either a noisy or a quiet environment.

So this is a three-way ANOVA with a total of eight different conditions (2 ages × 2 sexes × 2 different noise levels). The dependent variable is the number of errors on a numerical memory test in the different conditions. The main features of this research are presented in Table 24.1.

The sheer number of comparisons possible between sections of the data causes problems. These comparisons are:

1. The main effect of sex – that is comparing males and females irrespective of age or noise.

2. The main effect of age – that is comparing young and old irrespective of sex or noise.

3. The main effect of noise – that is comparing noisy and quiet conditions irrespective of age or sex.

4. The interaction of age and sex – that is comparing age and sex groups ignoring the noise conditions. This would look like Table 24.2.

5. The interaction of age and noise – that is comparing age and noise groups ignoring sex. This is shown in Table 24.3.

6. The interaction of noise and sex – that is comparing noise and sex groups ignoring age. This is shown in Table 24.4.

7. There is a fourth interaction – the interaction of noise and sex and age which is represented by Table 24.5. Notice that the cell means of each of the conditions are involved in this.

Table 24.3   Interaction of age and noise

	Young	Old
Noisy conditions	. . .	. . .
Quiet conditions	. . .	. . .

Table 24.4   Interaction of noise and sex

	Noisy conditions	Quiet conditions
Males	. . .	. . .
Females	. . .	. . .

Table 24.5   Interaction of noise, sex, and age

	Noisy conditions		Quiet conditions	
	Young	Old	Young	Old
Males	. . .	. . .	. . .	. . .
Females	. . .	. . .	. . .	. . .

Although Table 24.5 looks like the format of the original data table (Table 24.1), the scores in the cells will be very different because all of the other sources of variation will have been removed.

The steps in calculating this three-way analysis of variance follow the pattern which we demonstrated in Chapter 22 but with extra layers of complexity:

1. The error term is calculated in the usual way by subtracting the cell mean from each score in a particular cell. The variance estimate of this table can then be calculated.

2. The main effect of sex is calculated by substituting the male mean for each of the male scores and the female mean for each of the female scores. The variance estimate of this table can then be calculated.

3. The age main effect is arrived at by substituting the mean score of the young people for each of their scores and substituting the mean score of the old people for each of their scores. The variance estimate of this table can then be calculated.

4. The noise main effect is arrived at by substituting the mean score in the noisy conditions for each score in the noisy conditions and substituting the mean score in the quiet conditions for each score in the quiet conditions. The variance estimate of this table can then be calculated.

5. The interaction of age and sex is arrived at by taking the table of scores with the error removed and then removing the age and sex difference simply by taking away the column mean and then the row mean. This is the same procedure as we applied to get the interaction in the two-way analysis of variance. The variance estimate of this table can then be calculated.

6. We arrive at the interaction of age and noise by drawing up a similar table and then taking away the appropriate age and noise means in turn. The variance estimate of this table can then be calculated.

7. We arrive at the interaction of noise and sex by drawing up a similar table and then taking away the appropriate noise and sex means in turn. The variance estimate of this table can then be calculated.

8. The three-way interaction (age × noise × sex) is obtained by first of all drawing up our table of the age × noise × sex conditions. We then take away the main effects by subtracting the appropriate age, noise and sex means from this table. But we also have to take away the two-way interactions of age × noise, age × sex, and noise × sex by subtracting the appropriate means from the above table. Whatever is left is the three-way interaction. The variance estimate of this final table can then be calculated.

24.3 Mixed designs and repeated measures

Repeated measures designs have the same subjects (or matched groups of subjects) measured in *all* conditions just as in the repeated measures one-way analysis of variance except that there are two or more independent variables. The repeated measures design is intended to increase the precision of research by measuring the error variance (residual variance) in a way which excludes the individual differences component. The individual differences component is obtained from the general tendency of individual participants to score relatively high or relatively low, say, irrespective of the experimental condition. The trend for each individual can simply be deducted from the error scores to leave (residual) error.

Fully repeated measures designs are uncommon in multifactorial ANOVA. Some independent variables do not allow for repeated measures – sex, for example, is not a repeated measure since a person cannot change sex during the course of an experiment. Only where matching of groups on the basis of sex has been carried out is it possible to have sex as a repeated measure.

Much more common in psychology are *mixed designs* in which the repeated measure is on just some of the independent variables. Mixed designs are two- or more-way analyses of variance in which participants are measured in more than one experimental condition but not *every* experimental condition. (This means that *for at least one of the independent variables* in a mixed design, scores on different participants will be found in the different levels of this independent variable.) Usually you will have to check through the experimental design carefully in order to decide whether a researcher has used a mixed design, although many will stipulate the type of design.

One common mixed design is the pre-test/post-test design. Participants are measured on the dependent variable before *and* after the experimental treatment. This is clearly a related design since the same people are measured twice on the same dependent variable. However, since the experimental and control groups consist of different people, this comparison is unrelated. Hence this form of the pre-test/post-test design is a mixed design. This sort of design is illustrated in Table 24.6. Imagine that the dependent variable is self-esteem measured in children before *and* after the experimental manipulation. The experimental manipulation involves praising half of the children (the experimental group) for good behaviour but telling the other half (the control group) nothing. Obviously this sort of design allows the researcher to test whether the two groups are similar prior to the experimental manipulation by comparing the experimental and control groups on the pre-test measure. The hypothesis that praise affects self-esteem suggests that the post-test measure should be different for the two groups. (Notice that the hypothesis predicts an interaction effect in which the related and unrelated independent variables interact to yield rather different scores for the experimental group and the control group on the post-test.)

In virtually all respects, the computation of the mixed design is like that for the two-way (unrelated) ANOVA described in Chapter 22. Both main effects *and* the interaction are calculated in identical fashion. The error is treated differently though. Although the *total* error is calculated by subtracting the cell mean from each of the data scores to leave the error score (as in Chapter 22), in the mixed design this error is then sub-divided into two component parts: (a) the individual differences component, and (b) the (residual) error component. Actually we have done this before for the related one-way ANOVA in Chapter 21. The slight difference is that in Chapter 21 we removed the individual differences component of error to leave the (residual) error which was then used as an 'improved' error term in calculating the significance of the main effect of what was a related measures independent variable. In a mixed design, the (residual) error term is calculated and used for the error term when examining the effects of the related independent variable (this error term is often called 'B × subjects within groups'); what is new is that the error due to individual differences is calculated and then used as the error term for the *unrelated* independent variable (this error term is often called 'subjects within groups').

Note the slight amendments made to the tables compared to those given in Chapter 22; columns headed *subject* and *subject mean* have been added. If there is variation in the *subject mean* column it shows that there is still an individual differences component in the scores in the main body of the table. Careful examination of (a) the column means and row means, (b) the cell means, (c) the subject means and (d) the individual scores in the cells, will hint strongly whether there remains any variation due to respectively (a) the main effects, (b) interaction, (c) individual differences, and (d) (residual) error.

Table 24.6   **Example of a mixed ANOVA design**

	Subject	Pre-test measure		Post-test measure		Subject mean	
Control	S1	6	Mean = 5.000	5	Mean = 6.000	5.500	Mean = 5.500
	S2	4		6		5.000	
	S3	5		7		6.000	
Experi-mental	S4	7	Mean = 5.667	10	Mean = 11.000	8.500	Mean = 8.333
	S5	5		11		8.000	
	S6	5		12		8.500	
			Mean = 5.333		Mean = 8.500	Overall mean = 6.917	

If you feel confident with the two-way unrelated ANOVA described in Chapter 22, we suggest that you need to concentrate on Step 2 and Step 7 below as these tell you how to calculate the error terms. The other steps should be familiar.

In Table 24.6 the variance estimate for $N-1$ degrees of freedom $= \frac{76.92}{11} = 6.99$. N is the number of scores, i.e. 12.

> Just to remind you, 6.99 is the variance estimate (or mean square) based on the 12 scores in Table 24.6. To avoid repetitious calculations with which you should now be familiar, we have given only the final stages of the calculation of the various variance estimates. This is to allow you to work through our example and check your calculations.

In the mixed-design ANOVA the following steps are then calculated.

Step 1: Between subjects scores

Between subjects scores are the data but with the pre-test/post-test difference eliminated. In other words, each subject's score in the pre-test and post-test conditions is replaced by the corresponding subject mean. Thus the column means for the pre-test and post-test have the (residual) error removed since the remaining variation within the cells is due to individual differences. However, there still remains variation within the table due to individual differences as well as the main effects and interaction. To be absolutely clear, the first entry of 5.500 for both the pre-test and post-test measure is obtained by averaging that first person's scores of 5 and 6 in Table 24.7.

Table 24.7   **Between subjects scores (i.e. with (residual) error removed)**

	Subject	Pre-test		Post-test		Subject mean	
Control	S1	5.500	Mean = 5.500	5.500	Mean = 5.500	5.500	Mean = 5.500
	S2	5.000		5.000		5.000	
	S3	6.000		6.000		6.000	
Experi-mental	S4	8.500	Mean = 8.333	8.500	Mean = 8.333	8.500	Mean = 8.333
	S5	8.000		8.000		8.000	
	S6	8.500		8.500		8.500	
			Mean = 6.917		Mean = 6.917	Overall mean = 6.917	

Table 24.8   **Subjects within groups scores (i.e. error due to individual differences removed)**

	Subject	Pre-test	Post-test	Subject mean	
Control	S1	5.500 – 5.500 = 0.000	0.000	0.000	Mean = 0.000
	S2	5.000 – 5.500 = –0.500	–0.500	–0.500	
	S3	6.000 – 5.500 = 0.500	0.500	0.500	
Experi-mental	S4	0.167	0.167	0.167	Mean = 0.000
	S5	–0.333	–0.333	–0.333	
	S6	0.167	0.167	0.167	
		Mean = 0.000	Mean = 0.000	Overall mean = 0.000	

In Table 24.7 the variance estimate for the between subjects scores $= \frac{25.41}{5} =$ 5.08 (df = number of subjects – 1, i.e. 6 – 1 = 5).

Step 2: Subjects within groups scores (i.e. individual difference component)

If we take away the cell mean from the scores in Table 24.7, we are left with the individual difference component for each subject for each score. Thus, S2's scores are on average –0.500 below the row mean. Table 24.8 gives the individual difference component of every score in the original data.

In Table 24.8 the variance estimate for the subjects within groups scores = $\frac{1.32}{4} = 0.33$ (df = number of subjects – number of rows of data, i.e. 6 – 2 = 4).

You will see that these individual difference scores seem rather like error scores – they add to zero for each cell. Indeed they are error scores – the individual differences component of error. The variance estimate of the individual differences is used as the error variance estimate for calculating the significance of the control/experimental comparison (i.e. the *unrelated* independent variable).

Step 3: Experimental/control scores: main effect

The best estimate of the effects of the experimental versus the control condition involves simply replacing each score for the control group with the control group mean (5.500) and each score for the experimental group by the experimental group mean (8.333). This is shown in Table 24.9.

In Table 24.9 the variance estimate for the experimental/control main effect $= \frac{24.09}{1} = 24.09$ (df = number of rows of data − 1, i.e. 2 − 1 = 1).

The statistical significance of the main effect of the experimental versus control manipulation independent variable involves the variance estimate for the main effects scores in Table 24.9 and the variance estimate for the (residual) error scores in Table 24.8. By dividing the former by the latter variance estimate, we obtain the *F*-ratio for testing the effects of the experimental versus control conditions. If this is significant then there is an overall difference between the control and experimental group scores.

Step 4: Within subjects scores

Subtract the between subjects scores (Table 24.7) from the data table (Table 24.6) and you are left with the within subjects scores. In other words, the scores in Table 24.10 are what is left when the effects of the experimental/control comparison and the individual difference component of the scores are removed. Notice that the subject means in Table 24.10 are all zero as are the row means. This indicates that there are no individual differences or differences due to the experimental/control comparison remaining in Table 24.10.

Table 24.9   **Main effect (experimental/control comparison)**

	Subject	**Pre-test**	**Post-test**	**Subject mean**	
Control	S1	5.500	5.500	5.500	Mean = 5.500
	S2	5.500	5.500	5.500	
	S3	5.500	5.500	5.500	
Experi-mental	S4	8.333	8.333	8.333	Mean = 8.333
	S5	8.333	8.333	8.333	
	S6	8.333	8.333	8.333	
	Mean = 6.917	Mean = 6.917		Overall mean = 6.917	

Table 24.10 **Within subjects scores (i.e. the scores with individual differences and control/experimental differences eliminated)**

	Subject	Pre-test measure	Post-test measure	Subject mean	
Control	S1	0.5	−0.5	0.000	Mean = 0.000
	S2	−1.0	1.0	0.000	
	S3	−1.0	1.0	0.000	
Experi-mental	S4	−1.5	1.5	0.000	Mean = 0.000
	S5	−3.0	3.0	0.000	
	S6	−3.5	3.5	0.000	
	Mean = −1.583		Mean = 1.583	Overall mean = 0.000	

Table 24.11 **Main effects of the pre-test/post-test comparison**

	Subject	Pre-test measure	Post-test measure	Subject mean	
Control	S1	5.333	8.500	6.917	Mean = 6.917
	S2	5.333	8.500	6.917	
	S3	5.333	8.500	6.917	
Experi-mental	S4	5.333	8.500	6.917	Mean = 6.917
	S5	5.333	8.500	6.917	
	S6	5.333	8.500	6.917	
	Mean = 5.333		Mean = 8.500	Overall mean = 6.917	

In Table 24.10 the variance estimate $= \frac{51.48}{6} = 8.58$ (df = number of scores − number of subjects = 12 − 6 = 6).

Step 5: Within subjects independent variable main effect: pre-test/post-test scores

This is the main effect of the repeated measure. It is is obtained simply by substituting the appropriate column average from the data table (Table 24.6) for each of the scores (Table 24.11).

In Table 24.11 the variance estimate for the pre-test/post-test main effect $= \frac{30.14}{1} = 30.14$ (df = number of columns of data − 1, i.e. 2 − 1 = 1).

Step 6: Interaction of experimental/control with pre-test/post-test

The calculation of the interaction is much as for the two-way unrelated ANOVA (Chapter 22):

1. We can eliminate error by making every score in the data table the same as the cell mean (Table 24.12).

2. We can eliminate the effect of the control versus experimental treatment by simply taking the corresponding row means away from all of the scores in Table 24.12 (Table 24.13).

3. Notice that Table 24.13 still contains variation between the pre-test and the post-test columns. We eliminate this by subtracting the corresponding column mean from each of the scores in the Pre-test and Post-test columns (Table 24.14). Table 24.14 contains the scores for the interaction. The variance estimate for the interaction = $\frac{14.08}{1}$ = 14.08 (df = number of rows of data − 1 × number of columns of data −1, i.e. $(2 − 1) \times (2 − 1) = 1 \times 1 = 1$).

Table 24.12   **Removing (total) error from the data table**

	Subject	Pre-test	Post-test	Subject mean	
Control	S1	5.000	6.000	5.500	Mean = 5.500
	S2	5.000	6.000	5.500	
	S3	5.000	6.000	5.500	
Experi-	S4	5.667	11.000	8.333	Mean = 8.333
mental	S5	5.667	11.000	8.333	
	S6	5.667	11.000	8.333	
	Mean = 5.333	Mean = 8.500		Overall mean = 6.917	

Table 24.13   **Removing experimental/control main effect ((total) error removed in previous step)**

	Subject	Pre-test	Post-test	Subject mean	
Control	S1	5.000 − 5.500 = −0.500	0.500	0.000	Mean = 0.000
	S2	−0.500	0.500	0.000	
	S3	−0.500	0.500	0.000	
Experi-	S4	−2.666	2.667	0.000	Mean = 0.000
mental	S5	−2.666	2.667	0.000	
	S6	−2.666	2.667	0.000	
		Mean = −1.584	Mean = 1.584	Overall mean = 0.000	

Table 24.14 **Removing pre-test/post-test differences (error and experimental/ control main effect already removed in previous two steps)**

	Subject	Pre-test	Post-test	Subject mean	
Control	S1	$-0.500 - (-1.584) = 1.084$	-1.084	0.000	Mean = 0.000
	S2	1.084	-1.084	0.000	
	S3	1.084	-1.084	0.000	
Experi-	S4	-1.082	1.083	0.000	Mean = 0.000
mental	S5	-1.082	1.083	0.000	
	S6	-1.082	1.083	0.000	
		Mean = 0.000	Mean = 0.000		Overall mean = 0.000

Step 7: Pre-test/post-test × subjects within groups

Earlier we explained that pre-test/post-test × subjects within groups is an error term which is essentially the (residual) error that we calculated in Chapter 21. It is actually quite easy to calculate the (residual) error simply by (a) drawing up a total error table by subtracting the cell means from each score in the data table (Table 24.6) as we did for the two-way unrelated ANOVA in Chapter 22, and then (b) taking away from these (total) error scores the corresponding (residual) error in Table 24.8. In other words, (residual) error = (total) error – individual difference error. Most statistical textbooks present a rather more abstract computational approach to this which obscures what is really happening. However, to facilitate comparisons with other textbooks, if required, we will present the calculation using essentially the computational method.

The calculation of this error term involves taking the data (Table 24.6) and then (a) subtracting the interaction score (Table 24.14), (b) subtracting the individual differences score (Table 24.7), and (c) adding the between subjects score (Table 24.11). Notice that the scores in Table 24.15 are just as we would expect of error scores – the cells all add up to zero. It is (residual) error since there is no variation left in the subject mean column.

In Table 24.15 the variance estimate for the pre-test/post-test × subjects within groups (or residual error) = $\frac{7.37}{4}$ = 1.84 (df = (number of subjects – number of rows) × (number of columns – 1) = $(6 - 2) \times (2 - 1) = 4 \times 1 = 1$).

This (residual) error term is used in assessing the significance of the pre-test/ post-test comparison as well as the interaction.

Table 24.15 **Pre-test/post-test × subjects within groups scores (i.e. (residual) error)**

	Subject	Pre-test	Post-test	Subject mean	
Control	S1	6 − 5.000 − 5.500 + 5.500 = 1.000	5 − 6.000 − 5.500 + 5.500 = −1.000	0.000	Mean = 0.000
	S2	4 − 5.000 − 5.000 + 5.500 = −0.500	6 − 6.000 − 5.000 + 5.500 = 0.500	0.000	
	S3	5 − 5.000 − 6.000 + 5.500 = −0.500	7 − 6.000 − 6.000 + 5.500 = 0.500	0.000	
Experimental	S4	7 − 5.667 − 8.500 + 8.333 = 1.167	10 − 11.000 − 8.500 + 8.333 = −1.167	0.000	Mean = 0.000
	S5	5 − 5.667 − 8.000 + 8.333 = −0.334	11 − 11.000 − 8.000 + 8.333 = 0.333	0.000	
	S6	5 − 5.667 − 8.500 + 8.333 = −0.834	12 − 11.000 − 8.500 + 8.333 = 0.833	0.000	
		Mean = 0.000	Mean = 0.000	Overall mean = 0.000	

Table 24.16 **Analysis of variance summary table (using basic concepts)**

Source of variation	Sums of squares	Degrees of freedom	Variance estimate	*F*-ratio
Unrelated: Main effect (unrelated variable)	24.09	1	24.09	$\dfrac{24.09}{0.33} = 73.00*$
Individual differences error	1.32	4	0.33	
Related: Main effect (related variable)	30.14	1	30.14	$\dfrac{30.14}{1.84} = 16.38*$
Interaction (related × unrelated variables)	14.08	1	14.08	$\dfrac{14.08}{1.84} = 7.65*$
(Residual) error	7.37	4	1.84	

* Significant at 5% level.

Table 24.17   Analysis of variance summary table (conventional textbook version)

Source of variation	Sums of squares	Degrees of freedom	Variance estimate	F-ratio
Between subjects:				
A (praise)	24.09	1	24.09	$\frac{24.09}{0.33} = 73.00^*$
Subjects within groups	1.32	4	0.33	
Within subjects:				
B (time)	30.14	1	30.14	$\frac{30.14}{1.84} = 16.38^*$
AB	14.08	1	14.08	$\frac{14.08}{1.84} = 7.65^*$
B × subjects within groups	7.37	4	1.84	

* Significant at 5% level.

The various calculations in Steps 1 to 7 can be made into an analysis of variance summary table. Table 24.16 is a summary table using the basic concepts we have included in this book. Table 24.17 is the same except that it uses the conventional way of presenting mixed designs in statistics textbooks.

You might be wondering about the reasons for the two error terms. The (residual) error is merely that with no individual differences remaining, and in Chapter 21 we examined how removing individual differences helps to control error variation in related designs. Not surprisingly, it is used for the main effect and interaction which include related components. However, since the individual differences error contains only that source of variation, it makes a good error term for the unrelated scores comparison. After all, by getting rid of 'true' error variation the design allows a 'refined' error term for the unrelated comparison.

Perhaps we ought to explain why conventionally rather unusual names are used for the error terms in mixed ANOVAs. The reason is that the individual differences component of the scores cannot be estimated totally independently of the interaction between the main variables since they are both dependent on pre-test/post-test differences. Consequently the estimate of individual differences cannot be totally divorced from the interaction. It follows from this that both error terms ought to be labelled in ways which indicate this fact. On balance, then, you would be wise to keep to the conventional terminology.

> **Design consideration:** This sort of mixed design requires a significant interaction for the experimental hypothesis to be supported but does have the drawback that essentially the main effect of the pre-test/post-test comparison may well be affected by this interaction. (Remember that ANOVA takes out main effects first and interactions can be confused with these.) Furthermore, the unrelated comparison can also be affected in the same way. A simpler, although not so thorough, analysis of these same data would be a *t*-test comparing the differences between the pre-test and post-test scores for the experimental and control groups.

The 'risks' in related subjects designs

The advantage of related designs is that the error component of the data can be reduced by the individual differences component. Similarly, in matched-subject designs the matching variables, if they are carefully selected because they correlate with the dependent variable, reduce the amount of error in the scores. However, there is a trade-off between reducing the error term and the reduction in degrees of freedom involved (Glantz and Slinker, 1990) since the degrees of freedom in an unrelated ANOVA error term are higher than for the related ANOVA error term. If one's matching variables are poorly related to the dependent variable or if the individual differences component of error is very small, there may be no advantage in using the related or matched ANOVA. Indeed, there can be a reduction in the power of the related ANOVA to reject your null hypothesis. This is a complex matter. The practical advice is (a) not to employ matching unless you know that there is a strong relationship between the matching variables and the dependent variable (e.g. it is only worth matching subjects by their sex if you know that there is a sex difference in scores on the dependent variable), and (b) to do whatever you can to reduce the error variance by standardising your methods and using highly reliable measures of the dependent variable.

24.4 Unequal sample sizes

Human ingenuity features heavily in the variety of analysis of variance designs available. Some of the conventionally accepted 'rules' of the analysis of variance can be bypassed with a degree of imagination. Although one does not need equal sample sizes in the *one-way* unrelated analysis of variance, generally it is believed that other ANOVAs are not possible with unequal sample sizes. You can calculate virtually any ANOVAs with unequal cell sizes but they get somewhat cumbersome and really are best done on a computer. The main problem in unequal sample sizes is that they distort the main effects and lower order (number of variables) interactions, so unequal cell sizes make such simple averages misleading. Analysis of variance for unequal sample sizes has to make an adjustment for this. Even having no scores in some cells does not totally prevent you doing an analysis of variance!

Furthermore, you can even do analyses of variance when you have only one subject per condition but here we are approaching the surreal. Since the error variance estimate is dependent on variation within a cell, there is no error variance if there is only one score in a cell. In these circumstances one of the complex interactions is used as the error term. Presumably the assumption is that the interaction is an inflated estimate of the error (i.e. it includes error and the interaction effect) but better than no estimate of the error at all. Although these techniques are available for extreme circumstances, most of us should regard them as statistical trainspotting – of interest only to completist collectors of the statistically obscure. Most of us would do better to spend our time getting decent data in the first place.

24.5 Fixed versus random effects

The issue of fixed versus random effects is a typical analysis of variance misnomer. It really means fixed or random choice of the different levels of an independent variable. The implication is that you can select the levels of a treatment (independent variable) either by a systematic decision or by choosing the levels by some random procedure.

Most psychological research assumes a *fixed effects* model and it is hard to find instances of the use of random effects. A fixed effect is where the researcher chooses or decides to fix what the different values of the independent variable are going to be. In some cases you have no choice at all – a variable such as sex gives you no discretion and your sex variable has just two different values (male and female). Usually we just operate as if we have the choice of the different treatments for each independent variable. We simply decide that the experimental group is going to be deprived of sleep for five hours and the control group not deprived of sleep at all.

But there are many different possible amounts of sleep deprivation – no hours, one hour, two hours, three hours and so forth. Instead of just selecting the number of hours of sleep deprivation on the basis of a particular whim, practicality or any other similar basis, it is possible to choose the amounts of sleep deprivation *at random*. We could draw the amount out of a hat containing the possible levels. In circumstances like these we would be using a *random* effects model. Because we have selected the hours of sleep deprivation at random, it could be said that our ability to generalise from our experiment to the effects of sleep deprivation in general is enhanced. We simply have chosen an unbiased way of selecting the amount of sleep deprivation, after all.

Since the random effects model rarely corresponds to practice in psychological research, it is pointless getting very concerned about it. Psychologists' research is more likely to be the result of agonising about time, money and other practical constraints on the choices available.

24.6 Analysis of covariance

The analysis of covariance (ANCOVA) is very much like the analysis of variance. The big difference is that it allows you to take account of any variable(s) which might correlate with the dependent variable (apart, of course, from any independent variables in your analysis of variance design). In other words, it is possible to adjust the analysis of variance for differences between your groups which might affect the outcome. For example, you might find that social class correlates with your dependent variable, and that social class differs for the groups in your ANOVA. Using ANCOVA you can adjust the scores on your dependent variable for these social class differences. This essentially is to equate all of the groups so that their mean social class is the same. Although it is possible to do ANCOVA by hand, we would recommend the use of a computer since you are likely to want to equate for several variables, not just one. Furthermore, you should check to see that your covariate does, in fact, correlate with the dependent variable otherwise your analysis becomes less sensitive, not more so.

Table 24.18 gives data which might be suitable for the analysis of variance. The study is of the effects of different types of treatment on the dependent variable depression. For each participant, a pre-test measure of depression given prior to therapy is also given. Notice that the pre-test scores of Group 3, the no-treatment control group, tend to be larger on this pre-measure. Therefore, it could be that the apparent effects of therapy are to do with pre-existing differences between the three groups. Analysis of covariance could be used to allow for these pre-existing differences.

Table 24.18 **Example of analysis of covariance data**

Group 1 Psychotherapy		Group 2 Anti-depressant		Group 3 No-treatment control	
Independent variable	Covariate	Independent variable	Covariate	Independent variable	Covariate
Depression	Pre-test	Depression	Pre-test	Depression	Pre-test
27	38	30	40	40	60
15	32	27	34	29	52
22	35	24	32	35	57

24.7 Notes and recommendations

■ Often complex experimental designs which would necessitate using these complicated analysis of variance procedures are very cumbersome to implement. You should employ them only after careful deliberation about what it is you really want to know from your research.

■ Avoid the temptation to include basic demographic variables such as age and sex routinely as independent variables in the analysis of variance. If they are key factors then they should be included, otherwise they can merely lead to complex interactions which may be hard to interpret and not profitable when you have done so.

Recommended further reading

Glantz, S.A., and Slinker, B.K. (1990). *Primer of Applied Regression and Analysis of Variance*. New York: McGraw-Hill.

Chapter 25

Statistics and the analysis of experiments

Preparation

Make sure that you understand hypotheses (Chapter 10), and nominal category data versus numerical score data (Chapter 1).

25.1 Introduction

Feeling jaded and listless? Don't know what stats to use to analyse your experiment? Make money from home. Try Professor Warburton's Patent Stats Pack. All the professional tricks revealed. Guaranteed not to fail. Gives hope where there is no hope. Professor Warburton's Stats Pack troubleshoots the troubleshooters.

Since the death of Professor Warburton in 1975, through thrombosis of the wallet, his Patent Stats Pack had been feared lost. Libraries on three continents were searched. Miraculously it was discovered after many years in Australia in a trunk under the bed of a dingo farmer. Auctioned recently at Sotheby's to an unknown buyer – reputedly a German antiquarian – it broke all records. Controversy broke out when scholars claimed that Professor Warburton was a fraud and never held an academic appointment in his life. To date, it has not been possible to refute this claim.

These are vile slurs against Professor Warburton who many regard as the founder of the post-modernist statistics movement and the first person to deconstruct statistics. Judge for yourself.

25.2 The Patent Stats Pack

Principle 1: Practically nothing needs to be known about statistical calculations and theory to choose appropriate procedures to analyse your data. The characteristics of your research are the main considerations – not knowledge of statistics books.

Principle 2: Ideally you should not undertake research without being able to sketch out the likely features of your tables and diagrams.

Principle 3:   You *can* make a silk purse out of a sow's ear. First catch your silk pig . . . A common mistake is thinking that the data as they are collected are the data as they will be analysed. Sometimes, especially when the statistical analysis has not been planned prior to collecting data, you may have to make your data fit the available statistical techniques. Always remember that you may need to alter the format of your data in some way in order to make it suitable for statistical analysis. These changes include:

(a)   adding scores from several variables to get a single overall or composite variable, and

(b)   separating a variable into several different components (especially where you have collected data as frequencies in nominal categories and have allowed multiple answers).

25.3 Checklist

The following are the major considerations which will help you choose an appropriate statistical analysis for your data.

1.   Write down your hypothesis. Probably the best way of doing this is to simply fill in the blanks in the following:

'My hypothesis is that there is a relationship between
Variable 1 _____ and Variable 2 _____'

Do not write in the names of more than two variables. There is nothing to stop you having several hypotheses. Write down as many hypotheses as seems appropriate – but only *two* variable names per hypothesis. Treat each hypothesis as a separate statistical analysis.

If you cannot name the two variables you see as correlated then it is possible that you wish only to compare a single sample with a population. In this case check out the single-sample chi-square (Chapter 14) or the single-sample t-test (Chapter 12).

2.   If you cannot meet the requirements of 1 above then you are possibly confused about the purpose of the research. *Go no further until you have sorted this out* – do not blame statistics for your conceptual muddle. Writing out your hypotheses until they are clear may sound like a chore but it is an important part of statistical analysis.

3.   Classify each of the variables in your hypothesis into either of the following two categories:

(a)   Numerical score variables

(b)   Nominal (category) variables – and count the number of categories.

4.   Based on 3, decide which of the following statements is true of your hypothesis:

(a)   I have *two* numerical score variables: Yes/No
(if yes then go to 5)

(b)   I have *two* nominal category variables: Yes/No
(if yes then go to 6)

(c)   I have *one* nominal category variable and *one* numerical score variable: Yes/No
(if yes then go to 7)

5.   If you answered yes to 4(a) above (i.e. you have two numerical score variables) then your statistical analysis involves the correlation coefficient. This might include Pearson Correlation, Spearman Correlation or Regression. Turn to Chapter 29 on the analysis of questionnaire research for ideas of what is possible.

6.   If you answered yes to 4(b), implying that you have two nominal category variables, then your statistical analysis has to be based on contingency tables using chi-square or closely related tests. The range available to you is as follows:

(a)   Chi-square

(b)   Fisher Exact Test for 2 × 2 or 2 × 3 contingency tables, especially if the samples are small or expected frequencies low

(c)   The McNemar Test if you are studying *change* in the same sample of people.

The only problem which you are likely to experience with such tests is if you have allowed the participants in your research to give more than one answer to a question. If you have, then the solution is to turn each category into a separate variable and code each individual according to whether or not they are in that category. So, for example, in a frequency table such as Table 25.1 it is pretty obvious that multiple responses have been allowed since the total of the frequencies is in excess of the sample size of 50. This table could be turned into four new tables:

■ Table 1: The number of vegetarians (19) versus the number of non-vegetarians (31)

■ Table 2: The number of fast food preferrers (28) versus the non-fast food preferrers (22)

■ Table 3: Italian preferrers (9) versus Italian non-preferrers (41)

■ Table 4: Curry preferrers (8) versus non-curry preferrers (42)

7.   If you answered yes to 4(c) then the nominal (category) variable is called the *independent* variable and the numerical score variable is called the *dependent* variable. The number of categories for the independent variable partly determines the statistical tests you can apply:

Table 25.1   **Food preferences of a sample of 50 teenagers**

Food type	Frequency
Vegetarian	19
Fast food	28
Italian	9
Curry	8

(a) If you have *two* categories for the independent (nominal category) variable then:

- the *t*-test is a suitable statistic (Chapters 12 and 13)
- the one-way Analysis of Variance (ANOVA) is suitable (Chapters 20 and 21)

The choice between the two is purely arbitrary as they give equivalent results. Remember to check whether your two sets of scores are independent or correlated/related. If your scores on the dependent variable are correlated then it is appropriate to use the related or correlated versions of the *t*-test (Chapter 12) and the Analysis of Variance (Chapter 21).

(b) If you have *three or more* categories for the independent (nominal category) variable then your choice is limited to the one-way Analysis of Variance (ANOVA). Again, if your dependent variable features correlated or related scores, then the related or correlated one-way Analysis of Variance can be used (Chapters 19 and 20).

> If it becomes clear that the basic assumptions of parametric tests are violated by your data (which for all practical purposes means that the distribution of scores is *very* skewed), then you might wish to employ a nonparametric equivalent (Chapter 18 and Appendix C).

Sometimes you may decide that you have *two or more independent* variables for each dependent variable. Here you are getting into the complexities of the analysis of variance and you need to consult Chapters 22 and 24 for advice.

25.4 Special cases

Multiple items to measure the same variable

Sometimes instead of measuring a variable with a single question or with a single technique, that variable is measured in several ways. Most likely is that a

Table 25.2 An aid to selecting appropriate statistical analyses for different experimental designs

Type of data	One sample compared with known population	Two independent samples	Two related samples	Two or more independent samples	Two or more related samples	Two or more independent variables
Nominal (category) data	One-sample chi-square	Chi-square	McNemar Test	Chi-square	Not in this book*	Chi-square
Numerical score data	One-sample t-test	Unrelated t-test, unrelated one-way ANOVA	Related t-test, related one-way ANOVA	Unrelated ANOVA	Related ANOVA	Two-way etc. ANOVA
Numerical score data which violates assumptions of parametric tests	Not in this book*	Mann–Whitney U-Test	Wilcoxon Matched Pairs Test	Kruskal–Wallis (Appendix C)	Friedman (Appendix C)	Not in this book*

* These are fairly specific non-parametric tests which are rarely used.

questionnaire has been used which contains several questions pertaining to the same thing. In these circumstances you will probably want to combine these questions to give a single numerical score on that variable. The techniques used to do this include the use of standard scores and factor analysis (which are described in Chapters 5 and 26). Generally by combining these different indicators of a major variable together to give a single score you improve the reliability and validity of your research. The combined scores can be used as a single variable and analysed with *t*-tests or analyses of variance, for example.

Assessing change over time

The simplest way of studying change over time is to calculate the difference between the first testing and the second testing. This is precisely what a repeated measures *t*-test, for example, does. However, these difference scores can themselves be used in whatever way you wish. In particular, it would be possible to compare difference scores from two or more different samples in order to assess if the amount of change over time depended on sex or any other independent variable. In other words, it is unnecessary to have a complex analysis of variance design which includes time as one independent variable and sex as the other.

25.5 Notes and recommendations

- Nobody ever learned to play a musical instrument simply by reading a book and never practising. It takes a little time to become confident in choosing appropriate statistical analyses.

- Simple statistical analyses are not automatically inferior to complex ones.

- Table 25.2 should help you choose an appropriate statistical procedure for your experimental data. It is designed to deal only with studies in which you are comparing the *means* of two or more groups of scores. It is not intended to deal with correlations between variables.

Part 4

More advanced correlational statistics

Chapter 26

Partial correlation

Spurious correlation, third variables, suppressor variables

Preparation

Revise the Pearson Correlation Coefficient (Chapter 7) if necessary. What do we mean by a causal relationship?

26.1 Introduction

The partial correlation coefficient is particularly useful when trying to make causal statements from field research. It is not useful in experimental research where different methods are used to establish causal relationships. Look at the following research outlines taking as critical a viewpoint as possible:

- **Project 1**: Researchers examine the published suicide rates in different geographical locations in the country. They find that there is a significant relationship between unemployment rates in these areas and suicide rates. They conclude that unemployment causes suicide.

- **Project 2**: Researchers examine the relationship between shoe size and liking football matches. They find a relationship between the two but claim that it would be nonsense to suggest that liking football makes your feet grow bigger.

Although both of these pieces of research are superficially similar, the researchers draw rather different conclusions. In the first case it is suggested that unemployment *causes* suicide whereas in the second case the researchers are reluctant to claim that liking football makes your feet grow bigger. The researchers in both cases may be correct in their interpretation of the correlations but should we take their interpretations at face value? The short answer is 'no' since correlations do not prove causality in themselves.

In both cases, it is possible that the relationships obtained are spurious (or artificial) ones which occur because of the influence of other variables which the researcher has not considered. So, for example, the relationship between shoe size

273

and liking football might be due to gender – men tend to have bigger feet than women and tend to like football more than women do. So the relationship between shoe size and liking football is merely a consequence of gender differences. The relationship between unemployment and suicide, similarly, could be due to the influence of a third variable. In this case the variable might be social class. If we found, for example, that being from a lower social class was associated with a greater likelihood of unemployment *and* with being more prone to suicide, this would suggest that the relationship between unemployment and suicide was due to social class differences, not because unemployment leads directly to suicide.

Partial correlation is a statistically precise way of calculating what the relationship between two variables would be if one could take away the influence of one (or more) additional variables. Sometimes this is referred to as *controlling for a third variable* or *partialling out a third variable*. Essentially it revises the value of your correlation coefficient to take into account third variables.

> **Design consideration:**   Partial correlation can never prove that causal relationships exist between two variables. The reason is that partialling out a third, fourth or fifth variable does not rule out the possibility that there is an additional variable which has not been considered which is the cause of the correlation. However, partial correlation may be useful in examining the validity of claims about specified variables which might be causing the relationship. Considerations of causality are a minor aspect of partial correlation.

26.2 Theoretical considerations

Partial correlation can be applied to your own data if you have the necessary correlations available. However, partial correlation can also be applied to published research without necessarily obtaining the original data itself – so long as the appropriate correlation coefficients are available. All it requires is that the values of the correlations between your two main variables and the possible third variable are known. It is not uncommon to have the necessary tables of correlations published in books and journal articles although the raw data (original scores) are rarely included in published research.

A table of correlations between several variables is known as a correlation matrix. Table 26.1 is an example featuring the following three variables: numerical intelligence test score (which we have labelled X in the table), verbal intelligence test score (which we have labelled Y in the table), and age (which we have labelled C in the table) in a sample of 30 teenagers.

Notice that the diagonal from top left to bottom right consists of 1.00 repeated three times. This is because the correlation of numerical score with itself, verbal score with itself, and age with itself will always be a perfect relationship ($r = 1.00$) –

Table 26.1 **A correlation matrix involving three variables**

	Variable X Numerical score	Variable Y Verbal score	Variable C Age in years
Variable X Numerical score	1.00	0.97	0.80
Variable Y Verbal score	0.97	1.00	0.85
Variable C Age in years	0.80	0.85	1.00

it has to be since you are correlating exactly the same numbers together. Also notice that the matrix is symmetrical around the diagonal. This is fairly obvious since the correlation of the numerical score with the verbal score has to be exactly the same as the correlation of the verbal score with the numerical score. More often than not a researcher would report just half of Table 26.1, so the correlations would look like a triangle. It doesn't matter which way of doing things you choose.

Remember that we have used the letters X, Y and C for the different columns and rows of the matrix. The C column and C row are the column and row respectively for the *control* variable (age in this case).

Not only is partial correlation an important statistical tool in its own right, it also forms the basis of other techniques such as multiple regression (Chapter 28).

26.3 The calculation

The calculation of the partial correlation coefficient is fairly speedy so long as you have a correlation matrix ready made. Assuming this, the calculation should cause no problems. Computer programs for the partial correlation will normally be capable of calculating the correlation matrix for you, if necessary. Calculation 26.1 works out the relationship between verbal and numerical scores in the above table controlling for age ($r_{XY.C}$).

Calculation 26.1

Partial correlation coefficient

The calculation is based on the correlations found in Table 26.1.

Formula:

$$r_{XY.C} = \frac{r_{XY} - (r_{XC} \times r_{YC})}{\sqrt{1 - r_{XC}^2} \ \sqrt{1 - r_{YC}^2}}$$

Key:

$r_{XY.C}$ = correlation of verbal and numerical scores with age controlled as denoted by .C

r_{XY} = correlation of numerical and verbal scores (= 0.97)

r_{XC} = correlation of numerical scores and age (the control variable) (= 0.80)

r_{YC} = correlation of verbal scores and age (the control variable) (= 0.85)

Using the values taken from the correlation matrix in Table 26.1 we find that:

$$r_{XY.C} = \frac{0.97 - (0.80 \times 0.85)}{\sqrt{1 - 0.80^2} \ \sqrt{1 - 0.85^2}}$$

$$= \frac{0.97 - (0.68)}{\sqrt{1 - 0.64} \ \sqrt{1 - 0.72}}$$

$$= \frac{0.29}{\sqrt{0.36} \ \sqrt{0.28}}$$

$$= \frac{0.29}{0.6 \times 0.53}$$

$$= \frac{0.29}{0.32}$$

$$= 0.91$$

Thus controlling for age has hardly changed the correlation coefficient – it decreases only very slightly from 0.97 to 0.91.

26.4 Interpretation

What does this mean? Well, the original correlation between numerical and verbal scores of 0.97 is reduced to 0.91 when we control for age. This is a very small amount of change and we can say that controlling for age has no real influence on the original correlation coefficient.

The following is the original pattern of relationships between the three variables:

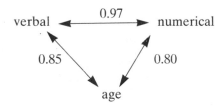

The partial correlation essentially removes all the variation between verbal scores and age and also between numerical scores and age. This is rather like making these correlations zero. But, in this case, when we make these correlations zero we still find that there is a very substantial correlation between verbal and numerical scores:

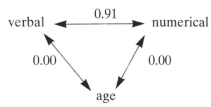

This is an important lesson since it suggests that controlling for a third variable does not always affect the correlation, despite the fact that in this case the control variable age had quite substantial relationships with both verbal and numerical ability scores! *This should be a warning that simply showing that two variables are both correlated with a third variable does not in itself establish that the third variable is responsible for the main correlation.* Such arguments in tutorials therefore can be a waste of breath.

Despite this, often the partial correlation coefficient substantially changes the size of the correlation coefficient. Of course, it is important to know that a third variable does not change the correlation value. In contrast, the next example shows a major change following partialling.

Calculation 26.2

Statistical significance of the partial correlation

This should be calculated exactly in the same way as the statistical significance of the non-partialled correlation with one slight difference. The degrees of freedom are N minus the total number of variables in the partial correlation. That is, as we are controlling for just one additional variable the degrees of freedom are $N - 3$. So in Calculation 26.1 which was based on scores from 30 teenagers, the degrees of freedom are $30 - 3 = 27$. As you can see from Significance Table 26.1 this partial correlation coefficient remains extremely statistically significant after partialling.

Significance Table 26.1   **5% Significance values for the partial correlation (two-tailed test)**

The degrees of freedom are the sample size minus the number of variables in the partial correlation. Thus, if you are controlling for just one variable the degrees of freedom are $N - 3$.

If the number of degrees of freedom you want is not listed, take the next lower tabulated value. Alternatively extrapolate from listed values.

Degrees of freedom	Significant at 5% level Accept hypothesis						
3	−0.81	to	−1.00	*or*	+0.81	to	+1.00
4	−0.75	to	−1.00	*or*	+0.75	to	+1.00
5	−0.71	to	−1.00	*or*	+0.71	to	+1.00
6	−0.67	to	−1.00	*or*	+0.67	to	+1.00
8	−0.60	to	−1.00	*or*	+0.60	to	+1.00
10	−0.55	to	−1.00	*or*	+0.55	to	+1.00
12	−0.51	to	−1.00	*or*	+0.51	to	+1.00
15	−0.47	to	−1.00	*or*	+0.47	to	+1.00
20	−0.41	to	−1.00	*or*	+0.41	to	+1.00
25	−0.37	to	−1.00	*or*	+0.37	to	+1.00
30	−0.34	to	−1.00	*or*	+0.34	to	+1.00
40	−0.30	to	−1.00	*or*	+0.30	to	+1.00
50	−0.27	to	−1.00	*or*	+0.27	to	+1.00
60	−0.25	to	−1.00	*or*	+0.25	to	+1.00
100	−0.19	to	−1.00	*or*	+0.19	to	+1.00

The above table has been adapted and extended from Table VII of R.A. Fisher and F. Yates (1974). *Statistical Tables for Biological, Agricultural and Medical Research*. London: Longman. With the kind permission of the publisher.

26.5 Multiple control variables

It may have struck you that there might be several variables that a researcher might wish to control for at one and the same time. For example, a researcher might wish to control for age and social class at the same time, or even age, social class and sex. This can be done relatively easily on a computer but is rather cumbersome to do by hand.

There are a number of terms that are used which are relatively simple if you know what they mean:

1. *Zero* order correlation – the correlation between your main variables (e.g. r_{XY}).

2. *First* order partial correlation – the correlation between your main variables controlling for just *one* variable (e.g. $r_{XY.C}$).

3. *Second* order partial correlation – the correlation between your main variables controlling for *two* variables at the same time (the symbol for this might be $r_{XY.CD}$).

Not surprisingly, we can extend this quite considerably; for example, a *fifth* order partial correlation involves *five* control variables at the same time (e.g. $r_{XY.CDEFG}$). The principles remain the same no matter what order of partial correlation you are examining.

26.6 Suppressor variables

Sometimes you might find that you actually obtain a low correlation between two variables which you had expected to correlate quite substantially. In some instances this is because a third variable actually has the effect of reducing or suppressing the correlation between the two main variables. Partial correlation is useful in removing the inhibitory effect of this third variable. In other words, it can sometimes happen that controlling the influence of a third variable results in a *larger* correlation. Indeed, it is possible to find that an initially negative correlation becomes a positive correlation when the influence of a third variable is controlled.

26.7 An example from the research literature

Baron and Straus (1989) took the officially reported crime rates for rapes from most US states and compared these with the circulation figures for soft-core pornography in these areas. The correlation between rape rates and the amounts of pornography over these states was 0.53. (If this confuses you, the correlations are calculated 'pretending' that each state is like a person in calculating the

Table 26.2   **Correlation between rape, pornography and divorce**

	Variable X Rape rates	Variable Y Pornography circulation	Variable C Proportion of divorced men
Variable X Rape rates	1.00	0.53	0.67
Variable Y Pornography circulation		1.00	0.59
Variable C Proportion of divorced men			1.00

correlation coefficient.) The temptation is to interpret this correlation as suggesting that pornography leads to rape. Several authors have done so.

However, Howitt and Cumberbatch (1990) took issue with this. They pointed out that the proportions of divorced men in these areas also correlated substantially with both pornography circulation rates and rape rates. The data are listed in Table 26.2.

It might be the case that rather than pornography causing rape, the apparent relationship between these two variables is merely due to the fact that divorced men are more likely to engage in these 'alternative sexual activities'. It is a simple matter to control for this third variable, as set out in Calculation 26.3.

Calculation 26.3

Partial correlation coefficient for rape and pornography controlling for proportion of divorced men

Formula:

$$r_{XY.C} = \frac{r_{XY} - (r_{XC} \times r_{YC})}{\sqrt{1 - r_{XC}^2}\ \sqrt{1 - r_{YC}^2}}$$

Key:

$r_{XY.C}$ = correlation of rape rates with pornography controlling for proportion of divorced men

r_{XY} = correlation of rape and pornography (= 0.53)

r_{XC} = correlation of rape and proportion of divorced men (= 0.67)

r_{YC} = correlation of pornography and proportion of divorced men (= 0.59)

Using the values taken from the correlation matrix in Table 26.2 we find that:

$$r_{XY.C} = \frac{0.53 - (0.67 \times 0.59)}{\sqrt{1 - 0.67^2}\ \sqrt{1 - 0.59^2}}$$

$$= 0.22$$

In this case, the correlation when the third variable is taken into account has changed substantially to become much nearer zero. It would be reasonable to suggest that the partial correlation coefficient indicates that there is *no* causal relationship between pornography and rape – quite a dramatic change in interpretation from the claim that pornography causes rape! The argument is not necessarily that the proportion of divorced men directly causes rape and the purchase of pornography. However, since it is an unlikely hypothesis that rape and pornography *cause* divorce then the fact that partialling out divorce reduces greatly the correlation between rape and pornography means that our faith in the original 'causal' link is reduced.

26.8 An example from a student's work

It is becoming increasingly common to teach children with special educational needs in classrooms along with other children rather than in special schools. Butler (1995a) measured the number of characteristics a sample of 14 teachers possessed which have been held to be of special importance in the effective teaching of special needs children. These qualities would include 'empathy towards special needs children', 'attitude towards integrating special needs children' and about ten others.

In order to assess the quality of the learning experience, the student researcher time-sampled children's task-centred behaviour. By this is meant the number of time periods during which the child was concentrating on the task in hand rather than, say, just wandering around the classroom causing a nuisance. The researcher rated one special needs child and one 'normal' child from each teacher's class. She found that there was a very high correlation of 0.96 between the number of qualities that a teacher possessed and the amount of time that the special needs children spent 'on task' (df = 12, $p<0.01$). Interestingly the correlation of the measure of teacher qualities with the behaviour of normal children in the class was only 0.23. The student used partial correlation to remove the task-oriented behaviour of the 'normal' children in order to control for the extent to which teacher qualities had a beneficial effect on ordinary teaching. This made absolutely no difference to the correlation between the number of qualities the teacher possessed and the amount of time special needs children spent on educational tasks. In other words, the student could be confident that she had identified qualities of teachers which were especially beneficial to special needs children.

In terms of the research design there might be some worries, as the student was well aware. In particular, in an ideal research design there would be a second observer rating the behaviour of the children in order to check the consistency of the ratings between different observers.

26.9 Notes and recommendations

■ If you are doing a *field* rather than a laboratory project check your research hypotheses. If they appear to suggest that one variable *causes* another then do consider using partial correlation. It can potentially enhance one's confidence about making causal interpretations if a significant correlation remains after partialling. However, caution should still be applied since there always remains a risk that an additional variable suppresses the relationship between your two main variables.

■ Do not forget that even after partialling out third variables, any causal interpretation of the correlation coefficient remaining has to be tentative. No correlation coefficient (including partial correlation coefficients) can establish causality in itself. You establish causality largely through your research design, not the statistics you apply.

■ Do not overlook the possibility that you may need to control more than one variable.

■ Do not assume that partial correlation has no role except in seeking causal relationships. Sometimes, for example, the researcher might wish to control for male–female influences on a correlation without wishing to establish causality. Partial correlation will reveal the strength of a non-causal relationship having controlled for a third variable. Causality is something the researcher considers; it is not something built into a correlation coefficient as such.

■ Do not forget to test the statistical significance of the partial correlation – as shown above, it is very easy.

Chapter 27

Factor analysis

Simplifying complex data

Preparation
Review variance (Chapter 5), correlation coefficient (Chapter 7), and correlation matrix (Chapter 26).

27.1 Introduction

Researchers frequently collect large amounts of data. Sometimes, speculatively, they add extra questions to a survey without any pressing reason. With data on so many variables, it becomes difficult to make sense of the complexity of the data. With questionnaires, one naturally seeks patterns in the correlations between questions. However, the sheer number of interrelationships makes this hard. Take the following brief questionnaire:

Item 1: It is possible to bend spoons by rubbing them
Agree strongly   Agree   Neither   Disagree   Disagree strongly

Item 2: I have had 'out of body' experiences
Agree strongly   Agree   Neither   Disagree   Disagree strongly

Item 3: Satanism is a true religion
Agree strongly   Agree   Neither   Disagree   Disagree strongly

Item 4: Tarot cards reveal coming events
Agree strongly   Agree   Neither   Disagree   Disagree strongly

Item 5: Speaking in tongues is a peak religious experience
Agree strongly   Agree   Neither   Disagree   Disagree strongly

Item 6: The world was saved by visiting space beings
Agree strongly   Agree   Neither   Disagree   Disagree strongly

Item 7: Most people are reincarnated
Agree strongly   Agree   Neither   Disagree   Disagree strongly

Item 8: Astrology is a science, not an art
Agree strongly   *Agree*   *Neither*   *Disagree*   *Disagree strongly*

Item 9: Animals have souls
Agree strongly   *Agree*   *Neither*   *Disagree*   *Disagree strongly*

Item 10: Talking to plants helps them to grow
Agree strongly   *Agree*   *Neither*   *Disagree*   *Disagree strongly*

Agree strongly could be scored as 1, agree scored as 2, neither as 3, disagree as 4, and disagree strongly as 5. This turns the words into numerical scores. Correlating the answers to each of these 10 questions with each of the others for 300 respondents, generates a large correlation matrix (a table of all possible correlations between all of the possible pairs of questions). Ten questions will produce 10^2 or 100 correlations. Although the correlation matrix is symmetrical about the diagonal from top left to bottom right, there remain 45 *different* correlations to examine. Such a matrix might be much like the one in Table 27.1.

It is not easy to make complete sense of this; the quantity of information makes overall interpretation difficult. Quite simply, large matrices are too much for our brains to comprehend. This is where factor analysis can be beneficial. It is a technique which helps you overcome the complexity of correlation matrices. Essentially, it takes a matrix of correlations and generates a much smaller set of 'supervariables' which characterise the main trends in the correlation matrix.

Table 27.1   **Correlation matrix of 10 items**

	Item 1	Item 2	Item 3	Item 4	Item 5	Item 6	Item 7	Item 8	Item 9	Item 10
Item 1	1.00	0.50	0.72	0.30	0.32	0.20	0.70	0.30	0.30	0.10
Item 2	0.50	1.00	0.40	0.51	0.60	0.14	0.17	0.55	0.23	0.55
Item 3	0.72	0.40	1.00	0.55	0.64	0.23	0.12	0.17	0.22	0.67
Item 4	0.30	0.51	0.55	1.00	0.84	0.69	0.47	0.44	0.56	0.35
Item 5	0.32	0.60	0.64	0.84	1.00	0.14	0.77	0.65	0.48	0.34
Item 6	0.20	0.14	0.23	0.69	0.14	1.00	0.58	0.72	0.33	0.17
Item 7	0.70	0.17	0.12	0.47	0.77	0.58	1.00	0.64	0.43	0.76
Item 8	0.30	0.55	0.17	0.44	0.65	0.72	0.64	1.00	0.27	0.43
Item 9	0.30	0.23	0.22	0.56	0.48	0.33	0.43	0.27	1.00	0.12
Item 10	0.10	0.55	0.67	0.35	0.34	0.17	0.76	0.43	0.12	1.00

These 'supervariables' or factors are generally much easier to understand than the original matrix.

27.2 A bit of history

Factor analysis is not a new technique – it dates back to shortly after the First World War. It is an invention largely of psychologists, originally to serve a very specific purpose in the field of mental testing. As you are probably aware, there are numerous psychological tests of different sorts of intellectual ability. The purpose of factor analysis was to detect which sorts of mental skills tend to go together and which are distinct abilities. It has proven more generally useful and is used in the development of psychological tests and questionnaires. Personality, attitude, intelligence and aptitude tests are often based on it since it helps select which items from the tests and measures to retain. By using factors, it is possible to obtain 'purer' measures of psychological variables. Not surprisingly, then, some theorists have used it extensively. The personality theories of researchers Raymond Cattell and Hans Eysenck (Cramer, 1992) are heavily dependent on factor analysis. The development of high speed electronic computers has made the technique relatively routine since no longer does it require months of hand calculations.

27.3 Concepts in factor analysis

In order to understand factor analysis, it is useful to start with a simple and highly stylised correlation matrix such as the one in Table 27.2.

You can probably detect that there are *two* distinct clusters of variables. Variables A, C and E all tend to correlate with each other pretty well. Similarly, variables B, D and F all tend to correlate with each other. Notice that the

Table 27.2   **Stylised correlation matrix between variables A to F**

	Variable A	Variable B	Variable C	Variable D	Variable E	Variable F
Variable A	1.00	0.00	0.91	−0.05	0.96	0.10
Variable B	0.00	1.00	0.08	0.88	0.02	0.80
Variable C	0.91	0.08	1.00	−0.01	0.90	0.29
Variable D	−0.05	0.88	−0.01	1.00	−0.08	0.79
Variable E	0.96	0.02	0.90	−0.08	1.00	0.11
Variable F	0.10	0.80	0.29	0.79	0.11	1.00

Table 27.3 **Stylised correlation matrix with variable names added**

	Batting	Cross-words	Darts	Scrabble	Juggling	Spelling
Batting	1.00	0.00	0.91	−0.05	0.96	0.10
Crosswords	0.00	1.00	0.08	0.88	0.02	0.80
Darts	0.91	0.08	1.00	−0.01	0.90	0.29
Scrabble	−0.05	0.88	−0.01	1.00	−0.08	0.79
Juggling	0.96	0.02	0.90	−0.08	1.00	0.11
Spelling	0.10	0.80	0.29	0.79	0.11	1.00

members of the first cluster (A, C, E) do not correlate well with members of the second cluster (B, D, F) – they would not be very distinct clusters if they did. In order to make the clusters more meaningful, we need to decide what variables contributing to the first cluster (A, C, E) have in common; next we need to explore the similarities of the variables in the second cluster (B, D, F). Calling the variables by arbitrary letters does not help us very much. But what if we add a little detail by identifying the variables more clearly and relabelling the matrix of correlations as in Table 27.3?

Interpretation of the clusters is now possible. Drawing the clusters from the table we find:

■ 1st Cluster
  – Variable A = skill at batting
  – Variable C = skill at throwing darts
  – Variable E = skill at juggling
■ 2nd Cluster
  – Variable B = skill at doing crosswords
  – Variable D = skill at doing the word game 'Scrabble'
  – Variable F = skill at spelling

Once this 'fleshing out of the bones' has been done, the meaning of each cluster is somewhat more apparent. The first cluster seems to involve a general skill at hand–eye coordination; the second cluster seems to involve verbal skill.

This sort of interpretation is easy enough in clear-cut cases like this and with small correlation matrices. Life and statistics, however, are rarely that simple. Remember that in Chapter 26 on partial correlation we found that a zero correlation between two variables may become a large positive or negative correlation when we take away the influence of a third variable or a suppressor variable which is hiding the true relationship between two main variables. Similar sorts of

Table 27.4 **Factor loading matrix**

Variable	Factor 1	Factor 2
Skill at batting	0.98	–0.01
Skill at crosswords	0.01	0.93
Skill at darts	0.94	0.10
Skill at 'Scrabble'	–0.07	0.94
Skill at juggling	0.97	–0.01
Skill at spelling	0.15	0.86

things can happen in factor analysis. Factor analysis enables us to handle such complexities which would be next to impossible by just inspecting a correlation matrix.

Factor analysis is a mathematical procedure which reduces a correlation matrix containing many variables into a much smaller number of factors or 'supervariables'. A supervariable cannot be measured directly and its nature has to be inferred from the relationships of the original variables with the abstract 'supervariable'. However, in identifying the clusters above we have begun to grasp the idea of 'supervariables'. The abilities which made up Cluster 2 were made meaningful by suggesting that they had verbal skill in common.

The *output* from a factor analysis based on the correlation matrix presented above might look rather like the one in Table 27.4.

What does this table mean? There are two things to understand:

1. Factor 1 and Factor 2 are like the clusters of variables we have seen above. They are really variables but we are calling them 'supervariables' because they take a large number of other variables into account. Ideally there should only be a small number of factors to consider.

2. The numbers under the columns for Factor 1 and Factor 2 are called *factor loadings*. Really they are nothing other than correlation coefficients recycled with a different name. So the variable 'ability at batting' correlates 0.98 with the 'supervariable' which is Factor 1. 'Ability at batting' does not correlate at all well with the 'supervariable' which is Factor 2 (the correlation is nearly zero at –0.01). Factor loadings follow all of the rules for correlation coefficients so they vary from –1.00 through 0.00 to +1.00.

We interpret the meaning of Factor 1 in much the same way as we interpreted the clusters above. We find the variables which correlate best with the supervariable or factor in question by looking at the factor loadings for each of the factors in turn. Usually you will hear phrases like 'batting, darts and juggling load highly on Factor 1'. All this means is that they correlate highly with the supervariable, Factor 1. Since we find that batting, darts and juggling all correlate well with Factor 1, they must define the factor. We try to see what batting, darts and juggling have in common – once again we would suggest that hand–eye coordination is the common element. We might call the factor hand–eye coordination. Obviously there is a subjective element in this since not everyone would interpret the factors identically.

27.4 Decisions, decisions, decisions

This entire section can be ignored by the faint-hearted who are not about to carry out a factor analysis.

Now that you have an idea of how to interpret a factor loading matrix derived from a factor analysis, it is time to add a few extra complexities. As already mentioned, factor analysis is more subjective and judgemental than most statistical techniques you have studied so far. This is not solely because of the subjectivity of interpreting the meaning of factors. There are many variants of factor analysis. By and large these are easily coped with as computers do most of the hard work. However, there are four issues that should be raised as they underlie the choices to be made.

Rotated or unrotated factors

The most basic sort of factor analysis is the *principal components method*. It is a mathematically based technique which has the following characteristics:

1. The factors are extracted in order of magnitude from the largest to smallest in terms of the amount of variance explained by the factor. Since factors are variables they will have a certain amount of variance associated with them.

2. Each of the factors explains the *maximum amount* of variance that it possibly can.

The amount of variance 'explained' by a factor is related to something called the *eigenvalue*. This is easy to calculate since it is merely the *sum* of the *squared* factor loadings of a particular factor. Thus the eigenvalue of a factor for which the factor loadings are 0.86, 0.00, 0.93, 0.00, 0.91 and 0.00 is $0.86^2 + 0.00^2 + 0.93^2 + 0.00^2 + 0.91^2 + 0.00^2$ which equals 2.4.

But maximising each successive eigenvalue or amount of variance is a purely mathematical choice which may not offer the best factors for the purposes of understanding the conceptual underlying structure of a correlation matrix. For this reason, a number of different criteria have been suggested to determine the 'best' factors. Usually these involve maximising the number of high factor loadings on a factor and minimising the number of low loadings (much as in our stylised example). This is not a simple process because a factor analysis generates several factors – adjustments to one factor can adversely affect the satisfactoriness of the other factors. This process is called *rotation* because in pre-computer days it involved rotating (or twisting) the axes on a series of scattergrams until a satisfactory or 'simple' (i.e. easily interpreted) factor structure was obtained. Nowadays we do not use graphs to obtain this simple structure but procedures such as VARIMAX do this for us. Principal components are the unadjusted factors which explain the greatest amounts of variance but are not always particularly easy to interpret.

These are quite abstract ideas and you may still feel a little confused as to which to use. Experimentation by statisticians suggests that the rotated factors tend to reveal underlying structures a little better than unrotated ones. We would recommend that you use rotated factors until you find a good reason not to.

Orthogonal or oblique rotation

Routinely researchers will use *orthogonal rotations* rather than *oblique rotations*. The difference is not too difficult to grasp if you remember that factors are essentially variables, albeit 'supervariables':

1. Orthogonal rotation simply means that none of the factors or 'supervariables' are actually allowed to correlate with each other. This mathematical requirement is built into the computational procedures.

2. Oblique rotation means that the factors or 'supervariables' are allowed to correlate with each other (although they can end up uncorrelated) if this helps simplify the interpretation of the factors. Computer procedures such as PROMAX produce correlated or oblique factors.

There is something known as *second-order factor analysis* which can be done if you have correlated factors. Since the oblique factors are supervariables which correlate with each other, it is possible to produce a correlation matrix of the correlations between factors. This matrix can then be factor-analysed to produce new factors. Since second-order factors are 'factors of factors' they are very general indeed. You cannot get second-order factors from uncorrelated factors since the correlation matrix would contain only zeroes! Some of the controversy amongst factor analysts is related to the use of such second-order factors.

How many factors?

We may have misled you into thinking that factor analysis reduces the number of variables that you have to consider. It can, but not automatically so, because in fact without some intervention on your part you could have as many factors as variables you started off with. This would not be very useful as it means that your factor matrix is as complex as your correlation matrix. Furthermore, it is difficult to interpret all of the factors since the later ones tend to be 'junk' and consist of nothing other than error variance.

You need to limit the number of factors to those which are 'statistically significant'. There are no commonly available and universally accepted tests of the significance of a factor. However, one commonly accepted procedure is to ignore any factor for which the eigenvalue is less than 1.00. The reason for this is that a factor with an eigenvalue of less than 1.00 is not receiving its 'fair share' of variance by chance. What this means is that a factor with an eigenvalue under 1.00 cannot possibly be statistically significant – although this does not mean that those with an eigenvalue greater than 1.00 are actually statistically significant. For most purposes it is a good enough criterion although skilled statisticians might have other views!

Another procedure is the Scree test. This is simply a graph of the amount of variance explained by successive factors in the factor analysis. The point at which the curve flattens out indicates the start of the non-significant factors.

Getting the number of factors right matters most of all when one is going to rotate the factors to a simpler structure. If you have too many factors the variance tends to be shared very thinly.

Communality

Although up to this point we have said that the diagonal of a correlation matrix from top left to bottom right will consists of ones, an exception is usually made in factor analysis. The reason for this is quite simple if you compare the two correlation matrices in Tables 27.5 and 27.6.

Table 27.5   **Correlation matrix 1**

	Variable A	Variable B	Variable C
Variable A	1.00	0.50	0.40
Variable B	0.50	1.00	0.70
Variable C	0.40	0.70	1.00

Table 27.6   **Correlation matrix 2**

	Variable A	Variable B	Variable C
Variable A	1.00	0.12	0.20
Variable B	0.12	1.00	0.30
Variable C	0.20	0.30	1.00

You will notice that Matrix 1 contains substantially higher correlation coefficients than Matrix 2. Consequently the ones in the diagonal of Matrix 2 contribute a disproportionately large amount of variance to the matrix compared to the equivalent ones in Matrix 1 (where the rest of the correlations are quite large anyway). The factors obtained from Matrix 2 would largely be devoted to variance coming from the diagonal. In other words, the factors would have to correspond more or less to variables A, B and C. Hardly a satisfactory simplification of the correlation matrix! Since most psychological data tend to produce low correlations, we need to do something about the problem.

The solution usually adopted is to substitute different values in the diagonal of the correlation matrix in place of the ones seen above. These replacement values are called the *communalities*. Theoretically, a variable can be thought of as being made of three different types of variance:

1. Specific variance – variance which can only be measured by that variable and is specific to that variable.

2. Common variance – variance which a particular variable has in common with other variables.

3. Error variance – just completely random variance which is not systematically related to any other source of variance.

A correlation of any variable with itself is exceptional in that it consists of all of these types of variance (that is why the correlation of a variable with itself is 1.00), whereas a correlation between two different variables consists only of variance that is common to the two variables (common variance).

Communality is essentially the correlation that a variable would have with itself based solely on common variance. Of course, this is a curious abstract concept. Obviously it is not possible to know the value of this correlation directly since variables do not come ready broken down into the three different types of variance. All that we can do is estimate as best we can the communality. The highest correlation that a variable has with any other variable in a correlation matrix is used as the communality. This is shown in Table 27.7.

So if we want to know the communality of Variable A we look to see what its highest correlation with anything else is (in this case it is the 0.50 correlation with Variable B). Similarly we estimate the communality of Variable B as 0.70 since

Table 27.7 **Correlation matrix 1 (communality *italicised* in each column)**

	Variable A	Variable B	Variable C
Variable A	1.00	0.50	0.40
Variable B	*0.50*	1.00	*0.70*
Variable C	0.40	*0.70*	1.00

Table 27.8   **Correlation matrix 1 but using communality estimates in the diagonal**

	Variable A	Variable B	Variable C
Variable A	0.50	0.50	0.40
Variable B	0.50	0.70	0.70
Variable C	0.40	0.70	0.70

Table 27.9   **Part of a factor loading matrix**

	Factor 1	Factor 2
Variable A	0.50	0.70
Variable B	0.40	0.30

this is its highest correlation with any other variable in the matrix. Likewise the communality of Variable C is also 0.70 since this is its highest correlation in the matrix with another variable. We then substitute these communalities in the diagonal of the matrix as shown in Table 27.8.

These first estimates can be a little rough and ready. Normally in factor analysis, following an initial stab using methods like this, better approximations are made by using the 'significant' factor loading matrix in order to 'reconstruct' the correlation matrix. For any pair of variables, the computer multiplies their two loadings on each factor, then sums the total. Thus if part of the factor loading matrix was as shown in Table 27.9, the correlation between Variables A and B is $(0.50 \times 0.40) + (0.70 \times 0.30)$ $= 0.20 + 0.21 = 0.41$. This is not normally the correlation between Variables A and B found in the original data but one based on the previously estimated communality and the significant factors. However, following such a procedure for the entire correlation matrix does provide a slightly different value for each communality than our original estimate. These new communality estimates can be used as part of the factor analysis. The whole process can be repeated over and over again until the best possible estimate is achieved. This is usually referred to as a process of *iteration* – successive approximations to give the best estimate.

Actually, as a beginner to factor analysis you should not worry too much about most of these things for the simple reason that you could adopt an 'off the peg' package for factor analysis which, while not satisfying every researcher, will do the job pretty well until you get a little experience and greater sophistication.

27.5 Exploratory and confirmatory factor analysis

So far, we have presented factor analysis as a means of simplifying complex data matrices. In other words, factor analysis is being used to explore the structure (and, as a consequence, the meaning) of the data. This is clearly a very useful analytical tool. Of course, the danger is that the structure obtained through these essentially mathematical procedures is assumed to be the basis for a definitive interpretation of the data. This is problematic because of the inherent variablity of most psychological measurement which suggests that the factors obtained in exploratory factor analysis may themselves be subject to variability.

As a consequence, it has become increasingly common to question the extent to which exploratory factor analysis can be relied upon. One development from this is the notion of confirmatory factor analysis. Put as simply as possible, confirmatory factor analysis is a means of confirming that the factor structure obtained in exploratory factor analysis is robust and not merely the consequence of the whims of random variability in one's data. Obviously it would be silly to take the data and re-do the factor analysis. That could only serve to check for computational errors. However, one could obtain a new set of data using more or less the same measures as in the original study. Then it is possible to factor-analyse these data to test the extent to which the characteristics of the original factor analysis are reproduced in the fresh factor analysis of fresh data. In this way, it may be possible to confirm the original analysis.

27.6 An example of factor analysis from the literature

Butler (1995b) points out that children at school spend a lot of time looking at the work of their classmates. Although the evidence for this is clear, the reasons for their doing so are not researched. She decided to explore children's motives for looking at the work of other children and proposed a four-component model of the reasons they gave. Some children could be mainly concerned about learning to do the task and develop their skills and mastery of a particular type of task; other children might be more concerned with the quality of the product of their work. Furthermore, a child's motivation might be to evaluate themselves (self-evaluation); on the other hand, their primary motivation might be in terms of evaluating the product of their work on the task. In other words, Butler proposed two dichotomies which might lead to a four-fold categorisation of motivations for looking at other children's work as in Table 27.10.

Based on this sort of reasoning, the researcher developed a questionnaire consisting of 32 items, 'Why I Looked at Other Children's Work'. Raters allocated

Table 27.10   **Butler's model of reasons to look at the work of others**

	Product improvement	Self-improvement
Performance oriented	Doing better than others with little effort	Comparing task skills with those of others
Mastery oriented	Wanting to learn and improve	Checking whether own work needs improving

a number of items to each of the above categories and the best eight items in each category were chosen for this questionnaire. An example of a question from this questionnaire is:

I wanted to see . . . if my work is better or worse than others

The children's answers had been coded from 1 to 5 according to their extent of agreement with the statements.

Each child was given a page of empty circles on which they drew many pictures using these circles as far as possible. When this had been completed, they answered the 'Why I Looked at Other Children's Work' questionnaire. The researcher's task was then to establish whether her questionnaire actually consisted of the four independent 'reasons' for looking at the work of other children during the activity.

An obvious approach to this questionnaire is to correlate the scores of the sample of children on the various items on the questionnaire. This produced a 32 × 32 correlation matrix which could be factor-analysed to see whether the four categories of motives for looking at other children's work actually emerged:

> 'Principal-components analysis[1] with oblique rotation[2] yielded five factors with eigenvalues greater than 1.0[3] which accounted for 62% of the variance[4] . . . Three factors corresponded to the mastery-oriented product improvement (MPI), performance-oriented product improvement (PPI), and performance-oriented self-evaluation (PSE) categories, but some items loaded high on more than one factor[5]. Items expected a priori to load on a mastery-oriented self-evaluation (MSE) category formed two factors. One (MSE) conformed to the original conceptualization, and the other (checking procedure [CP]) reflected concern with clarifying task demands and instructions.' (Butler, 1995b, p. 350, superscripts added)

The meaning of the superscripted passages is as follows:

1. Principal components analysis was the type of factor analysis employed – it means that communalities were *not* used. Otherwise the term 'principal axes' is used where communalities have been estimated.

2. Oblique rotation means that the factors may well correlate with each other. That is, if one correlates the factor loadings on each factor with the factor loadings on each of the other factors, a correlation matrix would be produced in which the correlations may differ from zero. Orthogonal rotation would have produced a correlation matrix of the factors in which the correlation coefficients are all zero.

3. This means that there are five factors which are potentially statistically significant – the minimum value of a potentially significant eigenvalue is 1.0 although this is only a *minimum* value and no guarantee of statistical significance.

Table 27.11 Butler's factor loading matrix

Item: I wanted to see . . .	Performance-oriented self-evaluation	Mastery-oriented product improvement	Checking procedures	Performance-oriented product improvement	Mastery-oriented self-evaluation
Who had the most ideas	0.61				
Whose work was best	0.74				
If others had better ideas than me	0.68				
Whether there were ideas I hadn't thought of		0.68		-0.37	0.34
Ideas which would help me develop my own ideas		0.68			
If I'd understood what to do			0.85		
Whether my drawings were appropriate			0.86		
If I was working at the appropriate speed					0.63
How I was progressing on this new task					0.70
I didn't want to hand in poor work				0.67	
I didn't want my page to be emptier than others'				0.74	

Factor loadings with absolute values less than 0.30 are not reported. Table adapted from Butler (1995b).

4. These five factors explain 62% of the variance, apparently. That is, the sum of the squared factor loadings on these five factors is 62% of the squared correlation coefficients in the 32 × 32 correlation matrix.

5. In factor analysis, some items may load on more than one factor – this implies that they are measuring aspects of more than one factor.

Table 27.11 gives an adapted version of the factor analysis table in which some items have been omitted for simplicity's sake in the presentation.

You will notice from Table 27.11 that many factor loadings are missing. This is because the researcher has chosen not to report low factor loadings on each factor. This has the advantage of simplifying the factor loading matrix by emphasising the stronger relationships. The disadvantage is that the reporting of the analysis is incomplete and it is impossible for readers of the report to explore the data further. (If the original 32 × 32 correlation matrix had been included then it would be possible to reproduce the factor analysis and carry out variants on the original analysis.)

The researcher has inserted titles for the factors in the matrix. Do not forget that these titles are arbitrary and the researcher's interpretation. Consequently, you may wish to consider the extent to which her titles are adequate. The way to do this is to examine the set of questions which load highly on each of the factors to see whether a radically different interpretation is possible. Having done this you may feel that Butler's interpretations are reasonable. Butler's difficulty is that she has five factors when her model would predict only four. While this means that she is to a degree wrong, her model is substantially correct because the four factors she predicted appear to be present in the factor analysis. The problem is that some of the questionnaire items do not appear to measure what she suggested they should measure.

Some researchers might be tempted to re-do the factor analysis with just four factors. The reason for this is that the proper number of factors to extract in factor analysis is not clear-cut. Because Butler used a minimal cut-off point for significant factors (eigenvalues of 1.0 and above), she may have included more factors than she needed to. It would strengthen Butler's argument if such a reanalysis found that four factors reproduced Butler's model better. However, we should stress that factor analysis does not lead to hard-and-fast solutions and that Butler would be better confirming her claims by the analysis of a fresh study using the questionnaire.

27.7 Notes and recommendations

■ Do not be afraid to try out factor analysis on your data. It is not difficult to do if you are familiar with using simpler techniques on a computer.

■ Do not panic when faced with output from a factor analysis. It can be very lengthy and confusing because it contains things that mere mortals simply do not want to know. Usually the crucial aspects of the factor analysis are to be found towards the end of the output. If in doubt, don't hesitate to contact your local expert – computer output is not always user friendly.

- Take the factor analysis slowly – it takes a while to build your skills sufficiently to be totally confident.
- Do not forget that interpreting the factors can be fairly subjective – you might not always see things as other people do and it might not be you who is wrong.
- Factor analysis can be applied only to correlations calculated using the Pearson Correlation formula.

Recommended further reading

Child, D. (1970). *The Essentials of Factor Analysis*. London: Holt, Rinehart and Winston.

Chapter 28

Multiple regression and multiple correlation

Preparation

Revise Chapter 8 on simple regression and the standard error in relation to regression. You should also be aware of standard scores from Chapter 5 and the co-efficient of determination for the correlation coefficient in Chapter 7. Optimal understanding of this chapter is aided if you understand the concepts of partial correlation and zero-order correlation described in Chapter 26.

28.1 Introduction

Traditionally, psychologists have assumed that the primary purpose of research is to isolate the influence of one variable on another. So researchers might examine whether paternal absence from the family during childhood leads to poor mathematical skills in children. The fundamental difficulty with this is that other variables which might influence a child's mathematical skills are ignored. In real life, away from the psychology laboratory, variables do not act independently of each other. An alternative approach is to explore the complex pattern of variables which may relate to mathematical skills. Numerous factors may be involved in mathematical ability including maternal educational level, the quality of mathematical teaching at school, the child's general level of intelligence or IQ, whether or not the child went to nursery school, the sex of the child and so forth. We rarely know all the factors which might be related to important variables such as mathematical skills before we begin research; so we will tend to include variables which turn out to be poor predictors of the criterion. Multiple regression quite simply helps us choose empirically the most effective set of predictors for any criterion.

Multiple regression can be carried out with scores or standardised scores (*z*-scores). Standardised multiple regression has the advantage of making the regression values directly analogous to correlation coefficients. The consequence of this is that it is easy to make direct comparisons between the influence of different variables. In unstandardised multiple regression the variables are left in their original form. Standardised and unstandardised multiple regression are usually done simultaneously by computer programs.

28.2 Theoretical considerations

> The techniques described in this chapter concern *linear* multiple regression which assumes that the relationships between variables essentially fall on a straight line.

Multiple regression is an extension of simple (or bivariate) regression (Chapter 8). In simple regression, a single dependent variable (or criterion variable) is related to a single independent variable (or predictor variable). For example, marital satisfaction may be regressed against the degree to which the partners have similar personalities. In other words, can marital satisfaction be predicted from the degree of personality similarity between partners? In multiple regression, on the other hand, the criterion is regressed against several potential predictors. For example, to what extent is marital satisfaction related to various factors such as socio-economic status of both partners, similarity in socio-economic status, religious affiliation, similarity in religious affiliation, duration of courtship, age of partners at marriage and so on? Of course, personality similarity might be included in the list of predictors studied.

Multiple regression serves two main functions:

1. To determine the minimum number of predictors needed to predict a criterion. Some of the predictors which are significantly related to the criterion may also be correlated with each other and so may not all be necessary to predict the criterion. Say, for example, that the two predictors of attraction to one's spouse and commitment to one's marriage both correlate highly with each other and that both these variables were positively related to the criterion of marital satisfaction (although marital commitment is more strongly related to marital satisfaction than is attraction to the spouse). If most of the variation between marital satisfaction and attraction to the spouse was also shared with marital commitment, then marital commitment alone may be sufficient to predict marital satisfaction. Another example of this would be the industrial psychologist who wished to use psychological tests to select the best applicants for a job. Obviously a lot of time and money could be saved if redundant or very overlapping tests could be weeded out, leaving just a minimum number of tests which predict worker quality.

2. To explore whether certain predictors remain significantly related to the criterion when other variables are controlled or held constant. For example, marital commitment might be partly a function of religious belief so that those who are more religious may be more satisfied with their marriage. We may be interested in determining whether marital commitment is

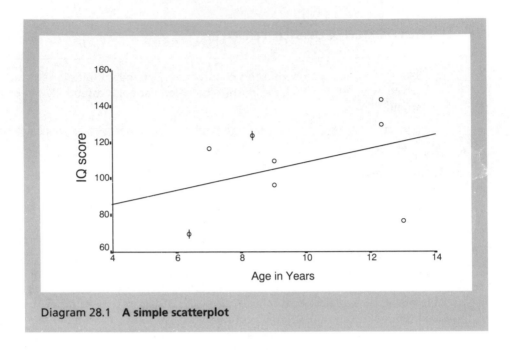

Diagram 28.1   **A simple scatterplot**

still significantly related to marital satisfaction when strength of religious belief is controlled.

To explain multiple regression, it is useful to remember the main features of simple regression:

1. Simple regression can be represented by the scatterplot in Diagram 28.1 in which values of the criterion are arranged along the vertical axis and values of the predictor are arranged along the horizontal axis. For example, marital satisfaction may be the criterion and personality similarity the predictor. Each point on the scatterplot indicates the position of the criterion and predictor scores for a particular individual in the sample. The relationship between the criterion and the predictor is shown by the slope of the straight line through the points on the scattergram. This 'best fitting' straight line is the one which minimises the (squared) distances between the points and their position on the line. This slope is known as the regression coefficient.

2. The intercept constant is the point at which the regression line intersects or cuts the vertical axis, in other words, the value on the vertical axis when the value on the horizontal axis is zero.

3. To determine the predicted score of the criterion from a particular score of the predictor, we draw a line parallel to the vertical axis from the score on the horizontal axis to the regression line. From here we draw a second line

parallel to the horizontal axis to the vertical axis, which gives us the predicted score of the criterion.

4. Unless there is a perfect relationship between the predictor and the criterion, the predicted score of the criterion will usually differ from the actual score for a particular case.

5. Unlike the correlation coefficient, regression is dependent on the variability of the variables involved. This makes regressions on different samples and different variables very difficult to compare. However, we can standardise the scores on the predictor and the criterion variables. By expressing them as standard scores (i.e. z-scores), each variable will have a mean of 0 and a standard deviation of 1. Furthermore, the intercept or intercept constant will always be 0 in these circumstances.

Regression equations

Simple regression is usually expressed in terms of the following regression equation:

$$Y \quad = \quad a \quad + \quad bX$$

| predicted score on criterion variable | intercept constant | regression coefficient × predictor score |

In other words, to predict a particular criterion score, we multiply the particular score of the predictor by the regression coefficient and add to it the intercept constant. Note that the values of the intercept constant and the regression coefficient remain the same for the equation, so the equation can be seen as describing the relationship between the criterion and the predictor.

When the scores of the criterion and the predictor are standardised to z-scores, the regression coefficient is the same as Pearson's correlation coefficient and ranges from +1.00 through 0.00 to –1.00.

In multiple regression, the regression equation is the same except that there are several predictors and each predictor has its own (partial) regression coefficient:

$$Y = a + b_1X_1 + b_2X_2 + b_3X_3 + \ldots$$

A partial regression coefficient expresses the relationship between a particular predictor and the criterion controlling for, or partialling out, the relationship between that predictor and all the other predictors in the equation. This ensures that each predictor variable provides an independent contribution to the prediction.

The relationship between the criterion and the predictors is often described in terms of the percentage of variance of the criterion that is *explained* or *accounted for* by the predictors. (This is much like the coefficient of determination for the correlation coefficient.) One way of illustrating what the partial regression coefficient means is through a Venn diagram (Diagram 28.2) involving the criterion Y and the two predictors X_1 and X_2. Each of the circles signifies the amount of variance of one of the three variables. The area shaded in Diagram 28.2(a) is common only to

X_1 and Y and represents the variance of Y that it shares with variable X_1. The shaded area in Diagram 28.2(b) is shared only by X_2 and Y and signifies the amount of variance of Y that it shares with variable X_2. Often a phrase such as 'the amount of variance explained by variable X' is used instead of 'the amount of variance shared by variable X'. Both terms signify the amount of overlapping variance.

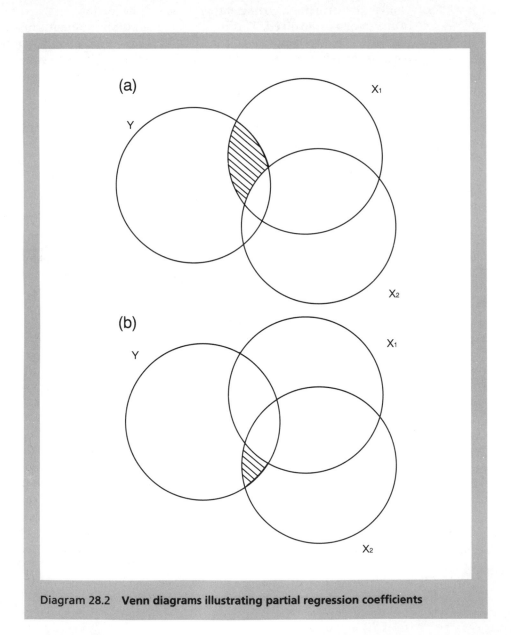

Diagram 28.2   **Venn diagrams illustrating partial regression coefficients**

The number of regression equations that can be compared in a multiple regression increases exponentially with the number of predictors. With only *two* predictors, the maximum number of regression equations that can be examined is three – the two predictors on their own and the two combined:

1. $Y = a + b_1X_1$
2. $Y = a + b_2X_2$
3. $Y = a + b_1X_1 + b_2X_2$

With *three* predictors (X_1, X_2 and X_3) the number of regression equations that can be looked at is seven – three with only one predictor, three with two predictors and one with all three predictors:

1. $Y = a + b_1X_1$
2. $Y = a + b_2X_2$
3. $Y = a + b_3X_3$
4. $Y = a + b_1X_1 + b_2X_2$
5. $Y = a + b_1X_1 + b_3X_3$
6. $Y = a + b_2X_2 + b_3X_3$
7. $Y = a + b_1X_1 + b_2X_2 + b_3X_3$

To work out the number of regression equations that can be compared with any number of predictors, we raise 2 to the power of the number of predictors and subtract 1 from the result. In the case of three predictors this is 7 ($2^3 - 1 = 8 - 1 = 7$).

Design considerations: Regression can involve the raw scores or standard scores. Computers will usually print out both sorts.

1. Regression involving 'standard scores' gives regression coefficients which can more readily be compared in terms of their size since they range between +1.0 and –1.0 like simple correlation coefficients (i.e. Pearson Correlation). In other words, the predictor variables are comparable irrespective of the units of measurement on which they were originally based. This is just like any other standard scores (Chapter 5).

2. Regression involving 'non-standard scores' or raw scores is about the 'nuts and bolts' of prediction. Like our account of simple regression, it provides predicted numerical values for the criterion variable based on an individual's scores on the various predictor variables. However, the size of the regression coefficient is no indication of the importance of the unstandardised predictor since the size is dependent on the units of measurement involved.

Selection

Since multiple regression is particularly useful with a large number of predictors, such an analysis involves many regression equations. Obviously the complexity of the analysis could be awesome. In order not to have to look at every potential equation, a number of different approaches have been suggested for selecting and testing predictors. These approaches include *hierarchical* (or *blockwise*) *selection* and *stepwise selection*. Hierarchical selection enters predictors into the regression equation on some practical or theoretical consideration. Stepwise selection employs statistical criteria to choose the smallest set of predictors which best predict the variation in the criterion. In contrast to these methods, entering all predictors into the regression equation is known as *standard* multiple regression. Finally, comparing all possible sets of predictors is called *setwise* regression.

1. In hierarchical selection predictors are entered singly or in blocks according to some practical or theoretical rationale. For example, potentially confounding variables such as socio-demographic factors may be statistically controlled by entering them first into the regression equation. Alternatively, similar variables may be grouped (or 'blocked') together and entered as a block, such as a block of personality variables, a block of attitude variables and so on. The computer tells us the net influence of each block in turn.

2. Stepwise selection: The predictor with the highest zero-order correlation is entered first into the regression equation if it explains a significant proportion of the variance of the criterion. The second predictor to be considered for entry is that which has the highest partial correlation with the criterion. If it explains a significant proportion of the variance of the criterion it is entered into the equation. At this point the predictor which was entered first is examined to see if it still explains a significant proportion of the variance of the criterion. If it no longer does so, it is dropped from the equation. The analysis continues with the predictor which has the next highest partial correlation with the criterion. The process stops when no more predictors are entered into or removed from the equation.

28.3 Stepwise multiple regression example

Since we will need to use hierarchical multiple regression to carry out path analysis in the next chapter, we will illustrate stepwise multiple regression in the present chapter. Our example asks whether a person's educational achievement (the criterion variable) can be predicted from their intellectual ability, their motivation to do well in school and their parents' interest in their education (the predictor variables). The minimum information we need to carry out a multiple regression is the number of people in the sample and the correlations between all the variables. It has been suggested that with stepwise regression it is desirable to

Table 28.1   **Correlation matrix for a criterion and three predictors**

	Educational achievement	Intellectual ability	School motivation
Intellectual ability	0.60		
School motivation	0.40	0.30	
Parental interest	0.20	0.20	0.30

Table 28.2   **The regression output**

Predictor variables	r	B	Beta	R^2 increments
Intellectual ability	.60	.84	.53	.36
School motivation	.40	.24	.24	.05

$$R^2 = .41$$
$$\text{Adjusted } R^2 = .40$$
$$R = .64$$

NB   B weights can only be calculated with data on means and standard deviations.

have 40 times more cases than predictors. Since we have three predictors, we will say that we have a sample of 120 cases. (However, much reported research fails to follow this 'rule of thumb'.) In order to interpret the results of multiple regression it is usually necessary to have more information than this but for our purposes the fictitious correlation matrix presented in Table 28.1 should be sufficient.

The calculation of multiple regression with more than two predictors is complicated and so will not be shown. However, the basic results of a stepwise multiple regression analysis are given in Table 28.2. What this simple example shows is that only two of the three 'predictors' actually explain a significant percentage of variance in educational achievement.

These two variables are intellectual ability and school motivation. The first variable to be considered for entry into the regression equation is the one with the highest zero-order correlation with educational achievement. This variable is intellectual ability. The *proportion* of variance in educational achievement explained or predicted by intellectual ability is the square of its correlation with educational achievement which is 0.36 ($0.6^2 = 0.36$). The next predictor to be considered for entry into the regression equation is the variable which has the highest partial correlation with the criterion. These partial correlations have not been presented; however, school motivation is the predictor variable with the highest partial correlation with the criterion variable educational achievement.

School motivation explains a further significant increment of 0.05 in variance. The two predictors together explain 0.41 of the variance of educational achievement. The figure of the total proportion of variance explained is arrived at either by adding together the increments for R^2 (the multiple correlation squared) which are 0.36 and 0.05 or by squaring the overall R (the multiple correlation) which is 0.64^2 or 0.41. The multiple correlation is likely to be bigger the smaller the sample and the more predictors. Consequently, this figure is usually adjusted for the size of the sample and the number of predictors, which reduces it in size somewhat. Furthermore, as can seen from Table 28.2, R^2 also can be expressed as increments. Finally, the partial regression or beta coefficients for the regression equation containing the two predictors are also shown in Table 28.2 and are 0.53 for intellectual ability and 0.24 for school motivation. We can write this regression equation as follows:

$$\text{Educational achievement} = a + 0.53 \times \text{intellectual ability} + 0.24 \times \text{school motivation}$$

According to our fictitious example, the weight of intellectual ability is greater than that of school motivation in predicting educational achievement.

Design consideration: There is a concept, *multicollinearity*, which needs consideration when planning a multiple-regression analysis. This merely refers to a situation in which several of the predictor variables correlate with each other very highly. This results in difficulties because small sampling fluctuations may result in a particular variable appearing to be a powerful predictor while other variables may appear to be relatively weak predictors. So Variables A and B, both of which predict the criterion, may correlate with each other at, say, 0.9. However, because Variable A, say, has a *minutely* better correlation with the criterion it is selected first by the computer. Variable B then appears to be a far less good predictor. When the intercorrelations of your predictor variables are very high, perhaps above 0.8 or so, then the dangers of multicollinearity are also high. In terms of research design, it is a well-known phenomenon that if you measure several different variables using the same type of method then there is a tendency for the variables to intercorrelate simply because of that fact. So, if all of your measures are based on self-completion questionnaires or on ratings by observers then you may find strong intercorrelations simply because of this. Quite clearly care should be exercised if possible to ensure that your predictor measures do not intercorrelate highly. If multicollinearity is apparent then be very careful about claiming that one of the predictors is far better than another.

The main things you need to consider in relation to the analysis are:

1. The R^2 increments tell you how much your prediction improved as the computer adds in more variables at a time. In the above example, we can see that intellectual ability is by far the most useful predictor.

2. Be careful not to be confused by the unstandardised regression coefficients (B) and the standardised regression coefficients (beta). We are using beta values in the above. Beta regression coefficients are rather like correlation coefficients since they are calculated by effectively transforming each score on a variable into a standard score (Chapter 5). However, because of other adjustments made, the beta regression coefficients are closer to partial correlation coefficients. Nonetheless, it is best to use the standardised regression coefficients (betas) as they are easy to interpret, each regression coefficient being comparable to the other. You would use the unstandardised (B) regression coefficients if you are trying to make predictions from the values of the predictor variable to the criterion variable.

28.4 An example from the published literature

Munford (1994) examined the predictors of depression in African–Americans. The research involved her administering the following measures:

1. The Beck Depression Inventory

2. The Rosenberg Self-Esteem Scale

3. The Hollingshead Two-Factor Index of Social Position. This is a measure of the occupational social class and educational standards (i.e. a measure of social class)

4. The gender (self-reported sex) of the individual

5. The Racial Identity Attitude Scale which measures several different stages in the development of racial identity:

   (a) Pre-Encounter: the stage before black people become exposed to racism. It is the stage at which they accept the definitions of themselves imposed by the white racist community

   (b) Encounter: essentially the stage where identity is challenged by direct experiences of racism

   (c) Immersion: the individual is learning to value their own race and culture

   (d) Internalisation: the individual has achieved a mature and secure sense of their own race and identity.

As one might expect, Munford was interested in the relationship between depression as measured by the Beck Depression Inventory (the criterion variable)

Table 28.3   Summary of stepwise multiple regression: self-esteem, gender, social class and racial identity attitudes as predictors of depression

Predictor	R^2 increments	R^2 (adj) total	Beta F
Self-Esteem	.37	.37	134.10
Pre-Encounter	.02	.39	8.97
Encounter	.01	.41	4.71
Gender	.01	.42	4.77

(Adapted from Munford, 1994)

and the remaining variables (the predictor variables). She computed a correlation matrix between all of the variables, but as this involved 28 different correlation coefficients it is obvious that she needed a means of simplifying its complexity. She subjected her correlation matrix to a stepwise regression which yielded the outcome shown in Table 28.3.

As you can see, many of the predictors are not included in the table, indicating that they were not significant independent predictors of depression (thus social class and internalisation, for example, are excluded). Self-esteem is the best predictor of depression – those with the higher self-esteem tended to have lower depression scores. One cannot tell this directly from the table as it presents squared values which would have lost any negative signs. *We have to assess the direction of the relationship from the correlation matrix of all of the variables together.* The correlation matrix (not shown) reveals a negative correlation (–0.61) between self-esteem and depression.

Although pre-encounter, encounter and gender all contribute something to the prediction, the increment in the amount of variation explained is quite small for each of them. Thus R^2 for pre-encounter is only 0.02 which means (expressed as a percentage) that the increase in variation explained is only 2% (i.e. $0.02 \times 100\%$).

Beta F essentially reports F-ratios (Chapter 19) for each of the predictor variables. All of those presented are statistically significant since otherwise the variable in question would not correlate significantly with the depression.

28.5 Notes and recommendations

■ Multiple regression is only practicable in most cases using a computer since the computations are numerous.

■ Normally one does not have to compute the correlation matrix independently between variables. The computer program usually does this on the raw scores. There may be a facility for entering correlation matrices which might be useful once in a while when you are re-analysing someone else's correlation matrix.

■ Choose hierarchical selection for your multiple regression if you are essentially trying to test out theoretical predictions or if you have some other rationale. One advantage of this is that you can first of all control for any social or demographic variables (sex, social class, etc.) which might influence your results. Then you can choose your remaining predictors in any order which you think meets your needs best.

■ Choose stepwise selection methods in circumstances in which you simply wish to choose the best and smallest set of predictors. This would be ideal in circumstances in which you wish to dispense with time-consuming (and expensive) psychological tests, say in an industrial setting involving personnel selection. The main considerations here are entirely practical.

Recommended further reading

Glantz, S.A., and Slinker, B.K. (1990). *Primer of Applied Regression and Analysis of Variance*. New York: McGraw-Hill.

Chapter 29

Path analysis

Preparation

Path analysis requires that you understand the basic principles of multiple regression (Chapter 27).

29.1 Introduction

As modern psychology has increasingly drawn from real problems and non-laboratory research methods, the problems of establishing what variables affect other variables have changed. Laboratory experiments in which causal linkages are determined by random assignment of individuals to an experimental and control group have been supplemented by a wish to understand people better in their natural environment. Causal modelling is merely a generic name for attempts to explore the patterns of interrelationships between variables in order to suggest how some variables might be causally influencing others. Of course, some suggestions might be rather better than others; some theoretical links might not fare well against actual data. In path analysis it is possible to estimate how well a particular suggested pattern of influences fits the known data. The better the model or causal pattern fits the actual data then the more likely we are to believe that the model is a useful theoretical development.

There is no suggestion intended that this will inevitably provide indisputable evidence that a particular causal model is the only possibility. Path analysis simply seeks to describe a particular path which explains the relationships among the variables well, and precisely; variables which we failed to include in our analysis might be rather better. Of course, we can exclude some causal pathways on logical grounds. For example, childhood experiences might possibly influence our adult behaviour. So it is reasonable to include childhood experiences as influences on adult behaviour. However, the reverse pattern is not viable. Our childhood experiences cannot possibly be caused by our adult behaviour; the temporal sequence is wrong. In other words, some causal models are not so viable as others for logical reasons.

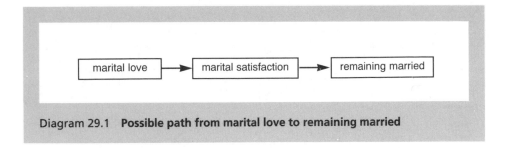

Diagram 29.1   **Possible path from marital love to remaining married**

29.2 Theoretical considerations

Path analysis involves specifying the assumed causal relationships among several variables. Take, for example, the variables (1) marital satisfaction, (2) remaining married, and (3) the love between a couple. A reasonable assumption is that couples who love one another are more likely to be satisfied with their marriage and consequently are more likely to stay together. This pattern of assumed relationships is described as a causal model. Such a pattern of influences (or causal model) can be presented as a *path diagram* as in Diagram 29.1. In this, variables to the left (marital love) are thought to influence variables towards the right (marital satisfaction and remaining married). Right-facing arrows between variables indicate the causal direction. So marital love causes marital satisfaction which in turn is responsible for remaining married.

However, relationships between variables in themselves do not establish that marital love really causes marital satisfaction. There are four possible causal relationships between two variables:

1. As suggested by our model, marital love may increase marital satisfaction.

2. The opposite effect may occur with marital satisfaction heightening marital love.

3. Both variables may affect each other, marital love bringing about marital satisfaction and marital satisfaction enhancing marital love. This kind of relationship is variously known as a *two-way*, *bidirectional*, *bilateral*, *reciprocal* or *non-recursive* relationship.

4. The relationship may not really exist but may appear to exist because both variables are affected by some further confounding factor(s). For example, both marital love and marital satisfaction may be weaker in emotionally unstable people and stronger in emotionally stable people. This creates the impression that marital love and marital satisfaction are related when they are not, because emotionally unstable people are lower in both marital love and marital satisfaction while emotionally stable people are higher in both. This fourth sort of relationship is known as a *spurious* one.

In path analysis a distinction is often made between *exogenous* and *endogenous* variables:

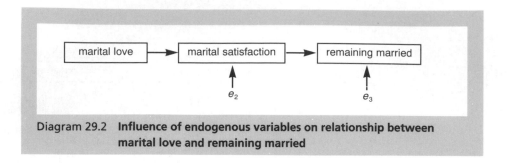

Diagram 29.2   Influence of endogenous variables on relationship between marital love and remaining married

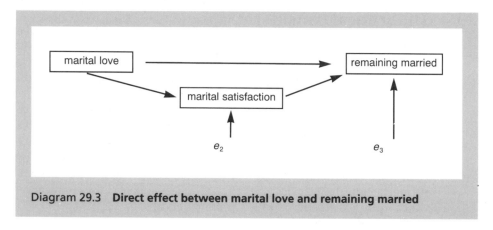

Diagram 29.3   Direct effect between marital love and remaining married

(a)   An exogenous variable is one whose assumed causes have not been measured or tested.

(b)   An endogenous variable is one for which one or more possible causes have been measured and have been posited in the causal model.

So in the above model, marital love is an exogenous variable while marital satisfaction and remaining married are endogenous variables.

There will be some variation in endogenous variables which is unaccounted for or unexplained by causal variables in the model. This unexplained variance in an endogenous variable is indicated by vertical arrows pointing towards that variable as shown in the path diagram in Diagram 29.2. For example, the variance in marital satisfaction *not* explained by marital love is represented by the vertical arrow from e_2. Similarly, the variance in remaining married unaccounted for by marital satisfaction is depicted by the vertical arrow from e_3. The e stands for *error* – the term used to describe unexplained variance. The word *residual* is sometimes used instead to refer to the variance that remains to be explained.

In this model marital love is assumed to have an *indirect* effect on remaining married through its effect on marital satisfaction. However, marital love may also have a *direct* effect on remaining married as shown in the path diagram of Diagram 29.3.

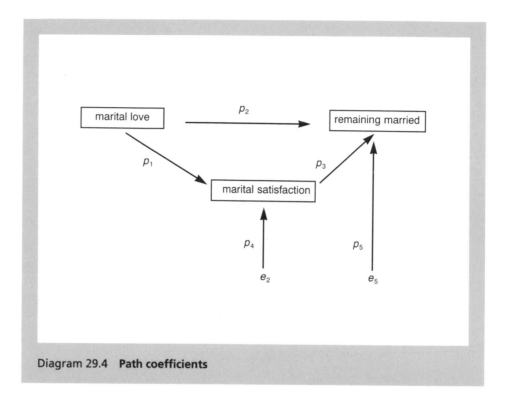

Diagram 29.4 **Path coefficients**

Path coefficients

The values of the direct effects are known as *path coefficients*. They are usually the standardised beta coefficients taken from multiple regression analyses (see Chapter 28). In other words, they are essentially correlation coefficients. The values of the paths reflecting error (or residual) variance are known as error or residual path coefficients.

We will use the symbol p_1 for the path coefficient for the direct effect of marital love on marital satisfaction, p_2 for the direct effect of marital love on remaining married, and p_3 for the direct effect of marital satisfaction on remaining married. We will refer to the paths reflecting error variance for marital variance and remaining married respectively as p_4 and p_5. These are shown in Diagram 29.4.

To calculate these path coefficients we need to calculate the following two regression equations:

Marital satisfaction $= a + p_1$ marital love

Remaining married $= b + p_2$ marital love $+ p_3$ marital satisfaction

(In the above equations a and b are intercept coefficients for the regression equations. Intercept coefficients are the points at which the regression lines cut

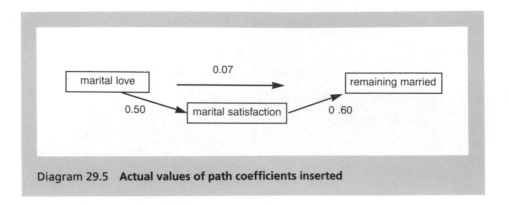

Diagram 29.5   Actual values of path coefficients inserted

the vertical axis. They are identified with different symbols simply because they will have different values. We can largely ignore them for the present purposes.)

Suppose that the correlation between marital love and marital satisfaction is 0.50, between marital love and remaining married 0.40 and between marital satisfaction and remaining married 0.70 for a sample of 100 couples. The path coefficients are the standardised beta coefficients for these two equations which are:

Marital satisfaction = a + 0.50 marital love

Remaining married = b + 0.07 marital love + 0.67 marital satisfaction

In other words the path coefficient for p_1 is 0.50, for p_2 0.07 and for p_3 0.67 as shown in Diagram 29.5.

Since there is only one predictor variable in the first regression, the standardised beta coefficient of 0.50 is the same as the zero-order correlation of 0.50 between marital love (the predictor variable) and marital satisfaction (the criterion variable). (If there are several predictors then partial correlation coefficients would be involved.) Note that the path coefficient between marital love and remaining married is virtually zero (0.07) and statistically not significant. This means that marital love does not directly affect remaining married. The path coefficient (0.67) between marital satisfaction and remaining married differs little from the correlation (0.70) between them. This indicates that the relationship between marital satisfaction and remaining married is not due to the spurious effect of marital love.

To determine an indirect effect (such as that between marital love and remaining married which is mediated by marital satisfaction), the path coefficient between marital love and marital satisfaction (0.50) is multiplied by the path coefficient between marital satisfaction and remaining married (0.67). This gives an indirect effect of 0.335 (0.50 × 0.67 = 0.335). To calculate the total effect of marital love on remaining married, we add the direct effect of marital love on remaining married (0.07) to its indirect effect (0.335) which gives a sum of 0.405. The total effect of one variable on another should be, within rounding error, the same as the zero-order correlation between the two variables. As we can see, the total effect of marital love on remaining married is 0.405, which is very close to the value of the zero-order correlation of 0.40. In other words, path analysis breaks down or decomposes the correlations between the endogenous and exogenous variables into their component parts, making it easier to see what might be happening. So, for example, the correlation between marital love and remaining married is decomposed into (a) the indirect effect of marital love on remaining married, and (b) the direct effects of marital love on marital satisfaction and of marital satisfaction on remaining married. Doing this enables us to see that although the correlation between marital love and remaining married is moderately strong (0.40), this relationship is largely mediated indirectly through marital satisfaction.

The correlation between marital satisfaction and remaining married can also be decomposed into the direct effect we have already calculated (0.67) and a spurious component due to the effect of marital love on both marital satisfaction and remaining married. This spurious component is the product of the direct effect of marital love on marital satisfaction (0.50) and of marital love on remaining married (0.07) which gives 0.035 (0.50 × 0.07 = 0.035). This is clearly a small value. We can reconstitute the correlation between marital satisfaction and remaining married by summing the direct effect (0.67) and the spurious component (0.035) which gives a total of 0.67 + 0.035 = 0.705. This value is very similar to the original correlation of 0.70.

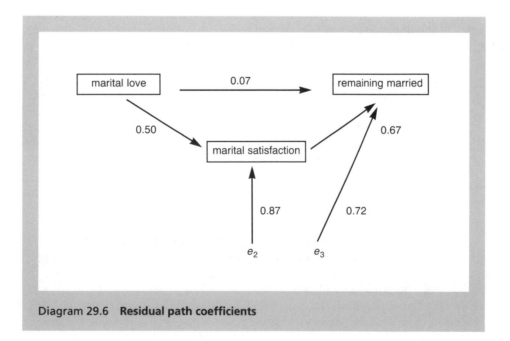

Diagram 29.6   **Residual path coefficients**

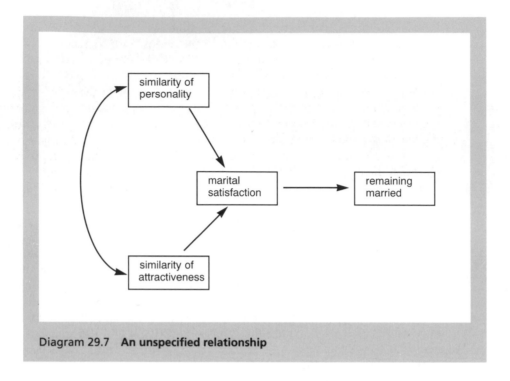

Diagram 29.7   An unspecified relationship

To calculate the proportion of variance not explained in an endogenous variable we subtract the adjusted multiple R squared value for that variable from 1. The adjusted multiple R squared value is 0.24 for marital satisfaction and 0.48 for remaining married. So 0.76 (1 − 0.24 = 0.76) or 76% of the variance in marital satisfaction is not explained, and 0.52 (1 − 0.48) or 52% of the variance in remaining married is not explained. In path analysis it is assumed that the variables representing error are unrelated to any other variables in the model (otherwise it would not be error). Consequently, the error path coefficient is the correlation between the error and the endogenous variable which can be obtained by taking the square root of the proportion of unexplained variance in the endogenous variable. In other words, the residual path coefficient is 0.87 ($\sqrt{0.76}$ = 0.87) for marital satisfaction and 0.72 ($\sqrt{0.52}$ = 0.72) for remaining married (Diagram 29.6).

Where there is a relationship between two variables whose nature is not known or specified, this relationship is depicted in a path diagram by a curved double-headed arrow. Suppose, for example, the two exogenous variables of similarity in personality and similarity in physical attractiveness, which were assumed to influence marital satisfaction, were known to be related but this relationship was thought not to be causal. This relationship would be shown in a path diagram as in Diagram 29.7.

The correlation between these two exogenous variables is not used in calculating the effect of these two variables on marital satisfaction and remaining married.

Table 29.1 **Original and recomposed correlations**

Pairs of variables	Original correlations	Recomposed correlations
Marital love and marital satisfaction	0.50	0.500
Marital love and remaining married	0.40	0.405
Marital satisfaction and remaining married	0.70	0.705

Table reproduced from Wagner and Zick (1995) with the kind permission of the publisher, John Wiley and Son.

Generalisation

To determine whether our path analysis is generalisable from the sample to the population, we calculate how well our model reflects the original correlation matrix between the variables in that model using the large sample chi-square test. This will not be described here other than to make these two points:

1. If this chi-square test is statistically significant, then this means that the model does not fit the data.

2. Other things being equal, the larger the sample, the more likely it is that the chi-square test is statistically significant and the model is to be rejected.

In terms of our model in Diagram 29.6, we can see that the recomposed correlations for the model are very similar to the original correlations between the three variables as shown in Table 29.1.

Not all models will demonstrate this feature. It is always true when the model is just-identified. Identification is an important concept in path analysis. However, it is somewhat complex and so can only be presented in outline here. There are three types of identification:

1. Just-identified. This means that all the variables in the path analysis are connected by unidirectional paths (single-headed arrows). Actually even with the arrows entirely reversed in direction this would still be the case. Since the standardised beta coefficients are essentially correlation coefficients, this entirely reversed model would fit our data just as well as our preferred model. In other words, the recomposed correlations for this reversed just-identified model are just the same as for the forward model. *The reconstituted correlations for any just-identified model are similar to the original correlations. Consequently it is not possible to use the match between the model and the data as support for the validity of the model.*

2. Under-identified. In this there are assumed to be one or more bidirectional pathways (double-headed arrows between variables). For example, the relationship between marital love and marital satisfaction may be thought of as

being reciprocal, both variables influencing each other. Since it is impossible to provide an estimate of the influence of marital love on marital satisfaction which is entirely independent of the influence of marital satisfaction on marital love, it is not possible to say what the unique estimate for these pathways would be. Consequently we would need to modify our model to avoid this. That is, we need to respecify it as a just-identified or an over-identified model.

3. Over-identified. In an over-identified model it is assumed that some pairs of variables do not relate. Using our example, an over-identified model assumes that there is no relationship between two pairs of variables. For instance, take the following model which postulates that marital love does not lead directly to remaining married:

marital love → marital satisfaction → remaining married

This is over-identified since there are two ways in which the path coefficients could be estimated:

(a) The path coefficient between marital satisfaction and remaining married could simply reflect the correlation between these two variables (i.e. 0.70).

(b) Alternatively, the correlation between marital satisfaction and remaining married could be estimated by dividing the correlation between marital love and remaining married (0.40) by that between marital love and marital satisfaction (0.50).

29.3 An example from published research

Path analysis can be as simple or as complex as the researchers' theories about the interrelationships between variables in their research. Increasing the numbers of variables under consideration accelerates the complexity in the path diagram. Not only does the analysis look more daunting if many variables are involved, but the path diagram becomes harder to draw. In this section we will discuss a path analysis by Wagner and Zick (1995) of the causes of blatant ethnic prejudice. It is fairly well known and established that there is a relationship between people's level of formal education and their expressions of prejudice: the more prejudiced tend to have the least formal education. This suggests that there is something about education which leads to less prejudice but what is the mechanism involved? Does education act directly to reduce prejudice or does it do so indirectly through some mediating variable (Diagram 29.8)?

Thus there are two possible paths: (1) the *direct* path from formal education to blatant prejudice, and (2) the *indirect* path which involves a mediating variable(s).

Of course, the apparent complexity of this path diagram can be increased if several mediating variables are used rather than just one. Furthermore, if several direct variables are used instead of just formal education, the diagram will become increasingly complex. Wagner and Zick (1995) collected information in a

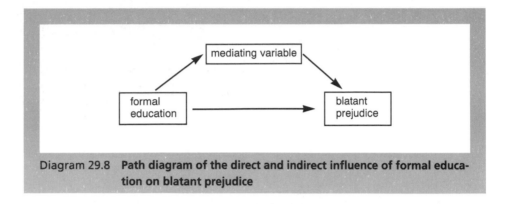

Diagram 29.8 **Path diagram of the direct and indirect influence of formal education on blatant prejudice**

number of European countries on several potential mediating variables linking formal education and blatant prejudice:

1. Individual (relative) deprivation: the feeling of an individual that he or she is economically deprived compared to other people.

2. Group (relative) deprivation: the feeling that one's social group (e.g. ethnic group) have fared badly economically compared to the rest of society.

3. Perceived incongruency: the incompatibility between an ethnic group's values and those dominant in society.

4. Political conservatism: the individual's position on the political left-wing to right-wing dimension.

5. National pride: pride in being a member of the national group (e.g. French or German).

6. Contact with foreign people: the numbers of foreign people living in one's neighbourhood.

Although this list of mediating variables far from exhausts the possibilities, it does provide measures of a number of variables which empirical studies have related to blatant ethnic prejudice.

In addition, the researchers had other measures which they could have included in the path diagram (e.g. sex and age) but omitted because the researchers did not consider them relevant to their immediate task. However, they were used by the researchers as control variables, as we shall see. There was another variable, *Social Strata*, which was a measure of social class. This was included in the path diagram by the researchers as social class was actually affected by a person's level of education.

There is no mystery about the path diagram; it is merely one of several path diagrams which the researchers could have studied. Most of the possibilities were ignored and the researchers concentrated on why those with the most formal education tend to express the least blatant prejudice. Drawing the

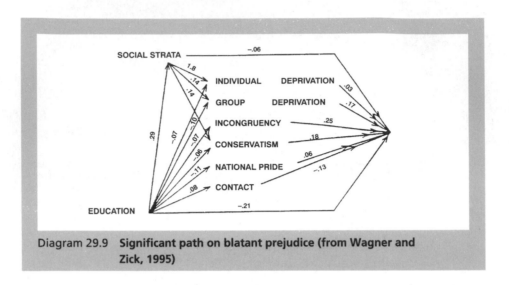

Diagram 29.9   **Significant path on blatant prejudice (from Wagner and Zick, 1995)**

diagram is a paper-and-pencil task based on elaborating the simple path diagram in Diagram 29.8. Wagner and Zick's path diagram is shown in Diagram 29.9. It includes both direct and indirect (mediated) relationships. Arrows pointing more or less towards the right are the only ones included as these indicate possible causal directions. Having drawn the elaborated diagram, the researchers inserted the values of the relationships between the variables (i.e. path coefficients which are essentially correlation coefficients) next to the appropriate arrows. The researchers omitted arrows (pathways) when the path coefficient did not reach statistical significance. However, because the sample was big ($N = 3788$), very small values were significant at the 5% level. The square of $E = 0.83$ in Diagram 29.9 indicates how much variation in blatant prejudice is *unexplained* by the path diagram.

The path coefficients themselves were taken from Table 29.2. As you can see, this contains a lot of information. The following are the main considerations:

1. A zero-order correlation is merely the Pearson Correlation Coefficient as described in Chapter 7. First-order, second-order, etc., correlations are partial correlations as described in Chapter 26.

2. The upper triangle of the matrix in the table is merely a correlation matrix involving the range of measures in the path diagram with age and sex added.

3. Because the sample size was very large ($N = 3788$), many of the correlations account for very little variance although they are statistically significant; the correlation of 0.04 is statistically significant but its coefficient of determination or amount of variation shared by the two variables is 0.04^2 or 0.0016 or 0.16%.

4. Correlation coefficients are not used in the path analysis but are used in a multiple regression to obtain the beta weights.

Table 29.2   Zero-order correlations between variables (upper part) and results of a path analysis (lower part)

	Age	Sex	Educ.	Strata	Ind. dep.	Group dep.	Incongr.	Conser.	Pride	Contact	Prejud.
Age		-0.02	-0.28*	-0.01	0.07*	0.03†	0.06*	0.13*	0.18*	-0.24*	0.23*
Sex	-0.02		-0.07*	-0.02	0.04†	0.02	-0.02	0.02	-0.01	-0.14*	0.04*
Education	-0.28*b	-0.08*b		0.27*	-0.13*	-0.14*	-0.08*	-0.05*	-0.15*	0.17*	-0.34*
Social strata	0.07*b	0.01b	0.29*b		-0.20*	-0.17*	-0.02	0.13*	-0.02	0.34†	-0.14*
Individual deprivation	0.05*b	0.03b	-0.07†b	-0.18*b		0.30*	0.01	-0.09*	-0.07*	-0.08*	0.12*
Group deprivation	0.01b	0.01b	-0.10*b	-0.14*b	0.28*c		0.12*	0.01	0.03†	0.01	0.25*
Incongruency	0.04†b	-0.02b	-0.07*b	-0.00b	-0.02c	0.11*c		0.09*	0.04†	-0.01	0.32*
Conservatism	0.12*b	0.02b	-0.06†b	0.14*b	-0.07*c	-0.03c	0.08*c		0.23*	-0.10*	0.24*
National pride	0.15*b	-0.01b	-0.11*b	0.01b	-0.09*c	0.04c	0.01c	0.20*c		-0.09*	0.18*
Contact	-0.22*b	-0.13*b	0.09*b	0.01b	-0.08*c	0.06†c	0.01c	-0.07*c	-0.03c		-0.21
Blatant prejudice	0.08*b	0.00b	-0.21*b	-0.06*b	0.03†b	0.17*b	0.25*b	0.18*b	0.06*b	-0.13*b	

b: beta-coefficient from a simultaneous regression.

c: partial correlation with the effects of age, sex, education and social strata partialled out unless otherwise indicated: Pearson correlation coefficient.

$*p \leq 0.01$; $†p \leq 0.05$.

Table reproduced from Wagner and Zick (1995) with the kind permission of the publisher, John Wiley and Son.

5. Wagner and Zick (1995) carried out a simultaneous multiple regression on the correlation matrix in order to predict blatant prejudice from age, sex, formal education, social strata and the mediating variables (individual deprivation, group deprivation, etc.).

6. The beta weights from this multiple regression are indicated by a letter *b* in the lower half of the matrix in Table 29.2.

7. The coefficients marked *c* in the lower half of the matrix in Table 29.2 are partial correlations which take away the effects of age, sex, education and social strata from the relationships between the pairs of variables. That is, one needs to insert in the *indirect* pathways the correlations having removed the influence of age, sex, education and social strata. In other words, the coefficients marked *c* are the fourth-order correlation coefficients (partial correlations) controlling for age, sex, education and social strata simultaneously. Although this procedure is perfectly adequate, it is more conventional to use hierarchical multiple regression to achieve much the same end.

The authors describe the results of their path analysis as follows:

'The path analysis shows that the predictors of ethnic prejudice mentioned above are determined by formal education, even though some of the direct paths from education are relatively weak. However, for individual and group relative deprivation and for political conservatism, social strata mediates part of the determination by formal education. The influence of mediating variables means that the covariation of formal education and ethnic prejudice can be partially explained especially by variations in social strata, group deprivation, incongruency, conservatism, and acceptance of contact with foreigners. In addition to this, the path analysis indicates a strong direct path from education to blatant prejudice which cannot be explained by the mediation variables measured. A chi-square analysis shows that a restricted model without the assumption of a direct path from education to prejudice is significantly worse than the full model presented (Chi-square = 84.02, df = 1). Thus, the path analysis demonstrates that part of the educational differences in ethnic outgroup rejection can be accounted for by the mediating psychological variables, even though a substantial proportion of the covariance of respondents' education and outgroup rejection remained unexplained.' (Wagner and Zick, 1995, pp. 53–54)

Major points which might clarify the above paragraph include:

1. Education influences variables which influence blatant prejudice. Often the influences are very weak. Most studies would use far smaller sample sizes so the tiny coefficients sometimes obtained in the study would be dismissed as not significant.

2. The chi-square tests whether the indirect paths model is significantly improved by adding in the direct path from formal education to blatant

prejudice. The results of the analysis suggest that the direct + indirect effects model is superior to the indirect effects alone model.

29.4 Notes and recommendations

■ Path analysis requires a degree of mastery of statistical concepts which many students will not achieve during their degree course. Anyone who is convinced that it is appropriate for their research will need to consult supplementary sources and any local expert who might be available.

■ The complexity of path analysis should not be allowed to interfere with one's critical faculties. A path analysis cannot be any better than the quality of the data which go into it.

■ Path analysis involves exploring data in ways which seem alien to those who feel that statistics should be a hard-and-fast discipline in which there is only one right way of doing things. It is an example of a statistical technique which is an exploratory tool rather than a fixed solution to a fixed problem.

Recommended further reading

Pedhazur, E. (1982). *Multiple Regression in Behavioral Research*. Fort Worth: Harcourt Brace.

Chapter 30

The analysis of a questionnaire/survey project

Preparation
Review correlation (Chapter 8) and regression (Chapter 9).

30.1 Introduction

This chapter examines the analysis of questionnaire and/or survey projects. A lot of research planned by students adopts this style. The key feature is the number of variables involved; this type of research tempts researchers to write lengthy questionnaires with numerous items. It takes little effort to write a question, even less to write a poor question. Still less time is required to answer the questions if they are in a closed-ended format in which just one alternative is circled. An exploratory or pilot study will not always identify faulty questions and, more often than not, the pressures on students' time are such that pilot studies are rudimentary and based on very few individuals.

Some students, wanting to get closer to the experiences of the participants in their research, choose to ask the questions themselves rather than have a self-completion questionnaire. However, the basic problem remains very much the same – too much data. The difference is that with the open-ended interview approach the data have to be coded in a form suitable for statistical analysis. The coding process has its own problems – largely what coding categories to use and whether the categories used are easily used by the coders. Profound disagreements between the coders suggest either that the categories are inadequate or that they have been very poorly defined.

Of course, there are student projects which utilise ready-made questionnaires purchased from a supplier of psychological tests and measures. Although there are numerous questions involved, these are reduced to a single 'score' or measurement (or sometimes a small number of 'subscores'). The groundwork of turning the questionnaire into a small number of 'scores' has already been done by its writers and will not be elaborated upon here.

30.2 The research project

Sarah Freeman is a bright young psychology student who has partied for most of her time at university. So when it is time to plan a research project she has little background knowledge of psychological research and theory. Stuck for a final-year project she designs a piece of research based on her main interest in life – thinking about sex. Her project explores the hypothesis that a religious upbring-ing leads to sexual inhibitions. Naturally, her supervisor is reluctant to let Sarah loose on the public at large and so insists that the research is carried out on a consenting sample of fellow-students. Pressured by deadlines for coursework essays, she hastily prepares a questionnaire which she pushes under bedroom doors in the Elisha Briggs Hall of Residence. Participants in the research are to return the completed questionnaires to her via the student mail system.

Her questionnaire is a simple enough affair. Sarah's questions – with spelling corrected – are as follows.

(1) My gender is
    Male   *Female*

(2) My degree course is _____

(3) I am _____ years of age

(4) My religion is _____

(5) I would rate my religious faith as:
    Very strong   *Strong*   *Neither*   *Weak*   *Very weak*

(6) I attend a place of worship _____ per year

(7) My faith in God is important to me
    Strongly agree   *Agree*   *Neither*   *Disagree*   *Strongly disagree*

(8) I am a virgin
    Agree   *Disagree*

(9) I am sexually promiscuous
    Strongly agree   *Agree*   *Neither*   *Disagree*   *Strongly disagree*

(10) I fantasise about sex with several partners at the same time
    Strongly agree   *Agree*   *Neither*   *Disagree*   *Strongly disagree*

(11) I feel guilty after sex with more than three people at the same time
    Strongly agree   *Agree*   *Neither*   *Disagree*   *Strongly disagree*

(12) Oral sex is an abomination
    Strongly agree   *Agree*   *Neither*   *Disagree*   *Strongly disagree*

(13) Sadomasochism is appealing to me
    Strongly agree   *Agree*   *Neither*   *Disagree*   *Strongly disagree*

(14) I like sex
   *Once a week   Twice a week   Every day   Every morning   All the time
                                             and evening*

(15) Pornography
   Is disgusting   Is a stimulant   Is best home made

Suddenly Sarah sees the light of day – just a few months before she finishes at university and is launched onto the job market. Despite being due for submission, the project is in a diabolical mess. No more partying for her – she has become a serious-minded student (well, sort of) and she is determined to resurrect her flagging and ailing attempts at research. No longer does she burn the candle at one end – she now burns it at both ends trying to make sense of statistics and research methods books. Pretty dry stuff it all is. If only she had spent some time on statistics in her misspent youth she would not have been in this hole. Can she get out of the mess?

The short answer is 'no'; the longer answer is that she could improve things considerably with a well-thought-out analysis of her data. Research has to be carefully planned to be at its most effective. She needed to consider her hypotheses, methods and statistical analysis in advance of even collecting the data. Sarah is paying for the error of her ways. One positive aspect of all this is that Sarah can at least show that she is aware of the major issues and problems with her sort of research.

30.3 The research hypothesis

Although statistics is not particularly concerned about the details of the hypotheses underlying research, a clear statement of the purposes of the research often transforms the analysis of haphazardly planned research. Of course, it is by far the best to plan meticulously before doing your research. However, this does not always happen in research – even in research by professionals.

Simply stated, Sarah's research aims to find out whether there is a relationship between religious upbringing and sexual inhibitions. The trouble with this is that it is unclear quite what is meant by a religious upbringing – does it matter which sort of religion or how intensely it is part of family life? Furthermore, it is unclear what she means by sexual inhibitions – for example, not carrying out certain activities might be the result of inhibitions but it may also be that the person does not find them arousing.

Given the limited range of questions which Sarah included in her questionnaire, we might suggest to her that she has several measures of religiousness:

1. The first is what religion they claim to be. The range is wide and includes fundamentalist, Roman Catholic, Protestant, Muslim and a variety of other religions. Is it possible for Sarah to make suggestions as to which religions are most likely to encourage sexual repression – perhaps she thinks that Roman Catholicism, Islam and fundamentalism are the religions most likely

to inculcate sexual inhibitions. If so, she could formulate a hypothesis which relates aspects of the religion to sexual inhibition.

2. There is a question about actual attendance at church. It could be that involvement in the religious community is a key variable in the influence of religion on sexual inhibitions. This might be specified as a hypothesis.

3. There are two questions which involve the importance of religious beliefs in the lives of the respondents. Again, a hypothesis might specify religious beliefs as the important element in the possible relationship.

In terms of her measures of sexual activity, there are some very obvious things to point out. The first is that it is very difficult to relate any of the sex questions to sexual inhibition as such. Some of the questions deal with frequency of sexual activities, some deal with sexual fantasy, and others deal with somewhat 'unusual' sexual practices. Probably Sarah is stuck with a fatal flaw in her research – that is, she failed to *operationalise* her concept properly; she may not have turned her *idea* of sexual inhibitions into a *measure* of that thing. It may or may not be that her measures do reflect sexual inhibitions. This is really a matter of the validity of her measures for her purposes. At the level of superficial validity of the questions we may have our doubts. Clearly Sarah might have done better to include some questions which ask about sexual inhibitions. In the circumstances it might be appropriate for Sarah to reformulate her hypotheses to suggest that religious upbringing influences sexual behaviours and sexual fantasy. At least this might make more sense in terms of her questionnaire. Unfortunately there is a downside to this – sexual inhibition seemed to be a psychologically interesting concept.

30.4 Initial variable classification

It is useful for the novice researcher to classify the variables that they have collected into category variables and numerical scores:

1. You should remember that psychologists frequently turn answers on a verbal scale into numerical scores. So questions 5, 7, 9, 10, 11, 12, 13 and 14 all have fixed answer alternatives. Although they do not involve numbers, it is conventional in psychological research to impose a numerical scale of 1 to 5 onto these answer categories. The reason for this is that the categories have verbal labels which imply increasing quantities of something. Scaling from 1 to 5 is arbitrary but has been shown to work pretty well in practice.

2. Some variables which appear at first to be just nominal categories can be turned into numerical scores simply and easily. The classic example of this in research is the variable gender which consists of just two categories – male and female. Innumerable research reports code the gender variable numerically as 1 = male and 2 = female. The logic is obvious, the numerical codings implying different quantities of the variable femaleness (or maleness). However, such variables can legitimately be treated in either way.

Table 30.1   Sarah's 15 questions classified as category or score variables

Nominal or category variables	Numerical score variables	Other
Question 1: Gender* Question 2: Degree course	Question 1: Gender*	
	Question 3: Age	
Question 4: Religion		
	Question 5: Faith	
	Question 6: Attend	
	Question 7: God	
	Question 8: Virgin	
	Question 9: Promiscuous	
	Question 10: Fantasise	
	Question 11: Guilty	
	Question 12: Oral	
	Question 13: Sadomasochism	
	Question 14: Like sex	
Question 15: Pornography		

* Means that the variable may be placed in more than one column.

So, with these points in mind, we can classify each of our variables as 'category' or 'numerical score' or 'other' – meaning anything we are uncertain about (as in Table 30.1).

This is quite promising in terms of statistical analysis as 12 out of the 15 variables can be classified as numerical scores. This allows some of the more powerful correlational statistical techniques to be used if required. This still leaves three variables classified as categories. These are the degree course the student is taking, their religion and their views on pornography. These are probably quite varied in terms of their answers anyway. So, Sarah may find that there may be 20 or more different degree courses included in the list of replies with only a few students in each of these 20 or more categories. Similarly, the religion question could generate a multiplicity of different replies. *As they stand, these three variables are of little use in statistical analysis – they need to be recoded in some way.*

30.5 Further coding of data

It is difficult to know why Sarah included the degree course question – it does not seem to have much to do with the issues at hand – so one approach is to discreetly ignore it. Probably a better approach is to recode the answers in a simple but appropriate way. One thing which could be done is to recode them as *Science* or *Arts* degree courses. In other words, the degree course could be coded as 1 if it is science and 2 if it is arts. If this is done then the variable could be classified as a numerical score much as the gender variable could be.

The religion question is more of a problem. Given that the answers will include Catholics, Mormons, Baptists, and many more, the temptation might be to classify the variable simply as *religion given* versus *no religion given*. However, this may not serve Sarah's purposes too well since it may be that the key thing is whether the religion is sexually controlling or not. One approach that Sarah could take is to obtain the services of people who are knowledgeable about various religions. They could be asked to rate the religions in terms of their degree of sexual control over their members. This could be done on a short scale such as:

| *Very sexually controlling* | *Sexually controlling* | *Not sexually controlling* |

This would transform the religion variable into a numerical scale if ratings were applied from 0 to 2, for example. Those not mentioning a religion might be deemed to be in the 'not sexually controlling' category. Obviously Sarah should report the degree of agreement between the raters of the religion (i.e. the inter-rater reliability).

Of course, Sarah might decide to categorise the religions in a category form:

1. None
2. Fundamentalist
3. Catholic
4. Protestant
5. Muslim
6. Other

Unfortunately, this classification retains the nominal category characteristics of the original data although reducing the numbers of categories quite substantially.

The question about pornography seems to be a natural nominal category variable given the response alternatives. Perhaps it is best to treat it as such although it could be recoded in such a way that the 'is a stimulant' and 'is best home made' answers are classified together as being pro-pornography while the 'is disgusting' answer is given a different score. There are no hard and fast rules about these decisions and at some stage you have to come to terms with the fact that some choices seem almost arbitrary. That does not mean that you should not try to base your decisions on rational arguments as far as possible.

30.6 Data cleaning

There is little point in retaining variables in your research which contain little or no variance. It is particularly important with analyses of questionnaire-type materials to systematically exclude useless variables since they can create misleading impressions at a later stage.

The important steps are as follows:

1. Draw up or print out frequency counts of the values of each variable you have. This can be done as frequency tables or histograms/bar charts. It should become obvious to you if virtually every participant in the research gives much the same answer to a question. Consider deleting such non-discriminating questions.

2. In the case of variables which have a multiplicity of different values, you might consider recoding these variables into a small number of ranges. This might apply in the case of the age question in Sarah's research.

3. Where you find empty or virtually empty response categories then consider combining categories. Some categories may contain just a few cases. These are probably useless for your overall analysis.

30.7 Data analysis

A relatively simple approach

If Sarah follows our advice, all or virtually all of the variables will be coded as numerical scores. Any variables not coded in this way essentially will have to be analysed by statistics suitable for category data – this might be the chi-square but more likely they will be treated as different values of the independent variable for the analysis of variance or a similar test. We would recommend, as far as possible within the requirements of your hypotheses, that all variables are transformed into numerical scores.

Accepting this, it would be a relatively simple matter to calculate the correlations between all of the variables in Sarah's list and each other. The trouble with this is that this results in a rather large correlation matrix of 15×15 correlation coefficients – in other words a table of 225 coefficients. Although the table will be symmetrical around the diagonal of the matrix, this still leaves over 100 different correlations. It is not the purpose of statistical analysis to pour complexity on your research; statistics are there to simplify as far as is possible.

In Sarah's research, the sex questions are quite numerous. She has eight different questions about sexual matters. Obviously it would be satisfactory if there were some way of combining these different answers together in order that a single measure of 'sexual inhibition' could be developed. One simple thing that might be done is simply to add the scores on the questions together. This would require the following:

1. That the different questions are scored in the same direction. Looking at Sarah's questionnaire we see that, for example, the question 'I like sex' if

scored numerically from left to right would give a bigger score to those who liked sex most often. However, the answers to the question on sadomasochism if scored numerically from left to right would give a lower score to those who liked sadomasochistic sex. It is necessary to recode her answers in such a way that they are consistent. In this case all the answers which are more sexual could be rescored as necessary to make the high scores pro-sex.

2. That the standard deviations of scores on questions to be added together are similar, otherwise the questions with the biggest standard deviations will swamp the others. If they differ radically, then it is best to convert each score on a variable to a standard score and then add up answers to several questions (Chapter 5).

A similar sort of thing could be done with the three religious questions although it might be equally appropriate, given their relatively small number, to treat them as three separate variables.

In order to test her hypotheses, Sarah could correlate the sex and religion variables together. A significant relationship in the predicted direction would support Sarah's hypotheses. (It would be equally appropriate to apply *t*-tests or analyses of variance with religion as the independent variable and sex questions as the dependent variables.)

The advantage of using correlations is that it is then possible to control for (or partial out) obvious background variables which might influence the relationships found. In this study gender and age are of particular interest since both of them might relate to our main variables of interest. Partial correlation could be used to remove the influence of gender and age from the correlation between religion and sexual inhibition.

A more complex approach

Given the number of questions Sarah has included on her questionnaire, it is arguable that she ought to consider using factor analysis on the sex questions to explore the pattern of interrelations between the variables. She may well find that the answers to the sex questions tend to cluster together to form small groups of questions which tend to measure separate aspects of sex. For example, questions which deal with unusual sexual practices might group together.

Factor analysis would identify the important clusters or factors. In addition, factor analysis will usually give factor scores which are weighted scores for each individual on each factor separately. These are expressed on the same scale and so are comparable. In other words, they have already been expressed in terms of standard scores.

It is then possible to relate scores on the religion variable(s) with scores on each of the factors just as before. Partialling out gender and age might also be appropriate.

An alternative complex approach

One could also employ multiple regression (Chapter 28). Probably the best approach is to use religion as the dependent (criterion) variable(s) and the separate sex variables as the independent (predictor) variables. In this way it is possible to find out which of the sex variables contribute to the prediction of the religious experiences of the participants in childhood. Sarah may find that only certain of the questions are particularly and independently related to religion. Actually, Sarah could control for age and sex by forcing them into the regression early in the analysis.

30.8 Notes and recommendations

- Although statistics can help structure poor data, it is impossible to remedy all faults though statistics. Research design and planning is always vital.

- Statistics is useful in simplifying complex data into a small number of variables. Unfortunately, for most practical purposes it is impossible to do this without resorting to computer analysis. This is because of the sheer number of variables to be analysed.

- Do not let your partying outstrip your studying.

Chapter 31

Statistical power analysis

Do my findings matter?

Preparation

Significance testing and the correlation coefficient are the basic ideas. Since this chapter contrasts with much of current practice in the use of statistics by academic psychologists, a degree course at the University of Real Life might help.

One of the most neglected questions in statistical analysis is that of whether or not the researcher's findings are of any real substance. Obviously part of the answer to this question depends very much on the particular research question being asked. One needs to address issues such as (a) Is this a theoretically important issue? (b) Is this an issue of social relevance? and (c) Will this research actually help people? None of these are statistical matters. Statistics can help quantify the strength of the relationships established in the research. Very few research publications seriously discuss this issue with respect to the research they describe.

31.1 Statistical significance

Students sometimes get confused as to the meaning of significance in statistics. Perhaps it is a pity that the word significance was ever used in this context since all that it actually means is that it is reasonable to generalise from your sample data to the population. That is to say, significance merely tells you the extent to which you can be confident that your findings are not simply artifacts of your particular sample or samples. It has absolutely nothing to do with whether or not there are really substantial trends in your data. Researchers tend to keep a little quiet about the substance of their findings, preferring merely to report the statistical significance. It is common – but bad – practice to dwell on statistical significance, but this is encouraged by the fact that publication of one's research in psychology depends very much on obtaining statistical significance.

The size of the samples being used has a profound effect on the statistical significance of one's research. A correlation of 0.81 is needed to be statistically significant at the 5% level with a sample size of 6. However, with a much larger sample size (say, 100), one only requires a correlation of 0.20 to be statistically significant at the 5% level. In other words, with a large enough sample size quite small relationships can be statistically significant.

We have already seen that the *squared* correlation coefficient basically gives us the proportion of the total variance shared by two variables. Sometimes r^2 is referred to as the *coefficient of determination*. With a correlation of $r = 1.00$ the value of r^2 is still 1.00 (i.e. the total amount of variance). That means that all of the variation in one of the variables is predictable from the other variable. In other words, 100% of the variation on one variable is determinable from the variation in the other variable. Expressed graphically it would mean that all of the points on a scattergram would fit perfectly on a straight line. If, however, the correlation between two variables is 0.2 then this means that r^2 equals 0.04. That is to say that the two variables have only 4% of their variance in common. This is not very much at all despite the fact that such a small correlation may well be statistically significant if the sample size is large enough. The scatterplot of such a small correlation has points which tend to scatter quite a lot from the best-fitting straight line between the points – in other words there is a lot of error variance compared to the strength of the relationship between the two variables.

31.2 Method and statistical power

Before going any further, we should emphasise that the quality of your research methods is an important factor determining the strength of the relationships found in your research. Sloppy research methods or poor measurements are to be avoided at all costs. Anything which introduces measurement error into your research design will reduce the apparent trends in the research. So, for example, a laboratory experimenter must take scrupulous care in standardising her or his procedures as far as possible.

This is clearly demonstrated if we consider a researcher trying to assess the relationship between children's ages and their heights in a sample of pre-school children. An excellent method for doing this would be to obtain each child's birth certificate to obtain his or her age and to take the child down to the local clinic to have the child's height precisely measured by the clinic nurse who is experienced at doing so. In these circumstances there is probably very little we can do further to maximise our chances of assessing the true relationship between age and height in children.

A much sloppier way of doing this research on the relation between children's ages and heights might be as follows. The researcher asks the child's nursery teacher to estimate the child's height and tells them to guess if they complain that they do not know. The children's ages are measured by asking the children themselves. It is pretty obvious that these measures of age and height are a little rough and ready. Using these approximate measures we would expect rather poor correlations between age and height – especially compared to the previous,

very precise method. In other words, the precision of our measurement procedures has an important influence on the relationships we obtain.

The difference between the two studies is that the second researcher is using
very unreliable measures of height and age compared with the very reliable
measures of the first researcher. There are a number of ways of measuring
reliability in psychology including interrater reliability which is essentially the
correlation between a set of measurements taken by person A with those taken
by person B. So, for example, we would expect that the birth certificate method
of measuring age would produce high correlations between the calculations of
two different people, and that asking the children themselves would not produce
very reliable measures compared with the answer we would get from the same
·children even the next day.

If you can calculate the reliability of your measurements, it is possible to
adjust the correlation between two measures. This essentially inflates the reliability coefficients to equal 1.00. In other words, you get the correlation between
age and height assuming that the measures were totally reliable. The formula for
doing this is:

$$r_{x\infty y\infty} = \frac{r_{xy}}{\sqrt{r_{xx} r_{yy}}}$$

The symbol $r_{x\infty y\infty}$ is the coefficient of attenuation. It is merely the correlation
between variables x and y if these variables were perfectly reliable. The symbols
r_{xx} and r_{yy} are the reliability coefficients of the variables x and y.

Often in research we do not have estimates of the reliability of our measures
so the procedure is not universally applicable.

31.3 Size of the effect in studies

Although it is relatively easy to see the size of the relationships in correlation
research, it is not quite so obvious in relation to experiments which have been
analysed using t-tests, chi-square, or a nonparametric test such as the Wilcoxon
Matched Pairs. One of the approaches to this is to find ways of turning each of
these statistics into a correlation coefficient. Generally this is computationally
easy. The resulting correlation coefficient makes it very easy to assess the size of
your relationships as it can be interpreted like any other correlation coefficient.

Chi-square

It is easy to turn a 2×2 chi-square into a sort of correlation coefficient by
substituting the appropriate values in the following formula:

$$r_{\text{phi}} = \sqrt{\frac{\text{chi-square}}{N}}$$

r_{phi} is simply a Pearson correlation coefficient for frequency scores. In fact, it is merely a special name for the Pearson correlation coefficient formula used in these circumstances. Interpret it more or less like any other correlation coefficient. It is always positive because chi-square itself can only have positive values. Remember that N in the above formula refers to the number of subjects and *not* to the degrees of freedom.

If your chi-square is bigger than a 2 × 2 table, you can calculate the *contingency coefficient* instead. The formula for this is:

$$\text{Contingency coefficient} = \sqrt{\frac{\text{chi-square}}{\text{chi-square} + N}}$$

As above, N in this case is the sample size, *not* the number of degrees of freedom.

It is possible to interpret the contingency coefficient *very approximately* as if it were a Pearson correlation coefficient. But avoid making precise parallels between the two.

The *t*-test

Essentially what is done here is to turn the *independent variable* into numerical values. That is to say, if the research design has, say, an experimental and a control group we code one group with the value 1 and the other group with the value 2. Take the research design in Table 31.1, for example, which compares men and women in terms of level of job ambition (the dependent variable).

Of course, normally we would analyse the difference between the means in terms of the *t*-test or something similar. However, we can correlate the scores on the dependent variable (job ambition) if we code the independent variable as 1 for a man and 2 for a woman (Table 31.2). The two sets of scores can then be correlated using a Pearson correlation. This should be a simple calculation for

Table 31.1   **Scores of men and women on a dependent variable**

Men	Women
5	2
4	1
9	3
6	2
4	1
7	6
5	2
1	2
4	

Table 31.2 **Arranging the data in Table 31.1 so that the sex can be correlated with the dependent variable**

Score on dependent variable (job ambition)	Score on independent variable sex (men coded as 1, women coded as 2)
5	1
4	1
9	1
6	1
4	1
7	1
5	1
1	1
4	1
2	2
1	2
3	2
2	2
1	2
6	2
2	2
2	2

you. However, if you have already worked out your t-values for the t-test you can use the following formula to enable you to calculate the correlation quicker:

$$r_{bis} = \sqrt{\frac{t^2}{t^2 + df}}$$

where t is the value of the t-statistic and df equals the degrees of freedom for the t-test.

Do not worry too much about r_{bis} since it is merely the Pearson correlation coefficient when one variable (e.g. sex) has just one of two values.

31.4 An approximation for nonparametric tests

We have to approximate to obtain a correlation coefficient for nonparametric tests such as the Mann–Whitney U-test. One possible procedure is to work out the statistic (e.g. Mann–Whitney U-test), check its probability value (significance level), and then look up what the value of the t-test would be for that same significance level and sample size. For example, if we get a value of the Mann–Whitney U of 211 which we find to be significant at the 5% level (two-tailed test) on a sample of 16 subjects, we could look up in the t-table the value of t which would be significant at the 5% level (two-tailed test) on a sample of 16 subjects (i.e. the degrees of freedom = 14). This value of t is 2.15 which could be substituted in the formula:

$$r_{bis} = \sqrt{\frac{t^2}{t^2 + df}}$$

31.5 Analysis of variance (ANOVA)

It is possible to compute from analysis of variance data a correlation measure called *eta*. This is analogous to a correlation coefficient but describes a curvilinear rather than the linear relationship which the Pearson correlation coefficient does. It is of particular use in the analysis of variance since it is sometimes difficult to know which of the independent variables explains the most variance. The probability value of an F-ratio in itself does not enable us to judge which of the independent variables accounts for the largest amount of the variance of the dependent variable. Table 31.3 is a summary table from an analysis of variance considering the influence of intelligence and social class on a dependent variable. It is difficult to know from the table whether intelligence or social class explains more of the variance.

In order to calculate the value of eta for any of the variables all we need to do is substitute in the following formula:

$$eta = \sqrt{\frac{treatment\ df \times F\text{-}ratio}{(treatment\ df \times F\text{-}ratio) + within\ df}}$$

So, for example, if we take intelligence then we substitute the values from Table 31.3 in the formula:

$$eta = \sqrt{\frac{2 \times 8.9}{(2 \times 8.9) + 108}}$$

$$= \sqrt{\frac{17.8}{17.8 + 108}}$$

Table 31.3 **Analysis of variance summary table**

Source of variance	Sums of squares	Degrees of freedom	Mean square	*F*-ratio	Significance
Intelligence	1600	2	800	8.9	1%
Social class	2400	3	800	8.9	1%
Interaction	720	6	120	1.3	Not significant
Within (error)	9720	108	90		

Table 31.4   **Analysis of variance summary table with values of eta added**

Source of variance	Sums of squares	Degrees of freedom	Mean square	*F*-ratio	Signifi-cance	Eta
Intelligence	1600	2	800	8.9	1%	0.38
Social class	2400	3	800	8.9	1%	0.44
Interaction	720	6	120	1.3	Not significant	0.26
Within (error)	9720	108	90			

$$= \sqrt{\frac{17.8}{125.8}}$$

$$= \sqrt{0.1415}$$

$$= 0.38$$

If we do a similar calculation for the two other sources of variation we can extend our summary table to include eta (Table 31.4). What this extra information tells us is that social class accounts for more variation in the dependent variable than does either intelligence or the interaction.

31.6 Notes and recommendations

- *Do not* expect the things in this chapter to feature regularly in other researchers' reports. They tend to get ignored despite their importance.

- *Do* be aware of the need to assess the degree of explanatory power obtained in your research as part of your interpretation of the value of your findings. All too frequently psychologists seek statistical significance and forget that their findings may be trivial in terms of the amount of variance explained.

- *Do* try to design your research in such a way that the error and unreliability are minimised as far as possible.

Appendix A

Testing for excessively skewed distributions

The use of nonparametric tests (Mann–Whitney U-test, Wilcoxon Matched Pairs test) rather than parametric tests (Unrelated *t*-test, Related *t*-test) is conventionally recommended by some textbooks when the distribution of scores on a variable is significantly skewed (Chapter 18). There are a number of difficulties with this advice, particularly just how one knows that there is too much skew. It is possible to test for significant skewness. One simply computes a formula for the skewness and then divides this by the standard error of the skewness. If the resulting value equals or exceeds 1.96 then your skewness is significant at the 5% level (two-tailed test) and the null hypothesis that your sample comes from a symmetrical population should be rejected.

A.1 Skewness

The formula for skewness is:

$$\text{Skewness} = \frac{(\Sigma d^3) \times N}{\text{sd}^3 \times (N-1) \times (N-2)}$$

Notice that much of the formula is familiar: N is the number of scores, d is the deviation of each score from the mean of the sample, and sd is the estimated standard deviation of the scores (i.e. you use $N-1$ in the formula for standard deviation as described in Chapter 11).

What is different is the use of cubing. To cube a number you multiply it by itself twice. Thus the cube of 3 is $3 \times 3 \times 3 = 27$. A negative number cubed gives a negative number. Thus the cube of –4 is $(-4) \times (-4) \times (-4) = -64$.

We will take the data from Table 5.1 in Chapter 5 to illustrate the calculation of skewness. For simplicity's sake we will be using a definitional formula which involves the calculation of the sample mean. Table A1 gives the data in column 1 as well as the calculation steps to be followed. The number of scores, N, equals 9.

Table A1   **Steps in the calculation of skewness**

	Column 1 Age (years)	Column 2 (scores – sample mean)	Column 3 (square values in column 2)	Column 4 (cube values in column 2)
	20	20 – 23 = –3	9	–27
	25	25 – 23 = 2	4	8
	19	19 – 23 = –4	16	–64
	35	35 – 23 = 12	144	1728
	19	19 – 23 = –4	16	–64
	17	17 – 23 = –6	36	–216
	15	15 – 23 = –8	64	–512
	30	30 – 23 = 7	49	343
	27	27 – 23 = 4	16	64
ΣX = sum of scores = 207			Σd^2 = 354	Σd^3 = 1260
$\overline{X}$ = mean score = 23				

For Table A1,

$$\text{Estimated standard deviation (sd)} = \sqrt{\frac{\Sigma d^2}{N-1}}$$

$$= 6.652$$

Substituting this value and the values from the table in the formula for skewness we get:

$$\text{Skewness} = \frac{1260 \times 9}{6.652^3 \times (9-1) \times (9-2)}$$

$$= \frac{11340}{16483.322}$$

$$= {}^{\bullet}0.688$$

(Skewness could have a negative value.)

A.2   Standard error of skewness

The standard error of skewness involves calculating the value of the following formula for our particular sample size ($N = 9$):

$$\text{Standard error of skewness} = \sqrt{\frac{6 \times N \times (N-1)}{(N-2) \times (N+1) \times (N+3)}}$$

$$= \sqrt{\frac{432}{840}}$$

$$= \sqrt{0.514}$$

$$= 0.717$$

The significance of skewness involves a z-score:

$$z = \frac{\text{skewness}}{\text{standard error of skewness}}$$

$$= \frac{0.688}{0.717}$$

$$= 0.96$$

This value of z is lower than the minimum value of z (1.96) required to be statistically significant at the 5% level with a two-tailed test. Thus the scores are *not* extremely skewed. This implies that you may use parametric tests rather than nonparametric tests for comparisons involving this variable. Obviously you need to do the skewness test for the other variables involved.

For the related *t*-test, it is the skewness of the *differences* between the two sets of scores which needs to be examined, not the skewnesses of the two different sets of scores.

Appendix B

Large sample formulae for the nonparametric tests

Sometimes you may wish to do a nonparametric test when the sample sizes exceed the tabulated values of the significance tables in Chapter 18. In these circumstances we would recommend using a computer. The reason is that ranking large numbers of scores is extremely time consuming and you risk making errors. However, if a computer is not available to do the analyses, you can make use of the following large sample formulae for nonparametric tests.

B.1 Mann–Whitney U-test

$$z = \frac{U - \dfrac{n_1\, n_2}{2}}{\sqrt{\left(\dfrac{n_1\, n_2}{N\,(N-1)}\right)\left(\dfrac{N^3 - N}{12} - \Sigma\, \dfrac{t^3 - t}{12}\right)}}$$

U is as calculated in Chapter 18. n_1 and n_2 are the sizes of the two samples, and N is the sum of n_1 and n_2. t is a new symbol in this context: the number of scores tied at a particular value. Thus if you have three scores of 6 in your data, $t = 3$ for the score 6.

Notice that Σ precedes the part of the formula involving t. This indicates that for every score which has ties you need to do the calculation for the number of ties involved *and* sum all of these separate calculations. Where there are no ties, this part of the formula reduces to zero.

The calculated value of z must equal or exceed 1.96 to be statistically significant with a two-tailed test.

B.2 Wilcoxon Matched Pairs test

$$z = \frac{T - \dfrac{N\,(N+1)}{4}}{\sqrt{\dfrac{N(N+1)\,(2N+1)}{24}}}$$

T is the value of the Wilcoxon Matched Pairs statistic as calculated in Chapter 18. N is the number of pairs of scores in that calculation.

As before, z must equal or exceed 1.96 to be statistically significant with a two-tailed test.

Appendix C

Nonparametric tests for three or more groups

Several nonparametric tests were described in Chapter 18. However, these dealt with circumstances in which only two sets of scores were compared. If you have three or more sets of scores there are other tests of significance which can be used. These are nowhere near so flexible and powerful as the Analyses of Variance described in Chapters 20 to 24.

C.1 The Kruskal–Wallis three or more unrelated conditions test

The Kruskal–Wallis test is used in circumstances where there are *more than two* groups of independent or unrelated scores. All of the scores are *ranked* from lowest to highest irrespective of which group they belong to. The average rank in each group is examined. If the null hypothesis is true, then all groups should have more or less the same average rank.

Table C1 **Reading scores under three different levels of motivation**

High motivation	Medium motivation	Low motivation
17	10	3
14	11	9
19	8	2
16	12	5
18	9	1
20	11	7
23	8	6
21	12	
18	9	
	10	

Table C2   **Scores in Table C1 ranked from smallest to largest**

Row	High motivation	Medium motivation	Low motivation
	20	12.5	3
	18	14.5	10
	23	7.5	2
	19	16.5	4
	21.5	10	1
	24	14.5	6
	26	7.5	5
	25	16.5	
	21.5	10	
		12.5	
A	Mean rank $= \dfrac{198}{9} = 22.00$	Mean rank $= \dfrac{122}{10} = 12.20$	Mean rank $= \dfrac{31}{7} = 4.43$
B	Sum of ranks² $= 198^2 = 39204$	Sum of ranks² $= 122^2 = 14884$	Sum of ranks² $= 31^2 = 961$
C	Mean rank² $= \dfrac{39204}{9} = 4356.00$	Mean rank² $= \dfrac{14884}{10} = 1488.40$	Mean rank² $= \dfrac{961}{7} = 137.29$
D	R = sum of calculations in Row C = 4356.00 + 1488.40 + 137.29 = 5981.69		

Imagine that the reading abilities of children are compared under three conditions: (1) high motivation, (2) medium motivation, and (3) low motivation. The data might be as in Table C1. Different children are used in each condition so the data are unrelated. The scores on the dependent variable are on a standard reading test.

The scores are ranked from lowest to highest, ignoring the particular group they are in. Tied scores are given the average of the ranks they would have been given if they were different (Chapter 18). The results of this would look like Table C2, which also includes:

■ Row A: the mean rank in each condition

■ Row B: the square of the sum of the ranks in each condition

■ Row C: the square of the sum of ranks from Row B divided by the number of scores in each condition

■ Row D: R which equals the sum of the squares of the sums of ranks divided by the sample size, i.e. the sum of the figures in Row C.

The statistic, H, is calculated next using the following formula:

$$H = \frac{12R}{N(N+1)} - 3(N+1)$$

where R is the sum of the mean rank^2 in Row D in Table C2, and N is the number of scores ranked. Substituting,

$$H = \frac{12 \times 5981.69}{26\,(26 + 1)} - 3\,(26 + 1)$$

$$= \frac{71780.28}{702} - 81$$

$$= 102.251 - 81$$

$$= 21.25$$

The distribution of H approximates that of chi-square. The degrees of freedom is the number of different groups of scores minus 1. Thus the significance of H can be assessed against Significance Table 14.1 which tells us that our value of H needs to equal or exceed 6.0 to be significant at the 5% level (two-tailed test). Thus we reject our null hypothesis that reading was unaffected by levels of motivation.

C.2 The Friedman three or more related samples test

This test is used in circumstances in which you have three or more *related* samples of scores. The scores for each participant in the research are ranked from smallest to largest separately. In other words the scores for Joe Bloggs are ranked from 1 to 3 (or however many conditions there are), the scores for Jenny Bloggs are also ranged from 1 to 3, and so forth for the rest. The test essentially examines whether the average ranks in the several conditions of the experiment are more or less equal as they should be if the null hypothesis is true.

Table C3 gives the scores in an experiment to test the recall of pairs of nonsense syllables under three conditions – high, medium and low distraction. The same participants were used in all conditions of the experiment.

Table C4 shows the scores ranked from smallest to largest for each participant in the research separately. Ties are given the average of the ranks that they would have otherwise been given.

Table C3 **Scores on memory ability under three different levels of distraction**

	Low distraction	**Medium distraction**	**High distraction**
John	9	6	7
Mary	15	7	2
Shaun	12	9	5
Edmund	16	8	2
Sanjit	22	15	6
Ann	8	3	4

Table C4   **Scores ranked separately for each participant**

	Low distraction	**Medium distraction**	**High distraction**
John	3	1	2
Mary	3	2	1
Shaun	3	1	1
Edmund	3	2	1
Sanjit	3	2	1
Ann	3	1	2
Row A	Sum of ranks = 18	Sum of ranks = 9	Sum of ranks = 8
Row B	Square = 18^2 = 324	Square = 9^2 = 81	Square = 8^2 = 64
Row C	R = sum of above squares = 324 + 81 + 64 = 469		

- Row A gives the sums of the ranks for each condition or level of distraction
- Row B gives the square of each sum of ranks for each conditon
- Row C gives the total, R, of the squared sums of ranks from Row B.

The value of R is entered in the following formula:

$$\chi_r^2 = \frac{12\,R}{nK\,(K+1)} - 3n\,(K+1)$$

where n is the number of participants (i.e. of rows of scores) = 6, and K is the number of columns of data (i.e. of different conditions) = 3. Therefore

$$\chi_r^2 = \frac{12 \times 469}{6 \times 3 \times (3+1)} - 3 \times 6 \times (3+1)$$

$$= \frac{5628}{72} - 72$$

$$= 6.17$$

The statistical significance of χ_r^2 is assessed using the chi-square table (Significance Table 14.1). The degrees of freedom are the number of conditions − 1 = 3 − 1 = 2. This table tells us that a value of 6.0 or more is needed to be statistically significant at the 5% level (two-tailed test). Thus, it appears that the null hypothesis that the conditions have no effect should be rejected in favour of the hypothesis that levels of distraction influence memory.

Appendix D

Tables for one-tailed significance at 5% level

This appendix contains tables of the one-tailed significance values at the 5% level. In general you should bear in mind the following points:

- It is only practicable to do one-tailed tests if you have just two outcomes to compare with each other. Tests such as the t-test, the Wilcoxon Matched Pairs (Signed Ranks) test, the Mann–Whitney U-test, and the correlation coefficients are suitable for one-tailed significance testing if the other requirements for one-tailed testing are met. However, chi-square is only suitable if you have just *one* degree of freedom. Similarly, the Analysis of Variance can only be used if the independent variable being tested has only *one* degree of freedom.

- One-tailed testing requires that you predict the direction of the outcome of the test *prior* to collecting your data and that there are strong theoretical and/or previous research reasons for predicting the outcome.

- Once you have decided upon a one-tailed test of significance *do not* revert to two-tailed testing if your hypothesis fails.

- These tables could also be used for two-tailed tests at the 10% level of significance.

- The significance levels for the two-tailed tests presented elsewhere in this book can be used to give additional one-tailed significance levels. So tables of significance for two-tailed tests at the 5% level are identical in all other respects to tables of significance for one-tailed tests at the 2.5% level of significance. Tables of significance for two-tailed tests at the 1% level are otherwise identical to tables of significance for one-tailed tests at the 0.5% level.

Significance Table D1   **5% Significance values of the Pearson correlation coefficient (one-tailed test)**

Your value must be in the listed ranges for your sample size to be significant at the 5% level (i.e. to accept the hypothesis at the 5% level). However, remember that you must also have predicted accurately the sign of the correlation, positive or negative.

If your required sample size is not listed, then take the nearest *smaller* sample size. Alternatively extrapolate from listed values.

Sample size	Significant at 5% level: accept hypothesis
5	−0.81 to −1.00 *or* +0.81 to +1.00
6	−0.73 to −1.00 *or* +0.73 to +1.00
7	−0.67 to −1.00 *or* +0.67 to +1.00
8	−0.62 to −1.00 *or* +0.62 to +1.00
9	−0.58 to −1.00 *or* +0.58 to +1.00
10	−0.55 to −1.00 *or* +0.55 to +1.00
11	−0.52 to −1.00 *or* +0.52 to +1.00
12	−0.50 to −1.00 *or* +0.50 to +1.00
13	−0.48 to −1.00 *or* +0.48 to +1.00
14	−0.46 to −1.00 *or* +0.46 to +1.00
15	−0.44 to −1.00 *or* +0.44 to +1.00
16	−0.43 to −1.00 *or* +0.43 to +1.00
17	−0.41 to −1.00 *or* +0.41 to +1.00
18	−0.40 to −1.00 *or* +0.40 to +1.00
19	−0.39 to −1.00 *or* +0.39 to +1.00
20	−0.38 to −1.00 *or* +0.38 to +1.00
25	−0.34 to −1.00 *or* +0.34 to +1.00
30	−0.29 to −1.00 *or* +0.29 to +1.00
40	−0.25 to −1.00 *or* +0.25 to +1.00
50	−0.23 to −1.00 *or* +0.23 to +1.00
60	−0.21 to −1.00 *or* +0.21 to +1.00
100	−0.16 to −1.00 *or* +0.16 to +1.00

The above table has been adapted and extended from Table VII of R.A. Fisher and F. Yates (1974). *Statistical Tables for Biological, Agricultural and Medical Research*. London: Longman. With the kind permission of the publisher.

Significance Table D2   **5% Significance values of the Spearman correlation coefficient (one-tailed test)**

Your value must be in the listed ranges for your sample size to be significant at the 5% level (i.e. to accept the hypothesis at the 5% level). However, remember that you must also have predicted accurately the sign of the correlation, positive or negative.

If your required sample size is not listed, then take the nearest *smaller* sample size. Alternatively extrapolate from listed values.

Sample size	Significant at 5% level: accept hypothesis					
5	−0.90	to	−1.00	*or*	+0.90	to	+1.00
6	−0.83	to	−1.00	*or*	+0.83	to	+1.00
7	−0.71	to	−1.00	*or*	+0.71	to	+1.00
8	−0.64	to	−1.00	*or*	+0.64	to	+1.00
9	−0.60	to	−1.00	*or*	+0.60	to	+1.00
10	−0.56	to	−1.00	*or*	+0.56	to	+1.00
11	−0.54	to	−1.00	*or*	+0.54	to	+1.00
12	−0.51	to	−1.00	*or*	+0.51	to	+1.00
13	−0.49	to	−1.00	*or*	+0.49	to	+1.00
14	−0.46	to	−1.00	*or*	+0.46	to	+1.00
15	−0.45	to	−1.00	*or*	+0.45	to	+1.00
16	−0.43	to	−1.00	*or*	+0.43	to	+1.00
17	−0.42	to	−1.00	*or*	+0.42	to	+1.00
18	−0.40	to	−1.00	*or*	+0.40	to	+1.00
19	−0.39	to	−1.00	*or*	+0.39	to	+1.00
20	−0.38	to	−1.00	*or*	+0.38	to	+1.00
25	−0.34	to	−1.00	*or*	+0.34	to	+1.00
30	−0.31	to	−1.00	*or*	+0.31	to	+1.00
40	−0.26	to	−1.00	*or*	+0.26	to	+1.00
50	−0.23	to	−1.00	*or*	+0.23	to	+1.00
60	−0.21	to	−1.00	*or*	+0.21	to	+1.00
100	−0.16	to	−1.00	*or*	+0.16	to	+1.00

The above table has been adapted and extended from G.J. Glasser and R.F. Winter (1961). Critical values of the coefficient of rank correlation for testing the hypothesis of independence. *Biometrika*, **48**, 444–448. With the kind permission of the Biometrika Trustees.

Significance Table D3   **5% Significance values of *t* (one-tailed test)**

Your value must be in the listed ranges for your degrees of freedom to be significant at the 5% level (i.e. to accept the hypothesis). Remember that you must also have predicted accurately which mean of the two sets of scores would have been the higher.

If your required degrees of freedom are not listed, then take the nearest *smaller* listed values. Alternatively extrapolate from listed values.

Degrees of freedom	Significant at 5% level Accept hypothesis
3	±2.35 or more extreme
4	±2.13 or more extreme
5	±2.02 or more extreme
6	±1.94 or more extreme
7	±1.90 or more extreme
8	±1.86 or more extreme
9	±1.83 or more extreme
10	±1.82 or more extreme
11	±1.80 or more extreme
12	±1.78 or more extreme
13	±1.77 or more extreme
14	±1.76 or more extreme
15	±1.75 or more extreme
18	±1.73 or more extreme
20	±1.73 or more extreme
25	±1.71 or more extreme
30	±1.70 or more extreme
40	±1.68 or more extreme
60	±1.67 or more extreme
∞	±1.65 or more extreme

The above table has been adapted and extended from Table III of R.A. Fisher and F. Yates (1974). *Statistical Tables for Biological, Agricultural and Medical Research*. London: Longman. With the kind permission of the publisher.

Significance Table D4   5% Significance values of chi-square (one-tailed test)

Your value must be in the listed ranges for your degrees of freedom to be significant at the 5% level (i.e. to accept the hypothesis). In addition, you must have predicted which two cells have the high frequencies.

Since you can only carry out a one-tailed chi-square test if you have 1 degree of freedom, most of this table is unnecessary for one-tailed testing. However, it is of use to those interested in other uses of the table.

Degrees of freedom	Significant at 5% level Accept hypothesis
1	2.71 or more
2	4.61 or more
3	6.25 or more
4	7.78 or more
5	9.24 or more
6	10.64 or more
7	12.02 or more
8	13.36 or more
9	14.68 or more
10	15.99 or more
11	17.28 or more
12	18.55 or more

The above table has been adapted and extended from Table IV of R.A. Fisher and F. Yates (1974). *Statistical Tables for Biological, Agricultural and Medical Research*. London: Longman. With the kind permission of the publisher.

Significance Table D5   5% Significance values for the sign test (one-tailed test)

T is the smaller of the sum of the positive signs and the sum of the negative signs. Your value of T must be in the listed ranges for your sample size to be significant at the 5% level (i.e. to accept the hypothesis). In addition, you must have predicted in advance whether there will be more pluses than minuses or vice versa.

Number of pairs of scores (ignoring any tied pairs)	Significant at 5% level Accept hypothesis
5–7	0 only
8–10	0 to 1
11–12	0 to 2
13–15	0 to 3
16–17	0 to 4
18–20	0 to 5
21–22	0 to 6
23–25	0 to 7
26–27	0 to 8
28–29	0 to 9
30–32	0 to 10
33–34	0 to 11
35–36	0 to 12
37–39	0 to 13
40–41	0 to 14
42–43	0 to 15
44–46	0 to 16
47–48	0 to 17
49–50	0 to 18

The above table has been adapted and extended from Table M of R.P. Runyon, A. Haber and K.A. Coleman (1994). *Behavioural Statistics: The Core*. New York: McGraw-Hill. With the kind permission of the publisher.

Significance Table D6   **5% Significance values for the Wilcoxon Matched Pairs test (one-tailed test)**

Your value must be in the listed ranges for your sample size to be significant at the 5% level (i.e. to accept the hypothesis). In addition, you should have predicted which group of scores would have the smaller sum of ranks.

If your required number of pairs of scores (ignoring any tied pairs) is not listed, then take the nearest *smaller* listed values. Alternatively extrapolate from listed values.

Number of pairs of scores (ignoring any tied pairs)	Significant at 5% level Accept hypothesis
5	0 only
6	0 to 2
7	0 to 3
8	0 to 5
9	0 to 8
10	0 to 10
11	0 to 13
12	0 to 17
13	0 to 21
14	0 to 25
15	0 to 30
16	0 to 35
17	0 to 41
18	0 to 47
19	0 to 53
20	0 to 60
21	0 to 67
22	0 to 75
23	0 to 83
24	0 to 91
25	0 to 100

The above table has been adapted and extended from Table J of R.P. Runyon and A. Haber (1989). *Fundamentals of Behavioural Statistics*. New York: McGraw-Hill. With the kind permission of the publisher.

Significance Table D7   **5% Significance values for the Mann–Whitney U-test (one-tailed test)**

Your value must be in the listed ranges for your sample sizes to be significant at the 5% level (i.e. to accept the hypothesis). In addition, you should have predicted which group would have the smaller sum of ranks.

Sample size for smaller group	Sample size for larger group											
	5	6	7	8	9	10	11	12	13	14	15	20
5	0–4	0–5	0–6	0–8	0–9	0–11	0–12	0–13	0–15	0–16	0–18	0–25
	21–25	25–30	29–35	32–40	36–45	39–50	43–55	47–60	50–65	54–70	57–75	75–100
6	0–5	0–7	0–8	0–10	0–12	0–14	0–16	0–17	0–19	0–21	0–23	0–32
	25–30	29–36	34–42	38–48	42–54	46–60	50–66	55–72	59–78	63–84	67–90	88–120
7	0–6	0–8	0–11	0–13	0–15	0–17	0–19	0–21	0–24	0–26	0–28	0–39
	29–35	34–42	38–49	43–56	48–63	53–70	58–77	63–84	67–91	72–98	77–105	101–140
8	0–8	0–10	0–13	0–15	0–18	0–20	0–23	0–26	0–28	0–31	0–33	0–47
	32–40	38–48	43–56	49–64	54–72	60–80	65–88	70–96	76–104	81–112	87–120	113–160
9	0–9	0–12	0–15	0–18	0–21	0–24	0–27	0–30	0–33	0–36	0–39	0–54
	36–45	42–54	48–63	54–72	60–81	66–90	72–99	78–108	84–117	90–126	96–135	126–180
10	0–11	0–14	0–17	0–20	0–24	0–27	0–31	0–34	0–37	0–41	0–44	0–62
	39–50	46–60	53–70	60–80	66–90	73–100	79–110	86–120	93–130	99–140	106–150	138–200
11	0–12	0–16	0–19	0–23	0–27	0–31	0–34	0–38	0–42	0–46	0–50	0–69
	43–55	50–66	58–77	65–88	72–99	79–110	87–121	94–132	101–143	108–154	115–165	151–220
12	0–13	0–17	0–21	0–26	0–30	0–34	0–38	0–42	0–47	0–51	0–55	0–77
	47–60	55–72	63–84	70–96	78–108	86–120	94–132	102–144	109–156	117–168	125–180	163–240
13	0–15	0–19	0–24	0–28	0–33	0–37	0–42	0–47	0–51	0–56	0–61	0–84
	50–65	59–78	67–91	76–104	84–117	93–130	101–143	109–156	118–169	126–182	134–195	176–260
14	0–16	0–21	0–26	0–31	0–36	0–41	0–46	0–51	0–56	0–61	0–66	0–92
	54–70	63–84	72–98	81–112	90–126	99–140	108–154	117–168	126–182	135–196	144–210	188–280
15	0–18	0–23	0–28	0–33	0–39	0–44	0–50	0–55	0–61	0–66	0–72	0–100
	57–75	67–90	77–105	87–120	96–135	106–150	115–165	125–180	134–195	144–210	153–225	200–300
20	0–25	0–32	0–39	0–47	0–54	0–62	0–69	0–77	0–84	0–92	0–100	0–138
	75–100	88–120	101–140	113–160	126–180	138–200	151–220	163–240	176–260	188–280	200–300	262–400

The above table has been adapted and extended from Table I of R.P. Runyon and A. Haber (1989). *Fundamentals of Behavioural Statistics*. New York: McGraw-Hill. With the kind permission of the publisher.

Significance Table D8   **5% Significance values of the *F*-distribution for testing differences in variance estimates between two samples (one-tailed test)**

Your value has to equal or be larger than the tabulated value to be significant at the 5% level (i.e. to accept the hypothesis). In addition, you should have predicted which of the variance estimates is the larger.

Additional values are to be found in Significance Table D9.

Degrees of freedom for smaller variance estimate (denominator)	**Degrees of freedom for larger variance estimate (numerator)**					
	5	**7**	**10**	**20**	**50**	**∞**
5	3.5 or more	3.4	3.3	3.2	3.2	3.1
6	3.1	3.0	2.9	2.8	2.8	2.7
7	2.9	2.8	2.7	2.6	2.5	2.5
8	2.7	2.6	2.5	2.4	2.3	2.3
10	2.5	2.4	2.3	2.2	2.1	2.1
12	2.4	2.3	2.2	2.1	2.0	1.9
15	2.3	2.2	2.1	1.9	1.8	1.8
20	2.2	2.0	1.9	1.8	1.7	1.6
30	2.1	1.9	1.8	1.7	1.6	1.5
50	2.0	1.8	1.7	1.6	1.4	1.3
100	1.9	1.8	1.7	1.5	1.4	1.2
∞	1.9	1.7	1.6	1.4	1.3	1.0

The above table has been adapted and extended from Table D of R.P. Runyon and A. Haber (1989). *Fundamentals of Behavioural Statistics*. New York: McGraw-Hill. With the kind permission of the publisher.

Significance Table D9   **5% Significance values of the F-ratio for ANOVA (one-tailed test)**

Your value has to equal or be larger than the tabulated value to be significant at the 5% level (i.e. to accept the hypothesis). You should also have predicted which group of scores has the highest mean. Only the *column* for one degree of freedom should be used for one-tailed testing.

Additional values are to be found in Significance Table D8.

Degrees of freedom for error or within-cells mean square (or variance estimate)	Degrees of freedom for between-treatments mean square (or variance estimate)					
	1	2	3	4	5	∞
1	39.9 or more	49.5	53.6	55.8	57.2	63.3
2	8.5	9.0	9.2	9.2	9.3	9.5
3	5.5	5.5	5.4	5.3	5.3	5.1
4	4.5	4.3	4.2	4.1	4.1	3.8
5	4.1	3.8	3.6	3.5	3.5	3.1
6	3.8	3.5	3.3	3.2	3.1	2.7
7	3.6	3.3	3.1	3.0	2.9	2.5
8	3.5	3.1	2.9	2.8	2.7	2.3
9	3.4	3.0	2.8	2.7	2.6	2.2
10	3.3	2.9	2.7	2.6	2.5	2.1
13	3.1	2.8	2.6	2.4	2.4	1.9
15	3.1	2.7	2.5	2.4	2.3	1.8
20	3.0	2.6	2.4	2.3	2.2	1.6
30	2.9	2.5	2.3	2.1	2.1	1.5
60	2.8	2.4	2.2	2.0	2.0	1.3
∞	2.7	2.3	2.1	1.9	1.9	1.0

The above table has been adapted and extended from Table D of R.P. Runyon and A. Haber (1989). *Fundamentals of Behavioural Statistics*. New York: McGraw-Hill. With the kind permission of the publisher.

Significance Table D10   **5% Significance values for the partial correlation (one-tailed test)**

The degrees of freedom are the sample size minus the number of variables in the partial correlation. Thus, if you are controlling for just one variable the degrees of freedom are $N - 3$.

Your value must be in the listed ranges for your sample size to be significant at the 5% level (i.e. to accept the hypothesis).

If the number of degrees of freedom you want is not listed, take the next lower tabulated value. Alternatively extrapolate from listed values.

Degrees of freedom	Significant at 5% level Accept hypothesis					
3	−0.73	to −1.00	or	+0.73	to	+1.00
4	−0.67	to −1.00	or	+0.67	to	+1.00
5	−0.62	to −1.00	or	+0.62	to	+1.00
6	−0.58	to −1.00	or	+0.58	to	+1.00
8	−0.52	to −1.00	or	+0.52	to	+1.00
10	−0.48	to −1.00	or	+0.48	to	+1.00
12	−0.44	to −1.00	or	+0.44	to	+1.00
15	−0.40	to −1.00	or	+0.40	to	+1.00
20	−0.35	to −1.00	or	+0.35	to	+1.00
25	−0.32	to −1.00	or	+0.32	to	+1.00
30	−0.29	to −1.00	or	+0.29	to	+1.00
40	−0.25	to −1.00	or	+0.25	to	+1.00
50	−0.23	to −1.00	or	+0.23	to	+1.00
60	−0.21	to −1.00	or	+0.21	to	+1.00
100	−0.16	to −1.00	or	+0.16	to	+1.00

The above table has been adapted and extended from Table VII of R.A. Fisher and F. Yates (1974). *Statistical Tables for Biological, Agricultural and Medical Research*. London: Longman. With the kind permission of the publisher.

Appendix E

1% Significance values for two-tailed tests

Significance Table E1 **1% Significance values of the Pearson correlation coefficient (two-tailed test)**

Your value must be in the listed ranges for your sample size to be significant at the 1% level (i.e. to accept the hypothesis at the 1% level).

If your required sample size is not listed, then take the nearest *smaller* sample size. Alternatively extrapolate from listed values.

Sample size	Significant at 1% level: accept hypothesis					
5	−0.96	to	−1.00	*or*	+0.96	to	+1.00
6	−0.92	to	−1.00	*or*	+0.92	to	+1.00
7	−0.87	to	−1.00	*or*	+0.87	to	+1.00
8	−0.83	to	−1.00	*or*	+0.83	to	+1.00
9	−0.80	to	−1.00	*or*	+0.80	to	+1.00
10	−0.77	to	−1.00	*or*	+0.77	to	+1.00
11	−0.74	to	−1.00	*or*	+0.74	to	+1.00
12	−0.71	to	−1.00	*or*	+0.71	to	+1.00
13	−0.68	to	−1.00	*or*	+0.68	to	+1.00
14	−0.66	to	−1.00	*or*	+0.66	to	+1.00
15	−0.64	to	−1.00	*or*	+0.64	to	+1.00
16	−0.62	to	−1.00	*or*	+0.62	to	+1.00
17	−0.61	to	−1.00	*or*	+0.61	to	+1.00
18	−0.59	to	−1.00	*or*	+0.59	to	+1.00
19	−0.58	to	−1.00	*or*	+0.58	to	+1.00
20	−0.56	to	−1.00	*or*	+0.56	to	+1.00
25	−0.51	to	−1.00	*or*	+0.51	to	+1.00
30	−0.46	to	−1.00	*or*	+0.46	to	+1.00
40	−0.40	to	−1.00	*or*	+0.40	to	+1.00
50	−0.36	to	−1.00	*or*	+0.36	to	+1.00
60	−0.33	to	−1.00	*or*	+0.33	to	+1.00
100	−0.26	to	−1.00	*or*	+0.26	to	+1.00

The above table has been adapted and extended from Table VII of R.A. Fisher and F. Yates (1974). *Statistical Tables for Biological, Agricultural and Medical Research*. London: Longman. With the kind permission of the publisher.

Significance Table E2   **1% Significance values of the Spearman correlation coefficient (two-tailed test)**

Your value must be in the listed ranges for your sample size to be significant at the 1% level (i.e. to accept the hypothesis at the 1% level).

If your required sample size is not listed, then take the nearest *smaller* sample size. Alternatively extrapolate from listed values.

Sample size	Significant at 1% level: accept hypothesis				
5	Cannot be significant at 1%				
6		−1.00	*or*	+1.00	
7	−0.93	to −1.00	*or*	+0.93	to +1.00
8	−0.88	to −1.00	*or*	+0.88	to +1.00
9	−0.83	to −1.00	*or*	+0.83	to +1.00
10	−0.79	to −1.00	*or*	+0.79	to +1.00
11	−0.74	to −1.00	*or*	+0.74	to +1.00
12	−0.71	to −1.00	*or*	+0.71	to +1.00
13	−0.68	to −1.00	*or*	+0.68	to +1.00
14	−0.66	to −1.00	*or*	+0.66	to +1.00
15	−0.64	to −1.00	*or*	+0.64	to +1.00
16	−0.62	to −1.00	*or*	+0.62	to +1.00
17	−0.61	to −1.00	*or*	+0.61	to +1.00
18	−0.59	to −1.00	*or*	+0.59	to +1.00
19	−0.58	to −1.00	*or*	+0.58	to +1.00
20	−0.56	to −1.00	*or*	+0.56	to +1.00
25	−0.51	to −1.00	*or*	+0.51	to +1.00
30	−0.48	to −1.00	*or*	+0.48	to +1.00
40	−0.40	to −1.00	*or*	+0.40	to +1.00
50	−0.36	to −1.00	*or*	+0.36	to +1.00
60	−0.33	to −1.00	*or*	+0.33	to +1.00
100	−0.26	to −1.00	*or*	+0.26	to +1.00

The above table has been adapted and extended from G.J. Glasser and R.F. Winter (1961). Critical values of the coefficient of rank correlation for testing the hypothesis of independence. *Biometrika*, **48**, 444–448. With the kind permission of the Biometrika Trustees.

Significance Table E3   **1% Significance values of _t_ (two-tailed test)**

Your value must be in the listed ranges for your degrees of freedom to be significant at the 1% level (i.e. to accept the hypothesis at the 1% level).

If your required degrees of freedom are not listed, then take the nearest _smaller_ listed values. Alternatively extrapolate from listed values.

Degrees of freedom	Significant at 1% level Accept hypothesis
3	±5.84 or more extreme
4	±4.60 or more extreme
5	±4.03 or more extreme
6	±3.71 or more extreme
7	±3.50 or more extreme
8	±3.36 or more extreme
9	±3.25 or more extreme
10	±3.17 or more extreme
11	±3.11 or more extreme
12	±3.06 or more extreme
13	±3.01 or more extreme
14	±2.98 or more extreme
15	±2.95 or more extreme
18	±2.88 or more extreme
20	±2.85 or more extreme
25	±2.79 or more extreme
30	±2.75 or more extreme
40	±2.70 or more extreme
60	±2.66 or more extreme
∞	±2.58 or more extreme

The above table has been adapted and extended from Table III of R.A. Fisher and F. Yates (1974). _Statistical Tables for Biological, Agricultural and Medical Research_. London: Longman. With the kind permission of the publisher.

Significance Table E4   **1% Significance values of chi-square (two-tailed test)**

Your value must be in the listed ranges for your degrees of freedom to be significant at the 1% level (i.e. to accept the hypothesis).

Degrees of freedom	Significant at 1% level Accept hypothesis
1	6.7 or more
2	9.2 or more
3	11.3 or more
4	13.3 or more
5	15.1 or more
6	16.8 or more
7	18.5 or more
8	20.1 or more
9	21.7 or more
10	23.2 or more
11	24.7 or more
12	26.2 or more

The above table has been adapted and extended from Table IV of R.A. Fisher and F. Yates (1974). *Statistical Tables for Biological, Agricultural and Medical Research*. London: Longman. With the kind permission of the publisher.

Significance Table E5   **1% Significance values for the sign test (two-tailed test)**

T is the smaller of the sum of the positive signs and the sum of the negative signs. Your value of T must be in the listed ranges for your sample size to be significant at the 1% level (i.e. to accept the hypothesis).

Number of pairs of scores (ignoring any tied pairs)	Significant at 1% level Accept hypothesis
6–8	Cannot be significant
9–11	0 only
12–14	0 to 1
15–17	0 to 2
18–20	0 to 3
21–23	0 to 4
24–25	0 to 5
26–28	0 to 6
29–31	0 to 7
32–33	0 to 8
34–36	0 to 9
37–38	0 to 10
39–41	0 to 11
42–43	0 to 12
44–46	0 to 13
47–49	0 to 14
50	0 to 15

The above table has been adapted and extended from Table M of R.P. Runyon, A. Haber and K.A. Coleman (1994). *Behavioural Statistics: The Core*. New York: McGraw-Hill. With the kind permission of the publisher.

Significance Table E6   **1% Significance values for the Wilcoxon Matched Pairs test (two-tailed test)**

Your value must be in the listed ranges for your sample size to be significant at the 1% level (i.e. to accept the hypothesis at the 1% level).

If your required number of pairs of scores (ignoring any tied pairs) is not listed, then take the nearest *smaller* listed values. Alternatively extrapolate from listed values.

Number of pairs of scores (ignoring any tied pairs)	Significant at 1% level Accept hypothesis
6	Cannot be significant at 1%
7	Cannot be significant at 1%
8	0 only
9	0 to 1
10	0 to 3
11	0 to 5
12	0 to 7
13	0 to 9
14	0 to 12
15	0 to 15
16	0 to 19
17	0 to 23
18	0 to 27
19	0 to 32
20	0 to 37
21	0 to 42
22	0 to 48
23	0 to 54
24	0 to 61
25	0 to 68

The above table has been adapted and extended from Table J of R.P. Runyon and A. Haber (1989). *Fundamentals of Behavioural Statistics*. New York: McGraw-Hill. With the kind permission of the publisher.

Significance Table E7   **1% Significance values for the Mann–Whitney U-test (two-tailed test)**

Your value must be in the listed ranges for your sample sizes to be significant at the 1% level (i.e. to accept the hypothesis at the 1% level).

Sample size for smaller group	Sample size for larger group											
	5	6	7	8	9	10	11	12	13	14	15	20
5	0	0–1	0–1	0–2	0–3	0–4	0–5	0–6	0–7	0–7	0–8	0–13
	25	29–30	34–35	38–40	42–45	46–50	50–55	54–60	58–65	63–70	67–75	87–100
6	0–1	0–2	0–3	0–4	0–5	0–6	0–7	0–9	0–10	0–11	0–12	0–18
	29–30	34–36	39–42	44–48	49–54	54–60	59–66	63–72	68–78	73–84	78–90	102–120
7	0–1	0–3	0–4	0–6	0–7	0–9	0–10	0–12	0–13	0–15	0–16	0–24
	34–35	39–42	45–49	50–56	56–63	61–70	67–77	72–84	78–91	83–98	89–105	116–140
8	0–2	0–4	0–6	0–7	0–9	0–11	0–13	0–15	0–17	0–18	0–20	0–30
	38–40	44–48	50–56	57–64	63–72	69–80	75–88	81–96	87–104	94–112	100–120	130–160
9	0–3	0–5	0–7	0–9	0–11	0–13	0–16	0–18	0–20	0–22	0–24	0–36
	42–45	49–54	56–63	63–72	70–81	77–90	83–99	90–108	97–117	104–126	111–135	144–180
10	0–4	0–6	0–9	0–11	0–13	0–16	0–18	0–21	0–24	0–26	0–29	0–42
	46–50	54–60	61–70	69–80	77–90	84–100	92–110	99–120	106–130	114–140	121–150	158–200
11	0–5	0–7	0–10	0–13	0–16	0–18	0–21	0–24	0–27	0–30	0–33	0–48
	50–55	59–66	67–77	75–88	83–99	92–110	100–121	108–132	116–143	124–154	132–165	172–220
12	0–6	0–9	0–12	0–15	0–18	0–21	0–24	0–27	0–31	0–34	0–37	0–54
	54–60	63–72	72–84	81–96	90–108	99–120	108–132	117–144	125–156	134–168	143–180	186–240
13	0–7	0–10	0–13	0–17	0–20	0–24	0–27	0–31	0–34	0–38	0–42	0–60
	58–65	68–78	78–91	87–104	97–117	106–130	116–143	125–156	135–169	144–182	153–195	200–260
14	0–7	0–11	0–15	0–18	0–22	0–26	0–30	0–34	0–38	0–42	0–46	0–67
	63–70	73–84	83–98	94–112	104–126	114–140	124–154	134–168	144–182	154–196	164–210	213–280
15	0–8	0–12	0–16	0–20	0–24	0–29	0–33	0–37	0–42	0–46	0–51	0–73
	67–75	78–90	89–105	100–120	111–135	121–150	132–165	143–180	153–195	164–210	174–225	227–300
20	0–13	0–18	0–24	0–30	0–36	0–42	0–48	0–54	0–60	0–67	0–73	0–105
	87–100	102–120	116–140	130–160	144–180	158–200	172–220	186–240	200–260	213–280	227–300	295–400

The above table has been adapted and extended from Table I of R.P. Runyon and A. Haber (1989). *Fundamentals of Behavioural Statistics*. New York: McGraw-Hill. With the kind permission of the publisher.

Significance Table E8   **1% Significance values of the *F*-distribution for testing differences in variance estimates between two samples (two-tailed test)**

Your value has to equal or be larger than the tabulated value to be significant at the 1% level for a two-tailed test (i.e. to accept the hypothesis).

Additional values are to be found in Significance Table E9.

Degrees of freedom for smaller variance estimate (denominator)	Degrees of freedom for larger variance estimate (numerator)					
	5	7	10	20	50	∞
5	10.97 or more	10.5	10.1	9.6	9.2	9.0
6	8.8	8.3	7.9	7.4	7.1	6.9
7	7.5	7.0	6.6	6.2	5.9	5.7
8	6.6	6.2	5.8	5.4	5.1	4.9
10	5.6	5.2	4.9	4.4	4.1	3.9
12	5.1	4.7	4.3	3.9	3.6	3.4
15	4.6	4.1	3.8	3.4	3.1	2.9
20	4.1	3.7	3.4	2.9	2.6	2.4
25	3.9	3.5	3.1	2.7	2.4	2.2
30	3.7	3.3	3.0	2.6	2.2	2.0
50	3.4	3.0	2.7	2.3	1.9	1.7
100	3.2	2.8	2.5	2.1	1.7	1.4
∞	3.0	2.6	2.3	1.9	1.5	1.0

The above table has been adapted and extended from Table D of R.P. Runyon and A. Haber (1989). *Fundamentals of Behavioural Statistics*. New York: McGraw-Hill. With the kind permission of the publisher.

Significance Table E9   **1% Significance values of the *F*-ratio for ANOVA (two-tailed test)**

Your value has to equal or be larger than the tabulated value to be significant at the 1% level for a two-tailed test (i.e. to accept the hypothesis).

Additional values are to be found in Significance Table E8.

Degrees of freedom for error or within-cells mean square (or variance estimate)	Degrees of freedom for between-treatments mean square (or variance estimate)					
	1	**2**	**3**	**4**	**5**	**∞**
1	4052 or more	4999	5403	5625	5764	6366
2	98.5	99.0	99.2	99.3	99.3	99.5
3	34.1	30.8	29.5	28.7	27.9	26.1
4	21.2	18.0	16.7	16.0	15.5	13.5
5	16.3	13.3	12.1	11.4	11.0	9.0
6	13.7	10.9	9.8	9.2	8.8	6.9
7	12.3	9.6	8.5	7.9	7.5	5.7
8	11.3	8.7	7.6	7.0	6.6	4.9
9	10.6	8.0	7.0	6.4	6.1	4.3
10	10.0	7.6	6.6	6.0	5.6	3.9
13	9.1	6.7	5.7	5.2	4.9	3.2
15	8.7	6.4	5.4	4.9	4.6	2.9
20	8.1	5.9	4.9	4.4	4.1	2.4
30	7.6	5.4	4.5	4.0	3.7	2.0
60	7.1	5.0	4.1	3.7	3.3	1.6
∞	6.6	4.6	3.8	3.3	3.0	1.0

The above table has been adapted and extended from Table D of R.P. Runyon and A. Haber (1989). *Fundamentals of Behavioural Statistics*. New York: McGraw-Hill. With the kind permission of the publisher.

Significance Table E10   **1% Significance values for the partial correlation (two-tailed test)**

The degrees of freedom are the sample size minus the number of variables in the partial correlation. Thus, if you are controlling for just one variable the degrees of freedom are $N - 3$.

Your value must be in the listed ranges for your sample size to be significant at the 1% level (i.e. to accept the hypothesis at the 1% level).

If the number of degrees of freedom you want is not listed, take the next lower tabulated value. Alternatively extrapolate from listed values.

Degrees of freedom	Significant at 1% level Accept hypothesis					
3	−0.92	to	−1.00	*or*	+0.92	to	+1.00
4	−0.88	to	−1.00	*or*	+0.88	to	+1.00
5	−0.83	to	−1.00	*or*	+0.83	to	+1.00
6	−0.80	to	−1.00	*or*	+0.80	to	+1.00
8	−0.74	to	−1.00	*or*	+0.74	to	+1.00
10	−0.68	to	−1.00	*or*	+0.68	to	+1.00
12	−0.64	to	−1.00	*or*	+0.64	to	+1.00
15	−0.59	to	−1.00	*or*	+0.59	to	+1.00
20	−0.53	to	−1.00	*or*	+0.53	to	+1.00
25	−0.48	to	−1.00	*or*	+0.48	to	+1.00
30	−0.42	to	−1.00	*or*	+0.42	to	+1.00
40	−0.39	to	−1.00	*or*	+0.39	to	+1.00
50	−0.35	to	−1.00	*or*	+0.35	to	+1.00
60	−0.33	to	−1.00	*or*	+0.33	to	+1.00
100	−0.25	to	−1.00	*or*	+0.25	to	+1.00

The above table has been adapted and extended from Table VII of R.A. Fisher and F. Yates (1974). *Statistical Tables for Biological, Agricultural and Medical Research*. London: Longman. With the kind permission of the publisher.

Appendix F

Index of Significance tables

The standard normal z-distribution: Significance Table 5.1, page 48

	5% two-tailed test	5% one-tailed test	1% two-tailed test
Pearson correlation	10.1, page 103	D1, page 350	E1, page 360
Spearman correlation	10.2, page 105	D2, page 351	E2, page 361
t-test	12.1, page 122 13.1, page 134	D3, page 352	E3, page 362
Chi-square	14.1, page 145*	D4, page 353	E4, page 363
Sign test	18.1, page 175	D5, page 354	E5, page 364
Wilcoxon Matched Pairs	18.2, page 177	D6, page 355	E6, page 365
Mann–Whitney U-test	18.3, page 180	D7, page 356	E7, page 366
F for differences	19.1, page 186	D8, page 357	E8, page 367
F for ANOVA	20.1, page 196 21.1, page 218 22.1, page 237	D9, page 358	E9, page 368
Partial correlation	26.1, page 278	D10, page 359	E10, page 369

* Also lists 1% significance values (two-tailed test).

References

Baron, L., and Straus, M. (1989). *Four Theories of Rape: A State-Level Analysis*. New Haven, CT: Yale University Press.

Blalock, H.M. (1972). *Social Statistics*. New York: McGraw-Hill.

Butler, C. (1995a). Teachers' qualities, resources and involvement of special needs children in mainstream classrooms. Unpublished thesis, Department of Social Sciences, Loughborough University.

Butler, R. (1995b). Motivational and informational functions and consequences of children's attention to peers' work. *Journal of Educational Psychology*, **87**(3), 347–360.

Cramer, D. (1992). *Personality and Psychotherapy*. Milton Keynes: Open University Press.

Crighton, D., and Towl, G. (1994). The selection and recruitment of prison officers. *Forensic Update: A Newsletter for Forensic Psychologists*, **39**, 4–7.

Donnerstein, E. (1980). Aggressive erotica and violence against women. *Journal of Personality and Social Psychology*, **39**(2), 269–277.

Gillis, J.S. (1980). *Child Anxiety Scale Manual*. Institute of Personality and Ability Testing, Champaign, Illinois.

Howitt, D., and Cumberbatch, G. (1990). *Pornography: Impacts and Influences*. London: Home Office Research and Planning Unit.

Johnston, F.A., and Johnston, S.A. (1986). Differences between human figure drawings of child molesters and control groups. *Journal of Clinical Psychology*, **42**(4), 638–647.

Kerlinger, F.N. (1986). *Foundations of Behavioural Research*. New York: Holt, Rinehart & Winston.

Munford, M.B. (1994). Relationship of gender, self-esteem, social class and racial identity to depression in blacks. *Journal of Black Psychology*, **20**, 157–174.

Rosenthal, J.A. (1988). Patterns of reported child abuse and neglect. *Child Abuse and Neglect*, **12**, 263–271.

Szostak, H. (1995). Competitive performance, anxiety and perceptions of parental pressure in young tennis players. Unpublished thesis, Department of Social Sciences, Loughborough University.

Wagner, U., and Zick, A. (1995). The relation of formal education to ethnic prejudice: its reliability, validity and explanation. *European Journal of Social Psychology*, **25**, 41–56.

Index